Oracle Certified Professional DBO Certification Exam Guide

Jason S. Couchman

Osborne/**McGraw-Hill**

Berkeley New York St. Louis San Francisco
Auckland Bogotá Hamburg London Madrid
Mexico City Milan Montreal New Delhi Panama City
Paris São Paulo Singapore Sydney Tokyo Toronto

Osborne/**McGraw-Hill**
2600 Tenth Street
Berkeley, California 94710
U.S.A.

For information on translations or book distributors outside the U.S.A., or to arrange bulk purchase discounts for sales promotions, premiums, or fund-raisers, please contact Osborne/**McGraw-Hill** at the above address.

Oracle Certified Professional DBO Certification Exam Guide

1234567890 DOC DOC 019876543210

Book P/N 0-07-212359-1 and CD P/N 0-07-212360-5
parts of
ISBN 0-07-212361-3

Publisher
Brandon A. Nordin

Associate Publisher and Editor-in-Chief
Scott Rogers

Acquisitions Editor
Jeremy Judson

Project Editors
Ron Hull and Lisa Theobald

Acquisitions Coordinator
Monika Faltiss

Technical Editors
Alan Haensgen and Susan Jang

Copy Editor
Nancy Crumpton

Proofreader
Linda Medoff

Indexer
Irv Hershman

Computer Designers
Jani Beckwith and Gary Corrigan

Illustrators
Beth Young and Robert Hansen

Series Design
Jani Beckwith

This book was composed with Corel VENTURA™ Publisher.

To my parents

About the Author...

Jason S. Couchman is a database consultant and the author of *Oracle8 Certified Professional DBA Certification Exam Guide*, also from Oracle Press. He is frequently invited to present on Oracle topics at Oracle user conferences. His work has been published by *Oracle Magazine*, Harvard Business School Publishing, and Gannett Newspapers.

About the Oracle8 Database Operator Certification Exam

The demand for well-trained information technology (IT) professionals is high and the competition for jobs is intense. Individuals, experienced or new to the profession, need to know what skills make them attractive to employers. Employers look for ways to distinguish employees and prospective employees who have the solid foundation of skills needed for effective performance. The Oracle Certified Professional (OCP) program helps the IT industry make these distinctions by establishing a standard of competence in specific job roles. An OCP certification is a valuable, industry-recognized credential that signifies a proven level of knowledge and ability on Oracle technologies.

In today's increasingly complex system environments, a new role has emerged as an integral part of efficient, successful database administration. This is the role of the Database Operator (DBO)—an individual who performs routine, operational tasks on an Oracle database and who has an introductory knowledge of database software and the graphical utilities associated with managing the database. DBOs provide valuable support to Database Administrators (DBAs) in the management of the database. Because they have the ability to execute routine administrative tasks on the database independently, DBOs enable enterprise DBAs to concentrate on mission-critical operations, including making strategic decisions about database design, maintenance, and tuning, as well as diagnosing and troubleshooting complex database issues.

Upon completing the requirements for certification, Oracle Certified Professionals receive a certificate in recognition of their accomplishment and are also eligible to include the Oracle Certified Professional logo on their business card or resume.

Requirements for Certification

To become an Oracle Certified Database Operator, you must pass only one test. This test challenges you to apply specific knowledge that you have gained through recommended Oracle University training, self-study, and on-the-job experience. The knowledge that you will be tested on includes essential aspects of the SQL language; installation of an Oracle database; creation and configuration of databases; loading data; setting up and managing users; installing applications; and high-level backup, recovery, and performance tuning.

The certification process requires that you pass the following exam:

Oracle8 Database Operator (Exam #1Z0-401)

If you fail the exam, you must wait at least 30 days before you can retake the exam. You may attempt to retake the exam up to three times in a 12-month period.

Recertification

Oracle is committed to keeping the OCP Program current with the latest technology. To ensure the value of your Oracle Certified Professional credential, you may upgrade your certification to the latest version. Oracle announces the requirements for upgrading your certification based on the release of new products and upgrades. Oracle will give six months' notice announcing when an exam version is expiring.

Exam Format

The test is delivered by computer and consists of multiple-choice, free response, and interactive graphical questions. A brief tutorial precedes each test to familiarize you with the test delivery system. The test consists of 60 to 90 questions that must be completed in 90 minutes.

Exam Special 10% Discount Offer

You can qualify for a special 10% discount when you register for the OCP exam by contacting the number listed below. You must specifically request the discount and mention extension 46. Offer valid through December 31, 2000. To register for your Oracle8 Database Operator exam and be eligible for the 10% discount, please call the Sylvan Prometric Regional Service Center nearest you:

- Asia-Pacific Regional Service Center (Sydney, Australia). . . . . +61.2.9414.3663
- Europe Regional Service Center (Lelystad, Netherlands) . . . . +31.320.23.9894
- Japan Regional Service Center . . . . +813.3269.9620
- Latin America Regional Service Center . . . . +1.410.843.4300
- North America Regional Service Center . . . . +1.800.891.3926

Please visit **http://education.oracle.com/certification** to obtain an OCP Candidate Guide for information on specific exam objectives and recommended preparation methods. You may also obtain recommendations on exam preparation courses and materials from your local Oracle University representative.

Contents at a Glance

Contents

Preface

y interest in Oracle certification began in 1996 when I read about the Oracle DBA certificate offered by the Chauncey Group. I found it difficult to prepare for that certification exam for two reasons. First, there was an absence of readily available practice questions. Second, preparation for the exam involved reviewing six or seven different manuals and Oracle Press books, none of which were particularly suited to the task. Judging from the response to this book so far, it would seem others have had similar experiences. Since then, Oracle has released OCP exam tracks for developers, financial apps, and database operations, the topic of the book you are about to read.

This book is divided into ten chapters, the first nine of which cover technical content tested in the Oracle8 DBO certification track from Oracle. The remaining chapter is dedicated to covering new question formats found on the DBO exam that have not appeared on OCP exams up until now. The body of each chapter follows the format described in this preface.

Within each chapter, there are several section discussions. These section discussions correspond directly to subject areas tested in the OCP exams. The discussion presents facts about the Oracle database. Commands and keywords that the user enters are presented in `Courier`, while new terms or emphasized facts are presented in *italics*. Particularly important facts and suggestions are set apart from regular text. They are preceded by the word *TIP*, and a special icon appears in the margin next to them.

At the end of each section are some exercises for review. Designed to reinforce the material you just read, these exercises are short-answer questions. You should try to do *all* the exercises at the end of each discussion. If you can, try to answer the question without reviewing the chapter material and write the answer in the book for later review.

A summary of the material presented appears near the end of each chapter. This digest information is designed for quick review after reading the chapter and doing the exercises. In the days prior to your OCP exam, you can re-read the chapter summary to familiarize yourself with the information covered.

After the chapter summary, you'll find a short list of the key facts about Oracle presented in the chapter. This list, called a "Two-Minute Drill," is designed to be your final review for the OCP exam in the subject area covered in the chapter. Go over the Two-Minute Drill for each chapter in the unit covering your OCP exam the night before you take your exam as a memory jogger and memorization list.

The chapter also contains questions patterned after the actual exam. These questions will familiarize you with the style of OCP questions. They will also test your knowledge of the Oracle material presented in the chapter. You should attempt to answer these questions after reviewing the chapter material. Finally, to help you understand the test material, each chapter contains the answers to the chapter questions, along with an explanation of each answer.

In order to get the most from this book, you need to answer the following question: what is your level of Oracle experience? There are two ways to use this book. If you are a professional with a beginner or intermediate level of Oracle experience, you should use the standard method of studying the material in this book. Start at the beginning of each chapter, read it from start to finish, and *do the exercises*. Review the material by reading the chapter summary and Two-Minute Drill, and then answer the practice questions. The standard method for reading the book should give you the facts you need to understand to pass the OCP exam. Information is presented in several different ways to help you retain the facts you need to know. If you have reviewed the material thoroughly, answering the exercise questions and studying the chapter summary and the drill for all chapters in the unit, you should do well on the OCP exam.

However, advanced users of Oracle seeking to prepare for OCP exams quickly can also use the book's *accelerated reading method*. Skip directly to the chapter summary and read it to understand the content of the chapter. Then, review the Two-Minute Drill and try the chapter questions. If you find yourself getting most of the questions right, you may be ready to take the test. Even if you are missing questions, you will probably have a better idea of the areas you need to review. You can then flip back to the specific area in the chapter content to help refresh your memory. Given the introduction of Oracle8 topics and concepts that may be unfamiliar to readers, however, I discourage all but the most advanced users of Oracle reading this book from employing the accelerated reading method.

Finally, a note about errata. Because OCP covers such vast ground in a short time, this has become a living text. If you feel you have encountered difficulties due to errors, you can either check out www.exampilot.com to find the latest errata or send me an email directly at jcouchman@mindspring.com.

Good luck!

Acknowledgments

here are many people I would like to thank for their help in writing this book. My first and most heartfelt thanks goes to the dedicated readers of my other books, who took time out of their busy schedules to send feedback. I have listened to your praise and constructive criticism, and made every effort to correct and amplify my work based on the points you made. Please, keep the email coming—it is by far the most effective way to make my work better!

Next, a note of gratitude to the folks at Oracle who made the book possible. Thanks to Brad Saffer and Julia Johnson who have always been extremely helpful in informing me about the OCP program. Thanks also to the technical reviewers at Oracle Education for their feedback and assistance with the technical content review and with the material covering Oracle8. Thanks also to the fine folks at Osborne—Scott Rogers, Jeremy Judson, and Monika Faltiss. Special thanks to the folks in production as well—Ron Hull and especially Lisa Theobald, who stepped in at the end to pull it all together. A heartfelt thanks to Nancy Crumpton as well, for her dedication to the work and to painstaking details. As always, thanks to my wife, Stacy.

Finally, thanks to my parents. Without their attention, I never would have gotten to where I am today.

Introduction

he Oracle Certified Professional DBO Certification Exam is the latest credential from Oracle Corporation. Called OCP, it represents the culmination of many people's requests for objective standards in one of the hottest markets in the software field, Oracle database administration. The presence of OCP on the market indicates an important reality about Oracle as a career path. Oracle is mature, robust, and stable for enterprise-wide information management. However, corporations facing a severe shortage of qualified Oracle professionals need a measurement for Oracle expertise.

The OCP certification core track for DBOs consists of one test on Oracle8. As of this printing, each test consists of about 70 multiple-choice questions pertaining to the recommended usage of Oracle databases. You have about 90 minutes to take the exam. The current content of the exam covers Oracle8. Obtaining DBO certification for Oracle8 through the core track is contingent on taking and passing the core examination.

Why Get Certified?

If you are already an Oracle professional, you may wonder, "Why should I get certified?" Perhaps you have a successful career as an Oracle professional, enjoying the instant prestige your resume gets with that one magic word on it. With market forces currently in your favor, you're right to wonder. But, while no one is saying you don't know Oracle when you put the magic word on your resume, can you prove how well you *do* know Oracle without undergoing a technical interview? I started asking myself that question last year when Oracle certification began to emerge. I was surprised to find out that, after years of using Oracle, developing Oracle applications, and administering Oracle databases for Fortune 500 companies, there were a lot of things about Oracle I *didn't* know. And the only reason I know them now is because I took the time and effort to become certified.

If you're looking for another reason to become certified in Oracle, consider the example of computer professionals with Novell NetWare experience in the late 1980s and early 1990s. It seemed that anyone with even a little experience in NetWare could count on a fantastic job offer. Then Novell introduced its CNE/CNA programs. At first, employers were hiring professionals with or without the certificate. As time went on, however, employers no longer asked for computer professionals with Novell NetWare experience—they asked for CNEs and CNAs. A similar phenomenon can be witnessed in the arena of Microsoft Windows NT, where the MCSE has already become the standard by which those professionals are measuring their skills. If you want to stay competitive in the field of Oracle database administration, your real question shouldn't be *whether* you should become certified, but *when*.

If you are not in the field of Oracle database management, or if you want to advance your career using Oracle, there has never been a better time to do so. OCP is already altering the playing field by changing the focus of the Oracle skill set from "how many years have you used it" to "*how well* do you know how to use it?" That shift benefits organizations using Oracle as much as it benefits the professionals who use Oracle because the emphasis is on *performance*, not attrition.

Managers who are faced with the task of hiring Oracle professionals can breathe a sigh of relief with the debut of OCP as well. By seeking professionals who are certified, managers can spend less time trying to determine if the candidate knows Oracle well enough to do the job, and more time assessing the candidate's work habits and compatibility with the team.

How Should You Prepare for the Exam?

If you spend your free time studying things like how to back up your database using OEM Backup Manager, you are probably ready to take the DBO exam now. For the rest of us, Oracle and other companies offer classroom- and computer-based training options to learn Oracle. Now, users have another option—this book! By selecting this book, you demonstrate two excellent characteristics—you are committed to a superior career in the field of Oracle database operations, and you care about preparing for the exam correctly and thoroughly.

Oracle Certification Past and Present

Oracle certification started in the mid 1990s with the involvement of the Chauncey Group International, a division of Educational Testing Service. With the help of many Oracle DBAs, Chauncey put together an objective, fact-based, and scenario-based examination on Oracle database administration. This test did an excellent job of measuring knowledge of Oracle7, versions 7.0 to 7.2. Consisting of 60 questions, Chauncey's exam covered several different topic areas, including backup and recovery, security, administration, and performance tuning, all in one test.

Oracle Corporation has taken certification several giant leaps ahead with the advent of OCP. The DBO certification examination is one test consisting of about 70 questions. Oracle has also committed to including scenario-based questions on the OCP examinations, and preparation material for these new questions is included in this book as well. Scenario-based questions require you not only to know the facts about Oracle, but also to understand how to apply those facts in real-life situations involving interactive use of GUI tools.

Taking the Oracle Assessment Test

It is essential that you begin your preparation for the OCP DBO certification exams by taking the Oracle Assessment Test. The Oracle Assessment Test is a mock-up of the real exam, with questions designed to help you identify your personal areas of strength and weakness with Oracle. You can load the Oracle Assessment Test from the Oracle Education Web site; its URL is http://education.oracle.com/certification. You should load it onto your Windows-based computer and take the exams to determine which areas you need to study. You should also download the OCP Candidate Guide for the DBO track, which publishes the topic areas for each exam corresponding to chapter and section discussions in this book.

Figure I-1 is a diagram of the Oracle Assessment Test graphical user interface. The features of the interface are indicated in the figure. Several of the main features of the assessment test interface are explained here. The assessment test interface is highly similar to the actual Sylvan Prometric OCP DBO test driver, with a few exceptions as noted. At the top, the interface tells you how much time has elapsed and the number of questions you have answered. On the actual OCP exam only, there is also a checkbox in the upper-left corner of the interface. You can use this checkbox to mark questions you would like to review later. In the main window of the interface is the actual production question, along with the choices. The interface generally allows the user to select only one answer, unless the question directs you to select more answers. In this case, the interface will allow you to select only as many answers as the question requests.

After answering a question, or marking the question for later review, the candidate can move onto the next question by clicking the appropriate button in the lower-left corner. The next button over on the bottom allows you either to print your score on the assessment test or to return to the previous question on the OCP exam. Next, in the assessment test only, you can score your questions at any time by pressing the grade test button on the bottom-right side. The final feature to cover is the exhibit button. In some cases, you may require the use of an exhibit to answer a question. If the question does not require use of an exhibit, the button will be grayed out.

The Oracle Assessment Test indicates your performance by means of a grade window, such as the one displayed in Figure I-2. It details the number of questions you answered correctly, along with your percentage score based on 100 percent. Finally, a bar graph indicates where your performance falls in comparison to the maximum score possible on the exam. The OCP exam reports your score

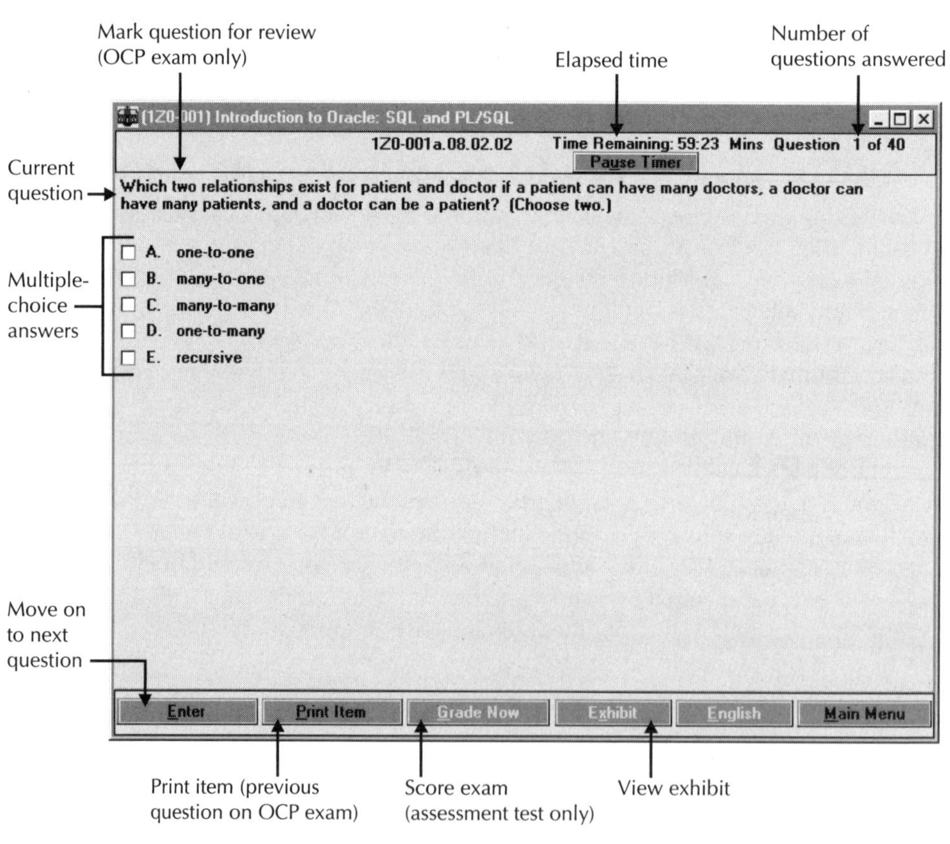

FIGURE I-1. *The Oracle assessment test user interface*

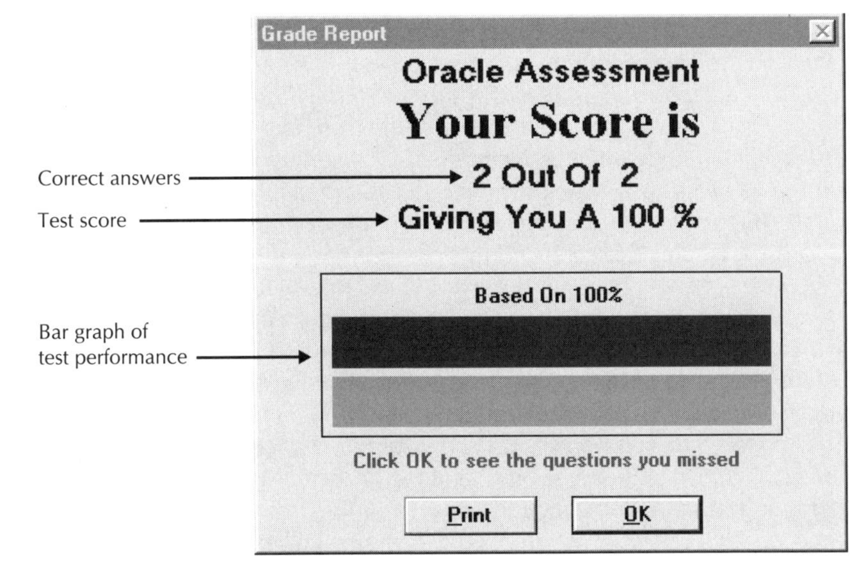

FIGURE 1-2. *Grading your test performance*

immediately after you exit the exam, so you will know right then whether or not you passed in a similar fashion as the assessment test. Both interfaces offer you the ability to print a report of your score.

Taking the OCP Exams

The score range for the DBO exam is between 0 and 70. Each question is worth about 1 point, and a passing score is about 50. Given the recent use of questions with two or even three correct answers on OCP exams, the scoring method for actual OCP exams may differ from my explanation somewhat. There is no penalty for wrong answers. The OCP DBO certification exam is administered at Sylvan Prometric test centers. To schedule your OCP exam in the United States, call Sylvan Prometric at 1-800-891-EXAM. For contact information outside the United States, refer to the assessment test software. For Oracle's official information about OCP certification, visit http://education.oracle.com/certification.

Some preliminary items are now identified for you to take the OCP exams. The first tip is, *don't wait until you're the world's foremost authority on Oracle to take the OCP exam.* The passing score for most exams is approximately 50. You have to get 50 questions right, or about 75 to 80 percent of the exam. So, if you are getting about four questions right out of five on the assessment test or in the chapters (more on chapter format in a minute), you should consider taking the OCP exam. Remember, you're certified if you pass with a 50 or a 70.

The next item is, *if you can't answer the question within 30 seconds, mark it with the checkbox in the upper-left corner of the OCP interface for review later.* The most significant difference between the OCP interface and the assessment test interface is a special screen appearing after you answer all the questions. This screen displays all your answers, along with a special indicator next to the questions you marked for review. This screen also offers a button for you to click in order to review the questions you marked. You should use this feature extensively. If you spend only 30 seconds answering each question in your first pass on the exam, you will have at least an hour to review the questions you're unsure of, with the added bonus of knowing you answered all the questions that were easiest first.

Third, *there is no penalty for guessing.* If you answer the question correctly, your score goes up ten points; if not, your score does not change. If you can eliminate any choices on a question, you should take the chance in the interest of improving your score. In some questions, the OCP exam requires you to specify two or even three choices—this can work in your favor, meaning you need to eliminate fewer choices to get the question right.

Each subsequent chapter of the guide builds on information presented in the previous chapters. As such, you should read the guide from beginning to end and take the test accordingly. Taking the exams in this manner will maximize your use of the guide and improve your results on the tests.

The New Scenario-Based Questions on the OCP Exam

Oracle Corporation has announced its intention to include scenario-based questions in the OCP DBO certification exam series. These questions require you to apply the facts about Oracle to real-life situations portrayed on the exam—complete with exhibits and documents to substantiate the example—and determine the correct answer based on those exhibits and documents. In order to assist you better in preparation for these new test questions, the questions in this book have been designed to replicate scenario-based exam questions. Chapter 10 focuses on new question formats in detail as well.

Finally, if you have comments about the book or would like to contact me about it, please do so by email at jcouchman@mindspring.com. You can also find related information such as posted corrections and amplifications at www.exampilot.com.

CHAPTER 1

A DBO's Introduction to Oracle Software

his chapter introduces the following topic areas of Oracle software:

- What an Oracle database is
- Tools for accessing Oracle
- Role of the DBO

Welcome to the exciting world of Oracle databases. Oracle is widely acknowledged as the most popular database software in the world today. It finds its roots in relational database theory conceived by E. F. Codd in the 1950s, and extends those theories into an infinite variety of directions, such as data warehousing, online transaction processing, and Web-enabled applications. Undoubtedly, the popularity of this software is part of the reason you are reading this book. This book has the answers to your questions about what an Oracle database is, how it works, and what you can do with it. If I do my job right as the author of this book, it will also give you a glimpse of what those strange people running around in most organizations calling themselves *database administrators* do as well. By reading this book, and taking and passing the OCP DBO exam offered by Oracle Corporation, you may even find this to be a first step in your journey to become one of those strange people. At the very least, this book can help you assist DBAs with the everyday tasks of running Oracle on popular Windows operating systems.

What an Oracle Database Is

This section answers the following questions you may have about an Oracle database system:

- RDBMS versus flat file systems
- Tasks of the RDBMS
- Components of the Oracle database
- Logical and physical database structure
- Common database terms

This section explains the basic features of an Oracle database system, what it is, and what it is not. You will compare the Oracle relational database management system, or RDBMS, to flat file systems and other methods historically used for data management. You will learn what tasks the RDBMS accomplishes. You will cover the components of an Oracle database as well. The section will touch on the logical and physical database structure of Oracle; and, finally, it will identify and define some basic database terms used in conjunction with Oracle.

For the first version of the OCP DBO exam, released March 1999, you are required to understand concepts presented in the "Oracle DBO Candidate Guide" available from Oracle Education at http://education.oracle.com/certification. Be sure you understand these concepts as they pertain to Oracle8 releases 8.0.3 to 8.0.6, SQL*Plus releases 3.3 to 8.0.6, Net8 releases 8.0.3 to 8.0.6, and Oracle Enterprise Manager up to release 1.6. Certain materials that pertain to Oracle Enterprise Manager Tuning Pack, Oracle Enterprise Manager Diagnostics Pack, and Oracle Expert are presented in this book, according to their usage in conjunction with Oracle8*i* release 8.1.5 and Oracle Enterprise Manager release 2.0.4—which shouldn't be a problem, as the usage of those tools in OEM 2.0.4 is similar to their usage in earlier versions of Enterprise Manager. To better assist you in preparing for evolving scenario-based and short-answer question types presented in the DBO exam, Chapter 10 covers approaches to answering those questions with hands-on examples.

RDBMS versus Flat File Systems

Software development companies have taken many different approaches to information management. In years gone by, the more popular software packages for data storage and retrieval focused on flat file systems as the storage means of choice, while simultaneously requiring you to define how information is stored and retrieved, using a programming language such as COBOL. Some early breeds of flat file systems included hierarchical storage systems, in which data records were stored in a hierarchy similar to the hierarchical directory structure you might see on your PC's hard drive in Windows Explorer. These applications ran on mainframes, and brand names of these older data management packages include IMS from IBM and IDMS from Computer Associates. The language most often used to develop mechanisms to add or manage data in those systems was COBOL.

Those older flat file systems were great for certain tasks like defining parent/child relationships. A parent/child relationship might include the relationship of salespeople within a food service distribution company to the company's customers, or the tracking number for an invoice as it relates to product line items on the customer's order from that food service distribution company. However, some drawbacks to flat file systems stem from the fact that a parent/child relationship cannot model. Within the food service company example, a customer's order may list many different products. Each of those products themselves will probably appear on many different orders. In this case of a "many products to many orders" relationship, which way should the hierarchy be designed? What should be the parent and what should be the child? The usual solution was to create two separate hierarchies, one with product as parent, the other with order as parent. Unfortunately, this often meant maintaining much of the same information in two places. Keeping data content consistent across multiple places where it is kept makes storage and retrieval complex. Another shortcoming of hierarchical databases using flat file systems is that they are not easily adaptable to changing business needs. If the food service distributor creates a new sales system that calls for joint ownership of customer accounts by multiple salespeople, the hierarchical database will need to be redesigned.

Motivated by dissatisfaction with the cumbersome characteristics of hierarchical flat file databases, E. F. Codd, a computer scientist working for IBM in the 1950s, developed an alternative: the *relational* model. Instead of storing data in hierarchies, Codd proposed storing related data items, such as control numbers and ordered products, in tables. If the tables were designed according to a few simple principles, Codd discovered, they were both intuitive and extremely efficient in storing data. A single data item could be stored in only one place. Over time, many software makers recognized the significance of Codd's work and began developing products that adhered to Codd's model. Since the 1980s, virtually all database software products (including Oracle's) conform to the relational model.

RDBMS versus Flat File System Quick Reference

Table 1-1 shows a quick comparison of flat file systems to relational database management systems.

For Review

Be sure you can describe the features, advantages, and disadvantages of flat file systems and relational database management systems.

Task	Flat File System	RDBMS
Handles parent/child data relationships?	Yes	Yes
Handles other types of data relationships?	Not well	Yes
Handles data manipulation easily?	No	Yes
Easily adaptable to changing business needs?	No	Yes
Handles data retrieval easily?	Sometimes	Yes
Handles data retrieval quickly?	Sometimes	Sometimes

TABLE 1-1. *Comparing Features of Flat File Systems to RDBMS*

Tasks of the RDBMS

Central to the success of the relational model is the use of a relational database management system, or RDBMS, for storing, retrieving, and manipulating data in a database. Earlier products required organizations to have many COBOL programmers on staff to code mechanisms for managing data retrieval routines that interact directly with the files of the database. In contrast, the RDBMS handles these tasks automatically using a functional programming language called SQL (pronounced either "sequel" or as the letters spelled out). SQL stands for "structured query language," and it allows users to request the data they want according to strict comparison criteria. The following code block shows a typical SQL statement:

```
SELECT EMPID, FIRSTNAME, SALARY FROM EMP WHERE LASTNAME = 'FARBISSINA';
```

Behind the scenes, an RDBMS translates this statement into a series of operations that retrieve the actual data from a file somewhere on the machine hosting your database. This step is called *parsing*. After parsing is complete, the RDBMS executes the series of operations to complete the requested action. That series of operations may involve some or all of the following tasks:

- Implicit datatype conversion
- Disk reads or disk writes
- Filtering table data according to search criteria
- Index lookups for faster response time
- Sorting and formatting data returned

TIP
An index is a special database object that can be used to enhance performance of certain RDBMS operations. You will learn more about indexes in Chapter 9.

For Review

Understand the tasks an RDBMS completes behind the scenes when users request certain pieces of data.

Components of the Oracle Database

Although every relational database offers an RDBMS that accepts basically the same types of SQL statements, not all databases have the same components. An Oracle database is considerably more complicated than some other databases you may have seen, such as Access or even SQL Server. The components of an Oracle database are broken into three basic areas, corresponding to the three basic areas of host machines that run Oracle databases. In this section, pay close attention to how each component in each part of the Oracle database interacts with a component in another part. Figure 1-1 illustrates the various elements of the Oracle database, while the following discussions identify and describe each component. The components are

- **Memory** The Oracle System Global Area, or SGA
- **Disk** Oracle datafiles, redo logs, control files, password files, and parameter files
- **CPU** Threads in the Oracle background process, and the server process.

Oracle SGA

Oracle's memory component, the System Global Area or SGA, consists of several elements, each of which is designed for a specific purpose.

BUFFER CACHE The buffer cache stores Oracle data in memory for users to view or change data. In this way, users never make changes directly to disk files. Instead, Oracle reads the appropriate data into memory for the user process to change, and writes the changes back to disk at some point later. Components of the buffer cache include the *keep pool* for persistent storage of data; the *recycle pool* for storage of data to be eliminated from memory quickly; and the *default pool*, which follows a modified *least-recently used* or *LRU* algorithm to determine when data in this area will be eliminated.

LOG BUFFER The log buffer stores special information called *redo*, which helps Oracle reconstruct data changes in the event of a system failure. Redo information is written to the log buffer by users making data changes and is stored in the log buffer until Oracle can write the redo information to disk.

SHARED POOL The shared pool stores many items that are "mission critical" to the operation of your Oracle database. Components of the shared pool include the *library cache* for storing parsed SQL statements for reuse by other users, the *dictionary* or *row cache* for storing Oracle data dictionary information in memory where it can be accessed quickly, and latches and other database control mechanisms.

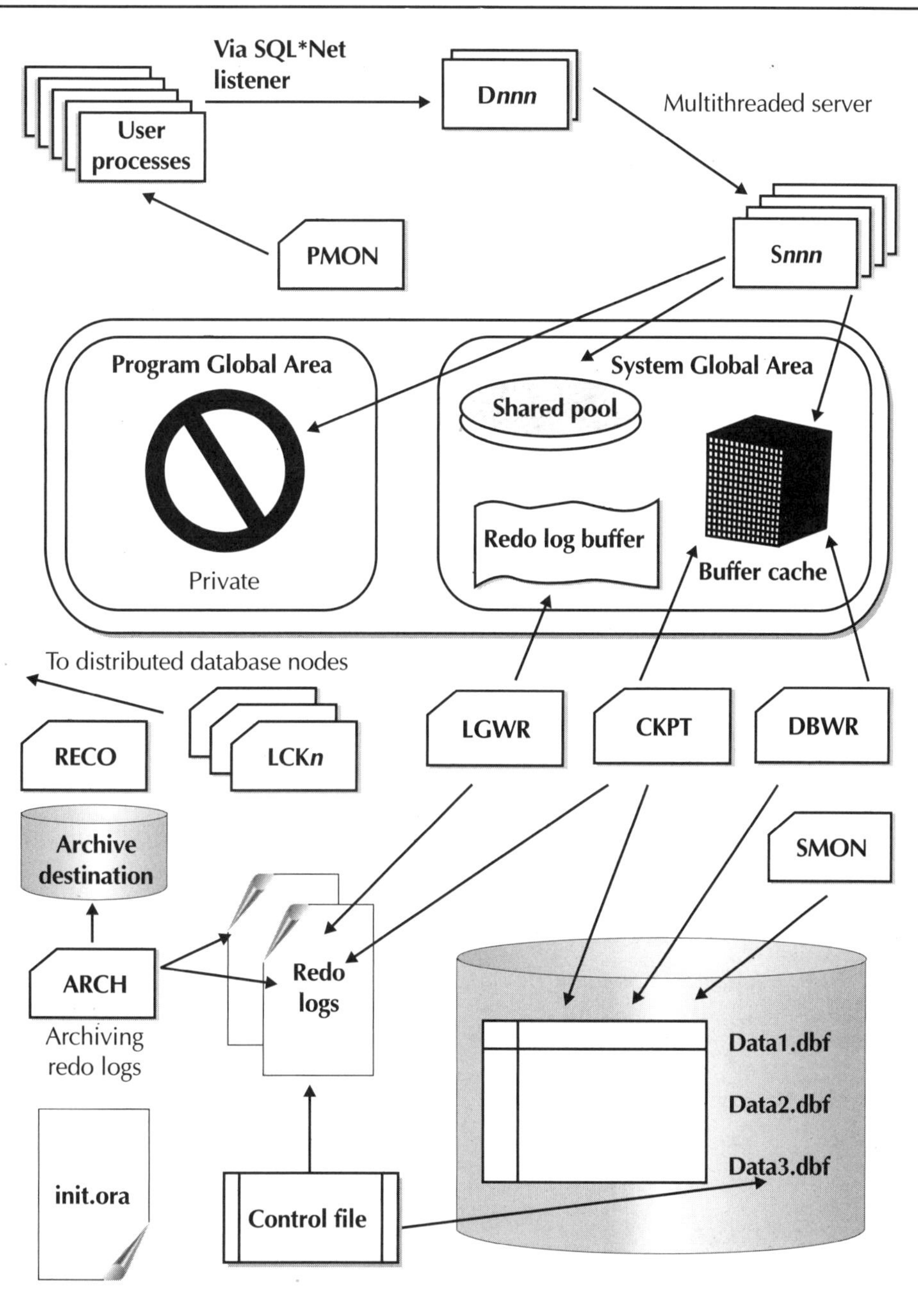

FIGURE 1-1. *Oracle server architecture*

TIP
The Oracle data dictionary is a set of information stored in Oracle that tells you all kinds of important things about your database. The data dictionary is used frequently by users and Oracle processes alike, so it is important for overall database performance to store dictionary information in memory when possible. Hence, you can see the need for the dictionary cache in your shared pool.

LARGE POOL The fourth and less-frequently used component of Oracle's SGA is the large pool, which is used to support parallel database operations and parallel database recovery. Introduced in Oracle8, this component is optional for Oracle database operation.

Oracle Disk Components

The Oracle disk components store all kinds of vital information in your Oracle database. You cannot run Oracle without having all your disk components (except password files) in their place.

DATAFILES This mandatory disk component is used for storing Oracle dictionary and application database objects. These components often grow extremely large in size. Information in the buffer cache and the dictionary cache in memory comes from datafiles on disk.

REDO LOGS This mandatory disk component is used for storing redo information on disk. Information from the log buffer in memory eventually gets written here.

CONTROL FILES This mandatory disk component is used for storing vital information about the location of Oracle disk components on the host system. The physical location of datafiles and redo logs in the server's file system are both stored in your control file. There can be one or many control files in an Oracle database. If there is more than one control file, each will be an identical copy. Oracle reads the control files every time you start the database and updates the control files when redo logs or datafiles are added or moved.

PASSWORD FILES This optional disk component is used for securing privileged user connection information to allow the database to be managed remotely via Enterprise Manager, Oracle's database management tool. Without a password file, you may only administer your database by connecting directly to the machine hosting the Oracle database and using management tools like Server Manager or SQL*Plus directly from the host machine.

PARAMETER FILES This mandatory disk component is used for configuring how Oracle will operate while it is running. The parameter file contains many parameters with values set for those parameters. Oracle reads the parameter file when you start the database. Some Oracle professionals refer to the parameter file as the `init.ora` file. You may maintain one or many parameter files for a database, corresponding to different instance configurations you may want to implement at various times.

Oracle Server and Background Process

The final components of Oracle to be covered are the set of elements that comprise Oracle on your host system's CPU. The Oracle server process reads data from datafiles into the buffer cache on behalf of user processes. It can either be shared between multiple users or be dedicated to one user. The Oracle database also has one background process in Windows environments—`oracle80.exe`. If you press CTRL-ALT-DELETE on your system hosting the Oracle database, click on the Task Manager button to bring up the Task Manager, and then click on the Processes tab, you will see this process running on your Windows machine. In Windows, this process has many threads that handle other important activities your database is engaged in at all times in the background. The following discussions identify those threads.

DBW0 This thread writes changed or "dirty" data blocks from the buffer cache to datafiles on disk at specified intervals (every three seconds) or whenever LGWR tells it to.

LGWR This thread writes redo information from the log buffer to redo logs on disk. This process is usually very busy on online transaction-processing systems because users are always making changes to data.

CKPT This thread helps LGWR perform key operations on the Oracle database when redo logs fill. For example, CKPT tells DBW0 to write dirty buffers to disk, and updates datafile headers when LGWR starts writing a fresh redo log.

ARCH This thread copies a filled redo log to an archive destination. By archiving redo logs, ARCH assists in allowing your Oracle database to be recoverable while simultaneously automating the activity of saving filled redo logs for later use during recovery. More information about backup, recovery, and archiving will be given in Chapter 6.

...his thread monitors server processes whose users may have ...nnected abnormally or died. If this happens, PMON performs cleanup activities and releases resources the dead process may have acquired.

SMON This thread periodically coalesces smaller chunks of free space in datafiles into larger chunks of free space, and also handles instance recovery after the Oracle database crashes.

For Review

Know the three components of the Oracle database, and be able to name each of the elements in each component.

Logical and Physical Database Structure

You have already covered the objects comprising the physical storage structure of your Oracle database. Now, you will cover the logical storage structure. The three elements of the logical storage structure of an Oracle database are *tablespaces, segments*, and *extents*. A tablespace is an area consisting of many Oracle datafiles in which users and Oracle can store application and dictionary database objects, such as tables. Segments are chunks of space in a tablespace used for storing the actual database object, be it a table or some other object. If, in the course of adding data to a table in the Oracle database, the segment runs out of space to store the data, it may allocate extra space called an *extent* for housing the overflow. A quick listing of the items comprising the logical and physical database structures of the Oracle database is shown here:

Logical Database Structures

- Tablespaces
- Segments
- Extents

Physical Database Structures

- Datafiles
- Redo logs
- Control files
- Password files
- Parameter files

The logical and physical database structures are closely intertwined. However, there are many subtle differences you should understand before proceeding as a DBO. Some elements of the logical database structure have physical database structure cousins, while others do not. The following list shows the elements of both logical and physical database structures and how they relate to one another.

Physical Database Structures	**Logical Database Structure**
■ Datafiles	■ Tablespaces
■ Data blocks	■ Segments Extents
■ Redo logs Control files Password files Parameter files	■ (No equivalent)

The relationship itself that exists between physical and logical database structures may be a one-to-many relationship or a one-to-one relationship. A "one-to-one" relationship means that, for every one unit of an item, there is one and only one unit of another. A good example of this relationship is human heads to human bodies—there is one and only one human body for every human head. A "one-to-many" relationship means that, for every one unit of an item, there could be one or more units of another item. A good example of one-to-many relationships is human hands to human fingers—for every one hand, there are one or many fingers. This relationship of one-to-one or one-to-many is called *ordinality*. The ordinality of the relationships that exist between logical and physical database structures is explained in the following bullets, and a diagram to help you interpret the inter-relationships between the following items appears in Figure 1-2.

- The relationship of tablespaces to datafiles is one-to-many because a tablespace is composed of one or more datafiles. Each datafile can belong to one and only one tablespace.
- Data blocks are subsets of datafiles. Each datafile will contain many data blocks, each of which is exactly the same size (usually 2K, 4K, 8K, or 16K, though sometimes larger).
- The relationship of segments and/or extents to data blocks is one-to-many because segments and extents are composed of one or more data blocks from the datafile.

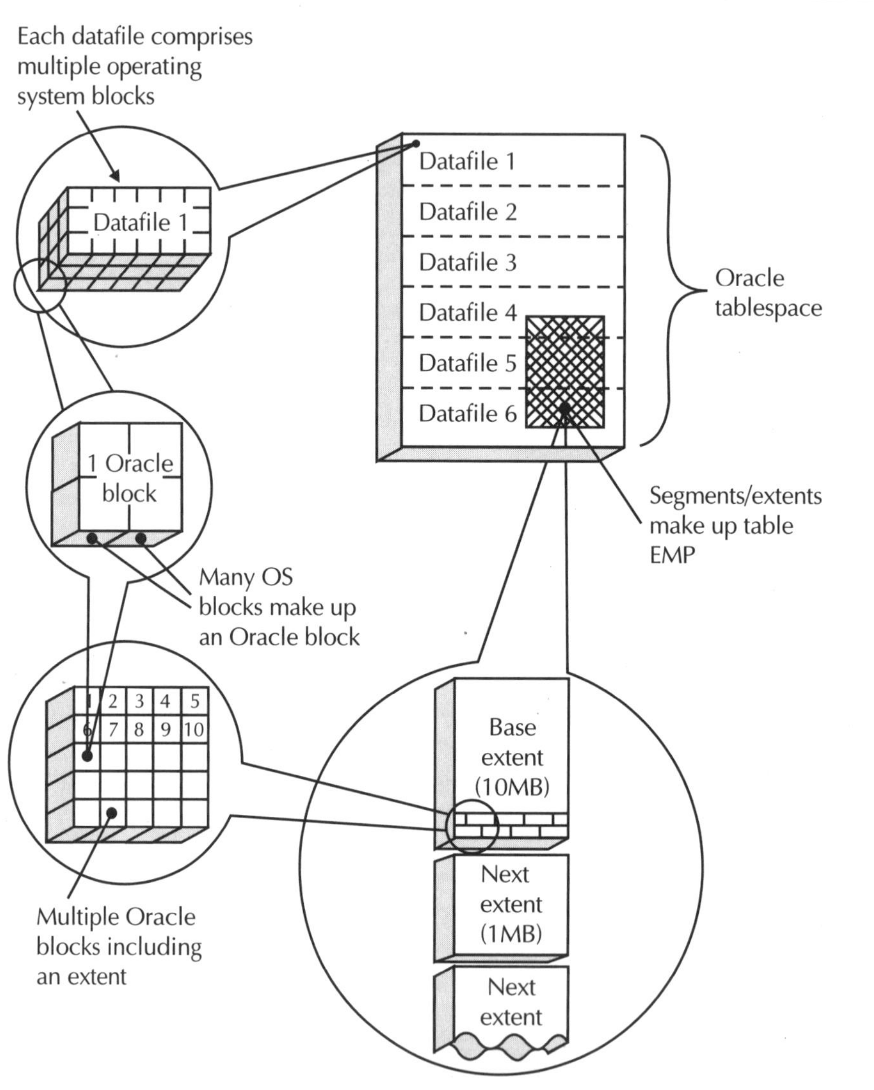

FIGURE 1-2. *Relationships among storage structures in an Oracle database*

For Review

1. Understand the elements composing the logical and physical database structures.
2. Be able to define which logical database objects correspond to which physical database objects.
3. Understand the ordinality of relationships between physical and logical database objects.

Common Database Terms

The following is a list of common terms you will encounter throughout this book, and in your activities as an operator of the Oracle database. The terms are broken out into conceptual areas. Each conceptual area is prefaced with a heading and short description.

Global Database Terms

The following terms should be understood in a global sense. You will use these terms frequently when talking about or describing Oracle databases at a high level.

- **Instance** A running Oracle database.
- **Oracle SID** The system identifier or unique name for an Oracle database on a host machine. Usually is the same as the global database name.
- **Host system** The Windows server machine on which the Oracle database resides.
- **OFA** Stands for "optimal flexible architecture" or "Oracle flexible architecture." Represents a standard for which the directory layout of your Oracle database installation should conform to ensure minimal difficulty for Oracle support and other entities in determining location of important files in your Oracle database.
- `init.ora` A special file containing initialization parameters that define how Oracle configures itself to run when the instance starts.
- **Trace file** Log files maintained by Oracle background processes and user processes. You can review the actions leading up to a process failure, or application performance, using the contents of a trace file.

- **ALERT file** A special log file maintained by Oracle to notify the DBO of system-wide events of interest, including database startup, shutdown, and errors.
- **Event** Something that occurs that causes change throughout the Oracle database, such as startup or shutdown.
- **Service** A mechanism in Enterprise Manager or the Windows operating system allowing automated execution of certain tasks.
- **OLTP** Stands for "online transaction processing," a type of database application where many users enter data into the database frequently.
- **DSS** Stands for "decision support system," a type of database application where a few users access mostly static historical data for reporting purposes. Commonly used DSS applications include data warehouses and data marts.

Oracle Processes

The following terms describe important running programs or *processes* in your Oracle database that you should be aware of.

- **Session** A user connection to the Oracle database.
- **Background process** A program executing behind the scenes taking care of key tasks for an operating Oracle instance.
- **Server process** A program executing on behalf of sessions connected to Oracle that actually obtain information from the database for the session.

Oracle Memory and Control Structures

The following terms describe aspects of memory structures that are important to know about in Oracle as the DBO for your database.

- **SGA** The System Global Area, Oracle's memory component.
- **V$ views** A special set of views containing data about a running Oracle instance.
- **Locks** Elements in the Oracle database that ensure that only one user at a time can make a change to any particular item of data.
- **Latches** Elements in the Oracle database that manage or restrict usage of key items in the database, such as memory or other system resources.

Users and Privileges

The following terms relate to users and privilege management. This topic is covered extensively in Chapter 5.

- **User** An ID for someone who can access the Oracle database.
- **Authentication** Use of password or other secure information to ensure that only one user can access Oracle via a particular ID.
- **Role** A database object to which privileges can be granted, that allows for simplified privilege management.
- **Schema** A logical grouping of database objects according to the user owning the objects.
- **SYS** An Oracle-generated user that owns key resources in the Oracle database, including dictionary views, tables, `V$` views, and Oracle-supplied packages.
- **INTERNAL** A special privileged alias for the SYS user that is commonly used to start and stop the Oracle database.
- **`sysdba`** A privileged role granted to database users allowed to start and stop the Oracle database.
- **SYSTEM** An Oracle-generated user that owns key resources in the Oracle database, such as tool repositories.

Database Objects

The following terms are objects that exist in Oracle databases. You will learn more about these objects throughout the text.

- **Table** An object in the Oracle database akin to a spreadsheet, containing rows and columns of data.
- **Index** An object in the Oracle database that allows high-speed access to table information.
- **Sequence** An object in Oracle that generates numbers.
- **Rollback segment** An object in the Oracle database that stores data changes prior to the end of a transaction, allowing users to discard changes made, and to provide read-consistent versions of data for long-running transactions.

- **Constraints** Objects in Oracle that ensure data entering the database conforms to a specified set of rules.
- **Data dictionary** A set of tables and views in the Oracle database owned by the SYS user, which contains key information about the contents of the Oracle database.
- `catalog.sql` A file run by user SYS when a database is created that generates objects in the data dictionary.
- **Oracle-supplied packages** Special PL/SQL blocks provided with the Oracle software release that allow you to perform advanced operations in the database.
- `catproc.sql` A file run by user SYS when a database is created that generates Oracle-supplied packages and other items used in PL/SQL.
- **DDL** SQL statements in Oracle that allow creation, change, and removal of tables, indexes, and other objects.
- **DML** SQL statements in Oracle that allow creation, change, and removal of data in tables.
- **Data load** An occurrence in which a large amount of new information is introduced into an Oracle database using a tool or process.

Backup, Recovery, and Archiving

The following terms apply to Oracle backup, recovery, and archiving transaction information. Concepts identified here are described in detail in Chapter 6.

- `archivelog` A mode for running your Oracle database that allows recovery of data up to the point in time of database failure.
- **Backup** A spare copy of an Oracle database used for ensuring that database failure does not cause user data to be lost.
- **System crash** An event when the Oracle database terminates abnormally, possibly leading to data loss and the need for system recovery.
- **Recovery** The act of re-creating an Oracle database using backup information when the database is lost or corrupted for any reason.
- **RMAN** A tool that handles backup and recovery for Oracle databases.

Management Tools and Tasks

The following terms describe Oracle management tools and tasks that will be described and used extensively throughout the text.

- **Oracle Enterprise Manager** Sometimes referred to as OEM, this is the tool for managing and administering your Oracle database.
- **Repository** A set of database objects created and maintained by tools like Oracle Enterprise Manager that help the tool perform its job.
- **Database Assistant** A graphical interface tool used for creating Oracle databases.
- **Tuning** The act of adjusting Oracle's configuration so that the database runs faster.
- **Oracle Expert** An OEM tool used for high-level tuning. The tool is available with the purchase of the Oracle Enterprise Manager Tuning Pack.

Oracle Networking

The following terms apply to Oracle networking tools, processes, and components. Configuring Oracle networking is covered extensively in Chapter 3.

- **Net8** An Oracle software product that ensures connectivity between users and the Oracle database.
- **Net8 Assistant** A graphical interface tool used for configuring Oracle networking.
- **Net8 Easy Config** A graphical interface tool used for configuring locally managed database network name resolution.
- `tnsnames.ora` A file stored locally on an Oracle client used for local management of database network name resolution.

For Review

Be able to define all the terms given in this section.

Tools for Accessing Oracle

This section shows you the tools used for accessing the Oracle database:

- SQL and PL/SQL: an introduction
- Oracle has a tool for everyone

So far, you have seen the Oracle that handles data management for you behind the scenes. You may, at this point, still be unfamiliar with the face of an Oracle database and the language it speaks. You may even consider yourself a stranger in a strange land of software, wandering through a desert of bits and bytes swirling around you like sand in the Kashmir, or else perhaps a driving blizzard in the Yukon. This section will change that. In this section, you will learn to recognize some familiar faces of Oracle usage. You will also learn the language an Oracle database speaks. The material in this chapter will lay a foundation for later work you will accomplish throughout the book. First, you will learn the basic components of the languages of Oracle: SQL, PL/SQL, and, increasingly, Java. This foundation will be expanded in Chapters 8 and 9. Second, you will cover the tools different users employ for working with the Oracle database, depending on their job role. Pay particular attention to the tool used by DBOs and DBAs in this discussion—Oracle Enterprise Manager. You will cover this tool extensively throughout the rest of the book.

SQL and PL/SQL: An Introduction

Historically, two languages have been used in the operation and usage of an Oracle database. They are SQL and PL/SQL. You have already been lightly exposed to SQL, the functional programming language the Oracle RDBMS understands and translates into operations for extracting data from the Oracle database according to user requests. You will learn more about actually coding in SQL in Chapters 8 and 9 of this book. There are four basic subsets of commands in SQL for performing operations in the Oracle database. They are

- **DDL operations** These are commands used for creating, redefining, or removing objects from the Oracle database, such as tables or other objects.
- **DML operations** These are commands used for creating, redefining, or removing data from objects like tables in the Oracle database.
- **DCL operations** These are special commands for data access, control, and management in the Oracle database.
- **Queries** Commands used for retrieving data from the Oracle database.

PL/SQL: SQL's Programmatic Extension

Oracle also uses a language that adds many programmatic extensions to SQL, like `if-then` commands, looping constructs, and variable declarations. This language is called PL/SQL and is roughly equivalent to T-SQL in SQL Server, though PL/SQL is far more powerful. There are two basic types of PL/SQL "blocks," or listings of code. They are *named PL/SQL blocks* and *unnamed* or *anonymous PL/SQL blocks.* The rest of the discussion identifies the differences between the two, with some examples.

TIP

Don't worry if you don't understand everything that the PL/SQL code block examples are doing in this section. You won't be tested on the specifics of coding PL/SQL on the OCP DBO exam. The code blocks are provided for example purposes only.

Named PL/SQL: Procedures, Functions, Triggers, and Packages

Named blocks or modules of PL/SQL code are blocks of code that can be stored and referenced by name by other PL/SQL blocks, or by the user from the SQL*Plus command line. When you submit a named block of code to Oracle, the database will parse and compile the block, and store it associated to the name you gave the block. You can run the block later by referencing it by name in another PL/SQL block, or by using the `execute` command in SQL*Plus. For example, if you had a named PL/SQL procedure called `money_converter( )`, you could execute it in SQL*Plus as follows:

```
SQL> execute money_converter;
```

Named blocks of PL/SQL code are divided into four categories. Those categories are stored procedures, functions, packages, and triggers. The four types of named PL/SQL code blocks are described in the following paragraphs, and examples are given to show you what these different code blocks look like.

PROCEDURE A *procedure* is a named block of PL/SQL code that consists of a series of statements accepting and/or returning zero or more variables.

```
PROCEDURE money_converter
(amount         IN NUMBER,
from_currency   IN VARCHAR2,
to_currency     IN VARCHAR2,
return_val      IN OUT NUMBER
```

```
) IS    /* denotes beginning of declaration section. */
   my_new_amt number(10) := 0;
   bad_data exception;
BEGIN    /* begins the executable section of a code block. */
     IF my_new_amt > 3 THEN
       DBMS_OUTPUT.PUT_LINE('Do this');
     ELSE
       DBMS_OUTPUT.PUT_LINE('Do that');
     END IF;
     return_val := my_new_amt;
EXCEPTION  /*Begins the Exception Handler */
     WHEN bad_data THEN
       DBMS_OUTPUT.PUT_LINE('Error condition');
END;
```

FUNCTION A *function* is a named block of PL/SQL code that consists of a series of statements accepting zero or more variables and returning one value.

```
FUNCTION convert_money
(amount           IN NUMBER,
from_currency     IN VARCHAR2,
to_currency       IN VARCHAR2
) RETURN NUMBER IS    /* denotes beginning of declaration section. */
   my_new_amt number(10) := 0;
   bad_data exception;
BEGIN    /* begins the executable section of a code block. */
     IF my_new_amt > 3 THEN
       DBMS_OUTPUT.PUT_LINE('Do this');
     ELSE
       DBMS_OUTPUT.PUT_LINE('Do that');
     END IF;
     RETURN my_new_amt;
EXCEPTION  /*Begins the Exception Handler */
     WHEN bad_data THEN
       DBMS_OUTPUT.PUT_LINE('Error condition');
END;
```

PACKAGE A *package* is a named block of PL/SQL code that consists of a collection of named procedures and functions and has two parts. The first part is a *specification*, listing available procedures and functions and their parameters, constants, and user-defined type declarations. The second part is a *body*, containing the actual code for the procedures and functions.

```
-- Package Specification
CREATE OR REPLACE PACKAGE money_pkg IS
/************/
  EOF constant varchar2(30) := '~~+~~+~~';
/************/
  FUNCTION convert_money
  (amount          IN NUMBER,
   from_currency   IN VARCHAR2,
   to_currency     IN VARCHAR2
  ) RETURN NUMBER;
/************/
  PROCEDURE money_converter
  (amount          IN NUMBER,
   from_currency   IN VARCHAR2,
   to_currency     IN VARCHAR2,
   return_val      IN OUT NUMBER
  );
/************/
END;

-- Package Body
CREATE OR REPLACE PACKAGE BODY money_pkg IS
/************/
 FUNCTION convert_money
  (amount          IN NUMBER,
   from_currency   IN VARCHAR2,
   to_currency     IN VARCHAR2
  ) RETURN NUMBER
 IS   /* denotes beginning of declaration section. */
     my_new_amt number(10) := 0;
     bad_data exception;
  BEGIN   /* begins the executable section of a code block. */
    IF my_new_amt > 3 THEN
      DBMS_OUTPUT.PUT_LINE('Do this');
    ELSE
      DBMS_OUTPUT.PUT_LINE('Do that');
    END IF;
    RETURN my_new_amt;
```

```
  EXCEPTION  /*Begins the Exception Handler */
    WHEN bad_data THEN
      DBMS_OUTPUT.PUT_LINE('Error condition');
 END;
/***************/
  PROCEDURE money_converter
  ( amount          IN NUMBER,
    from_currency   IN VARCHAR2,
    to_currency     IN VARCHAR2,
    return_val      IN OUT NUMBER
  ) IS   /* denotes beginning of declaration section. */
   my_new_amt number(10) := 0;
   bad_data exception;
  BEGIN   /* begins the executable section of a code block. */
    IF my_new_amt > 3 THEN
      DBMS_OUTPUT.PUT_LINE('Do this');
    ELSE
      DBMS_OUTPUT.PUT_LINE('Do that');
    END IF;
    return_val := my_new_amt;
  EXCEPTION  /*Begins the Exception Handler */
    WHEN bad_data THEN
      DBMS_OUTPUT.PUT_LINE('Error condition');
  END;
/************/
END;
```

TRIGGER A *trigger* is a named block of PL/SQL code that consists of a series of PL/SQL statements attached to a database table. Whenever a triggering event (a DML statement such as `update`, `insert`, `delete`, which you'll learn more about in Chapter 9) occurs, the event's corresponding trigger will occur. For example, an `update` trigger will fire whenever an `update` statement occurs, but not when an `insert` statement occurs. Triggers can be defined to fire once for an entire table when the triggering event occurs, or for each row modified by the triggering event. Triggers can also be set to fire only when one column in a row changes.

```
CREATE OR REPLACE TRIGGER rate_hist_trigger_01
BEFORE delete ON exch_rate
BEGIN
   INSERT INTO exch_rate_hist (chg_user, chg_date_time, comment)
   VALUES (user, to_char(sysdate,'YYYY-MM-DD HH:MIAM'),
          'Exchange rates removed from table on this date');
END;
```

Anonymous PL/SQL Blocks

In addition to named blocks of PL/SQL, you can have unnamed or anonymous PL/SQL blocks. An anonymous PL/SQL block is the second type of code block, consisting of several PL/SQL commands that are submitted to Oracle for parsing and execution all at the same time. Anonymous blocks are not stored in the Oracle database the way named blocks are. Instead, Oracle parses and executes the statements when you submit the block. The following code listing contains an anonymous PL/SQL block:

```
DECLARE /* begins the declaration section in an anonymous block */
    my_convert_amt          NUMBER(10);
    my_convert_currency     VARCHAR2(5);
    my_old_currency         VARCHAR2(5);
    bad_data                EXCEPTION;
BEGIN /* begins the executable section of a code block. */
IF my_convert_amt=6 THEN
     . . .
    ELSE
     . . .
    END IF;
EXCEPTION  /*Begins the Exception Handler */
    WHEN bad_data THEN
      DBMS_OUTPUT.PUT_LINE('Error condition');
END;
```

For Review

1. Be able to identify the types of SQL statements defined in this section.
2. Be able to identify the different types of named PL/SQL blocks, and understand what an anonymous block is.

Oracle Has a Tool for Everyone

There are tools available from Oracle for handling virtually every aspect of database usage and management, regardless of what role you play in the organization. Those tools, and examples of what the tools look like, are given in this section.

Tools for Designers

Designers of applications using Oracle databases have tools at their disposal for doing their job of data modeling and system design. The primary tools available from Oracle for this purpose are Oracle*CASE and Designer. Figure 1-3 shows a screen shot of Designer for Windows.

Tools for Developers

Application developers also have a wealth of tools at their disposal for coding robust and thin-client applications and reports designed by application designers. These tools include Developer and JDeveloper. Figure 1-4 shows a screen shot of Developer. Furthermore, Oracle also makes available plenty of runtime environments and precompilers for programming languages for developing applications that integrate well with Oracle. Those runtime environments include the PL/SQL engine and the Java Runtime Environment. The precompilers include Pro*C, SQL*J, Pro*COBOL, Pro*Fortran, and Pro*Ada.

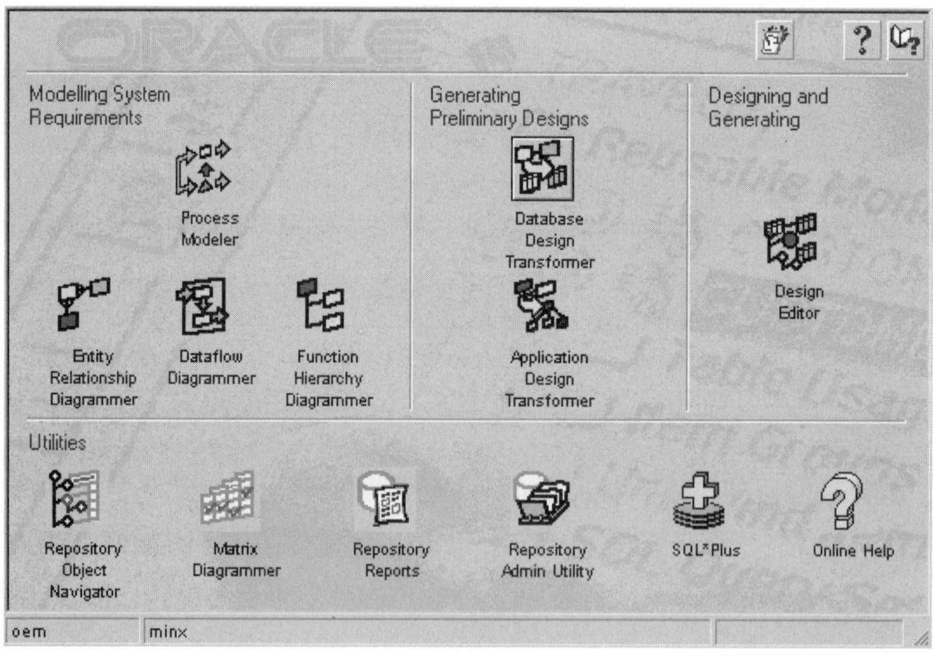

FIGURE 1-3. *Designer for Windows*

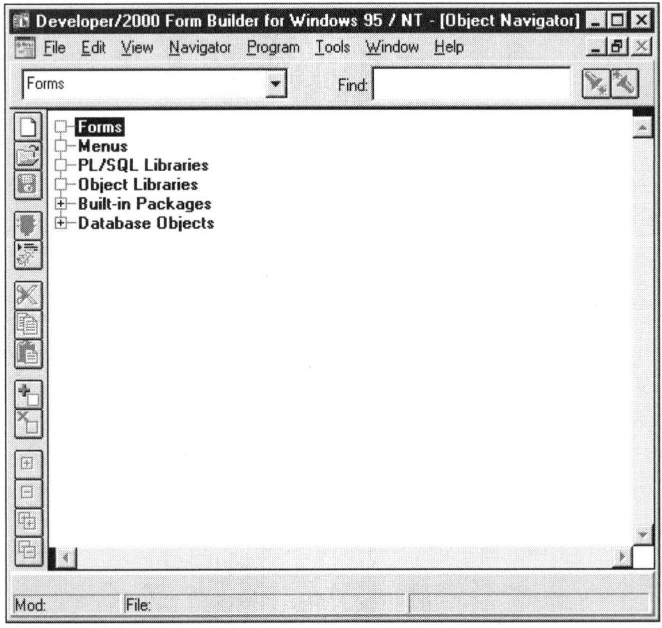

FIGURE 1-4. *Developer for Windows*

Tools for End Users

There are a myriad of tools for end users of Oracle databases. Many of those tools are developed by designers and developers using tools already mentioned. However, Oracle also makes a special tool available for viewing data in tables directly. This tool is called SQL*Plus. Figure 1-5 shows SQL*Plus in action.

```
SQL*Plus: Release 8.0.5.0.0 - Production on Sun Sep 19 15:7:13 1999

(c) Copyright 1998 Oracle Corporation.  All rights reserved.


Connected to:
Oracle8i Enterprise Edition Release 8.1.5.0.0 - Production
With the Partitioning and Java options
PL/SQL Release 8.1.5.0.0 - Production

SQL>
```

FIGURE 1-5. *SQL*Plus for Windows*

Tools for DBAs and DBOs

The final set of tools to consider are the database management tools available for DBAs and DBOs to administer an Oracle database. By far, the most powerful of all these tools is Oracle Enterprise Manager, Oracle's graphical interface tool for administration tasks. Figure 1-6 shows the Enterprise Manager console. Also available for database administrative tasks are Server Manager and SQL*Plus. These tools are also powerful, though somewhat more difficult to use because they require the user to perform administrative tasks using commands issued at a command-line prompt. Typically, only more experienced users will employ these tools.

For Review

Be able to identify on sight the tools that Oracle makes available for designers, developers, end users, DBAs, and DBOs.

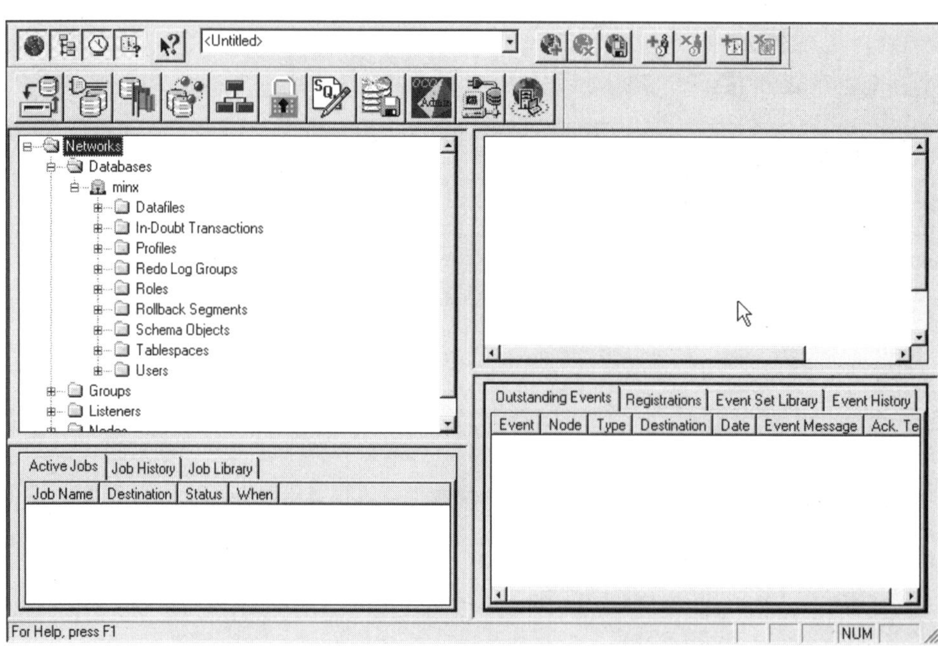

FIGURE 1-6. *Oracle Enterprise Manager console*

Role of the DBO

This section will explain the duties of the Oracle database operator:

- Main DBO job tasks
- Where to find other Oracle products

Okay, so now you probably know at least what an Oracle database is, and how people work with it. Now what? Well, as my father used to say, now you get your marching orders. This section explains the main tasks a DBO accomplishes in an organization. Be aware, however, that your experience may differ—just as Windows is a relative newcomer to the world of server operations, the DBO role in Oracle database operation is also comparatively new. Next, you will cover other tools that can be used in conjunction with Oracle technology. These other technologies do not come bundled with Oracle database software, so not every organization may have the products identified and described here.

Main DBO Tasks

You may think of the work done by a DBO as a scaled-down version of the work performed by DBAs. Typically, the difference between the job of the DBO and that of the DBA is that a DBO handles more operational procedures, and a DBA handles more strategic efforts. The main tasks DBOs perform on Oracle databases are listed and defined in the following bullets of this section. They are

- Install Oracle software, including Oracle Server, Net8, OEM, and SQL*Plus.
- Create Oracle databases and services on Windows, including password files.
- Monitor the database operation by reviewing critical trace files and ALERT logs.
- Start and stop the Oracle database.
- Implement logical and physical structures in the Oracle database.
- Set up users for applications.
- Create objects to store application data.
- Secure application data manipulation.
- Back up and recover the Oracle database.
- Load data into Oracle databases.

- Perform basic troubleshooting activities and set up alerts.
- Solve blocking situations.
- Perform basic performance tuning with Oracle Expert.
- Understand how to formulate basic SQL queries in SQL*Plus.
- Understand how to formulate basic SQL DML and DDL in SQL*Plus.

For Review

Be sure you can identify the tasks normally associated with the role of the DBO in Oracle.

Where to Find Other Oracle Products

Oracle offers many advanced products for managing and using your Oracle database besides the ones already identified. For example, Oracle Enterprise Manager comes with a basic Management Pack that includes some useful tools like Oracle TopSessions and Oracle Performance Monitor for tuning and monitoring the operation of your Oracle database. However, more advanced tuning tools such as Oracle Expert, which is a component tested on the OCP DBO exam, is available only as optional add-on software in the OEM Tuning Pack from Oracle, purchased under separate license. Other management products are available for Oracle as well. You may find other software useful for the purpose of managing your organization's databases at the Oracle Web site at www.oracle.com.

For Review

Understand the difference between the basic Management Pack and Tuning Pack available in conjunction with Oracle Enterprise Manager.

Chapter Summary

This chapter introduced many important areas of administering the Oracle database. You learned what an Oracle database is, and what differences exist between the Oracle RDBMS and a flat file system. You also covered the tasks handled by the Oracle RDBMS, and how the RDBMS simplifies many activities formerly engaged in by programmers. You defined the components of an Oracle database, including memory, CPU, and disk components, and learned how to distinguish the logical database components from the physical database components. A dictionary of important terms was given for your information as well.

This chapter also defined the SQL and PL/SQL languages. You learned about the different subsets of SQL, and what the differences between them are. You also learned about named and anonymous PL/SQL blocks, and what the four types of named PL/SQL blocks are. Then, the chapter covered the various tools available for designers, developers, end users, DBAs, and DBOs, showing you what the various applications look like. The final area covered in this chapter was a listing of the main tasks for a DBO and a brief explanation of the other software that you might need to administer your Oracle database.

Two-Minute Drill

- Advantages of the Oracle RDBMS over flat file systems include
  - Easier to change system in the event of changing business requirements
  - Flexibility to model data relationships other than parent/child
  - Permits easier data manipulation and retrieval using SQL
- The RDBMS in an Oracle database handles the following tasks:
  - Implicit datatype conversion
  - Disk reads or disk writes
  - Filtering table data according to search criteria
  - Index lookups for faster response time
  - Sorting and formatting data returned
- The memory components of an Oracle database include the Oracle System Global Area, or SGA, consisting of
  - Buffer cache for storing data requested by and changed by users
  - Redo log buffer for storing redo information generated by user data changes
  - Shared pool for storing dictionary information, parsed SQL statements, latches, and other mission-critical database control mechanisms
  - Large pool for supporting parallel SQL and recovery operations
- Components of the buffer cache include the keep pool, recycle pool, and default pool. Data is phased out of the buffer cache using a modified LRU algorithm.

- The disk components of the Oracle database include
  - Datafiles for storing application and dictionary data
  - Redo logs for storing redo information
  - Control files for storing physical database layout on host system
  - Password files for storing authentication information for remote system administration
  - Parameter files (sometimes called `init.ora`) for startup configuration of the Oracle database.
- Oracle's CPU components include server processes for obtaining data for user processes from datafiles and one background process for executing various tasks to keep Oracle running.
- The threads handled by the Oracle background process in Windows environments include
  - DBW0 for writing data changes from buffer cache to datafiles
  - LGWR for writing redo information from log buffer to redo logs
  - CKPT for assisting LGWR in performing tasks associated with when an online redo log fills.
  - ARCH for copying filled redo log information to the archive destination.
  - PMON for handling user process and/or associated server process failure and cleanup.
  - SMON for coalescing free space in datafiles and for instance recovery after instance failure.
- Logical database components in the Oracle database include
  - Tablespaces for storing database objects like tables
  - Segments and extents for housing actual data in database objects like tables

- Logical and physical database components map into each other in the following ways:
  - The relationship of tablespaces to datafiles is one-to-many because a tablespace is composed of one or more datafiles. Each datafile can belong to one and only one tablespace.
  - Data blocks are subsets of datafiles. Each datafile will contain many data blocks, each of which is exactly the same size (usually 2K, 4K, 8K, or 16K, though sometimes larger).
  - The relationship of segments and/or extents to data blocks is one-to-many because segments and extents are composed of one or more data blocks from the datafile.
- Review and *be sure you understand all* of the common database terms provided in this chapter for the OCP DBO exam.
- SQL is the language used by Oracle users to communicate what data they would like to see, create, change, or remove from the Oracle database. These are DML commands and queries.
- SQL also contains commands that allow you to create, change, or remove database objects like tables, and commands for managing the database. These are DCL and DDL commands.
- PL/SQL is Oracle's programmatic extension to SQL, allowing you to code control structures, loops, and variable declarations around SQL operations.
- Two types of PL/SQL blocks are available in Oracle—named blocks and anonymous blocks.
- The four types of named PL/SQL blocks are procedures, functions, packages, and triggers.
- There are many different tools available to the various types of users in the Oracle database, including the following:
  - **Designers** Oracle*CASE, Designer
  - **Developers** Developer, Pro*C, Pro*COBOL, Pro*Ada, Pro*Fortran, SQL*J, PL/SQL
  - **End users** Applications developed using previously listed tools, SQL*Plus
  - **DBAs and DBOs** Oracle Enterprise Manager, Server Manager, SQL*Plus

- The main tasks of a DBO include
  - Install Oracle software, including Oracle Server, Net8, OEM, and SQL*Plus.
  - Create Oracle databases and services on Windows, including password files.
  - Monitor the database operation by reviewing critical trace files and ALERT logs.
  - Start and stop the Oracle database.
  - Implement logical and physical structures in the Oracle database.
  - Set up users for applications.
  - Create objects to store application data.
  - Secure application data manipulation.
  - Back up and recover the Oracle database.
  - Load data into Oracle databases.
  - Perform basic troubleshooting activities and set up alerts.
  - Solve blocking situations.
  - Perform basic performance tuning with Oracle Expert.
  - Understand how to formulate basic SQL queries in SQL*Plus.
  - Understand how to formulate basic SQL DML and DDL in SQL*Plus.

Chapter Questions

1. **Look at the application shown in Figure 1-7. Figure 1-7 shows the application graphical user interface tool used primarily by which of the following types of database users:**

   A. Designers

   B. End users

   C. Developers

   D. DBOs

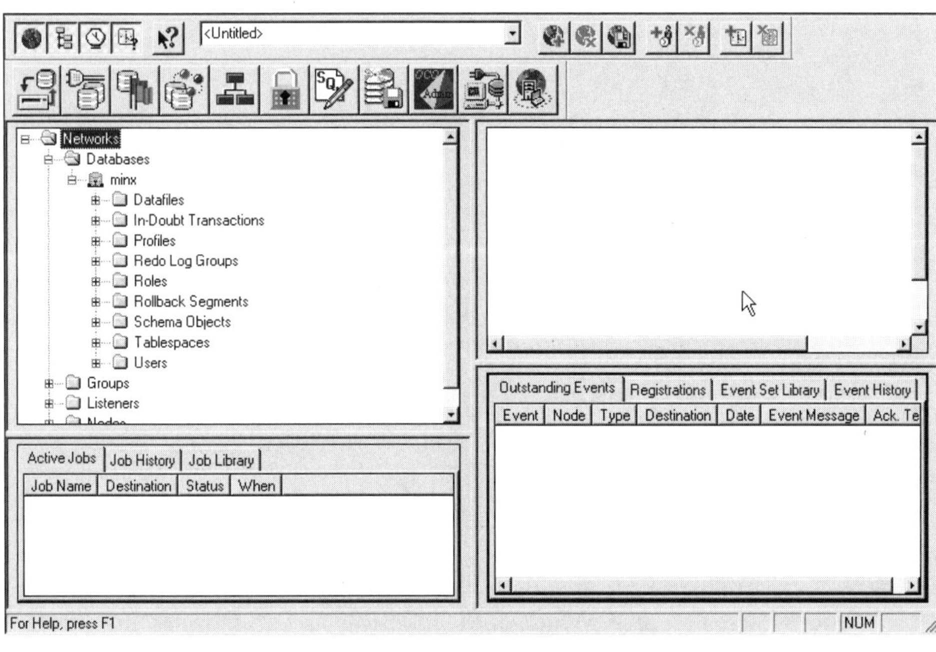

FIGURE 1-7. *Exhibit for Question 1*

2. **You are a DBO determining the tasks you will need to perform as part of your job description. Which three of the following choices may apply? (Choose three.)**

   A. Design logical data models for applications.

   B. Back up the Oracle database.

   C. Write applications in Pro*C.

   D. Debug a Developer report.

   E. Install drivers for Java-based applications to run against Oracle.

   F. Create a tuning session with Oracle Expert to determine performance bottlenecks.

   G. Develop a routine in PL/SQL that sends invoices to a payroll application.

3. You are attempting to identify the uses for SQL on your Oracle database. Which of the following choices identify a component of SQL?

A. Control structures for looping

B. Methods for variable declaration

C. `If-then` statements

D. `create table` statements

4. You are associating physical database components with logical database components in your Oracle8 database. Which of the following choices identifies the physical component of Oracle that maps to extents?

A. Blocks

B. Datafiles

C. Segments

D. Parameters

5. You are attempting to determine the location of certain files pertaining to your Oracle database. Which of the following terms identifies a set of standards that simplifies the task of determining where Oracle database files reside across many different host systems?

A. SGA

B. OFA

C. SID

D. SYS

6. Which of the following tasks does the developer of an application not have to worry about when using a relational database management system or RDBMS to handle data storage on behalf of that application?

A. Handling user login and authentication

B. Locating data on disks

C. Reading data into memory

D. Parsing SQL statements

7. You are determining what products are necessary for successful application usage in conjunction with an Oracle database environment. Which of the following products are required to ensure connectivity between an Oracle Forms application running on a client machine and the database running on a server?

A. Oracle8 Server

B. Net8

C. Oracle Enterprise Manager

D. Developer

E. Designer

8. You are attempting to identify components of an Oracle database. Which part of Oracle does the dictionary cache reside in?

A. Datafile

B. Redo log

C. Oracle background process

D. SGA

E. LGWR thread

Answers to Chapter Questions

1. D. DBOs

Explanation The tool in Figure 1-7 is Oracle Enterprise Manager, Oracle's tool for administering the Oracle database. This tool is used primarily by DBOs and DBAs for execution of tasks like backup and recovery, creating new database objects, startup and shutdown of the database, and so on. Choice A is incorrect because the tool used primarily by designers is Designer or Oracle*CASE, while choice B is incorrect because the tool used by end users is SQL*Plus or a tool developed by a developer. Developers use any of the development suites available from Oracle like Developer or JDeveloper, or any of the programming languages or precompilers available with the Oracle server, eliminating choice C.

2. B, E, *and* F.

Explanation DBOs handle tasks like backup and recovery, installation of new software components, and tuning with Oracle Expert. Thus, choices B, E, and F are all correct answers. Logical data models are the domain of database designers and sometimes DBAs, eliminating choice A. Writing applications in Pro*C, debugging reports written in Developer, or developing routines in PL/SQL to handle application functionality are all the domain of developers, making choices C, D, and E wrong.

3. D. `create table` statements

Explanation SQL is used for creating, modifying, and removing database objects like tables, as well as creating, modifying, and removing data from those objects. The two subsets for these purposes are DDL and DML, respectively. The `create table` statement falls within the realm of DDL, so it is a SQL statement. Control structures for looping, methods for variable declaration, and `if-then` statements are all part of PL/SQL, Oracle's programmatic extension to SQL, which makes choices A, B, and C all incorrect.

4. A. Blocks

Explanation The physical database component that corresponds to both extents and segments is the data block, which is an atomic unit of measure of datafiles in your Oracle database. Datafiles themselves map to tablespaces on the logical database structure side, however, making choice B incorrect. Segments themselves are part of the logical database structure, so choice C is wrong as well. Finally, while parameters define the size of Oracle data blocks, parameters are not the part of the physical database configuration that actually maps to segments and extents, so choice D is incorrect.

5. B. OFA

Explanation OFA stands for "optimal flexible architecture," and it is Oracle's set of standards for ensuring that DBOs can easily locate files on different Oracle databases, even if the DBO didn't set up the Oracle database. SGA stands for "System Global Area," Oracle's memory component, making choice A incorrect. SID is the Oracle system identifier, the unique name for the Oracle database on that host machine. This does nothing to help locate database files, so choice C is also wrong. Finally, SYS is a privileged user of the Oracle database created when you create your database. Although you could log in to Oracle and look up the location of important database files in the Oracle data dictionary, knowledge of and conformity to the OFA is by far the easiest way to locate Oracle files on a server. Thus, choice D is incorrect as well.

6. A. Handling user login and authentication

Explanation Developers of applications that use relational databases are spared the torture of coding many low-level operations required for flat file systems and hierarchical databases from years gone by. These operations include choices B, C, and D, so those choices are incorrect. However, the developer of the application still needs to provide some way for users of the application to log in to Oracle in order to view and manipulate data, so choice A is correct.

7. B. Net8

Explanation Net8 is the software component used for connectivity between clients and servers in an Oracle network application. Oracle8 Server is the actual database software that runs on the server to store the data for an application. No connectivity is provided strictly with that tool; however, most Oracle8 distributions include Net8, even though it is a separate product. Thus, choice A is incorrect. Oracle Enterprise Manager is used for database administration, and itself usually needs Oracle Net8 to be installed for connectivity purposes, thus making choice C incorrect. Both Designer and Developer need Net8 in order to connect to the database, so choices D and E are wrong as well.

8. D. SGA

Explanation The dictionary cache is part of the Oracle shared pool on the Oracle server, which in turn is part of the System Global Area or SGA, Oracle's memory component. Datafiles and redo logs are disk components of Oracle, and thus choices A and B are incorrect. Oracle background processes and the LGWR thread are both CPU components of Oracle, thus making choices C and E incorrect as well.

CHAPTER 2

Oracle Installation and Configuration

n this chapter, you will cover the following fundamentals of using Oracle products:

- Installing Oracle database software
- Creating Oracle databases and services
- Locating Oracle files on your machine

Oracle often has been compared to the Jann, or Genie, from the story of Alladin and the magic lamp in *1001 Arabian Nights,* translated by Captain Sir Richard Francis Burton. This is because your wish for data storage and retrieval is Oracle's command. It would be great if all you had to do to set up Oracle was rub on the side of your computer with a handful of sand, but unfortunately, setup is a little more complex than that. In this chapter, you will learn how to install Oracle database software for the Windows platform. You will also learn how to create an Oracle database and automate Oracle startup and shutdown via Windows services. Finally, you will learn the location of important Oracle files on your machine, which is useful in supporting multiple Oracle instances in your organization.

Installing Oracle Database Software

This section will teach you how to install Oracle software, covering the following topics:

- Using the Oracle Installer to install Oracle
- Installing the Oracle server software
- Installing Net8
- Installing client software

The Oracle Installer software is used for setting up Oracle on your Windows machine. Although the use of InstallShield hides some of the complexity in unloading files from the CD-ROM onto your machine, you must still give a fair amount of information to the Oracle Installer in order to set up your Oracle database. You will learn in this section how to use the Oracle Installer to set up Oracle on your machine, along with the steps required to install the Oracle server software, Net8, and your Oracle client software. By "client software," we mean Oracle SQL*Plus, Net8 Client, and Oracle Enterprise Manager.

Using the Oracle Installer to Install Oracle

The Oracle Installer is sometimes also referred to as the Oracle Software Asset Manager, or SAM. SAM tells you what Oracle software already exists on this machine, allowing you to install new components or remove old ones in a graphical interface. You can access SAM in one of several ways:

- SAM will begin running automatically after you insert the Oracle8 Server for Windows CD-ROM into your computer (using the `autorun.exe` program on your CD-ROM).
- From Windows Explorer, drill down into the node representing your CD-ROM drive after the Oracle8 Server for Windows CD-ROM is placed in your machine. In the CD-ROM's root directory, double-click on `setup.exe`.
- Click on Start | Run from your Windows desktop, and type in **`x:\setup.exe`**, where *x* is the letter representing your CD-ROM drive.

Installing Oracle8 from Autorun

When installing Oracle8 from Autorun, the first screen you see will offer you three options to proceed, as shown in Figure 2-1. You can

- **Begin Installation** Autorun will proceed with installing Oracle software components.
- **Browse Information** Autorun will allow you to see various Readme files detailing important information about this release of Oracle software.
- **Explore CD** Autorun will assist in letting you explore the contents of your CD.

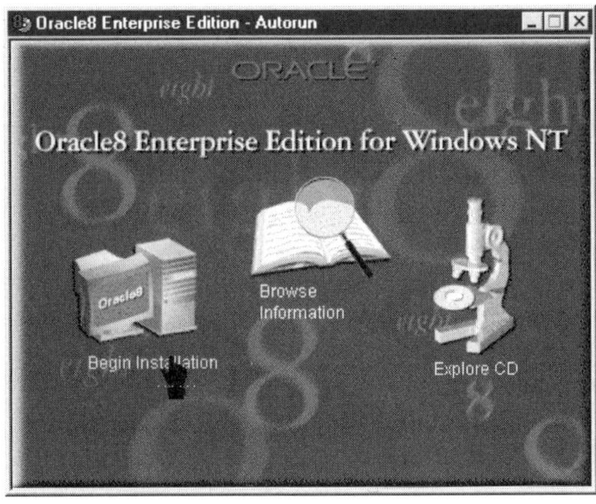

FIGURE 2-1. *Oracle Installer Autorun screen*

Beginning Installation

You can click on the Begin Installation icon now in Autorun to begin the installation of your Oracle software. Or, if you chose to install Oracle using the `setup.exe` program, you will proceed with Oracle installation at this point. The Oracle Installer will then prompt you to enter a company name for the organization that will own this Oracle software. Next, the Oracle Installer will prompt you to enter an Oracle software home directory, often referred to by Oracle users as `ORACLE_HOME`, as shown here:

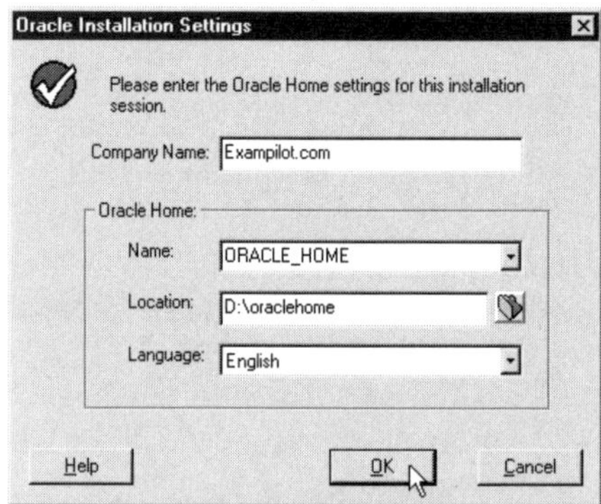

Most of the time, the Oracle software home directory you will want to use is `c:\orant`. However, if you will have multiple Oracle databases running on your machine, you may want to create separate `ORACLE_HOME`s for each instance—in which case you should come up with some sort of naming convention for each Oracle software home directory. Finally, if the Oracle software home directory you specified does not exist already, Oracle will prompt you as to whether or not it is okay for Oracle Installer to create one.

TIP
*This explanation for installing Oracle covers Oracle8 and earlier Oracle software releases. For Oracle8*i *and later software releases, the Oracle Installer looks and works slightly different from the information presented here.*

Oracle Installer will then prompt you to select whether you want to perform a typical installation or whether you want to perform a custom installation, as shown here:

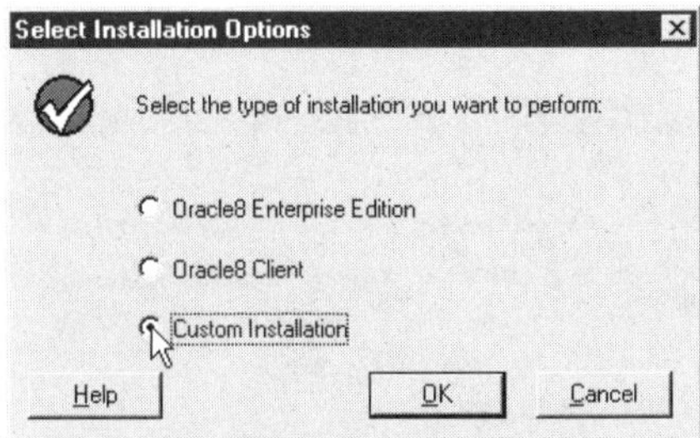

If you select Oracle8 Enterprise Edition or Oracle8 Client, Oracle Installer will choose the software components typically installed for you from the list of available products in Software Asset Manager. If you select Custom Installation, you will be free to choose the components yourself. For purposes of familiarization with the products you will install again and again as Oracle database operator, the next discussion will assume you selected Custom Installation.

For Review

Know the things you must specify to Oracle Installer up to this point of your Oracle installation. Also, know the differences between installing Oracle via Autorun and via `setup.exe`.

Installing the Oracle Server

At this point, the Software Asset Manager screen will appear, looking as it is shown in Figure 2-2. The main items on this interface to be aware of include the following:

- Available Products text box, listing available software on CD-ROM
- Products Installed text box, listing software already installed
- Space Requirements text area, identifying space requirements for selected software

TIP

You should be aware of the amount of space available on the drive where you want to install Oracle software. A typical Oracle software installation requires about 700MB of space. This does not include the space required to store your Oracle database, either!

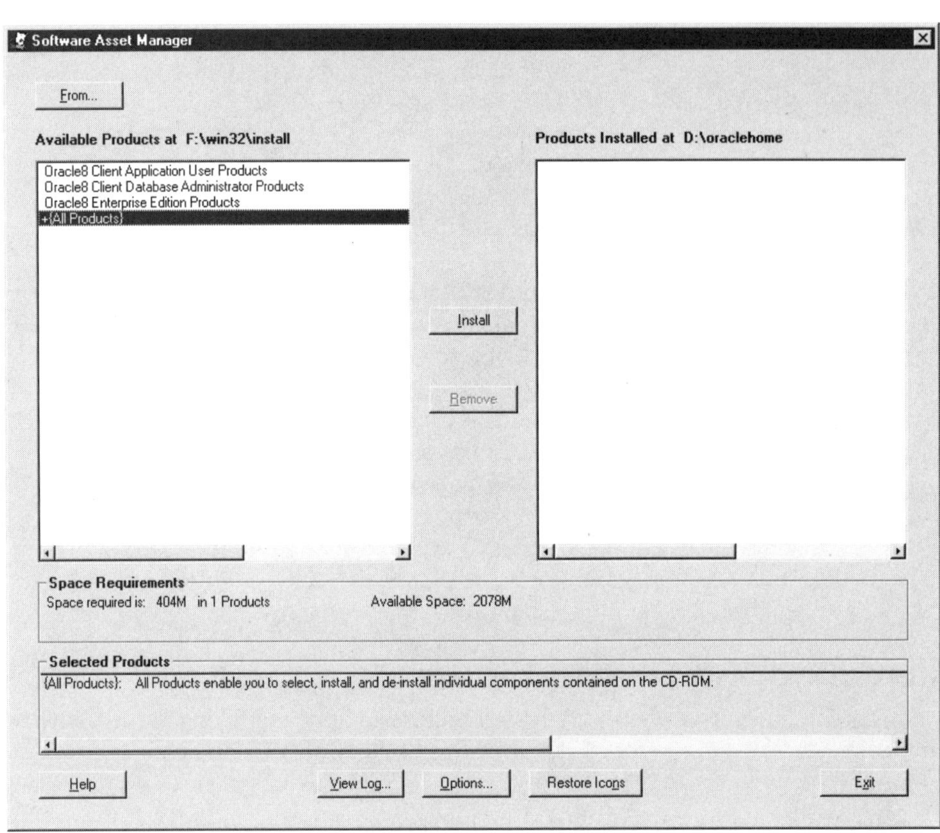

FIGURE 2-2. *Software Asset Manager screen*

A less-important area of SAM is the Selected Products area that offers a description for each product selected for installation. If you need to review the usage of the product you are intending to install, you can look in this area. Another component of SAM to be aware of is the From button in the upper-left corner of the interface. You may use this button to point SAM to another area to install Oracle software from, such as a staging area on your machine or network where Oracle installation software has been preloaded for easy access. You may use this button when applying patches to your Oracle software release that you download from Oracle METALink.

Selecting Software to Install

For this discussion, you will be installing Oracle8 Enterprise Edition from your Oracle8 Server for Windows CD-ROM. You can select this software component in the SAM Available Products window by clicking on the Oracle8 Enterprise Edition 8.0.5.0.0 listing, as shown in Figure 2-3. If you want to install multiple software

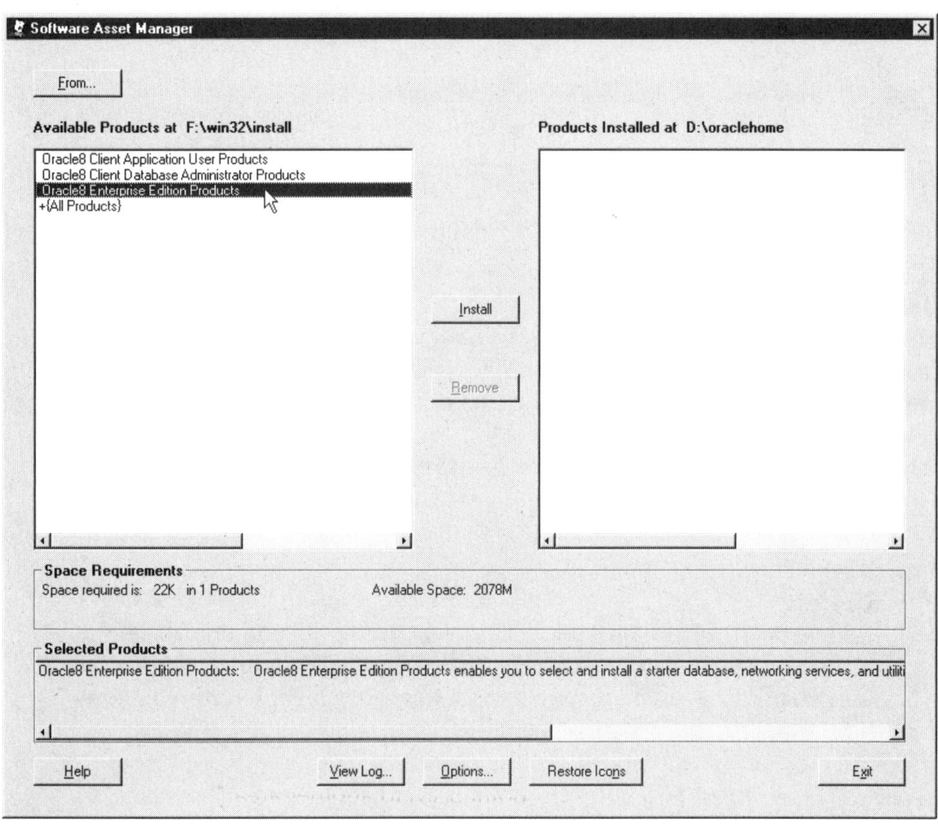

FIGURE 2-3. *Selecting Oracle8 Server software for installation*

components, you must hold down the CTRL key on your keyboard at the same time you click on the software components to install. Some other software components you may want to install include

- Intelligent Agent
- Oracle8 utilities
- Oracle8 cartridges (optional)
- Net8 (installation explained in an upcoming section)
- Oracle8 client software (installation explained in an upcoming section)

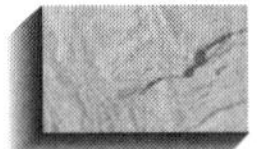

TIP
Some items in the Available Products listing may have a plus sign (+) next to them, which indicates that there are subcomponents to that software product. To view those subcomponents, you can click on the + sign next to the component.

Proceeding with Installation

When you are finished with selecting the Oracle8 software components you want to install, you click on the Install button, toward the top-middle part of the SAM interface, between the Available Products and Products Installed windows. SAM will then display installation progress along with important information about the software installed, as shown in Figure 2-4. When finished, Oracle Installer returns you to the SAM screen. If you have finished installing Oracle software, click on the Exit button in the lower-right portion of the SAM interface.

For Review

Identify all components you must select in SAM to properly install the Oracle database server software. When finished installing a particular software component, remember that Oracle Installer returns you to the Software Asset Manager screen.

Installing Net8

As you already learned in the previous section, you don't need to install Net8 as a separate step from installing the Oracle server, because you can select multiple

FIGURE 2-4. *Installation progress*

software components by holding the CTRL key while clicking on a software listing in the Available Products window of SAM. However, it is useful to install Net8 as a separate component at least once when installing Oracle software, to reinforce the point that *Net8 is a separate software product from Oracle8 Server.* To install Net8, scroll through the listing of Available Products in SAM until you find the listing for Net8, shown in Figure 2-5. Click on that listing, and then press the Install button. Just as before, Oracle Installer will show you progress. When Oracle Installer has finished, it will return to the Software Asset Manager screen.

For Review

Understand how to install Net8 software using Oracle Installer.

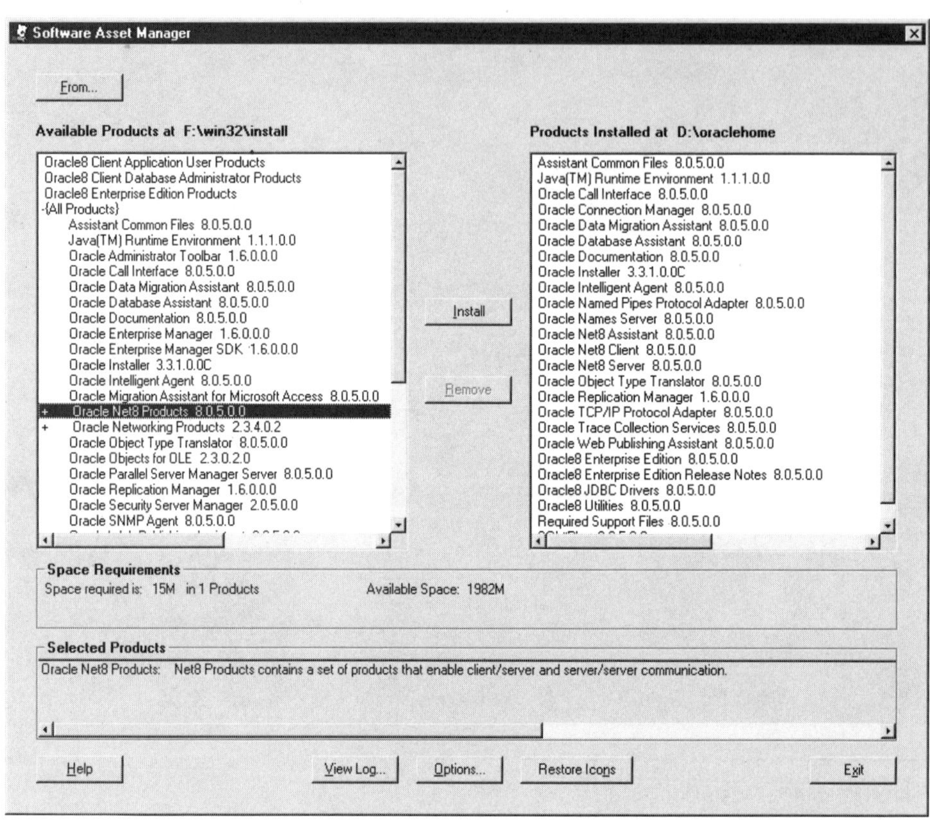

FIGURE 2-5. *Installing Net8*

Installing Client Software

A final component you will want to install is the Oracle8 client software. This software includes SQL*Plus, Net8 for client machines, and in some cases, Enterprise Manager as well. These tools are all useful for accessing the Oracle database from a client machine, or for accessing the Oracle database running locally on the server. Like Net8, *Oracle8 client software is separate from the Oracle8 database.* To install client software, select the Oracle8 Client listing in the Available Products window of the SAM, as shown in Figure 2-6, and press the Install button.

For Review

Know which software component to select if you want to install Oracle8 client software on your machine.

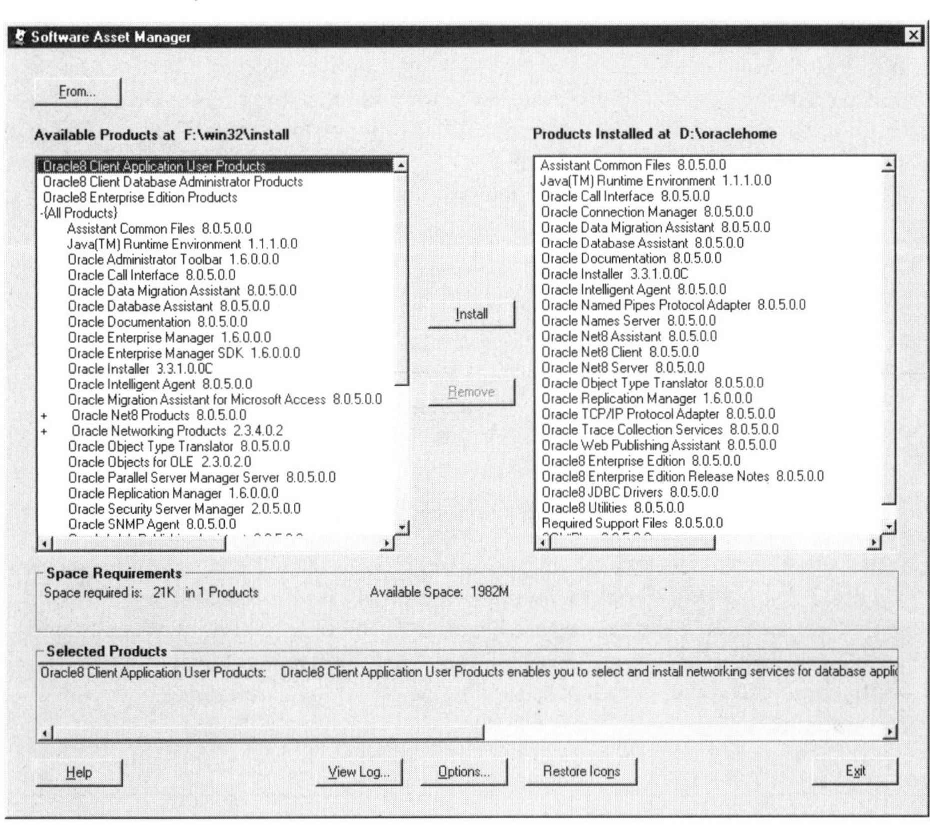

FIGURE 2-6. *Installing Oracle8 client software*

Creating Oracle Databases and Services

In this section, you learn the following topics on creating Oracle databases and services:

- Finding database files on your host system
- Creating a database with the Database Assistant
- Identifying files required to open Oracle databases
- Understanding the Oracle database service

When performing a typical Oracle software installation, the Oracle Installer will create a default database for you. However, when you install Oracle software using custom installation, as we did in the previous section, you will not have an Oracle database created automatically for you. Instead, you must create your own database using Oracle Database Assistant. You should also understand where to find different files required for your Oracle database. Finally, you may need to automate the startup and shutdown of your Oracle database to occur when you reboot the server. This section explains all these things.

Finding Database Files on Your Host System

Most Oracle database installations follow similar directory structures when storing the files that comprise an Oracle database. This allows you as a database operator to easily maintain many different Oracle databases residing on many different machines. By understanding the layout of Oracle files on your file system, you can make assumptions about where different database components are stored when moving from machine to machine, thus cutting down on your search time when trying to diagnose problems on an Oracle database you have never worked with before.

Figure 2-7 shows the directory layout of a typical Oracle database installation. Note that not all Oracle directories are listed, only the ones you may typically find yourself exploring. In addition, Table 2-1 shows the filename extensions and file types for some of the directories noted in Figure 2-7 for easy reference and understanding.

Directory	Typical Filename Extension and Type
`C:\orant\bin`	Program executables and shared libraries—`.exe`, `.dll`
`C:\orant\database`	Initialization files—`.ora` Database files—`.dat`, `.dbf`, `.ora` Control files—`.ctl`, `.ora` Redo logs—`.log`, `.ora` Windows command files—`.cmd`
`C:\orant\net80\admin`	Network configuration files—`.ora`
`c:\orant\net80\agent`	Agent configuration files—`.tcl`

TABLE 2-1. *Oracle8 Filename Extensions and Types*

Directory	Typical Filename Extension and Type
`c:\orant\net80\log`	Network log files—`.log`
`c:\orant\rdbms80\admin`	Database configuration files—`.sql`, `.plb`
`c:\orant\rdbms80\loader`	SQL*Loader sample control files—`.ctl` SQL*Loader sample parameter files—`.par` SQL*Loader sample data files—`.dat`
`c:\orant\rdbms80\trace`	Database trace files—`.trc`

TABLE 2-1. *Oracle8 Filename Extensions and Types* (continued)

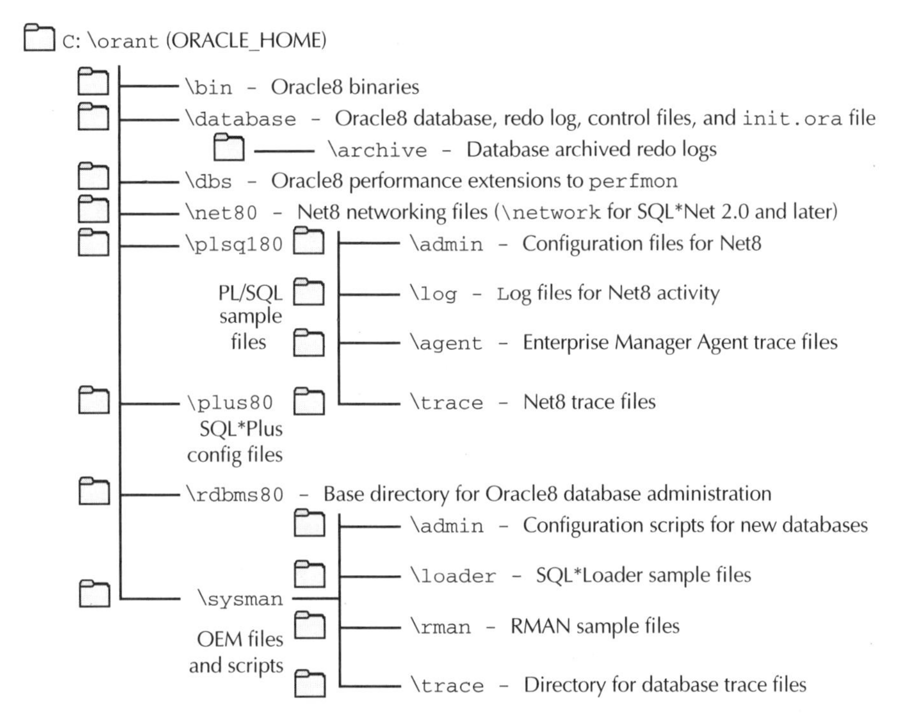

FIGURE 2-7. *Oracle8 directory structure*

For Review

Be sure you understand the directory structure of an Oracle database installation. Also, know the main types of files you might find on an Oracle software installation, along with their extensions.

Creating a Database with the Database Assistant

When using the custom installation method given with Oracle Installer, you will not create a database automatically. Therefore, to create your first Oracle database (as well as subsequent databases you might store on this server), you can use the Oracle Database Assistant. This tool allows you to create your Oracle database using a GUI interface tool. Start the Oracle Database Assistant from your Windows desktop by clicking on Start | Programs | Oracle for Windows | Oracle Database Assistant. Follow these steps to create your Oracle database with Database Assistant:

1. The base screen is shown here. Select the "Create a database" radio button in that interface. Then click Next.

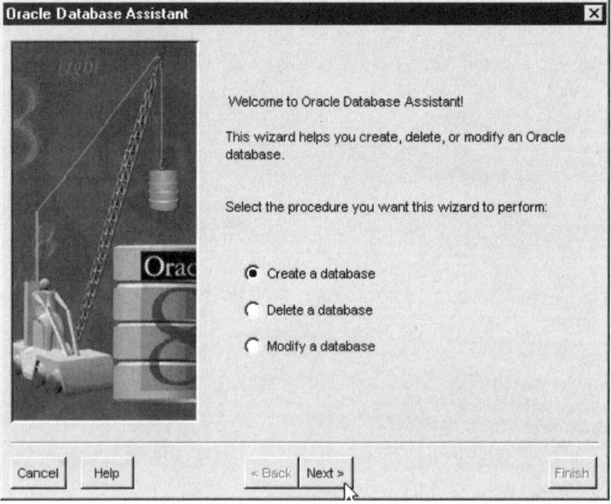

2. The next screen you will see in Database Assistant looks like this:

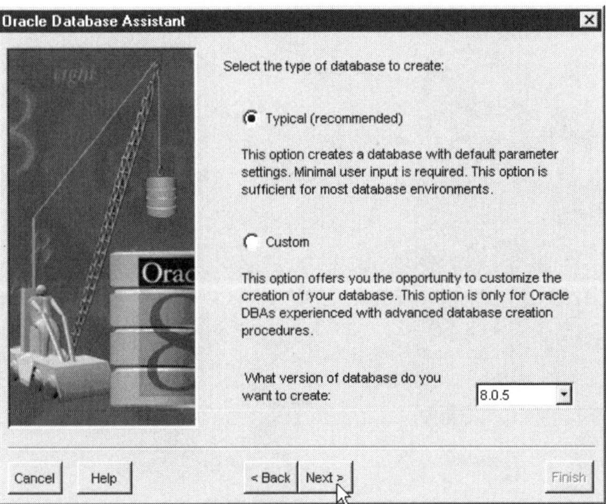

If you have never created an Oracle database before, you can select the Typical radio button in the next screen shown in Database Assistant, and the wizard will define most components of your new database for you. The rest of the discussion assumes you are performing a typical installation. Now click Next.

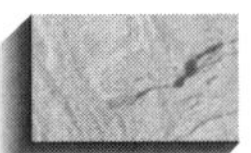

TIP

If you have created a database before, you can select the Custom radio button. Also, be sure you create the type of database appropriate to the Oracle8 software version installed on your machine.

3. In the Database Assistant screen, shown next, select the data cartridges you want to include with your database by clicking the checkbox next to each appropriate cartridge. If a cartridge listing is grayed out, that means this cartridge is not available with your Oracle8 software installation. If you want to make that cartridge available, you should return to the Oracle Installer Software Asset Manager and install the appropriate cartridge(s). Then click Next.

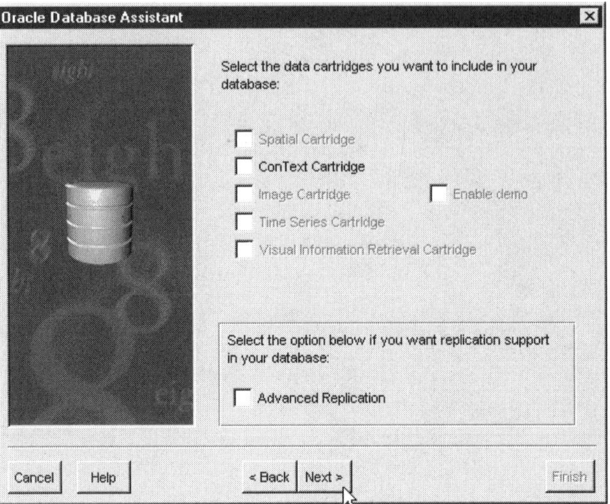

4. The next Database Assistant screen, shown below, prompts you to select whether you want the Assistant to copy database files from the CD-ROM or create new ones. Copying database files from the CD-ROM is faster. If you choose to create new database files, the installation of your new database could take several minutes. When ready to create your new database, click Finish.

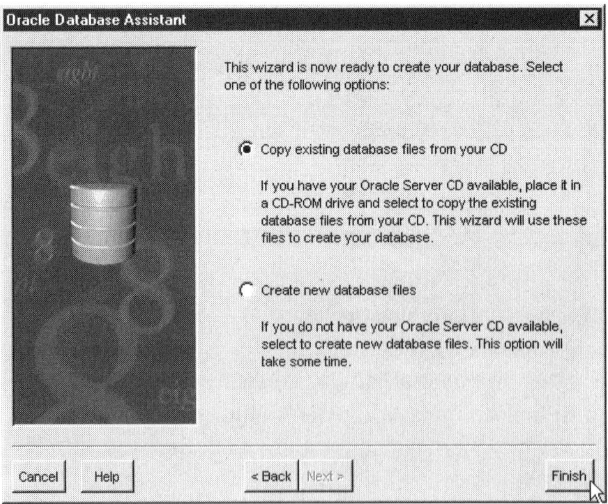

5. You will see some prompts from the Database Assistant indicating it will now create your database. Click OK or Yes to proceed. You may also be prompted to indicate whether you want this new database SID added to

your `listener.ora` file. The Database Assistant displays a progress indicator screen, as shown here.

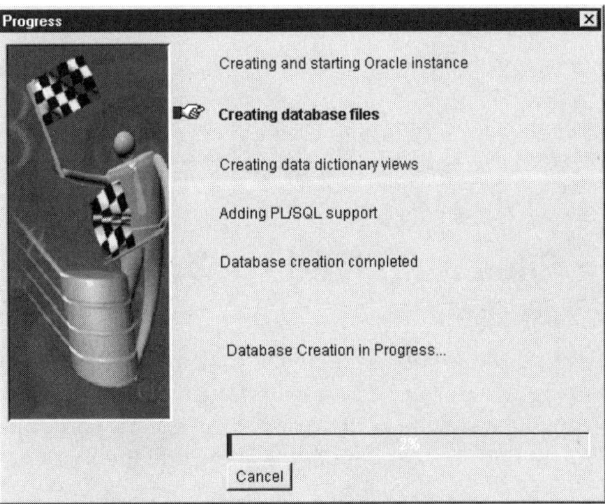

TIP
You can review the database creation process executed by Database Assistant by looking in the `c:\orant\database\spoolmain.log` file.

Modifying Your Windows Registry

Once your new database is created, you can see important configuration information about it in your Windows registry by opening a DOS prompt on your desktop and typing **regedit** at the prompt. Here is what the Windows registry looks like:

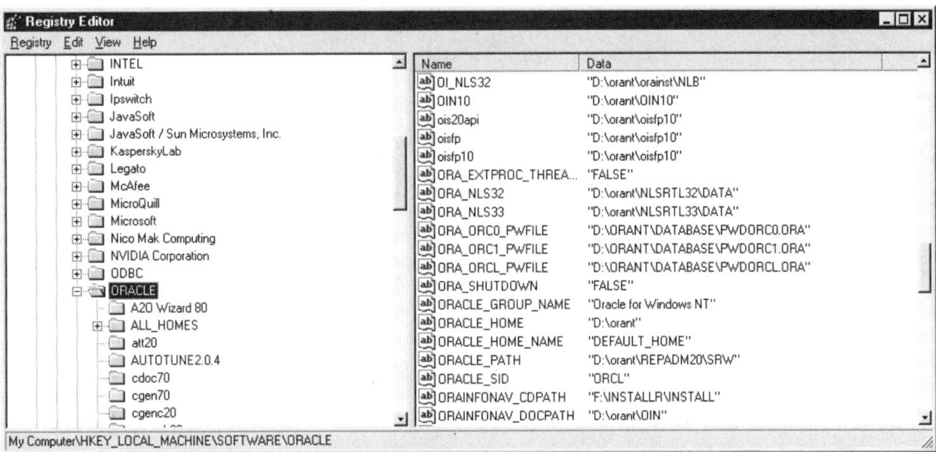

Inside the Registry Editor, you can drill down into the My Computer | HKEY_LOCAL_MACHINE | SOFTWARE | ORACLE node to view settings for `ORACLE_HOME` and `ORACLE_SID` values. `ORACLE_HOME` should be the same as you set in the Oracle Installer and `ORACLE_SID` should be `ORCL`.

For Review

Understand all steps required to create a new database using the Oracle Database Assistant. Also, be sure you understand how to configure your registry settings.

Identifying Files Required to Open Oracle Databases

Once your Oracle database is created, you can look at the files that comprise your Oracle database in the `d:\orant\database` folder on your machine. Notice that many of the files on your machine contain `ORACLE_SID` as part of their name. The various files you might find in a typical database include the following.

Datafiles

These files store Oracle table and index data. One or more datafiles can comprise an Oracle tablespace. You will learn more about Oracle storage structures in Chapter 4. The following bullets and descriptions will help you understand the contents of various datafiles that exist in your database.

- The `sysorcl.ora` file contains important system database objects like the data dictionary.
- The `rbsorcl.ora` file contains rollback segments.
- The `temporcl.ora` file stores temporary segments used for sorting.
- The `dataorcl.ora` contains application data.
- The `indxorcl.ora` file contains index data.
- The `usrorcl.ora` file contains user database objects.

Redo Logs

These files store online redo information for every transaction made against the Oracle database. Every database must have at least two online redo log files. Database

Assistant, by default, will create four redo log files: `redo1orcl.ora`, `redo2orcl.ora`, `redo3orcl.ora`, and `redo4orcl.ora`.

Control Files

These files store the physical layout of your Oracle database. They also store the database name, creation timestamp, current log sequence number, checkpoint information, and other key points regarding redo logs. The control files created by Database Assistant for this database include `ctl1orcl.ora` and `ctl2orcl.ora`.

Parameter Files

This file stores parametric information used when an Oracle database is started. The filename is `initorcl.ora`.

Password Files

Called `pwdorcl.ora` by default, this file contains password information for users having the privilege to start and stop the Oracle database remotely.

TIP

Depending on how many databases you may have already created on this machine, the default `ORACLE_SID` assigned when you create a new one could be ORC0, ORC1, and so on, altering the names of the datafiles, redo logs, control files, parameter files, and password files according to the pattern `pwd<SID>.ora`.

All datafiles, redo logs, and control files that were created when the database was created and/or were online the last time the Oracle database was shut down are required when the database is started. Oracle *cannot* start if even one of these files is missing. In addition, you will also need a parameter file to configure how the instance will operate and to specify whether or not the password file is required.

A Sample init.ora

This file is read at the startup of your Oracle instance and defines aspects of database operation, including memory available to the database components, physical database attributes, and whether a password file is required for database operation. The parameter file also specifies the location of your control files, archive logs, and trace files. This file also specifies how many rollback segments will be acquired at database startup. The following code listing shows you a sample of what your init.ora file might look like, while Table 2-2 explains the meaning of many important initialization parameters you should be aware of:

```
db_name = orcl
db_files = 1024
control_files = ("D:\orant\database\ctl1orcl.ora",
                 "D:\orant\database\ctl2orcl.ora")
db_file_multiblock_read_count = 8
db_block_buffers = 200
shared_pool_size = 10000000
log_checkpoint_interval = 10000
processes = 59
dml_locks = 100
log_buffer = 8192
sequence_cache_entries = 10
sequence_cache_hash_buckets = 10
#audit_trail = true
#timed_statistics = true
background_dump_dest = D:\orant\rdbms80\trace
user_dump_dest = D:\orant\rdbms80\trace
db_block_size =2048
compatible = 8.0.5.0.0
sort_area_size = 65536
log_checkpoint_timeout = 0
remote_login_passwordfile = shared
max_dump_file_size = 10240
```

Parameter Name	Meaning
DB_NAME	The name of your database. Should be the same as ORACLE_SID. The difference between DB_NAME and ORACLE_SID is that DB_NAME is the name of the database used within Oracle, while ORACLE_SID is an environment variable.
DB_FILES	The maximum number of files that can be associated with this database.

TABLE 2-2. *Initialization Parameters and Their Meanings*

Parameter Name	Meaning
DB_BLOCK_BUFFERS	The number of buffers that will comprise your buffer cache, an area of shared memory in your Oracle database known as the System Global Area, or SGA. The size of your buffer cache in bytes is determined by multiplying this number by DB_BLOCK_SIZE, which is explained later in this table.
SHARED_POOL_SIZE	The size of your shared pool in bytes, another component of the Oracle SGA, used in part to store parsed SQL statements for reuse.
PROCESSES	The maximum number of OS processes that may connect to this database at the same time.
LOG_BUFFER	The size in bytes of your redo log buffer, another component of the Oracle SGA.
AUDIT_TRAIL	Set to TRUE or FALSE, corresponding to whether or not you want to enable database auditing. Setting this to TRUE degrades overall database performance.
TIMED_STATISTICS	Set to TRUE or FALSE, corresponding to whether or not you want to enable statistics collection on your database. Setting this to TRUE degrades overall database performance.
ROLLBACK_SEGMENTS	Specifies by name the rollback segments your database will acquire at startup.
MAX_DUMP_FILE_SIZE	The maximum size in bytes of your Oracle database core dumps.

TABLE 2-2. *Initialization Parameters and Their Meanings* (continued)

Parameter Name	Meaning
LOG_ARCHIVE_START	Set to TRUE or FALSE, depending on whether you want to archive your filled online redo logs automatically.
LOG_ARCHIVE_DEST	The directory where you want archived redo logs written to.
LOG_ARCHIVE_FORMAT	The naming convention you want automatic archiving to use when copying logs to their archive destination.
BACKGROUND_DUMP_DEST	The location on your file system of background process trace and/or dump files.
USER_DUMP_DEST	The location on your file system of user process trace and/or dump files.
DB_BLOCK_SIZE	The size in bytes of data blocks for your Oracle database. This parameter is specified once at database creation time. After that point, this parameter must remain the same.
REMOTE_LOGIN_PASSWORDFILE	Set to NONE, EXCLUSIVE, or SHARED to indicate whether password files are required for this instance.
COMPATIBLE	Version of Oracle software with which this instance is compatible.

TABLE 2-2. *Initialization Parameters and Their Meanings* (continued)

For Review

Know the use of a parameter file and when it is read. Also, be sure you understand the use of every parameter identified in Table 2-2.

Understanding the Oracle Database Service

Windows services are used for starting processes that will run on the server in the background. These services are then available to other machines connecting to this server via the network. When an Oracle database is created, Database Assistant also creates two services that can be used for starting and stopping the Oracle database. These services can be started either from the Windows Control Panel or from a DOS prompt. The services are

- **OracleStart<SID>** Starts the OracleService<SID> service when Windows starts.
- **OracleService<SID>** Starts the Oracle database.

Starting Oracle Services from the Control Panel

Use the following steps to start Oracle services from the Control Panel:

1. From the Windows desktop, click on Start | Settings | Control Panel. In the Control Panel, click on the Services icon.
2. The Services window is shown next. In it, find the OracleStart<SID> service, click on it once to highlight, and press the Start button. Windows then attempts to start Oracle.

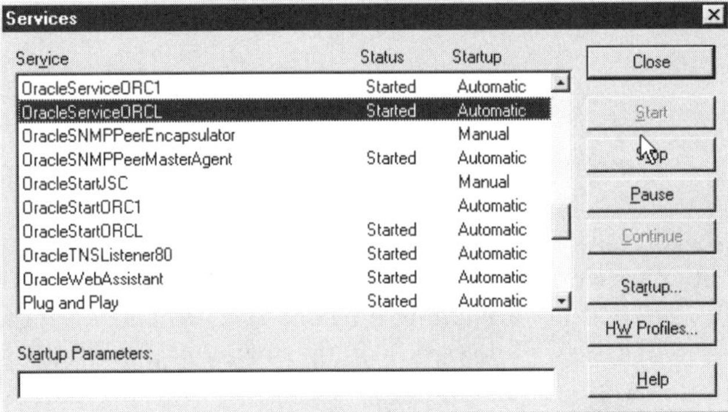

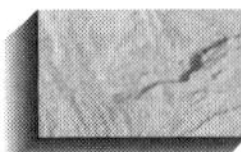

TIP

To stop a running Oracle database from the Services window, follow the same procedures identified previously, except click the Stop button instead of clicking the Start button.

Starting Oracle Services from DOS

Follow these steps to start Oracle services from your DOS prompt:

1. From the Windows desktop, click on Start | Programs | Command Prompt.
2. Type **`net start OracleService<SID>`** at the command line.

TIP
For stopping Oracle services at the command prompt, follow the same procedures identified previously, except type **`net stop OracleService<SID>`** *instead of entering the* `net start` *command.*

For Review

Understand what a service is. Also, understand how to start and stop Oracle as a service, both from the Control Panel | Services window and from a DOS prompt.

Locating Oracle Files on Your Machine

Here, you will learn where to find important and useful Oracle files on your machine:

- What password files are and how to create them
- What trace files are and how to use them

In Figure 2-7, you have already seen the directory layout of a typical Oracle database installation. In this section, you will learn the few remaining files that comprise the Oracle architecture, where they are located, and what they are for. The first of these two is the Oracle password file. You will learn how to create an Oracle password file using Oracle utilities. The use and location of trace files in your Oracle database are both covered in this section as well.

What Password Files Are and How to Create Them

Access to the database for specific administrative tasks is managed with special privileges called `sysdba` and `sysoper`. The `sysdba` privilege is the most powerful privilege in the database, allowing the grantee the ability to create databases, start or stop databases, and perform all kinds of database recovery operations. The other privilege, `sysoper`, is a subset of `sysdba`, allowing the grantee to start and stop the database and perform complete recovery operations.

When many users exist who can administer the Oracle databases, it is sometimes effective to give every user his or her own username for doing so. This way, the activities of every privileged user can be tracked with more granularity than if several users are given the same username and password for performing the same activities. Authentication of many users having `sysdba` or `sysoper` privileges is handled through the use of a password file. When a user is granted these privileges, that user is added to the password file. When the password file is created, a maximum limit is set to the number of privileged users. A special user, called SYS, is created with every database. This user is given the `sysdba` privilege. This user is also called INTERNAL.

TIP
After creating a typical database using Database Assistant, the default password for SYS/INTERNAL when connecting as a regular user is CHANGE_ON_INSTALL. To connect as a user with `sysdba` *privileges, the SYS/INTERNAL password is ORACLE.*

You can find the password file for the database you created earlier in the chapter by checking in the Windows registry for that file's location. Do so by drilling down to the My Computer | HKEY_LOCAL_MACHINE | SOFTWARE | ORACLE node and then looking on the right side of the interface for the value set for the registry entry called ORA_<SID>_PWFILE. You can then find the file in Windows Explorer. Sometimes, this file might be hidden. Don't bother trying to open this file in WordPad, because it is a binary file.

Creating Your Password File

To create a new password file for your database, you must first remove the old one. Do so by clicking once on the password file in Windows Explorer and pressing the DELETE key, or by changing to the directory containing your password file in a DOS prompt and typing **del PWD<SID>.ora**. The `orapwd80.exe` utility is used to create password files in Oracle. At the command line, type **orapwd80 file=*filename* password=*passwd* entries=*num***. The *filename* is the name of your new password file, *passwd* is the new password for the SYS/INTERNAL user, and *num* is the maximum number of users that may be given the `sysdba` or `sysoper` privilege for administering this database. The following code block illustrates what you type at the DOS prompt to create your password file:

```
C:\ORANT\DATABASE> orapwd80 file=pwdorcl.ora password=jason entries=20
```

Password files also allow users to manage the database remotely. That is to say, users who are entered into the password file can start, stop, and recover the Oracle database from Oracle Enterprise Manager running on a remote client, instead of from the machine hosting the Oracle database. To specify use of a password file, the `REMOTE_LOGIN_PASSWORDFILE` `init.ora` parameter must be set to EXCLUSIVE and the instance must be restarted. The other settings for this parameter are SHARED, meaning that only SYS/INTERNAL can connect to Oracle remotely for startup and shutdown, or NONE, meaning that any user wanting to start or stop Oracle must do so from the machine hosting the Oracle database.

Granting sysdba to Other Users

To grant the `sysdba` privilege to another user, you must first connect as the SYS/INTERNAL user to Oracle by way of either Oracle Enterprise Manager or Server Manager line mode. Then, grant the privilege to another user via the `grant` command. The following code block shows how:

```
C:\ORANT> svrmgr30
Oracle Server Manager Release 3.0.5.0.0 - Production
(c)1997, Oracle Corporation. All rights reserved.
Oracle8 Enterprise Edition Release 8.0.5.2.1 - Production
PL/SQL Release 8.0.5.2.1 - Production
SVRMGR> connect internal
Connected.
SVRMGR> grant sysdba to jason
Grant succeeded.
```

or

```
C:\ORANT> svrmgr30
Oracle Server Manager Release 3.0.5.0.0 - Production
(c)1997, Oracle Corporation. All rights reserved.
Oracle8 Enterprise Edition Release 8.0.5.2.1 - Production
PL/SQL Release 8.0.5.2.1 - Production
SVRMGR> connect sys as sysdba;
Connected.
SVRMGR> grant sysdba to jason
Grant succeeded.
```

Now, user JASON can connect to Oracle as `sysdba` and start or stop Oracle.

For Review

Understand the functionality offered by a password file. Know the initialization parameter that must be set in order to use a password file, and its three settings. Know how to create a password file. Know what the `sysdba` and `sysoper` privileges are. Know how to use the Windows registry to find your password file.

What Trace Files Are and How to Use Them

A trace file is a file that the Oracle database maintains with key information about its own operation. The DBA or DBO often can examine the contents of a trace file to see what is happening on the database at a specific point in time. If an error occurs in the database, information is written into the trace file about that error. Each thread of the main process in Oracle, the `oracle80.exe` process, will create its own trace file in the event that something causes that thread to fail. In addition, the main Oracle process will maintain a database-wide trace file called the ALERT file, which contains information about regular database activities such as database starts and stops; settings for initialization parameters; redo log switches; and database, tablespace, and rollback segment creation. Errors, such as locking errors, corruptions, and the like, are logged to the ALERT file as well. Some errors you might find in an ALERT file include `ORA-00600` (internal error—call Oracle Support), `ORA-00060` (deadlocks), and `ORA-01578` (block corruption).

By default, all ALERT files can be found in the `c:\orant\rdbms80\admin` directory. The ALERT file can be found in the directory specified by the `BACKGROUND_DUMP_DEST` initialization parameter, and the name of your ALERT file will be `<SID>alrt.log`. Oracle will write alert information to the same ALERT file for the life of that database. If your database exists for a long time, the ALERT file could grow quite large. It is important to move your ALERT file to another destination periodically and compress it to save room. If the ALERT file doesn't exist the next time Oracle needs to write information to it, Oracle will simply create a new one.

Chapter Summary

This chapter covered a lot of important information tested on the OCP DBO exam in three main areas. Those areas were how to install Oracle software, how to create an Oracle database, and where to find important Oracle files. The first topic covered was installing Oracle software. You learned about the significance of the Oracle Installer program for this task and the different ways you can start the Oracle Installer. You learned how to install Oracle8 Server, Net8, and Oracle8 client software as well. The next section covered how to create Oracle databases using the Database Assistant tool. The files required for opening a database—namely, datafiles, redo logs, and control files—were each explained. The use of the initialization file and its contents were covered as well. You also learned about the special use of the Oracle password file, how to create it, and how to maintain it. The use of services to start and stop Oracle were also explained. Finally, you covered how to find the ALERT file and what its contents are.

Two-Minute Drill

- Three ways to start Oracle Installer are
    - Put the Oracle8 CD-ROM in your machine (Autorun).
    - Type **`x:\setup.exe`**, where *x* is your machine's CD-ROM drive.
    - Open Windows Explorer, drill down into the CD-ROM drive node, and double-click on `setup.exe`.
- SAM stands for Software Asset Manager and is the component of Oracle Installer that tells you the different Oracle software components installed on your machine.
- You have to specify an Oracle software home directory, or `ORACLE_HOME`, where your software will be installed.
- Your database also has an `ORACLE_SID`, which is usually your database name.
- If you choose Typical Installation, Oracle chooses the software to install for you. If you choose Custom Installation, you choose your own software.
- Software components like Oracle8 Enterprise Edition, Intelligent Agent, cartridges, Net8, and Oracle8 Client are all listed as separate software components in the Available Products window in SAM.
- Components of the Oracle Installer SAM interface include
    - Available Products text box
    - Installed Products text box
    - Space Requirements text area
- A complete Oracle software installation can require 700MB or more space on your hard drive, not counting files that actually comprise the Oracle database.

- To select multiple software components for installation, hold down the CTRL key while clicking on the software name in SAM.
- A software component that has subcomponents will be listed with a + sign next to it in the Available Products window of SAM.
- Understand that Net8 and Oracle8 client software are software components separate from the Oracle8 server.
- Review Figure 2-7 to understand the file system architecture for a typical Oracle installation on Windows platforms.
- Review Table 2-1 to understand the different file types and filename extensions you might find in your Oracle file system architecture, and where you might find those files.
- Understand the process of creating a database using Database Assistant.
- A log of Database Assistant's activities can be found in `c:\orant\database\spoolmain.log`.
- Information about Oracle components is entered into the Windows registry. You can find this information under HKEY_LOCAL_MACHINE | SOFTWARE | ORACLE in the registry.
- The files required to open your Oracle database include datafiles, redo logs, control files, parameter files, and password files.
- Review the chapter to understand the names of different datafiles created by Database Assistant when a database is created.
- A tablespace can be comprised of one or more datafiles.
- Location of control files is specified by the parameter file.
- The control file then identifies the location of all other files in the Oracle database.
- Redo logs contain transaction information generated by every data change operation that takes place on the database.
- Parameter files contain parameter settings for configuring how the Oracle database will behave.
- Password files contain the names of and passwords for those users allowed to start and stop the Oracle database.
- Be sure you know the use for every parameter listed in Table 2-2.

- A service is a special setup allowing a program to start and run in the background, available to any user connecting to the server.
- Database Assistant creates two services along with a new database:
  - `OracleStart<SID>` Starts the OracleService<SID> service when Windows starts.
  - `OracleService<SID>` Starts the Oracle database.
- You can start a service using the Start | Settings | Control Panel | Services interface, or from a DOS prompt using the `net start` command.
- A password file is created using the `orapwd80.exe` program. Review the command-line parameters for use when running this program to create a password file.
- You can find the location of your password file using the Windows registry.
- The privileges that allow users to start up and shut down the Oracle database are `sysdba` and `sysoper`. `sysoper` is a subset of `sysdba`.
- Trace files keep track of error messages encountered by Oracle background processes.
- A special trace file called the ALERT file logs system-wide errors encountered by the database.

Chapter Questions

1. **To perform administrative tasks on the database using Oracle password authentication, the DBA should have the following two privileges granted to them:**

   A. `sysdba` or `sysoper`

   B. CONNECT or RESOURCE

   C. `restricted session` or `create session`

2. **Which component of the SGA stores parsed SQL statements used for process sharing?**

   A. Buffer cache

   B. Program Global Area

   C. Redo log buffer

   D. Shared pool

3. **The `initsid.ora` parameter that indicates the size of each buffer in the buffer cache is the**

   A. DB_BLOCK_BUFFERS

   B. BUFFER_SIZE

   C. DB_BLOCK_SIZE

   D. ROLLBACK_SEGMENTS

4. **The datafiles named in a `create database` statement are used as storage for which of the following database components?**

   A. SYSTEM tablespace

   B. `init.ora` file

   C. Redo log member

   D. ALERT log

5. **Changing the password used to manage the password file changes the password for which of the following?**

   A. SYSTEM

   B. RPT_BATCH

   C. CONNECT

   D. `internal`

   E. `audit`

6. **The default password for the SYS user when connecting normally to the database is which of the following choices?**

   A. CHANGE_ON_INSTALL

   B. NO_PASSWORD

   C. MANAGER

   D. ORACLE

   E. NULL

7. **DBAs who are planning to administer a database remotely should use all of the following choices, except**

   A. ORAPWD

   B. `REMOTE_LOGIN_PASSWORDFILE` set to `exclusive`

   C. `OS_AUTHENT_PREFIX` set to OPS$

   D. A password file

8. **Which of the following administrative tools in OEM can be used to view the initialization parameter settings for Oracle?**

   A. Schema Manager

   B. Instance Manager

   C. Security Manager

   D. Data Manager

   E. Software Manager

Answers to Chapter Questions

1. A. `sysdba` or `sysoper`

Explanation Choices B and C are incorrect. Each privilege listed has some bearing on access, but none of them give any administrative ability. Refer to the discussion of choosing an authentication method.

2. D. Shared pool

Explanation Choice A is incorrect because the buffer cache is where data blocks are stored for recently executed queries. Choice B is incorrect because the program global area is where the actual values returned from a query are stored, not the parse information for the query. Choice C is incorrect because the redo log buffer stores redo entries temporarily until LGWR can write them to disk. Refer to the discussion of Oracle architecture.

3. C. `DB_BLOCK_SIZE`

Explanation Since each buffer in the buffer cache is designed to fit one data block, the size of buffers in the database block buffer cache will be the same size as the blocks they store. The size of blocks in the database is determined by `DB_BLOCK_BUFFERS`. Refer to the discussion of initialization parameters to be changed during database creation.

4. A. SYSTEM tablespace

Explanation Since datafiles can only be a part of tablespaces (more on this in Chapter 4), all other choices must be eliminated immediately. Another reason to eliminate at least choices B and D is that neither the `init`*`sid`*`.ora` file nor the ALERT log are created in the `create database` statement. So, as long as you know that redo logs are composed of online redo log members, and tablespaces like SYSTEM are composed of datafiles, you should have no problem getting a question like this one right.

5. D. `internal`

Explanation Choice A is incorrect because the SYSTEM password has no affiliation with the password for the password file. SYS and `internal` do. Choice B is incorrect because RPT_BATCH is not a password created by Oracle in a `create database` statement. Choice C is incorrect because CONNECT is a role, not a user. Choice E is incorrect because `audit` is a command, not a user. Refer to the discussion of creating the password file as part of choosing user authentication.

6. A. CHANGE_ON_INSTALL

Explanation This is a classic piece of Oracle trivia. Memorize it, along with the SYSTEM password, which incidentally is MANAGER. This is all fine for OCP, but beware of others who may also have memorized these facts. Don't let a hacker use this information against you. Make sure you change the default passwords for SYS and SYSTEM after creating your database. And, remember that `oracle` is the password for SYS or INTERNAL when connecting to Oracle as `sysdba`.

7. C. OS_AUTHENT_PREFIX set to OPS$

Explanation A DBA should use password file authentication when planning to administer a database remotely. This action consists of a password file, the ORAPWD utility, and setting the `REMOTE_LOGIN_PASSWORDFILE` parameter to `exclusive`. The `OS_AUTHENT_PREFIX` parameter is used to alter the prefix Oracle requires on Oracle users when operating system authentication is being used. This one, obviously, is not required for Oracle password authentication.

8. B. Instance Manager

Explanation The Instance Manager tool handles all instance-related tasks, including display and modification of initialization parameters set in the `init`*`sid`*`.ora` file. Schema Manager handles tasks involving database object creation and modification, eliminating choice A. Security Manager handles user privilege and role management, which eliminates choice C. Data Manager handles the loading and unloading of data from EXPORT binary or flat file format, eliminating choice D. Finally, Software Manager handles enterprise deployment of Oracle software, eliminating choice E.

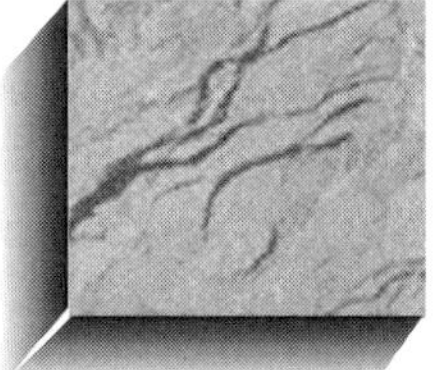

CHAPTER 3

Networking and Database Availability

In this chapter, you will cover the following topics related to Oracle networking and database availability:

- Oracle networking and OEM configuration
- Startup and shutdown of Oracle databases

Oracle databases are meant to be used. In most organizations, this fact means that the Oracle database must be available to many users across a local area network. It also means that the database must be created, the instance must be running, and that users can connect to it. This chapter will teach you how to accomplish all three with Oracle running on Windows environments. By the end of it, you will be able to identify the purpose of and configure various Oracle networking files. You will also be able to use Enterprise Manager to open and close your Oracle database, and store your initialization parameters normally found in the `initsid.ora` file in Instance Manager instead.

Oracle Networking and OEM Configuration

This section covers the following topics on Oracle networking and OEM configuration:

- Purpose and structure of Net8
- Net8 files for configuration
- Generating Net8 files with Net8 Assistant
- Creating the OEM repository
- Using OEM console navigator

The discussions in this section will explain the purpose and structure of Net8. You will learn the basics of how Oracle connects clients to the database server using Net8. You will also learn how to configure it using key configuration files on both client and server. The special purpose of Net8 Assistant for automatic generation of these files will also be explained. Recall in Chapter 2 that you learned how to install Oracle Enterprise Manager. Well, in reality, you were only shown half the installation. The other half is learning how to create the repository of tables in Oracle that OEM uses to operate normally. This section will explain how to create that OEM repository. Finally, you will learn more about the OEM console navigator, and what it allows you to do. The purpose of a special piece of software called the Intelligent Agent, which resides on the server side to assist in OEM console tasks, will be covered as well.

Purpose and Structure of Net8

Whatever your network, Net8 can help you connect your users to the Oracle database. There are versions of Net8 that run on TCP/IP, DECnet, IPX, and many other LAN or WAN products. Moreover, it is possible for Net8 to handle users on multiple networks attempting to connect to the same Oracle database. Networked computing has seen three distinct trends in the last 40 years of organizational use of computers:

- **Mainframe computing** Paradigm that uses mainframe computers to solve business problems. Mainframes feature powerful processing capacity at high speeds but have the drawbacks of unwieldy interfaces, complex programming, and inflexibility for changing business requirements.
- **Client/server computing** Paradigm that uses personal computers and servers, each running their own software, to solve business problems. Advantages include great looking user interfaces and flexibility for changing business needs, but has the drawback of slow operation and distributed data storage that require synchronization activity to guarantee data reliability.
- **Internet computing** Paradigm that uses servers and personal computers, each running their own software, to solve business problems. The differentiating characteristic of PC software in this case is the use of Web browser technology as a universal client. Advantages include centralized storage of data, fast user processing times, great looking user interfaces, and simplified choice process for client software. Disadvantages include security (perceived or real) and dependence on network availability for operation.

Benefits of Net8 for Client/Server and Internet Computing

Net8 is Oracle's networking software that allows both Internet computing and client/server architecture to be used in your database applications. The key component of Net8 includes database name and location resolution, locally or with an Oracle Names server. Net8 does not, however, do any hostname resolution. The resolution of a name you have given to a server to its network IP address; Net8 counts on the underlying network to handle that.

Thus, Net8's basic purpose includes communication of user requests from client to server. Note the use of *communication*—not *transport*—in that description. Net8 is *not* a stand-alone networking protocol. In other words, if you aren't using TCP/IP, DECnet, IPX, or some other networking protocol already, Net8 alone won't make all your computers magically start talking to one another. Net8 simply runs over the top of an existing network to make all the Oracle-related components talk to each other, using something called the Transparent Network Substrate, or TNS, to form connections between clients and servers. TNS allows Net8 to communicate with

Oracle clients and servers across many different network protocols using a uniform interface. TNS also allows connectivity between Oracle clients and servers on different network types (such as TCP/IP and DECnet), even where no lower-level bridging connectivity exists, using the Oracle Connection Manager. TNS also allows client software like SQL*Plus and Oracle8 Enterprise to run and connect with one another on the same machine. The connectivity provided by TNS allows communication between client processes and server processes, and it allows communication between two servers. Finally, Net8 also integrates with security options available on your network.

Other Features of Net8

Net8 also offers several other features in several different areas. For handy reference, the following bullets identify these Net8 features:

- Net8 offers scalability with connection pooling and connection concentration.
- Net8 provides independence from standard networking protocols with the use of Oracle Protocol Adapters.
- Net8 can handle connections from multiple network protocols for the same Oracle server using Oracle Connection Manager.
- Net8 simplifies network administration via Net8 Assistant, running stand-alone or from the OEM console.
- Net8 reduces reliance on both local and third-tier name resolution on TCP/IP networks through the use of host-naming.
- Native Naming Adapters provide interconnectivity with third-party vendor standard name services.

Procedure Net8 Uses to Establish Server Connection

You should understand how Net8 connects user processes to Oracle. Note that the entire process described here can be found in Figure 3-1. Two operations, *open* and *close*, are involved in connection. When you want to open a connection to Oracle from your client, such as when you start SQL*Plus, you must supply a username, password, and a *connect string*. This string is usually a short name that uniquely identifies the database you want to connect to.

In order for Net8 to recognize the connect string you provide as a valid representation for a database somewhere on the network, your connect string must map to a *connect descriptor*, which is a description of the Oracle service you want to connect to. A connect descriptor has several components that are network specific, including a host machine name/address, ORACLE_SID, and specific Net8 listener port number (we're being fairly TCP/IP specific here) for connecting to

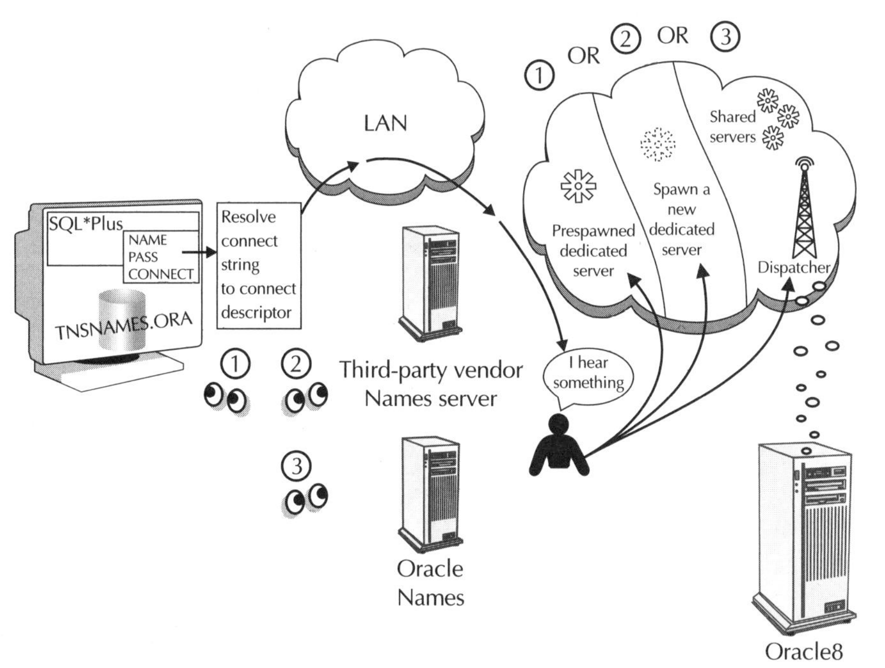

FIGURE 3-1. *How Net8 connects client to server*

Oracle. The mapping of connect string to connect descriptor can be found in one of three places on your network:

- Locally on your client machine in the `tnsnames.ora` file
- On a Names server running somewhere on your computer network
- On some other kind of network naming service made by a third-party vendor

Net8 then travels the network, looking for the host machine named in the descriptor. Once found, Net8 calls on that host machine using the specific port identified in the connect descriptor. A *listener* process should be running on the server, tuned into that particular port, waiting for user processes to call. The listener process knows what port to listen to because that port is identified in the connect descriptor. When the listener hears the incoming connection, the listener will either refuse or allow the connection. A listener will refuse connection if the user process requests connection to an Oracle database that this listener does not listen for, if the user authentication information provided isn't valid, or if the Oracle database is not available.

Once Connection Is Established

If the connection is allowed, one of three things happen, depending on whether you are using shared or dedicated servers to handle user process data requests. A server process on Oracle acts on behalf of user processes to obtain data from the database. If you are using dedicated server processes to handle user requests for data, the listener generates or *spawns* a new dedicated server for that user process to use and then hands or *bequeaths* the user process to that dedicated server. The user process then requests the dedicated server to obtain data on its behalf, and the dedicated server does what it is told. When the user process ends, the dedicated server also ends.

In some cases, you may have prespawned dedicated server processes running on the machine hosting the Oracle database as well. If this is the case, the listener gives the address in memory of the prespawned dedicated server back to the user process, who then establishes connection to that dedicated server process directly. The listener process also keeps track of which prespawned dedicated servers are active and idle at any given time. The listener process may also prespawn a new dedicated server process to replace the one that was just assigned a user process. This happens when the value for the `init.ora` parameter `PRESPAWN_MAX` is not exceeded by the number of prespawned dedicated servers already running on the host. For both types of dedicated server processing, Net8 supports synchronous data transfer of SQL statements from client to server and data returned from server to client.

If the multithreaded server (MTS) architecture is being used, the listener process replies to the user process with the address in memory of the least busy *dispatcher* process, and the user process then establishes connection with the dispatcher directly. The dispatcher process maintains a queue for user processes to place their data requests on. The least busy dispatcher process is the one with the shortest queue. More than one dispatcher process may be running on the host machine. The dispatcher has a number of *shared server* processes working with it that pull requests of the queue in *first in, first out* order and process the request to return data to the user process. The dispatchers and shared servers will stay running even after user processes go away. For shared server processing, Net8 supports asynchronous data transfer of SQL requests from client to dispatcher queue and then results from server to client.

Ending Connection to a Server Process

Ending connection to a server process can happen voluntarily or involuntarily. For example, you may terminate your SQL*Plus session by typing **`exit`**, and your connection with the shared or dedicated server process will be severed. If you are connected to Oracle via OEM, SQL*Plus, or another tool, and attempt to establish a new connection to Oracle as a different user, the tool you are using will usually disconnect your current session first before establishing a new one. This fact explains why you are disconnected from Oracle after failing to attempt another connection, as shown in the following code block:

```
SQL> connect jason/jason
Connected.
SQL> connect jason/jasoin
ERROR:
ORA-01017: invalid username/password; logon denied
Warning: You are no longer connected to ORACLE.
```

Your session may also be ended involuntarily for many reasons, usually owing to the fact that some process died. For example, if your client machine hangs and you reboot, then your session has been ended involuntarily. Also, if your dedicated server fails for some reason, your session is also disconnected involuntarily. Note also that if you have already established connection to a dispatcher or dedicated server, and the listener process fails, Net8 and Oracle behavior for connected users may become highly erratic, from user connections being terminated to your being unable to restart the listener until all connected users have been disconnected.

For Review

1. Identify how a user process establishes connection with a shared or dedicated server via Net8. What is a listener process, and what file is involved in its configuration?
2. What is a connect string? What is a connect descriptor? Where are three locations where the mapping between the two can be found?
3. How are user processes disconnected from their servers?

Net8 Files for Configuration

This section will cover all the files you need to know about as a DBO in order to establish and maintain connectivity within Oracle databases. The following discussions will identify each of the files involved in Oracle networking, explain the purpose of the file, and even show you an example of what the file might look like in real life. You can generally find these files in the `c:\orant\net80\admin` or the `c:\orant\network\admin` directory on the client or server machine.

Using tnsnames.ora

The tnsnames.ora file is used by Oracle tools like SQL*Plus on the client side to resolve the connect string you provide when you attempt to log in to the database. When you issue your SQL*Plus startup command in Windows, either you will provide a connect string in the text box at the bottom of the login prompt, or you will attach the connect string to the end of your username (and password) information at the DOS prompt. The following code block illustrates this:

```
C:\ORANT> plus80 jason@minx
SQL*Plus 8.0.5 Enterprise Edition for Windows NT
Copyright (c)1997 Oracle Corporation. All rights reserved.
Password: ******
Connected to Oracle 8.0.5.1.0 Enterprise Edition
With the partitioning and objects options.
PL/SQL 8.0.5.1.0 Enterprise Edition
SQL>
```

That @minx on the end of your username passed as an argument to SQL*Plus indicates that you want to connect as user JASON to the database corresponding to the MINX connect string in your tnsnames.ora file. The name of your connect string in that file needn't correspond to either the name of the machine hosting your Oracle database or to the SID for that database. However, it might help to establish standards for your organization's TNS naming resolution connect strings, particularly if you have a lot of users connecting to Oracle that use local naming you will support. The following code block shows a sample tnsnames.ora file.

```
#This is a SQL*Net Configuration file generated by SQL*Net Easy Configuration.
#Attention: Do not modify this file yourself.
#If you do, your SQL*Net Easy Configuration may not function properly.

Beq-local.world =
  (DESCRIPTION =
    (ADDRESS_LIST =
        (ADDRESS =
          (COMMUNITY = beq.world)
          (PROTOCOL = BEQ)
          (PROGRAM = oracle73)
          (ARGV0 = oracle73ORCL)
          (ARGS = '(DESCRIPTION=(LOCAL=YES)(ADDRESS=(PROTOCOL=beq)))')
        )
    )
    (CONNECT_DATA = (SID = ORCL)
    )
  )
minx.world =
  (DESCRIPTION =
    (ADDRESS_LIST =
        (ADDRESS =
          (COMMUNITY = tcp.world)
          (PROTOCOL = TCP)
          (Host = 2.3.4.5)
```

```
          (Port = 1521)
        )
    )
    (CONNECT_DATA = (SID = minx)
    )
  )
Example2.world =
  (DESCRIPTION =
    (ADDRESS_LIST =
        (ADDRESS =
          (COMMUNITY = spx.world)
          (PROTOCOL = SPX)
          (Service = Server_lsnr)
        )
    )
    (CONNECT_DATA = (SID = ORCL)
    )
  )
Example3.world =
  (DESCRIPTION =
    (ADDRESS_LIST =
        (ADDRESS =
          (COMMUNITY = nmp.world)
          (PROTOCOL = NMP)
          (Server = FinanceServer1)
          (Pipe = ORAPIPE)
        )
    )
    (CONNECT_DATA = (SID = ORCL)
    )
  )
```

By default, Oracle will always prefer to use `tnsnames.ora` for hostname resolution. In some situations, you might want to consider host-naming (available on TCP/IP networks only) or Oracle Names as an alternative to locally managed name resolution with `tnsnames.ora`. For more information on configuring host-naming or Oracle Names, consult the *Oracle8 Certified Professional DBA Certification Exam Guide* or your Oracle8 documentation that came with the Oracle software distribution CD.

Using sqlnet.ora

The `sqlnet.ora` file is used to specify whether client-side tracing is enabled, and the default naming conventions for the default domain and directory path specifying your client's preferred name resolution methods, in order. Though not required, it is usually wise to configure `sqlnet.ora`, particularly when you are using default domain names in the `tnsnames.ora` file. The default domain name in `tnsnames.ora` can be found appended to the end of the connect string in that file. If you review the previous code block, notice that the MINX connect string has `.world` attached to the end of it. This is your default domain. If you do not have a `sqlnet.ora` file setup, or if your default domain in that file is not set to `world`, you may receive the `tns-12154: could not resolve service name` error when you try to connect to the Oracle database specified by that connect descriptor. The following code block shows you a sample of the `sqlnet.ora` file:

```
AUTOMATIC_IPC = OFF
TRACE_LEVEL_CLIENT = OFF
names.directory_path = (TNSNAMES, HOSTNAME, ONAMES)
names.default_domain = world
name.default_zone = world
```

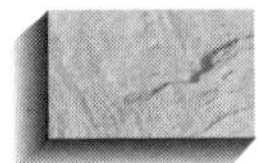

TIP
Ideally, the default domain for your Oracle network should also be the domain of the machine hosting the Oracle database. Thus, if your machine's domain is `.couchman.com`, the default domain may also be `.couchman.com`. Often, however, Oracle customers simply set the default domain for their Oracle network to `.world`.

Using listener.ora

The final file to consider is the `listener.ora` file. This file configures particulars about the Net8 listener residing on the Oracle server, so you will find this file on the machine hosting the Oracle database. The default name for your Net8 listener is LISTENER, but this file contains the nondefault name of the Net8 listener if you have defined it. It also contains the SIDs of all the Oracle databases on the host machine that the listener handles connection requests for, and the protocol the listener will tune into. If you want your database to support connections across multiple protocols, you may either run multiple listeners, one for each protocol, or simply configure one listener to listen for every protocol. A single listener can listen for network connections for many networks and for many databases, all at the same time. However, more databases and network protocols mean more work for the Oracle Net8 listener process, which may create a network bottleneck for busy databases. The following code block demonstrates the contents of a typical `listener.ora` file.

```
LISTENER =
  (ADDRESS_LIST =
        (ADDRESS= (PROTOCOL= IPC)(KEY= minxbase))
        (ADDRESS= (PROTOCOL= IPC)(KEY= PNPKEY))
        (ADDRESS= (PROTOCOL= TCP)(Host= 1.2.3.4)(Port= 1521))
  )
SID_LIST_LISTENER =
  (SID_LIST =
    (SID_DESC =
      (GLOBAL_DBNAME= coolmack.)
```

```
      (ORACLE_HOME= /usr2/app/oracle/product/8.1.5)
      (SID_NAME = belly)
    )
    (SID_DESC =
      (GLOBAL_DBNAME= workstation2.)
      (ORACLE_HOME= /u01/app/oracle/product/8.0.4)
      (SID_NAME = tstminx)
    )
    (SID_DESC =
      (GLOBAL_DBNAME= workstation1.)
      (ORACLE_HOME= /u01/app/oracle/product/8.0.5)
      (SID_NAME = minxbase)
    )
  )
STARTUP_WAIT_TIME_LISTENER = 0
CONNECT_TIMEOUT_LISTENER = 10
TRACE_LEVEL_LISTENER = OFF
```

For Review

Be sure you can name all files used for Oracle network connectivity and describe their usage. Know whether the file named is stored on the client or on the server. Also, be able to identify that file on sight.

Generating Net8 Files with Net8 Assistant

This section covers how you generate your Net8 files with Net8 Assistant. You will learn the steps required to create and edit all the files just described, using this GUI tool provided by Oracle in Oracle8 and later releases.

Configuring Net8 Files and Using Local Naming Method

You can continue to use locally configured and maintained `tnsnames.ora` files. Net8 has enhanced the Easy Config utility to improve your ability to configure this file by offering modifications in several areas. For example, now you can configure more components in the connect descriptor stored in the `tnsnames.ora` file. In TCP/IP, this includes the ability to configure a port on the host machine other than 1521, where a listener might exist. To configure a part in SQL*Net 2.*x*, you had to make the modification to the actual `tnsnames.ora` file, violating the rule that users should never modify their `tnsnames.ora` files directly and preventing further use of the Easy Config utility with that `tnsnames.ora` file. You can also test your connection from within Easy Config to ensure that the connect descriptor generated is correct. In previous versions, you had to close Easy Config and attempt opening a session with a tool such as SQL*Plus in order to test the connection, and if the information was wrong, you had to go back into Easy Config to fix `tnsnames.ora`.

Using Net8 Assistant to Set Up tnsnames.ora

You can continue to use locally configured and maintained `tnsnames.ora` files. Net8 has the Net8 Assistant utility to improve your ability to configure this file. This discussion covers how to use Net8 Assistant for this purpose. Note that you can use Net8 Easy Config to configure your local names file, as you might have done with SQL*Net 2.3. However, Oracle has not committed to supporting Net8 Easy Config, given that Net8 Assistant also provides this functionality.

To set up your `tnsnames.ora` file using Net8 Assistant, follow these steps:

1. Start Net8 Assistant on your client. In Windows, do this by clicking Start | Programs | Oracle for Windows | Oracle Net8 Assistant. You may be informed that your file contains comment information that may be overwritten. Click Yes to specify that it is okay to do so.
2. Drill down to the Network | Service Names node, and click on the Add button, which contains the small plus sign (+) at the top of the interface. You will then see the Net8 Assistant Service Name Wizard. First, you define your service name, which is the same as the connect string used to logically identify the database. Figure 3-2 displays the Net8 Assistant Service Name Wizard window with a new service being configured. To proceed to the next screen, click Next.

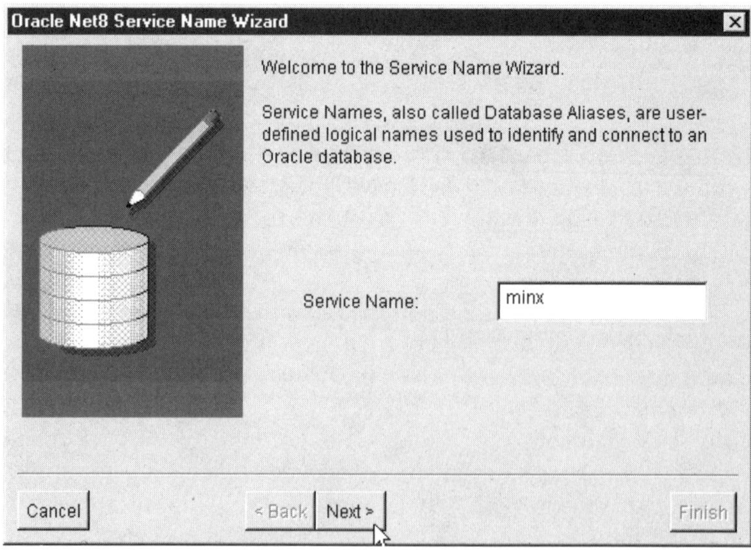

FIGURE 3-2. *Net8 Assistant with new service being configured*

3. The next screen is where you select the networking protocol to be used in support of the new service being configured. The list box in the center of the screen will reflect all the protocols installed on your client, such as TCP/IP, SPX, or Named Pipes. You may have additional network protocols on your own machine, as well. Two other protocols that you should always see listed are Bequeath (local database) and IPC (interprocess communication) for other local processes, such as EXTPROC. Figure 3-3 shows the networking-protocol selection screen in Net8 Assistant Service Name Wizard.
4. You can select your networking protocol for this connect string and then click Next to move to the next screen, where you define the network-specific information for connecting to your host using this protocol. For example, if you selected TCP/IP as the networking protocol, this next screen asks that you define the name of the machine hosting Oracle and the port number on which the listener exists. After configuring this information, click Next.
5. The next screen is where you define the SID for your Oracle database on the host you designated in the previous step. Enter your SID in the text box provided, and click Next.

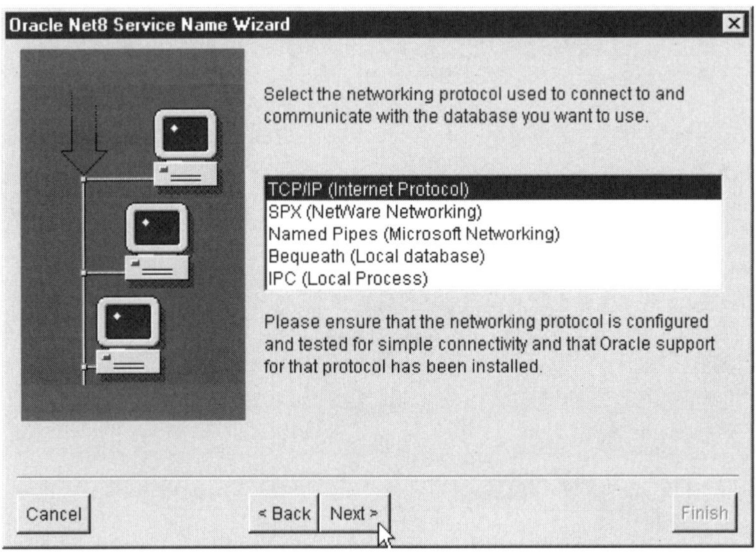

FIGURE 3-3. *Net8 Assistant with networking protocol being configured*

6. The following screen is where you can test your service configuration. Click the Test button to do so, and a new screen will appear where Net8 Assistant will attempt to execute a test connection to the listener. Enter a username and password for Net8 to use, and click Test. The results of your test will be shown in the text box, as shown in Figure 3-4. When testing is finished, click Done.
7. You will now be back to the screen you saw in step 6. If the test succeeded, proceed to the next screen by clicking the Next button, and skip ahead to step 8. If the test didn't succeed, click the Back button to return to steps 3, 4, and 5 to reconfigure your network or Oracle SID information to correct the problem. After that, return to step 6 and retest. Keep doing this until your test succeeds.
8. At this point, your configuration is finished, so click the Finish button.

Using Net8 Assistant to Identify Client Preferences

The final area you need to understand in this chapter is how to use Net8 Assistant to identify client preferences for connection to your database. This tool includes a

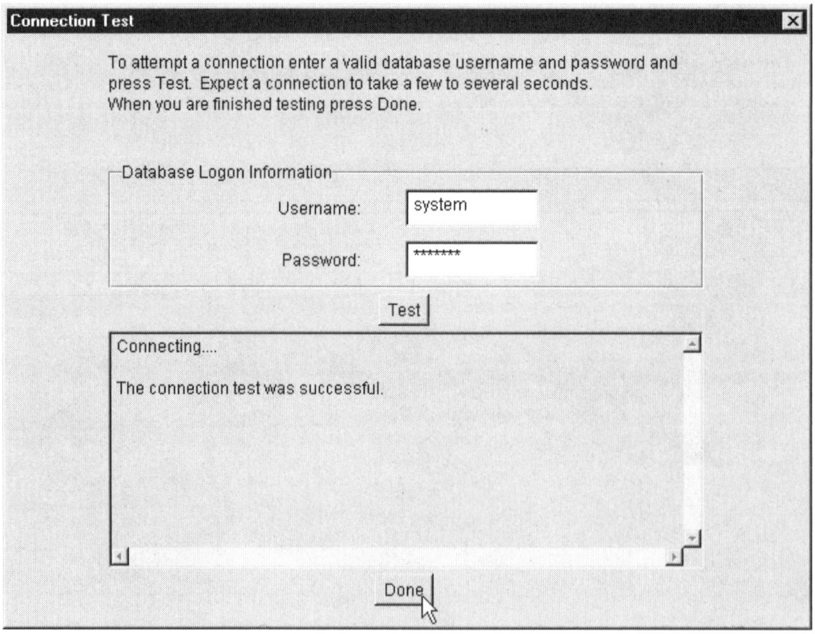

FIGURE 3-4. *Net8 Assistant test interface*

node that you can drill down into called Profiles, where you can define how your client will attempt to connect to the Oracle server. You can open this node by clicking on Network | Profile in the drill-down area on the left side of Net8 Assistant. When you do so, the work area on the right will show a drop-down list box in which you can set up different profile areas for your client. Available areas in that list box are Naming, General, Preferred Oracle Names Servers, Oracle Security Server, and Advanced Networking Options.

Figure 3-5 shows you what you should see in the work area if you select Naming from the drop-down list box. Three tab interfaces are available, representing the three ways you can set up how clients find servers in the Oracle network. Those tab interfaces are Methods, Oracle Names, and External. The Methods tab interface is where you set all the methods you want available to your client. The available methods are shown in Figure 3-5 and should be self-explanatory. The Selected Methods window on the left shows you what methods your client will attempt to use in order to connect to Oracle. You can add or take away methods from the Available Methods window on the right using the arrow buttons between the two windows.

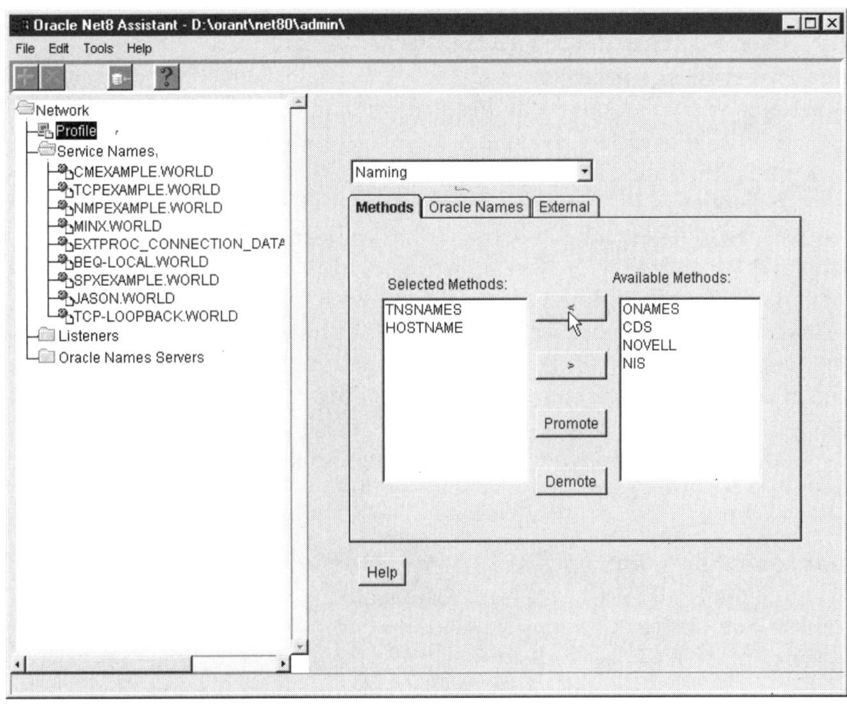

FIGURE 3-5. *Net8 Assistant Naming work area with Methods tab interface shown*

Setting Order of Preference for Naming Methods

The list of Selected Methods also indicates the order of preference your client will use in attempting to locate a host. In Figure 3-5, you see that this client will attempt to use local naming first. If the client cannot find a local `tnsnames.ora` file, it will attempt to use Oracle Names. If the client cannot find `tnsnames.ora` or an Oracle Names server, the client will attempt to use host-naming. You can set the order of preference you want your client to use when attempting to find a host. First, click on the method in the Selected Methods window whose preference you want to set. Second, click on Promote to move the method up or Demote to move it down in the list. By doing so, you change the order that Net8 uses to determine the location of Oracle databases on the network for this client.

TIP

By default, Net8 will attempt to resolve a service name lookup using the following methods in this order: local naming with `tnsnames.ora`, Oracle Names, host-naming.

Using Net8 Assistant to Set General Client Preferences in sqlnet.ora

The other area you will focus on in this discussion is setting general client preferences in Net8 Assistant. Note that these changes get written to the `sqlnet.ora` file. Setting general preferences for your client is accomplished by clicking on General in the drop-down list in the Profiles work area. When you do so, you will see four new tab interfaces in that work area, called Tracing, Logging, Routing, and Advanced. Figure 3-6 shows the Net8 Assistant Tracing tab interface. The Tracing tab interface allows you to define where client-side and server-side trace files are kept, while the Logging tab interface handles the setup of client-side log file/directory and server-side log directory information. The Routing tab interface has check boxes where you can specify whether this client wants to use dedicated servers, IPC addresses, or source routing addresses. Finally, the Advanced tab interface allows you to configure advanced features like a client registration ID and TNS timeout in seconds.

UsingNet8 Assistant to Set Up the Network Listener

To configure the Net8 listener on your host machine, you must first start Net8 Assistant. When Oracle is running on Windows, this is accomplished by clicking Start | Programs | Oracle for Windows | Oracle Net8 Assistant. You may be asked whether it is okay to continue due to comment information being detected in your network configuration file. Click Yes, and you will then see the Net8 Assistant window, shown in Figure 3-7. As you can see from the figure, this utility is laid out

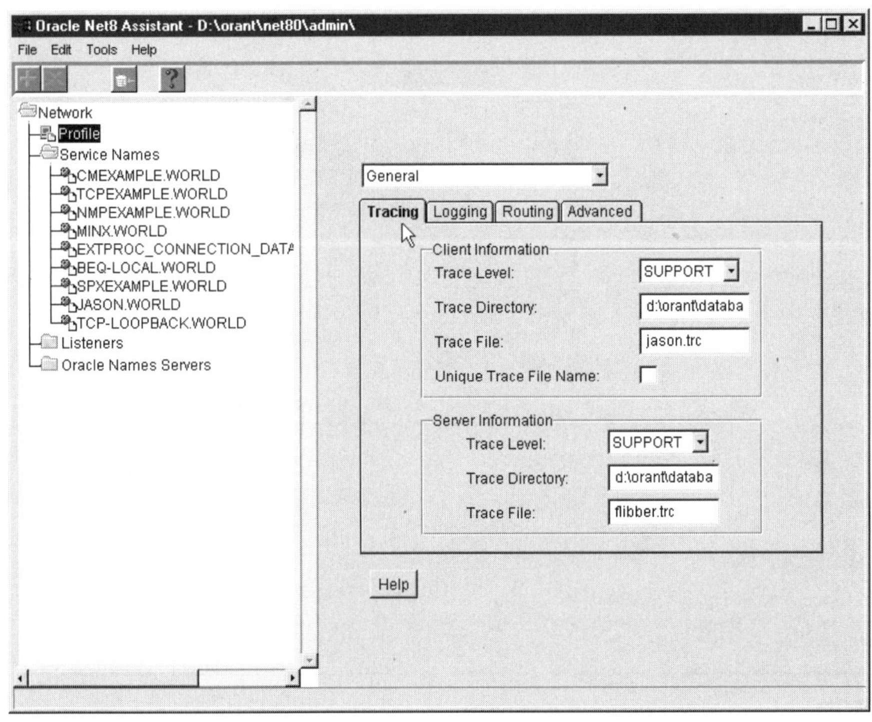

FIGURE 3-6. *Net8 Assistant Tracing tab interface*

like most Oracle utilities, with the drill-down interface on the left and the work area on the right.

The default name for your network listener process is LISTENER. You can configure the default listener by drilling down to the Network | Listeners | LISTENER node. In the work area on the right, you should see the listener configuration interface, shown in Figure 3-7. You can configure your Net8 listener in four different areas, specified by the drop-down list box in the upper-left corner of the Net8 Assistant work area. These four areas are General Parameters, Listening Locations, Database Services, and Other Services. These areas will each be explained in some detail.

Configuring General Parameters

The General Parameters configuration area allows you to configure general listener properties, including delay on startup, saving configuration on shutdown, logging and tracing properties such as log and trace files, and whether authentication is

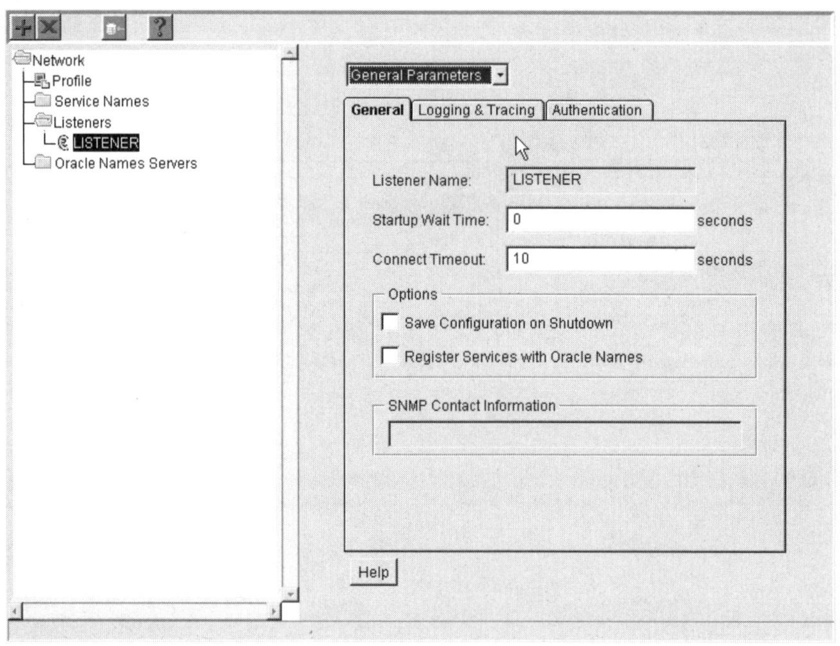

FIGURE 3-7. *Net8 Assistant interface*

required to perform listener startup and shutdown. There are three tab interfaces: General, Logging & Tracing, and Authentication (shown in Figure 3-7).

The General tab has several text boxes in which you can set values for Startup Wait Time, Connect Timeout, and SNMP Contact Information. The tab also contains a pair of check boxes in which you can indicate whether you want your configuration saved on listener-process shutdown and whether any of the services this listener tunes in for should be registered with Oracle Names. If you are running Names, you should click this check box.

Many operations performed by LSNRCTL, such as stopping the listener, require a password by default. You may find it easier if you configure the listener not to require a password. This is accomplished by clicking the Authentication tab in the General Parameters work area for your listener. In the Authentication tab, click the Do Not Require a Password for Listener Operations radio button, as shown in Figure 3-8. Then select the File | Save Network Configuration menu option to save this setup.

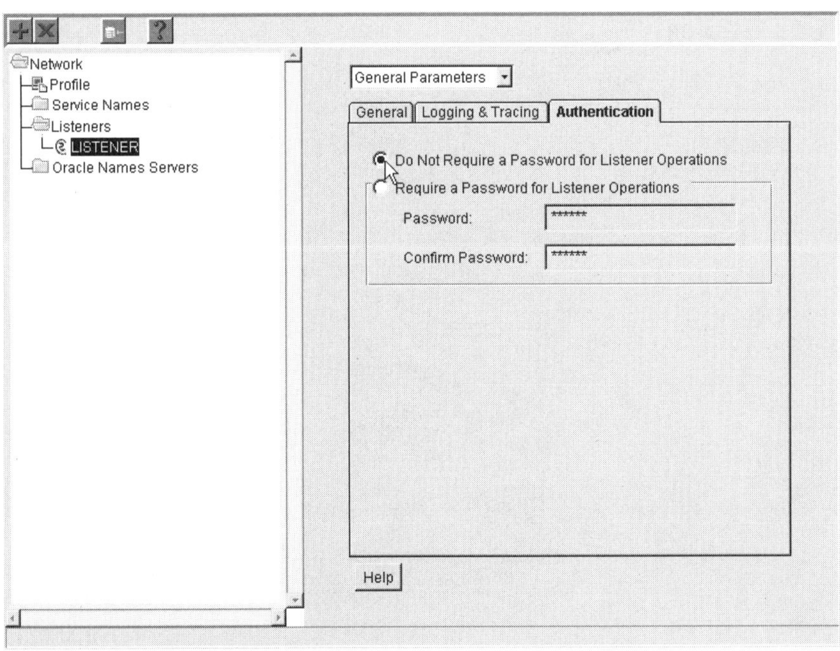

FIGURE 3-8. *Net8 Assistant Authentication tab*

Configuring Listening Locations

The Listening Locations configuration area allows you to specify where this listener will listen for connections. Available addresses are shown as tab interfaces, as shown in Figure 3-9, and in each tab, you select a protocol for the location and either host/port or key information. Buttons at the bottom of the window allow you to add or remove listening locations. You can include setups for all the networks from which users may attempt to access Oracle, each as a separate address in this interface.

Each Address tab will have a Protocol drop-down list box, in which you can select from available protocols. The appearance of any other text boxes in this interface depends on the protocol you choose. If you choose TCP, you will see Host and Port text boxes for setting the hostname/IP address and the port the listener should tune into. If you choose NMP (named pipes), you will see Machine Name and Pipe Name text boxes. If you choose IPC (interprocess communication, used when client and server run on the same node), you will see a Key text box. If you choose SPX, you will see a Service Name text box. Selecting other protocols will cause other text

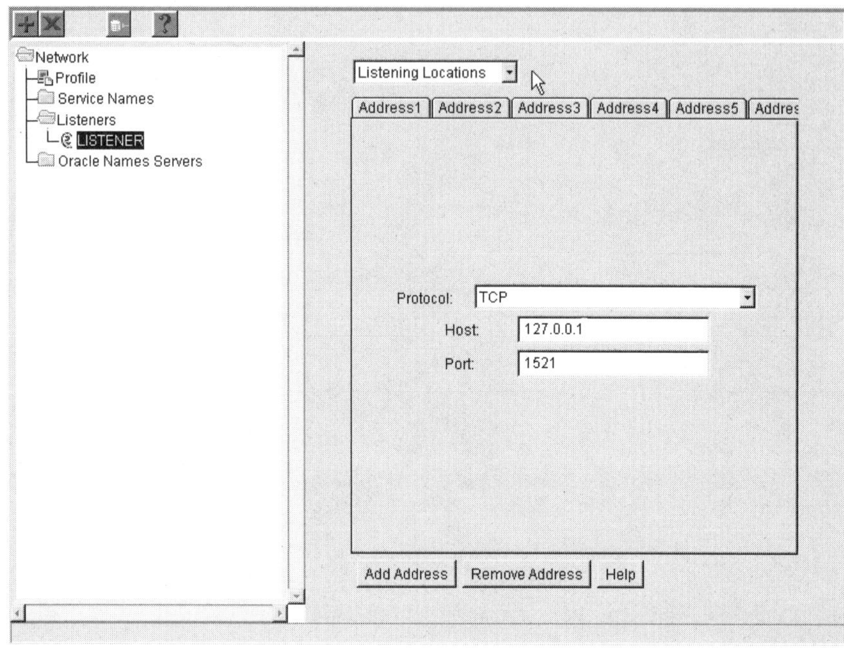

FIGURE 3-9. *Listening Locations tab interface*

boxes to appear that capture relevant information for establishing how the listener process tunes into incoming user sessions.

Configuring Database Services

The Database Services tab is where you configure which database this listener will listen for connections to. (Figure 3-10 shows you the Database Services tab interface.) Many organizations run only one Oracle database on a host machine, meaning that a listener will listen for connections to only one database. But, if you plan to run multiple Oracle8 databases on one host, you may need to manipulate the number of databases the listener will listen for connections to, using the Add Database and Remove Database buttons.

For each database your listener serves, you will define a Global Database Name, Oracle Home Directory, and SID, all in the appropriate text boxes in the interface. You can also choose to have the listener prespawn or not prespawn dedicated servers for this database by clicking the appropriate radio button. If you choose to prespawn, you will need to select the number of dedicated servers that

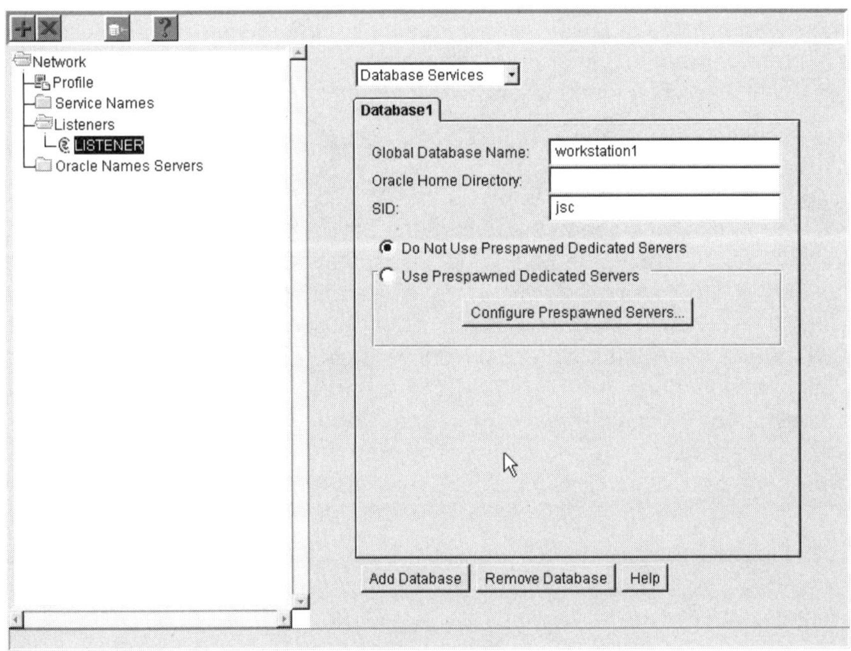

FIGURE 3-10. *Database Services tab interface*

the listener should prespawn for each of the network protocols the listener tunes in to; to do this, click the Configure Prespawned Servers button, and enter appropriate values in the Configure Prespawned Servers interface.

Configuring Other Services

The Other Services area is where you configure the Net8 listener to listen for services other than databases that might have users connecting to them. Figure 3-11 shows this interface. The most common example of another service that your listener might listen for connections to is EXTPROC. Other examples include Web or other application servers.

For each other service you configure, you will need to enter several pieces of information in the text boxes in the interface. The first text box, Global Service Name, is the global name for this service. Any valid service name is okay. The next text box, Program Name, is the name of the executable program running the service. The third text box, Program Argument Zero, is the first internal argument or command-line argument that makes the program run (known in C programming as *argv0*). Next, the Program Arguments text box identifies any other command-line arguments in the form `argument=value`. The Environment text box is used to identify any environment variables that must be defined before starting the service. Finally, the SID text box identifies the system identifier for this service.

Naming the Listener

One aspect of listener configuration you can do outside of Net8 Assistant is to name the listener. Be careful when manually editing network configuration files. For some releases of Oracle7, Oracle did not support manually changed configuration files.

The default name for your network listener is LISTENER, but it can have any name you want. If you want to change the name of your network listener, you must do so using the listener configuration file that Net8 Assistant helps to write. In most Oracle installations on Windows, the `net80/admin` subdirectory under your Oracle software home directory contains a file called `listener.ora`. This is the listener configuration file. If you do not find the `net80` directory on your installation, you can look in other directories, such as `network/admin`. Once you find it, you can open and modify

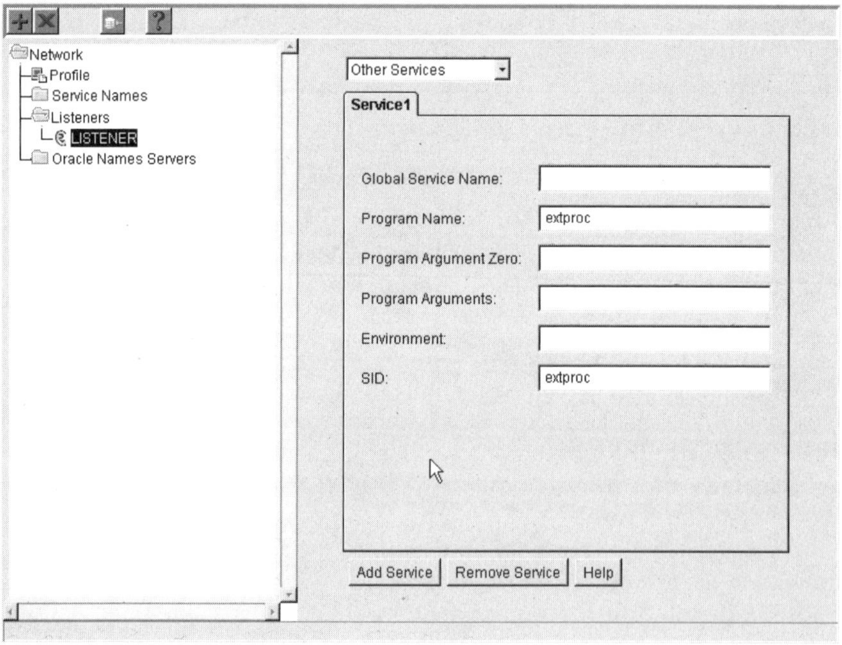

FIGURE 3-11. *Other Services tab interface*

`listener.ora` using your favorite text editor, such as Notepad. To name the listener something besides LISTENER, add the parameter `MYLISTENER = name`, where *name* is a small alphanumeric text string.

Starting the Network Listener

LSNRCTL is the Listener Control utility, a tool that helps you manipulate the listener process. Once the listener is configured, you can start it with LSNRCTL. LSNRCTL is similar to SQL*Plus or Server Manager running in line mode in that you can run this utility interactively and in batch mode.

To operate LSNRCTL interactively, simply enter the name of the LSNRCTL executable at the host-system command prompt. Once in the LSNRCTL interactive application, you can enter a command that LSNRCTL understands. To start your listener, use the `start` command, as shown here for Windows environments:

```
D:\orant\NET80\ADMIN> lsnrctl80
LSNRCTL80 for 32-bit Windows: Version 8.0.5.0.0
Production on 05-MAY-99 11:58:39
(c) Copyright 1997 Oracle Corporation.  All rights reserved.
Welcome to LSNRCTL, type help for information.
LSNRCTL> start
Starting tnslsnr80: please wait
Service OracleTNSListener80 start pending.
Service OracleTNSListener80 started.
TNSLSNR80 for 32-bit Windows: Version 8.0.5.0.0 Production
System parameter file is D:\orant\NET80\admin\listener.ora
Log messages written to D:\orant\NET80\log\listener.log
Listening on: (ADDRESS=(PROTOCOL=ipc)
(PIPENAME=\\.\pipe\oracle.worldipc))
Listening on: (ADDRESS=(PROTOCOL=ipc)
(PIPENAME=\\.\pipe\EXTPROC0ipc))
Listening on: (ADDRESS=(PROTOCOL=nmp)
(PIPENAME=\\WORKSTATION1\pipe\ORAPIPE))
Listening on: (ADDRESS=(PROTOCOL=tcp)
(DEV=164)(HOST=11.11.11.11)(PORT=1521))
Listening on: (ADDRESS=(PROTOCOL=tcp)
(DEV=124)(HOST=11.11.11.11)(PORT=1526))
Listening on: (ADDRESS=(PROTOCOL=tcp)
(DEV=140)(HOST=127.0.0.1)(PORT=1521))
Listening on: (ADDRESS=(PROTOCOL=ipc)
(PIPENAME=\\.\pipe\JSCipc))
Connecting to (ADDRESS=(PROTOCOL=IPC)
(KEY=oracle.world))
STATUS of the LISTENER
----------------------
Alias                     LISTENER
```

```
Version                       TNSLSNR80 for 32-bit Windows:
                              Version 8.0.5.0.0 Production
Start Date                    05-MAY-99 11:58:47
Uptime                        0 days 0 hr. 0 min. 2 sec
Trace Level                   off
Security                      ON
SNMP                          OFF
Listener Parameter File       D:\orant\NET80\admin\listener.ora
Listener Log File             D:\orant\NET80\log\listener.log
Services Summary
  JSC            has 1 service handler(s)
  extproc        has 1 service handler(s)
The command completed successfully
LSNRCTL>
```

To operate LSNRCTL in batch, you issue the name of the Listener Control utility executable, followed by the command you want executed on your listener, followed by the listener name. If you have not renamed your listener, you needn't include the name of your listener, because LSNRCTL will assume LISTENER is the name of your listener. For example, to start the listener on UNIX, issue **`lsnrctl start`**. For Windows, the name of the LSNRCTL executable is `lsnrctl80`, as shown in the following code block:

```
D:\orant\NET80\ADMIN> lsnrctl80 start
LSNRCTL80 for 32-bit Windows: Version 8.0.5.0.0
Production on 05-MAY-99 12:00:39
(c) Copyright 1997 Oracle Corporation.  All rights reserved.
Starting tnslsnr80: please wait
Service OracleTNSListener80 start pending.
Service OracleTNSListener80 started.
TNSLSNR80 for 32-bit Windows: Version 8.0.5.0.0 Production
System parameter file is D:\orant\NET80\admin\listener.ora
Log messages written to D:\orant\NET80\log\listener.log
Listening on: (ADDRESS=(PROTOCOL=ipc)
(PIPENAME=\\.\pipe\oracle.worldipc))
Listening on: (ADDRESS=(PROTOCOL=ipc)
(PIPENAME=\\.\pipe\EXTPROC0ipc))
Listening on: (ADDRESS=(PROTOCOL=nmp)
(PIPENAME=\\WORKSTATION1\pipe\ORAPIPE))
Listening on: (ADDRESS=(PROTOCOL=tcp)
(DEV=164)(HOST=11.11.11.11)(PORT=1521))
Listening on: (ADDRESS=(PROTOCOL=tcp)
(DEV=124)(HOST=11.11.11.11)(PORT=1526))
Listening on: (ADDRESS=(PROTOCOL=tcp)
(DEV=140)(HOST=127.0.0.1)(PORT=1521))
Listening on: (ADDRESS=(PROTOCOL=ipc)
(PIPENAME=\\.\pipe\JSCipc))
```

```
Connecting to (ADDRESS=(PROTOCOL=IPC)
(KEY=oracle.world))
STATUS of the LISTENER
----------------------
Alias                     LISTENER
Version                   TNSLSNR80 for 32-bit Windows:
                          Version 8.0.5.0.0 Production
Start Date                05-MAY-99 12:01:07
Uptime                    0 days 0 hr. 0 min. 2 sec
Trace Level               off
Security                  ON
SNMP                      OFF
Listener Parameter File   D:\orant\NET80\admin\listener.ora
Listener Log File         D:\orant\NET80\log\listener.log
Services Summary
  JSC          has 1 service handler(s)
  extproc      has 1 service handler(s)
The command completed successfully
D:\orant\NET80\ADMIN>
```

Using LSNRCTL to Stop the Listener

Stopping your listener using LSNRCTL is best accomplished with LSNRCTL running in interactive mode because this operation requires a password by default. To stop the listener interactively in Windows, start LSNRCTL using the `lsnrctl80` command, set the password for the session using `set password`, and then issue the `stop` *name* command, where *name* is the name of your listener and is optional if your listener name is LISTENER. The following code block illustrates stopping the listener:

```
D:\orant\NET80\ADMIN> lsnrctl80
LSNRCTL80 for 32-bit Windows: Version 8.0.5.0.0
Production on 05-MAY-99 12:05:39
(c) Copyright 1997 Oracle Corporation.  All rights reserved.
Welcome to LSNRCTL, type help for information.
LSNRCTL> set password
Password:
The command completed successfully
LSNRCTL> stop
Connecting to (ADDRESS=(PROTOCOL=IPC)(KEY=oracle.world))
The command completed successfullY
LSNRCTL>
```

Troubleshooting Listener Shutdown

If you want to start and stop your listener in batch mode, you may find it easier to do so if you configure the listener not to require password authentication using Net8 Assistant. To configure the listener not to require password authentication for startup and shutdown, you can do so within Net8 Assistant by selecting the Do Not Require a Password for Listener Operations radio button, in the General Parameters menu, on the Authentication tab.

You may experience some problems with stopping your network listener process in batch if you use the default password authentication requirement, as shown in the following code block:

```
D:\orant\NET80\ADMIN> lsnrctl80 stop
LSNRCTL80 for 32-bit Windows: Version 8.0.5.0.0 -
Production on 05-MAY-99 12:10:03
(c) Copyright 1997 Oracle Corporation.  All rights reserved.
Connecting to (ADDRESS=(PROTOCOL=IPC)(KEY=oracle.world))
TNS-01169: The listener has not recognized the password
```

A `TNS-01169` error simply means you should run LSNRCTL interactively, issue the `set password` command for the LSNRCTL session, and then issue the `stop` command. If running LSNRCTL interactively seems too frustrating, you should set up your listener not to require password authentication at all using Net8 Assistant.

Finally, if your listener is not started when you attempt to stop it, you will receive a long set of output. Don't worry, you simply need to remember that you must have your listener started before you stop it. The output that will result when you try to stop a stopped listener looks approximately like the following code block:

```
D:\orant\NET80\ADMIN> lsnrctl80
LSNRCTL80 for 32-bit Windows: Version 8.0.5.0.0
Production on 05-MAY-99 12:20:39
(c) Copyright 1997 Oracle Corporation.  All rights reserved.
Welcome to LSNRCTL, type help for information.
LSNRCTL> set password jason
The command completed successfully
LSNRCTL> stop
Connecting to (ADDRESS=(PROTOCOL=IPC)(KEY=oracle.world))
TNS-12224: TNS:no listener
 TNS-12541: TNS:no listener
  TNS-12560: TNS:protocol adapter error
   TNS-00511: No listener
    32-bit Windows Error: 2: No such file or directory
```

Additional LSNRCTL Commands

Although your use of LSNRCTL will be primarily for starting and stopping the listener, you can accomplish several other listener-management tasks with it. The basic format for all commands is `lsnrctl` *`command name`*, where *`command`* is replaced by the command you want to use, and *`name`* is replaced with the name of the listener you wish to administer. If you want to work on the default listener named LISTENER, *name* is optional. The table below shows the available LSNRCTL commands. Note that, by default, these operations require you to supply a password. The following code block gives an example of using LSNRCTL commands:

```
D:\orant\NET80\ADMIN> lsnrctl80
LSNRCTL80 for 32-bit Windows: Version 8.0.5.0.0
Production on 05-MAY-99 12:30:39
(c) Copyright 1997 Oracle Corporation.  All rights reserved.
Welcome to LSNRCTL, type help for information.
LSNRCTL> services
Connecting to (ADDRESS=(PROTOCOL=IPC)(KEY=oracle.world))
Services Summary...
  JSC          has 1 service handler(s)
    DEDICATED SERVER established:0 refused:0
      LOCAL SERVER
  extproc      has 1 service handler(s)
    DEDICATED SERVER established:0 refused:0
      LOCAL SERVER
The command completed successfully
```

The following table lists the LSNRCTL commands:

LSNRCTL Command	**Description**
`change_password`	Changes the password required for authenticated listener activities, such as stopping the listener.
`dbsnmp_start`	Starts the Simple Network Management Protocol agent for Oracle running on that host machine.
`dbsnmp_status`	Returns current status for the Simple Network Management Protocol agent for Oracle running on that host machine.
`dbsnmp_stop`	Stops the Simple Network Management Protocol agent for Oracle running on that host machine.
`help`	Lists all the commands available; use the `help` command to get specific information about a particular LSNRCTL command.
`quit` `exit`	Terminates this session with LSNRCTL; only used when LSNRCTL is run in interactive mode.
`reload`	Reconfigures your listener without stopping it by shutting down all aspects of your listener except listener addresses, then reloading `listener.ora`.

LSNRCTL Command	Description
save_config	Updates listener.ora with any configuration changes made in the LSNRCTL interactive session, and also makes a copy of your configuration file called listener.bak.
services	Shows information about connections established and refused for dedicated servers, prespawned servers, and dispatchers that listener works with.
spawn *program* (*arguments*)	Starts the *program* named as a parameter to this command. The *program* should correspond to an alias defined by settings for the SID_LIST_LISTENER parameter in the listener.ora file.
status	Displays listener version, start time, run duration, trace enabled, and listener.ora file used for startup.
trace (*option*)	Starts tracing for the listener; valid values for *option* include off, user, admin, and support.
version	Displays listener and Oracle Protocol Adapter versions.

LSNRCTL SET and SHOW Commands

The set and show commands allow you to establish and display LSNRCTL session-wide values for various options. You have already seen one example of a set command, and that was set password. Every option you can specify for the set command has an equivalent show command option, except for set password.

The syntax for set and show commands are set *option* and show *option*, respectively. Available set and show options are shown on the facing page. Examples of using set and show are given in the following code block:

```
D:\orant\NET80\ADMIN> lsnrctl80
LSNRCTL80 for 32-bit Windows: Version 8.0.5.0.0
Production on 05-MAY-99 12:58:39
(c) Copyright 1997 Oracle Corporation.  All rights reserved.
Welcome to LSNRCTL, type help for information.
LSNRCTL> set log_file logfile1;
Connecting to (ADDRESS=(PROTOCOL=IPC)(KEY=oracle.world))
LISTENER parameter "log_file" set to logfile1.log
The command completed successfully
LSNRCTL> show log_file
Connecting to (ADDRESS=(PROTOCOL=IPC)(KEY=oracle.world))
LISTENER parameter "log_file" set to logfile1.log
The command completed successfully
```

The following table lists the `set` and `show` command options:

set/show Option	**Description**
`connect_timeout` *`seconds`*	Specifies seconds to be the amount of time that the listener will wait for connection request after the connection is started.
`current_listener` *`name`*	Specifies *`name`* to be the listener being manipulated during this LSNRCTL session; useful when multiple listeners are available on the machine.
`log_directory` *`path`*	Sets *`path`* to be the default log directory where listener process logs are written.
`log_file` *`filename`*	Changes the default log filename to *`filename`*.
`log_status` *`status`*	Changes logging status, where *`status`* can be `on` or `off`.
`save_config_on_stop` *`status`*	Defines whether LSNRCTL should save listener configuration changes made this session to `listener.ora`; valid values for *`status`* are `on` and `off`.
`startup_waittime` *`seconds`*	Specifies *`seconds`* to be how long the listener will wait before responding to a `start` command.
`trc_directory` *`path`*	Specifies *`path`* to be the default directory where trace files for this listener will be written.
`trc_file` *`filename`*	Changes the default trace filename for this listener to *`filename`*.
`trc_level` *`option`*	Sets tracing for this listener; valid values for *`option`* are `off`, `user`, `admin`, and `support`.
`use_plug_and_play` *`status`*	Tells the current listener to register with a Names server running on the network, and the listener will look for Names servers on established ports; valid values for *`status`* are `on` and `off`.

NET START and NET STOP: LSNRCTL Alternatives

From the DOS command line, you can also start and stop your Net8 listener with the `net start` and `net stop` commands, respectively. Observe in the following code block the syntax for doing so:

```
C:\orant> net start MYLISTENER
```

or

```
C:\orant> net stop MYLISTENER
```

For Review

1. Identify the commands that can be used to determine the current listener version running on a machine. What are some other commands that can be used with LSNRCTL? What are `set` and `show` commands? Identify some different options that can be defined and displayed with `set` and `show` commands.
2. How do you stop your network listener process? How can you change the authentication requirement for stopping the listener? What command is used to identify a password for LSNRCTL operations? What is LSNRCTL? How is it used? What is it used for?
3. What are the three arguments for running LSNRCTL from the command line? Which of these arguments is optional, and under what circumstances? What are the four areas for configuring your Net8 listener in the Net8 Assistant? Identify the method of navigating through the Net8 Assistant interface to configure the listener.
4. What is the default name for your listener? How do you name the listener something besides its default name?

Creating the OEM Repository

For versions of Oracle Enterprise Manager prior to OEM 2.0, you will need to create an OEM repository on every database you want to administer prior to actually using OEM for that purpose on that database. In OEM 2.0 and later, you need to create only one repository on one database for all databases you want to administer.

Here's a little information on what the repository is used for. OEM keeps a set of database objects like tables, indexes, sequences, views, and so on, for the purpose of providing certain key functionality in the OEM repository. Before creating the OEM repository, it is usually a good idea to create a new user on your database to own the repository and a separate tablespace for storing these objects as well, though certain items like PL/SQL source code always get stored in the SYSTEM tablespace. Certain OEM software bundles (Oracle calls them *packs*, as in Tuning Pack or Management Pack) create more objects in the repository than others, particularly Tuning Pack, which stores a great deal of information in your repository. You shouldn't need to do much to administer this tablespace, unless you use some of these more repository-intensive packs and/or do a lot of performance monitoring with these Oracle tools. If you are using these tools a lot (like Oracle Expert), you should monitor the size of the tablespace storing your OEM repository and ensure it does not run out of space.

TIP

Repositories are only required for using the OEM console. If you want to run any OEM application such as Instance Manager or Storage Manager stand-alone, connected directly to a database, you can do so without creating a repository on that database. However, the enhanced functionality provided via the OEM console will not be available to you—only the functions provided by the application running stand-alone.

Creating the OEM Repository: Step-by-Step

The following instructions show you how to create that repository on your Oracle database:

1. In SQL*Plus, create a user to house the OEM repository. For versions of Oracle prior to 8.1.5, click Start | Programs | Oracle for Windows | SQL*Plus. For Oracle 8.1.5 and later, click Start | Programs | Oracle – ORACLE_HOME | Development | SQL*Plus. Log in to your database as SYS, and issue the following commands, noting that you may want to choose a different pathname depending on where your Oracle datafiles are located:

```
create tablespace oem_repository
datafile 'e:\orant\oradata\minx\oemrep01.dbf' size 50M reuse
default storage (initial 50K next 50K pctincrease 0)
online;

create user oem
identified by oem
default tablespace oem_repository
temporary tablespace temp;
```

2. Click Start | Programs | Oracle Enterprise Manager | Enterprise Manager to start the OEM console. You will need to provide the username, password, and connect string for the user you just created to connect. Once you have done so, OEM will prompt you that this is a new database and that you need to create a repository using the window shown here. Click OK to permit OEM to do this.

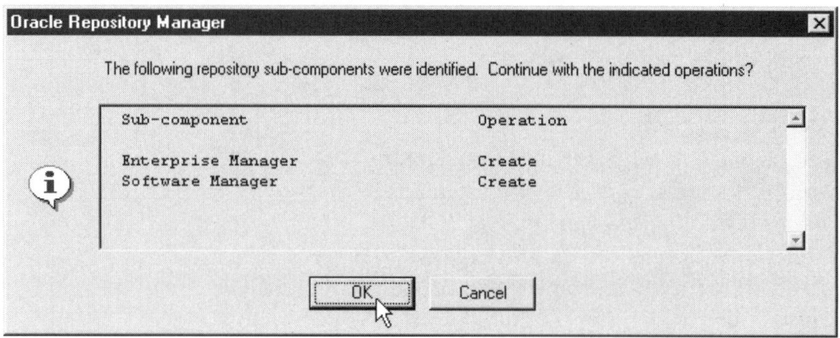

3. After that, OEM will show you its progress in creating the new repository, using the window shown next.

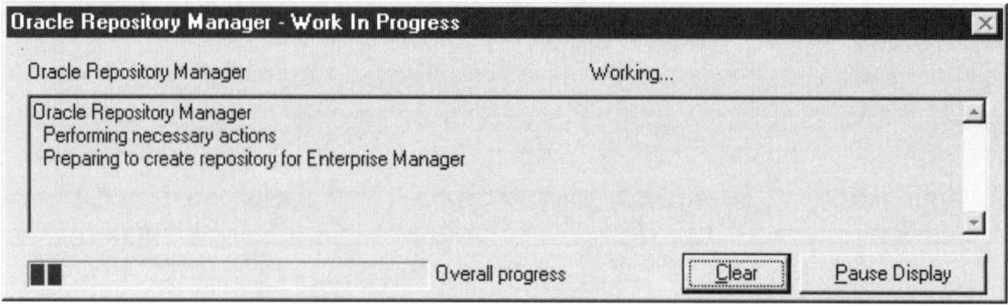

4. When complete, Oracle will show you the OEM console, as in Figure 3-12.

Intelligent Agent and Service Discovery

You're not finished yet. After creating the database repository, OEM still needs some stuff to allow you the ability to administer your Oracle database. OEM needs to see what databases are out there running. To do so, Oracle Intelligent Agent must be running in conjunction with that Oracle database. Intelligent Agent uses two configuration files, `snmp_ro.ora` and `snmp_rw.ora`, to handle all its configuration needs. These files are created the first time Intelligent Agent is run and placed in the

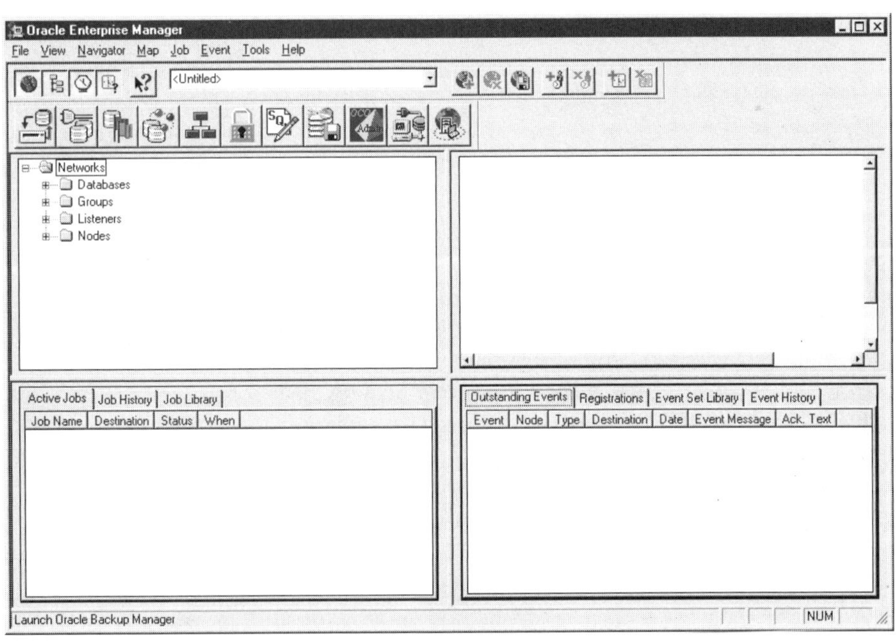

FIGURE 3-12. *Oracle Enterprise Manager console*

network/admin or net80/admin subdirectory under ORACLE_HOME. The following code block shows the contents of your snmp_ro.ora file:

```
snmp.visibleservices = (listener, minx)
snmp.shortname.listener = LISTENER
snmp.longname.listener = listener_workstation1
snmp.configfile.listener = E:\orant\network\admin\listener.ora
snmp.oraclehome.listener = E:\orant
snmp.servicename.listener_workstation1 =
OracleORACLE8I_HOMETNSListener
snmp.SID.minx = MINX
snmp.oraclehome.minx = e:\orant
snmp.address.minx = (ADDRESS=
                             (PROTOCOL=BEQ)
                             (PROGRAM=ORACLE)
                             (ARGV0=ORACLEMINX)

(ARGS='(DESCRIPTION=(LOCAL=YES)(ADDRESS=(PROTOCOL=beq)))')
                     )
ifile = E:\orant\network\admin\snmp_rw.ora
```

The last parameter in the snmp_ro.ora file points to the snmp_rw.ora file. The following code block shows the contents of snmp_rw.ora:

```
snmp.contact.listener = ""
snmp.index.listener = 1
snmp.contact.minx = ""
snmp.index.minx = 2
```

You shouldn't normally need to mess with the contents of these files. However, in some situations, you might have problems setting up your Intelligent Agent process, particularly if the problem relates to assigning a value for the TNS_ADMIN environment variable within the Windows registry. To resolve these issues, check out the readme.txt file in the network/agent/doc or net80/agent/doc directory under ORACLE_HOME on the server hosting the Oracle database for more information about setting registry parameters and configuring Windows services.

Starting Intelligent Agent

The following steps show how to start Intelligent Agent:

1. Click Start | Settings | Control Panel.
2. In the Control Panel, click the Services icon.
3. Scroll down until you find the Oracle<ORACLE_HOME>Agent or OracleAgent80 entry, as shown in Figure 3-13. Click that entry once to highlight it, and then click the Start button.

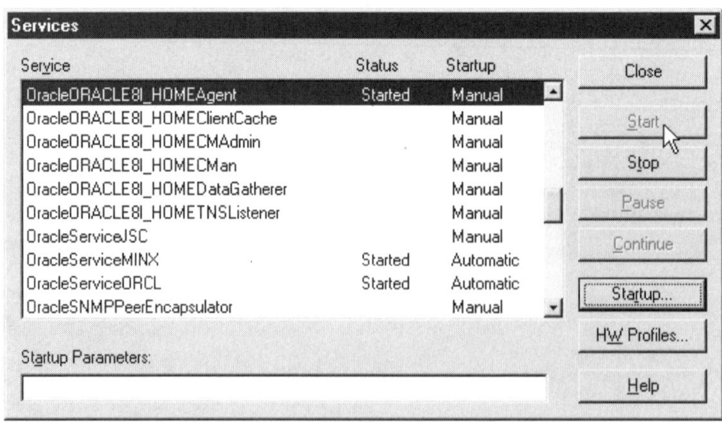

FIGURE 3-13. *Intelligent Agent startup using Windows services*

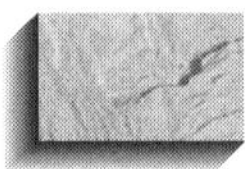

TIP
You can also configure Intelligent Agent to start automatically when the Windows machine boots by clicking the Startup button; and in the Service window under Startup Type, select the Automatic radio button; then click OK.

Discovering Databases in OEM

Once Intelligent Agent is running for your Oracle database, OEM can discover those databases automatically using the following steps:

1. In OEM, click the Navigator | Service Discovery | Discover New Services menu option. A wizard will appear telling you OEM can discover databases running Intelligent Agent automatically. Click Next.
2. Enter the name of the machine hosting the Oracle database in the text box labeled New Node; then click the Add button. Do this for all host machines running Oracle databases (and corresponding Intelligent Agents), as shown in Figure 3-14. Then click Next.

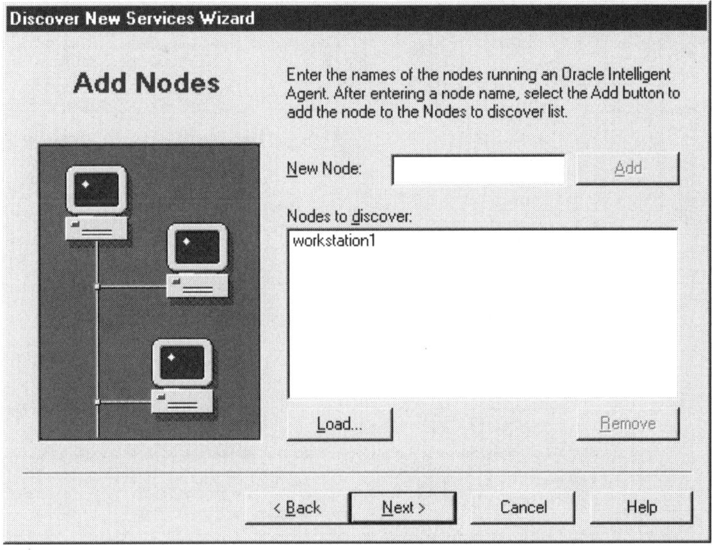

FIGURE 3-14. *Defining host machines in Discover New Services Wizard*

3. Specify that OEM should retrieve information automatically after the wizard completes by clicking the Immediately after Wizard Completion radio button in the next window. Then click Next.

4. A summary window appears. To proceed, click the Finish button, and OEM will set about discovering your Oracle database. The Service Discovery Status window will indicate successful database discovery by showing a check mark next to the host you specified. When finished, click Close. Back in the OEM console, you should now see your database listed as a drill-down node in the upper-left interface. Drill down into your database to see the options available to you via OEM, as shown in Figure 3-15.

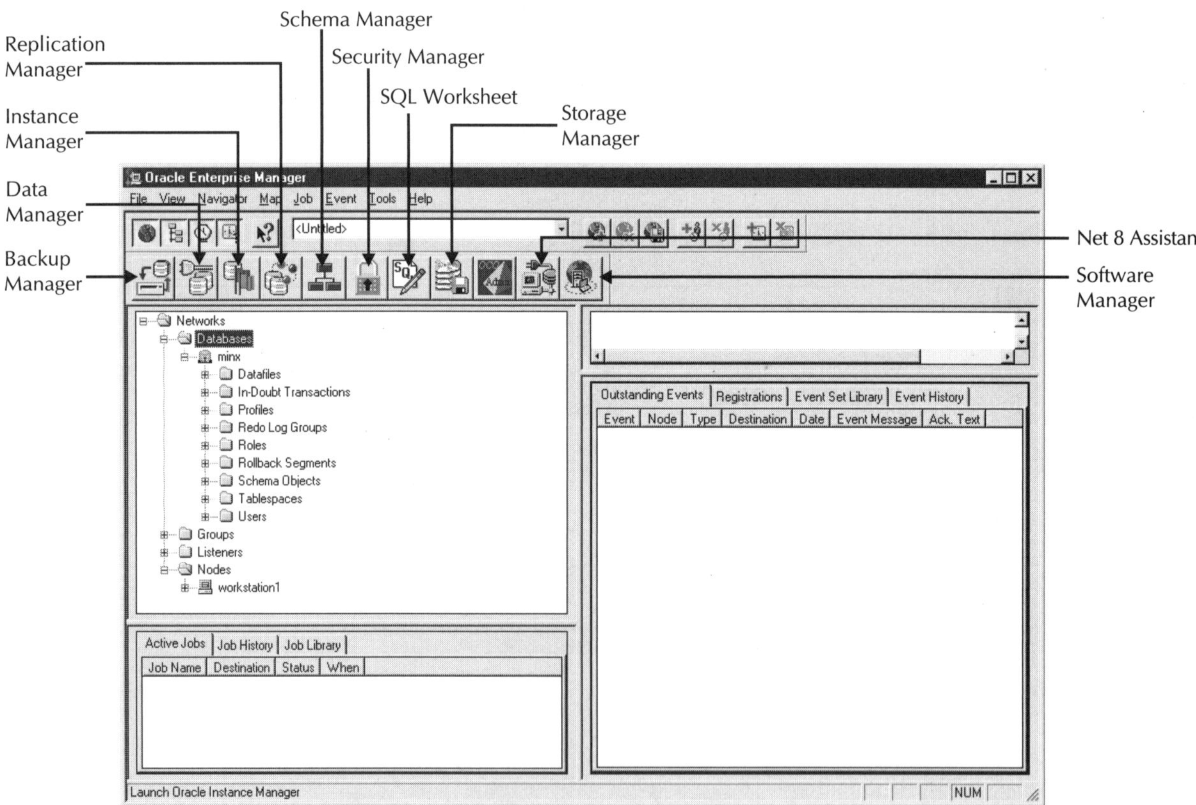

FIGURE 3-15. *OEM with database service discovered*

For Review

Understand the steps for creating an OEM repository for the first time on your Oracle database. Be sure you know how to start Intelligent Agent and the importance of using Intelligent Agent in conjunction with OEM. Also, be sure you can discover a new database in OEM automatically using Intelligent Agent.

Using OEM Console Navigator

Once your OEM software is installed, the repository created, and a database is discovered in OEM, you now can use the console to handle virtually every Oracle DBO task laid out for the Oracle Certified Professional (OCP) exam. This brief discussion should set the stage for items discussed in the rest of this chapter, as well as in Chapters 4, 5, 6, and 7, with respect to the following topics:

- Database startup and shutdown
- Physical and logical database structure maintenance
- Database user management and security
- Object management
- Backup, recovery, and data loading
- Event monitoring
- Contention and blocking issues
- Performance tuning

OEM Tools for Database Management

Oracle Enterprise Manager can simplify many areas of managing your database. OEM is usually run from your desktop. Assuming you use Windows, you can identify the tools at your disposal as part of OEM by looking either under Start | Programs | Oracle Enterprise Manager, or under the Tools | Applications menu within the Enterprise Manager application itself. The following list identifies the applications available for OEM, along with providing a brief description of their use:

- **Backup Manager** Handles automation of backup operations
- **Data Manager** Manages import, export, and loading of data into tables of an Oracle database

- **Instance Manager** Handles management of an Oracle instance, including session, in-doubt transaction, and initialization parameter information
- **Replication Manager** Manages configuration, scheduling, and administrative functions of replication between nodes on a network running Oracle databases
- **Schema Manager** Manages table, index, cluster, and other object creation and management in an Oracle database
- **Security Manager** Handles user access privileges and role administration
- **SQL Worksheet** Used to execute SQL statements from scripts in a graphical interface more advanced than SQL*Plus
- **Storage Manager** Handles configuration and management of logical and physical disk resources for the Oracle database
- **Net8 Assistant** Handles configuration and management of Net8 networking components
- **Software Manager** Used as part of an enterprise-wide management of Oracle software application design, distribution, and asset management

TIP
In addition to the administrator tools in the preceding list, other applications are available for different cartridges you may have installed on your Oracle database, such as ConText Cartridge System Administrator. Administrative tools accompany add-ins like the Diagnostic Pack as well, including Lock Manager and Performance Manager.

To start any of the tools available in OEM, you can either click the Tools | Applications | <TOOL> menu option, or click the button for the appropriate application labeled in Figure 3-15. In addition, the lower-right window in the OEM console navigator handles event monitoring and acceptance, while the Job and Event menus allow you to schedule jobs and set up events to happen automatically on your Oracle database. Furthermore, you can start selected OEM applications using the OEM Administrator toolbar, which runs on the desktop when you click Start | Programs | Oracle Enterprise Manager | Administrator Toolbar. Finally, you can even start many of the OEM applications stand-alone by clicking Start | Programs | Oracle Enterprise Manager | <TOOL>. You will begin your exploration of using OEM applications shortly.

For Review

Understand at a high level what the OEM application components are, and where you can perform job scheduling or event definition in the console navigator. Also, understand the four ways to start an OEM application.

Startup and Shutdown of Oracle Databases

You will learn the following topics in this section:

- Startup and shutdown modes defined
- Database shutdown with Instance Manager
- Database startup with Instance Manager
- Initialization parameters in Instance Manager

You can't get to your database if it is not running. This section covers how to start and stop your Oracle database remotely using OEM Instance Manager, a GUI tool that facilitates database operative management tasks. You will learn how to manage values set for your initialization parameters (normally kept in `init.ora`) using Instance Manager as well. Note that, unless you are running both your Oracle database and Oracle Enterprise Manager on the same Windows host machine, you cannot use Instance Manager to start or stop your Oracle database unless you first create a password file. This topic was covered toward the end of Chapter 2. If you haven't covered how to create a password file and how to tell Oracle to use that password file, stop now and review that material in Chapter 2. When finished, you may proceed to complete this section.

Startup and Shutdown Modes Defined

Oracle database startup and shutdown with either Server Manager (a command-line utility for administering the Oracle database) or Instance Manager can be conducted in several modes. All the options discussed for Server Manager are available via Instance Manager, except through a graphical user interface. You may also want to note that starting Oracle databases in Windows is not necessarily handled with Server Manager or even OEM, but instead may also be handled as a service. There are several different options for starting Oracle instances, with or without opening the database. For both database startup and shutdown, you must be logged in to Oracle as a privileged database user such as `INTERNAL`.

STARTUP NOMOUNT This option starts the instance without mounting the database. That means all the memory structures and background processes are in place, but no database is attached to the instance. You will use this option later, for creating the Oracle database. You can specify this option with or without specifying an `initsid.ora` file for the `PFILE` parameter. If you do not specify `PFILE`, Oracle usually looks in the `c:\orant\database` directory for the `initsid.ora` file for that instance. If Oracle cannot find an initialization file, then it will not start the database.

STARTUP MOUNT This option starts the instance and attaches the database but does not open it. You can't mount a database you haven't created yet. This option is useful in situations in which you have to move physical database files around on the machine hosting Oracle, or when database recovery is required. You should specify an `initsid.ora` file for the `PFILE` parameter when using this option; otherwise, Oracle will not use values you may have specified in your `initsid.ora` file. If the instance is already started but the database is not mounted, use `alter database mount` instead.

STARTUP OPEN This option starts your instance, attaches the database, and opens it. This is the default option for starting Oracle. It is used when you want to make your database available to users. You can't open a database you haven't created yet. The file you specify for the `PFILE` parameter must be an `initsid.ora` file. If the instance is started and the database is mounted, use `alter database open` instead.

Other Options Used in Conjunction with Startup Modes

Another database startup option in Oracle is `startup force`. This option forces the instance to start and the database to open. It is used in situations in which other `startup` options are met with errors from Oracle, and no `shutdown` options seem to work either. This is an option of last resort, and there is no reason to use it generally unless you cannot start the database with any other option. You can also use `startup restrict` to open the database while simultaneously preventing all users but the DBA from accessing database objects.

Options for Stopping Oracle

Shutdown of the Oracle instance works in much the same way as starting the instance. You must be logged in to Oracle either as `internal` or as a user with `sysdba` privileges. The task can be accomplished from Server Manager or OEM Instance Manager, or as a Windows service. Four priorities can be specified by the DBA for shutting down the database. They are `shutdown normal`, `shutdown immediate`, `shutdown abort`, and `shutdown transactional`. The next four sections will explain each of these options and give cases in which their use might be appropriate.

SHUTDOWN NORMAL This is the lowest priority shutdown. When `shutdown normal` is issued, Oracle will wait for users to log off before actually shutting down the instance and closing the database. Oracle follows three rules during `shutdown normal`. First, Oracle will not let new users access the database. Second, Oracle will not force users already logged in to the system to log off to complete the shutdown. Third, under normal shutdown situations, there is no need for instance recovery.

SHUTDOWN IMMEDIATE This is a higher-priority shutdown that the DBA can use when `shutdown normal` would take too long. The `shutdown immediate` command shuts down a database as follows. No new users will be able to connect to the database once the `shutdown` command is issued. Oracle will not wait for a user to log off as it does for `shutdown normal`, instead terminating user connections immediately and rolling back uncommitted transactions. Immediate database shutdown, though more drastic than `shutdown normal`, does not require any instance recovery.

SHUTDOWN ABORT This is the highest priority database shutdown command. In all cases in which this priority is used, the database will shut down immediately. All users are immediately disconnected, no transactions are rolled back, and media recovery will be required when the database starts up again. You will use this option only when media or disk failure has taken place on the machine hosting Oracle.

SHUTDOWN TRANSACTIONAL A transactional shutdown prevents clients from losing work. A transactional database shutdown proceeds with the following conditions: no client can start a new transaction on this particular instance, a client is disconnected when the client ends the transaction that is in progress, and a `shutdown immediate` occurs when all transactions have finished. The next startup will not require an instance recovery.

TIP
In most situations, you will use the `shutdown immediate` or `shutdown transactional` mode to shut down your database because they are the speediest and cleanest ways to do so. Avoid using the `shutdown abort` mode unless you plan to wait while Oracle executes instance recovery the next time you start your database.

For Review

1. What connection must be used for the task of database startup and shutdown?
2. What are the options for database startup and shutdown?

Using Instance Manager to Shut Down the Database

Within Server Manager, you can shut down your Oracle database in the following way:

1. From the command line on the host machine, start Server Manager, and log in as either `sysdba` or `internal`:

```
C:\orant> svrmgr30
Oracle Server Manager Release 3.0.5.0.0 - Production
(c)Copyright 1998, Oracle Corporation. All Rights Reserved.
Oracle8 Enterprise Edition Release 8.0.5 - Production
With the Partitioning and Objects options
PL/SQL Release 8.0.5 - Production
SVRMGR> connect internal
Connected.
SVRMGR>
```

2. From within Server Manager, use the `shutdown` *`option`* command to start the instance. Several options exist for *`option`*, including `immediate`, `normal`, or `abort`. An example of `shutdown immediate` is shown in the following code block:

```
SVRMGR> shutdown immediate
ORA-01507: database not mounted
ORACLE instance shut down.
SVRMGR>
```

Using Instance Manager to Stop an Oracle Database

To stop Oracle using Instance Manager, follow these steps:

1. Start Instance Manager either by clicking the Instance Manager button on the OEM console navigator, clicking the Tools | Applications | Instance Manager menu option, or clicking Start | Programs | Oracle Enterprise Manager | Instance Manager. You must log in to Oracle as a user who can start and stop the Oracle database, such as `internal`, connecting as `sysdba`, as shown here.

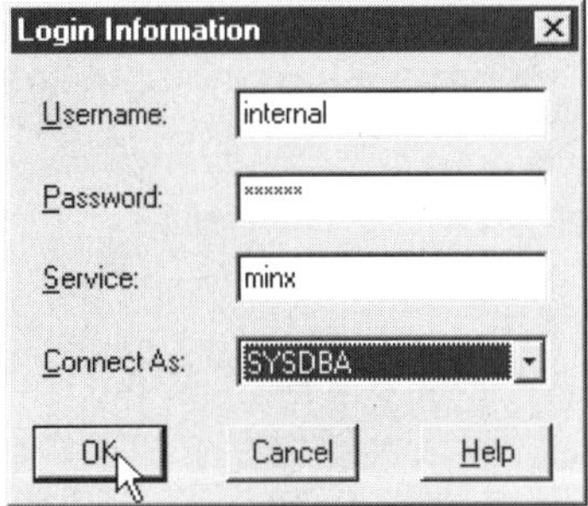

You will now see Instance Manager. Note there are two interfaces in the main window. The left is for navigation, and the right is for specifying and displaying information. At this time, you should note a green light indicating that your database is up and running. Figure 3-16 shows OEM Instance Manager.

2. There are two ways to stop Oracle. Either click the Shutdown radio button on the right side of the Instance Manager main window, or click the Database | Shutdown menu option. If you receive a message saying that no stored configuration exists for this database, don't worry: you'll create a stored configuration shortly. Simply click Yes.

   The Shutdown Options window appears asking you for the mode you want to shut down your database in:

   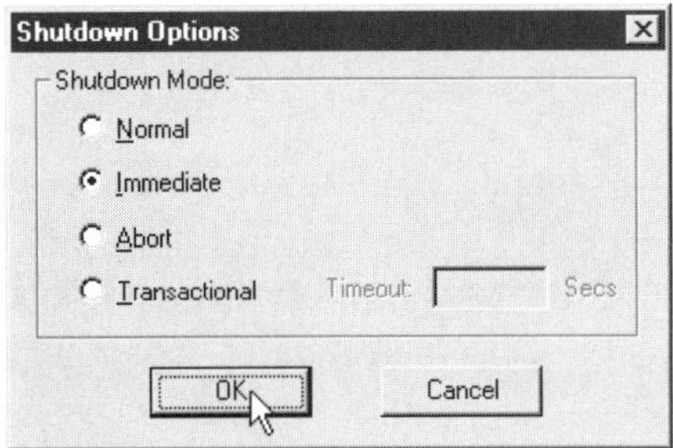

3. Pick your mode using information from the previous discussion by clicking the appropriate radio button. Note that for database shutdown in `transactional` mode only, you can also define a timeout in seconds. If users are still conducting transactions after that timeout expires, Instance Manager defaults to a `shutdown immediate` and forcibly disconnects those users, rolling back their transactions. After selecting the shutdown mode, click OK.

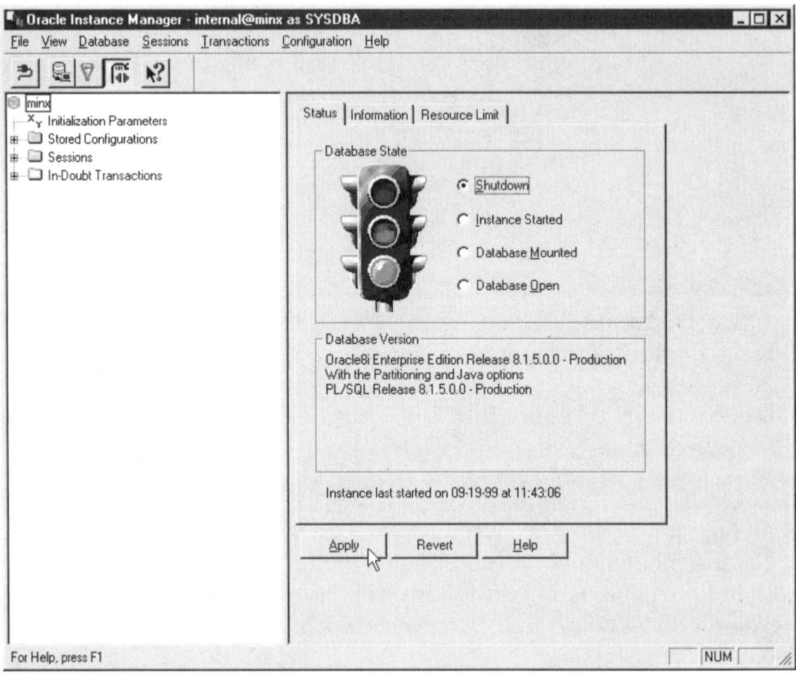

FIGURE 3-16. *OEM Instance Manager*

For Review

Understand how to shut down Oracle from within Instance Manager.

Using Instance Manager to Start the Database

To start the instance using Server Manager, follow these steps:

1. From the command line on the host machine, start Server Manager and log in either as `sysdba` or `internal`:

```
C:\orant> svrmgr30
Oracle Server Manager Release 3.0.5.0.0 - Production
(c)Copyright 1998, Oracle Corporation. All Rights Reserved.
Oracle8 Enterprise Edition Release 8.0.5 - Production
With the Partitioning and Objects options
```

```
PL/SQL Release 8.0.5 - Production
SVRMGR> connect internal
Connected.
SVRMGR>
```

2. From within Server Manager, use the `startup` *`start_option dbname`* `pfile=`*`init.ora`* command to start the instance. Several options exist for *`start_option`*, including `nomount`, `mount`, `open`, and `open force`. The `PFILE` parameter should be used to identify the exact `init`*`sid`*`.ora` file you want to use. An example of `startup nomount` is shown in the following code block:

```
SVRMGR> startup nomount pfile=initORGDB01.ora
ORACLE instance started.
Total System Global Area                        227174560 bytes
Fixed Size                                          42764 bytes
Variable Size                                    93999104 bytes
Database Buffers                                 81920000 bytes
Redo Buffers                                     51208192 bytes
SVRMGR>
```

Using Instance Manager to Start Oracle

To start an Oracle database using Instance Manager, click the Startup menu option at the top of Instance Manager. The Startup window appears, in which you specify the startup mode and associated options you want to use. If you have no initialization parameter configuration stored in your OEM repository, you will also need to specify the `init`*`sid`*`.ora` you want to use for database startup in the appropriate text box, as shown here:

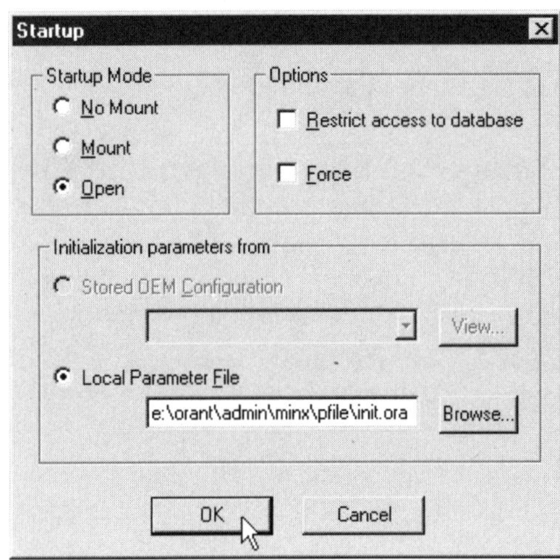

For Review

Know how to start your Oracle database in Instance Manager.

Initialization Parameters in Instance Manager

Once your instance is started, several different ways exist for obtaining the values set for the instance on initialization. The first and least effective way to view parameter values in your database is to look at the `init`*`sid`*`.ora` file. This choice does not give you all parameters, and what's more, the parameters in your parameter file may have changed since the last time you started Oracle. A much better way to obtain parameter values is to `select` them from a special view in Oracle called `V$PARAMETER`. Still another effective way for obtaining parameter values in Oracle is to use Server Manager. The `show parameter` command will list all parameters for the instance. Finally, you can use OEM Instance Manager to display instance parameters by clicking the Initialization Parameters node, as shown in Figure 3-17. Can you guess where Instance Manager and Server Manager draw their initialization parameter information from? If you said `V$PARAMETER`, you were right!

Setting parameters is done in one of two ways. By far, the most effective way to set a database parameter is to add the name of the parameter and the value to the `init`*`sid`*`.ora` file for your instance. After that, shut down and start up your instance using the `init`*`sid`*`.ora` file. Unfortunately, in the world of multiuser database environments, DBAs do not always have the luxury of bouncing the database whenever they want. You can always try to schedule this sort of thing or, if the need is not critical, wait until the weekend. Another method for setting parameters is with the `alter system` command. However, this is not an effective method for changing parameters because not all initialization parameters can be changed using this command. The ones that can be changed include `RESOURCE_LIMIT`, `GLOBAL_NAMES`, `AUDIT_TRAIL`, `TIMED_STATISTICS`, some of the MTS parameters, and some of the licensing parameters.

Using Instance Manager to Store Parameter Configurations

For performing database starts and stops remotely, you can save your initialization parameter configurations in Instance Manager to simplify and automate the startup and shutdown tasks. To do so, click the Save button on the bottom-right side of the Instance Manager interface. The Save Configuration window will appear, prompting you to enter a name for this saved configuration, along with comments (if any). After saving your configuration, you can see it by drilling down into the <SID> | Stored Configurations | <NAME> node on the left side of the Instance Manager interface, shown in Figure 3-18.

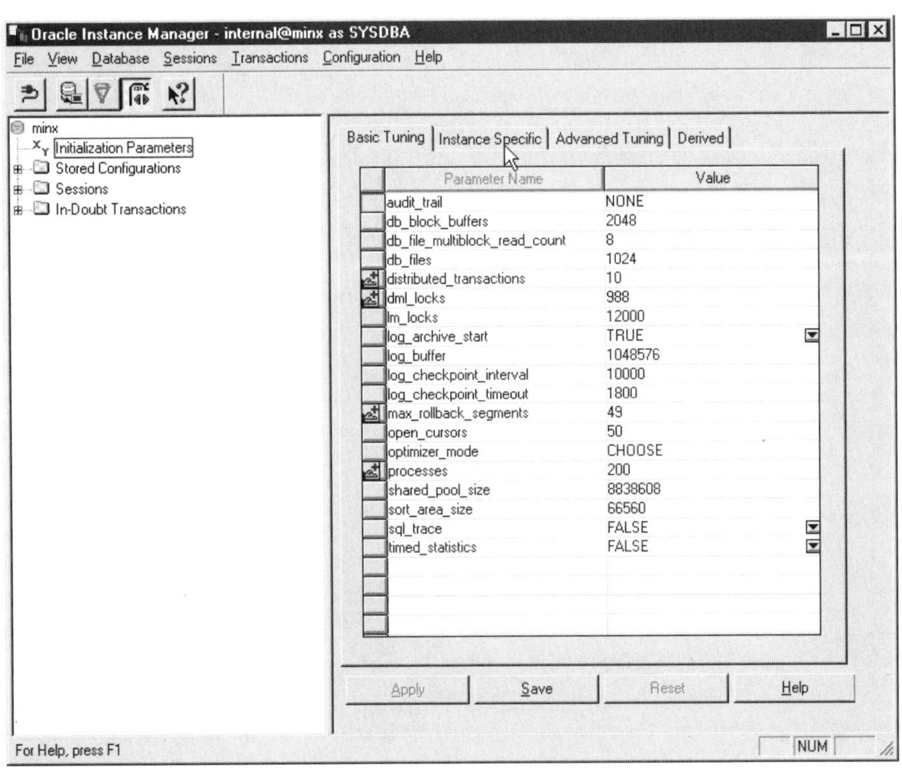

FIGURE 3-17. *Instance parameters in Instance Manager*

TIP

Once you have stored a configuration locally in Instance Manager, you can use that configuration when starting your database by selecting the Stored OEM Configuration radio button in the Startup Database window and then entering the name of your configuration in the appropriate text box.

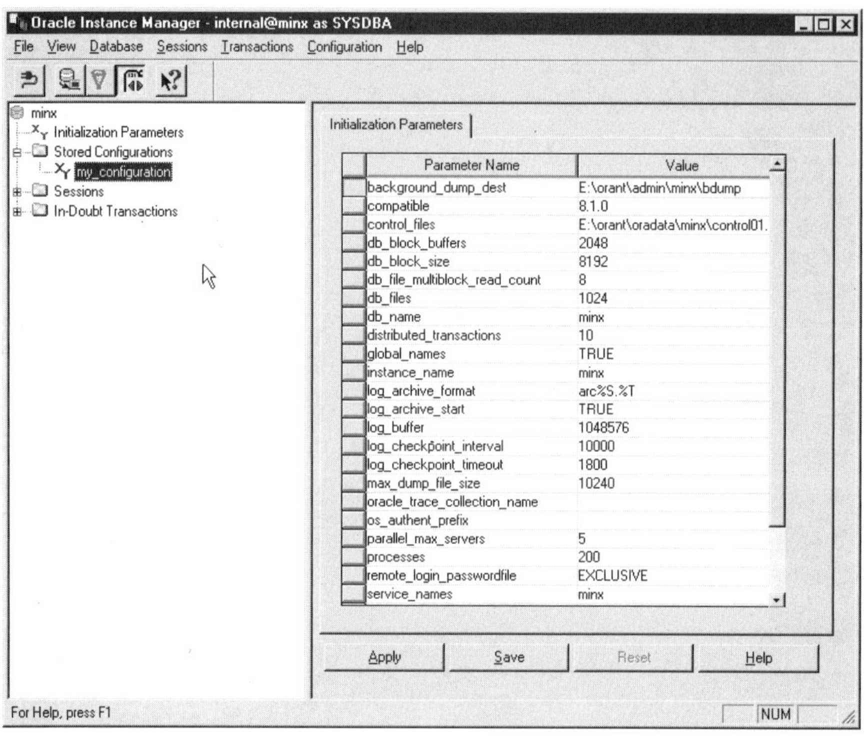

FIGURE 3-18. *Instance Manager saved configurations*

For Review

1. Identify some ways you can obtain instance parameters. Which of these ways is least effective? Which are most effective?
2. What methods are available for changing instance parameters before the instance is started? What about after the instance is started?
3. How do you save a configuration local to Instance Manager? When might it be useful to do so?

Chapter Summary

In this chapter, you covered many important concepts pertaining to Oracle8 networking, and startup and shutdown of your Oracle database using Oracle Enterprise Manager tools. You learned about the defined purpose of Net8 as a method of communication, not a networking protocol. Remember, Net8 needs TCP/IP or some other network software in order to work. You also learned about the location and purpose of most Net8 configuration files you will encounter as a DBO. The use of Net8 Assistant for the purpose of configuring your Net8 network was covered and illustrated as well. You learned what the OEM repository is and how to create it. The importance of Intelligent Agent as a tool for enabling OEM was discussed, along with how to actually start and use Intelligent Agent. Finally, you covered at a high level what the components of OEM are, and how they are used.

The chapter discussed startup and shutdown of your Oracle instance and database as well. You learned about the various startup modes for Oracle and what they mean. You also learned about two important options for starting your Oracle database that are used in conjunction with the basic startup modes. Also, you learned about the different modes for shutting down an Oracle database, and what situations are appropriate for the use of each. Finally, you saw how to start and stop your Oracle database from the DOS command line using Server Manager, and using Instance Manager within Oracle Enterprise Manager.

Two-Minute Drill

- The three types of networked computing that have been seen in business environments in the last 30 years are
  - *Mainframe computing*—centralized machine processing all software, all users hard-wired to one computer. Advantages are centralized data location and processing speed; disadvantages are hard-to-use interfaces and inflexibility for changing business requirements.
  - *Client/server computing*—decentralized machines processing software components that work together. Advantages include attractive interfaces that are easier to use; disadvantages are distributed data and slow processing speed.
  - *Internet computing*—centralized machines processing specialized software components accessed by generic browsers. Advantages are attractive interfaces that are easy to use and centralized data storage; disadvantages are security and dependence on network resources for correct use.

- Net8 handles communication (not raw transport) between Oracle clients and servers on a network. Net8 can be configured for client/server or Internet computing. Communication is handled between Oracle peers using Transparent Network Substrate, or TNS.
- Net8 needs a raw transport protocol, such as TCP/IP, IPX/SPX, or DECnet, in order to work.
- Features of Net8 include
  - Net8 offers scalability with connection pooling and connection concentration.
  - Net8 provides independence from standard networking protocols with the use of Oracle Protocol Adapters.
  - Net8 can handle connections from multiple network protocols for the same Oracle server using Oracle Connection Manager.
  - Net8 simplifies network administration via Net8 Assistant, running stand-alone or from the OEM console.
  - Net8 reduces reliance on both local and third-tier name resolution on TCP/IP networks through the use of host-naming.
  - Native Naming Adapters provide interconnectivity with third-party vendor standard name services.
- Net8 allows clients to connect to servers via connect strings. Connect strings are associated by Net8 with descriptors. A connect descriptor is a handle that Oracle associates with important pieces of information like the machine hosting Oracle, Oracle SID, connection protocol, and so on, for simplified connection.
- Connect descriptors can be found in one of three places:
  - Locally on your client machine in the `tnsnames.ora` file
  - On a Names server running somewhere on your computer network
  - On some other kind of network naming service made by a third-party vendor
- The steps in connecting Oracle clients to Oracle servers via Net8 are
  1. Entering username, password, and connect string
  2. Net8 resolving connect string into connect description

3. Sending connection request from client to server listener
4. Listener hearing request and connecting user process to a server process

- Net8 client-side configuration files are usually found in the `net80/admin` or `network/admin` directory under the Oracle software home directory. These files, along with their purposes, include
  - **`tnsnames.ora`** Configures connect string resolution into connect descriptor
  - **`sqlnet.ora`** Configures client preferences such as naming convention specification, enabling network traces, name resolution preferences, and others
- Net8 server-side configuration files are usually found in the `net80/admin` `or network/admin` directory under the Oracle software home directory. These files, along with their purposes, include
  - **`listener.ora`** Configures the behavior of the listener process
  - **`snmp_ro.ora`** `and` **`snmp_rw.ora`** Configures the Intelligent Agent process
- Review procedures for configuring your `listener.ora`, `tnsnames.ora`, and `sqlnet.ora` files using Net8 Assistant.
- Understand the three components of enabling use of Oracle Enterprise Manager on a database:
  - Creating the OEM repository on that database (in versions of OEM before 2.0)
  - Starting Intelligent Agent
  - Discovering databases on the Oracle network within OEM
- Understand how to create an OEM repository when logging in to a new database from OEM for the first time.
- Intelligent Agent enables OEM to perform automated service discovery, event monitoring, job scheduling, and other enhanced features that use of OEM stand-alone cannot do.
- Review procedure for starting Intelligent Agent on Windows using the Windows Services tool in the Control Panel.
- Review the step-by-step process of automatic database detection using Intelligent Agent within OEM.

- The applications within OEM for database management include
  - **Backup Manager** Handles automation of backup operations
  - **Data Manager** Manages import, export, and loading of data into tables of an Oracle database
  - **Instance Manager** Handles management of an Oracle instance, including session, in-doubt transaction, and initialization parameter information
  - **Replication Manager** Manages configuration, scheduling, and administrative functions of replication between nodes on a network running Oracle databases
  - **Schema Manager** Manages table, index, cluster, and other object creation and management in an Oracle database
  - **Security Manager** Handles user access privileges and role administration
  - **SQL Worksheet** Used to execute SQL statements from scripts in a graphical interface more advanced than SQL*Plus
  - **Storage Manager** Handles configuration and management of logical and physical disk resources for the Oracle database
  - **Net8 Assistant** Handles configuration and management of Net8 networking components
  - **Software Manager** Used as part of an enterprise-wide management of Oracle software application design, distribution, and asset management
- The OEM console navigator is where event monitoring and job scheduling can be set up.
- The ways OEM applications can be started are
  - From the Tools | Applications menu in OEM console navigator
  - From the button icon toolbar within OEM
  - Stand-alone from the Start menu in Windows

- From the OEM Administrator Toolbar (only Security Manager, Schema Manager, Storage Manager, SQL Worksheet, Instance Manager, and Net8 Assistant can be started this way)

- The startup modes in Oracle include
  - **`startup nomount`** Starts instance, does not mount database
  - **`startup mount`** Starts instance, mounts but does not open database
  - **`startup open`** Starts instance, mounts and opens database
- In addition, you can specify `restrict` to restrict access to an open database or `force` to force Oracle to open the database that did not shut down properly.
- The shutdown modes in Oracle are as follows:
  - **`shutdown normal`** No new existing connections are allowed, but existing sessions may take as long as they want to wrap up.
  - **`shutdown immediate`** No new connections are allowed, existing sessions are terminated, and their transactions are rolled back.
  - **`shutdown abort`** No new connections are allowed, existing sessions are terminated, and transactions are not rolled back.
  - **`shutdown transactional`** No new connections are allowed, and existing sessions are not terminated until current transaction completes.
- The `shutdown immediate` and `shutdown transactional` operations are the quickest and cleanest ways to shut down an Oracle database. Never use `shutdown abort` unless you are planning to perform media recovery the next time you start the database.
- Be sure you understand how to start up and shut down a database using Instance Manager, step-by-step.
- Initialization parameters are stored either in the init*sid*.ora file or as a stored configuration in OEM Instance Manager. Be sure you know how to save a stored configuration and manage parameters in Instance Manager for OCP.

Chapter Questions

1. **Power will disconnect on the machine running Oracle in two minutes, but user JASON has left for the day while still connected to Oracle. His workstation is locked, so he cannot be logged out from his desktop. How should the DBA shut down the instance?**

   A. `shutdown normal`

   B. `shutdown immediate`

   C. `shutdown abort`

   D. `shutdown force`

   E. `shutdown recover`

2. **You are about to start the Oracle database. Which of the following administrative tools in OEM can be used to view the initialization parameter settings for Oracle?**

   A. Schema Manager

   B. Instance Manager

   C. Security Manager

   D. Data Manager

   E. Software Manager

3. **You are analyzing project requirements in order to develop the appropriate Oracle networking implementation. Which two of the following choices do not indicate a benefit of a client/server system? (Choose two.)**

   A. Ease of application use

   B. Low distribution cost

   C. Use of client machine processing power

   D. Scalability

   E. Centralized code management

4. A design diagram for one application system shows several different nodes acting as servers. This "N-tier" implementation is most likely a model for which of the following types of architectures?

A. Client/server

B. Uniprocessor

C. Internet Computing

D. Mainframe

5. Net8's ability to manage connectivity between client and server through a uniform interface, independently of the underlying network protocol used to manage a network, is provided by which of the following components?

A. Oracle Call Interface

B. Transparent Network Substrate

C. Oracle Processing Interface

D. Network Interface

E. Oracle Protocol Adapter

6. An Oracle Forms application has just issued a `select` statement to the Oracle database. Which of the following components will be handled on the server within the RDBMS, rather than by Net8?

A. Two-Task Common

B. Transparent Network Substrate

C. Network Interface

D. Oracle Protocol Adapter

E. Oracle Call Interface

7. You are explaining the benefits of Net8 to a project manager as part of the rationale for converting corporate IT to an Oracle platform. Which of the following choices best describes the role of Oracle Connection Manager?

A. Centralizes management of naming services

B. Offers independence from standard networking protocols

C. Provides the ability to handle connections to one Oracle server from multiple networks

D. Implements high application scalability

E. Allows interconnectivity with external naming services

8. After establishing that a host exists using connect-descriptor information, Net8 encounters an error attempting to locate the Oracle database with SID information given. Which of the following choices identifies the stage of processing at which the connection failed?

A. Hostname resolution

B. Password authentication

C. Connect-string lookup

D. Listener-availability check

E. Oracle SID resolution

9. Prespawned servers are being used on Oracle to manage user process requests. After Net8 establishes a connection, which of the following processes will connect users to a prespawned server?

A. Listener

B. Dispatcher

C. Assistant

D. DBWR

10. The Network Routing component of Net8 handles routing data from client to server across a network. Which of the following OSI layers represents where this component resides in the Net8 architecture?

A. Physical

B. Link

C. Network

D. Transport

E. Session

11. Your attempt to shut down a running Net8 listener in batch results in an error. Which of the following commands would result in successful completion of the shutdown operation?

A. `lsnrctl start`, followed by `lsnrctl services`

B. `lsnrctl`, followed by `services`

C. `lsnrctl`, followed by `set password`, followed by `stop`

D. `lsnrctl set password`, followed by `lsnrctl stop`

E. `lsnrctl`, followed by `stop`, followed by `change_password`

12. You want to define a nondefault trace directory for your Net8 listener process. Using Net8 Assistant, in which of the following areas would you make the necessary changes?

A. General Parameters

B. Listening Locations

C. Database Services

D. Other Services

13. Your only listener on the host system is called SPACEMAN. You defined the name for the Net8 listener in which of the following areas?

A. `tnsnames.ora`

B. `sqlnet.ora`

C. `listener.ora`

D. Net8 Assistant

14. Issuing `LSNRCTL start` from the command line indicates you are running the utility in which of the following modes?

A. Interactive

B. Batch

C. Read-only

D. Write-protected

15. Your attempt to shut down the listener is met with `protocol adapter error` and `no listener` messages. This is most likely due to which of the following causes?

- **A.** The listener is running in protected mode.
- **B.** You didn't supply a password for this privileged operation.
- **C.** The version of LSNRCTL you are using is incompatible with the listener.
- **D.** The listener you attempted to stop isn't running.

16. You use LSNRCTL to issue a command that allows you to determine how many connections have been refused by the listener on every protocol the listener tunes in to. Which of the following commands is the one you issued?

- **A.** `help`
- **B.** `services`
- **C.** `reload`
- **D.** `spawn`
- **E.** `status`

17. Net8 host-naming services makes several assumptions about your network environment. Which of the following choices is *not* an assumption Net8 host-naming services makes?

- **A.** Your network protocol is TCP/IP.
- **B.** Your listener is listening to port 1521.
- **C.** Your database is using dedicated servers.
- **D.** Your global database name is the same as your hostname.

18. You are using local naming in your Oracle network. Which of the following contains connection information for databases available to your client?

- **A.** `tnsnames.ora`
- **B.** `sqlnet.ora`
- **C.** `listener.ora`
- **D.** Net8 Assistant

Answers to Chapter Questions

1. B. `shutdown immediate`

Explanation A power outage can cause damage to an Oracle instance if it is running when the power goes out. But choice C is just too drastic, given that you are basically treating the situation as if it required media recovery. After all, you know that JASON is not executing a transaction, so no additional time to finish the `rollback` will be required before shutdown. Choice A will not do it either, though, because `shutdown normal` will wait all night for JASON to come in and log off. Choice B is the logical choice. Choices D and E are not valid options for shutting down a database instance.

2. B. Instance Manager

Explanation The Instance Manager tool handles all instance-related tasks, including display and modification of initialization parameters set in the init*sid*.ora file. Schema Manager handles tasks involving database object creation and modification, eliminating choice A. Security Manager handles user privilege and role management, which eliminates choice C. Data Manager handles the loading and unloading of data from EXPORT binary or flat file format, eliminating choice D. Finally, Software Manager handles enterprise deployment of Oracle software, eliminating choice E.

3. B *and* E. Low distribution cost *and* centralized code management

Explanation Choices A, C, and D all describe features of client/server applications. Their visual design makes them easy to use, their substantial application size puts client machine resources to work, and their use of networking makes them as scalable as the server side can handle. They are not inexpensive to distribute to your user populations, however, and the code is distributed over every single client machine, making code management difficult, if not impossible, to centralize.

4. C. Internet Computing

Explanation N-tier applications with multiple application servers all handling specialized tasks reserved for clients in client/server or two-tier architecture are part of the Oracle Internet Computing. Mainframes make sure all processing happens on one centralized machine, while, as noted, client/server is typically referred to as *two-tier architecture*. Uniprocessor architecture usually denotes that clients and servers all run on the same machine.

5. B. Transparent Network Substrate

Explanation The ability Net8 has to manage connections independent of any network protocol other than its own is gained with the Transparent Network Substrate, or TNS. Oracle Call Interface is part of the client side that applications call to handle data processing operations. Oracle Processing Interface is part of the server side that handles RDBMS operations. Network Interface is part of Net8 that establishes the session layer and accepts information from the client OCI or server OPI and passes that information to the transport layer. Oracle Protocol Adapters are at the link layer and pass data transmission requests from the Transparent Network Substrate to the network protocol on the physical layer.

6. A. Two-Task Common

Explanation The Two-Task Common process handles converting character-set and datatype information at the presentation layer, within the RDBMS rather than by Net8. Choices B, C, and D all identify components from Net8, which you were supposed to exclude, according to the question. Also, because the question mentions server-side, not client-side, processing, you should eliminate choice E because the Oracle Call Interface is part of client-side application processing.

7. C. Provides the ability to handle connections to one Oracle server from multiple networks

Explanation The Oracle Connection Manager utility in Net8 provides the ability to handle connections for one Oracle server that come in from multiple networks. Oracle Names is used to centralize management of naming services, eliminating choice A. TNS offers independence from standard networking protocols, eliminating choice B. High application scalability can be implemented with connection pooling and concentration, eliminating choice D. Native Naming Adapters are meant to allow interconnectivity between Oracle and external naming services, eliminating choice E.

8. E. Oracle SID resolution

Explanation Because the question basically says that the error was encountered while trying to resolve the Oracle SID, the answer has to be Oracle SID resolution. The question states that the hostname resolved successfully, eliminating choice A. Because connect-string lookup happens before hostname resolution, choice C must be eliminated as well. Because the Oracle SID has not been resolved, no password authentication has taken place, eliminating choice B. And because listener availability is checked before the SID is resolved, and the failure was with the SID, you can assume a listener was available on the specified port, eliminating choice D.

9. A. Listener

Explanation The listener process connects user processes with prespawned servers. A dispatcher is only used when the multithreaded server architecture is in place, eliminating choice B. The DBWR process is not involved in networking, eliminating choice D, while the Assistant process is fiction, eliminating choice C.

10. D. Transport

Explanation The Network Routing component of Net8 resides at the transport layer of the OSI network model. No Net8 component resides at the physical layer, eliminating choice A. Oracle Protocol Adapters handle tasks at the link layer, eliminating choice B. TNS handles things at the network layer, eliminating choice C. The Network Interface completes tasks at the session layer, eliminating choice E.

11. C. `lsnrctl`, followed by `set password`, followed by `stop`

Explanation By issuing only the `lsnrctl` command by itself on the command prompt, you run LSNRCTL in interactive mode, which is required to stop the listener because of the password requirement. First, you issue the `set password` command, and then you issue the `stop` command. Choice A starts a listener and therefore is incorrect. Choice B simply lists the running services and therefore is incorrect. Choice D is almost correct; but because you run both commands in batch mode, your second iteration doesn't actually have the password you set available to it, since the `set password` command sets it only session-wide.

12. A. General Parameters

Explanation Trace directory and filename information are both set in the General Parameters list box of Net8 Assistant. Listening Locations is used to determine what host machine addresses the listener will tune in to for connection requests and therefore is incorrect. Database Services is used to determine the databases this listener will connect users to, while Other Services is used to determine what nondatabase services, such as application servers, the listener will connect users to.

13. C. `listener.ora`

Explanation Because the default listener name is LISTENER, having your only listener named SPACEMAN means you changed the name of the listener. The way to do so is to set the `MYLISTENER` parameter equal to something in your `listener.ora` file. Neither the `tnsnames.ora` nor the `sqlnet.ora` files will assist in setting the listener name because these files handle client configuration while the listener resides on the server side. Likewise, Net8 Assistant is used to set up your `tnsnames.ora` file, a client file.

14. B. Batch

Explanation When you issue the LSNRCTL command from the command line, along with the name of the LSNRCTL executable, you are running LSNRCTL in batch. Interactive execution means you issued the executable from the command line only and are now at an LSNRCTL prompt. Choices C and D are not valid modes of LSNRCTL operation.

15. D. The listener you attempted to stop isn't running

Explanation "No listener" messages mean only one thing—there is no listener running by the name of the one you just tried to stop. Choice A is incorrect because there really is no such thing as protected mode when it comes to the listener. Choice B is incorrect because if you didn't supply a password, the errors would state that the addresses associated with that listener didn't recognize the password. You wouldn't receive "no listener" errors if the LSNRCTL and listener versions were incompatible.

16. B. `services`

Explanation The `services` command gives you information about the connections that were successful and the ones refused for each address. The `help` command lists all LSNRCTL commands and gives basic syntax for each, eliminating choice A. The `reload` command reloads `listener.ora` information without stopping the listener, eliminating choice C. The `spawn` command starts another process, such as a dedicated server, eliminating choice D. The `status` command gives listener version, start time, run duration, trace enabled, and the name of the file used to initialize the listener, but no information about connections accepted and refused, eliminating choice E.

17. C. Your database is using dedicated servers

Explanation Host-naming makes no assumptions about whether you are using MTS or dedicated servers. Choices A, B, and D, however, are all things that host-naming does make assumptions about.

18. A. `tnsnames.ora`

Explanation Whenever local naming is used, all Oracle database hostnames are stored in the `tnsnames.ora` file on the client machine. The `listener.ora` file is used for configuration on the server, eliminating choice C, while `sqlnet.ora` is used to configure client preferences, eliminating choice B. Choice D is wrong because Net8 Assistant is used to configure client preferences and listener services, but not local client hostname-lookup information. Net8 Assistant is used for that purpose.

CHAPTER 4

Database Structure and Object Creation

n this chapter, you cover the following topics related to creating the Oracle database and related application structure:

- Implementing logical and physical storage structure
- Creating objects for application data

This chapter continues you on your way to understanding Oracle from the database system architecture and related perspectives. You will learn in this chapter how to implement the logical and physical storage structure of an Oracle database using Storage Manager, a tool within the Oracle Enterprise Manager suite. You will also learn about creating objects for application data using a tool called SQL*Plus Worksheet, which is a GUI version of the SQL*Plus command-line application.

Implementing Logical and Physical Storage Structure

In this section, you cover the following points about implementing your logical and physical Oracle database storage structure:

- Components of Oracle database applications
- Required structures for creating new applications
- Using Storage Manager for application management
- Using Oracle tablespaces
- Creating and managing rollback segments

This section covers implementing a logical and physical Oracle database storage structure. You will learn what the components of Oracle database applications are, and what structures are required for creating new applications. The use of Storage Manager is critical for performing these tasks as a DBO because it reduces the need to remember complex commands, and you will learn how to use Storage Manager as well. Next, you will learn about the use of Oracle tablespaces for various purposes. Finally, you will learn about creation and management of rollback segments in Oracle, and why they are sometimes called the "problem children" of an Oracle database.

Components of Oracle Database Applications

So far we've spent a lot of time talking about the Oracle database, but not a lot of time talking about why organizations and people get Oracle databases. Oracle databases don't exist for their own sake; they exist to support an application. Your organization may have one or many applications floating around. You may have even supported or developed one. Here's a nifty shorthand way to think of an application: An application essentially boils down to a repeatable process or collection of processes that model reality. The reality being modeled could be anything, from sales forecasting to payroll processing to selling pineapples on the Web. From the database perspective, Oracle supports the data storage needs of an application by providing

- Tables to store data
- Indexes to get to data quickly
- Handles called *usernames* that allow people to access data
- Rules called *privileges* that restrict the way people get to the data

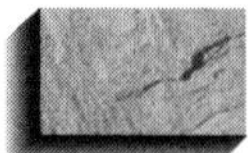

TIP
Users can access data, and they can even own the data. Sometimes, the data in one application is referred to as being part of a single domain.

An Example: Warehouse Freight Distribution

Tennessee is home to a great deal more than country music. Because of its central location, many trucking and warehouse freight distribution companies have made their home here. These freight distribution companies make a great case study example for the idea of logical and physical distribution. Let's say you are supervisor of the loading docks. When forklifts come out of the warehouse, the forklift operator tells you where the load is going, and you tell the forklift operator which truck is headed there. Figure 4-1 illustrates this basic concept.

This example shows two concepts behind the storage of those actual objects being shipped—a logical storage location and a physical location. The physical location is where the objects will end up; in Figure 4-1, you can see that the objects on the forklift will wind up in California. However, the logical location is far more immediate for both you and the forklift operator. That logical location is the truck.

Required Structures for Creating New Applications

The same reality applies to storing data on an Oracle database for an application. You have *logical* storage structures and *physical* structures.

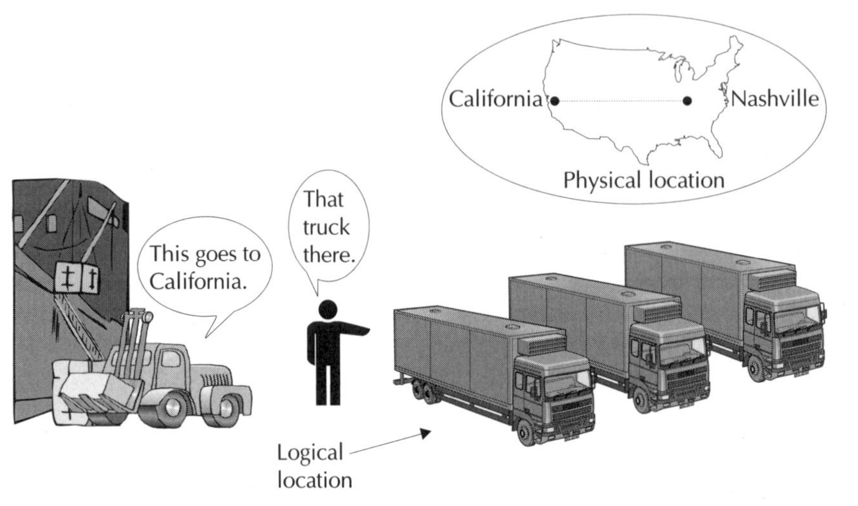

FIGURE 4-1. *Shipping and distribution*

Logical Database Structures

The logical structures are called *tablespaces*, *segments*, and *extents*:

- A *tablespace* is a logical database structure that is designed to store other logical database structures. Oracle sees a tablespace just like the loading dock supervisor sees the trucks: a large area of space into which objects can be placed.
- A *segment* is like a box of things being placed on the truck—an allocation of space used to store the data of a table, index, rollback segment, or temporary object. Space in tablespaces is allocated in segments. Like real boxes, segments can be different sizes.
- An *extent* is similar to a segment in that the extent stores information corresponding to a table, index, rollback segment, or temporary object. When the database object runs out of space in its segment and needs to add more data, Oracle allows it to allocate more space in the form of an extent. Getting an extent to store the data overflow is just like getting another box to store the excess of something that didn't fit in the last box.

Physical Database Structures

The other perspective you will have on your Oracle database is the *physical* structure—the disk space provided by the host machine. Physical structures for data storage are blocks and datafiles. Figure 4-2 illustrates the relationship of physical storage structures to logical storage structures.

- The *block* is the cornerstone of physical storage underlying the logical storage of objects in Oracle. Segments and extents are composed of data blocks. You specify the size of all blocks in a database when you create that database as a value in bytes, with an initialization parameter called `DB_BLOCK_SIZE`. Block size is typically specified as a multiple of operating system block size. Oracle blocks are 2K, 4K, 8K, and sometimes 16K.

- The *datafile* is a collection of blocks. One or more datafiles taken together can comprise a tablespace. Objects in a tablespace like tables and indexes can be stored by Oracle anywhere within the one or multiple datafiles comprising the tablespace. And while a tablespace may have many datafiles, each datafile can belong only to one tablespace.

Managing Space Within Tablespaces

Within tablespaces, Oracle manages free space by coalescing it into contiguous segments. This coalescing activity is handled automatically by the system monitor (or SMON) thread that runs as part of the main `oracle8.exe` background process in Windows. This way, lots of contiguous free space will be available when new database objects are created.

SYSTEM: A Special Tablespace

Every Oracle database contains a special tablespace, which in turn contains other special types of objects used constantly by both Oracle and its users. This tablespace is called `SYSTEM`. This tablespace contains objects that keep track of other objects being created in the database.

For Review

1. What items comprise the logical disk storage resources in Oracle? What items comprise the physical disk storage resources in Oracle?
2. How do physical disk storage resources map to logical disk storage resources in your Oracle database?
3. What process coalesces free space in your tablespace? What is the `SYSTEM` tablespace?

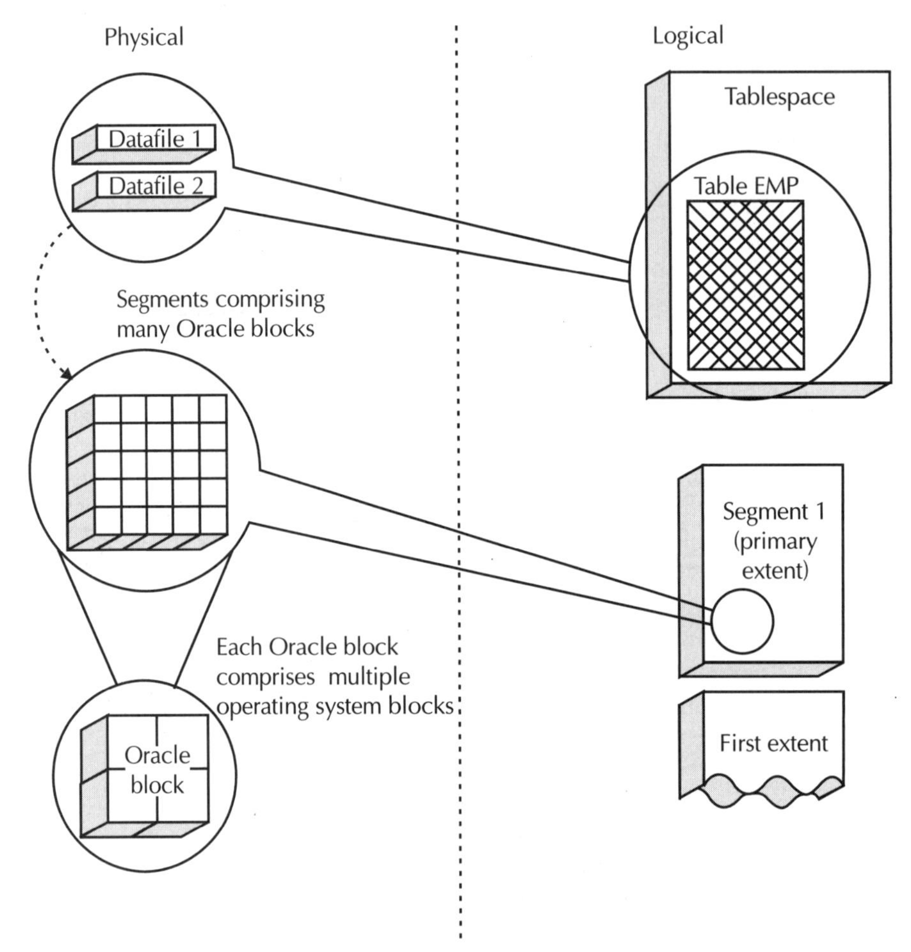

FIGURE 4-2. *Relationship between physical and logical storage structures*

Using Storage Manager for Application Management

Storage Manager is a tool in Oracle Enterprise Manager that is used to control Oracle's storage allocation. You create tablespaces in Storage Manager, which in turn creates datafiles on your host system. This lesson explains how to do it.

Creating Tablespaces

Tablespaces are created in several ways. The first way is by creating a database. Recall that in the `create database` statement, you named a few datafiles. These files made up the `SYSTEM` tablespace, which contains a bunch of important resources in your database, such as dictionary tables and the system rollback segment. Unfortunately, creating tablespaces in this way is a one-shot deal. Another way to create tablespaces is with Storage Manager.

Checking Tablespaces in Storage Manager

You can see all kinds of information about tablespaces using Storage Manager. By drilling down to the <SID> | Tablespaces node, you can see the utilization of space for each tablespace in your database. If you drill down further, into the <TBLSPC_NAME> | Datafiles node, you can see the datafile(s) allocated to the tablespace. By drilling into the Rollback Segments node instead, you can see any rollback segments created in that tablespace (for more information on rollback segments see "Creating and Managing Rollback Segments," later in the chapter). Figure 4-3 shows Storage Manager with this information displayed.

Creating Tablespaces in Storage Manager

To create a tablespace using Storage Manager, perform the following tasks:

1. Click on the <SID> | Tablespaces node. Then, click on the Create button. The Create button is the one with the plus sign (+) on it, identified in Figure 4-3.
2. In the Create Tablespace window, shown here, are two tabs, General and Extents. In the General tab, enter a name for your new tablespace in the appropriate text box. Click on the Online radio button to tell Storage Manager you want the tablespace to be online upon creation. Then click on the Permanent radio button to specify that this tablespace will house permanent objects like tables, indexes, and so on.

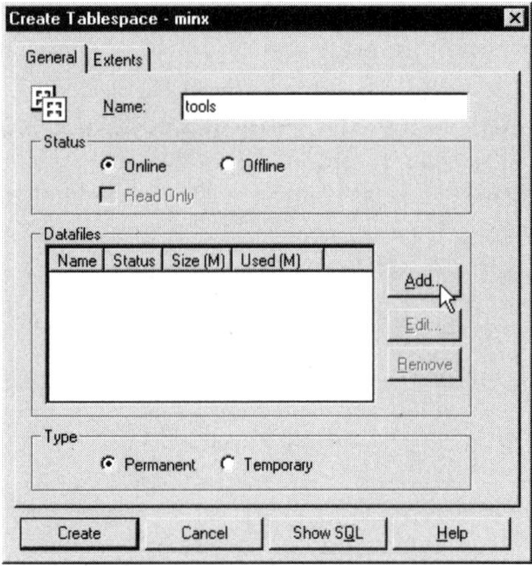

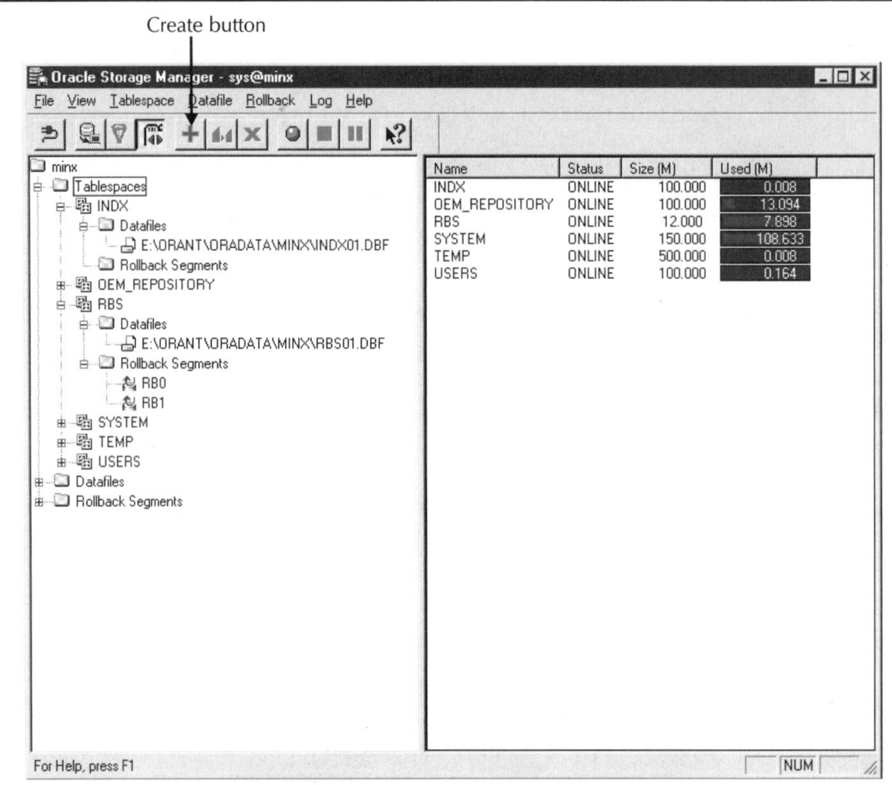

FIGURE 4-3. *Storage Manager interface*

3. Click on the Add button in the Create Tablespace interface. Here, you identify the name of the datafile(s) that comprise your tablespace. Enter an absolute pathname in the Name text box and the size of the file in kilobytes or megabytes. If the file already exists, click the Reuse Existing Datafile checkbox to overwrite it, as shown next. If you want to allow Oracle to dynamically extend the size of your datafile whenever the tablespace runs out of room, go to step 4. If not, skip ahead to step 5.

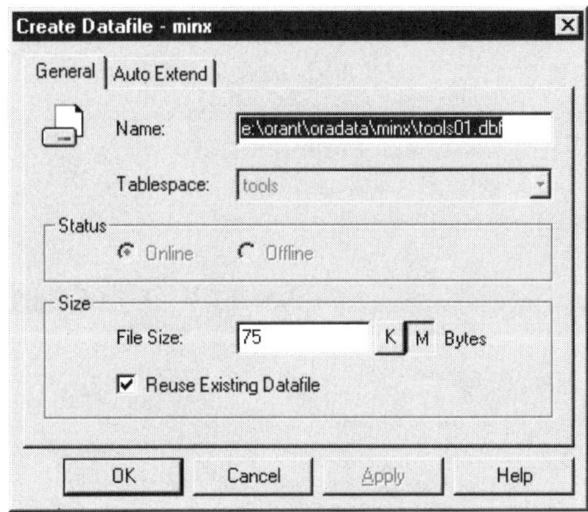

TIP
Be careful about using the Reuse Existing Datafile option when creating tablespaces to ensure you don't corrupt another database by overwriting its datafiles!

4. If you want to enable the Auto Extend option for your tablespace datafiles, click on the Auto Extend tab in the active window. Click the Enable Auto Extend checkbox, as shown here, and then specify how large each file extension should be and the maximum size this datafile is allowed to grow.

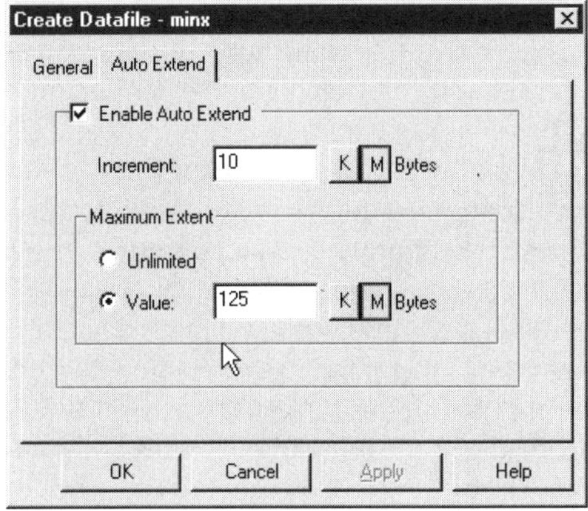

5. Click OK in the active window to return to the main Create Tablespace window. If you would like to add more datafiles, return to step 3. Otherwise, click the Extents tab to set the default storage settings. If you would like to override the default values set by Storage Manager, click the appropriate checkbox, as shown here. Otherwise, click the Create button, and Storage Manager will create your tablespace.

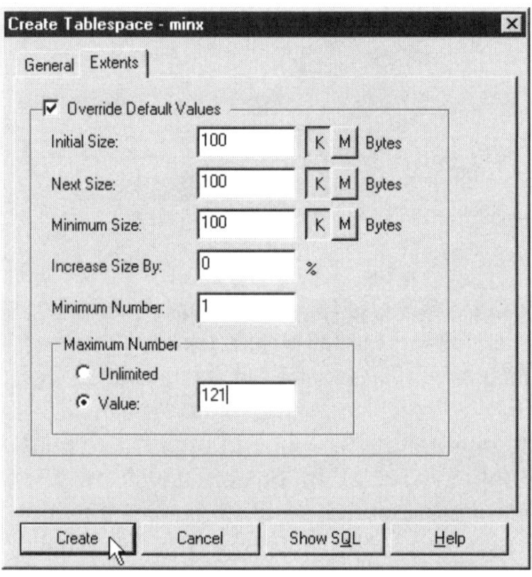

Special Note on Creating Temporary Tablespaces

Most of your tablespaces on the database will house permanent objects, or objects that will stick around in your database for a long time. Thus, when creating those tablespaces in Storage Manager, you will click on the Permanent radio button in the General tab in the Create Tablespace interface. However, sometimes you may want a special tablespace for housing temporary segments, or segments that get created and purged dynamically by Oracle when needed for certain types of operations (disk sorts, for example). Thus, when creating these types of tablespaces, you will click on the Temporary radio button in the General tab in the Create Tablespace interface. You don't need to do this in order to use this tablespace as your temporary tablespace, but it adds some protection against users trying to put tables and other permanent objects in an area where permanent objects are not meant to go.

TIP

More information about different types of tablespaces appears later in this section.

Storage Manager Is a Command Builder

Behind the scenes, Storage Manager creates tablespaces in Oracle with the `create tablespace` statement. If you click on the Show SQL button in the Create Tablespace interface, you can see the command used to create your tablespace. It should be similar to the one shown in the following code block:

```
CREATE TABLESPACE TOOLS DATAFILE
'E:\orant\oradata\minx\tools01.dbf' SIZE 75M
AUTOEXTEND ON NEXT 10M MAXSIZE 125M
MINIMUM EXTENT 150K
DEFAULT STORAGE
( INITIAL 100K NEXT 100K MINEXTENTS 1
  MAXEXTENTS 121 PCTINCREASE 0 )
ONLINE;
```

As you can see, the `create tablespace` statement has several components that match all the information you defined in the Storage Manager interface. First, you specify the datafiles your tablespace will own, using absolute pathnames. After that, you specify the `default storage` clause to set options that will be applied to database object creation if the `create` statement does not have storage parameters defined for it.

Default Storage Options Defined

The `default storage` clause defines storage options that will be applied to newly created database objects if the `create` statement does not have storage parameters defined for it. The `initial` and `next` options specify the size of the object's initial segment and next allocated extent, respectively. If `minimum extent` is defined for the tablespace you put your object in, and the value specified for `next` on your database object is less than `minimum extent`, Oracle rounds up to the next highest multiple for `minimum extent` and creates the initial or next extent as that size. This feature can reduce the amount of fragmentation in a tablespace.

The `minextents` and `maxextents` options specify the minimum and maximum number of extents the object can allocate in the tablespace. If you specify `minextents` greater than one and the tablespace has more than one datafile, Oracle will tend to spread extents over multiple datafiles, which can improve performance if those datafiles are also located on different disk resources.

Finally, `pctincrease` allows you to specify a percentage increase in the amount of space allocated for the next extent in the object. For example, if `next` is set to 200K, and `pctincrease` is 50, the second extent would be 200K in size, the third extent would be 300K (50 percent more than the second extent), the fourth extent would be 450K (50 percent more than the third extent), and so on. The minimum value is 0, and the default value is 50. The calculated value is rounded up to the next data block, which is a multiple of five times DB_BLOCK_SIZE. To make all extents the same size, specify pctincrease to be 0.

One storage option, when defined in a tablespace, cannot be overridden. That option is minimum extent, which ensures that every extent size used in the tablespace is a multiple of the specified integer value. Finally, you request that Oracle put your tablespace in the online and available state after creating it. If you omit the online keyword from your create tablespace statement, you can ensure it is online later by issuing alter tablespace *tblspc_name* online (the default is online).

Exercises

1. Identify two ways that tablespaces are created in Oracle.
2. Name some different aspects of tablespaces you can define with the create tablespace statement. Describe the meaning of each storage option. How are tablespace default storage options used?

Using Various Methods to Change Tablespace Size

There are a few different ways to modify the size of a tablespace. The first is by adding new datafiles to the tablespace. This task is accomplished within Storage Manager. To modify tablespace configuration in Storage Manager, do the following tasks:

1. Drill down to the <SID> | Tablespaces | <TBLSPC_NAME> node. On the right side of the Storage Manager interface, you should see the same set of tabs that you saw in the Create Tablespace window. Figure 4-4 shows the interface.
2. You can add more datafiles by clicking on the Add button and following steps already outlined for defining datafiles in Storage Manager.

Another method for adding datafiles is with the alter tablespace add datafile statement. Increasing the size of your tablespace by adding datafiles is accomplished with the statement in the following code block:

```
ALTER TABLESPACE orgdbdata ADD DATAFILE
'G:\Oracle\orgdbdata03.dat' SIZE 50M;
```

The number of datafiles you add to a tablespace is subject to two restrictions. First, you cannot add datafiles that will exceed the physical size of your disk resources (that one's pretty straightforward). Second, you cannot add more datafiles to your database than the limit set by the MAXDATAFILES clause in the create database statement.

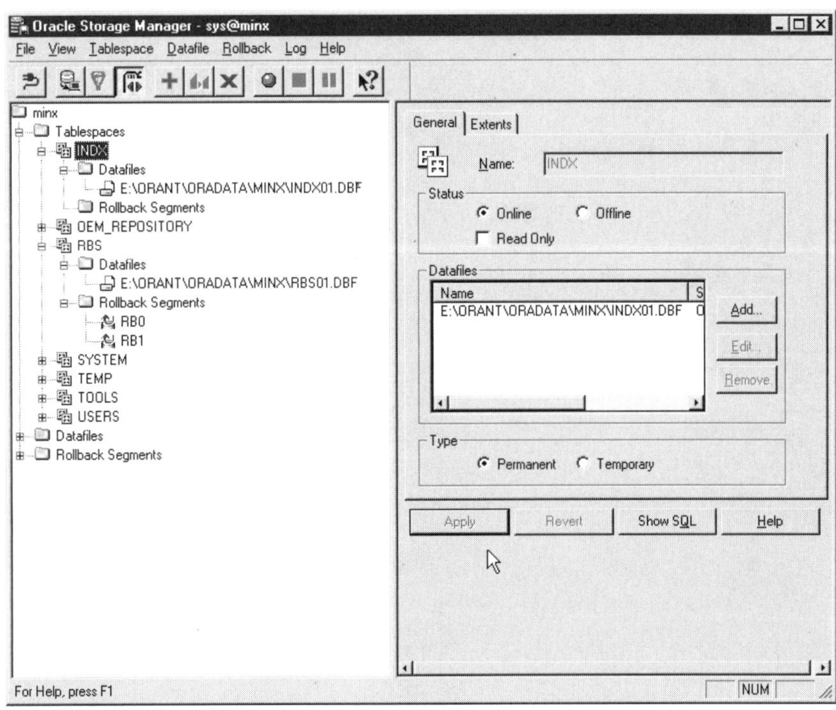

FIGURE 4-4. *Storage Manager tablespace redefinition interface*

Increasing Tablespaces by Resizing Datafiles

Another way to increase the size of a tablespace is to expand the size of existing datafiles manually. Resizing a datafile upward rarely meets with difficulty under Windows, unless you want to expand a datafile to a size larger than there is real space on disk to store it. To resize a datafile in Storage Manager, perform the following tasks:

1. Drill down to the <SID> | Tablespaces | <TBLSPC_NAME> | Datafiles | <FILENAME> node.
2. On the right side of the Storage Manager interface, click on the File Size text box, and modify the number that appears in it. Be sure to specify whether the size is in K or M by clicking the appropriate button next to the text box. Figure 4-5 illustrates.
3. Click the Apply button.

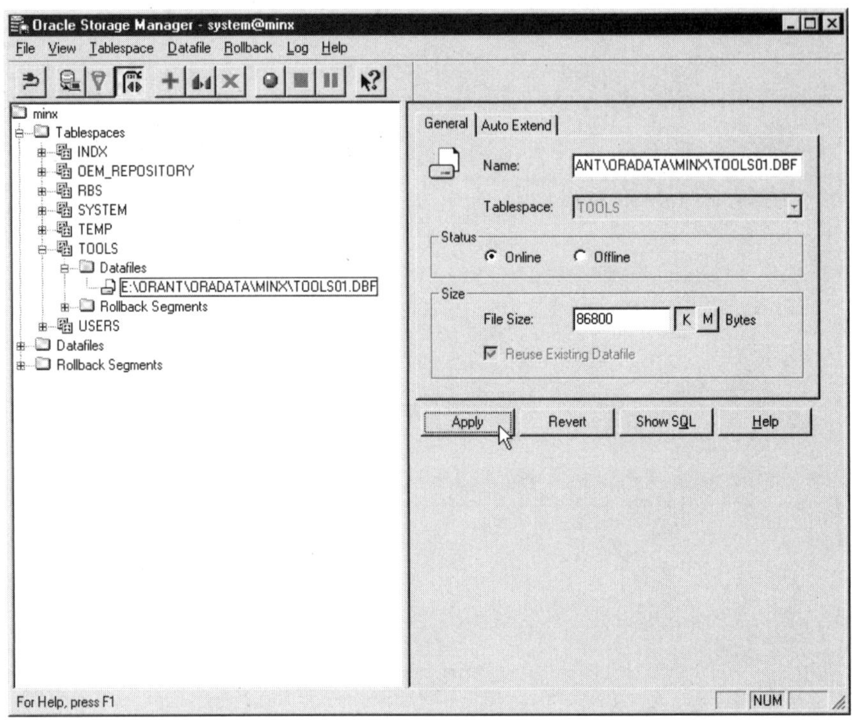

FIGURE 4-5. *Resizing tablespace datafiles with Storage Manager*

Behind the scenes, Storage Manager issues a command similar to the following statement:

```
ALTER DATABASE DATAFILE 'D:\Oracle\orgdbdata03.dat' RESIZE 1088M;
```

To enable automatic extension of your datafile, execute the following statement:

```
ALTER DATABASE DATAFILE 'D:\Oracle\orgdbdata03.dat'
AUTOEXTEND ON NEXT 10M MAXSIZE 50M;
```

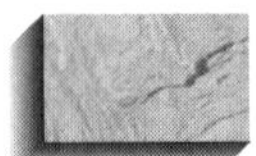

TIP
You usually can also resize a datafile to be smaller. This is not always safe, however, especially if the datafile contains segments or extents owned by database objects. Be careful when attempting this sort of activity.

Using Datafile Autoextend Feature to Expand Tablespaces

Increasing the size of your tablespace by allowing datafiles to allocate more space automatically is allowed as well. This is accomplished with the following steps in Storage Manager:

1. Drill down to the <SID> | Tablespaces | <TBLSPC_NAME> | Datafiles | <FILENAME> node.
2. On the right side of the Storage Manager interface, click the Auto Extend tab. In that interface, click the Enable Auto Extend checkbox. All text entry fields should no longer be grayed out.
3. Identify how much space Autoextend should allocate every time a datafile wants to increment in the Increment text box. Be sure to specify K or M. Then, enter the maximum size you want your datafile to be limited to by clicking the appropriate radio button and entering that size in bytes. Figure 4-6 illustrates.
4. Click the Apply button.

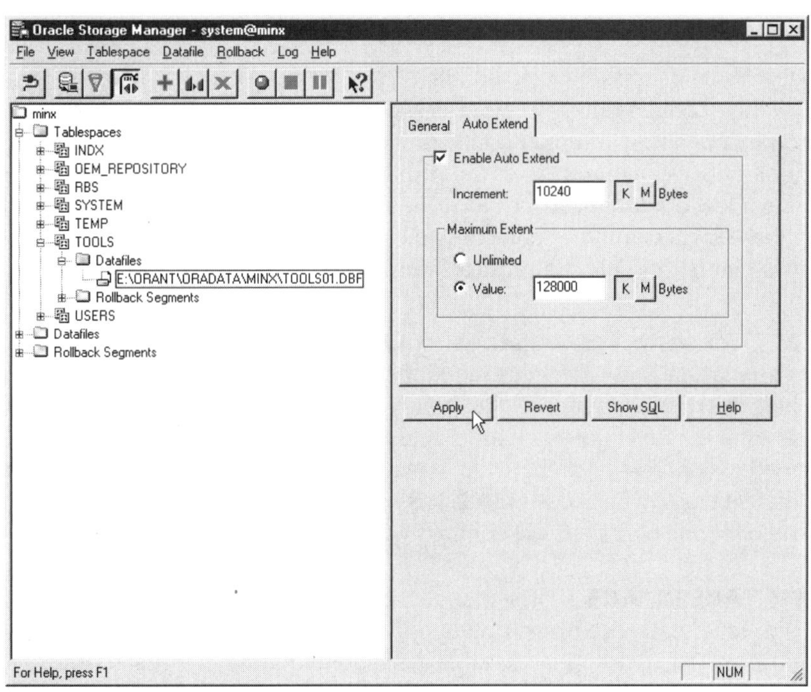

FIGURE 4-6. *Specifying Autoextend*

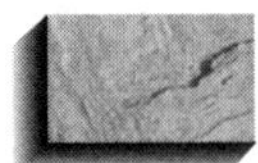

TIP
If you want to remove a tablespace, you can do so by drilling down to the <SID> | Tablespaces | <TBLSPC_NAME> node and clicking on the Remove button. This is the button with the big red X on it. Note, however, that you cannot remove a tablespace that has online active rollback segments in it. A later section, "Dropping a Rollback Segment in Storage Manager," explains how to take rollback segments offline and remove them.

For Review

1. Identify some ways that the size of a tablespace can be changed in Oracle.
2. Issuing the `alter database datafile` *`filename`* `offline drop` statement has what effect on your tablespace size?
3. How is a tablespace removed?

Using Oracle Tablespaces

When an Oracle database is created, the `SYSTEM` tablespace is created automatically. Though the `SYSTEM` tablespace can store any database object, it is not recommended that you put objects in it other than the dictionary objects and the system rollback segment. To avoid problems with your database, you will need to prepare a few other tablespaces to store different types of database objects. By placing these objects in other databases designed to fit their storage needs, the DBO prevents a number of potential storage problems.

Role of Different Tablespaces in Oracle

One of your first database activities should be to create separate tablespaces to store tables, indexes, rollback segments, temporary segments, and segments associated with database administrative tools such as Oracle Enterprise Manager. The tablespaces necessary for your Oracle database are explained in the following discussions. Each of these different types of database objects has its own unique behavior, and sometimes the behavior of one type of object conflicts with another.

SYSTEM TABLESPACE The `SYSTEM` tablespace contains tables, indexes, views, and other database objects owned by user SYS. These objects comprise the data dictionary. Also, the `SYSTEM` tablespace contains the `SYSTEM` rollback segment. Do not place any other objects in this tablespace.

DATA TABLESPACE The `DATA` tablespace contains all tables associated with an application. A system may contain many of these tablespaces, for lookup tables containing mostly static data, for work tables containing records added to an online system, or for history tables containing records for a data warehouse.

INDEX TABLESPACE The `INDEX` tablespace contains indexes for tables in a `DATA` tablespace. It is good to break tables and their associated indexes into separate tablespaces, to improve system manageability. You can also place `DATA` and `INDEX` tablespace datafiles on separate disks to improve overall system performance as well.

RBS TABLESPACE The `RBS` tablespace (sometimes called `ROLLBACK`) is used for storing rollback segments on an Oracle database. A rollback segment is a database object that aids in transaction processing on a system by storing old copies of uncommitted data changes for user processes. Storage of these objects is highly volatile and can interfere with other objects like application tables. Thus, it's best to keep rollback segments in their own tablespace.

TOOLS TABLESPACE Many tools like Oracle Enterprise Manager have a set of objects called a *repository* that contains information needed for the tool's operation. These objects are usually stored in a `TOOLS` tablespace to avoid conflict with application and/or user data. `TOOLS` tablespaces generally do not need to be very large.

USERS TABLESPACE Some users need the ability to create database objects in a database. For example, a user wanting to obtain performance information for SQL statements may need to create a special table called `PLAN_TABLE`. A `USER` tablespace is like a `TOOLS` tablespace in that it prevents user tables from getting mixed in with application tables.

TEMP TABLESPACE When users issue certain types of statements on Oracle, the database must write some information to disk for temporary use in order to perform a sort operation. This behavior in Oracle is highly volatile in terms of disk utilization, and has a tendency to fragment and interfere with growth of permanent database objects like tables. Thus, it is highly important to ensure that Oracle has a `TEMP` tablespace for disk sorts, and that all users use no tablespace besides `TEMP` for this purpose. The types of statements that produce sorts include

- `select` statements containing `order by` or `group by` clauses
- `create index` statements
- Set operations like `union all`
- Computing or estimating statistics for cost-based optimization, a DBA task

For Review

1. What tablespace is created with every Oracle database?
2. What additional tablespaces are necessary for correct Oracle operation? What sorts of database objects will these tablespaces eventually support?
3. How and when is a `TEMP` tablespace used?

Creating and Managing Rollback Segments

Before learning how to create and manage rollback segments, here's a short primer on what they are. Collections of data changes called *transactions* occurring on the Oracle database need rollback segments to store their unsaved data changes. Transactions are assigned to rollback segments in one of two ways. You can assign a transaction to a rollback segment explicitly with the `set transaction use rollback segment` *`rollback_seg`* statement within the transaction. Or, if no rollback segment is explicitly defined for the transaction, Oracle assigns the transaction to the rollback segment that currently has the lightest transaction load in round-robin fashion. Thus, more than one transaction can use the same rollback segment, but each block in the rollback segment houses data from one and only one transaction.

Rollback segments are used as follows. A rollback segment usually has several extents allocated to it at any given time, and these extents are used sequentially. After the database is started, the first transaction will be assigned to the first rollback segment, and it will store its data changes in extent #1 of the rollback segment. As the transaction progresses (a long-running batch process with thousands of `update` statements, let's say), it places more and more data into rollback segment extent #1. An extent containing data from a transaction in progress is called an *active* extent. More and more transactions are starting on the database, and some of those other transactions may be assigned to this rollback segment. Each transaction will fill extent #1 with more and more change data until the transactions `commit`.

If extent #1 fills with data changes before the transactions `commit`, the transactions will begin filling extent #2 with data. Transactions with data changes "spilling over" to a new extent are said to be performing a *wrap*. A special marker called a rollback segment *head* moves from extent #1 to extent #2 to indicate the extent where new and existing transactions assigned to the rollback segment can write their next data change. As soon as the transaction `commit`s its data changes, the space in extent #1 used to store its data changes is no longer required. If extent #1 is filled with data change information from only committed transactions, then extent #1 is considered *inactive*. Figure 4-7 displays the rollback segment behavior as described here.

To effectively use rollback segment space, the rollback segment allocates only a few extents, and those extents are reused often. The ideal operation of a rollback

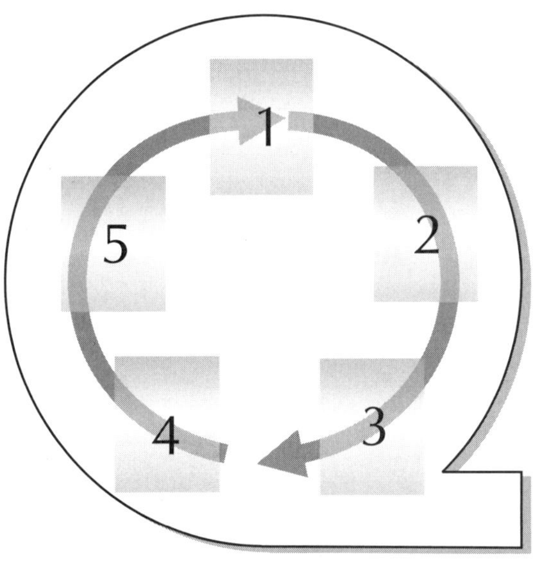

FIGURE 4-7. *A rollback segment containing five reusable extents*

segment with five extents is as follows: Transactions assigned to the rollback segment should fill extent #5 a little after transactions with data changes in extent #1 commit. Thus, extent #1 becomes inactive just before transactions in extent #5 need to wrap into it. However, this behavior is not always possible. If a transaction goes on for a long time without committing data changes, it may eventually fill all extents in the rollback segment. When this happens, the rollback segment acquires extent #6 and wraps data changes from the current transaction into it. The rollback segment head moves into extent #6, as well. Figure 4-8 illustrates how Oracle obtains or allocates more extents for a rollback segment.

If a transaction causes the rollback segment to allocate many extents for storing the long transaction's data changes—as determined by the `maxextents` storage option defined when the rollback segment is created—the rollback segment becomes enormously stretched out of shape. Oracle has an `optimal` option available in rollback segment storage that permits rollback segments to deallocate extents after long-running transactions cause them to acquire more extents than they really need. The `optimal` clause specifies the ideal size of the rollback segment in kilobytes or megabytes. This value tells Oracle the ideal number of extents the rollback segment should maintain. If `optimal` is specified for a rollback segment,

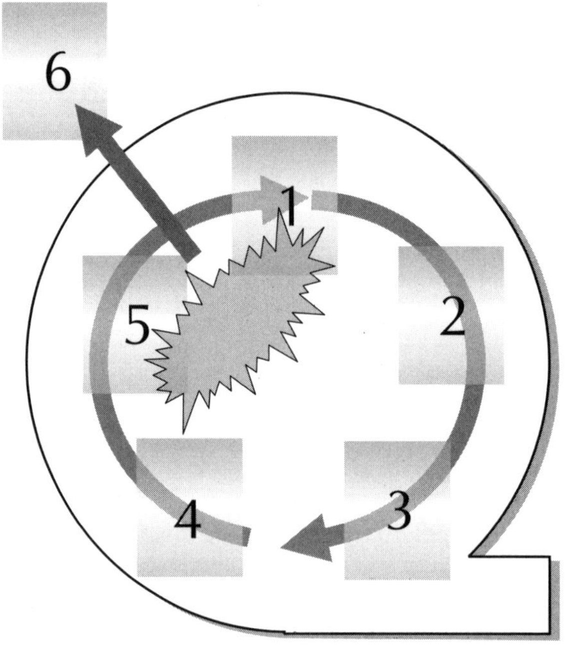

FIGURE 4-8. *How a rollback segment acquires more extents*

that object will deallocate space *when the rollback segment head moves from one extent to another,* if the current size of the rollback segment exceeds `optimal` and if there are contiguous adjoining inactive extents. Figure 4-9 illustrates rollback segment extent deallocation.

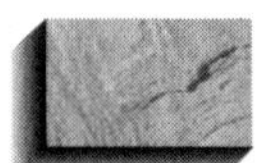

TIP

Extent deallocation as the result of `optimal` *has nothing whatsoever to do with transactions committing on the database. The deallocation occurs when the rollback segment head moves from one extent to another. Oracle does not deallocate extents currently in use (even if the total size exceeds* `optimal`*) and always attempts to deallocate the oldest inactive extents first.*

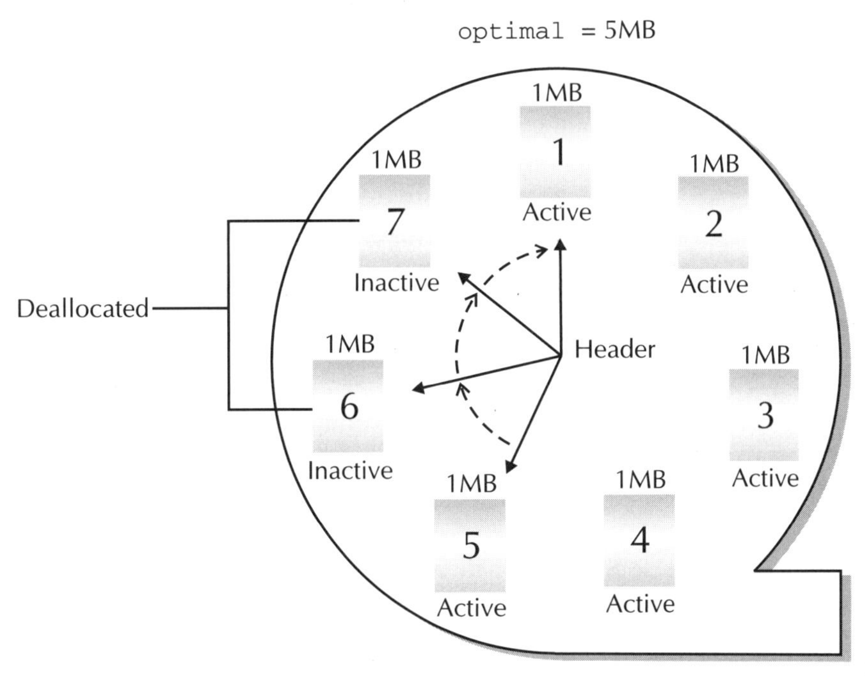

FIGURE 4-9. *Rollback segment extent deallocation*

The Rule of Four to Plan Rollback Segment Numbers for OLTP Systems

Oracle's recommended strategy for planning the appropriate number of rollback segments for most online transaction processing (OLTP) systems is here called the *Rule of Four,* for easy recollection. Take the total number of transactions that will hit the database at any given time and divide by 4 to decide how many rollback segments to create. Consider this example. You have a database that will be used for a small user rollout of an OLTP application. About 25 concurrent transactions will happen on the database at any given time. By applying the Rule of Four, you determine that about 6 rollback segments are required. Shortly, you will see the additional calculation required for determining rollback segment size.

Two exceptions exist to the Rule of Four. The first is if the quotient is less than 4 + 4, round the result of the Rule of Four up to the nearest multiple of 4 and use that number of rollback segments. In this case, the result would be rounded from 6 to 8. The second exception to the Rule of Four is that Oracle generally doesn't recommend more than 50 rollback segments for a database. If the Rule of Four determines that more than 50 rollback segments are needed, the DBA should start by allocating 50 and spend time monitoring the rollback segment wait ratio to determine whether more should be added later.

Planning Rollback Segment Numbers for Batch System Processing

When planning the number of rollback segments required on the batch transaction processing system, you need to make a small number of large rollback segments available to support long-running processes that make several data changes. You should monitor the database to see how many transactions your batch processes execute concurrently and apply the Rule of Four to determine the number of rollback segments needed, just as you would with an OLTP application. The next topic will demonstrate how to calculate the size for rollback segments supporting both OLTP and batch transactions.

Creating a Rollback Segment in Storage Manager

Storage Manager shows all kinds of information about rollback segments. Drill down to the <SID> | Tablespaces | SYSTEM | Rollback Segments node in Storage Manager. There are already some rollback segments in this tablespace, so you can investigate the type of information Storage Manager provides on rollback segments in this way. You can create a rollback segment in Storage Manager in the following way:

1. Drill down to the <SID> | Tablespaces | SYSTEM | Rollback Segments node, and click on the Create button. You will now see the Create Rollback Segment interface, as shown in here.

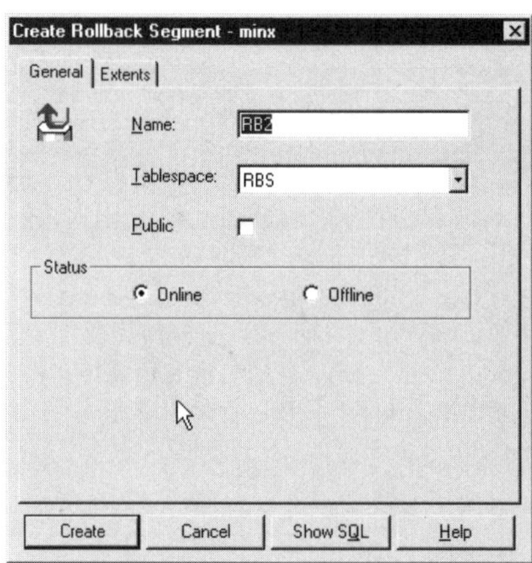

2. Enter the name of your new rollback segment in the Name text box. Try to be consistent with naming conventions on your rollback segments when creating new ones.

3. Choose the RBS tablespace to store your new rollback segment from the Tablespace list box.

4. Click the Public checkbox only if you want to create a public rollback segment (only important if you are using Oracle Parallel Server). Also, click on the Online radio button so that the rollback segment you create is online and available for use after creation.

5. Click on the Extents tab. You can choose any value for Initial Size and Next Size, such as 1MB, being careful to specify K or M. Just make sure you specify the same value for both Initial and Next. For Minimum Number, you should enter a number between 10 and 20, to indicate the number of extents your rollback segment will have. You can set Optimal Size to the size in MB of the rollback segment with minimum number of extents allocated. For Maximum Number, pick a number that is high enough to accommodate large transactions, but not so large that you will fill your RBS tablespace. The following illustration shows some settings.

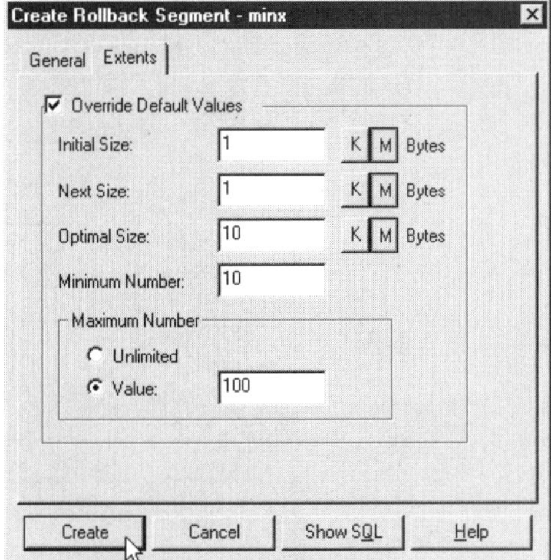

Resizing a Rollback Segment in Storage Manager

You can manually resize the maximum number of extents a rollback segment can have by performing the following steps in Storage Manager:

1. Drill down to the <SID> | Tablespaces | <TBLSPC_NAME> | Rollback Segments | <RBS_NAME> node.

2. Click on the Extents tab. Alter the Value tab in the Maximum Number section of the Extents tab work area. Then, click Apply. Figure 4-10 illustrates.

Dropping a Rollback Segment in Storage Manager

To remove a rollback segment from your database, you should execute the following tasks:

1. Drill down to the <SID> | Tablespaces | <TBLSPC_NAME> | Rollback Segments | <RBS_NAME> node.
2. Click the Offline radio button. Then, click Apply.
3. Drill down to the <SID> | Tablespaces | <TBLSPC_NAME> | Rollback Segments | <RBS_NAME> node.
4. Click the Remove button. Then, click Apply.

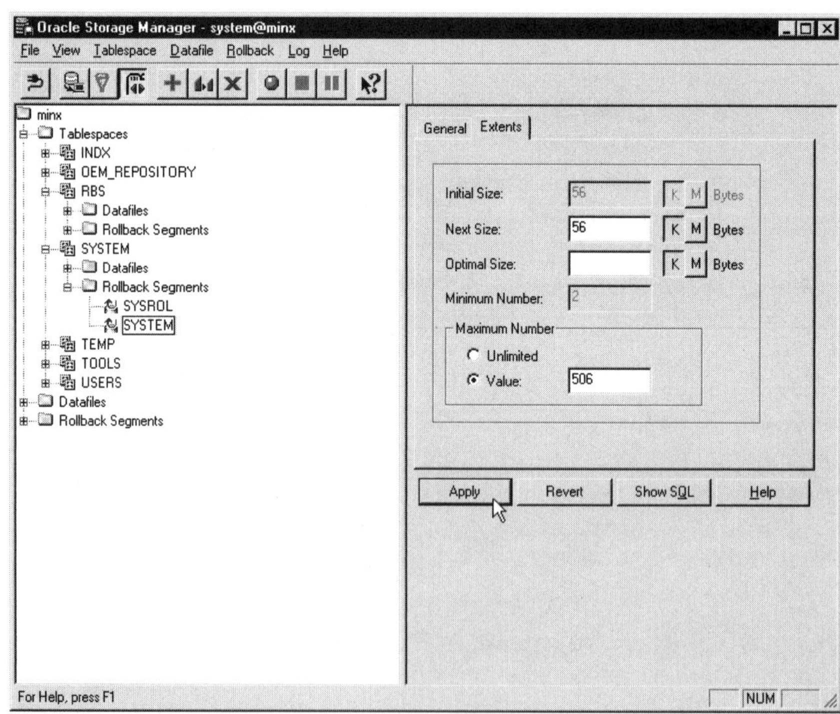

FIGURE 4-10. *Resizing rollback segments*

For Review

Understand what a rollback segment is, how it is used, and how to use Storage Manager to perform various activities on rollback segments.

Creating Objects for Application Data

In this section, you cover how to create objects to store application data:

- Running application scripts with SQL Worksheet
- Listing application objects with Schema Manager
- Using Storage Manager to control object storage

Once the storage structures of your Oracle database are in place, you can create the actual objects used within an application. These objects usually include tables, indexes, sequences, users, privileges, PL/SQL blocks, and other database objects. Most applications out there don't have just a few objects; they usually have many objects. An application sometimes will even have hundreds of objects. If you don't want to sit there and interactively create hundreds of database objects, you need to have a script on hand that does this for you. Many suppliers of packaged applications provide such scripts. In this chapter, you will learn how to use the SQL Worksheet provided with Oracle Enterprise Manager (OEM) for running these scripts. You will also learn how to use Schema Manager to view information about objects in your database. Finally, you will cover how to manage space allocation using Storage Manager.

Running Application Scripts with SQL Worksheet

Objects can be created from scripts in an Oracle database using a tool in OEM called SQL Worksheet. This tool is handy for creating applications in that it saves you the time of having to interact with a GUI tool to create those application objects. You will see the benefit of script execution, particularly in situations where the application has many, many objects stored in it. To start SQL Worksheet, click on Start | Programs | Oracle Enterprise Manager | SQL Worksheet. Figure 4-11 shows you the SQL Worksheet interface.

You will now walk through the steps required to run an application script with SQL Worksheet. The CD-ROM included with this book contains an application creation script called `chapter8.sql`. The following code block reproduces the contents of that script. If, for some reason, you have trouble using the `chapter8.sql` script, you can copy the following code block into a file using Notepad or WordPad on your Windows machine, and then rename the file `chapter8.sql` from a DOS prompt. It is important that you rename the file from a DOS prompt and not by using the File | Save As menu

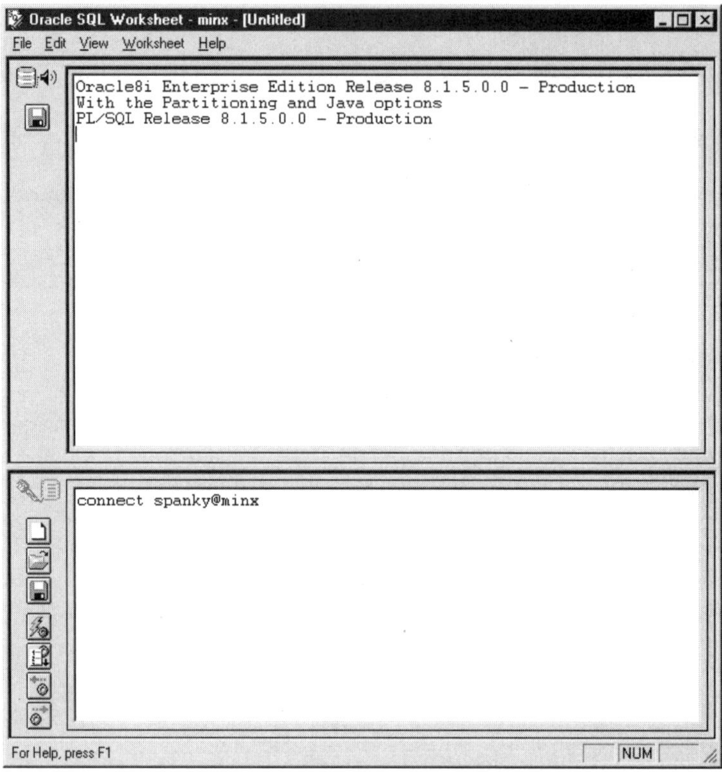

FIGURE 4-11. *SQL Worksheet*

option in your text editor. This is because the text editor will most likely try to attach a `.txt` extension to your file, making the file hard to find later when you want to run it.

```
create table emp
( EMPID                          VARCHAR2(20) primary key,
 LASTNAME                                VARCHAR2(30),
 FIRSTNAME                               VARCHAR2(30),
 SALARY                                  NUMBER,
 DEPT                                    VARCHAR2(10),
 HIRE_DATE                               DATE )
/
insert into EMP (EMPID, LASTNAME, FIRSTNAME,
SALARY, DEPT, HIRE_DATE )
```

```
Values
('02039', 'WALLA', 'RAJENDRA', 60000, '604B', '01-JAN-96')
/
insert into EMP (EMPID, LASTNAME, FIRSTNAME,
SALARY, DEPT, HIRE_DATE )
Values
('39334', 'SMITH', 'GINA', 75000, '604B', '15-MAR-97')
/
insert into EMP (EMPID, LASTNAME, FIRSTNAME,
SALARY, DEPT, HIRE_DATE )
 Values
('60403', 'HARPER', 'ROD', 45000, '504A', '30-APR-79')
/
insert into EMP (EMPID, LASTNAME, FIRSTNAME,
SALARY, DEPT, HIRE_DATE )
Values
('49539', 'QIAN', 'LEE', 90000, '504A', '25-MAY-99')
/
insert into EMP (EMPID, LASTNAME, FIRSTNAME,
SALARY, DEPT, HIRE_DATE )
Values
('49392', 'SPANKY', 'STACY', 10000, '604B', '14-FEB-98')
/
insert into EMP (EMPID, LASTNAME, FIRSTNAME,
SALARY, DEPT, HIRE_DATE )
Values
('12345', 'BUGGY', null, 55000, null, null)
/
commit
/
create table dept
(DEPT                              VARCHAR2(20) primary key,
 DEPT_HEAD                                 VARCHAR2(30),
 DEPT_BUDGET                               NUMBER)
/
insert into dept (DEPT, DEPT_HEAD, DEPT_BUDGET) values
('604B','SMITHERS',34000000)
/
insert into dept (DEPT, DEPT_HEAD, DEPT_BUDGET) values
('504A','ROSE',50000)
/
insert into dept (DEPT, DEPT_HEAD, DEPT_BUDGET) values
('404Z','BOESKY',56000000000)
/
commit
/
create view emp_vw
as select empid, lastname, firstname, salary
```

```
from emp
/
CREATE SEQUENCE countdown_20
START WITH 20
INCREMENT BY -1
MAXVALUE 20
MINVALUE 0
CYCLE
ORDER
CACHE 2
/
create synonym employee
for emp
/
create user spanky
identified by spanky
/
create user athena
identified by athena
/
```

TIP
For this exercise, you must login to SQL Worksheet as a user with `create table`, `create view`, `create synonym`, `create sequence`, and `create user` privileges. See your DBA about setting up a user with these privileges for you to use.

Running SQL Worksheet

Follow these steps to load application objects into your Oracle database from the `chapter8.sql` script:

1. Copy the script to the `c:\` directory on your computer.
2. Open SQL Worksheet.
3. In SQL Worksheet, click on the Open icon in the lower-left side of the interface. In the Browse window, find the `chapter8.sql` script on your machine. When finished, click the Open button. The contents of the script should appear in the lower window, as shown in Figure 4-12.
4. Click on the Execute button in the lower-left side of the SQL Worksheet window. The Execute button is the one with the lightning bolt on it, highlighted in Figure 4-13.

FIGURE 4-12. *SQL Worksheet with script contents shown*

TIP
Once you create an object, such as a table in a database, you own it and you are responsible for letting others use it. You are the only user who can grant access to data in that object to other users.

For Review

Be sure you know how to execute application creation scripts using SQL Worksheet.

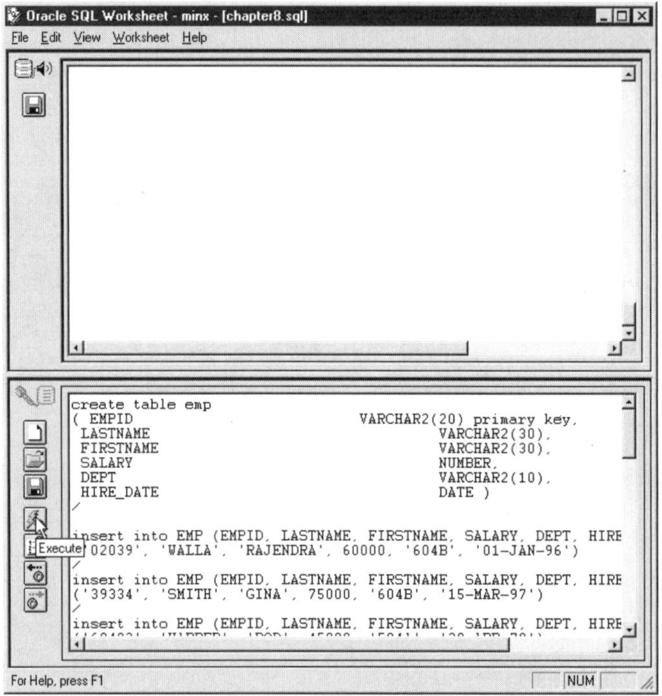

FIGURE 4-13. *SQL Worksheet with Execute button highlighted*

Listing Application Objects with Schema Manager

Once objects actually exist in your database, you can see what's out there using Schema Manager. This tool shows your database objects by object and by schema owner. Figure 4-14 shows Schema Manager.

Objects in Oracle That Require Storage Space

A key differentiation should be made at this point between objects of a database application and the segments that are used to store them. An object is stored somewhere in a tablespace datafile. This storage used in the datafile is called a *segment*. Segments can be used to store other database objects. Some database objects that might be stored in tablespace segments include

- **Tables** Collections of information structured into columns and rows of data. Ideally, tables are stored in `DATA` tablespaces.

- **Indexes** Objects that speed access to table data by storing a particular set of table columns and associated disk location information in hierarchical fashion. Ideally, indexes are stored in `INDEX` tablespaces.
- **Clusters** Collection of tables stored together in one segment. Ideally, clusters are stored in `DATA` tablespaces.
- **Snapshots** Copies of table data stored in distributed environments to reflect the way table data looked at a point in time. Ideally, snapshots are stored in `DATA` tablespaces.

TIP
In addition to the tablespaces previously described, all database objects in Oracle require some space for storage of their object definitions in tables owned by user `SYS`. This space is allocated in the `SYSTEM` tablespace.

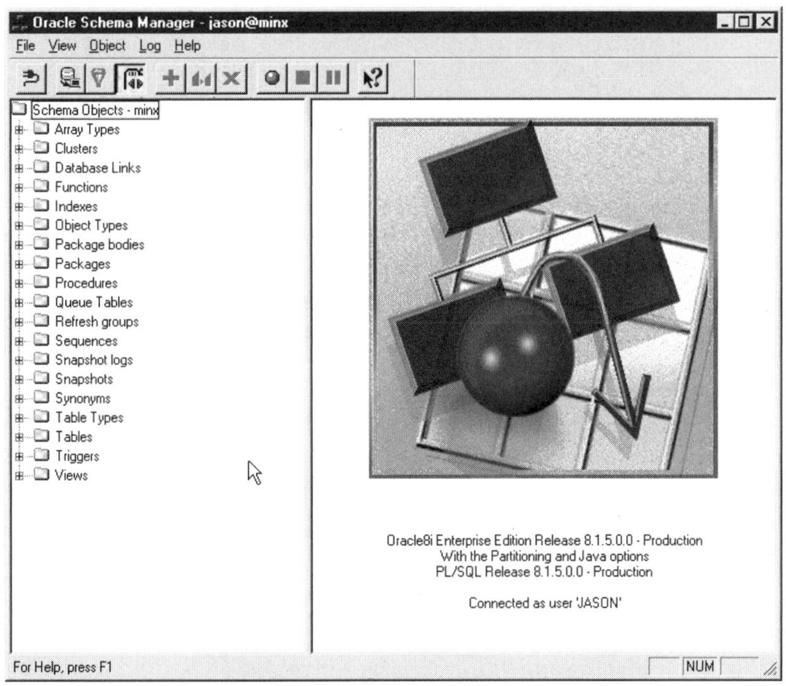

FIGURE 4-14. *Schema Manager interface*

Objects That Don't Require Storage Space

Objects in an Oracle database that do not require storage space in any tablespace other than `SYSTEM` include the following:

- **Views** Objects that show data from tables, but do not actually contain any data themselves. A view might be created to prevent users from seeing sensitive data in a table, such as salary information on other employees in the EMP table.
- **Sequences** Objects that incrementally generate numbers based on rules defined by the user.
- **Synonyms** Objects that are simply a name associated with another database object, like a table or view.
- **Database links** Objects that store connection information to other Oracle databases.
- **PL/SQL blocks** Stored code in Oracle that performs a specified task. Types of PL/SQL blocks include packages, procedures, functions, and triggers.

Viewing Information About Objects in Schema Manager

If you refer to Figure 4-14, you will see that on the left side of the interface, database objects are grouped by object. However, notice that by drilling down to the node referencing particular types of database objects, you can see the objects broken down by schema owner. For example, in Figure 4-15, you can see under the Schema Objects | Tables node several other nodes indicating users on the database who own tables. Drilling down further, into the Schema Objects | Tables | <OWNER> | <TABLENAME> node (where OWNER is the owner of the table, and TABLENAME is the name of a table), you can see several other nodes that indicate the particulars of the table in question, such as Indexes for associated constraints, Partitions, Snapshot logs, and Triggers.

By clicking on the <TABLENAME> node, as has been done in Figure 4-15 for the table BASEBALL_BAT owned by JASON, you can see on the right side of the interface several tab interfaces where you can see or modify information about the object. The tab interfaces you see will depend on the object you are looking at.

For Review

Know how to use Schema Manager to find information about database objects in your Oracle database.

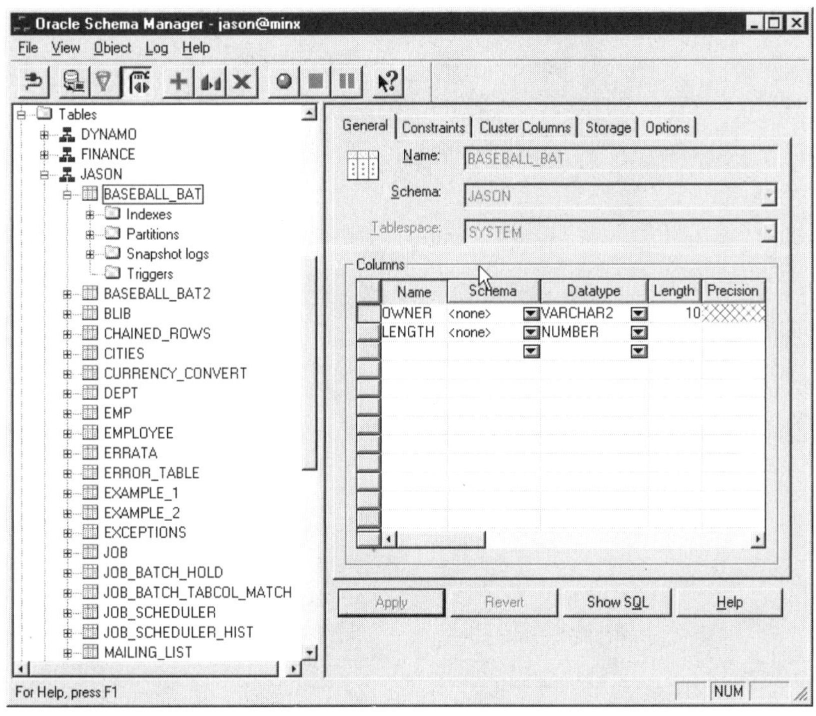

FIGURE 4-15. *Schema Manager interface*

Using Storage Manager to Control Object Storage

Finally, realize that you must monitor the growth of your database application in order to ensure you don't run out of space. Tables, clusters, indexes, and rollback segments can all grow over time; and since they are objects that require space in a tablespace, you must ensure they have the space they need to grow. To monitor the growth of tablespaces, you can use Storage Manager. To show the space used by tablespaces, datafiles, and rollback segments in Storage Manager, you click on the node corresponding to each of those items, respectively, and Storage Manager displays the overall space allocation for all those objects in your database, along with the space used, in a visual format. Figure 4-16 shows an example using rollback segments.

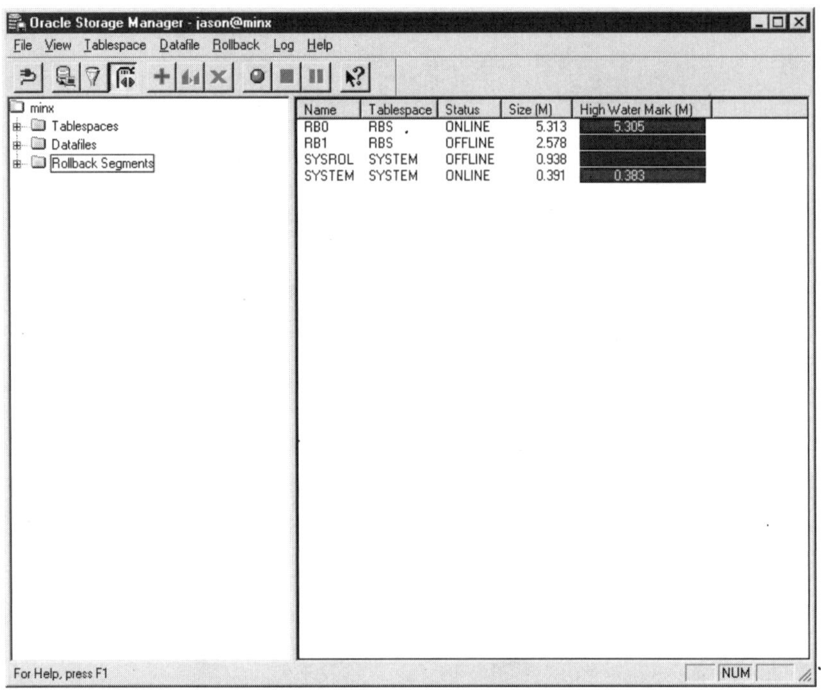

FIGURE 4-16. *Rollback segment storage allocation in Storage Manager*

For Review

Know the three object types that Storage Manager can graphically display space used and space available for.

Chapter Summary

In this chapter, you learned about creating applications in Oracle and the structures that underlie them. You covered how to implement a logical and physical database structure of your Oracle database application. You learned about tablespaces and datafiles, the fundamental storage structures that comprise Oracle database applications. You learned about tables, indexes, and other objects that are used in Oracle database applications. The use of Storage Manager for application management and storage object creation was explained as well. You learned about the tablespaces usually included in an Oracle database, and what purpose each has. You learned about creating and managing rollback segments as well.

Creating the actual objects used in an Oracle application was covered as well. You learned that, with a script containing all database object storage definitions, you can create your applications using SQL Worksheet. You also learned how to view information about the objects in your application using Schema Manager. Finally, the chapter covered how to monitor the space utilization of tablespaces, datafiles, and rollback segments using Storage Manager.

Two-Minute Drill

- Physical database storage structures include
  - **Datafiles** Files used for storing Oracle data
  - **Blocks** Fundamental unit of storage in an Oracle database
- Logical storage structures include
  - **Tablespaces** An area of storage comprised of one or more datafiles
  - **Segments** A collection of blocks used for storing Oracle objects
  - **Extents** Extra space allocated for an Oracle object when a segment fills
- Understand how tablespaces and datafiles relate to one another. A tablespace can have many datafiles, but each datafile can associate with only one tablespace.
- At database creation, there is one tablespace—`SYSTEM`.
- Don't place all database objects into the `SYSTEM` tablespace because their storage needs often conflict with each other.
- Instead, create multiple tablespaces for the different segments available on the database and place those objects into those tablespaces.
- The different types of tablespaces an application may need, and their uses, are
  - **DATA** Stores table data for an application
  - **INDEX** Stores indexes associated with table data for an application
  - **RBS** Stores rollback segments for an application
  - **TEMP** Stores temporary information associated with disk sorts
  - **USERS** Stores user database objects

- **TOOLS** Stores database objects associated with tools like the OEM repository.

- There are two types of tablespaces, temporary and permanent. A temporary tablespace cannot house permanent database objects, but a permanent tablespace can house temporary objects.
- Tablespaces can be created with Storage Manager. Understand how to create tablespaces in this way.
- Understand the use of default storage specifications in a tablespace.
- Know how to monitor storage allocation in Storage Manager. You can monitor storage allocation for the following object types:
  - Tablespaces
  - Datafiles
  - Rollback segments
- Rollback segments allow transaction processing to occur by storing the old version of data that has been changed but not committed by the users.
- Rollback segments should consist of equally sized extents.
- The `pctincrease` option is not permitted on rollback segments.
- Rollback segments must be brought online in order to use them.
- A rollback segment cannot be taken offline until all active transactions writing rollback entries have completed. This same restriction applies to tablespaces containing active rollback segments.
- Specific private rollback segments can be allocated at startup if they are specified in the `ROLLBACK_SEGMENTS` parameter in `init`*`sid`*`.ora`.
- The number of rollback segments required for an instance is determined by the Rule of Four—divide concurrent user processes by 4; if the result is less than 4 + 4, round up to the nearest multiple of 4.

Chapter Questions

1. **How many rollback segments will be required if the value set for `TRANSACTIONS` is 20 and the value set for `TRANSACTIONS_PER_ROLLBACK_SEGMENT` is 4?**

   A. 2

B. 4

C. 8

D. 9

2. **When a rollback segment is created, its availability status is automatically set to which of the following by Oracle?**

   A. Online

   B. Pending online

   C. Offline

   D. Stale

3. **Which of the following choices best describes the methodology for sizing extents for the sort segments on your Oracle database?**

   A. TRANSACTIONS/TRANSACTIONS_PER_ROLLBACK_SEGMENT

   B. X * SORT_AREA_SIZE + DB_BLOCK_SIZE

   C. (avg_row_size – init_row_size) * 100/avg_row_size

   D. 100—`pctfree`—(avg_row_size * 100)/avail_data_space

4. **When determining the number of rollback segments in a database, which of the following choices identifies a factor to consider?**

   A. Concurrent transactions

   B. Size of typical transactions

   C. Size of rows in table most frequently changed

   D. Number of anticipated disk sorts

5. **All of the following choices indicate a way to resolve the `ORA-1555 Snapshot too old (rollback segment too small)` error, except one. Which choice is it?**

   A. Create rollback segments with a higher `optimal` value.

   B. Create rollback segments with higher `maxextents`.

   C. Create rollback segments with larger extent sizes.

   D. Create rollback segments with high `minextents`.

6. You need to determine the storage allocation used for certain objects in your Oracle database. Available space in which three of the following types of objects can be displayed using Storage Manager?

A. Tablespaces

B. Tables

C. Datafiles

D. Rollback segments

E. Indexes

F. Sequences

Answers to Chapter Questions

1. C. 8

Explanation Refer to the Rule of Four in creating rollback segments. Remember, the equation is `TRANSACTIONS/TRANSACTIONS_PER_ROLLBACK_SEGMENT`. In this case, the result is 5. This is a special case in the Rule of Four that gets rounded up to 8.

2. C. Offline

Explanation Once created, a rollback segment status is offline and must be brought online in order to be used. Refer to the discussion of rollback segments. In order to bring it online, you must issue the `alter rollback segment online` statement, eliminating choice A. Pending online is not a valid status for rollback segments in Oracle, eliminating choice B. Stale is a valid status for redo logs, but not rollback segments, eliminating choice D.

3. B. X * SORT_AREA_SIZE + DB_BLOCK_SIZE

Explanation If the data to be sorted was any smaller than the `init`*`sid`*`.ora` parameter `SORT_AREA_SIZE`, then the sort would take place in memory. Thus, you can be sure that all disk sorts will write data at least as great as `SORT_AREA_SIZE` to disk, so you should size your sort segment to be a multiple of that parameter. Since the sort segment will need a header block, adding in `DB_BLOCK_SIZE` is required to make the extra room for the header. Choices C and D are formulas for determining `pctfree` and `pctused`, respectively, so they are wrong. Choice A is used to determine the number of rollback segments your database needs, making that one wrong as well.

4. A. Concurrent transactions

Explanation The number of concurrent transactions is used in part to determine the number of rollback segments your database should have. Had the question asked which choice played a role in determining the size of extents or total rollback segment size, then choices B or C would have been correct. Since disk sorts have little to do with rollback segments, under no circumstances should you have chosen D.

5. B. Create rollback segments with higher `maxextents`.

Explanation Each of the choices offered will eliminate the `ORA-15555` error, except choice B. Refer to the discussion of indexes created in conjunction with integrity constraints.

6. A, C, *and* D. Tablespaces, datafiles, *and* rollback segments

Explanation Using Storage Manager, you can find space available in tablespaces, datafiles, and rollback segments. To see space allocated for a table or index, you must query the DBA_SEGMENTS dictionary view. Sequences have no storage allocation other than their definition in the `SYSTEM` tablespace.

CHAPTER 5

Oracle Usage and Database Security

n this chapter, you will cover the following important topics on Oracle users and database security:

- Setting up users for new applications
- Securing application data manipulation

Every organization wants secure data. The extent to which an organization is willing to ensure data security varies according to many factors, including data sensitivity, budget, and understanding of the security options available. It has often been said that the most secure applications are the ones with no users. However, usage is the main reason most applications are created! So, it is the balance between limiting usage and controlling access that marks security on the Oracle platform. In this chapter, you will learn both how to set up users for applications and how to secure their access to data in those applications. Whether you believe security is a denial of life or the key to ultimate success as a DBO is a decision you must make for yourself.

Setting Up Users for New Applications

In this section, you will cover the following topics related to managing privileges:

- Functions of different types of users
- Identifying system privileges
- Directly granting system privileges
- Using roles to manage system privileges
- Using Security Manager to manage system privileges

All access in an Oracle database requires database privileges. Access to connect to the database, the objects the user is permitted to see, and the objects the user is allowed to create are all controlled by privileges. Use of every database object and system resource is governed by privileges. Privileges are required to create objects, to access objects, to change data within tables, to execute stored procedures, to create users, and so on. Since access to every object is governed by privileges, security in the Oracle database is highly flexible in terms of what objects are available to which users.

Functions of Different Types of Users

Fundamental to the overall goal of securing your database usage is the task of categorizing your database users by function. In the most general sense, there are three basic types of users into which all other user types will fall:

1. Application users
2. Application developers
3. Database administrators and operators

Role of Application Users

Application users come in many shapes and sizes. There are data entry users, whose primary responsibilities include keying data into an application. There are also reporting users, whose primary responsibilities are to take existing data in an application and collect it into paper reports for others to review. Managers and executives may also be users of an application. For example, a time reporting application might forward entries from employees to their managers for review and approval. Business analysts might also use an application to review trends and forecast business results. The role of all these application users is to use the application to fulfill some aspect of a business's needs.

Generally speaking, application users need access to database objects like stored procedures and tables to do their jobs. These objects will usually exist in the application already. Application users generally don't need to have the ability to create objects in a database such as stored procedures or tables, but they might need the ability to add data to existing tables, to run certain procedures for reporting, and so on.

Role of Application Developers

The role of application developers is to create new applications and enhance existing ones to meet business needs. Application developers include users who program PL/SQL procedures and create database objects such as tables to conform to data models needed for business applications. An application developer might also include systems analysts who review technical process flow and recommend changes to improve that process flow.

Generally speaking, application developers need the ability to create new database objects in Oracle such as tables, indexes, sequences, views, stored procedures, and so on. The developers usually have the ability to alter existing database objects as well. Often, an IS organization might maintain two or more database environments for any given application, one for production usage by application users, and the other for development and testing of enhancements or changes, that will eventually be applied to a production system after all the glitches are worked out.

For purposes of control, application developers aren't usually allowed to create or alter database objects for the production version of an application. Instead, they are allowed to make changes and enhancements to a test or development version. This separation of test and production ensures that there is a single point of control over the changes made to production applications to minimize potential disruptions to application users, while simultaneously giving developers the freedom they need to experiment with various implementation approaches.

Database Administrators and Operators

There are usually only a limited number of DBAs or DBOs for any application. Typically, the DBOs role is to supplement the efforts of the DBA in operational or production areas like keeping production databases online. This division of labor allows the DBA to focus on more strategic goals like planning systems architecture and application growth.

In most organizations, DBAs and DBOs often have several databases they administer. The role of the DBA is to ensure that Oracle databases supporting applications operate at maximum efficiency and allow room for data growth. DBAs and DBOs are also responsible for ensuring that Oracle databases are available for use when application users and/or developers need them. DBAs and DBOs also ensure that Oracle databases are backed up so that, if some hardware failure or data corruption occurs, recovery is possible, quick, and requires minimal data reentry from users. DBAs usually have the added responsibility for overall systems architecture planning. Since many DBOs come to Oracle from systems engineering backgrounds in hardware, networking, and infrastructure, DBOs may assist DBAs in this responsibility. Some DBAs assist business and systems analysts in data modeling and table layout to ensure the best possible application performance as well.

Those things said, it is usually *not* the responsibility of a DBA or a DBO to understand the inner workings of an application. Application developers handle that task. DBAs and DBOs usually aren't intimately familiar with how an application handles its transaction processing, beyond what information is available from common performance reporting tools such as UTLBSTAT and UTLESTAT, Oracle Expert, and OEM Management and Tuning Packs. They might be familiar with the tables that grow the fastest or are accessed the most because they have operational responsibilities to ensure those tables have plenty of room to grow.

DBAs and DBOs need the most latitude in performing tasks on the Oracle database. For this reason, they usually have access to important user accounts like INTERNAL, SYS, or SYSTEM. DBAs and DBOs need the ability to shut down and restart production and test databases, and to create both logical disk components like tables and indexes and physical disk components like tablespaces and datafiles for both test and production databases. DBAs and DBOs need the ability to create, back up, and restore test and production databases as well. They may also need the ability to create users, perform basic tuning, and resolve locking and resource contention issues in a hurry. Furthermore, DBAs and DBOs need a strong understanding of how the Oracle database works to both solve problems related to Oracle very quickly and explain facets of Oracle usage to others in an organization.

For Review

Understand the differences between the roles of application users, developers, and DBAs and DBOs.

Creating New Database Users

One of the primary tasks early on in the creation of a new database is adding new users. However, user creation is an ongoing task. As users enter and leave the organization, so, too, must the DBO keep track of access to the database granted to those users. When using Oracle's own database authentication method, new users are created with the `create user` statement:

```
CREATE USER spanky
IDENTIFIED BY first01
DEFAULT TABLESPACE users_01
TEMPORARY TABLESPACE temp_01
QUOTA 10M ON users_01
PROFILE app_developer
PASSWORD EXPIRE
ACCOUNT UNLOCK;
```

This statement highlights several items of information that comprise the syntax and semantics of user creation, and these areas will be covered in the sections that follow.

CREATE USER This is the user's name in Oracle. If the DBO is using operating system authentication to allow users to access the database, then the usernames should, by default, be preceded with OPS$. In no other case is it recommended that a username contain a nonalphanumeric character, although both _ and # are permitted characters in usernames. The name should also start with a letter. On single-byte character sets, the name can be from 1 to 30 characters long, while on multibyte character sets, the name of a user must be limited to 30 bytes. In addition, the name should contain one single-byte character according to Oracle recommendations. The username is not case sensitive and cannot be a reserved word.

IDENTIFIED BY This is the user's password in Oracle. This item should contain at least three characters, and preferably six or more. Generally, it is recommended that users change their passwords once they know their usernames are created. Oracle enforces this with the `password expire` clause. Users should change their passwords to something that is not a word or a name and that preferably contains a numeric character somewhere in it. As is the case with the username, the password can be a maximum length of 30 bytes and cannot be a reserved word. If operating system authentication is being used, you would use the keywords `identified externally`.

DEFAULT TABLESPACE Tablespace management is a crucial task in Oracle. The `default tablespace` names the location where the user's database objects are created by default. This clause plays an important role in protecting the integrity of the SYSTEM tablespace. If no `default tablespace` is named for a user, objects that the user creates may be placed in the SYSTEM tablespace. Recall that SYSTEM contains many database objects, such as the data dictionary and the SYSTEM rollback segment, that are critical to database use. Users should not be allowed to create their database objects in the SYSTEM tablespace.

TEMPORARY TABLESPACE If `temporary tablespace` is not explicitly specified by the DBO when the username is created, the location for all temporary segments for that user will be the SYSTEM tablespace. SYSTEM, as you already know, is a valuable resource that should not be used for user object storage.

QUOTA A `quota` is a limit on the amount of space the user's database objects can occupy within the tablespace. If a user attempts to create a database object that exceeds that user's `quota` for that tablespace, then the object creation script will fail. Quotas can be specified either in kilobytes (K) or megabytes (M). A `quota` clause should be issued separately for every tablespace other than the temporary tablespace on which the user will have access to create database objects. If you want a user to have the ability to use all the space in a tablespace, `quota unlimited on` *`tblspcname`* can be specified.

TIP

Users need quotas on tablespaces to create database objects only. They do not need a quota on a tablespace to `update`, `insert`, or `delete` data in an existing object in the tablespace, as long as they do have the appropriate privilege on the object for data being inserted, updated, or deleted.

PROFILE Profiles are a bundled set of resource-usage parameters that the DBA can set in order to limit the user's overall host machine utilization. A driving idea behind their use is that many end users of the system only need a certain amount of the host machine's capacity during their session. To reduce the chance that one user could affect the overall database performance with, say, a poorly formulated ad hoc report that drags the database to its knees, you may assign profiles for each user that limit the amount of time they can spend on the system.

PASSWORD EXPIRE This clause enforces the requirement that a user change his or her password on first logging in to Oracle. This extra level of password security guarantees that not even you, the DBO, will know a user's password. If this clause is not included, then the user will not have to change the password on first logging in to Oracle.

ACCOUNT UNLOCK This is the default for user accounts created. It means that the user's account is immediately available for use. The DBA can prevent users from using their accounts by specifying `account lock` instead.

Guidelines for User-Account Management

The following list identifies several new guidelines to follow when managing user accounts. In many cases, these items are new for Oracle8 and enhance the management of user accounts:

- Use a standard password for user creation, such as `123abc` or `first1`, and use `password expire` to force users to change this password to something else the first time they log in to Oracle.
- Avoid OS authentication unless all your users will access Oracle while connected directly to the machine hosting your database (this second part is also not advised).
- Be sure to always assign `temporary tablespace` and `default tablespace` to users, such as developers, with the ability to create database objects.
- Give few users `quota unlimited`. Although it's annoying to have users asking for more space, it's even more annoying to reorganize tablespaces carelessly filled with database objects.
- Become familiar with the user-account management and other host machine limits that can be set via profiles. These new features take Oracle user-account management to new levels of security.

For Review

1. What statement is used to create users? Explain the need for tablespace quotas. Do users need tablespace quotas to `insert` data in existing tables? Explain.
2. What is the purpose of a temporary tablespace? What clause is designed to force users to change their passwords after initial login?

Altering and Dropping Existing Users

Once a user is created, there are a few reasons you'll need to modify that user. One is to expire the password if a user forgets it, so that the next time the user logs in, the password can be changed by the user. The `alter user identified by` statement is used to change the user's password:

```
ALTER USER athena
IDENTIFIED BY forgotpassword
PASSWORD EXPIRE;
```

In certain situations, as the result of user profiles, a user's account may become locked. This may occur if the user forgot his or her password and tried to log in using a bad password too many times. To unlock a user's account while also making it possible for the user to change the password, the following `alter user` statement can be used:

```
ALTER USER athena
IDENTIFIED BY forgotpassword
ACCOUNT UNLOCK
PASSWORD EXPIRE;
```

Other situations abound. In an attempt to prevent misuse, you may want to lock an account that has been used many times unsuccessfully to gain access to Oracle, with the following statement:

```
ALTER USER athena
ACCOUNT LOCK;
```

TIP
You should remember that changes to password, account lock status, or password expiration are applied only to subsequent user sessions, not the current one.

Changing User Tablespace Allocation

You may want to reorganize tablespaces to distribute I/O load and make more effective use of the hardware running Oracle. Perhaps this effort involves dropping some tablespaces and creating new ones. If the DBO wants to change a user's default tablespace, the `alter user default tablespace` statement can be used. As explained earlier, this change is good for preserving the integrity of the SYSTEM tablespace. Only newly created objects will be affected by this statement. Existing objects created in other tablespaces by that user will continue to reside in those tablespaces until they are dropped. Additionally, if the user specifies a tablespace in which to place a database object, that specification will override the default tablespace.

```
ALTER USER spanky
DEFAULT TABLESPACE overflow_tabspc01;
```

By the same token, you may want to reorganize the tablespace used for disk sorts as you move from permanent tablespaces to temporary tablespaces, and this is done using `alter user temporary tablespace`. Only the DBA can make these changes; the users cannot change their own temporary or default tablespaces.

```
ALTER USER spanky
TEMPORARY TABLESPACE temp_overflow_01;
```

A tablespace accessible to the user at user creation can have a quota placed on it. A quota can be altered by the DBA with the `alter user quota` statement. For example, the DBA may want to reduce the quota on the USERS_01 tablespace from 10MB to 5MB for user SPANKY. If the user has already created over 5MB worth of database objects in the tablespace, no further data can be added to those objects, and no new objects can be created. Only the DBA can change a user's tablespace quota; the users cannot change their own quotas.

```
ALTER USER spanky
QUOTA 5M ON users_01;
```

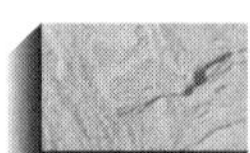

TIP

Specifying `quota 0 on` *SYSTEM for a user will prevent him from creating any object in the SYSTEM tablespace, even if that user still has his* `default tablespace` *set to SYSTEM. However, this restriction does not include the creation of packages, stored procedures, and functions.*

Aspects of User Accounts Changeable by Users

All aspects of the user's account covered already are the components that can be modified by the DBO. However, the aspects of the account that can be changed by the actual user are far more limited. A situation may arise in regular database use in which a user wants to change his or her password. This is accomplished with the following:

```
ALTER USER athena
IDENTIFIED BY mynewpassword;
```

TIP

Except for altering the password, the user can change nothing about their own user account, except in certain situations in which the `alter any user` privilege has been granted to that user.

Dropping User Accounts

As users come and go, their access should be modified to reflect their departure. To drop a user from the database, you execute the `drop user` statement. If a user has created database objects, the user cannot be dropped until the objects are dropped as well. In order to drop the user and all related database objects in one fell swoop, Oracle provides the `cascade` option.

```
DROP USER spanky CASCADE;
```

For Review

1. What statement is used for altering users?
2. What are the features of a user that the users themselves can change? What features can only the DBO change?
3. What statement is used to drop a database user? How can the objects created by the user be eliminated at the same time?

Monitoring Information About Existing Users

The DBO may periodically want to monitor information about users. Several data dictionary views may be used for the purpose of obtaining information about users. Some information a DBO may want to collect includes default and temporary tablespace information, objects created by that user, and the current account status for that user account. The following data dictionary views can be used to determine this information.

- **DBA_USERS** Contains username, Oracle-generated ID number, encrypted password, default and temporary tablespace information, and the user profile that was specified in the ID creation statements or any alteration that may have followed. Also, the view offers ACCOUNT_STATUS, which may be locked, open, or expired; GRACE_DATE, which identifies the date by which the user must change the password or the account will be locked; LOCK_DATE, which is the date the account was locked (NULL for open accounts); and EXPIRY_DATE, which is the date for account expiration.
- **DBA_OBJECTS** Contains specific information about every object in the database. The DBA can determine which objects belong to which users by using the OWNER column of this view.
- **DBA_TS_QUOTAS** Names all users and any tablespace quotas that have been created for them.

TIP
A value of –1 in MAX_BYTES or MAX_BLOCKS means that the user has unlimited space quota for that tablespace.

For Review

1. How can the DBA determine which users own which objects?
2. How can the DBA determine whether there are any quotas on tablespaces that a user has been granted access to?
3. What view contains user-account status and other account information?

Identifying System Privileges

There are two categories of privileges, *system privileges* and *object privileges.* System privileges control the creation and maintenance of many database objects, such as rollback segments, synonyms, tables, and triggers. Thus, system privileges will be granted mainly to application developers, DBAs, and DBOs. Additionally, the ability to use the `analyze` command to generate usage statistics for performance and the Oracle database `audit` capability to determine proper usage in practice is governed by system privileges. These latter system privileges are given mainly to DBAs and DBOs to handle database administrative tasks. You will learn about object privileges later in the chapterin the section "Securing Application Data Manipulation."

Categories of System Privileges

Generally speaking, several categories of system privileges relate to each object. Those categories determine the scope of ability that the privilege grantee will have. The classes or categories of system privileges are listed here. In the following sections, the privilege itself gives the ability to perform the action against your own database objects, while the `any` keyword refers to the ability to perform the action against any database object of that type in Oracle.

ADMIN FUNCTIONS These privileges relate to activities typically reserved for and performed by the DBA. Privileges include `alter system`, `audit system`, `audit any`, `alter database`, `analyze any`, `sysdba`, `sysoper`, and `grant any privilege`. You must have the `create session` privilege to connect to Oracle.

DATABASE ACCESS These privileges control who accesses the database, when they can access it, and what they can do regarding management of their own session. Privileges include `create session`, `alter session`, and `restricted session`.

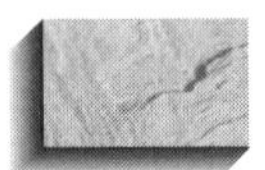

TIP
Note that every user created in Oracle must be given the `create session` privilege before the user can actually connect to the database.

TABLESPACES You already know that tablespaces are disk resources used to store database objects. These privileges, typically reserved for DBAs, determine who can maintain these disk resources. Privileges include `create tablespace`, `alter tablespace`, `manage tablespace`, `drop tablespace`, and `unlimited tablespace`. Note that you cannot grant `unlimited tablespace` to a role. More information on roles appears in the upcoming section, "Using Roles to Manage System Privileges."

USERS These privileges are used to manage users on the Oracle database. Typically, these privileges are reserved for DBAs or security administrators. Privileges include `create user`, `become user`, `alter user`, and `drop user`.

ROLLBACK SEGMENTS You already know that rollback segments are disk resources that make aspects of transaction processing possible. The privileges include `create rollback segment`, `alter rollback segment`, and `drop rollback segment`.

TABLES You already know that tables store data in the Oracle database. These privileges govern which users can create and maintain tables. The privileges include `create table`, `create any table`, `alter any table`, `backup any table`, `drop any table`, `lock any table`, `comment any table`, `select any table`, `insert any table`, `update any table`, and `delete any table`. The `create table` or `create any table` privilege also allows you to drop the table. The `create table` privilege also bestows the ability to create indexes and run the `analyze` command on the table. To be able to truncate a table, you must have the `drop any table` privilege granted to you.

CLUSTERS You already know that clusters are used to store tables commonly used together in close physical proximity on disk. The privileges include `create cluster`, `create any cluster`, `alter any cluster`, and `drop any cluster`. The `create cluster` and `create any cluster` privileges also allow you to alter and drop those clusters.

INDEXES You already know that indexes are used to improve SQL statement performance on tables containing lots of row data. The privileges include `create any index`, `alter any index`, and `drop any index`. You should note that there is no `create index` system privilege. The `create table` privilege also allows you to alter and drop indexes that you own and that are associated with the table.

SYNONYMS A synonym is a database object that allows you to reference another object by a different name. A public synonym means that the synonym is available to every user in the database for the same purpose. The privileges include `create synonym`, `create any synonym`, `drop any synonym`, `create public synonym`, and `drop public synonym`. The `create synonym` privilege also allows you to alter and drop synonyms that you own.

VIEWS You already know that a view is an object containing a SQL statement that behaves like a table in Oracle, except that it stores no data. The privileges include `create view`, `create any view`, and `drop any view`. The `create view` privilege also allows you to alter and drop views that you own.

SEQUENCES You already know that a sequence is an object in Oracle that generates numbers according to rules you can define. Privileges include `create sequence`, `create any sequence`, `alter any sequence`, `drop any sequence`, and `select any sequence`. The `create sequence` privilege also allows you to drop sequences that you own.

DATABASE LINKS Database links are objects in Oracle that, within your session connected to one database, allow you to reference tables in another Oracle database without making a separate connection. A public database link is one available to all users in Oracle, while a private database link is one that only the owner can use. Privileges include `create database link`, `create public database link`, and `drop public database link`. The `create database link` privilege also allows you to drop private database links that you own.

ROLES Roles are objects that can be used for simplified privilege management. You create a role, grant privileges to it, and then grant the role to users. Privileges include `create role`, `drop any role`, `grant any role`, and `alter any role`.

TRANSACTIONS These privileges are for resolving in-doubt transactions being processed on the Oracle database. Privileges include `force transaction` and `force any transaction`.

PL/SQL You have already been introduced to the different PL/SQL blocks available in Oracle. These privileges allow you to create, run, and manage those different types of blocks. Privileges include `create procedure`, `create any procedure`, `alter any procedure`, `drop any procedure`, and `execute any procedure`. The `create procedure` privilege also allows you to alter and drop PL/SQL blocks that you own.

TRIGGERS You know that triggers are PL/SQL blocks in Oracle that execute when a specified data manipulation activity occurs on the table to which the trigger is associated. Privileges include `create trigger`, `create any trigger`, `alter any trigger`, and `drop any trigger`. The `create trigger` privilege also allows you to alter and drop triggers that you own.

PROFILES You know that profiles are objects in Oracle that allow you to impose limits on resources for users on the machine hosting Oracle. Privileges include `create profile`, `alter profile`, `drop profile`, and `alter resource cost`.

SNAPSHOTS Snapshots are objects in Oracle that allow you to replicate data from a table in one database to a copy of the table in another. Privileges include `create snapshot`, `create any snapshot`, `alter any snapshot`, and `drop any snapshot`.

DIRECTORIES Directories in Oracle are objects that refer to directories on the machine hosting the Oracle database. They are used to identify a directory that contains objects Oracle keeps track of that are external to Oracle, such as objects of the BFILE type. Privileges include `create any directory` and `drop any directory`.

TYPES Types in Oracle correspond to user-defined types you can create in Oracle8 Objects Option. Privileges include `create type`, `create any type`, `alter any type`, `drop any type`, and `execute any type`. The `create type` privilege also allows you to alter and drop types that you own.

LIBRARIES A library is an object that allows you to reference a set of procedures external to Oracle. Currently, only C procedures are supported. Privileges include `create library`, `create any library`, `alter any library`, `drop any library`, and `execute any library`.

For Review

1. Name some system privileges on database objects. What are some objects that do not use system privileges to let users change the object definition or create the object?
2. What are some other system privileges used to manage certain operations on any database object? What is the `unlimited tablespace` privilege? What is the `restricted session` privilege?

Directly Granting System Privileges

Giving privileges directly to users is done with the `grant` command in SQL. SQL commands can be issued directly against the Oracle database in SQL*Plus, or by using a graphical interface like Security Manager within OEM. System privileges are first given to the SYS and SYSTEM users, and to any other user with the `grant any privilege` permission. As other users are created, they must be given privileges, based on their needs, with the `grant` command. For example, executing the following `grant` statement gives access to create a table to user SPANKY:

```
GRANT CREATE TABLE TO spanky;
```

TIP
*SQL*Plus is Oracle's command-line utility for working with the Oracle database. For more information on how to use SQL*Plus, check out Chapter 8.*

Giving Administrative Ability Along with Privileges

As the result of executing the `grant create table to SPANKY` SQL command, SPANKY will have the ability to execute the `create table` command in her user schema. However, SPANKY can't give this privilege to other users, nor can she relinquish them without the help of the DBO. In order to give user SPANKY some additional power to administer to other users the privileges granted to her, the DBO can execute the following query:

```
GRANT CREATE TABLE TO spanky WITH ADMIN OPTION;
```

The `with admin option` clause gives SPANKY the ability to give or take away the system privilege to others. Additionally, it gives SPANKY the ability to make other users administrators of that same privilege. Finally, if a role is granted to SPANKY `with admin option`, SPANKY can alter the role or even remove it. Only system privileges given `with admin option` can be administered by the grantee. All other privileges are administered by users with `grant any privilege`.

Revoking Users' System Privileges

There may come a time when users must have privileges revoked as well. This task is accomplished with the `revoke` command. Revoking the `create table` privilege also takes away any administrative ability given along with the privilege or role. No additional syntax is necessary for revoking a system privilege granted `with admin option`.

```
REVOKE CREATE TABLE FROM spanky;
```

Cascading Effects of Revoking System Privileges

When a system privilege is revoked, no cascading events take place along with it. Thus, if SPANKY created several tables while possessing the `create table` privilege, those tables are not removed when the privilege is revoked. The only effect is that SPANKY will not be able to create more tables. Only the `drop table` command will remove the tables. Also, if SPANKY had the `create table` privilege `with admin option`, any users SPANKY granted the `create table` privilege to will still have that privilege.

TIP

Understand the following scenario completely before continuing: User BOB has a system privilege granted to him `with admin option`. User BOB then grants the privilege to user PATEL, with administrative privileges. User PATEL does the same for user SASHA. Then BOB revokes the privilege from user PATEL. User SASHA will still have the privilege. Why? Because there is no cascading effect to revoking system privileges other than the fact that PATEL no longer can create tables!

For Review

1. What command is used to give privileges to users?
2. What special options are required for system and object privileges if the user is to have administrative capability along with the privilege?

Using Roles to Manage System Privileges

In large databases with lots of users, database objects, and procedures, privilege management and security can quickly escalate into a nightmarish effort requiring hundreds or even thousands of `grant` commands issued to create only one new user. Worse, if one privilege is missed, it can take a long time to figure out the problem. Instead of granting privileges directly to users, you can simplify the management of privileges with the use of a database object called a *role*. Roles ease the effort you will spend on password management in two ways: they act as a focal point for grouping the privileges to execute certain tasks, and they act as a "virtual user" of a database. Figure 5-1 shows conceptually how privileges are managed with roles. In order to use roles, you must do three things:

1. Logically group database users together according to common needs, and create roles for those needs. You restrict use of a role by password-protecting that role with the `identified by` clause.

   ```
   CREATE ROLE dev_dba_privs IDENTIFIED BY create#jr;
   CREATE ROLE programmers IDENTIFIED BY coder1;
   CREATE ROLE users IDENTIFIED BY enter#data;
   ```

2. Determine the activities each type of user will carry out, and list the privileges that each activity will require. These categories determine the access privileges that you give to each role on the database. For example, a development DBA might have the ability to create tables, indexes, triggers, and procedures. This step is more conceptual, and it is strongly recommended that you document your plan and get buy-in from everyone involved, including DBAs, managers, and users. (So, you can now see the importance of the exercise shown in the earlier section, "Functions of Different Types of Users.")

3. Grant required privileges for each job function to the associated role.

   ```
   GRANT CREATE TABLE TO dev_dba_privs WITH ADMIN OPTION;
   GRANT CREATE USER TO dev_dba_privs;
   GRANT CREATE PROCEDURE TO dev_dba_privs WITH ADMIN OPTION;
   ```

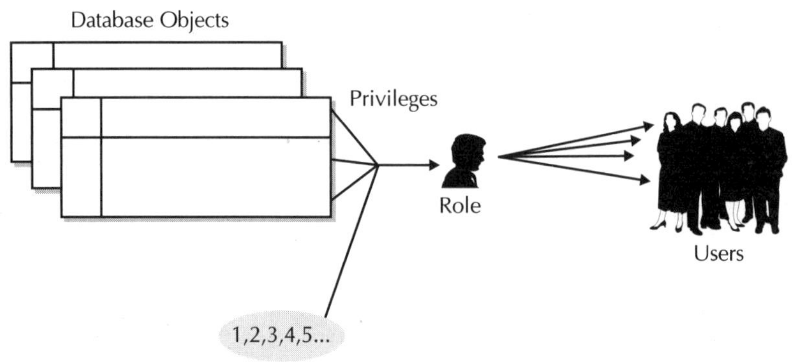

FIGURE 5-1. *Managing privileges with roles*

Once you establish this architecture of using roles as a "middle layer" for granting privileges, administration of user privileges is a simple matter of granting the appropriate role or roles to the users who need them.

```
GRANT dev_dba_privs TO athena;
GRANT dev_dba_privs TO spanky;
```

In order to use the privileges granted to a user via a role, the role must be enabled for that user. In order for the role to be enabled, it must be the default role for the user, or one of the default roles. The status of a role is usually enabled unless, for some reason, the role has been disabled. To change the status of a role for the user, the `alter user default role` statement can be issued. Some of the keywords that can be used in conjunction with defining roles are `all`, `all except`, and `none`; these keywords limit the roles defined for the `alter user` statement.

```
ALTER USER spanky DEFAULT ROLE ALL;
ALTER USER spanky DEFAULT ROLE ALL EXCEPT dev_dba_privs;
ALTER USER spanky DEFAULT ROLE dev_dba_privs;
ALTER USER spanky DEFAULT ROLE NONE;
```

Altering, Revoking, and Dropping Roles

Roles can be altered to require a password by using the `alter role identified by` statement. Roles can be deleted with the `drop role` statement. These two options may only be executed by those users with the `create any role`, `alter any role`, or `drop any role` privileges, or by the owner of the role. Privileges can be revoked from a role in the same way as they can be revoked from a user.

When a role is dropped, the associated privileges are revoked from the users granted that role. Alternatively, roles can also be revoked using the `revoke` statement, much like revoking privileges. This way, the role will still exist for other users while one user is no longer allowed to use privileges associated with the role:

```
-- spanky can no longer create tables, but has other
-- privileges given to DEV_DBA_PRIVS
REVOKE create table FROM dev_dba_privs;
-- spanky no longer has any privileges granted to DEV_DBA_PRIVS
REVOKE dev_dba_privs FROM SPANKY;
-- Neither spanky nor athena has any privileges granted to
DEV_DBA_PRIVS
DROP ROLE dev_dba_privs;
```

Predefined Roles in Oracle

In addition to the roles you might create yourself in the course of normal database operation, several roles are created by Oracle when the software is installed. These roles include

- **CONNECT** Can connect to the database and create clusters, links, sequences, tables, views, and synonyms. This role is good for table schema owners and development DBAs.
- **RESOURCE** Can connect to the database and create clusters, sequences, tables, triggers, and stored procedures. This role is good for application developers. It also has unlimited tablespace.
- **DBA** Can use any system privilege `with admin option`.
- **EXP_FULL_DATABASE** Can export all database objects to an export dump file.
- **IMP_FULL_DATABASE** Can import all database objects from an export dump file to the database.
- **DELETE_CATALOG_ROLE** Extends `delete` privileges on SYS-owned dictionary tables, in response to the new restriction on `delete any table` privileges that prevent grantees from removing rows from SYS-owned dictionary tables.
- **EXECUTE_CATALOG_ROLE** Allows grantee `execute` privileges on any SYS-owned package supplied with the Oracle software.
- **SELECT_CATALOG_ROLE** Allows grantee to `select` data from any SYS-owned dictionary table or view.

For Review

1. What is a role? How are privileges granted to a role?
2. What is a default role? Can a user exercise privileges granted through a role if the role is disabled? Explain.
3. What roles are created automatically on an Oracle database?

Using Security Manager to Manage System Privileges

If remembering all these commands and various privileges seems like a major hassle to you, take heart—Oracle Enterprise Manager simplifies the task of system privilege and role management via the Security Manager tool. This discussion centers around how to execute the same activities you just learned about—namely, granting privileges to users and roles, creating roles, and granting roles to users—using Security Manager.

You can start Security Manager in the following three ways. When doing so, be sure to log in to Security Manager as a user that can grant privileges to other users, such as SYSTEM, SYS, or the DBA for that database:

- By clicking Start | Programs | Oracle Enterprise Manager | Security Manager on your Windows desktop

- Within Oracle Enterprise Manager using the Security Manager button

- By clicking the Security button in the OEM Administrator Toolbar

Once inside Security Manager, you will see that the application is divided into two windows, one containing a drill-down tree listing users, roles, and profiles available on your Oracle database. A *profile* is a defined set of host system resource usage limits that you can impose on Oracle users to restrict their use of Oracle's underlying host system resources like CPU, I/O, connection idle time, and so on.

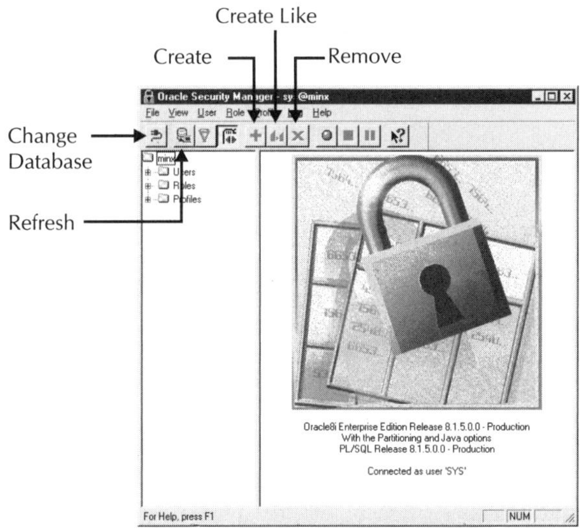

FIGURE 5-2. *Oracle Security Manager*

Figure 5-2 shows Security Manager with all users on your Oracle database listed and usage of various buttons defined.

Creating New Users in Security Manager

To create a new user in Security Manager, follow these steps:

1. Drill down to the Default Database | Users node on the left side of the Security Manager application window.
2. With the Users node highlighted, click the Create button identified in Figure 5-2.
3. You can enter the user information in the Create User interface shown in Figure 5-3.
4. When finished, click Create.

Granting System Privileges to Users with Security Manager

To grant privileges directly to a user, follow these steps:

1. For the user on your database you want to grant system privileges to, drill down to the Default Database | Users | <YOUR USER> | System Privileges

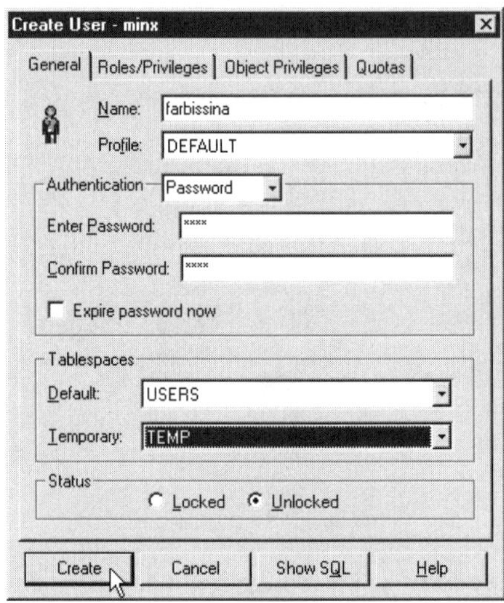

FIGURE 5-3. *Create User interface in Security Manager*

Granted node on the left side of the Security Manager application window, and you will see the system privileges this user currently has. For example, Figure 5-4 shows the system privileges granted to user ATHENA.

2. On the right side of the Security Manager application window, click the Roles/Privileges tab. Then, pull down the Privilege Type list box and click once on System Privileges to display the available system privileges. At the bottom of the right side of the Security Manager application window, you will see the system privileges granted to your user already, and whether or not the user can grant that privilege to other users. Again, Figure 5-4 illustrates.
3. To grant a system privilege to this user, scroll down to the appropriate system privilege and click once on the privilege to highlight. Then, click once on the down arrow button in the middle of the right side of the Security Manager interface. To grant more than one system privilege at a time, simply click once on each of the system privileges you want to grant to highlight before clicking the down arrow button. Finally, click the Apply button toward the bottom of the right side of the Security Manager interface. Figure 5-5 illustrates.

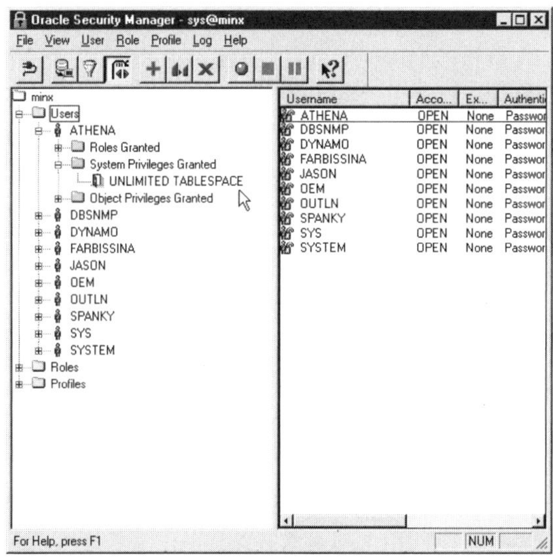

FIGURE 5-4. *Viewing system privileges with Security Manager*

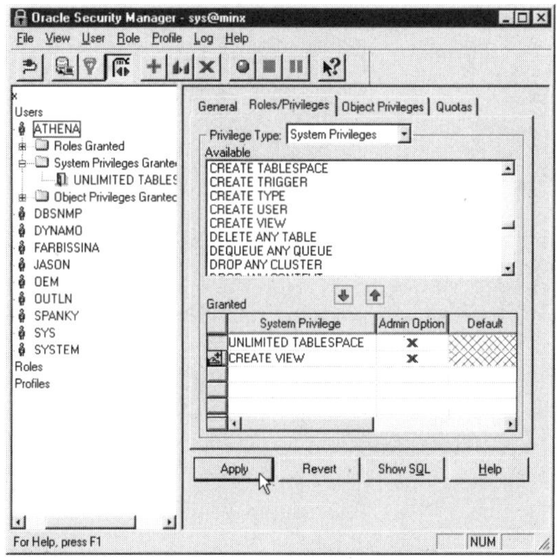

FIGURE 5-5. *Granting system privileges with Security Manager*

Creating Roles with Security Manager

To create roles within Security Manager, follow these steps:

1. Drill down to the Default Database | Roles node on the left side of the Security Manager interface, shown in Figure 5-6.
2. Click the Create button at the top of the Security Manager interface, pointed out in Figure 5-2. The Create Role interface will then appear as shown in Figure 5-7. Enter the name you want your new role to have, and whether you want to password-protect your new role. Then, click the Create button in the Create Role interface.

Granting Privileges to Roles with Security Manager

To grant privileges to a role after creating that role, follow these steps:

1. Drill down to the role you just created by clicking the Default Database | Roles | <YOUR ROLE> node. On the right side of the Security Manager window, you will see the same three tab interfaces presented when you created the role. Click the Roles/Privileges tab. Figure 5-8 illustrates what you will see in Security Manager.

FIGURE 5-6. *Default Database | Roles node in Security Manager*

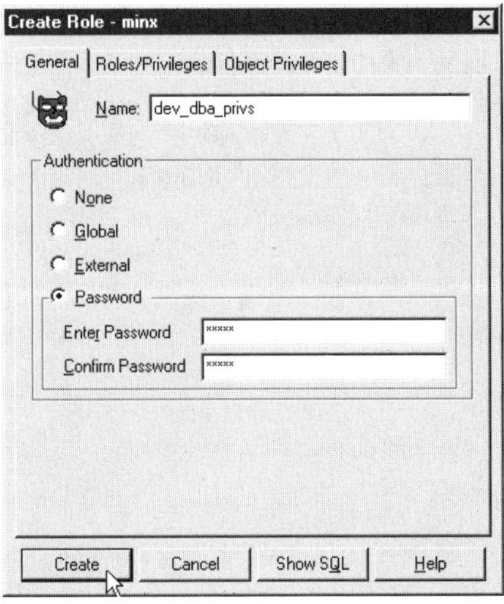

FIGURE 5-7. *Create Role interface in Security Manager*

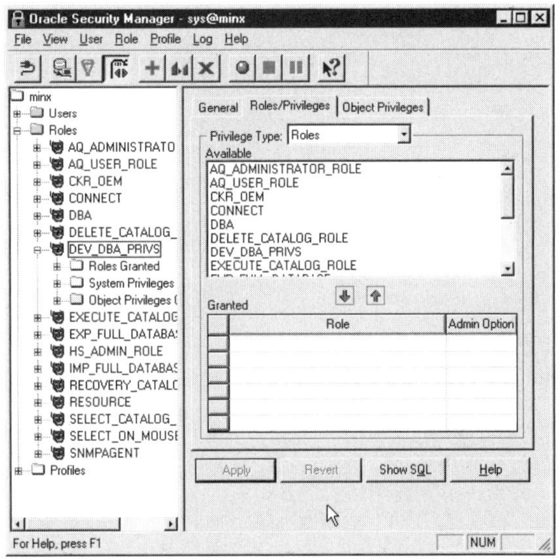

FIGURE 5-8. *Viewing system privileges for roles in Security Manager*

2. To grant a system privilege to this role, scroll down to the appropriate system privilege and click once on the privilege to highlight. Then, click once on the down arrow button in the middle of the right side of the Security Manager interface. To grant more than one system privilege at a time, simply click once on each of the system privileges you want to grant before clicking the down arrow button. Finally, click the Apply button toward the bottom of the right side of the Security Manager interface. Figure 5-9 illustrates.

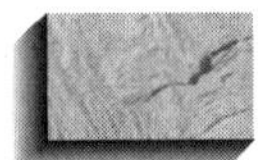

TIP
You can identify what privileges you want to grant your role before creating it as well, by clicking on the Roles/ Privileges tab and following the previous steps, before clicking the Create button, as shown in Figure 5-7.

Granting Roles to Users with Security Manager

To grant roles to users within Security Manager, follow these steps:

1. Drill down to the Default Database | Users | <YOUR USER> node on the left side of the Security Manager window. Click the Roles/Privileges tab

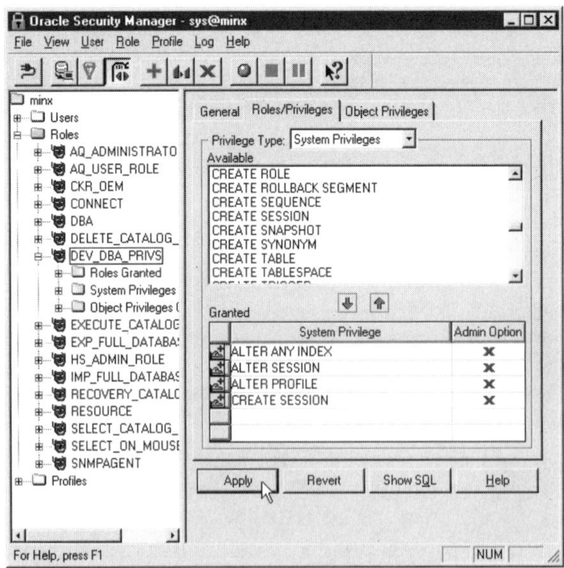

FIGURE 5-9. *Granting system privileges to roles in Security Manager*

interface on the right side of the Security Manager window. Ensure that Roles is displayed within the Privilege Type list box at the top of the right side of the Security Manager window. Figure 5-10 Illustrates.

2. To grant a role to this user, scroll down to the appropriate role and click once on the role to highlight. Then, click once on the down arrow button in the middle of the right side of the Security Manager interface. Finally, click the Apply button toward the bottom of the right side of the Security Manager interface. Figure 5-11 illustrates.

TIP
At any point in any of the previous steps, if you want to grant the privilege to a role, privilege to a user, or role to a user `with admin option`*, click the X shown in the Admin Option column in the bottom right side of Security Manager to change that X to a check mark. Then, click the Apply button.*

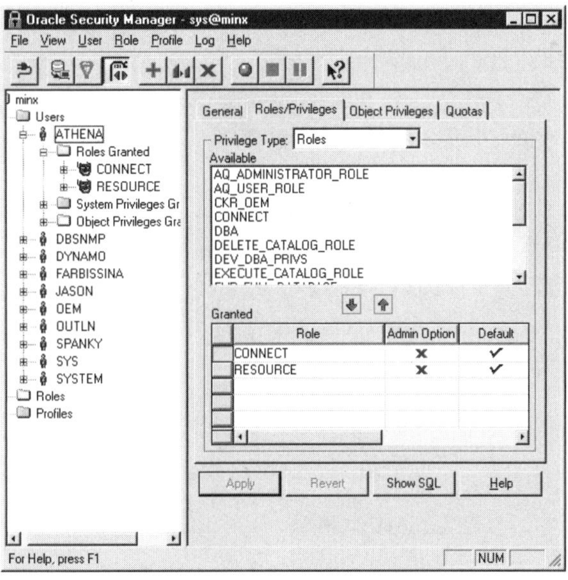

FIGURE 5-10. *Viewing roles granted to users with Security Manager*

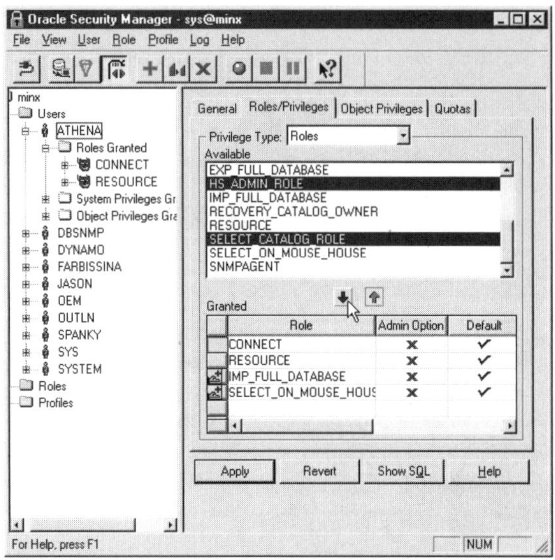

FIGURE 5-11. *Granting roles to users with Security Manager*

For Review

Understand how to create new roles, grant system privileges to users, grant system privileges to roles, and grant roles to users with or without administrative options within Security Manager. This takes practice.

Securing Application Data Manipulation

In this section, you will cover the following topics related to securing application data manipulation:

- Identifying object privileges
- Granting object privileges
- Granting object privileges with Security Manager

In this section of the chapter, you will cover how to secure the data manipulation operations users can execute on your application using object privileges. There are some significant differences between object privileges and system privileges. For one thing, Oracle has many more system privileges than object privileges. This fact makes object privileges much easier to remember than system privileges. Secondly, the methods used to grant and manage object privileges are very similar to those used for system privileges. Thus, if you understand how to grant a system privilege to users or to roles, you're already halfway there in understanding how to do the same with object privileges. In this section, you will learn what the object privileges are in Oracle and how to grant them.

Identifying Object Privileges

As mentioned earlier in the chapter, the other privilege category on the Oracle database is the set of *object privileges*. Object privileges manage access to objects within the application running on an Oracle database. Thus, object privileges are most often given to application users for the purpose of enabling or disabling their use or an application. The owner of database objects such as tables can administer access to those objects they own by granting object privileges to other users. There are eight types of object privileges, listed as follows:

- **`select`** Permits the grantee of this object privilege to access the data in a table, sequence, view, or snapshot.
- **`insert`** Permits the grantee of this object privilege to `insert` data into a table or, in some cases, a view.
- **`update`** Permits the grantee of this object privilege to `update` data into a table or view.
- **`delete`** Permits the grantee of this object privilege to `delete` data from a table or view.
- **`alter`** Permits the grantee of this object privilege to `alter` the definition of a table or sequence *only*, and only for the tables or sequences that have already been created. The `alter` privileges on all other database objects are considered system privileges.
- **`index`** Permits the grantee of this object privilege to create an index on a table already defined.
- **`references`** Permits the grantee to `create` or `alter` a table in order to create a `FOREIGN KEY` constraint against data in the referenced table.
- **`execute`** Permits the grantee to run a stored procedure, function, or package. The ability to execute a trigger associated with a table is implicitly given in association with the `insert`, `update`, or `delete` privilege granted to the user for that table.

TIP
A trick to being able to distinguish whether something is a system or object privilege is to memorize the object privileges since there are only eight of them. If you see a privilege that is not one of the eight object privileges, it is a system privilege.

For Review

What are some object privileges? What abilities do these privileges bestow?

Granting Object Privileges

As with system privileges, object privileges are granted to users with the `grant` SQL command. Usually, the owner of the database object is the user who grants object privileges to other users. The following code block shows how user ATHENA may give access to the EMP table in her schema to user SPANKY:

```
GRANT SELECT, UPDATE ON athena.emp TO spanky;
```

Granting Object Privileges to Users with Administrative Ability

As with system privileges, you can give users the ability to administrate an object privilege along with the ability to use that privilege themselves. The `with grant option` clause for object privileges gives SPANKY the same kind of ability as user ATHENA with respect to allowing other users on the database to `select` or `update` data in the EMP table owned by ATHENA. With the SQL command shown in the following code block, SPANKY can `select` and `update` data from EMP, and can give that ability to others as well:

```
GRANT SELECT, UPDATE ON emp TO SPANKY WITH GRANT OPTION;
```

Only object privileges given `with grant option` can be administered by the grantee. All others are administered by the owner of the database object. Additionally, there is a consolidated method for granting object privileges using the keyword `all`. Note that `all` in this context is not a privilege; it is merely a specification for all object privileges for the database object.

```
GRANT ALL ON emp TO spanky;
```

Granting Object Privileges to Roles

Object privileges can be granted to roles, just as system privileges can. The `grant` command is again used for this purpose.

```
GRANT ALL ON emp TO dev_dba_privs;
```

The general format for granting a privilege to a user or role is as follows:

```
GRANT privilege ON object TO user;
```

Revoking Object Privileges from Users or Roles

There may also come a time when users or roles may have privileges revoked. This task is accomplished with the `revoke` command. No additional syntax is necessary for revoking an object privilege granted `with grant option`.

```
REVOKE ALL ON emp FROM SPANKY;
REVOKE ALL ON emp FROM dev_dba_privs;
```

When an object privilege is revoked, there are some cascading events. For example, if SPANKY has the `update` privilege on ATHENA's EMP table, either granted directly to SPANKY or via a role, when ATHENA revokes the privilege, then SPANKY can no longer change records in the EMP table. However, the rows SPANKY already changed don't get magically transformed back the way they were before.

Cascading Effects of Revoking Object Privileges

There are several considerations to make when revoking object privileges. For instance, if a privilege has been granted `with grant option`, you cannot take away only the administrative ability while leaving the user with the object privilege unless you regrant the object privilege without administrative abilities. Also, if the user has been given the `references` privilege and used it to create a `FOREIGN KEY` constraint to another table, then some cascading must take place in order to complete the revocation of the `references` privilege.

```
REVOKE REFERENCES ON emp FROM spanky CASCADE CONSTRAINTS;
```

In the preceding example, not only is the privilege to create referential integrity revoked, but any instances in which that referential integrity was used on the database are also revoked. If a `FOREIGN KEY` constraint was created on the EMP table by user SPANKY, and the prior statement was issued without the `cascade constraints` clause, then the `revoke` statement will fail. Other cascading issues may appear after object privileges are revoked as well. In general, if an object privilege is revoked, then any item created by the user that relied on that object privilege may experience a problem during execution. To grant object privileges to others, you must own the database object, you must have been given the object privilege `with grant option`, or you must have the `grant any privilege` ability given to you.

Special Considerations for the execute Privilege

In versions of Oracle prior to Oracle8*i*, if a user has the ability to execute a stored procedure owned by another user, and the procedure accesses some tables, the object privileges required to access those tables must be granted *to the owner of the procedure*, not the user to whom `execute` privileges were granted. This is called *owner's rights execution*. What's more, the privileges must be granted directly to the user, not through a role. When a user executes a stored procedure, the user is able to use whatever privileges are required to execute the procedure.

For example, `execute` privileges are given to SPANKY on procedure `process_deposit( )` owned by ATHENA, and this procedure performs an `update` on the BANK_ACCOUNT table using an `update` privilege granted to ATHENA. SPANKY will be able to perform that `update` on BANK_ACCOUNT via the `process_deposit( )` procedure, even though the `update` privilege is not granted to SPANKY. However, SPANKY will *not* be able to issue an `update` statement on table BANK_ACCOUNT from SQL*Plus because the appropriate privilege was not granted to SPANKY directly.

In Oracle8*i* and later, the owner of a procedure has the option to define that procedure using *invoker's rights execution*. This means that, in the context of the previous example, if the invoker of the procedure or function does not have `update` privileges on the BANK_ACCOUNT table and the `process_deposit( )` procedure has been defined with invoker's rights execution, then the invoker won't be able to run that procedure even if the owner of the procedure has `update` privileges on the BANK_ACCOUNT table. The following code block shows source code for a stored procedure defined with invoker's rights. The clause that actually defines invoker's rights for this procedure is highlighted in bold:

```
CREATE or REPLACE PROCEDURE find_mouse (
  mouse_name in VARCHAR2,
  location out VARCHAR2
) AUTHID current_user
IS
 location varchar2(40);
BEGIN
 SELECT mouse_location
 INTO location
 FROM MOUSE_HOUSE
 WHERE name = mouse_name;
END;
```

Open to the Public

Another aspect of privileges and access to the database involves a special user on the database. This user is called PUBLIC. If a system privilege, object privilege, or role is granted to the PUBLIC user, then every user in the database has that privilege. Typically, it is not advised that the DBA should grant many privileges or roles to PUBLIC because if the privilege or role ever needs to be revoked, then every stored package, procedure, or function will need to be recompiled.

For Review

What cascading issues exist related to the `references` object privilege and the user PUBLIC?

Granting Object Privileges with Security Manager

Granting object privileges to users and roles with Security Manager is done in much the same way as granting system privileges to users and roles with Security Manager. The following discussions cover the step-by-step processes required for the tasks.

Granting Object Privileges to Users with Security Manager

To grant object privileges to users with Security Manager, follow these steps:

1. Drill down to Default Database | Users | <YOUR USER> in the left side of the Security Manager window. On the right side of the Security Manager window, click the Object Privileges tab. Security Manager should look like Figure 5-12.

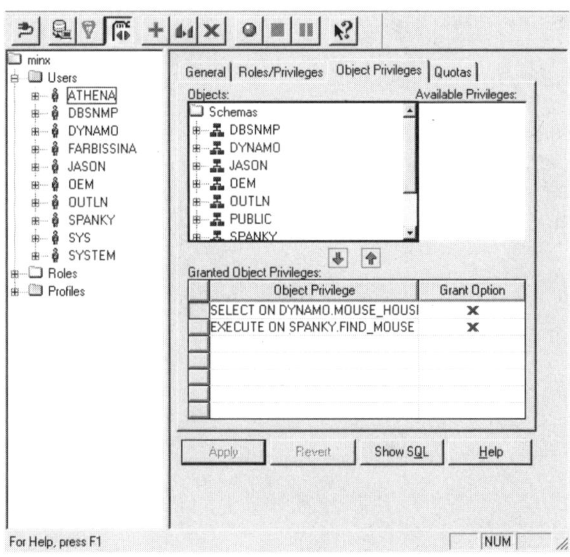

FIGURE 5-12. *Object Privileges tab within Security Manager*

2. On the top-right side of the Security Manager window, where it says "Objects:" and shows a set of drill-down nodes corresponding to users owning database objects on your database, drill down to the <USER> | <OBJECT TYPE> | <OBJECT NAME> node for the database object you want to grant object privileges on. On the right side in that top box, you should now see all the available object privileges associated with that database object. Figure 5-13 illustrates.

3. Click the object privilege you want to grant to the user. If you want to grant more than one, click all the object privileges you want to grant. Then, click the down arrow button to list the object privileges you are adding to that user. When finished, click the Apply button, as shown in Figure 5-14.

Granting Object Privileges to Roles with Security Manager

To grant object privileges to roles with Security Manager, follow these steps:

1. Drill down to Default Database | Roles | <YOUR ROLE> in the left side of the Security Manager window. On the right side of the Security Manager window, click the Object Privileges tab.

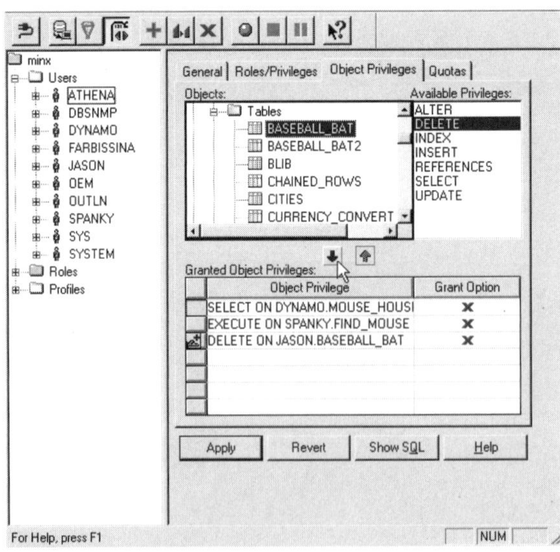

FIGURE 5-13. *Available object privileges on object selected*

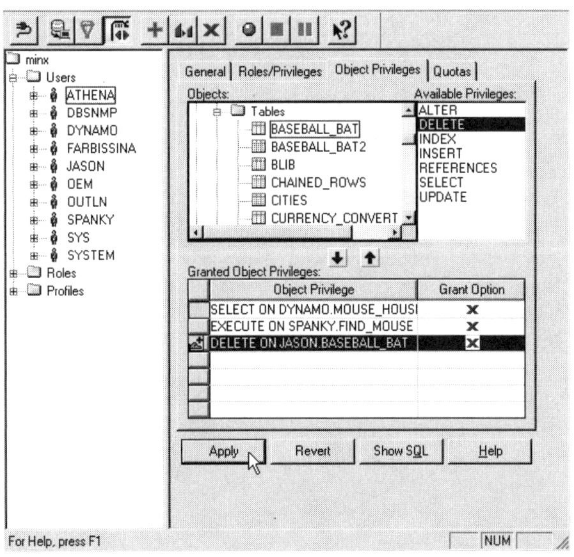

FIGURE 5-14. *Granting object privileges to users with Security Manager*

2. On the top-right side of the Security Manager window, where it says "Objects:" and shows a set of drill-down nodes corresponding to users owning database objects on your database, drill down to the <USER> | <OBJECT TYPE> | <OBJECT NAME> node for the database object you want to grant object privileges on. On the right side in that top box, you should now see all the available object privileges associated with that database object.
3. Click the object privilege you want to grant to the role. If you want to grant more than one, click all the object privileges you want to grant. Then, click the down arrow button to list the object privileges you are adding to that role. When finished, click the Apply button, as shown in Figure 5-15.

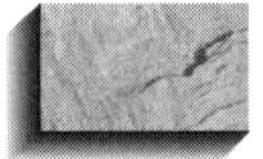

TIP

Granting roles with object privileges to users in Security Manager follows the same steps as granting roles with system privileges to users in Security Manager.

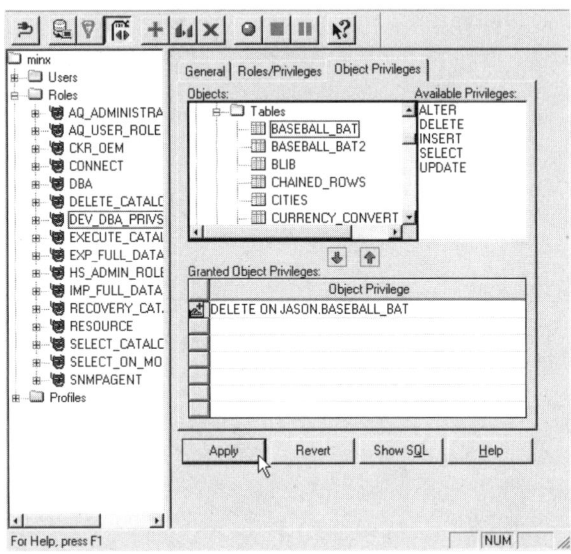

FIGURE 5-15. *Granting object privileges to roles in Security Manager*

For Review

Understand how to grant object privileges to users and roles in Security Manager.

Chapter Summary

In this chapter, you learned about the various aspects of user setup and privilege management. You learned how to categorize the three different types of users according to their needs, and how to create users in the Oracle database. You defined and discussed the system privileges available on an Oracle database, and gained an understanding of how to administer system privileges directly to users and via roles. You learned how to use Security Manager to create users and roles, how to grant system privileges to users and roles, and how to grant roles to users.

This chapter also discussed how object privileges are used to manage access to aspects of database applications. You defined and discussed the different object privileges available in Oracle. You learned the appropriate SQL commands and step-by-step operations in Security Manager for granting object privileges to roles and users. Finally, you learned how to revoke object privileges from users and roles as well.

Two-Minute Drill

- The three types of database users are
  - **Application users** People who utilize the objects within an Oracle database to view and manipulate data
  - **Application developers** People who add new objects to an Oracle database to enhance existing applications and develop new ones
  - **DBAs and DBOs** People who ensure that Oracle databases are available for use, backed up properly, running at optimum speed, and sized for growth
- New database users are created with the `create user` statement.
- A new user can have the following items configured by the `create user` statement:
  - Password
  - Default tablespace for database objects
  - Temporary tablespace
  - Quotas on tablespaces
  - User profile
  - Account lock status
  - Whether the user must specify a new password on first logging in
- User definitions can be altered with the `alter user` statement and dropped with the `drop user` statement. Users can issue the `alter user` statement only to change their passwords and default roles.
- Information about a database user can be found in the following data dictionary views:
  - DBA_USERS
  - DBA_PROFILES
  - DBA_TS_QUOTAS
  - DBA_OBJECTS
  - DBA_ROLE_PRIVS

   - DBA_TAB_PRIVS
   - DBA_SYS_PRIVS
- There are two categories of database privileges: *system privileges* and *object privileges.*
- System privileges allow for the creation of every object on the database, along with the ability to execute many commands and connect to the database.
- Object privileges allow for access to data within database objects.
- There are three basic classes of system privileges for some database objects: `create`, `alter`, and `drop`. These privileges give the grantee the power to create database objects in their own user schema.
- Some exceptions exist to the preceding rule. The `alter table` privilege is an object privilege, while the `alter rollback segment` privilege is a system privilege. The `create index` privilege is an object privilege as well.
- Three oddball privileges are `grant`, `audit`, and `analyze`. These privileges apply to the creation of all database objects and to running powerful commands in Oracle.
- The `any` modifier gives the user extra power to create objects or run commands on any object in the user schema.
- The final system privilege of interest is the `restricted session` privilege, which allows the user to connect to a database in `restricted session` mode.
- Object privileges give the user access to place, remove, change, or view data in a table or one column in a table, as well as to alter the definition of a table, create an index on a table, and develop `FOREIGN KEY` constraints.
- When system privileges are revoked, the objects a user has created will still exist.
- A system privilege can be granted `with admin option` to allow the grantee to administer others' ability to use the privilege.
- When object privileges are revoked, the data placed or modified in a table will still exist, but you will not be able to perform the action allowed by the privilege anymore.

- An object privilege can be granted `with grant option` to another user in order to make the user an administrator of the privilege.
- The `grant option` cannot be used when granting a privilege to a role.
- Roles are used to bundle privileges together and to enable or disable them automatically.
- A user can create objects and then grant the nongrantable object privileges to the role, which then can be granted to as many users as require it.
- There are roles created by Oracle when the software is installed:
  - **CONNECT** Can connect to the database and create clusters, links, sequences, tables, views, and synonyms. This role is good for table schema owners and development DBAs.
  - **RESOURCE** Can connect to the database and create clusters, sequences, tables, triggers, and stored procedures. This role is good for application developers. It also has unlimited tablespace.
  - **DBA** Can use any system privilege `with admin option`.
  - **EXP_FULL_DATABASE** Can export all database objects to an export dump file.
  - **IMP_FULL_DATABASE** Can import all database objects from an export dump file to the database.
  - **DELETE_CATALOG_ROLE** Extends `delete` privileges on SYS-owned dictionary tables, in response to the new restriction on `delete any table` privileges that prevent grantees from removing rows from SYS-owned dictionary tables.
  - **EXECUTE_CATALOG_ROLE** Allows grantee `execute` privileges on any SYS-owned package supplied with the Oracle software.
  - **SELECT_CATALOG_ROLE** Allows grantee to `select` data from any SYS-owned dictionary table or view.
- Roles can have passwords assigned to them to provide security for the use of certain privileges.
- Ensure you have a complete understanding of how to create users and roles using Security Manager.
- Ensure you have a complete understanding of how to grant privileges to users and roles, and how to grant roles to users, using Security Manager.

Chapter Questions

1. **You are eliminating some foreign key dependencies from the Oracle database prior to removal of some tables. When revoking the `references` privilege, the DBA must use which option to ensure success?**

   A. `with admin option`

   B. `with grant option`

   C. `cascade constraints`

   D. `trailing nullcols`

   E. `storage (initial 10M next 5M)`

2. **User BELL has just created a role on the Oracle database. As the creator of a role, BELL is granted which of the following privileges with respect to the role she has just created?**

   A. `grant any privilege`

   B. `create any role`

   C. `with admin option`

   D. `with grant option`

   E. `sysdba`

3. **You have been asked to remove a developer userid from the Oracle database. In order to find out how many database objects a user has created, which view would you query in the Oracle data dictionary, if you could query only one view?**

   A. DBA_USERS

   B. DBA_OBJECTS

   C. DBA_TS_QUOTAS

   D. DBA_TAB_PRIVS

   E. DBA_VIEWS

4. **A user cannot change aspects of their account configuration with the exception of one item. Which of the following choices identifies an area of**

the user's account that the user can change, using an `alter user` statement?

A. `identified by`

B. `default tablespace`

C. `temporary tablespace`

D. `quota on`

E. `profile`

F. `default role`

5. **The DBO must create a set of objects for a new application coming online. Which privilege would allow the DBO to connect to a database running in restricted mode?**

   A. `create table`

   B. `create user`

   C. `restricted session`

   D. `create session`

   E. `select any table`

6. **Which of the following statements is true about roles? (Choose three.)**

   A. Roles can be granted to other roles.

   B. Privileges can be granted to roles.

   C. Roles can be granted to users.

   D. Roles can be granted to synonyms.

   E. Users can be granted to roles.

   F. Roles are created when tablespaces are created.

   G. Privileges required for procedure execution can be granted through roles.

7. **User MANN has granted the `create any view with admin option` privilege to user SNOW. User SNOW granted the same privilege `with admin option` to user REED. User MANN revokes the privilege from user**

SNOW. Which statement is true about privileges granted to users REED, MANN, and SNOW?

A. REED and MANN have the privilege, but SNOW does not.

B. REED and SNOW have the privilege, but MANN does not.

C. MANN and SNOW have the privilege, but REED does not.

D. MANN has the privilege, but SNOW and REED do not.

E. Neither REED, MANN, nor SNOW have the privilege.

8. **You are granting `select` access on the BANK_ACCOUNT table to the `PROGRAMMER` role using Security Manager. Which of the following steps must be accomplished after selecting the BANK_ACCOUNT table in the appropriate interface? (Choose three.)**

A. Select the role to which the privilege will be given.

B. Click the Apply button.

C. Move the privilege to the list of privileges granted to that role.

D. Select the Object Privileges tab.

E. Select the appropriate privilege from the Privilege Type list box.

9. **You are trying to determine the available roles on a newly created Oracle database. Which three of the following are roles automatically granted by Oracle on your database? (Choose three.)**

A. SESSION

B. DBA

C. CREATE_ANY_DATABASE

D. SELECT_CATALOG_ROLE

E. RESOURCE

F. USER_PROFILE

G. EXECUTE

H. BECOME_ANY_USER

10. Which of the following choices identifies the aspect of a user that you cannot define when creating a user using SQL commands, but can define when creating a user via Security Manager?

A. Password

B. Default role

C. Default tablespace

D. Profile

E. Temporary tablespace

Answers to Chapter Questions

1. C. `cascade constraints`

Explanation If a `FOREIGN KEY` constraint is defined as the result of a `references` privilege being granted, then in order to revoke the `references` privilege, the `cascade constraints` option must be used. Choices A and B are incorrect because the `admin option` and `grant option` relate to the granting of system and object privileges, respectively, while this question is asking about the revocation of an object privilege. Choice D is incorrect because `trailing nullcols` refers to an option in the Data Manager control file covered in the next chapter. Finally, choice E is incorrect because the `storage` clause is not a component of user privilege management; it is a component of database table, index, and tablespace creation.

2. D. `with grant option`

Explanation Choice D is the correct answer because it is the appropriate administrative clause offered to the creator of a role in Oracle. The creator of a role can do anything they want with the role, including remove it. Choice C is incorrect because `with admin option` refers to the administrative clause for system privileges. Choices A, B, and E are incorrect because no privileges are given to a role on creation. Refer to the discussion of roles and the `with grant option`.

3. B. `DBA_OBJECTS`

Explanation The `DBA_OBJECTS` view lists all objects that are in the Oracle database, as well as the owners of those objects. Choice A is incorrect because `DBA_USERS` contains the actual user-creation information, such as encrypted password, default and temp tablespace, user profile, and default role. Choice C is incorrect because `DBA_TS_QUOTAS` identifies all the tablespace quotas that have been named for the user. Choice D is incorrect because `DBA_TAB_PRIVS` names all the table object privileges that have been granted and to whom they have been given. Finally, `DBA_VIEWS` will tell you what views this user has created, but the user may have created other objects in the database, so choice E is incorrect.

4. A. `identified by`

Explanation There is only one user creation option that the created user can modify. All others are managed by either a security administrator or the DBA. Although users can change the current role from the roles currently granted to them using the `set role` statement, they cannot issue the `alter user` statement to get the same result. Users cannot define their own profiles, default tablespaces, or temporary tablespaces, or grant themselves roles (unless, of course, they also own the role).

5. C. `restricted session`

Explanation Choice A is incorrect because the `create table` privilege allows the user to create a table, while choice B is incorrect for a similar reason—`create user` allows the user to create new users. Choice D is required for establishing connection to an open database, while choice C is the only privilege listed that allows the user to connect to a database in `restricted session` mode. Finally, the `select any table` privilege allows you to see all data in Oracle, but only if you can get into the database first, so choice E is also incorrect.

6. A, B, *and* C.

Explanation Roles can be granted to other roles, making choice A correct. Privileges can be given to roles, too, so choice B is also right. Finally, roles are given to users as a means of consolidating privilege management, making choice C the final correct choice. After that, everything's wrong. Roles cannot be granted to synonyms, making choice D wrong. Roles are granted to users, not the other way around, making choice E incorrect. A role is created if and only if the `create role` statement is issued, or when the database is created. Now, although the SYSTEM tablespace is also created when a database is created, note the imprecision of choice F—it states that roles are created when tablespaces are created, meaning when any tablespace is created. This is not true, and choice F is incorrect (though a little deceiving). Finally, with respect to choice G, the opposite is true. If a privilege is needed as part of the execution of a procedure (such as `update` access to a table), that privilege had better be granted to the owner of the procedure (under owner's rights execution) or to the invoker (under invoker's rights execution) directly—not through a role. Thus, choice G is also incorrect.

7. D. MANN has the privilege, but SNOW and REED do not.

Explanation If you've studied the question at all, you'll know immediately that someone still has the privilege, user MANN, because MANN is revoking it from everyone else. Thus, you can eliminate choice E right away. After that, the only result of revoking a system or object privilege in Oracle is that the user the privilege is revoked from is the only user who loses it. If the user has granted the privilege to someone else, that other user will still have the privilege. Of course, someone must review the discussion of cascading effects of granting privileges.

8. B, C, *and* E.

Explanation Since there are three correct answers here, you can work your way to the answer by process elimination if you're careful. First, you should know that the Apply button is the last thing you do, so getting choice B should be simple. From there, you should realize that selecting the role to be given privileges is the first thing you do, before selecting the BANK_ACCOUNT table from the Objects list. So, eliminate choice A. From there, you have a 33 percent chance of guessing the other step that happens before you select the BANK_ACCOUNT table, which will leave you with the other two steps that happen after selecting the BANK_ACCOUNT table. Recall that, in order to grant object privileges in Security Manager, you use the Object Privileges interface, selected with the appropriate tab. Thus, choice D can be eliminated because that step happens before picking the table. Choices C and E happen after, so they are correct answers.

9. B, D, *and* E. `DBA`, `SELECT_CATALOG_ROLE`, *and* `RESOURCE`.

Explanation Oracle provides you with several roles automatically when databases are created. Those roles include `RESOURCE`, `DBA`, and `SELECT_CATALOG_ROLE`, as well as `CONNECT`, `EXP_FULL_DATABASE`, `IMP_FULL_DATABASE`, `SYSDBA`, `DELETE_CATALOG_ROLE`, `SYSOPER`, and `EXECUTE_CATALOG_ROLE`. Choices A, C, F, G, and H are not among those roles automatically created by Oracle, so they must have been created later by users.

10. B. Default role

Explanation The password, default tablespace, profile, and temporary tablespace of a user can be defined by the `create user` statement. However, you cannot define a default role because none have been granted yet. However, when you create a user with Security Manager, the interface has a Roles/Privileges tab for granting system privileges and roles. In that tab, you can also check the roles you wish to be the default roles before clicking the Apply button. Thus, choice B is the correct answer.

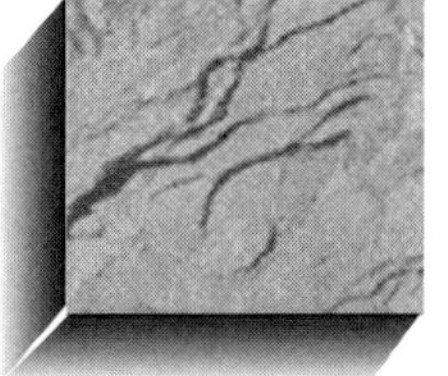

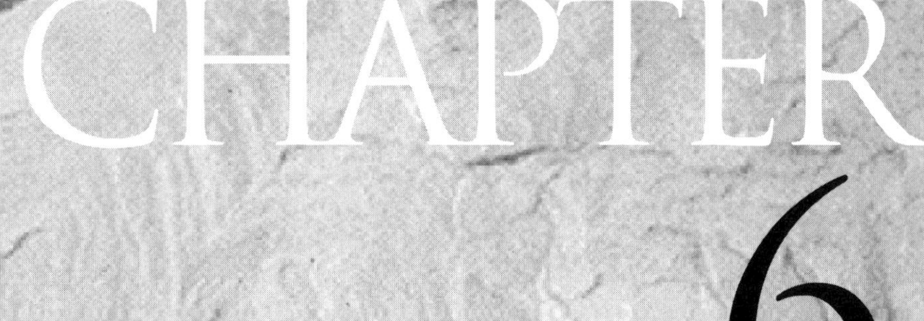

CHAPTER 6

Backup, Recovery, and Data Loads

his chapter explains the following critical concepts for Oracle database operation:

- Why and when to back up your database
- When and how to recover your database
- Loading non-Oracle data

Recoverability is anything but a cliché. Too bad many organizations treat it that way. Even organizations that spend a lot of money on RAID, mirroring, high availability, and other systems don't discover until too late that expensive systems are just as prone to data loss in the absence of a tested recoverability plan. To those who rush to deploy untested backup strategies, beware the results. If you don't take a little extra time up front, you will regret it later when the VP of your IT organization is breathing down your neck to get the system alive again. There's nothing safer than having your entire database backed up to tape as often as your production schedule allows. Here's a primer on how to avoid other headaches.

Why and When to Back Up Your Database

In this section, we'll explore these topics:

- Defining database backup frequency
- Backing up a database using various methods
- Performing full database backups
- Automating backups with OEM Job Scheduler

Point blank—you need to take backups of your database or else you are asking for trouble. This section will help you understand Oracle backup strategies. You will learn how to define the backup frequency of your Oracle database, corresponding to the frequency of data change your database experiences. You will also learn how to back up the Oracle database using various methods. The steps required to perform full database backups are covered in this section as well. Finally, you will learn how to automate database backups using Oracle Enterprise Manager.

Defining Database Backup Frequency

Before continuing, an important point must be made about Oracle's `archivelog` and `noarchivelog` modes of database operation. To understand the difference between these two modes of database operation, first understand Oracle's redo log architecture. Oracle records all changes made in the database (committed and uncommitted) in the online redo logs. Redo logs are of limited size. When one fills, Oracle starts writing to the next one in the sequence. Hence, this is the reason you must have at least two (and preferably more) online redo logs for your Oracle database. When the second one fills, Oracle overwrites the contents of the first one, and so on. If the database is running in `archivelog` mode, then Oracle will save the contents of a filled online redo log before allowing itself to overwrite the log's contents. If the database is running in `noarchivelog` mode, then Oracle will not save the contents of the filled online redo log before overwriting its contents. Archived redo information is useful in situations where you want to recover to the point of time a database failure occurred (as opposed to recovering only to a point in time when the backup was taken). That said, there are three ways to back up data in an Oracle database:

- **Cold backups** Copies of Oracle datafiles, control files, and redo logs are made when the database is shut down. Cold backups are great in situations where you want to take a benchmark backup copy of your database to a point in time and can afford the downtime required to take the backup. Archiving redo logs is optional, but you will need archives if you want the ability to recover to a point after the most recent cold backup is taken.
- **Hot backups** Copies of Oracle datafiles, control files, and redo logs are made when the database is open. Archiving redo logs is mandatory. Hot backups are great in situations where you want to take a benchmark backup copy of your database to a point in time but can't afford the downtime required to take the backup.
- **Binary exports** A binary copy of data in an Oracle database is made using the Data Manager tool while the database is open. Archiving redo logs is not relevant to this form of backup. This type of backup is often used for moving data between two different Oracle databases or when you want a backup copy of all data structures in your database.

When You Should Take Backups

The frequency you back up your database depends on how frequently data changes in that database. However, in high-volume transaction-processing environments, you might decide to back up your data twice a day, or even more frequently, depending on various factors such as how quickly the organization expects you to recover the data in that database in the event of failure. In less active database transaction environments, you might back up your data only once a day, or even less. For static or read-only environments, such as data warehouses, you may back up your database only after a data load completes. Figure 6-1 shows the spectrum of database volatility and associated suggested backup schedules. The bottom line is that there are two important questions to consider when defining the frequency of backups:

1. How important is recoverability to the point in time of database failure to your organization?
2. How much downtime is your organization prepared to accept if database recovery is required?

Recoverability to Point of Failure

Although many organizations tolerate users having to rekey some data in the event of system failure, most desire to see that effort kept to a bare minimum. To ensure recovery to a point in time as close as possible to the point of failure, the best option offered by Oracle is to take frequent backups in conjunction with redo log archiving. This level of recoverability is usually required for production databases. Other database environments for development or testing purposes don't usually require this level of recoverability. In this case, an organization may decide not to archive redo logs (which conserves disk space), opting instead to take cold backups of the database in conjunction with frequent exports of data.

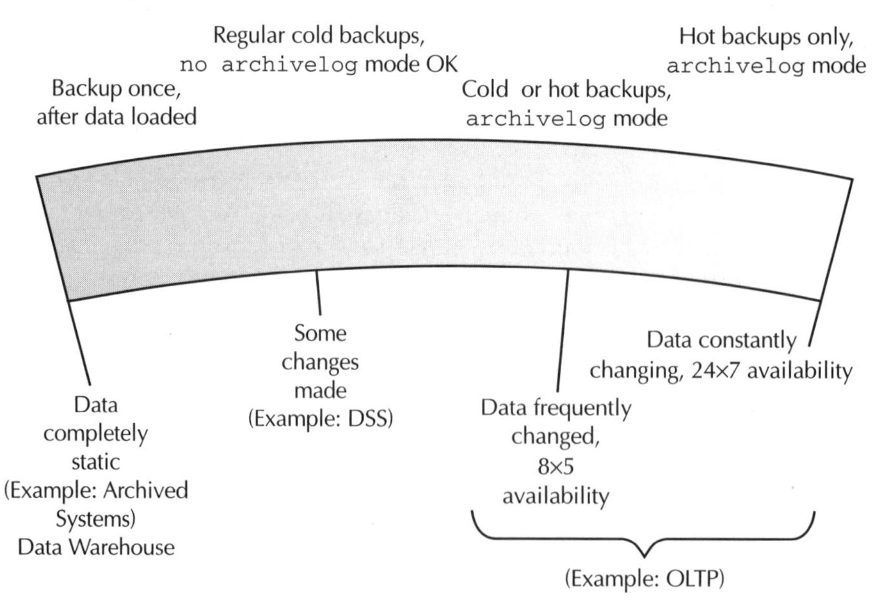

FIGURE 6-1. *Database volatility and associated backup strategies*

Backups and Recoverability Speed

Another benefit of frequent backups is reduced time spent handling recovery. The components of a recovery that take time are restoring backup datafile copies (either from tape or disk) and applying archived redo logs to the database. Databases with larger and more numerous datafiles will experience slower recoveries than databases with small and few datafiles, because it will take longer to restore those files from tape or to move them from one disk to another. Also, less frequent backups in conjunction with archiving redo logs means that more archive logs will need to be applied after datafiles are restored. Oracle can apply archived redo logs quickly, so this part of your recovery usually takes less time than restoring files from tape.

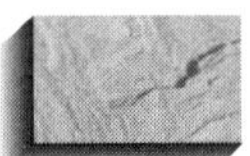

TIP

An ideal backup strategy is one that utilizes disk space as a staging area. Backup datafile copies and archived redo logs are copied out to the disk staging area. After being copied to tape, the files are left on disk for a day or two. This way, if a failure occurs, you will have at least one recent backup available on disk, reducing the time it takes to restore those files from tape.

A Note About Data Manager

Oracle has a useful tool called Data Manager that allows you to dump table and index data to a binary file and read the binary file to load data back into any Oracle database. This tool is useful for moving data between databases and complements a cold database backup strategy by backing up database objects in development and/or test environments. This tool shouldn't be relied on for production environments, however. Data Manager doesn't allow recovery to the point of database failure because they don't work in conjunction with archive logs. Data Manager also requires that you rebuild your Oracle physical/logical storage structures before database objects can be loaded. For production databases, only OEM tools like Backup Manager and Recovery Manager should be used. Recovery Manager is Oracle's server-side tool that allows you to script backup operations for storage in a recovery catalog database. For use of Recovery Manager as described in this chapter, you will need at least two databases in your organization—the main production database and the catalog database.

For Review

Understand the factors for making a decision about backup strategy.

Performing Full Database Backups

A full database backup is one in which all datafiles, online redo logs, control files, and archived redo logs (if archiving is enabled) are copied at the same time to an alternate location, usually to tape. It can be performed while the database is available to users (so long as you archive your redo logs) or when the database is shut down.

TIP
This chapter assumes that you have at least two separate databases available for backup and recovery—a recovery catalog database and the database containing actual data used by your organization. This is the recommended configuration for proper behavior when performing database backup and recovery.

Configuring Backups in OEM

As a DBO, you may find that your efforts are best served by taking backups with OEM Backup Manager. You can't log into Backup Manager as a standalone tool, though—only through the OEM console. To set up for taking a backup in this way, perform the following tasks:

1. Click on Start | Programs | Oracle Enterprise Manager | Enterprise Manager.
2. Connect to your OEM repository database as whatever user you created the repository with, on whatever database you created the repository in. Recall that in Chapter 3, we created a user called OEM to own the repository we created on MINX, so in Figure 6-2, OEM is used to log into the repository.

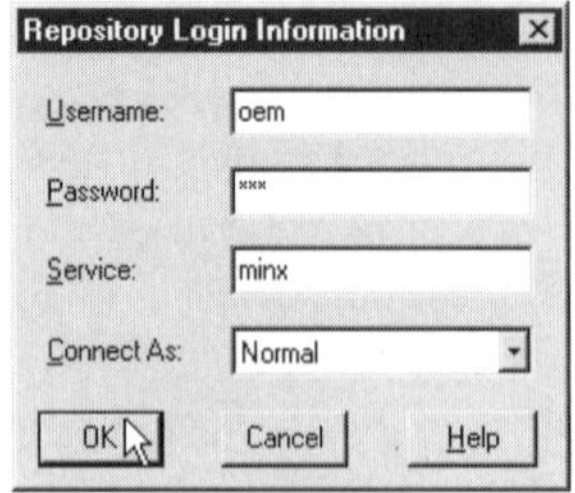

FIGURE 6-2. *Logging into the OEM repository*

3. When in the OEM console, drill down to the Networks | Databases | *dbname.dbdomain* node. In our case, the database name and domain will be MINX.WORLD, as shown in Figure 6-3.
4. Click on the File | Preferences menu option to modify the preferred login credentials for logging into the database you wish to back up. Figure 6-4 displays the appropriate window. In our case, the user is INTERNAL or SYS, the password is ORACLE (entered twice), and the role is SYSDBA. When finished, click OK.
5. A destination directory for backup copies of datafiles must exist before you attempt to back up your Oracle database. Using Windows Explorer or from the DOS prompt, create a directory on your machine where backup copies of datafiles can be stored. For this example, I use a directory called `e:\obackup`.
6. OEM will also need the ability to perform OS writes on the Windows machine hosting the Oracle database to copy the backup datafiles to their new destination. In the OEM console, click on the File | Preferences menu option to view the User Preferences interface.

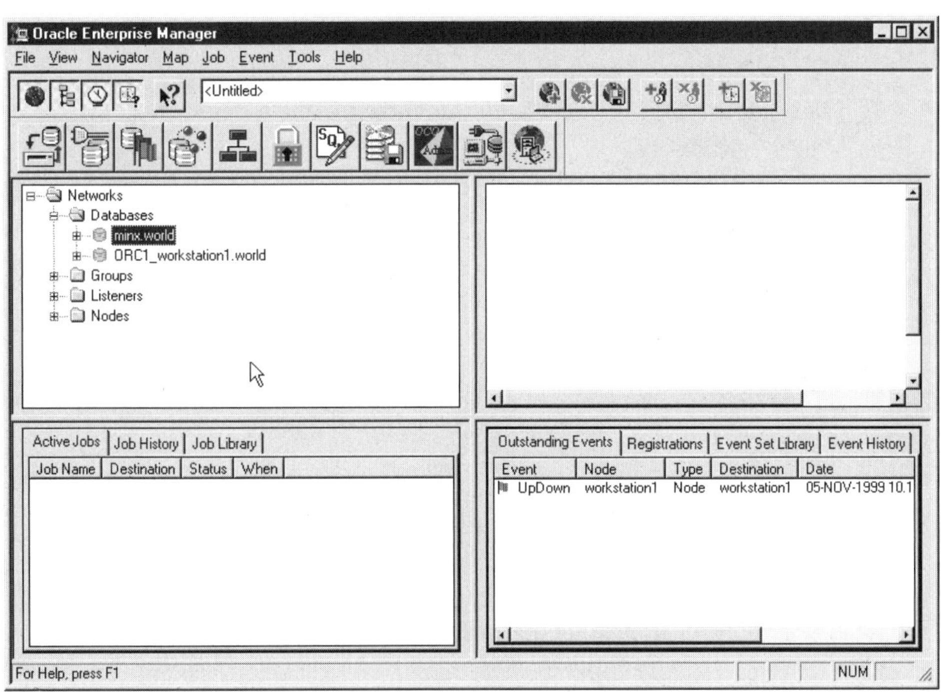

FIGURE 6-3. *MINX database in OEM console*

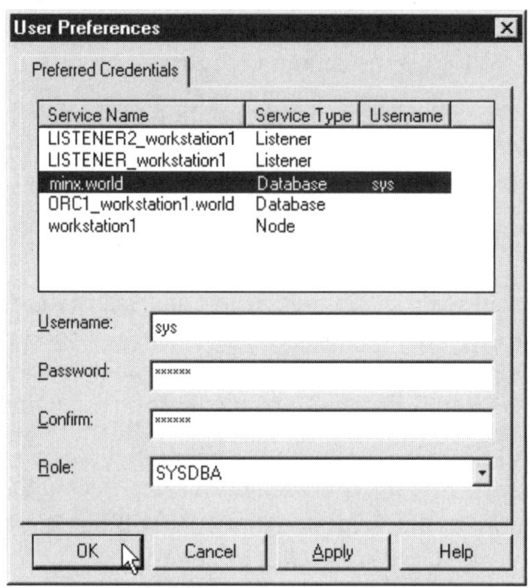

FIGURE 6-4. *MINX database login credentials*

7. Select the Service Name entry corresponding to the machine hosting your Oracle database.
8. Enter the username and password Oracle will use for writing files to the host machine, and then click OK. Figure 6-5 shows the User Preferences interface.
9. Next, you need to create a backup channel. Do so by clicking on the Channel | Create database option. The Create Channel interface is shown in Figure 6-6.
10. Give the channel a meaningful name.
11. Select Disk from the Channel Type drop-down list.
12. Enter the filename format you want Backup Manager to use for the Format text box. The %s value shown in Figure 6-6 will be explained later in the chapter.
13. Specify the backup destination directory you defined previously in step 5. In the example, the destination directory should be defined as `e:\obackup\`. *Be sure that you specify the trailing backslash at the end of the pathname,* as shown in Figure 6-6.

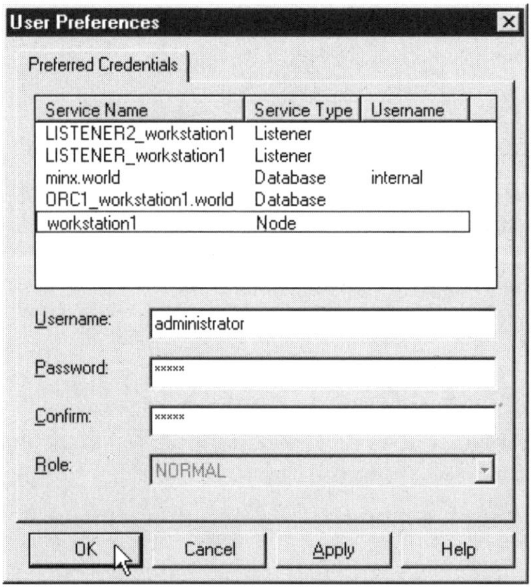

FIGURE 6-5. *User Preferences interface*

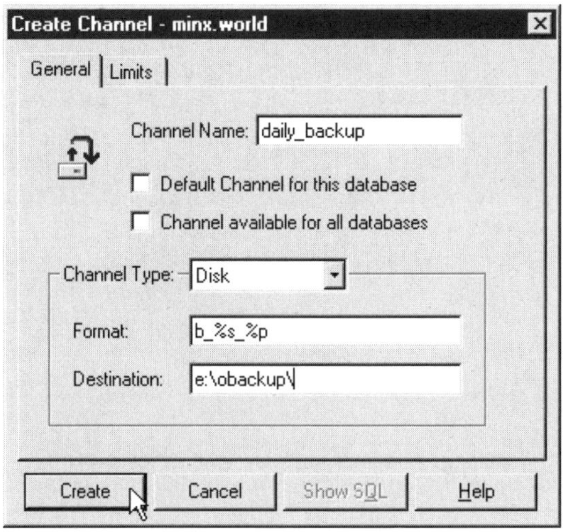

FIGURE 6-6. *Create Channel interface*

14. Click the Create button. Setup is now complete. You can view the channel you just created by drilling into the *dbname.dbdomain* | Channels node in Backup Manager, shown in Figure 6-7.

TIP
You may see a lot of strange ORA-3114 or ORA-12571 errors when you try to create a backup channel. If this occurs, be sure that your repository database is mounted and open when you try to create the channel. You cannot create a channel without having your repository database open and available.

Performing Offline Backups in Backup Manager

If the database is running in `noarchivelog` mode, backups performed using Backup Manager must be run with the database mounted but closed. If you attempt to run a backup of a `noarchivelog` mode database while that database is open, Oracle will give you the message `ORA-19062: cannot backup or copy active file in NOARCHIVELOG mode`. You *can*, however, take a backup of an

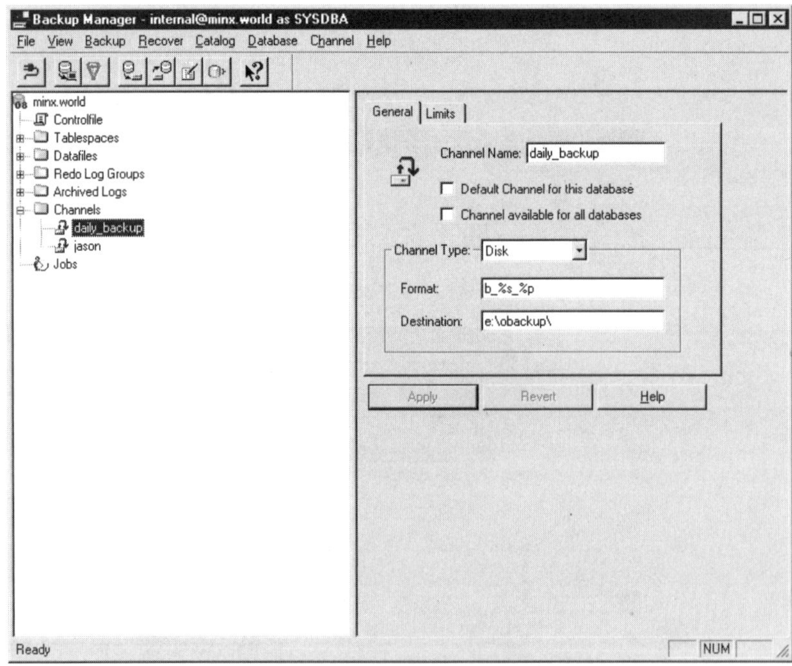

FIGURE 6-7. *Backup Manager interface with channels shown*

open database if that database is running in `archivelog` mode. Once you have completed the necessary setup tasks for backing up a database using Backup Manager, you can complete the following tasks for actually taking that backup:

1. While still in OEM and still drilled down to the Networks | Databases | Minx.World node, start Backup Manager by either clicking the Tools | Applications | Oracle Backup Manager menu option, or by clicking on the Backup Manager button.

2. You'll be prompted to select Operating System Backup subsystem or Oracle8 Recovery Manager subsystem for backing up your database, shown in Figure 6-8. The benefit of Oracle8 Recovery Manager is that it has more features, so choose it and click OK.
3. If your database is running in `noarchivelog` mode, Oracle will notify you that certain backup operations are not permitted. Click OK. At this point, only OEM console and Backup Manager should be running. In Backup Manager, change the database status to mounted, but not open, by clicking on the Database Mounted radio button and then clicking Apply, as shown in Figure 6-9.
4. Backup Manager will prompt you to select the shutdown mode to be used using the interface shown in Figure 6-10. Any option other than Abort will work, but Immediate will be the fastest. After selecting your shutdown option, click OK. A message will prompt you indicating that the instance has restarted. Click OK again.

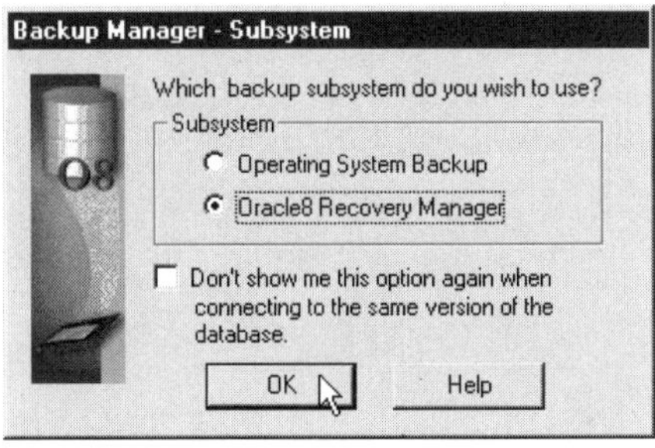

FIGURE 6-8. *Choosing Oracle8 Recovery Manager as the backup subsystem*

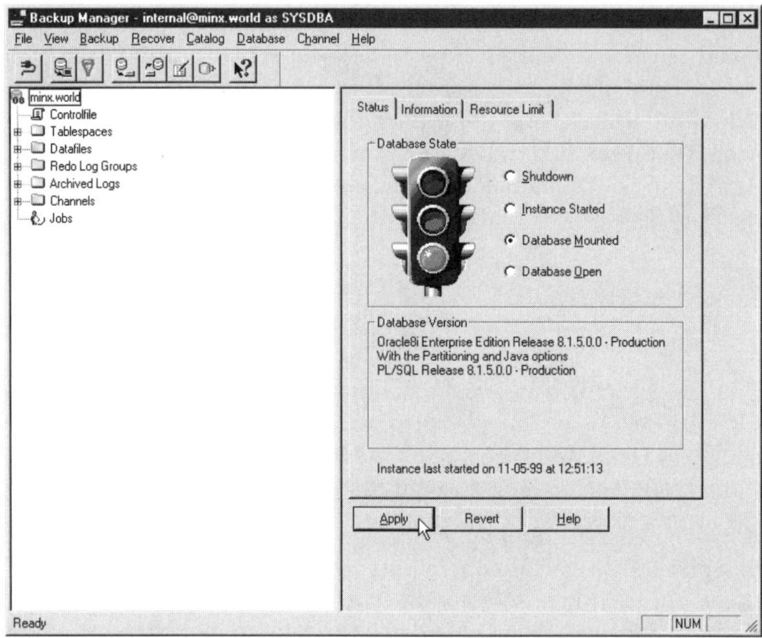

FIGURE 6-9. *Backup Manager interface*

5. Click on the Backup | Backup Wizard menu option to actually start the backup. The Backup Wizard is shown in Figure 6-11. The backup options available in Backup Wizard will depend on whether the database you're

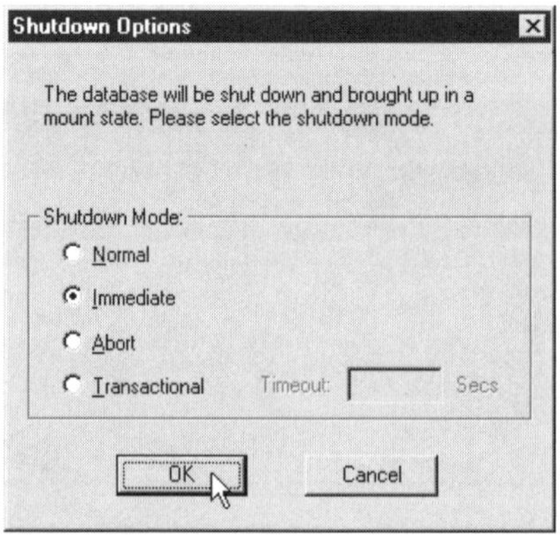

FIGURE 6-10. *Shutdown Options interface*

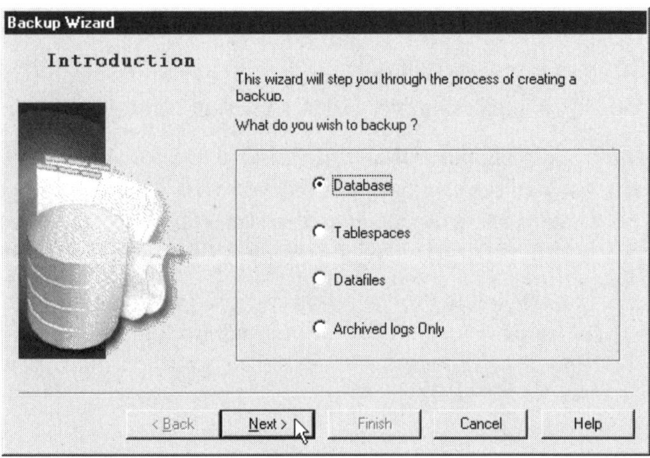

FIGURE 6-11. *Backup Wizard interface*

backing up is running in `archivelog` mode. For complete backup, choose the Database radio button and click Next.

6. Figure 6-12 displays the next screen in the Backup Wizard interface. Select the archived logs you want to include in your backup—none, all, or a subset

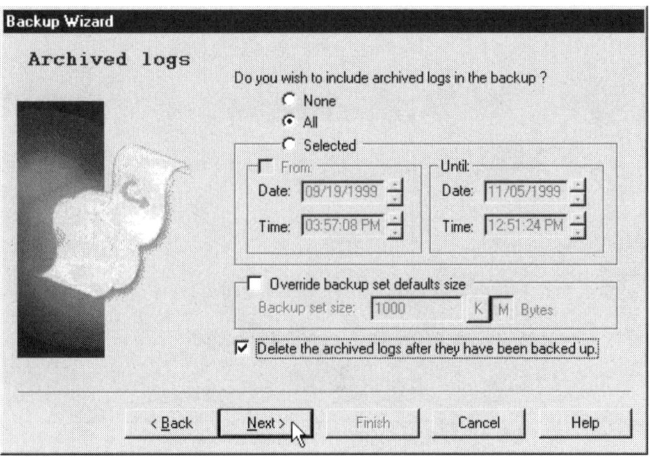

FIGURE 6-12. *Defining archived logs to back up in Backup Wizard*

based on time. If you choose All, you can also define whether Backup Manager deletes the archived logs after backing them up. Then click Next.

7. Choose whether Oracle will use a disk or tape channel for the backup, and then choose the backup name. This is shown in Figure 6-13. Then click Next.
8. Specify a backup tag name that is meaningful to you. When you attempt recovery, you can reference the backup you wish to use by way of the backup tag. Also, since you are taking a database backup, your backup increment level will default to 0. Figure 6-14 illustrates. Click Finish when complete.
9. Click OK after reviewing the summary, shown in Figure 6-15. The backup process will be submitted to the OEM Job Scheduler for execution. The status of that job's execution will appear in the OEM console, shown in Figure 6-16.

Performing Online Backups in Backup Manager

If the database is running in `archivelog` mode, backups performed using Backup Manager can be run with the database open or closed. You can use the same

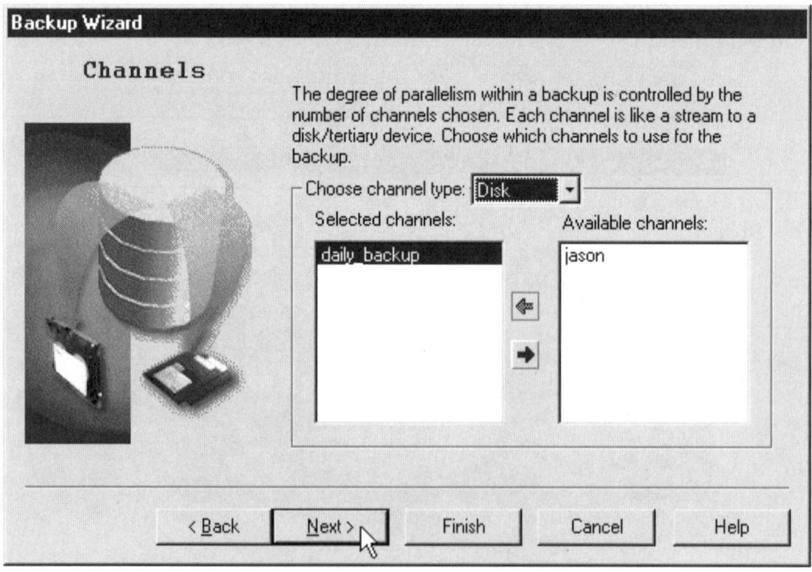

FIGURE 6-13. *Defining your backup channel*

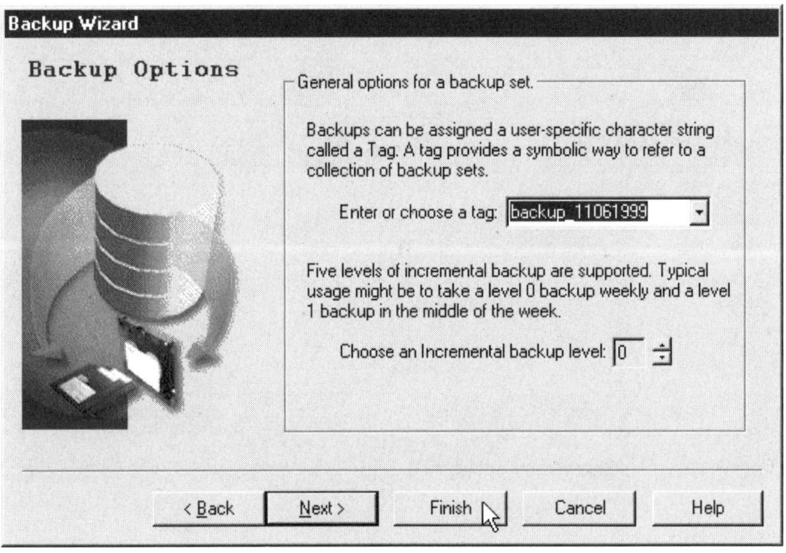

FIGURE 6-14. *Defining your backup tag*

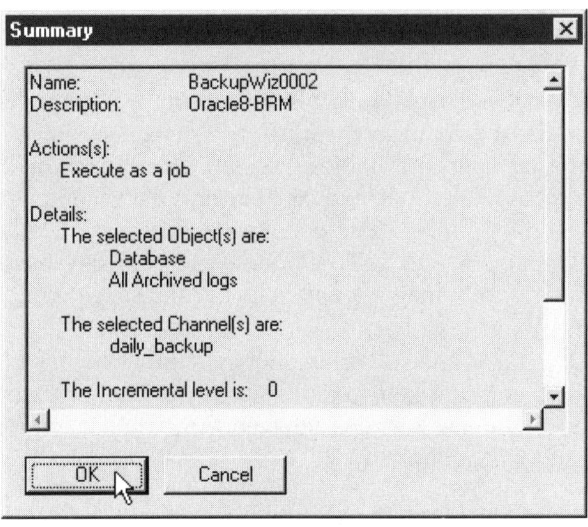

FIGURE 6-15. *Backup summary review*

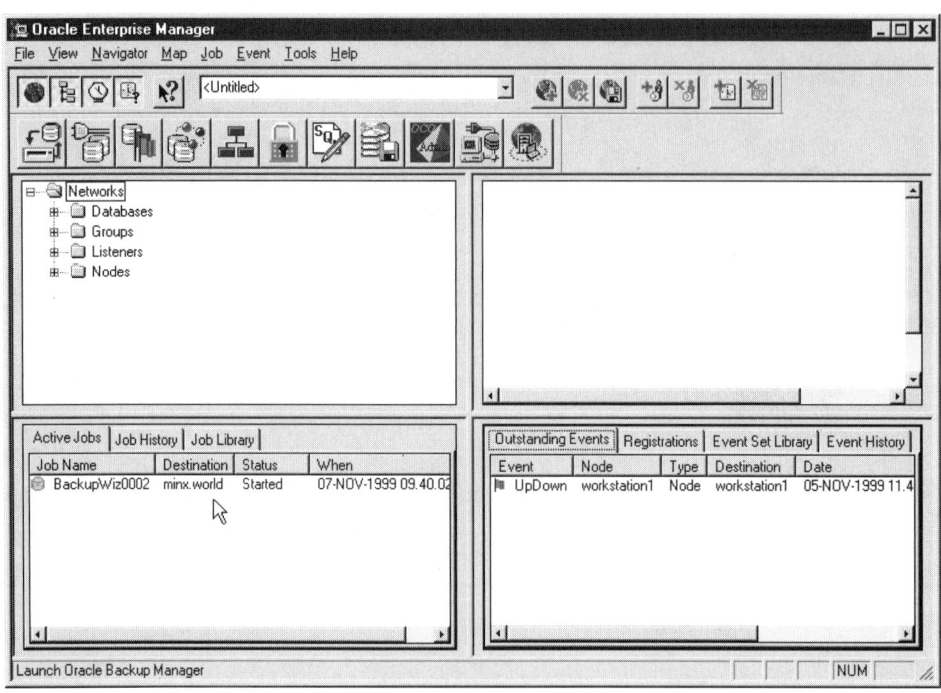

FIGURE 6-16. *Backup status in OEM console*

method for online database backups that is defined in the section "Performing Offline Backups in Backup Manager," earlier in this chapter. However, you can take online backups tablespace by tablespace, too. This discussion illustrates the method for doing so. Similarly, you can take backups of individual datafiles, or even of archived redo logs only. These options are normally grayed out if the database is not running in `archivelog` mode. Here are the steps for performing online backups in Backup Manager, tablespace by tablespace:

1. While still in OEM and still drilled down to the Networks | Databases | Minx.World node, start Backup Manager by either clicking the Tools | Applications | Oracle Backup Manager menu option, or by clicking on the Backup Manager button.
2. You'll be prompted to select Operating System Backup method or Oracle8 Recovery Manager method for backing up your database. The benefit of Oracle8 Recovery Manager is that it has more features, so choose it and click OK.

3. At this point, only OEM console and Backup Manager should be running. In Backup Manager, leave the database open.

4. Click on the Backup | Backup Wizard menu option to actually start the backup. The Backup Wizard is shown in Figure 6-17. The backup options available in Backup Wizard will depend on whether the database you're backing up is running in `archivelog` mode. Online backups can be taken using the Database option, or tablespace by tablespace. Since you have already seen how to take a full database backup, click the Tablespaces radio button and click Next.

5. Select the tablespace you wish to back up by clicking on it; then click on the down arrow button for all the tablespaces you want backed up. Click on the Include Control File With This Backup radio button to include the control file. Backing up the control file helps in situations when you must restore your database to a backup taken before a tablespace was added. Figure 6-18 illustrates. Then click Next.

6. Specify what Backup Manager should do with archive logs using the same method identified in step 6 and Figure 6-12 in the earlier section "Performing Offline Backups in Backup Manager." Then click Next.

7. Choose whether Oracle will use a disk or tape channel for the backup, and then choose the backup name, as you did in step 7 and Figure 6-13 in the earlier section "Performing Offline Backups in Backup Manager." Then click Next.

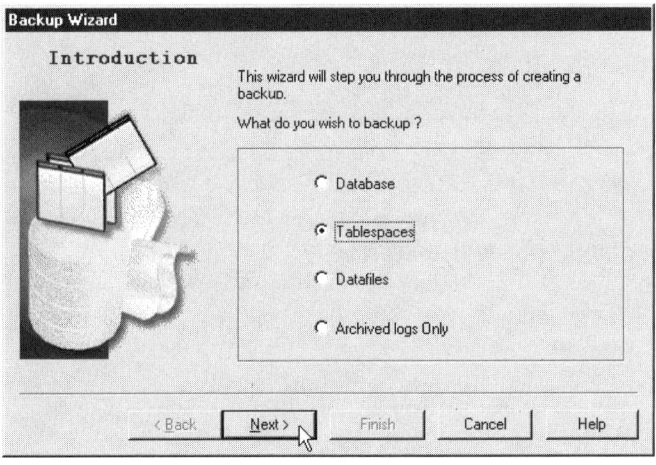

FIGURE 6-17. *Backup Wizard interface*

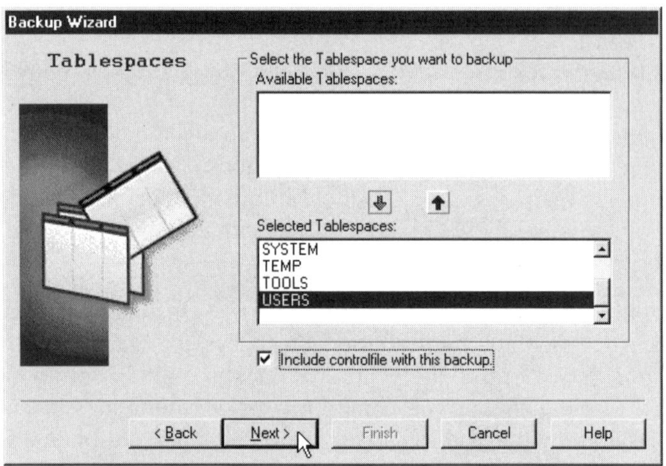

FIGURE 6-18. *Defining tablespaces and control files to back up in Backup Wizard*

8. Specify a backup tag name, as you did in step 8 and Figure 6-14 in the earlier section "Performing Offline Backups in Backup Manager." Then click Finish. When you attempt recovery, you can reference the backup you wish to use by way of the backup tag. Click Finish when finished, and then click OK after reviewing the summary.
9. The backup process will be submitted to the OEM Job Scheduler for execution. The status of that job's execution will appear in the OEM console.

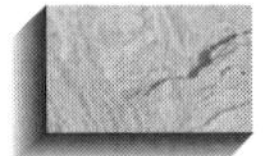

TIP
You may experience vague errors like `the database threw an exception` *running a backup if Backup Manager is open and running but the OEM console is not. Simply exit Backup Manager and restart the OEM console, then restart Backup Manager from within the console, and the errors should go away. Also, ensure that you have executed all setup steps before attempting a backup.*

For Review

Get some experience with the backup process in Backup Manager by setting up and executing different types of backup jobs.

Automating Backups with OEM Job Scheduler

You can automate the process of backing up your database using the Oracle Job Scheduler feature available in Oracle Enterprise Manager. Before doing so, you will need to be sure that the NT authentication required to perform an Oracle database backup is in place for the user who will actually need to perform the backup, or else the backup job will encounter errors when run. Follow these steps to perform that task:

1. Ensure that the NT user running the backup has the ability to log into NT as a batch job. Start by clicking on Start | Programs | Administrative Tools (Common) | User Manager to open the window shown in Figure 6-19.
2. In User Manager, click on the Policies | User Rights menu option. The User Rights Policy interface will appear. Ensure that the Show Advanced User Rights checkbox is selected. Select Log On As A Batch Job from the Right pull-down list. This is all shown in Figure 6-20.
3. Next, click the Add button to show the Add Users and Groups interface, displayed in Figure 6-21. The OEM client machine should appear in the List

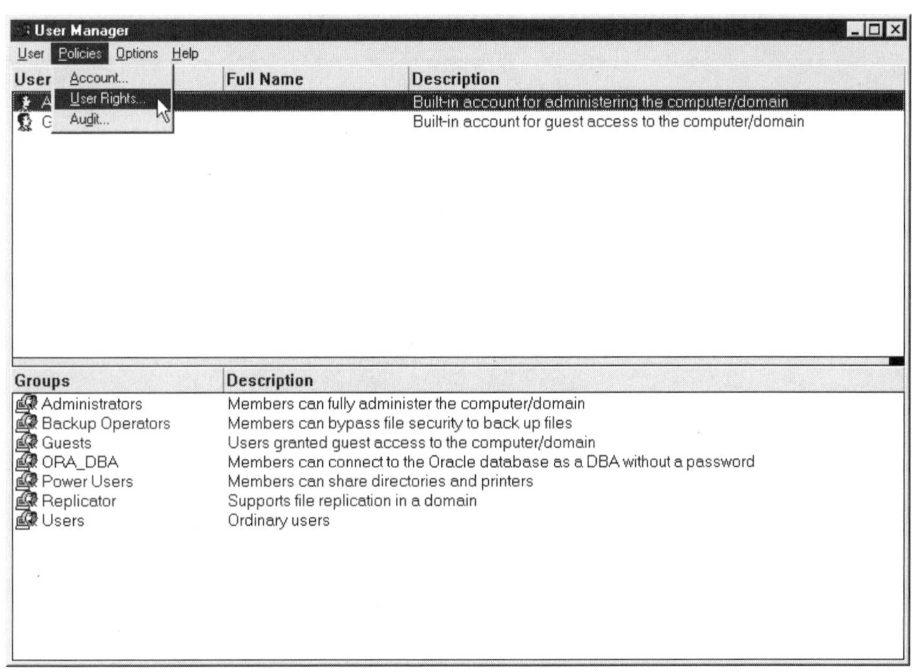

FIGURE 6-19. *User Manager interface*

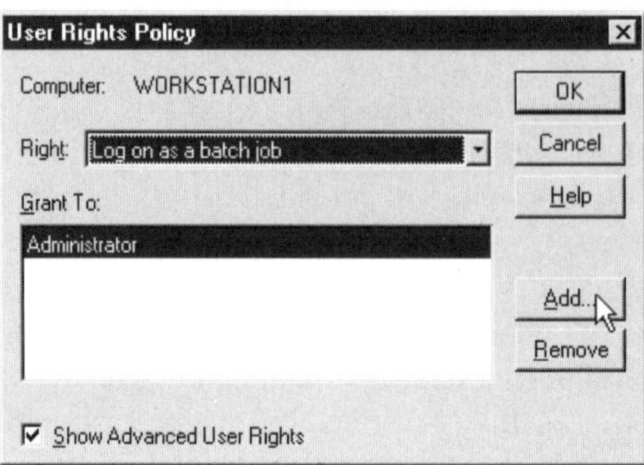

FIGURE 6-20. *User Rights Policy interface*

Names From drop-down box at the top of the interface. Click on the Show Users button.

4. Set who will perform backups by scrolling to the bottom of the Names window, where user names will appear. Then click Add, and then click OK. Click OK again. Then click File | Exit to exit the User Manager tool.

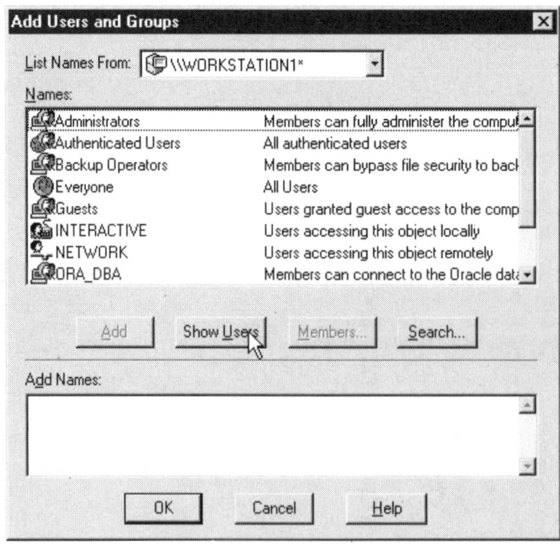

FIGURE 6-21. *Configuring batch login permissions in User Manager*

Configuring Automated Backups in Backup Manager

After completing up to step 8, in the process defined in either "Performing Offline Backups in Backup Manager" or "Performing Online Backups in Backup Manager," you can schedule your defined backup to be a regularly occurring backup process in the following way:

1. Instead of clicking Finish in step 8 of either process, click on Next twice instead. You will wind up in the Schedule interface.
2. Define the frequency of your backup by choosing an option from the Execute drop-down list.
3. Define the date when Backup Manager should start execution of this job as well.
4. When finished, click Finish and return to step 9 in either "Performing Offline Backups in Backup Manager" or "Performing Online Backups in Backup Manager" to finish defining your backup job.

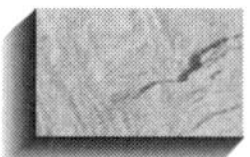

TIP

You can monitor the status of your executing job from within Backup Manager as well as in the OEM console. In Backup Manager, drill down to the dbname.dbdomain */ Jobs node. On the right side of the interface, click on the Job History tab. You will then see the history of all backup jobs executed for the database. If you see a "failed" status for any job, you can double-click on that listing to see the job output for debugging.*

For Review

Understand how to use Backup Wizard for automating periodic database backups.

When and How to Recover Your Database

The best way to learn how to recover your database is in a testing situation, but nobody ever listens to the voice of reason. Until then, we'll cover these topics:

- Different crash scenarios
- Complete recovery in `noarchivelog` mode

- No data loss and fast recovery with archive logs
- Turning on `archivelog` mode
- Recovery in `archivelog` mode

Recovering from the inevitable database crash is why you take backups. This section will teach you what you need to know about database crashes. You will learn first about the different types of crash scenarios and what they mean in terms of database recoverability. You will then learn about complete database recovery when your database is running in `noarchivelog` mode. After discovering the limitations of recovery in this mode, you will learn how to enable fast recovery and ensure zero data loss by archiving redo logs in Oracle's `archivelog` mode. You will then learn how to turn on `archivelog` mode in your Oracle database. Finally, you will learn how to recover your Oracle database running in `archivelog` mode.

Different Crash Scenarios

There are several different scenarios for failure in the Oracle database. These scenarios can be divided into five general categories. The five categories are statement failure, user-process failure, instance failure, user error, and media failure. Each of these categories has different implications for DBO intervention in recovering from the situation. Statement failure, user-process failure, and user error are discussed in this lesson.

TIP

It is beyond the scope of OCP exams and this text to discuss ways you can manage the human aspects of database failure situations. However technically adept you may become with your database administration, every DBO must still address the issue of customer service in making crisis situations more manageable. Depending on how high-stakes your organization's databases are, you might consider taking some training on effective communication as a means to round out your technical abilities in this area.

Statement Failure

When Oracle cannot process a statement issued by a user, this situation is generally known as *statement failure*. There are several causes for statement failure. First of all, a user may be attempting to issue a statement referencing a table that does not exist, or which they do not have permission to use. In this case, Oracle will issue the user an error that details both the area of the statement that contained the error and a reference to the Oracle error message code. Other types of statement failure include situations in which the statement is flawed, such as when a `select` statement has no `from` clause, or when the user tries to `insert` data into a table that exceeds their quota for doing so. Recovering from this error situation consists of Oracle immediately (and automatically) rolling back any changes made by the statement. The user may have to reissue the statement that failed with the proper syntax or table reference. You may have to alter the user's tablespace quotas or permissions as well.

User-Process Failure

The failure of a user process requires more intervention from the Oracle server. In some cases, the user may cancel or terminate the statement or process they are running with a CTRL-C command from SQL*Plus. Another cause might be if the client PC hangs while connected to Oracle. If a user process terminates, then the process monitor (PMON) background process intervenes, which saves the DBO some time and effort. PMON is there to handle automatic process recovery for the database: when PMON detects the process failure, PMON rolls back the failed process and releases locks on the tables.

User Error

Users occasionally make mistakes. Sometimes they accidentally delete data or drop database objects. This situation tests the limits of your backup and recovery strategy. If the problem is related to data change, the user may be able to recover using the `rollback` command. However, dropped tables or other objects may require DBA intervention and the use of Data Manager or other backup and recovery strategies. Usually, you need to recover the entire database to another machine, export the dropped or deleted object data, and restore the object to the appropriate environment. You may see this situation occur quite a bit in development environments where the developers are their own DBOs. You may want to consider informal or formal training (such as this book) for your developers if this situation gets aggravating. To avoid this problem in production, only the DBA or DBO should be allowed to create, alter, or drop database objects. By controlling the introduction, change, or removal of database objects in your production system, you reduce the likelihood that users become dependent on an unrecoverable database object.

Instance Failure

There are many possible causes of instance failure, including problems with the memory of the host system running Oracle, power outages, or background process failures. Although instance failure requires that you restart the database, the actual recovery is handled by Oracle via the system monitor (SMON) background process. After the DBO opens the database, SMON engages in the following steps to recover the instance:

1. SMON detects that instance recovery is required because checkpoint sequence numbers in the datafile headers are not synchronized.
2. DBW0 uses redo log information to write both uncommitted and committed data to datafiles. This is called the *roll-forward* process.
3. The database opens.
4. Either Oracle or user processes roll back all uncommitted work in progress at the time the instance failed, depending on who attempts to access the uncommitted data first.
5. After all uncommitted data is rolled back, the datafiles are again synchronized.

Oracle sometimes needs to keep certain online redo logs active after LGWR switches to a new one for the purpose of crash recovery. This situation is the crash you were learning about. After you start Oracle, SMON restores the instance to full operational capacity. It may take a while to recover the instance, depending on the transaction volumes on the database at the time of database failure. When instance recovery is complete, the users should be advised to reenter any transactions not committed at the time of database failure. You may also want to check the ALERT log to see what caused the failure. If the ALERT log contains an `ORA-00600` internal error, or another error that has generated core dumps of your Oracle SGA, or lists several numbers in square brackets (`[]`), call Oracle Worldwide Support. You will learn more about detecting high-severity issues and what to do when you find them in Chapter 7. For now, be aware of what to look for by reviewing the following code blocks:

```
Wed Nov 3 17:01:58 1999
Errors in file /u07/app/oracle/htprod/admin/htprod/bdump/
htprod_snp7_6109.trc:
ORA-07445: exception encountered:
core dump [npixfc()+596] [SIGSEGV] [Address not
mapped to object] [120] [] []
Wed Nov 3 17:04:02 1999
Restarting dead background process SNP7
SNP7 started with pid=23
```

```
Sun Oct 24 14:56:24 1999
Errors in file /u07/app/oracle/htprod/admin/htprod/bdump/
htprod_s000_3610.trc
ORA-00600: internal error code, arguments:
 [kghxhdr1], [], [], [], [], [], [], []
ORA-00600: internal error code, arguments:
 [729], [800], [space leak], [], [], [], [], []
Sun Oct 24 14:56:53 1999
found dead multi-threaded server 'S000', pid = (26, 1)
```

TIP
When recovering the instance, Oracle opens after the roll-forward process is complete in order to speed access to the database. Thus, uncommitted transactions may still be rolling back after the database is open and available for users.

Media Failure

Media failure means the loss of access to information on a disk due to data corruption, disk-head hardware failure, other types of I/O hardware failure, or accidental datafile deletion. Two types of media failure may occur on the database: temporary and permanent. If data on disk is temporarily unavailable (perhaps because a disk controller card failed), the problem can be corrected easily and quickly with a hardware replacement. If data on disk is permanently unavailable (perhaps because of physical or magnetic damage to the casing in which the disk is stored), the DBO must do two things:

1. Restore lost file(s) from backup copies of the database.
2. Apply database changes made after the most recent backup using archived redo log information (if archiving is used).

Backups and Recoverability

Your backup and recovery strategy is an insurance policy against problems in the database that render it unusable. Recovery usually requires a good understanding of both operating system–specific commands for physical file manipulation and Oracle's recovery mechanisms. The amount of time spent recovering the database depends on several factors:

- **Accessibility of backups** Both the physical location of backups (onsite or offsite) *and* the accessibility of backups on hardware storage media are factors. Disk is the fastest medium; tape is slower.

- **Frequency of backups** More frequent backups mean faster recovery because fewer archived redo logs need to be applied for the same amount of recovered data.
- **Type of failure** Some types of failure are easier to fix and less time consuming than others. For example, if the database lost one disk drive that contained only a few read-only tablespaces, the DBO would spend less time recovering than if the database lost several disks of volatile data that were backed up infrequently.
- **Type of backups** Physical backups provide better recoverability than logical exports, because archived redo can be applied to handle the changes made after the most recent backup was taken.

What Is Synchronization?

A point was made earlier that SMON will perform instance recovery if it detects that the datafiles are not synchronized. Part of the job Oracle performs during a checkpoint is to write the SCN to datafile headers and copy data in the buffer cache and log buffer to their respective disk files. This process synchronizes all Oracle files. If the instance crashes, these files will not be synchronized because Oracle did not have the opportunity to synchronize them before the instance failed. SMON will synchronize them for you automatically.

If media failure occurs, you will restore the lost datafiles from an earlier backup, and the headers for those files will have a different sequence number than the undamaged files. You will have to synchronize these datafiles yourself through the use of archived redo logs. Oracle will not open the database unless all datafiles are synchronized, except when the datafiles that are not synchronized are either offline or part of a read-only tablespace.

Recovery Implications of archivelog and noarchivelog Databases

There are several advantages to recovering databases running in `archivelog` mode over recovering databases running in `noarchivelog` mode. Perhaps the most important of these benefits is the ability to recover past the point of your most recent backup. You cannot recover past your most recent backup if your database is not running in `archivelog` mode. Thus, the major benefit of this setup is that no committed data need ever be lost in the event of media failure.

Another nice recovery benefit of `archivelog` databases is that the recovery in most cases can be performed while the database is open and available to your users. The only exceptions to this are when your database experiences media failure to the datafiles of the SYSTEM tablespace or a tablespace containing online rollback segments. In general, you need to restore those files that were damaged by the

Important Note: Using a Recovery Catalog Database
In this discussion, it is assumed that you have two separate databases available for use in the exercises, one acting as the recovery catalog database. For me, this is the MINX database. The other database is the one that is being recovered. This is the PUMA database, and it is running in `noarchivelog` mode. You can create a second database for yourself using the Oracle Database Assistant, covered in Chapter 2. You will need to perform a full backup on that new database before proceeding, so this is an excellent chance to review the tasks outlined for performing a backup in the previous section, "Performing Full Database Backups." For the rest of this section, assume that we have already taken a backup of the PUMA database using the methods presented in the next sections of the chapter.

media failure only when recovering `archivelog` databases. Recall that you needed to restore all database files from backup when recovering your `noarchivelog` database.

It takes longer to recover your database in `archivelog` mode than it takes to recover `noarchivelog` databases. This is because recovery time is a factor of the time it takes to restore the backup database files and archived redo logs from tape *plus* the time it takes to apply those archived redo logs to the lost database files. This isn't really an advantage or disadvantage, because although it generally takes less time to recover a `noarchivelog` database than an `archivelog` database, your recovery of an `archivelog` database yields greater data recoverability and user satisfaction.

Another disadvantage of recovering an `archivelog` database is the fact that you need to have every single archived redo log taken between the most recent backup and the present time in order to have complete recovery. If even one is missing, the best you can hope for is recovery to the point in time prior to the missing archived redo log. However, even this limitation usually means you will be able to recover to a point in time more recent than what you could get with the backup by itself.

Archived redo logs also take up space on disk, which can become a problem if you are working in development or test environments testing data loads or conversions. Working with Oracle running in `noarchivelog` mode is fine for development and test environments, where recovering the data is secondary to providing the architecture for application development.

For Review

1. What are the five types of failure that may occur on an Oracle database? How is instance failure detected? How is it resolved?
2. What is the difference between temporary media failure and permanent media failure? How is media failure resolved?
3. What is database synchronization? Why is it so important in detecting and resolving instance failure?
4. When is it appropriate to run Oracle in `noarchivelog` mode? Why? When would it be more appropriate to use Oracle in `archivelog` mode? Again, explain why.

Complete Recovery in noarchivelog Mode

"Restoring" is probably a more accurate way to describe database recovery when you operate your database in `noarchivelog` mode. For `noarchivelog` databases, you must recover every datafile, control file, and redo log from full backup to resolve media failure. Essentially, you are overwriting your current database with datafiles from an older version. For this reason, the database cannot be open for use during complete recovery. *You will also lose any data changes made between the time the last backup was taken and the time the failure occurred.* To illustrate a failure that may occur on your database, use Windows Explorer to rename a datafile on your database to something else. After that, the following steps are necessary for performing complete recovery:

1. Open the OEM console by clicking on Start | Programs | Oracle Enterprise Manager | Enterprise Manager. Connect as the repository software owner on the MINX database, which in our case is OEM.
2. Drill down to Networks | Databases | *dbname.dbdomain* (PUMA.WORLD, in our case) to specify that your next operation is to be executed on this database. Be sure you have already defined your INTERNAL or SYSDBA login preferences to that database in File | Preferences within the OEM console.
3. Click on the Backup Manager button, or on the Tools | Applications | Backup Manager menu item. Only one instantiation of Backup Manager can run at a time, so close any other Backup Manager windows that may be open.
4. Click on the Oracle8 Recovery Manager radio button to use that backup/recovery subsystem.

5. If your database is running in `noarchivelog` mode (the PUMA.WORLD database is), Backup Manager will inform you that certain backup and recovery operations will not be possible. Click OK to dismiss the message.

6. The database must be mounted, but not open, for database recovery. Click on the *dbname.dbdomain* node (PUMA.WORLD, in our case) on the left side of the interface. Click on the Database Mounted radio button. Then click on the Apply button. Backup Manager prompts you to select a shutdown mode. Any mode is fine, including `shutdown abort`. Then click OK.

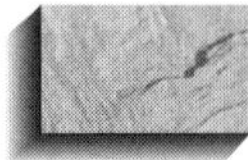

TIP
In real-life DBO situations, if it is necessary to fix any hardware as part of database recovery, shut down the database by clicking on the Shutdown radio button for step 6. Power off the machine that's hosting Oracle and replace any damaged hardware. Then turn the machine back on, repeat steps 1 through 6 to mount the database, and proceed from there.

7. In Backup Manager, click on Recover | Restore Wizard. For `noarchivelog` databases, you will only be able to perform full database recovery, as shown in Figure 6-22. Click Next in the wizard to proceed.

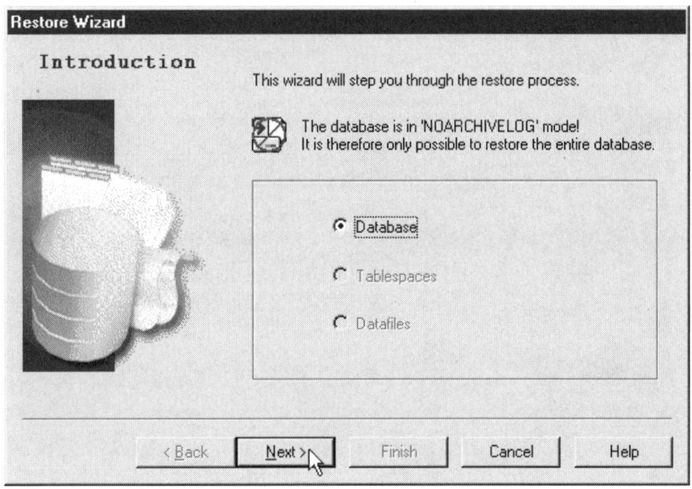

FIGURE 6-22. *Restore Wizard interface*

8. The next interface allows you to restore files to a new location. This screen is provided so that you can recover your database to different disks in the event that hardware cannot be fixed before recovering. Figure 6-23 shows the interface.
9. Select the channel you will use to recover using the interface you have already seen for backing up your database in Figure 6-13. Click Finish.
10. You will then be prompted to review the job you just defined. Click OK, and Backup Manager will submit your restore job.

TIP
Remember, because this database was running in `noarchivelog` mode, you will lose all data changes made to the database since the most recent backup was taken. To restore those changes, you will have to reenter the data manually.

For Review

Experiment with recovery using Backup Manager. Also, make sure you understand the data loss implications inherent with running your database in `noarchivelog` mode.

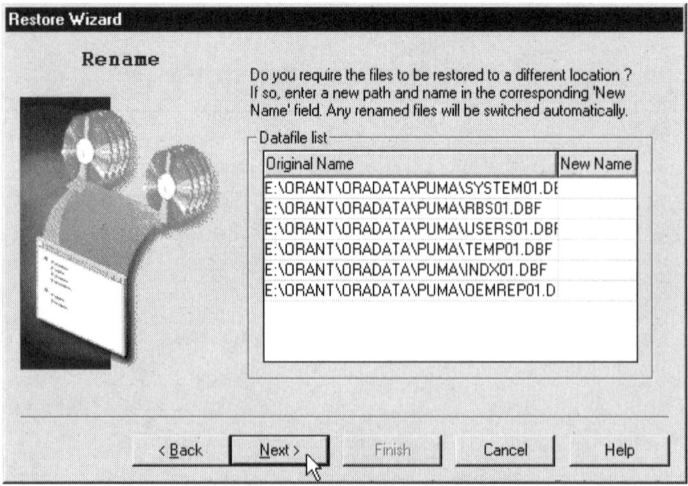

FIGURE 6-23. *Restoring datafiles to alternate locations in Restore Wizard*

No Data Loss and Fast Recovery with Archive Logs

In many situations, media failure for databases running in `noarchivelog` mode will be damaging. Remember, *all data changes made between the last backup and the failure will be lost.* If your database is characterized by heavy data-change activity by users, your recovery needs would be best served by archiving redo logs, because re-creating all the changes made by those users will be a time-consuming and frustrating process for them and you. Archiving your redo logs allows you to restore all data changes made to the database up to the point in time of the failure, in best-case situations, saving your users a great deal of time and aggravation.

Turning on archivelog Mode

You can use Instance Manager and the SQL*Worksheet tool to turn on `archivelog` mode in your Oracle database. To do so, you must perform the following tasks:

1. In OEM console, drill down to the Networks | Databases | *dbname.dbdomain* node for the database you want to put into `archivelog` mode (PUMA.WORLD, in this case).
2. Click on the Tools | Applications | Oracle Instance Manager menu item, or click on the Instance Manager button in the OEM toolbar.

3. In Instance Manager, click in the Database | Archive Log menu option. Your database must be mounted, but not open, for `archivelog` mode to be initialized. If your database is open, Instance Manager will prompt you to select the shutdown option you want to use. Choose any option other than `shutdown abort`.
4. You will be prompted whether you are sure you want to put the database into `archivelog` mode. Click Yes.
5. You will then be prompted to select whether you want to enable automatic archiving. This is when Oracle will automatically copy archived redo logs to your archive destination for you, behind the scenes, so you should click Yes.
6. The automatic archiving setting you define in step 5 will be valid only for the current run of the instance. If you restart Oracle later, automatic archiving will not be enabled. To set automatic archiving permanently on your instance, set the `LOG_ARCHIVE_START` parameter to TRUE in your `init.ora` file.

7. You will need to define an archiving destination for Oracle in your `init.ora` file using the `LOG_ARCHIVE_DEST` parameter. The value for this parameter is the absolute path for the archive destination directory on your host machine, such as the one listed in the following code block:

```
LOG_ARCHIVE_DEST='E:\orant\database\archive'
```

8. You will need to define the format of your archive log filenames in your `init.ora` file using the `LOG_ARCHIVE_FORMAT` parameter. The format for archived redo log names can include a static text string plus archive sequence formatting values shown in Table 6-1. However, since the archived redo logs will be created in a particular sequence, you can use some format conventions to identify your archived redo logs according to the data the logs contain. Many organizations find that `<SID>%S` works well in most situations. The following code block illustrates this:

```
LOG_ARCHIVE_FORMAT = PUMA_%S
```

9. Shut down your database completely in Instance Manager by clicking on the Shutdown radio button and clicking Apply. This step ensures that the new settings in your `init.ora` file take effect.
10. Open your database by clicking on the Database Open radio button in Instance Manager and clicking Apply.
11. In OEM console, open SQL Worksheet by clicking on the Tools | Applications | Oracle SQL Worksheet menu item, or by clicking on the SQL Worksheet button on the OEM toolbar. Ensure that you are logged into the database you just enabled archiving on as a privileged user like INTERNAL or with `sysdba` privileges.

12. In SQL Worksheet, issue the `alter system switch logfile` command. Figure 6-24 illustrates.
13. To verify that the location and filenaming format were specified correctly, you can open Windows Explorer, drill down to the directory you identified previously in step 7, and look for your newly archived redo log, as shown in Figure 6-25.

FIGURE 6-24. *SQL Worksheet with output from the* `switch logfile` *command*

FIGURE 6-25. *Windows Explorer with archive log displayed*

Format	Description
%S	Log sequence number, a sequential number representing the number of redo logs that have been written and archived since archiving began, the instance started, or the sequence was reset by resetlogs. When capitalized, the sequence number used to name the file will be padded to the left with zeros.
%s	Log sequence number, a sequential number representing the number of redo logs that have been written and archived since archiving began, instance started, or sequence reset by resetlogs, as in the preceding description. However, in this case, the value will not be padded to the left with zeros.
%T	Thread number for the redo logs of that instance within the Oracle Parallel Server architecture. When the format convention is capitalized, the thread number used in filenaming will be padded with zeros to the left. A thread is a running set of redo log information for one instance within a parallel database server.
%t	Thread number for the redo logs of that instance within the Oracle Parallel Server architecture, not padded to the left with zeros. Again, a thread is a running set of redo log information for one instance within a parallel database server.

TABLE 6-1. *LOG_ARCHIVE_FORMAT Formatting Characters*

TIP
Always shut down the database and take a full backup of it after enabling or disabling archivelog mode because the contents of the control file are changed. If you don't perform this step and you have to perform a complete recovery of your database using a cold backup taken when Oracle was running in noarchivelog mode, you will be unable to recover your database, even if you have the archived redo information.

For Review

1. What are the steps for putting a database into archivelog mode?

2. What `initsid.ora` parameters are involved in setting up archive redo logs, and what purpose does each serve?

3. What option for the `alter system` statement is used for switching redo logs in Oracle?

Recovery in archivelog Mode

Recovery when your database is running in `archivelog` mode happens in the following way. First, since you are archiving all transactions that occur against your Oracle database, you will not need to restore every datafile, only the one(s) that were lost in the media failure. For example, if you accidentally deleted the `users01.dbf` file corresponding to your USERS tablespace while the PUMA database was shut down, you do not need to restore every datafile in your database as you did with recovery of the PUMA database when it was running in `noarchivelog` mode. Instead, you need to restore only the lost database files and all archived redo logs generated since that backup datafile copy was taken from backup. After that, the recovery can take place. For this next exercise, assume we've already shut down the PUMA database and taken a complete backup of it (including archive logs). Note that the PUMA database should be mounted, but not open, when recovery is attempted. The steps for recovery of the `users01.dbf` file are as follows:

1. Open the OEM console by clicking on Start | Programs | Oracle Enterprise Manager | Enterprise Manager. Log in to the repository database (MINX) as the OEM repository owner (OEM).

2. Drill down in the OEM console to the Networks | Databases | *dbname.dbdomain* node for the database you wish to recover (PUMA). Click on SQL Worksheet.

3. Within SQL Worksheet, obtain current status for the missing `users01.dbf` file by issuing the `select name, status from v$datafile` command. The output is shown in Figure 6-26.

4. Bring the missing datafile offline within Oracle by issuing the `alter database datafile 'e:\orant\database\users01.dbf' offline` command.

5. Launch Backup Manager from the OEM console using the Backup Manager button on the toolbar, or with the Tools | Applications | Oracle Backup Manager menu option.

6. Click on the Oracle8 Recovery Manager backup/recovery subsystem radio button.

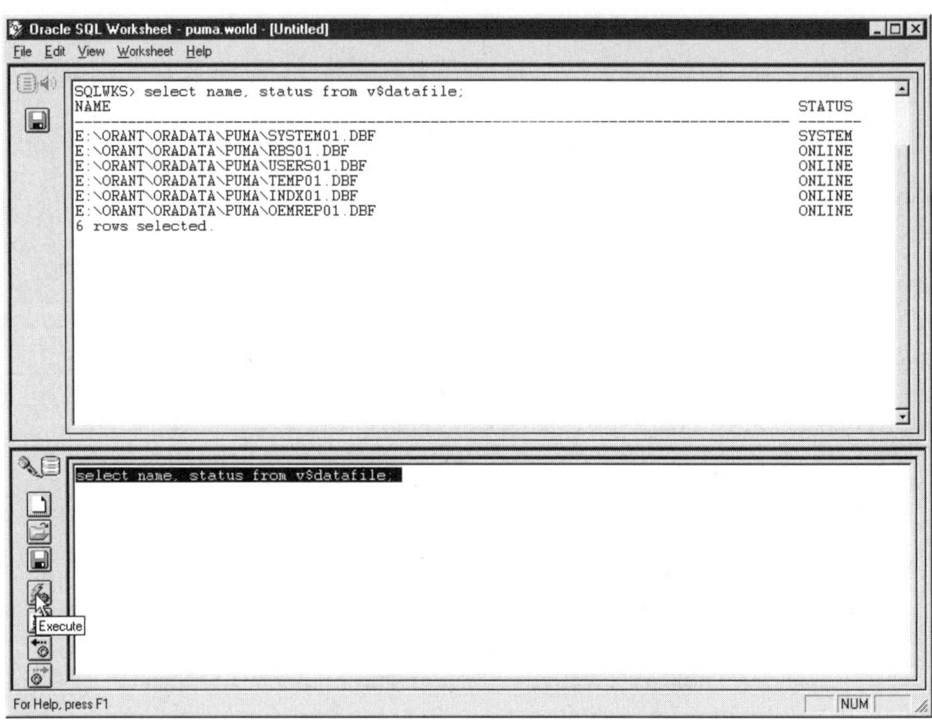

FIGURE 6-26. *Obtaining deleted datafile status within Oracle*

7. Backup Manager will then open. You will immediately be prompted that your `users01.dbf` datafile is missing and needs recovery, as shown in Figure 6-27. Click OK.

8. In Backup Manager, click on the Recover | Restore Wizard menu option. In the first interface of the wizard, select the Datafiles radio button, as shown in Figure 6-28.

9. Select the datafile you want to restore from the list of values (`users01.dbf`, in this case), and then click on the down arrow button. The interface is shown in Figure 6-29. When you've completed the selection of your datafiles, click Next.

10. If a disk has been lost, you can restore the datafile to a new location using the Restore Wizard interface shown in Figure 6-23. If you want to restore to the old location, just click Next.

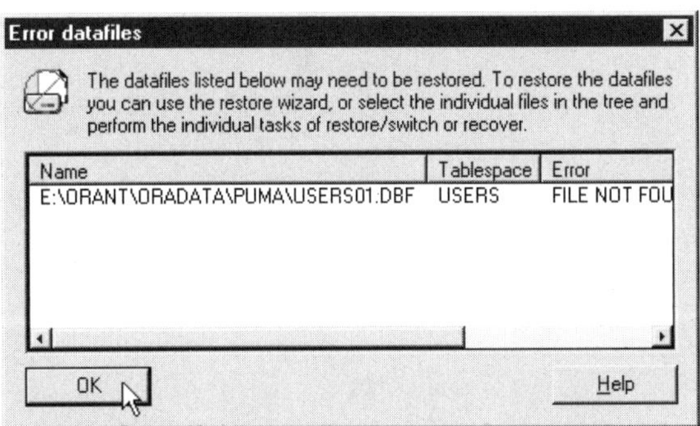

FIGURE 6-27. *Error datafiles prompt*

11. Select a channel to restore from using the Backup Wizard interface shown in Figure 6-13. Then click Finish.
12. Your restore job might take a short time to complete. When it does finish, you can return to the SQL Worksheet interface and issue the `alter database datafile 'e:\orant\database\users01.dbf' online` command.
13. In Instance Manager, click on the Database Open radio button and then on Apply to open your database. You might be prompted to confirm your request. Click Yes. The database should open normally.

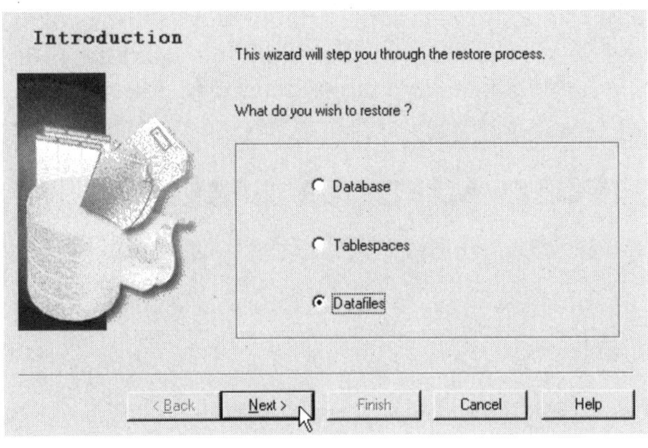

FIGURE 6-28. *Restore Wizard interface*

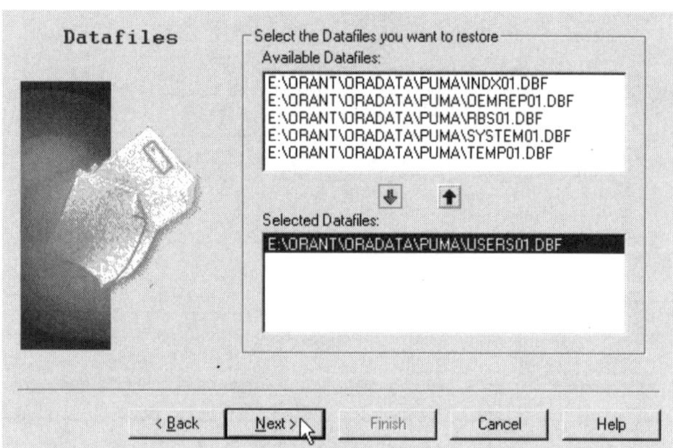

FIGURE 6-29. *Selecting datafiles to restore*

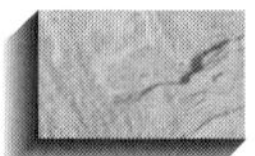

TIP
Since your database is running in `archivelog` *mode, every committed transaction should appear in your database up to the point in time of the media failure, not just changes made before the most recent database backup. This is a key point to know for the OCP DBO exam.*

For Review

Make sure that you understand that you can restore datafiles and tablespaces in addition to entire databases when running Oracle in `archivelog` mode. Also, you should understand the process for recovering said datafiles and tablespaces using the Backup Manager tool.

Loading Non-Oracle Data

No database exists in a vacuum, it seems, so we'll discuss getting other system data into Oracle:

- Types of table constraints
- Disabling constraints with Schema Manager
- Loading data with Data Manager

- Reenabling constraints with Schema Manager
- Automating data loads using OEM Job Scheduler

This section covers how to load data into Oracle databases. You will often need to do this, particularly if your work environment has many databases that feed information into each other. In this section, you will learn about different types of table constraints, and how to disable these constraints using Schema Manager. You will also learn how to use Data Manager, and how to reenable constraints after data loads using Schema Manager. Finally, you will learn about load automation using the Job Scheduler function in Oracle Enterprise Manager.

Types of Table Constraints

Before pursuing the topic of data loads, you should prepare yourself by ensuring that you understand what is meant by the term *constraint*. Tables created in an Oracle database can contain *integrity constraints*—rules that limit the type of data that can be placed in the table, row, or column. There are five types of integrity constraints: `PRIMARY KEY`, `UNIQUE`, `FOREIGN KEY`, `CHECK`, and `NOT NULL`. Two methods exist for defining constraints: the *table constraint method* and the *column constraint method*. The constraint is defined as a table constraint if the `constraint` syntax is part of the table definition, located away from the column datatype definition. The constraint is defined as a column constraint if the constraint definition syntax appears as part of a column definition. All constraints can be defined either as table constraints or as column constraints, except for `NOT NULL` constraints, which can be defined only as column constraints. The following code block displays two `create table` statements. The first shows definition of the `PRIMARY KEY` constraint defined as a table constraint, while the second shows definition of the primary key as a column constraint:

```
-- Table constraint definition
CREATE TABLE employee
(empid          NUMBER(10),
lastname        VARCHAR2(25),
firstname       VARCHAR2(25),
salary          NUMBER(10,4),
CONSTRAINT      pk_employee_01
PRIMARY KEY     (empid));

-- Column constraint equivalent definition
CREATE TABLE employee
(empid          NUMBER(10) primary key,
lastname        VARCHAR2(25),
firstname       VARCHAR2(25),
salary          NUMBER(10,4));
```

The main difference between use of table and column constraint definition methods is your ability to name your constraints yourself only when you define your constraint using the table constraint method. When you use the column constraint definition method, Oracle names the constraint for you. For simplicity, throughout the rest of the chapter, you will work with constraint definitions defined as table constraints. Later in the book, you may see constraints defined both as table and column constraints.

PRIMARY KEY Constraint Details

The definition of a column as the primary key in a table produces a few noticeable effects within the database itself. The term *primary key* refers to a special designation for a constraint that says to Oracle, "don't let any row insert a column value for EMPID that is NULL or that is the same as a column value that already exists for another row." Oracle will use some special methods to enforce this integrity constraint. Column values that are part of primary keys have a number of conditions enforced on them. First, any value in the column for any row must be unique. Second, no row can define the value in a column as NULL if that column is part of the primary key. So, in this example, no employee in the EMPLOYEE table can have a NULL value defined for EMPID.

TIP

Integrity constraints are rules that are defined on table columns that prevent anyone from placing inappropriate data in the column. There are five types of integrity constraints: `PRIMARY KEY`, `FOREIGN KEY`, `UNIQUE`, `NOT NULL`, and `CHECK`.

Take another moment to review the definition that was determined for the BANK_ACCOUNT table. Remember that the BANK_ACCOUNT table was supposed to have the BANK_ACCT_NO column be its primary key because that column defines the data that is unique about each row in the table. However, remember also that there is a special relationship between the BANK_ACCOUNT table and the EMPLOYEE table.

```
CREATE TABLE bank_account
(bank_acct_no         VARCHAR2(40),
empid                 NUMBER(10),
BANK_ROUTE_NO         VARCHAR2(40),
BANK_NAME             VARCHAR2(50),
CONSTRAINT            pk_bank_acct_01
PRIMARY KEY           (bank_acct_no),
CONSTRAINT            fk_bank_acct_01
FOREIGN KEY (empid) REFERENCES employee (empid));
```

FOREIGN KEY Constraint Details

Notice that in addition to the definition of a PRIMARY KEY constraint, this table also has a FOREIGN KEY constraint. The syntax for the definition allows the column to reference another table's column, of either the same or a different name. In order for a FOREIGN KEY constraint to be valid, the columns in both tables must have exactly the same datatypes. The designation FOREIGN KEY tells Oracle that the developer would like to create referential integrity between the EMPID columns in the BANK_ACCOUNT table and the EMPLOYEE table. This fact prevents a column in the child table (BANK_ACCOUNT) from containing a value that does not exist in the referenced column in the parent table (EMPLOYEE).

An option that can be specified along with the foreign key relates to the deletion of data from the parent. If someone attempts to `delete` a row from the parent table that contains a referenced value from the child table, Oracle will block the deletion unless the `on delete cascade` option is specified in the foreign-key definition of the `create table` statement. When the `on delete cascade` option is used, Oracle will not only allow the user to `delete` a referenced record from the parent table, but the deletion will cascade into the child table as well.

```
CREATE TABLE bank_acct
(bank_acct_no         VARCHAR2(40),
empid                 NUMBER(10),
BANK_ROUTE_NO         VARCHAR2(40),
BANK_NAME             VARCHAR2(50),
CONSTRAINT            pk_bank_acct_01
PRIMARY KEY           (bank_acct_no),
CONSTRAINT            fk_bank_acct_01
FOREIGN KEY (empid) REFERENCES employee (empid)
ON DELETE CASCADE);
```

UNIQUE Constraint Details

The definition of a UNIQUE constraint on HOME_PHONE prevents anyone from defining a row that contains a phone number that is identical to the phone number of anyone else already in the table. There are two weaknesses in this definition. The first is that having a UNIQUE constraint on a home phone number makes it difficult to store records for employees who are spouses or roommates with the same telephone number. Another point to be made about UNIQUE constraints, and FOREIGN KEY constraints for that matter, is that no data integrity is enforced if the column data value in a row is NULL. This is a special case scenario that applies only to NULL data in columns with FOREIGN KEY, UNIQUE, and CHECK constraints defined on them.

```
CREATE TABLE employee
(empid          NUMBER(10),
lastname        VARCHAR2(25),
firstname       VARCHAR2(25),
salary          NUMBER(10,4),
home_phone      number(15),
CONSTRAINT      pk_employee_01
PRIMARY KEY     (empid),
CONSTRAINT      uk_employee_01
UNIQUE          (home_phone));
```

TIP
FOREIGN KEY, CHECK, and UNIQUE integrity constraints for a column are not enforced on a row if the column data value for the row is NULL.

NOT NULL Constraint Details

Notice that in this table definition, *three* columns are defined to be NOT NULL, including the primary key. The two others are the LASTNAME and FIRSTNAME columns. The NOT NULL table constraint will be applied to the columns, preventing anyone from creating a row for this table that does not contain a first and last name for the employee. The NOT NULL constraint prevents the data value defined by any row for the column from being NULL. By default, primary keys are defined to be NOT NULL. All other constraints are nullable unless the developer explicitly defines the column to be NOT NULL.

CHECK Constraint Details

Notice also that the CHECK constraint has been created on this table. CHECK constraints have a number of limitations, all centering around the fact that the constraint can refer only to a specific set of constant values or operations on those values. A CHECK constraint cannot refer to another column or row in any table, including the one the constraint is defined on, and it cannot refer to special keywords that can have values in them, such as user, sysdate, or rowid. Thus, the CHECK constraint in the previous table definition is valid, but the one in the following excerpt from a table definition is not valid:

```
CREATE TABLE address
(...,
city    VARCHAR2(80)  check(city in (SELECT city FROM cities))
...);
```

CHECK constraints allow Oracle to verify the validity of data being entered on a table against a set of constants that act as valid values. For example, you could specify that the SALARY column not contain values greater than $500,000. If someone tries to create an employee row with a salary of $1,000,000 per year, Oracle would return an error message saying that the record data defined for the SALARY column has violated the CHECK constraint for that column.

```
CREATE TABLE employee
(empid          NUMBER(10),
lastname        VARCHAR2(25)      NOT NULL,
firstname       VARCHAR2(25)      NOT NULL,
salary          NUMBER(10,4)      CHECK(salary<500000),
home_phone      number(15),
CONSTRAINT      pk_employee_01
PRIMARY KEY     (empid),
CONSTRAINT      uk_employee_01
UNIQUE          (home_phone));
```

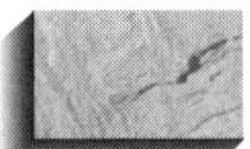

TIP
Some special keywords contain information about certain database conditions. These keywords, or pseudocolumns, are `user`, `sysdate`, and `rowid`. The `user` keyword gives the username of the owner of the current session. The `sysdate` keyword gives the current date and time at the time the statement is issued. The `rowid` keyword gives the ROWID of the row specified. These keywords cannot be used in conjunction with a `CHECK` constraint.

For Review

Understand the five types of constraints in an Oracle database.

Disabling Constraints with Schema Manager

Before you load data into an Oracle database table using Data Manager, you'll usually want to disable constraints on that table. This step usually improves the performance of the data load by reducing the overhead Oracle will usually perform to enforce whatever rules are associated with the constraint(s) in question. Schema Manager can be used to disable constraints in Oracle in the following way:

1. In the OEM console, click on the Tools | Applications | Oracle Schema Manager menu item, or click on the Data Manager button in the OEM toolbar.

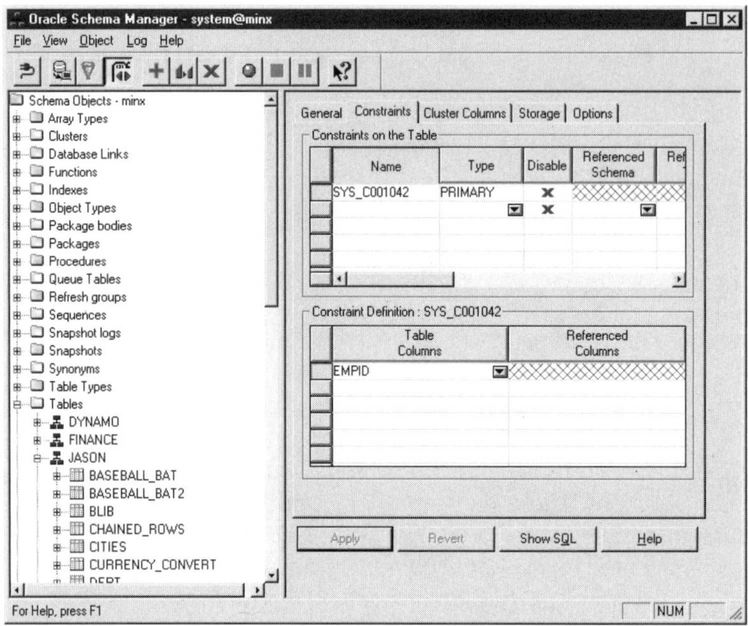

FIGURE 6-30. *Schema Manager Constraints tab interface*

2. Drill down to the Schema Objects—*SID* | Tables | *Schema* | *Tablename* node. In this case, the SID will be MINX, the schema JASON, and the tablename EMP. A set of tab interfaces will appear on the right. Click on the Constraints tab. Figure 6-30 illustrates what you should see.
3. In the top table appearing in the Constraints tab interface, click on the *X* that appears in the Disable column to indicate that you want to disable that constraint. Then click the Apply button. Figure 6-31illustrates.
4. Do this for all the constraints on the database object you are preparing to load.

For Review

Understand how to disable constraints in Schema Manager.

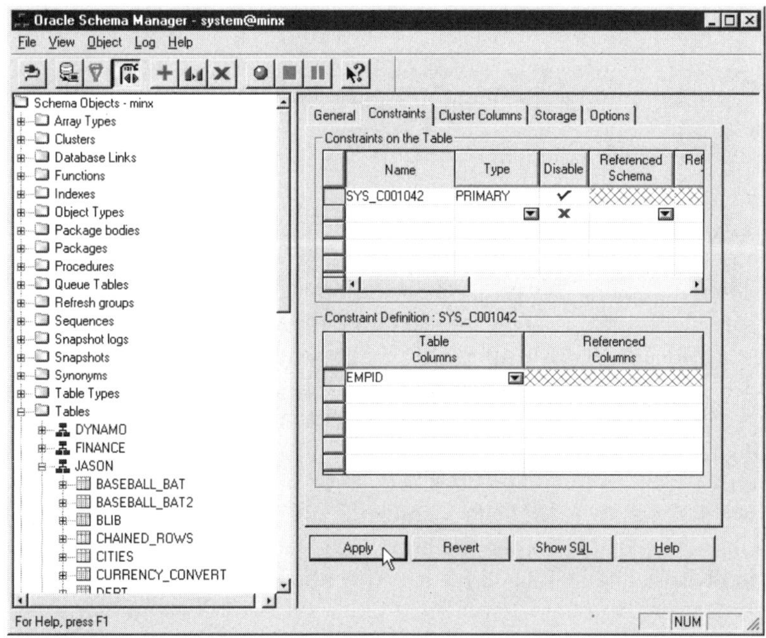

FIGURE 6-31. *Schema Manager with constraint being disabled*

Loading Data with Data Manager

If you are used to working with Oracle on the command line, Data Manager is a GUI tool in Oracle Enterprise Manager that is similar to SQL*Loader. It allows you to load data into an Oracle table from a flat file, where each row of information in the flat file will correspond to a row of data in a table. Before using Data Manager, you should understand its elements. The first is the data to be loaded, which is stored in a *datafile*. Don't confuse the Data Manager datafile with Oracle server datafiles that store database objects. The next is a set of controls for data loading that are defined in a *control file* (not to be confused with Oracle server's control file). These controls include specifications of how Data Manager should read and parse records, which columns should be loaded by data position, and other features.

Steps for Performing Data Loads

The key point to remember about data loads are the four steps you should take when performing a data load of any substantial degree:

1. Back up the existing data first. This step is optional but highly recommended in case of an error in the load.

2. Disable constraints on tables. This reduces the time Oracle spends maintaining indexes that support the constraint.
3. Load data from datafile. Oracle will know the format of incoming data based on the control file you provide for the load.
4. Reenable your table constraints.

Conventional versus Direct Path Data Loads

Data Manager provides two data paths for loading data. They are the *conventional* path and the *direct* path. Whereas the conventional path uses a variant of the SQL `insert` statement, with an array interface to improve data load performance, the direct path avoids the RDBMS altogether by converting flat file data into Oracle data blocks and writing those blocks directly to the database. Conventional-path data loads compete with other SQL processes and also require DBWR to perform the actual writes to database.

Figure 6-32 depicts the differences between conventional- and direct-path loads. In a conventional load, Data Manager reads multiple data records from the input file into a bind array. When the array fills, Data Manager passes the data to the Oracle RDBMS engine or optimizer for insertion. In a direct load, Data Manager reads records from the datafile, converts those records directly into Oracle data blocks, and writes them to disk, bypassing most of the Oracle database processing. Processing time for this option is generally faster than for a conventional load.

At the beginning of the direct-path load, Data Manager makes a call to Oracle to put a lock on the tables being inserted, and it makes another call to Oracle again at the end to release the lock. During the load, Data Manager makes calls to Oracle only to get new extents when necessary or to reset the highwatermark when data saves are required. A *highwatermark* is a marker in Oracle tables and other objects that indicates the maximum size the object has grown to.

A data save is the direct-path equivalent to a `commit`. A list of behaviors and actions the Data Manager direct path assumes and takes is given here:

- Partial data blocks are not used, so the server process is never required to do a database read of a "free list" to determine which blocks are available for storing more data.
- No SQL `insert` commands are used.
- The bind array is not used; Data Manager creates database blocks and writes them directly to storage. This feature allows the tool to avoid contending with other SQL statements for database buffer cache blocks.
- The direct path allows for presorting options, which enables the use of operating system high-speed sorting algorithms, if they are available. This speeds the creation of indexes and primary keys.

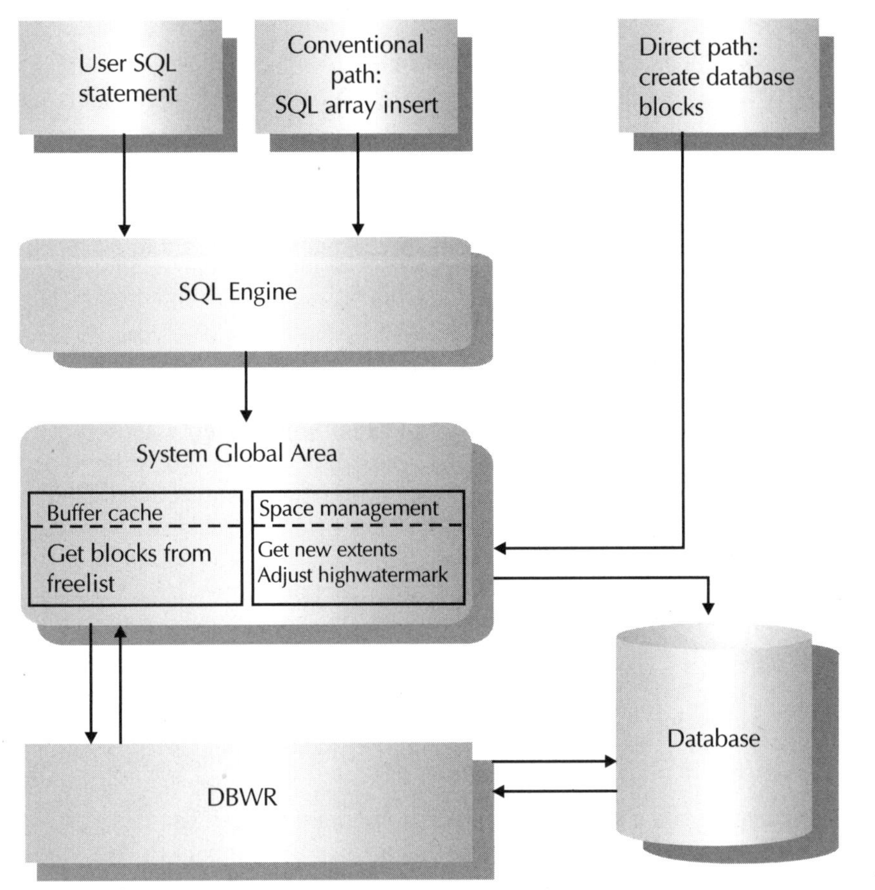

FIGURE 6-32. *Database paths for conventional and direct loads*

- Since Data Manager writes data directly to disk, in the event of instance failure, all changes made up to the most recent data save will be stored on disk, limiting the need for recovery.

Deciding to Use Direct-Path Load

Direct-path loading helps when a great deal of data must be loaded in a short period of time. Direct-path loads bypass the "customs inspectors" of the Oracle database—namely, integrity constraints, as well as the "post office," or table indexes, of the database. Unfortunately, the safety and performance conditions provided by indexes and integrity constraints must be met at some point. Therefore, the direct path operates on a "pay me later" principle; the index updates have to happen at some point, so after the DBO completes the direct-path load, developers will need to reapply the constraints and rebuild the indexes so as to put the Oracle database back together before users can access the data loaded in the direct path. Use the direct path in the following cases:

- When loading a large amount of data in a short time frame
- When increasing load performance by using parallel loading
- When loading a character set not supported in the current session (or when the conventional load of that character set produces errors)

Deciding to Use Conventional-Path Load

The advantages of conventional-path loading result from it being relatively nondisruptive to the underpinnings of a database table. Conventional-path loads work on the same principles that normal data inserts work, only much faster. Records in a conventional-path load pay their dues to the Oracle database as the records load; that is to say, the records loaded on the conventional path will update the associated indexes with a table and generally have the look and feel of normal online transaction processing. Use the conventional path in the following cases:

- When loading data across a network
- When loading data into a clustered table
- When loading a small amount of data into a large indexed table or a large table with many integrity constraints (it takes longer to drop and re-create a large index than to insert a few rows in the table and index)
- When applying single-row operations or SQL functions to data being loaded

Backing Up Table Data

Though optional, it is highly recommended that you back up the data in the table you are about to load *before* loading it. You never know when you might need to back out of a data change and restore old data. If running in `archivelog` mode, you can rely on the most recent backup plus applying archived redo logs to get your old data back; however, it could be a long process for recovery. If running in `noarchivelog` mode, you won't be able to get your old data back past the point of the most recent database backup. To export the data in a table, execute the following steps:

1. In the OEM console, launch Data Manager by clicking on the Tools | Applications | Oracle Data Manager menu item, or by clicking on the Data Manager button in the OEM toolbar.

2. In the Data Manager interface, drill down to the *SID* | Users | *Schema* | *Tablename* node. In this case, the SID is MINX, the schema Jason, and the tablename EMP. Right-click on this node, and select the Export option from the menu that appears. Figure 6-33 illustrates.
3. The first interface of the Data Manager Wizard asks you to define the location and name of your dump file, as shown in Figure 6-34. Click Next.

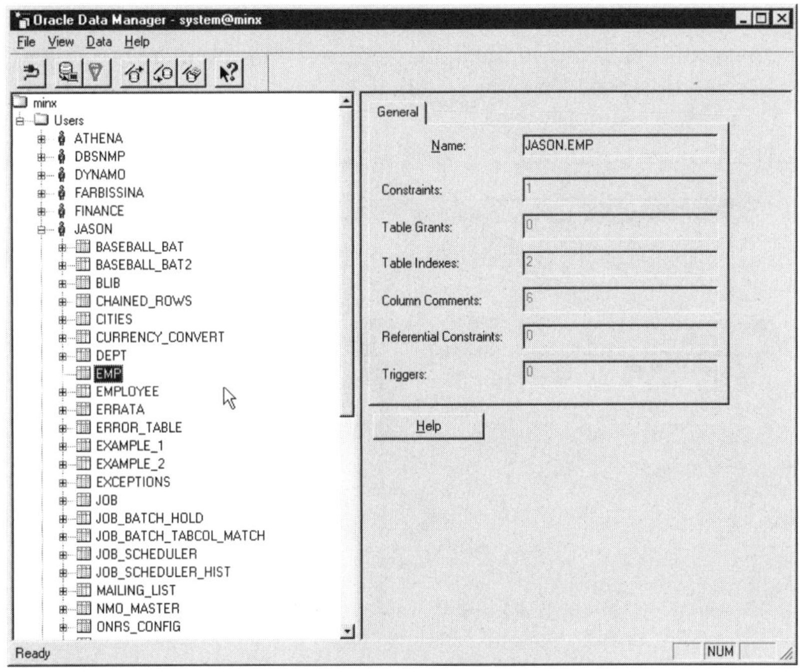

FIGURE 6-33. *Data Manager interface*

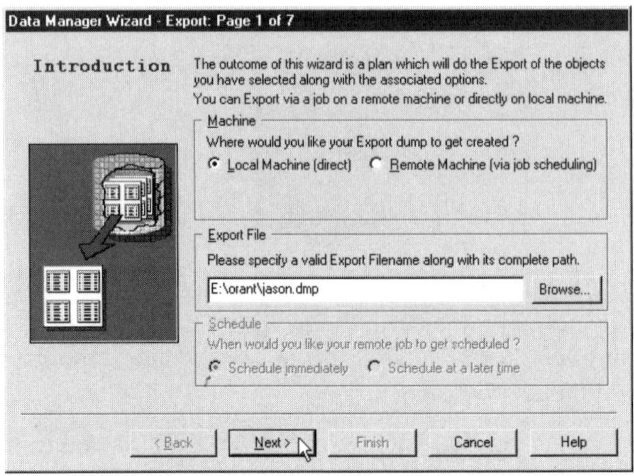

FIGURE 6-34. *Specifying export dump file location*

4. The next screen, shown in Figure 6-35, will show you the object you selected to export. You can either click Next to set advanced export options or simply click Finish.

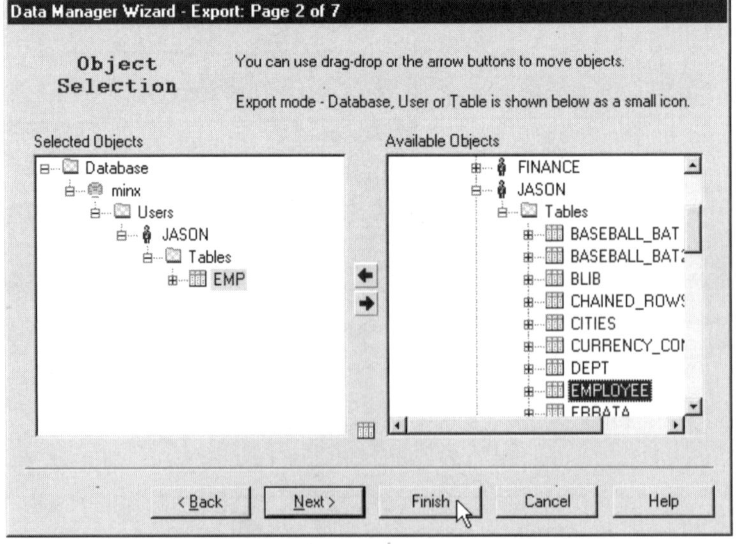

FIGURE 6-35. *Specifying object to be exported*

5. Review the export actions you just defined, and then click Finish again. Your data will then be exported. The progress and/or any errors encountered will be noted in an output window. When the export is finished, you can click Dismiss in the output window.

Removing Table Data Prior to Loading

In some cases, you may want to remove all data from the table you are about to load. This is accomplished using SQL Worksheet or SQL*Plus, using the `delete from` *`schema.tablename`* command, followed by `commit`. Alternatively, if the table is large (say, several hundred thousand rows or more), you may instead want to issue the `truncate table` *`schema.tablename`* command, which does not need to be followed by a `commit` command. The `truncate table` command can run much faster on large table data removal operations than the `delete` command.

TIP
The `truncate` or `replace` keyword in a Data Manager control file can be used as a way to eliminate the need for execution of this step entirely.

Defining Your Data Manager Control File

Once you have optionally saved your data and/or removed existing data from the table you want to load, you can execute the data load in Data Manager. You first need to define your control file, which in turn defines how Data Manager can expect to parse the information found in the data file. The control file provides the following information to Oracle for the purpose of the data load:

- Datafile name(s) and format
- Character sets used in the datafiles
- Datatypes of fields in those files
- How each field is delimited
- Which tables and columns to load

The following code block shows an example of a Data Manager control file. In this example, the control file itself can contain data. The control file does not always need to contain the data to be loaded, however.

```
LOAD DATA
INFILE *
INTO TABLE JASON.EMP
FIELDS TERMINATED BY "," OPTIONALLY ENCLOSED BY '"'
```

```
(empid, lastname, firstname, salary, dept, hire_date)
BEGINDATA
"02039", "WALLA","RAJENDRA",60000,"604B","01-JAN-96"
"39334", "SMITH","GINA",75000,"604B","15-MAR-97"
"60403", "HARPER","ROD",45000,"504A","30-APR-79"
"49539", "QIAN","LEE",90000,"504A","25-MAY-99"
"49392","SPANKY","STACY",100000,"604B","14-FEB-98"
```

TIP
You can find a control file containing the text in the prior code block on the CD-ROM that comes with this book, called `chapter6.ctl`*. Note that the schema owner of this table, JASON, may not exist on your database. Make sure you change it to the schema owner of the EMP table on your database before attempting this load.*

Comments can appear anywhere in the control file and need be delimited only by two dashes. Care should be taken not to place comments in the datafile or in the data portion of the control file.

The `load data` clause generally indicates the beginning of the contents of the control file. For all control files, the `infile` clause is required. It denotes where Data Manager can find the input data for this load. Using an asterisk (*) denotes that the data is in the control file.

The next line of the control file is the `into` table clause. It tells Data Manager the table to which the data will be loaded and the method by which it will be loaded. The `append` keyword denotes that these records can be inserted even if the table has other data. Other options include `insert`, which allows records to enter the table only if the table is empty; and `replace` and `truncate`, which delete all rows from the table before loading the new records.

The `fields terminated by` clause defines how columns will be delimited in the variable-length data records. The character that separates each data element is enclosed in double quotes. Also, an optional enclosure character is defined with the `optionally enclosed by` clause.

The next line begins with a parenthesis, and within the parentheses, the columns in the table to be loaded are specified. If a column from the table is not listed in this record, it will not be loaded with data from the datafile. The data loaded in each column will be selected from the data record positionally, with the first item in the record going into the first column, the second item into the second column, and so on.

Finally, in cases where the data is included in the control file, the `begindata` clause is mandatory for denoting the end of the control file and the beginning of the data. This clause need not be present if the data is in a separate file.

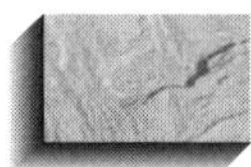

TIP
Put data in your control file only if you are doing a small data load. You can also find sample control files on the Oracle8 installation in the following directory: `x:\orant\rdbms80\loader`.

Loading Data into the Table

Using your control file taken either from CD-ROM or keyed into a text file using WordPad, you can load data into your table using Data Manager in the following way:

1. Open Data Manager from the OEM console, if it isn't open already, using the Tools | Applications | Oracle Data Manager menu option, or the Data Manager button on the OEM toolbar.
2. Drill down to the *SID* | *Users* | *Schema* | *Tablename* node in Data Manager, and then right-click on that node. Select the Load menu option. This is shown in Figure 6-36.
3. Identify the name of your control file by browsing for it in the Data Manager Wizard interface, shown in Figure 6-37. You can set more

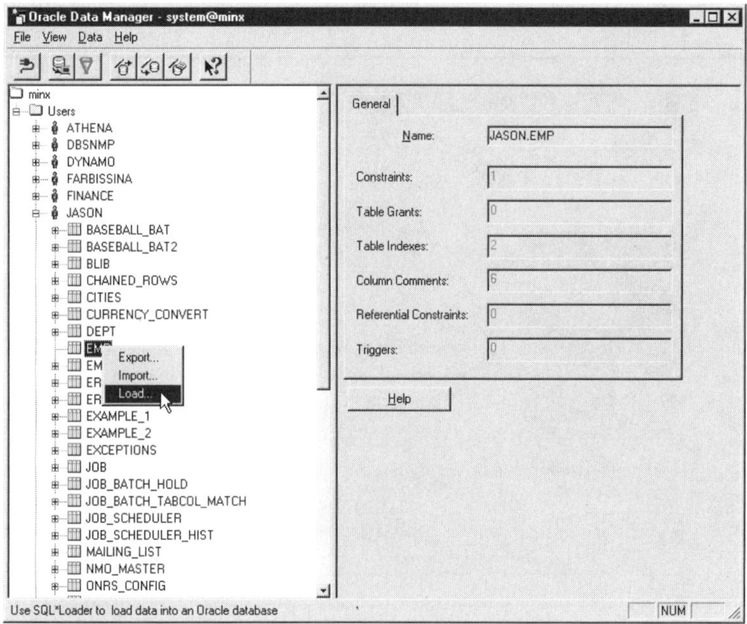

FIGURE 6-36. *Loading data using Data Manager*

advanced options for your data load, such as discard files, bad files, log files, and load path, by clicking Next to move through the other interface screens. Or you can simply run the load by clicking Finish twice.

4. Data Manager then displays the output messages it receives when attempting to load the data, shown in Figure 6-38. This will assist you in debugging the data load. You can click Dismiss when the load is complete.

TIP
*If you want to verify that your data really did load, you can do so by logging into Oracle via SQL*Plus, or using SQL Worksheet. If there are errors, you will see them in the output window or by looking in the log file generated by the data load.*

For Review

Be sure you understand the process for exporting data from Oracle and for loading data into Oracle via flat file.

Reenabling Constraints with Schema Manager

When loading is complete, you must reenable the constraints on your table using Schema Manager. This step is accomplished to prevent bad data from entering the

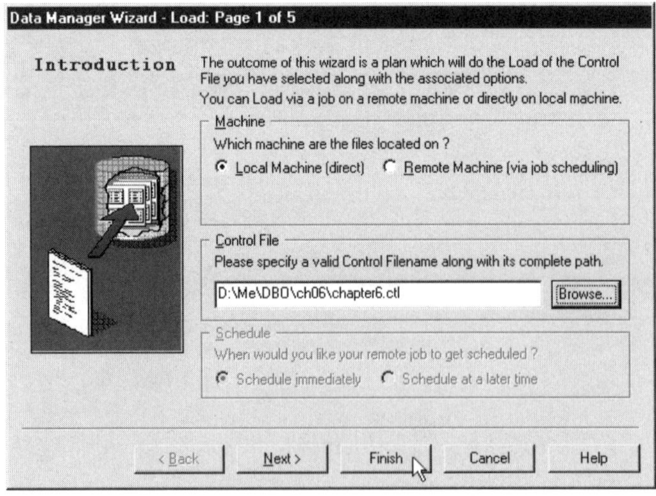

FIGURE 6-37. *Specifying control file location in Data Manager Wizard*

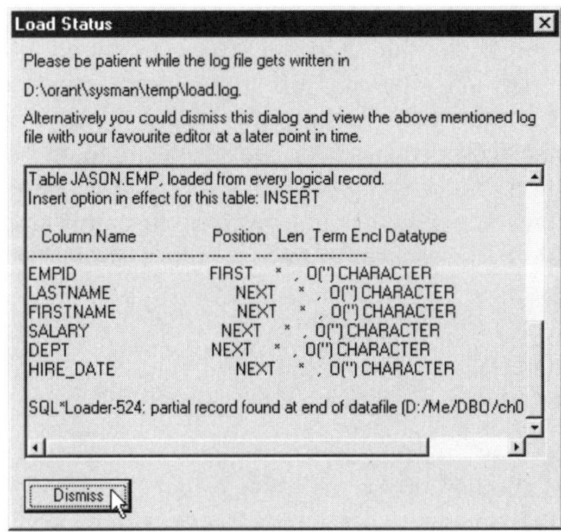

FIGURE 6-38. *Viewing load output*

table due to the constraints remaining disabled. To reenable the constraints, perform the following tasks:

1. From the OEM console, open Schema Manager using the Tools | Applications | Oracle Schema Manager menu option, or by clicking on the Schema Manager button on the OEM toolbar.
2. Drill down to the Schema Objects—*SID* | Tables | *Schema* | *Tablename* node (MINX, JASON, EMP, respectively). In the right side of the Schema Manager window, click on the Constraints tab interface.
3. In the top table, look for any constraints that have a checkmark in the Disable column. Click once on the checkmark to change it to an *X*. Then click Apply.
4. Do this for every constraint that is disabled for this object.

For Review

Be sure you remember that you always have to reenable constraints after disabling them for a data load, before the database is opened for general usage.

Automating Data Loads Using OEM Job Scheduler

You have already worked with the OEM Job Scheduler, albeit indirectly, when you learned how to automate a backup job in Backup Manager. In this section, you will learn how to automate a data load using the OEM Job Scheduler as well. The first task, setting up the "Log on as a batch job" privilege to an NT OS user, was explained in the section "Automating Backup with OEM Job Scheduler," earlier in this chapter. If you have questions about how to perform this task, you can refer to that previous discussion. The rest of the steps required for setting up a data load job are covered as follows:

1. From within the OEM console, click on the Job | Create Job menu item. The Create Job interface will appear. You will start off in the General tab in that interface.
2. Enter a name and description for your job in the appropriate text boxes. Then select the database you want this data load job to impact by clicking on that database listed in the Available Destinations window. Then click on the left arrow button to select that database. Figure 6-39 shows you the interface.
3. Click on the Tasks tab interface. From the list of available task names, select Load by clicking once on it and then clicking the left arrow button. Figure 6-40 shows you this interface.

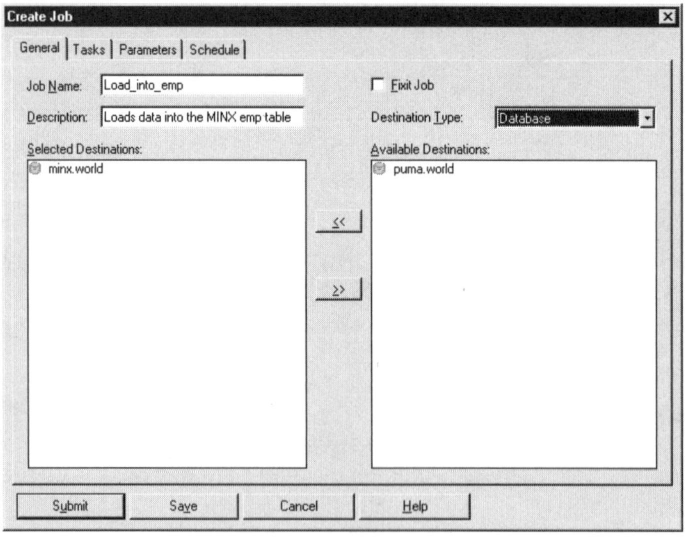

FIGURE 6-39. *Create Job interface*

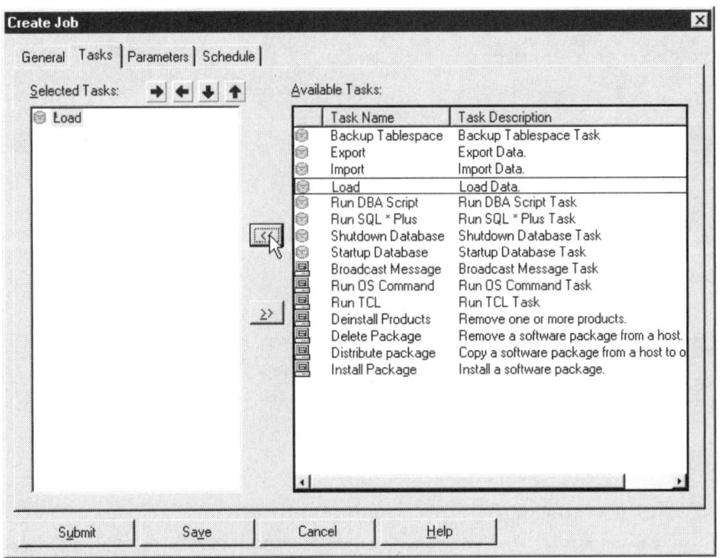

FIGURE 6-40. *Create Job Tasks interface*

4. Click on the Parameters tab interface. In the lower-right corner, you will see a text box in which you can specify a control file for this data load job. Browse for the `chapter6.ctl` control file you used earlier to enter data into the EMP table.

5. Click on the Create Job schedule interface. Here, you should define the job to execute periodically by selecting the Interval radio button. Then define when the first execution should be by choosing a date and time in the appropriate areas. Finally, specify the frequency with which the job should execute.

6. When finished, click the Save button. This will save the job under the Job Library tab in the lower-left window of the OEM console, shown in Figure 6-41.

7. If you want to execute the job, click on the job listing once under the Job Library tab interface. Then click on Job | Modify Saved Job. In the modification window, click the Submit button.

For Review

Know how to set up, save, and run a periodic data load using the OEM Job Scheduler.

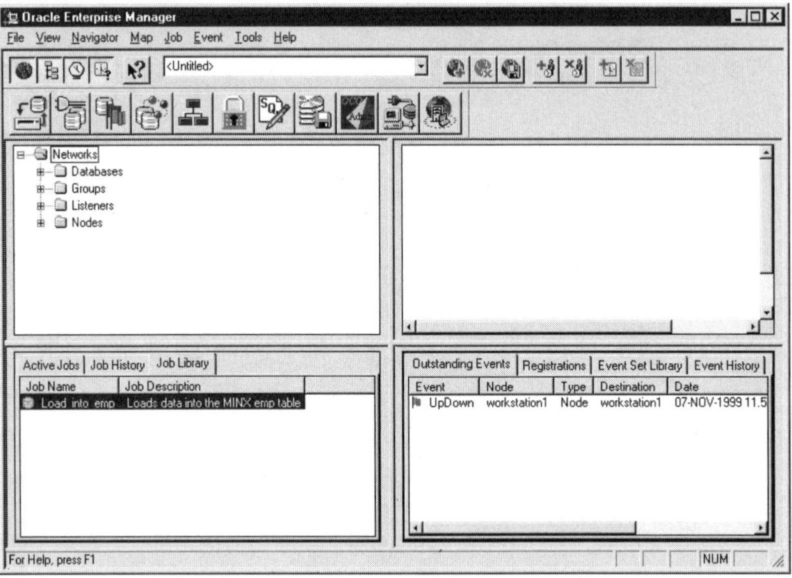

FIGURE 6-41. *OEM console with Job Library tab displayed*

Chapter Summary

This chapter covered a great deal of ground, judging from the number of interfaces into which you learned to enter data. You learned many topics having to do with database backup and recovery, as well as performing manual and automated data loads using the Data Manager tool in Oracle. You learned what factors come into play when trying to determine the frequency of database backups on your Oracle database. You also covered how to back up the database using OEM Backup Manager. The tasks for taking a full database backup were covered in some detail as well, along with the tasks required for automating backup of your Oracle database using the OEM job scheduling process.

Many tasks in the area of database recovery were covered in detail as well. You learned about the five different crash scenarios you can expect to encounter as an Oracle DBO, and what the recovery implications for each of those scenarios is as well. You learned about performing a complete recovery in Oracle when your database is running in `noarchivelog` mode. Then the chapter explained how Oracle's `archivelog` mode can eliminate data loss and provide flexibility in ensuring that production data is recoverable to the point of database failure. The tasks for putting Oracle into `archivelog` mode were covered in depth as well. The last area covered in the section on database recovery explained how to recover a database that is running in `archivelog` mode.

The final section of this chapter covered how to load non-Oracle data into your Oracle database using the Data Manager tool available through OEM. You covered the five different types of constraints on Oracle tables, and learned how and why to disable them before performing mass data loads. You learned about the conventional and direct paths Oracle can take for data loads, and how to decide which to use. The syntax and overall usage for Data Manager control files was covered in some depth as well. You learned the importance of and how to reenable table constraints after loading data into an Oracle table, and finally you covered how to automate the process of data loading using the OEM Job Scheduler.

Two-Minute Drill

- Data Manager loads data from a flat file to a table.
- There are several file components:
  - **Datafile** Contains all records to be loaded into the database
  - **Control file** Identifies how Data Manager should interpret the datafile
  - **Parameter file** Gives runtime options to be used by Data Manager
  - **Discard file** Holds records that Data Manager might reject, based on `when` conditions defined in the control file
  - **Bad file** Holds records that Data Manager might reject, based on constraint violations defined in your database
  - **Log file** Stores information about the execution of a Data Manager run, such as record counts and why records were rejected
- Data in the datafiles can be structured into fixed- or variable-length fields.
- The control file defines how Data Manager should interpret data from flat files, along with where Data Manager should put the data in the database.
- For variable-length data fields, appropriate delimiters must be specified.
- The two types of delimiters used are terminating delimiters and enclosing delimiters.
- There are two data load paths: *conventional* and *direct*.

- Conventional loads use the same SQL interface and other Oracle RDBMS processes and structures that other processes use.
- Conventional-path loading updates indexes as rows are inserted into the database, and also validates integrity constraints and fires triggers at that time.
- Direct-path loads bypass most of the Oracle RDBMS, writing full database blocks directly to the database.
- Direct-path loading disables indexes, insert triggers, and constraints until all data is loaded. Constraints and indexes are rechecked and built after data load.
- The direct-path load may occasionally leave an index in direct-path state. This often is due to load failure or the loading of a data record that violates the table's integrity constraints.
- Data Manager can export, or pull data out of, your Oracle database and put it into a file in binary format. Data Manager can also read the binary files it exports and load that data into the database.
- The three axioms of database backup and recovery for a DBO are these: maximize database availability, maximize recovery performance, and maximize data recoverability.
- Without backups, database recovery is not possible in the event of a database failure that destroys data.
- Three factors that should be considered when developing a backup strategy are the business requirements that affect database availability, whether the database should be recoverable to the point in time of the database failure, and the overall volatility of data in the database.
- Disaster recovery for any computer system can have the following impact: loss of time spent recovering the system, loss of user productivity correcting data errors or waiting for the system to come online again, the threat of permanent loss of data, and the cost of replacing hardware.
- The final determination of the risks an organization is willing to take with regard to their backup strategy should be handled by management. The DBO should advise management of any and all risks and the impact of any plan that management wants to enact regarding recovery.
- Complete recovery of data is possible in the Oracle database, but it depends on a good backup strategy.

- Testing backup and recovery strategy has three benefits: weaknesses in the strategy can be corrected, data corruption in the database that is being copied into the backups can be detected, and the DBO can improve their own skills and tune the overall process to save time.
- Physical backups are used to copy Oracle database files that are present from the perspective of the operating system. This includes datafiles, redo log files, control files, the password file, and the parameter file.
- There are two types of physical backups: offline backups and online backups.
- Offline backups are complete backups of the database taken when the database is closed. In order to close the database, use the `shutdown normal`, `shutdown transactional`, or `shutdown immediate` command.
- Archiving redo logs is crucial for providing complete data recovery to the point in time that the database failure occurs. Redo logs can be used only in conjunction with physical backups.
- When the DBO is not archiving redo logs, recovery is possible only to the point in time when the last backup was taken.
- Databases that must be available 24 hours a day generally require online backups because they cannot afford the database downtime required for logical backups or offline backups.
- Database recovery time consists of two factors: the amount of time it takes to restore a backup, and the amount of time it takes to apply database changes made after the most recent backup.
- If archiving is used, then the time spent applying the changes made to the database since the last backup consists of applying archived redo logs. If archiving is not used, then the time spent applying the changes made to the database since the last backup consists of users identifying and manually reentering the changes they made to the database since the last backup.
- The more changes made after the last database backup, the longer it generally takes to provide full recovery to the database.
- Shorter recovery time can be achieved with more frequent backups.
- Each type of backup has varied time implications. In general, offline physical database backups require database downtime.
- Only online database backups allow users to access the data in the database while the backup takes place.

- The more transactions that take place on a database, the more redo information is generated by the database.
- An infrequently backed-up database with many archived redo logs is just as recoverable as a frequently backed-up database with few online redo logs. However, the time spent handling the recovery is longer for the first option than the second.
- Read-only tablespaces need to be backed up only once, after the database data changes and the tablespace is set to read only.
- `init`*`sid`*`.ora` parameters involved in archiving include the following:
  - `LOG_ARCHIVE_DEST`, which identifies primary archive destination
  - `LOG_ARCHIVE_START`, which makes ARCH start running
  - `LOG_ARCHIVE_FORMAT`, which determines format conventions for archived redo logs
- A special trace file called the ALERT log contains information about several database-wide operations, including
  - Database startup and shutdown
  - `init`*`sid`*`.ora` parameter values
  - Tablespaces being created, altered, and dropped
  - Databases being altered
  - Rollback segments being created, altered, and dropped
  - Internal errors
  - Log switch activities
- Recovery when the database runs in `noarchivelog` mode is possible only to the point in time at which the most recent backup was taken.
- The advantage of running your database in `noarchivelog` mode, from a recovery perspective, is simplicity of backup and recovery.
- The disadvantage of `noarchivelog` mode is that you lose any data changes made after the most recent backup. This database operation mode is effective for development and testing environments.
- Database recovery for `noarchivelog` mode databases must be accomplished from full offline backups. *All* files must be restored from

backup, not just damaged ones, to ensure that the database is consistent at a single point in time.

- Review the step-by-step process for recovery of the database when running in `noarchivelog` mode, as it was outlined in the chapter.
- Recovery when the database runs in `archivelog` mode is possible to the point in time of media failure.
- The advantage of running your database in `archivelog` mode is that you have that additional level of recoverability and can run your database 24 hours a day, 7 days a week, while still being able to take backups.
- The disadvantage of `archivelog` mode is that recovery is somewhat more complex, and you need to make sure you have all the archived redo logs—from the time your backup was taken to the time of media failure. This database operation mode is effective for production database operation.
- Two components of database recovery when archiving is enabled are the database file backups and archived redo logs that can be applied in order to restore data changes made after the most recent backup.
- The types of database failure are user process error, statement failure, process failure, instance failure, and media failure.
- User error is when the user permanently changes or removes data from a database in error. Rollback segments give supplemental ability to correct uncommitted user errors, but usually the DBO will need to intervene for recovery.
- Statement failure occurs when something is syntactically wrong with SQL statements issued by users in the database. Oracle rolls back these statements automatically and issues an error to the user indicating what the statement problem was.
- Process failure occurs when the user session running against the database is terminated abnormally. Statement rollback, release of locks, and other process cleanup actions are performed automatically by PMON.
- Instance failure occurs when the instance is forced to shut down due to some problem with the host machine or an aborted background process. Recovery from this problem occurs when the instance is restarted. Instance recovery is handled automatically by the SMON process.
- Media failure occurs when there is some problem with the disks that store Oracle data, and the data is rendered unavailable. The DBO must manually intervene in these situations to restore lost data from backups.

- Temporary media failure usually results from the failure of hardware other than the actual disk drive. After the problem is corrected, the database can access its data again.
- Permanent media failure is usually the result of damage to data itself. Usually, the drive will need to be replaced and the DBO will need to recover the data on the disk from backup.
- Database backup and recovery is handled with OEM Backup Manager. Review how to conduct backups and recoveries using this tool.
- Data loads are handled with OEM Data Manager. Review how to conduct data loads and exports using this tool.

Chapter Questions

1. **After loading data into Oracle, you notice several rows are missing. Where would you look to see the data discarded by Data Manager when performing the load of data into the database?**

   A. Datafile

   B. Control file

   C. Command line

   D. Discard file

   E. Parameter file

2. **After running Data Manager with the conventional path, which file contains records that could not be loaded due to violating integrity constraints?**

   A. The parameter file

   B. The bad file

   C. The discard file

   D. The log file

3. **The DBO is planning a backup strategy for read-only tablespaces. A good plan for backups of a read-only tablespace may include which of the following?**

   A. Weekly offline backups and nightly online backups

B. Weekly online backups and monthly offline backups

C. Backing up the read-only tablespace once

D. Backing up the read-only tablespace once daily

4. The DBO has disabled archiving of redo logs in Oracle. Which of the following choices identifies the only recovery option available if the disk containing a data tablespace crashed?

A. Recovery to point of failure

B. Recovery to a point in time after the most recent offline backup

C. Recovery of data up to the point of the most recent offline backup

D. Recovery of data to the point of the most recent online backup

5. The DBO is evaluating backup and recovery strategies for a user population spread across 12 time zones. This user population is connected to the database 24 hours a day, 7 days a week. Which of the following backup strategies best accommodates the needs of this application?

A. Offline backups with archiving enabled

B. Online backups with archiving disabled

C. Online backups with archiving enabled

D. Offline backups with archiving disabled

6. Which of the following choices best identifies the task an Oracle DBO should perform before changing the archiving mode of an Oracle database?

A. Start the instance and mount but do not open the database

B. Back up the database

C. Take the tablespace offline

D. Issue the `archive log list` command from Server Manager

7. The DBO has just finished creating a database. Without putting the database into `archivelog` mode, the DBO can provide which of the following levels of service to users of the database in question?

A. 24-hour availability with guaranteed data recovery to the point of failure

B. Recoverability to the point of database failure

C. Recoverability to any point in time between the most recent backup and the failure

D. Recoverability to the point in time of the last backup

8. **Use of the `alter database rename file` command is most appropriate in which of the following situations?**

A. Recovery of unused damaged redo log files

B. Recovery when a disk cannot be replaced

C. Recovery when there is no backup datafile

D. Recovery when `noarchivelog` mode is used

9. **The DBO is about to execute a complete recovery from media failure. Three datafiles were damaged. Which of the following choices indicates the files the DBO should restore to perform this recovery if the database was running in `archivelog` mode?**

A. All datafiles in the database

B. All datafiles in tablespaces with damaged datafiles

C. All damaged datafiles only

D. All archived redo logs only

Answers to Chapter Questions

1. D. Discard file

Explanation The discard file contains records that you specified Data Manager should reject because of the `when` clause. Choice A is incorrect because the datafile can only contain data used for input. Choice B is incorrect because the control file actually contains the restriction, not the discarded records. Choice C is incorrect because the command line is used to define your parameters for the run. Choice E is incorrect because the parameter file is basically used for the same thing as choice C.

2. B. The bad file

Explanation The parameter file for Data Manager contains runtime parameters used to control the data load, eliminating choice A. The discard file is similar in function to the bad file but contains data rejected by user-defined reasons as part of the `when` clause, while the bad file contains rejected data for database-definition reasons, such as violating integrity constraints. This difference eliminates choice C. The log file contains information about the Data Manager run, such as the start and stop times and the number of records rejected, but not the records themselves. This eliminates choice D.

3. C. Backing up the read-only tablespace once

Explanation Since data cannot change in them, read-only tablespaces need to be backed up only once. All other backup strategies are recommended for more volatile databases.

4. C. Recovery of data up to the point of the most recent offline backup

Explanation Recovery to the point of your offline backup is the only option you have, because the only type of physical backup available to you when redo logs are not archived is offline backups. Thus, choice C is right. All other choices require that you archive your redo logs in Oracle.

5. C. Online backups with archiving enabled

Explanation A database with users in 12 time zones must be available 24 hours a day. With a user base so globally defined, the best option in this situation usually involves online backups. This narrows you down to choices B and C. However, choice C is correct because choice B is logically impossible—you cannot take online backups if redo logs are not archived.

6. A. Start the instance and mount but do not open the database

Explanation In order to change the archiving status of the database, the database must not be open. The instance has to be started and the database mounted, however, because the DBO is making a change to the control file. Choice B might be correct if the question asked for a task to complete after the archiving status is changed, but that's another question entirely. The other choices are simply wrong.

7. D. Recoverability to the point in time of the last backup

Explanation Without putting the database into `archivelog` mode, you can guarantee recoverability only to the point of the last database backup. This fact should be sufficient for you to eliminate choice A, which can be given only if archiving is enabled. Choice B is eliminated as well, because the choice basically describes complete recovery. Choice C is eliminated because the choice describes incomplete recovery. You should know by now that these two things are only possible once you start archiving your redo logs.

8. B. Recovery when a disk cannot be replaced

Explanation When you need to move your datafiles, as is the case when you cannot wait for hardware replacement to recover your database, you can use the `alter database rename file` command to make the change in your control file. Choice A is incorrect because recovering unused online redo logs requires a different set of commands. Choice C is incorrect because there is a separate set of procedures for re-creating your datafile for recovery when there is no backup. Choice D is incorrect because renaming files is neither appropriate nor inappropriate for situations in which you plan to recover a database that is not archiving its redo logs.

9. C. All damaged datafiles only

Explanation You would restore damaged datafiles only on databases running in `archivelog` mode because the application of archived redo information will make the database read consistent. Choices A and B are incorrect because although you can restore more datafiles than those that are damaged, your recovery will take longer because there will be more redo information to apply. Choice D is incorrect because you don't just need archived redo logs on hand for the recovery, you need datafiles, too.

CHAPTER 7

Database Tuning and Troubleshooting

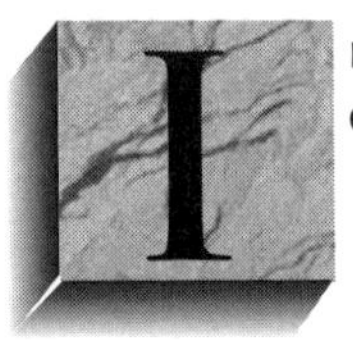

n this chapter, you will cover the following topics related to Oracle database tuning and troubleshooting:

- Anticipating Oracle issues
- Solving blocking situations
- Handling high-level performance tuning

In real-life Oracle database operation, it is highly advisable for you to ensure that your organization maintains OracleMETALS, the Web-, phone-, and consultant-based support service available from Oracle Corporation. METALink is available at http://metalink.oracle.com. Of course, there are lots of other things you need to know about troubleshooting Oracle tuning and other issues. In this chapter, you will learn how to anticipate Oracle issues such as database unavailability, space issues, and other conditions that may cause database outages. You will also learn how to solve blocking situations in Oracle. A blocking situation occurs when one user has been given access to a resource and other users are waiting for that resource to become free to continue their work. Finally, you will learn how to perform high-level performance tuning and the tools that Oracle makes available for this purpose.

Anticipating Oracle Issues

In this section, we will cover how to anticipate and troubleshoot the following Oracle issues:

- Troubleshooting: When the database is down
- Troubleshooting: Fixes for space allocation issues
- Troubleshooting: Resolutions for archive and trace issues
- Automating problem detection: OEM Job Scheduler
- Automating problem detection: OEM Event Service

You can troubleshoot problems with Oracle databases in two ways—by waiting for the problems to arise and then fight them, or by trying to see into the future to prevent problems. From numerous years of working with Oracle software, I can tell you that you will spend at least some of your time troubleshooting Oracle database problems in the first way—it's a computer system, so the unforeseen is inevitable. The key to your success as a DBO is how much time you can spend troubleshooting in the second way—by anticipating the problems and solving them in advance. This section covers the most common "serious problems" you might encounter as a DBO, and what to do to both resolve and prevent them.

Troubleshooting: When the Database Is Down

So many things can cause your database to fail that it isn't worth listing them all to have you try to prevent them. The key thing with database availability is figuring out a way to ensure that you will know right away when the database is down or unavailable to users. Once such way is through the use of event sets in the Oracle Enterprise Manager console. In order to use event sets in the console, your Oracle Intelligent Agent must be running on the server side. OEM console can detect what it needs to only if the Intelligent Agent is running. If you have an Oracle database in front of you that you've been working on through the examples in the book, ensure that your Intelligent Agent software is running on that database before proceeding through the rest of the chapter. You learned how to set up and start the Intelligent Agent in Chapter 3. If necessary, flip back to that chapter to refresh your understanding.

Once you've ensured that Intelligent Agent is running, you can begin working with event sets. Numerous event sets, predefined in OEM, can be used for detecting when the database is up or down, among other things. The following list shows you the predefined events in OEM and the activity they can handle for your database monitoring needs:

- **Oracle DB UpDown** Detects whether the database is up or down.
- **Oracle Host UpDown** Detects whether the machine hosting Oracle is up or down.
- **Oracle Listener UpDown** Detects whether the TNS listener is up or down.
- **Oracle DB Fault** Detects faults occurring on the database, such as a blocked user.
- **Oracle DB Resource** Detects resource issues in Oracle, such as full tablespaces.

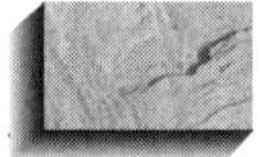

TIP
In addition to sending messages to the OEM console related to event detection, Intelligent Agent can also save messages when the OEM console is not running. The agent will keep checking to find a running OEM console, and when one is available again, the agent will send messages to that console.

Specifying Agent Polling Frequency

A key event set that ensures detection of database availability is the UpDown event set. As part of defining the UpDown event set, you must specify the frequency that Intelligent Agent will check for database availability at an interval that works for your organization. This is called the *polling frequency.* To check the polling frequency for a particular event set, perform the following tasks:

1. Start the OEM console by clicking on Start | Programs | Oracle Enterprise Manager | Enterprise Manager. Then log in to the OEM repository.
2. In the lower-right window of the OEM console, click on the Event Set Library tab. You should see a list of predefined available events from that library, as shown in Figure 7-1.
3. Double-click on the Oracle DB UpDown event set. Notice that there are some other event sets of interest, such as the Oracle Host UpDown set, which detects if the machine hosting the Oracle database has crashed, and the Oracle Listener UpDown set, which detects if the TNS listener is up or down. If the listener is down, you can restart it using the `lsnrctl` command or the `net start` command, or in the Control Panel | Services interface.
4. Figure 7-2 shows the Quick Edit Event Set interface, used for editing event sets. Click on the Parameters tab to determine if the value set for Frequency

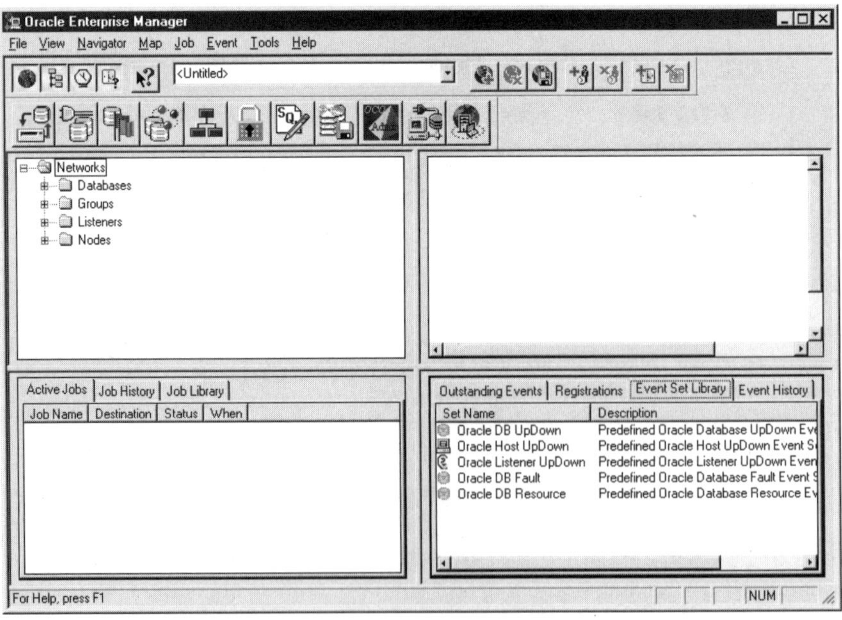

FIGURE 7-1. *OEM console Event Set Library tab*

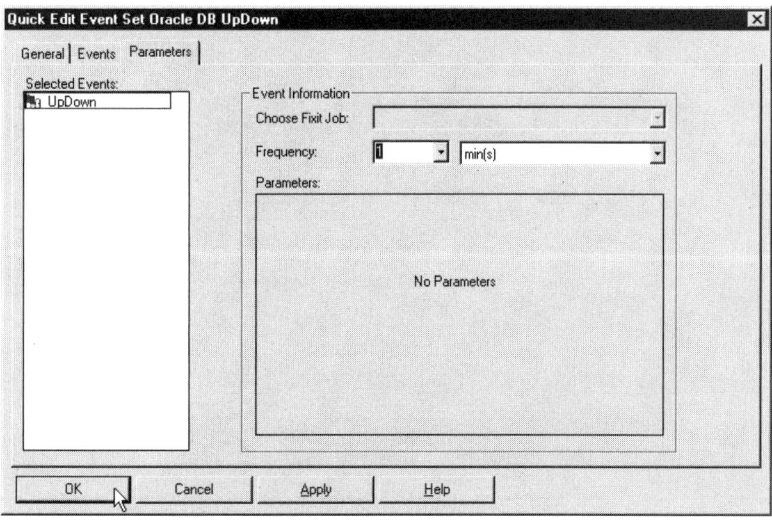

FIGURE 7-2. *Quick Edit Event Set interface*

is appropriate for your organization. The default is 5 minutes. If you would like to poll more or less frequently, modify the value and click OK. More frequent polling requires more system resources but also informs you of a problem more quickly.

Registering the DB UpDown Event Set for a Database

To allow OEM and Intelligent Agent to provide you with event detection information for a database, you must register the DB UpDown event set for that database. Assuming the OEM console is already opened from the prior set of instructions, follow these steps to register the DB UpDown event set for the PUMA database from Chapter 6:

1. Click on the Event | Register Event Set menu option within the OEM console. The Register Event Set interface will then appear. You will start your setup work for registering this event set in the General tab of that interface.
2. Ensure that the value set for Service Type is Database and that the value for Set Name is Oracle DB UpDown. Select the database you want to register the DB UpDown event set for from the list of available destinations by clicking on the available database once to highlight and then clicking the << button, or simply double-clicking on the database name. The proper setup is shown in Figure 7-3.

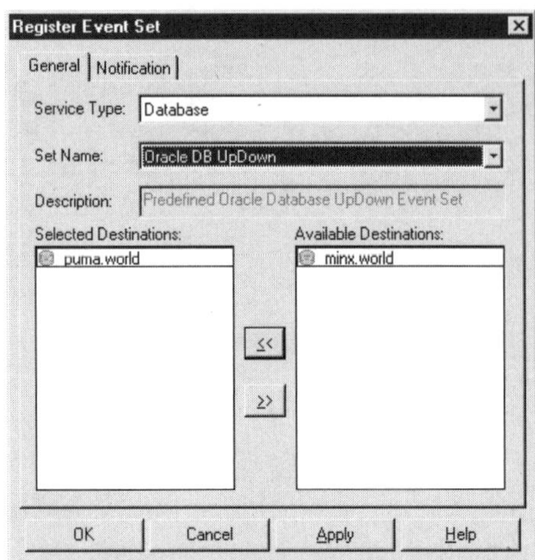

FIGURE 7-3. *Register Event Set interface, General tab*

3. Click OK to register the event set. OEM will then attempt to validate the destination. If this completes successfully, you will see a new entry in the Registrations tab back in the OEM console for your newly registered event set on the database you registered.

For Review

Understand what an event set is and the steps you need to perform to register a database to use a predefined event set.

Troubleshooting: Fixes for Space Allocation Issues

As mentioned earlier, many OEM events are available for detecting and fixing space allocation issues. A space allocation issue is when an Oracle storage structure fills to its capacity. You learned about the logical and physical storage structures available in Oracle in Chapter 4. If the datafiles associated with a particular tablespace are full, then your users will run into a space allocation issue on the database objects like tables and indexes that reside in that tablespace. If there is no space to accommodate user data entry into a table or index, then the user receives an error.

Causes for Space Allocation Issues

Three potential causes for space allocation issues on your system are listed here:

1. A database object's maximum storage limit was set too low and has been reached.
2. Users have added lots of data to a tablespace, the datafiles are now full, and the Auto Extend feature was not turned on.
3. The Auto Extend feature for a tablespace's datafiles was turned on, but the disk device itself ran out of space.

Errors Indicating Space Allocation Issues

When either you or the users of the Oracle database encounter the following errors, you will know you're dealing with a space allocation issue:

- **`ORA-01631: max # extents (`*`n`*`) reached in table`** ***`schema.name`*** An existing object's maximum number of extents has been reached, preventing the object from acquiring another extent. The cause is #1 in the previous list.
- **ORA-01653: `Unable to extend`** ***`object schema.name`*** **`by`** ***`x`*** **`in tablespace`** ***`tbsname`*** An existing object in a tablespace cannot grow anymore. The cause could be #2 in the previous list.
- **ORA-01658: `Unable to create INITIAL extent for segment in tablespace`** ***`name`*** A new object could not be created in a tablespace because the tablespace is out of room. This error is most likely caused by #2 or #3 in the previous list.

Detecting Space Allocation Problems

Often, the users of a database system will be the first to become aware of a space allocation issue. Unfortunately, by the time they become aware of the issue, it's already too late—you, the DBO, will then have to dedicate your time and effort to resolving the issue *right away*. A somewhat more proactive solution is either to monitor the space allocation on your Oracle database manually using OEM tools such as Storage Manager. With Storage Manager, you can see how much of your tablespace is allocated to database objects, broken out by tablespace as shown in Figure 7-4. To do so, drill down to the *dbname.dbdomain* | Tablespaces node. You can display storage allocation by datafile by drilling down to the *dbname.dbdomain* | Datafiles node instead.

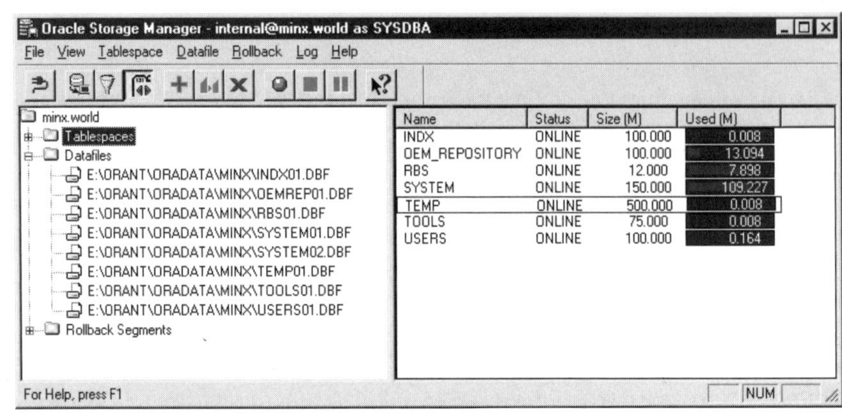

FIGURE 7-4. *Tablespace Manager storage allocation view*

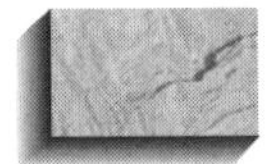

TIP

Of course, manual storage allocation monitoring implies that you actually have the time to manually check the storage allocation for your database, and most computer professionals don't have much time to spare. An alternative is to set up automatic detection of space allocation issues through the OEM console. You will learn how to perform this task later in the section, in "Automating Problem Detection: OEM Job Scheduler."

Resolving Problem #1: Object Space Allocation Issues

Resolution of space allocation issues is handled in different ways, depending on what issue it is that you're trying to resolve. If an existing object is having trouble acquiring the next extent it needs, even though there is enough room in the tablespace, you need to increase the maximum number of extents that the object can allocate. This is accomplished by issuing the `alter` *`object_type`* `object_name storage (maxextents [`*`n`*`|unlimited])` from SQL Worksheet, where *n* is a number larger than the maximum number of extents currently allocated to the object. The unlimited keyword is available as an alternative, allowing you to allocate the maximum number of extents possible for Oracle on the Windows platform. You can use Schema Manager in the following way:

1. Drill down to the Schema Objects | *Object_type* | *Schema* | *Object_name* node.

2. On the right side of the Schema Manager window, click on the Storage tab.
3. Find the Maximum Number label in the Storage tab interface, and click on the Unlimited radio button. This is shown in Figure 7-5.

Resolving Problem #2: Tablespace Storage Allocation Issues

Resolving space allocation issues when the tablespace is actually full is quite another matter. In this case, you can either issue the `alter tablespace` *`tblspc_name`* `add datafile 'x:\directory\filename' size n[K|M]` command. Or, you can perform the following tasks in Storage Manager:

1. Drill down to the *dbname.dbdomain* | Tablespaces | *Tblspc_name* node.
2. In the right side of the Storage Manager interface, where datafiles are listed, click on the Add button, as shown in Figure 7-6.

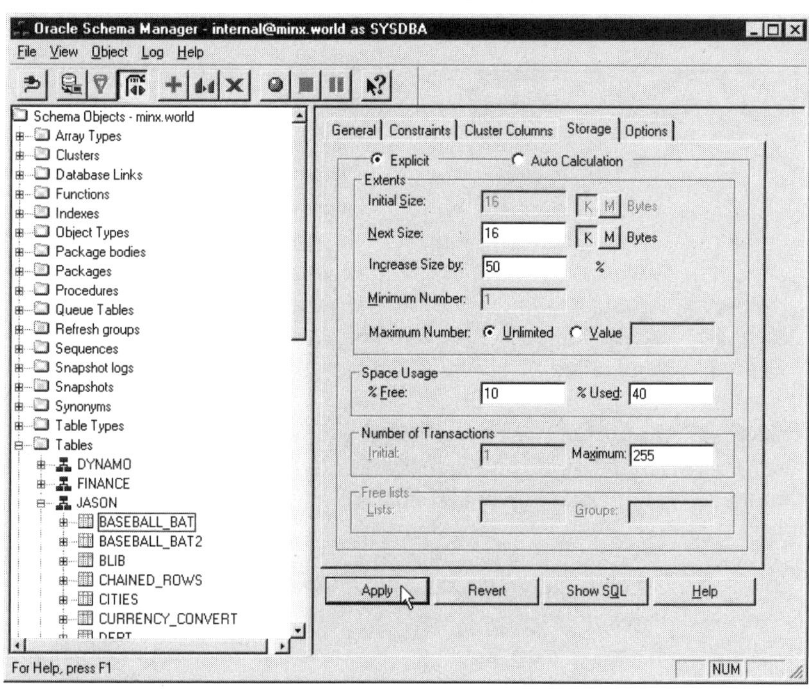

FIGURE 7-5. *Schema Manager Storage tab interface*

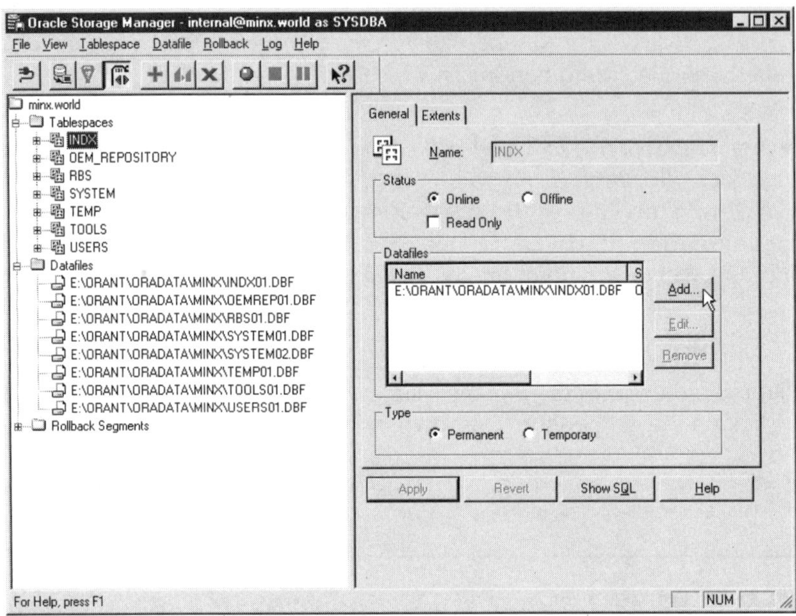

FIGURE 7-6. *Storage Manager interface*

3. The Create Datafile interface will appear, as shown in Figure 7-7. Enter the name of your new datafile, being sure to include the full pathname. If you are out of space on the same disk where your existing tablespace datafiles reside, then choose a different disk. Then specify the size of your new datafile. If the file already exists and you want to overwrite it, click the Reuse Existing Datafile checkbox. Then click OK.

ALTERNATIVE RESOLUTION TO PROBLEM #2 If space exists on the drive storing the Oracle datafile, and Auto Extend has not been enabled for the datafile(s) supporting the filled tablespace, you can enable Auto Extend as an alternative solution in the following way:

1. In the Storage Manager interface, click instead on the listing of an existing datafile.
2. Click the Edit button. In the Quick Edit Datafile interface shown in Figure 7-8, click on the Auto Extend tab. Click on the Enable Auto Extend checkbox.
3. Define the increment size that Oracle will allocate if this datafile fills. Then define the maximum size the datafile will be allowed to grow to (including

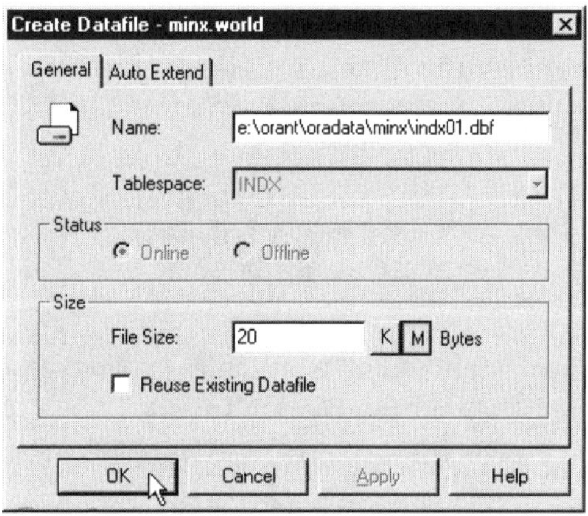

FIGURE 7-7. *Create Datafile interface*

its initial size allocation). If you want the datafile to grow until it consumes the entire disk, click the Unlimited radio button.

Resolving Problem #3: Disk Storage Allocation Issues

The resolution for this problem is essentially the same as that of problem #2. However, you will create your new datafile on another disk device. You may need to purchase additional hardware in the form of hard disks to accommodate this solution. Also, be aware of the performance impact of spreading datafiles across

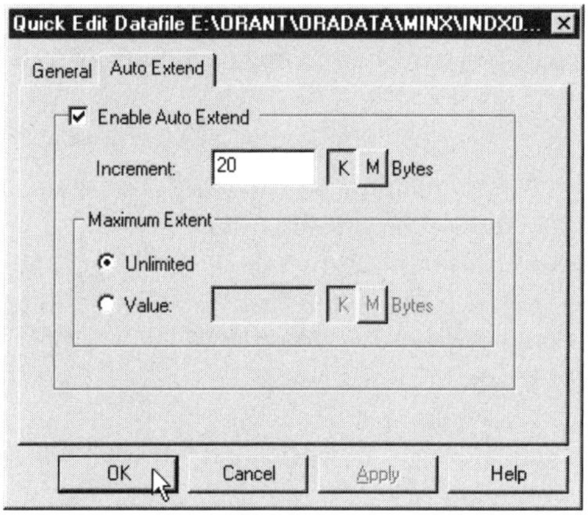

FIGURE 7-8. *Quick Edit Datafile interface*

separate drives, particularly when database objects that may contend with each other reside on the same physical volume.

Contention can arise between Oracle resources when Oracle needs to access two resources on the same disk at the same time, creating an I/O bottleneck. Those objects include

- **Tables contending with their associated indexes** Oracle will need to access these two objects at roughly the same time, so it's best to put them on separate disk devices.
- **Rollback segments contending with tables or indexes** Rollback segments are kept busy on an Oracle database. It's usually best to keep them on a disk resource separate from your permanent database objects.
- **Redo logs contending with anything** Redo logs are usually the most write-intensive disk resource on an Oracle database. You should keep them on a separate disk device from the rest of your database.

How Big Is Too Big?

When it comes to adding space to a tablespace, the question of how much space to add inevitably leaves many DBAs and DBOs stumped. The best answer to the question of when to add space comes only from understanding the nature of how data is added to the objects comprising the tablespace. For example, a tablespace containing objects that rarely have data added to them may not need space added often, even if that tablespace is 90 percent full. On the other hand, the tablespaces containing your most actively used tables in a customer order entry system may need space added when they are only 60 to 80 percent full, just as an added precaution against space allocation issues. Beware of overallocating empty space, however—the larger your datafiles, the harder they are to manage in the event of a problem. As a DBO, you will probably find the real challenge with respect to space allocation is finding the right balance of proactively adding space but not too much space.

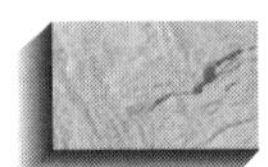

TIP
Communication is key to success when managing an Oracle database as a team. If you encounter space allocation issues that require increasing maximum extent allocations, adding datafiles, or turning on Auto Extend, be sure to communicate these issues to a DBA.

For Review

1. Make sure you understand the three space allocation scenarios described in this discussion. Know what the resolution is for each.
2. Be sure you can perform the tasks described in Schema Manager and Storage Manager for the DBO exam.

Troubleshooting: Resolutions for Archive and Trace Issues

In Chapter 6, you learned that archiving redo information is a great way to ensure that every committed data change made in Oracle up to the point of a media failure can be restored. Unfortunately, if not managed properly, archiving on an active Oracle database is also a great way to fill up a disk quickly. Figure 7-9 gives a pictorial representation of Oracle archiving its redo logs. Those archives are copied to the directory you specify using the `LOG_ARCHIVE_DEST` parameter in your `init.ora` file. You learned how to set this parameter in Chapter 6. Certain issues can arise when trace directories fill, too, though this situation is more of a silent but deadly variety, as you will soon learn.

Resolving Filled Archive Destination Issues

If the archive destination shown in Figure 7-9 fills, Oracle can no longer archive its online redo logs. If Oracle cannot archive its online redo logs, eventually all the

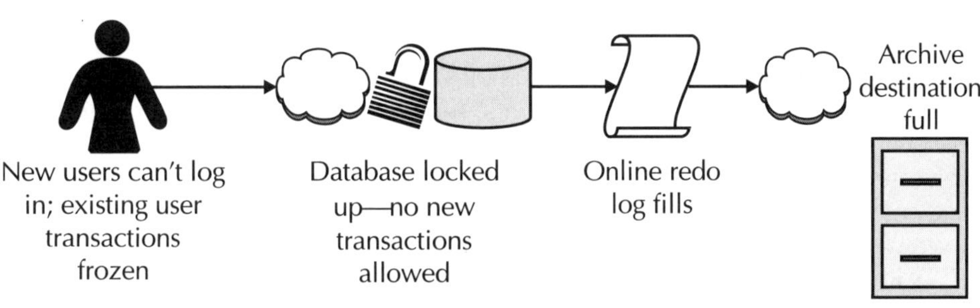

FIGURE 7-9. *When an archive destination fills*

online redo logs will fill, too. When all the online redo logs fill, Oracle stops letting new users connect to the database and stops letting connected users issue data changes too! However, Oracle won't issue any sort of error to existing users explaining the problem. Obviously, you can see from Figure 7-9 that users can quickly become frustrated with the Oracle database when this situation occurs. The resolution to this problem is as follows:

1. Copy archived redo logs in the archive destination to tape, if this hasn't been done already.
2. Remove older archived redo logs from the archive destination directory. "Older" can be taken to mean any archived redo logs that were created before the most recent backup was taken.
3. Tell Oracle to archive online redo logs so that new users can connect and existing users can make data changes. This is done in Instance Manager using the Database | Manually Archive | All menu option.

TIP
Recall from Chapter 6 that Backup Manager allows you to define what should be done with archive logs on disk after they have been backed up. It is strongly advisable for you to specify removal of those archive logs, though only after they have been saved to tape!

When a Trace File Destination Fills

Oracle also creates trace files for important background processes when those processes fail, which is useful for debugging the problems that occurred. Oracle maintains a system-wide trace file called the ALERT log as well, which contains information about events that occur while the database is running. You can find the location of these trace files by reviewing the setting for the `BACKGROUND_DUMP_DEST` initialization parameter. If the Oracle trace destination fills, Oracle will overwrite the ALERT log. Although it is not the immediate performance issue that a filled archive log destination is, a filled trace destination has an insidious way of causing headaches at the worst possible times. Because Oracle will overwrite the ALERT log quietly, you may not even realize that your trace file destination has filled until it's too late. Thus, you may lose valuable alert information without even knowing it, only to discover the problem later when you really need that tracing information. To resolve this issue, it's a good idea to periodically back up the trace file destination to tape and remove all files from that directory.

For Review

Know the signs of an archive or trace destination directory that has filled and how to resolve the issues associated with each situation.

Automating Problem Detection: OEM Job Scheduler

As mentioned earlier, it is a rare computer professional that has the time to manually monitor all the things they have to monitor in order to proactively avoid all issues users may bring to them for resolution. For this reason, Oracle Enterprise Manager allows you to set up jobs that run in the Job Scheduler to automate detection of problems by generating reports or performing certain actions at specified intervals. You can view the current job status by clicking on the Active Jobs tab interface in the lower-left window of the OEM console. Jobs that have been scheduled for execution in the Job Scheduler have three valid statuses:

1. **Submitted** The job has been submitted to the queue but has not been started.
2. **Scheduled** The submitted job is scheduled to run but has not started.
3. **Started** The job is running but has not finished.

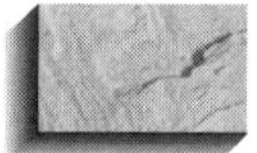

TIP
Once a job is complete, a listing of its execution will automatically be moved under the Job History tab. You can look here to determine whether or not your job runs properly. Clear your job history listing often, particularly if you have a lot of jobs you run this way, or a job you run frequently. Clearing the job history is done by clicking on the Job | Clear History menu option in OEM console.

Automating Detection of Objects Running Out of Extents

You can, for example, automate detection of objects running out of extents in your database by creating a job, which issues a basic SQL query designed to report those objects whose current number of allocated extents is close to the

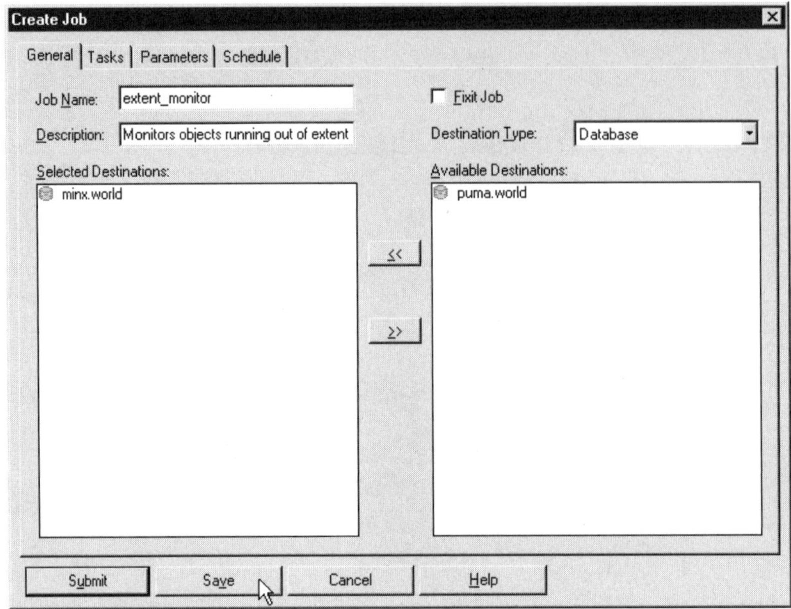

FIGURE 7-10. *The Create Job interface opens in the General tab*

maximum allowed number of extents. With OEM console open, you can define the job in the following way:

1. Click on the Job | Create Job menu option.
2. The Create Job interface will appear, as shown in Figure 7-10. This interface opens in the General tab. Enter a name and description for the job you want to run. Ensure that the value set for Destination Type is Database. Select the database you want to run the job against from the list of available destinations by double-clicking on the database.
4. Click on the Tasks tab in the Create Job interface. Select the Run SQL*Plus task from the list of available tasks by double-clicking on it.
5. Click on the Parameters tab. Enter the following SQL statement into the Script Text box, or simply browse the CD-ROM for the `chap7-1.txt` file to enter the SQL text that way.

```
select owner, segment_name, extents, max_extents
from dba_segments
where segment_type not in ('CACHE','ROLLBACK')
and max_extents - extents < 10
```

6. You can set the frequency the job will execute with by clicking on the Schedule tab and entering the execution interval.
7. Click on the Save button to make this job part of your OEM Job Library, visible using the Job Library tab interface in the lower-left side of the OEM console.
8. To run the job later, simply open the Job Library tab interface, double-click on the job listing to view the Create/Edit Job interface, and click the Submit button.

Automating Detection of Tablespaces Running Out of Space

You can define a job that detects whether your tablespace is running out of space in a way similar to the one in which you created a job that checked for objects running out of extents:

1. Click on the Job | Create Job menu item in the OEM console.
2. The Create Job interface appears. Enter the name of your job and its description. Ensure that the value set for Destination Type is Database. Select the database you want to run the job against from the list of available destinations by double-clicking on the database.
3. Click on the Tasks tab in the Create Job interface. Select the Run SQL*Plus task from the list of available tasks by double-clicking on it.
4. Click on the Parameters tab. Enter the following SQL statement into the Script Text box, or simply browse the CD-ROM for the `chap7-2.txt` file to enter the SQL text that way. Figure 7-11 illustrates.

```
select a.tablespace_name, nvl(a.total_bytes,0),
nvl(b.used_bytes,0), nvl(total_bytes-used_bytes,0)
"AVAILABLE_BYTES"
from
(select d.tablespace_name, sum(d.user_bytes) "TOTAL_BYTES"
from dba_data_files d
group by d.tablespace_name) a,
(select s.tablespace_name, sum(s.bytes) "USED_BYTES"
from dba_segments s
group by s.tablespace_name) b
where a.tablespace_name = b.tablespace_name (+)
```

5. You can set the frequency the job will execute with by clicking on the Schedule tab and entering the execution interval.
6. Click on the Save button to make this job part of your OEM Job Library, visible using the Job Library tab interface in the lower-left side of the OEM console.

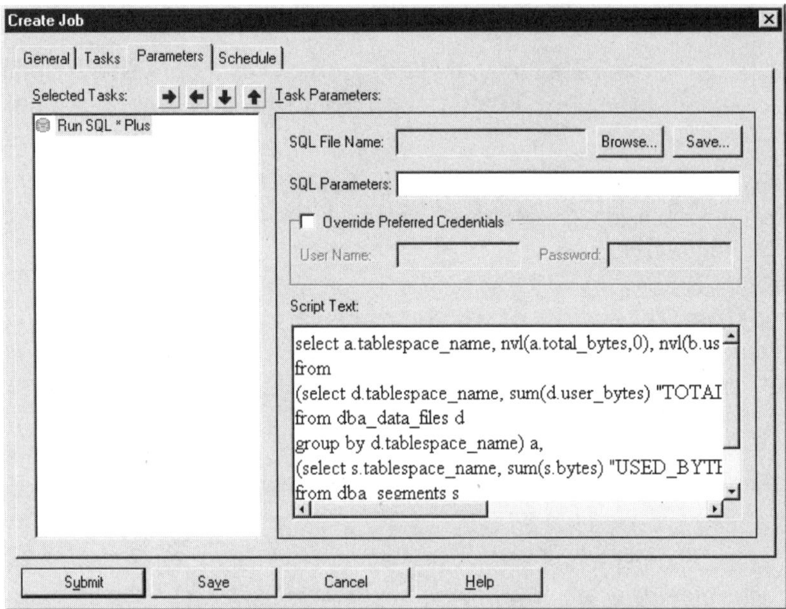

FIGURE 7-11. *Enter an SQL statement into the Script Text box in the Create Job interface*

7. To run the job later, simply open the Job Library tab interface, double-click on the job listing to view the Create/Edit Job interface, and click the Submit button.

Automating Trace File Cleanup

To automate cleanup of your trace files, you can set up a job using the Oracle OEM Job Scheduler in the following way:

1. Click on the Job | Create Job menu item in the OEM console.
2. The Create Job interface appears. Enter the name of your job and its description. Ensure that the value set for Destination Type is Node. Select the host machine you want to run the job against from the list of available destinations by double-clicking on the node. This is shown in Figure 7-12.
3. Click on the Tasks tab in the Create Job interface. Select the Run OS Command task from the list of available tasks by double-clicking on it.
4. Click on the Parameters tab. In the Command text box, enter **del**. In the Arguments text box, enter the directory set for the `BACKGROUND_DUMP_`

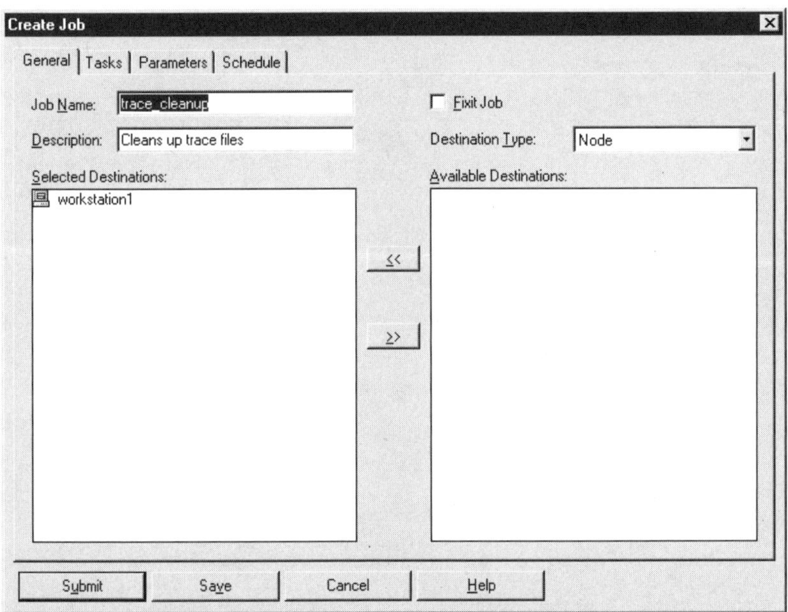

FIGURE 7-12. *Create Job interface with destination type set*

`DEST` initialization parameter, followed by an asterisk (*). For example, if the background dump destination was set to `c:\orant\rdbms80\trace`, enter **`c:\orant\rdbms80\trace\*`**. Figure 7-13 illustrates.

5. You can set the frequency the job will execute with by clicking on the Schedule tab and entering the execution interval.
6. Click on the Save button to make this job part of your OEM Job Library, visible using the Job Library tab interface in the lower-left side of the OEM console.
7. To run the job later, simply open the Job Library tab interface, double-click on the job listing to view the Create/Edit Job interface, and click the Submit button.

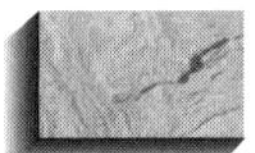

TIP
To avoid the delete confirmation presented by Windows, you can either issue the `del /Q` command or specify `*.log` or `*.trc` instead of the more general `*.*`.

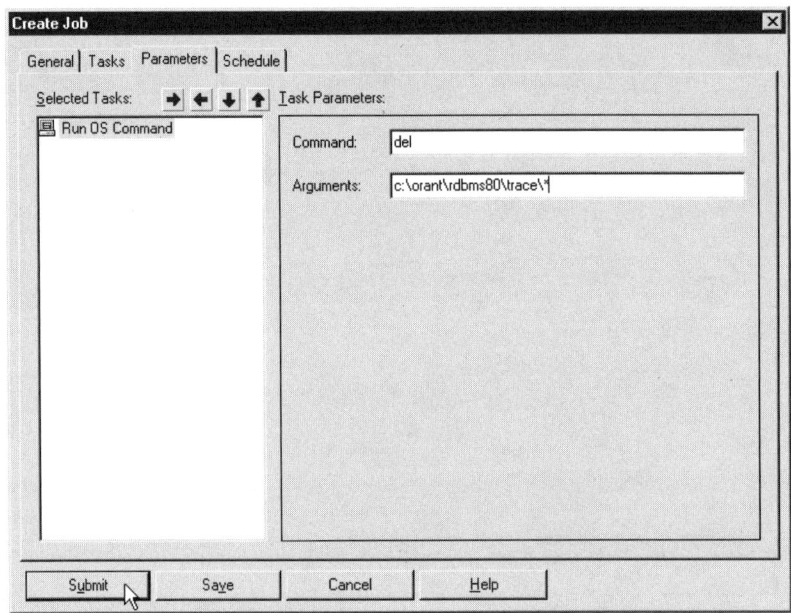

FIGURE 7-13. *Specifying the OS command*

For Review

Understand how to set up automated problem detection using job scheduling.

Automating Problem Detection: OEM Event Service

Rather than simply defining a routine job that generates reports, you can instead specify an event that will alert you only when there is a problem that you need to solve. For example, you might want to receive an email from OEM whenever it looks like a database object is running out of extents it can allocate. Another case is when you might want to be notified if a tablespace fills.

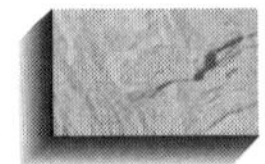

TIP

You may not see all the events described in this discussion if you only have OEM Standard Management Pack installed on your machine. To obtain these events, you should install the Diagnostics Pack.

Setting Up DB Resource Events for Objects Out of Extents

You can set up event detection for segments running out of extents in the following way:

1. In the OEM console, click on the Event | Create Event Set menu interface.
2. In the Create Event Set interface General tab, shown in Figure 7-14, give your new event set a name and ensure that the value set for Service Type is Database. You may also enter a description if you like.
3. Click on the Events tab in the Create Event Set interface. Select the Maximum Extents and Chunk Small events from the Available Events.
4. Click on the Parameters tab. This tab allows you to define red flag and yellow flag threshold percentages. At the time that tablespace fills to the threshold you set, you will receive the appropriate flag in the event window in the lower-right side of the OEM interface.

Setting Up DB Resource Events for Filled Tablespaces

You can set up event detection for filled tablespaces in the following way:

1. In the OEM console, click on the Event | Create Event Set menu interface.
2. In the Create Event Set interface General tab, give your new event set a name and ensure that the value set for Service Type is Database. You may also enter a description if you like.

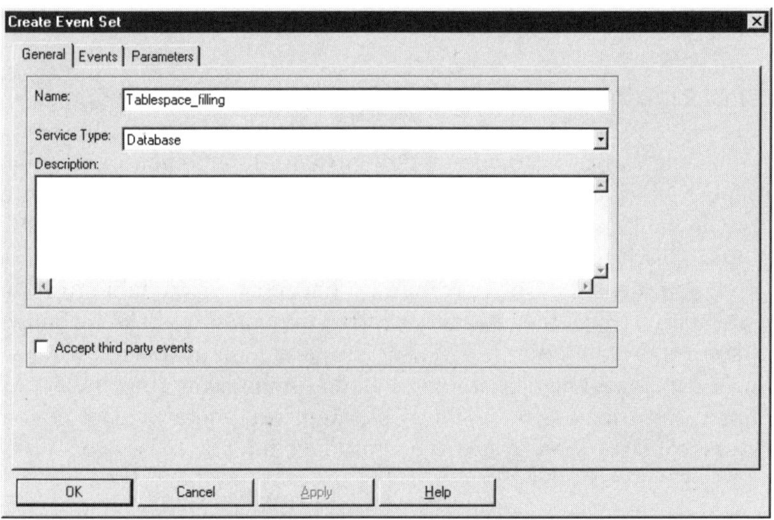

FIGURE 7-14. *Create Event Set interface*

3. Click on the Events tab in the Create Event Set interface. Select the Tablespace Full event from the Available Events.

4. Click on the Parameters tab. This tab allows you to define red flag and yellow flag threshold values for these events. At the time that the threshold you set is reached, you will receive the appropriate flag in the event window in the lower-right side of the OEM interface.

TIP
After creating the new event sets, you can then register them against databases using steps outlined in the beginning of the chapter in "Registering the DB UpDown Event Set for a Database."

For Review

Understand how to define event sets in Oracle to handle routine monitoring of various issues that may arise in the operation of your database.

Solving Blocking Situations

This section shows you how to determine and resolve blocking situations on your database:

- Determining why a session is blocked
- Detecting and releasing blocked sessions
- Understanding session deadlocks

One of Oracle's strengths as an RDBMS is that it provides users with the *integrity assurance* that only one user can make data changes to a table row at any given time. Oracle can also provide *read-consistency* to all other users while that one user makes the change. Sometimes, however, users encounter performance difficulties with the Oracle database that is associated with this feature. These incidents are collectively known as *blocking situations* in the Oracle database. Here's a common scenario. One user makes a data change to a table row, then forgets to *commit*, or save, the change. Another user wants to make a change to that same row but has to wait until the first user lets go of their access to that row by committing the change. Other examples abound. In this section, you will cover how to determine why a user session might be blocked. You will also learn how to detect and release blocked sessions. You will be introduced to Lock Manager, a tool in

OEM that quickly allows you to determine what locks are currently held by users in the system. Finally, you will learn about deadlocks and how they are resolved.

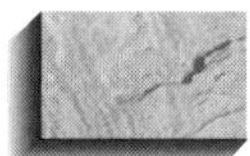

TIP
I based my material in this section on use of Lock Manager 1.6, part of the Oracle Performance Pack for OEM 1.6. Lock Manager is superceded by Performance Manager in OEM 2.0, but the functionality is largely transferable to previous versions.

Determining Why a Session Is Blocked

To begin, you need to understand the Oracle internals that provide users with the ability to make changes in the database. You have already learned about rollback segments, which store an original copy of uncommitted data changes for the purpose of allowing users to quickly back out of those changes in the event of a mistake. Another internal component of Oracle that allows data changes is the *lock*. In order to make data changes to any tables in Oracle, the user must first acquire the associated lock for that table. Locks exist at the table level in Oracle and, therefore, are sometimes called *table locks*.

Two Leading Causes for Blocked Sessions

A blocking situation occurs when two user sessions are trying to `update` or `delete` information in the same row in the same table. Following are the two leading causes for blocked sessions on an Oracle database:

- *Neglecting to handle transaction completion properly in an application.* It is the application developer's responsibility to ensure that transactions end by incorporating frequent use of `commit` and `rollback` statements. When this step does not take place, DBAs and DBOs often find themselves burdened with blocking and associated performance issues.
- *Abnormal termination of a user process, causing locks to be held by inactive processes until Oracle can clean them up.* This condition is often a by-product of the first cause, as users will often become impatient if their application appears to "hang." In this case, users sometimes reboot their PCs with the mistaken assumption that this action will somehow "clear things up." In reality, this step often exacerbates the problem because more and more "dead sessions" holding locks or attempting to acquire them pile up in the Oracle database, making more and more work for Oracle to clean up.

Acquiring Locks in Oracle

There are three different methods for acquiring locks on the Oracle database:

1. Oracle implicitly acquires the row share or row exclusive lock you require as part of the overall use of the `select for update` or `update` statements, respectively. Note that these two statements are able to acquire row-level locks only.
2. You can obtain a lock within PL/SQL code through the use of he `request( )` procedure in the DBMS_LOCK Oracle-supplied package.
3. Use the `lock table` *`name`* `in` *`lock`* `mode [nowait]` command, issued from SQL Worksheet or SQL*Plus, where *`name`* is the name of the table and *`lock`* is the table lock mode you want to lock the table in. Valid values for *`lock`* include the lock types described in the next few pages.

```
SQL> lock table survey in share update mode nowait;
Table(s) Locked.
SQL> lock table emp in exclusive mode;
Table(s) Locked.
```

Locks Are Held Until the Transaction Completes!

Once a lock is acquired on a table, your session will hold that lock until you end your transaction with `commit` or `rollback`, or by ending the session. Thus, if you acquire 700 locks, your session will hold *all 700* until your transaction completes. Consider the implication of this statement for a moment. Let's say you acquire a lock on a table row at 9:00, but it doesn't actually change any data. This can happen if you issue the `select for update` or `lock table` command.

Let's also say that you then acquire some other locks elsewhere in the database and take a hour to complete data changes. That original lock on the original table row you acquired at 9:00 is held for the whole transaction even though you aren't doing anything with it. If any other user attempts to make changes to the row you locked, then that user has to wait until you `commit` your transaction. Note also that if your locks were acquired as part of a PL/SQL block, the end of the block's execution does not implicitly end the transaction. Note that the `savepoint` command does not end a transaction either, so no locks will be released when you issue this command. The `savepoint` command in Oracle transaction processing allows you to define logical breakpoints in long-running transactions, which in turn allows you to discard part, but not all, of the changes made in that transaction.

Types of Locks in Oracle

Locks in Oracle are used for two basic purposes. The first purpose is for data-definition language (DDL) operations. DDL statements are those used in the Oracle architecture for defining tables, indexes, sequences, and other user-defined objects. Locks must be acquired to complete `create` or `alter` operations on database objects. The second purpose is for data-manipulation language (DML) operations. DML locks are acquired by user processes to make changes to object data. They allow transaction processing to take place within Oracle.

Related to the subject of transaction processing is the discussion of *transaction-level read consistency*. This term means that as a process executes a series of data-change statements that constitute a transaction, the process should have a version of the data that is consistent throughout the entire transaction. Locks support transaction-level read consistency by preventing two transactions from making changes to the same data in a table at the same time, without the other transaction knowing about the change. The following explanations present more information about each type of lock in Oracle.

EXCLUSIVE During the time an exclusive lock is held, the lock holder has exclusive access to change the table and its data. Other users may `select` data, but no other transaction can acquire any type of lock on the table or `insert`, `delete`, or `update` data in the table until the exclusive lock is released by the holder of that lock.

SHARE When one transaction has a share lock on a table, other transactions can also acquire a share, share-row, or share-update lock on that same table. However, other transactions will usually have to wait until the transaction holding a share lock completes in order to complete their own transactions. No transaction can acquire exclusive, row-exclusive, or share-row-exclusive locks on a table when another transaction already holds a share lock on that table. If two transactions hold a share lock on the same table, neither transaction can change data in the table until the other transaction gives up its lock. A transaction holding the only share lock on a table can make changes to that table that Oracle will process immediately. If other transactions hold share-row or share-update locks on the same table as a transaction holding a share lock, then data changes made by the transactions holding the share-row or share-update locks will have to wait until the transaction holding the share lock commits.

ROW EXCLUSIVE A row-exclusive lock held by a transaction allows other transactions to query any rows or `insert` new rows on the table while the row-exclusive lock is being held. In addition, transactions can concurrently process `update` or `delete` statements on rows other than those held under the row-exclusive lock in the same table. Therefore, row-exclusive locks allow multiple transactions to obtain simultaneous row-exclusive, share-row, or share-update locks for different rows in the same table. However, while one transaction holds a row-exclusive lock, no other transaction can make changes to rows that the first transaction has changed until the first transaction completes. Additionally, no transaction may obtain an exclusive, share, or share-row-exclusive lock on a table while another transaction holds a row-exclusive lock on that same table.

ROW SHARE A row-share lock held by a transaction allows others to query any rows or `insert` new rows on the table while the row-share lock is being held. In addition, transactions can process `update` or `delete` statements on rows other than those held under a row-share lock concurrently in the same table. Therefore, two or more transactions can make data changes to different rows in the same table at the same time, using row-share, row-exclusive, share-update, and share-row-exclusive locks. Other transactions can acquire share locks on a table when a transaction already has a row-share lock on that table. In this case, the transaction holding the row-share lock will now have to wait until the transaction holding the share lock completes before being able to proceed with its own changes. A transaction cannot acquire an exclusive lock on a table if another transaction has already acquired the row-share lock on that table.

SHARE ROW EXCLUSIVE A share-row-exclusive lock held by a transaction allows others to query rows while the share-row-exclusive lock is being held. Transactions can acquire share-row or share-update locks on the table while a transaction holds the share-row-exclusive lock, but any transaction that attempts to `insert`, `update`, or `delete` data will have to wait until the transaction holding the share-row-exclusive lock completes. No exclusive, share, share-row-exclusive, or row-exclusive locks can be acquired on a table until the transaction holding the share-row-exclusive lock completes. A share-row-exclusive table lock held by a transaction allows other transactions to query or lock specific rows using the `select for update` clause, but not to update the table.

SHARE UPDATE A share-update lock is acquired for making changes to data in table rows. When a transaction holds this lock, any other transaction can acquire any other type of lock on a table except for the exclusive lock. A share-update lock held by a transaction allows others to query any rows or `insert` new rows on the table while the share-update lock is being held. In addition, transactions can concurrently process `update` or `delete` statements on rows other than those held under share-update locks in the same table. Therefore, two or more transactions can make data changes to different rows in the same table at the same time using row-share, row-exclusive, share-update, and share-row-exclusive locks. Other transactions can acquire share locks on a table when a transaction already has a share-update lock on that table. In this case, the transaction holding the share-update lock will have to wait until the transaction holding the share lock completes before being able to proceed with its own changes.

For Review

1. Understand that locks provide integrity assurance and read consistency for users making changes to data in Oracle.
2. Know the causes of blocked sessions and how they relate to Oracle's locking mechanisms.

Detecting and Releasing Blocked Sessions

The key to resolving issues with blocked sessions is to be able to detect them. Tools such as Lock Manager in OEM allow you to perform this task. To release a blocked session, you can either force the blocking session to release the lock it holds that's blocking the other session, or you can kill the session. You will learn how to handle each of these situations shortly.

Blocked Sessions: A Demo

Resolving your blocked session situations in applications will most likely involve application developers who will review their code to find places where transactions have not been properly ended. To facilitate search and detection, you can use OEM Lock Manager to find the sessions holding locks on your database quickly and easily. Lock Manager is a tool found in the Oracle Enterprise Manager Diagnostics Pack available from Oracle Corporation. *If you have installed only Oracle Enterprise Manager Standard Management pack, you will not have Lock Manager on your system.* Lock Manager shows you the dependency trees formed between blocking and waiting sessions as well. For now, consider acquiring some hands-on knowledge. To see an example of blocking sessions, and using Lock Manager to detect blocking situations, follow these steps:

1. Open SQL*Plus by clicking Start | Programs | Oracle for Windows | SQL*Plus.
2. Log in to your database as a user with the ability to modify an existing table on the database. In my case, I'm logging in as user JASON to the MINX database, and I'm going to work with the EMP table.
3. Issue the `select * from EMP for update` statement in Oracle. You can substitute another table you have `select` and `update` privileges on.
4. Open another session to the same database from another SQL*Plus window, as a different user. In my case, I'll log in to Oracle as user SPANKY. You may want to substitute a different user, but for clarity sake, don't log in as the same user you used in step 2.

5. In SPANKY's session, issue an update statement against a row in the EMP table (or the table you substituted for step 3). SPANKY's session is now blocked.
6. Open Lock Manager by clicking on Start | Programs | Oracle Diagnostics Pack | Lock Manager. Log in to the Oracle database as a privileged user such as SYSTEM.
7. Lock Manager should now show that user JASON's first session is clearly blocking user SPANKY's session. Ensure that the pull-down menu in the center of the Lock Manager interface has Blocking/Waiting Locks displayed for this step.
8. Issue a `commit` statement in the first session you opened in step 1. SPANKY's session will now complete its transaction. Click on the Refresh button, and you will see that user JASON no longer holds a lock on the EMP table. User SPANKY's session is no longer blocked.
9. Issue a `rollback` command in SPANKY's session to ensure your change doesn't get saved. You can then refresh your view in Lock Manager to see that neither user JASON nor user SPANKY holds any locks on the EMP table anymore.

Other Methods for Resolving Blocked Sessions

With Lock Manager, you can employ another method for resolving a blocked session scenario as well—killing the blocking user session. This scenario works for situations in which you can't access the blocking session to issue a `commit` or `rollback` to end the current transaction. To end a blocking session using the Lock Manager tool, perform the following tasks:

1. Open Lock Manager by clicking on Start | Programs | Oracle Diagnostics Pack | Lock Manager.
2. Ensure that Blocking/Waiting Locks is displayed in the pull-down menu shown in the center of the interface.
3. Find the session that is blocking another session you wish to kill and click once on its listing to highlight. You will want to kill the blocking session, not the waiting session, because killing a waiting session does nothing to ensure that the blocking session will not cause another session to wait later.
4. With the blocking session highlighted, click on the Locks | Kill Session menu option in Lock Manager. At the confirmation prompt, click OK.

What Happens When You Kill a Session?

You will want to be sure you understand the following facts about what happens when you kill a session in Lock Manager (or Instance Manager, the other OEM tool that allows you to kill sessions):

- The active transaction in the blocking session is rolled back.
- The kill won't complete until that rollback is complete.
- The blocking session is terminated.
- All locks held by the blocking session are released.
- The waiting session will then be able to acquire the lock it was waiting for.

For Review

Understand the purpose of Lock Manager and the fact that it does not come with the OEM standard edition. You must order the Oracle Diagnostic Pack to have Lock Manager. Know also how to identify and resolve a blocking session both by ending the blocking session's transaction and by killing the blocking session.

Understanding Session Deadlocks

A *deadlock* is a situation in which two sessions both need a resource that is locked by the other session, and neither session can release its own resource without acquiring the resource held by the other. For this example, I will use the EMP table owned by user SPANKY, which I create using the `chapter8.sql` script you will use in the next chapter. The data stored in the SPANKY.EMP table is listed in the following code block:

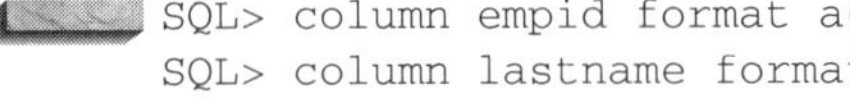

```
SQL> column empid format a6
SQL> column lastname format a10
SQL> column firstname format a10
SQL> column salary format 9999999
SQL> select * from spanky.emp;
EMPID  LASTNAME   FIRSTNAME    SALARY DEPT       HIRE_DATE
------ ---------- ---------- -------- ---------- ---------
02039  WALLA      RAJENDRA      60000 604B       01-JAN-96
39334  SMITH      GINA          75000 604B       15-MAR-97
60403  HARPER     ROD           45000 504A       30-APR-79
49539  QIAN       LEE           90000 504A       25-MAY-99
49392  SPANKY     STACY         10000 604B       14-FEB-98
12345  BUGGY                    55000
6 rows selected.
```

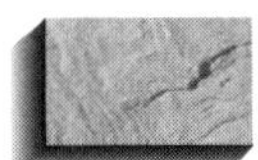

TIP
As indicated by the description, all database objects in Oracle have an owner. Objects can be logically grouped into "schemas" according to their owner. You will learn more about schemas and table ownership in Chapter 8.

A Deadlock Example

Deadlocking can be a devastating performance killer. Fortunately, Oracle has built-in deadlock detection for this situation. To illustrate how Oracle identifies a deadlock occurring between two sessions, and how Oracle intervenes, a deadlocking situation can be generated with the following steps:

1. Open two SQL*Plus sessions, as two different users. I do so as user JASON and SPANKY on the MINX database.
2. In JASON's session, issue the statement
   ```
   update emp set lastname = 'WALLAWALLA' where empid = '02039'
   ```
3. In SPANKY's session, issue the statement
   ```
   update emp set lastname = 'JONES' where empid = '39334'
   ```
4. In JASON's session, issue the statement
   ```
   update emp set salary = salary*1.08 where empid = '39334'
   ```
   SPANKY's session is now blocking JASON's, and JASON must wait for SPANKY to `commit` or `rollback` her transaction.
5. In SPANKY's session, issue the statement
   ```
   update emp set salary = salary*1.08 where empid = '02039'
   ```
   At this point, the `ORA-00060: deadlock detected while waiting for resource` error will appear in JASON's session blocking SPANKY's transaction. Notice that now SPANKY's session is waiting for JASON's current transaction to commit.
6. In JASON's session, issue the `select lastname from spanky.emp where empid = '02039'` statement. You will see that the prior change made in JASON's transaction is still present. Oracle only rolls back the change that initially caused the deadlock in JASON's transaction, not JASON's entire transaction.
7. In JASON's session, issue the `commit` statement to save changes made to the database and end the transaction. SPANKY's `update` is now complete as well.
8. In SPANKY's session, issue the `commit` statement to save changes made to the database and end the transaction. A transcript of both sessions side by side with a timeline is shown in Table 7-1.

Time	Transcript from JASON's Session	Transcript from SPANKY's Session

13:25:00	`SQL> update spanky.emp`
	`2 set lastname = 'WALLAWALLA'`
	`3 where empid = '02039';`
	`1 row updated.`
		[SPANKY connecting to database]

13:26:00	**[JASON preparing next update.]**	`SQL> update spanky.emp`
		`2 set lastname = 'JONES'`
		`3 where empid = '39334';`
		`1 row updated.`

13:27:00	`SQL> update spanky.emp`
	`2 set salary = salary*1.08`
	`3 where empid = '39334';`
		[Spanky preparing next update.]

13:28:00	**[Jason waits for SPANKY to complete transaction.]**	`SQL> update spanky.emp`
		`2 set salary = salary*1.08`
		`3 where empid = '02039';`

13:28:07	`Update spanky.emp`
	`*`
	`ERROR at line 1:`
	`ORA-00060: deadlock detected while waiting for resource`
	[Current statement rolled back, but JASON's transaction continues.]
		[Now SPANKY waits for JASON to complete transaction.]

13:29:00	`SQL> commit;`
	`Commit complete.`
		`1 row updated.`
		`SQL> commit;`
		`Commit complete.`

TABLE 7-1. *Transcript of Deadlocking Sessions*

TIP
If your process encounters a deadlock, you aren't required to commit or rollback immediately. However, it is usually a good idea to do so in order to avoid any continued blocking/waiting performance issues.

Finding Information About Deadlocks

After a deadlock occurs on your database, you can find information about it by looking for a session trace file in the directory specified by the USER_DUMP_DEST initialization parameter. In Oracle8, the default value for this directory is `X:\orant\rdbms80\trace`. In Oracle8*i*, this directory defaults to `X:\orant\admin\`*`SID`*`\udump`. The following code block shows an excerpt from the trace file generated when you run the previous example on an Oracle8*i* database. The trace file tells you which processes deadlocked and also tells you the rowid for the record they deadlocked on:

```
Dump file E:\orant\admin\minx\udump\ORA00209.TRC
Fri Nov 12 13:28:07 1999
ORACLE V8.1.5.0.0 - Production vsnsta=0
vsnsql=d vsnxtr=3
Windows NT V4.0, OS V5.101, CPU type 586
Oracle8i Enterprise Edition Release 8.1.5.0.0 - Production
With the Partitioning and Java options
PL/SQL Release 8.1.5.0.0 - Production
Windows NT V4.0, OS V5.101, CPU type 586
Instance name: minx
Redo thread mounted by this instance: 1
Oracle process number: 11
Windows thread id: 209, image: ORACLE.EXE
*** 1999.11.12.13.28.07.230
*** SESSION ID:(14.210) 1999.11.12.13.28.07.230
ksqded1:  deadlock detected via did
DEADLOCK DETECTED
Current SQL statement for this session:
update spanky.emp set salary = salary*1.08
where empid = '39334'
The following deadlock is not an ORACLE error. It is a
deadlock due to user error in the design of an application
or from issuing incorrect ad-hoc SQL. The following
information may aid in determining the deadlock:
Deadlock graph:
                       ---------Blocker(s)--------  ---------Waiter(s)---------
Resource Name          process session holds waits  process session holds waits
TX-0003005b-00000164        11      14     X             12      13           X
TX-00020012-00000163        12      13     X             11      14           X
session 14: DID 0001-000B-00000002      session 13: DID 0001-000C-00000002
session 13: DID 0001-000C-00000002      session 14: DID 0001-000B-00000002
Rows waited on:
Session 13: obj - rowid = 00001827 - AAABgnAAHAAAB2IAAA
Session 14: obj - rowid = 00001827 - AAABgnAAHAAAB2IAAB
```

For Review

1. Understand what is meant by the term *deadlock* and how one is generated in an Oracle database.

2. Know what happens when Oracle detects a deadlock.
3. Know where to look for the trace file produced when Oracle detects a deadlock.

Handling High-Level Performance Tuning

The final section in this chapter teaches you about basic performance tuning:

- Using Oracle Expert
- Creating a tuning session
- The steps of a tuning session
- Reviewing and implementing tuning recommendations

The final topic of this section covers high-level performance tuning. This is actually a huge topic area in Oracle, one that alone has been the subject of many books. Given the scope of the topic versus the relatively limited focus of what you need to know as a DBO for the OCP exam, this section focuses on how to use one of Oracle's newest tools for performance tuning. This tool is Oracle Expert. The idea behind Oracle Expert is for Oracle to combine a great deal of tuning expertise into one tool. In this section, you will cover how to use Oracle Expert for database tuning. You will learn how to create a tuning session with the tool, and what steps must be executed as part of a tuning session. Finally, you will learn how to review and implement the recommendations Oracle Expert provides to improve performance on your database.

Using Oracle Expert

When properly used, Oracle Expert can simplify the overall process of tuning an Oracle database. Its graphical interface should be intuitive if you have used Oracle Enterprise Manager for a while. Oracle Expert tunes your database in the following way:

1. You set up Oracle Expert for use and choose a database to tune.
2. You create the tuning session.
3. You specify scope for the tuning session. Some potential scopes for which you may want to limit Oracle Expert's tuning effort include application tuning, instance tuning, or storage structure tuning.
4. Oracle Expert collects statistics. Oracle Expert collects database, instance, schema, environment, and workload information as part of this process.

5. Oracle Expert analyzes statistics. This step can take a while.
6. You review Oracle Expert's recommendations.
7. You implement Oracle Expert's recommendations. You can decline some recommendations, but not all. Oracle Expert can generate scripts that will assist you in implementing those recommendations.

Setting Up Oracle Expert

To start using Oracle Expert, you need to execute the following setup steps:

1. Click on Start | Programs | Oracle Tuning Pack | Oracle Expert. You will need to connect to an Oracle Expert repository on the Oracle database you want to tune. To do so, provide contact information for a privileged user, such as SYSTEM.
2. If no repository exists on the database you specify, Oracle Expert will create one for you. Simply click OK in the Repository Manager screen, shown in Figure 7-15. Oracle Expert Repository Manager will display its progress. When finished, the repository creation will end automatically.
3. You will then see the Tuning Session Wizard interface, shown in Figure 7-16. You will be prompted to load the sample tuning session. Clear the Show This Wizard On Oracle Expert Startup checkbox by clicking on it. Then click Finish.
4. You will now see the Oracle Expert interface, shown in Figure 7-17. On the left side, notice the list of available databases to tune. Click on the Database node to add the database you want to tune to the list of available nodes. Right-click on the node and choose the New menu option.

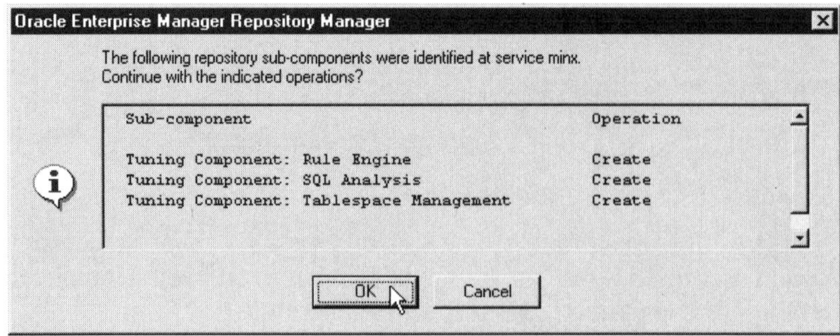

FIGURE 7-15. *Repository Manager interface*

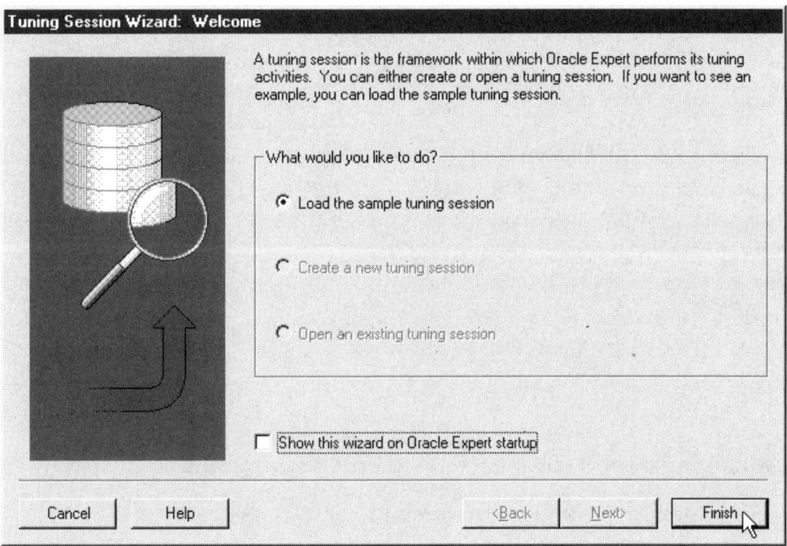

FIGURE 7-16. *Tuning Session Wizard interface*

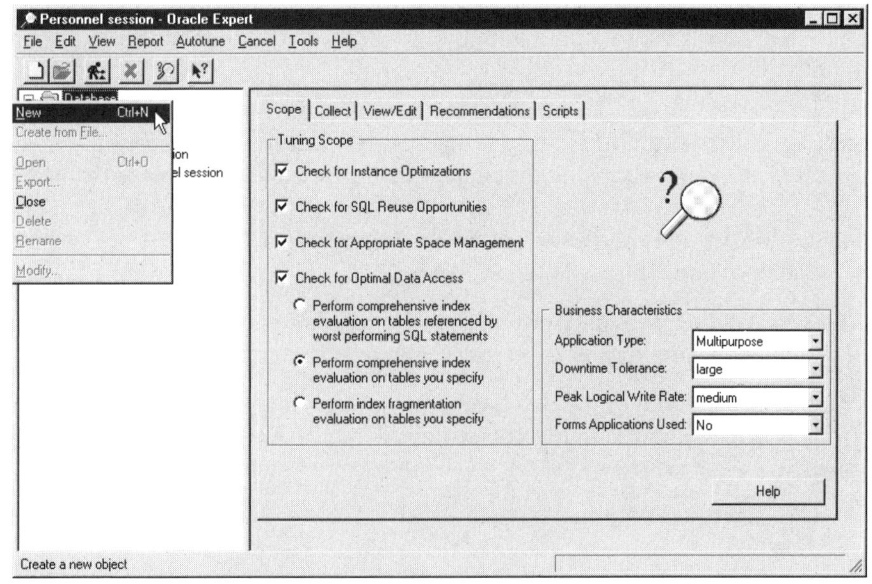

FIGURE 7-17. *Oracle Expert interface*

5. Log in to the database you wish to tune as a privileged user, such as SYSTEM. The database should now appear under the Database node on the left side of the Oracle Expert interface.

TIP
When using Oracle Expert to tune your database, you should ensure that Oracle Expert's tuning session runs at a time when peak usage is expected on your Oracle database. Otherwise, the information provided by Oracle Expert is likely to have only limited value.

For Review

1. Understand the steps of an Oracle Expert tuning session.
2. Understand how to perform the basic setup tasks associated with Oracle Expert.

Creating a Tuning Session

There are two ways to create a tuning session. You can create a tuning session in the Create Tuning Session Wizard that appears when you start Oracle Expert. Or, you can create a tuning session manually. The following two discussions cover each method.

Creating a Tuning Session Using the Wizard

Follow these steps to create a tuning session using the appropriate wizard:

1. In the Oracle Expert interface, click on the Tools | Tuning Session Wizard menu option. This is shown in Figure 7-18.
2. You will then see the Tuning Session Wizard. Click on the Create a New Tuning Session radio button in that wizard. Then click Next.
3. Select the name of the database you want to tune from the drop-down list. Then enter the name you would like to give your tuning session. Then click Finish.

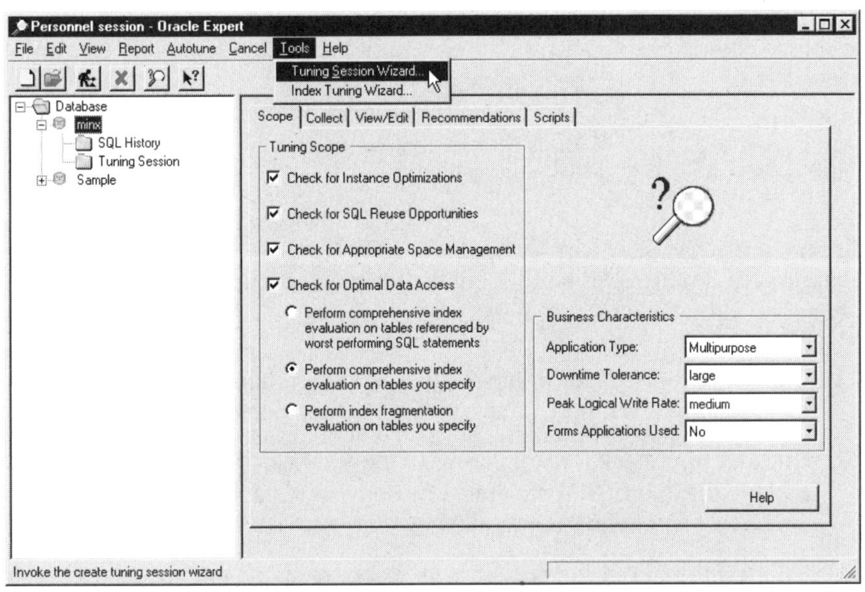

FIGURE 7-18. *Oracle Expert interface with Tuning Session Wizard shown*

Creating a Tuning Session Manually

However, this wizard will not appear if you followed the setup instructions and disabled that wizard's appearance at Oracle Expert startup. Instead, you can follow these steps to create a tuning session on your database using Oracle Expert:

1. Drill down to the Database | SID | Tuning Session node.
2. Click on the File | New menu option. A new tuning session node will appear.
3. You can then modify the name of the session if you like.

For Review

Understand how to perform the effort for creating a tuning session manually or via the Tuning Session Wizard.

The Steps of a Tuning Session

Once setup is complete, you have chosen your database, and a tuning session has been created, your effort for performing a tuning session focuses more on defining scope for statistics collecting and other setup aspects within the actual tuning session. Physically, you will focus more attention on the tab interfaces on the right side of the Oracle Expert interface as well.

Defining Tuning Session Scope

You define your tuning session scope in the Scope tab of the Oracle Expert interface. The following tasks are performed:

1. Click on the Check for Instance Optimizations checkbox if you want to include Oracle memory configuration in the scope of the tuning session.
2. Click on the Check for SQL Reuse Opportunities checkbox if you want to include the rate of SQL statement reuse in the Oracle shared pool library cache as part of your tuning session.
3. Click on the Check for Appropriate Space Management checkbox if you want Oracle Expert to investigate the storage structure layout of your database.
4. Click on the Check for Optimal Data Access checkbox if you want Oracle Expert to analyze index usage in the database. The method Oracle Expert employs to analyze index usage can be chosen using the radio buttons shown in Figure 7-19.
5. You can also identify the business characteristics of your database to Oracle Expert as a way to influence its recommendations.
    - For Application Type, you can specify OLTP, Data Warehouse, or Multipurpose. This indicates the type of application the database supports.
    - For Downtime Tolerance, you can specify None, Small, Medium, or Large. This specifies the amount of downtime tolerated for this database.
    - For Peak Logical Write Rate, you can specify Small, Medium, Large, or Huge. This specifies the volume of data written during peak periods of database usage.
    - For Forms Application Used, you can specify Yes or No. This specifies whether you run Oracle Forms as a front-end application to this database.

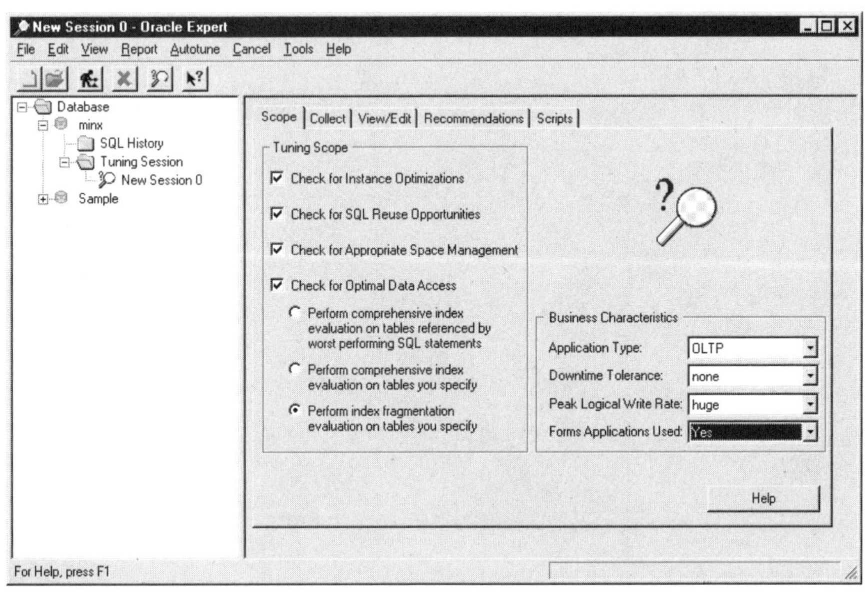

FIGURE 7-19. *Oracle Expert Scope tab*

Setting Up Collection Properties

After defining the scope of the tuning session, you can set up the collection properties for your session. First, click on the Collect tab. After doing so, you may notice that some of the options available in this interface are grayed out. The options available in this interface depend on the tuning scope you defined in the previous tab interface. The Collect interface is displayed in a table format, listing the collection property, the last time statistics were collected for this property, and whether all the options that need to be set are set. The Collect tab is shown in Figure 7-20. You can define collection properties using the following steps:

1. Click the Database Class checkbox to collect statistics in that class. Then click on the Options button to define options. The options are shown in Figure 7-21. You can include or exclude various statistics by checking options shown in the Options interface. When finished, click OK.
2. Click the Instance Class checkbox to collect statistics in that class. Then click on the Options button to define options. The options are shown in Figure 7-22. You can include or exclude various statistics by checking options shown in the Options interface. When finished, click OK.

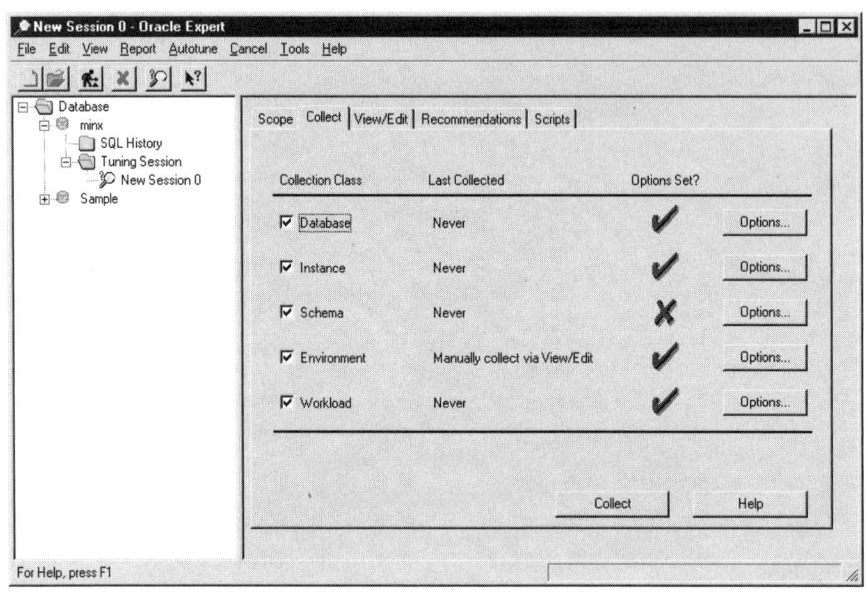

FIGURE 7-20. *Oracle Expert Collect tab*

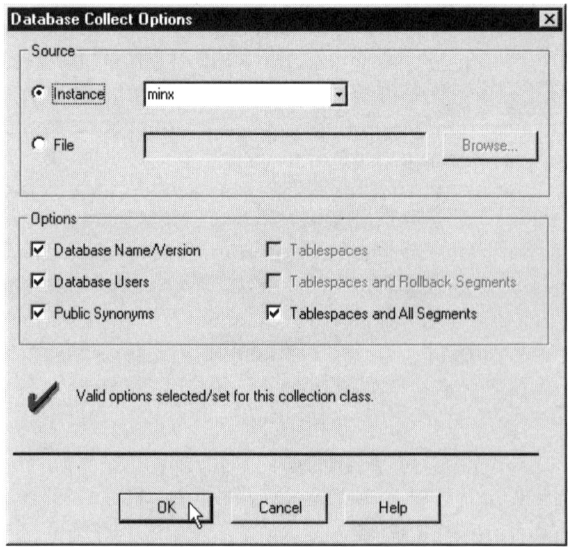

FIGURE 7-21. *Collect tab database Options interface*

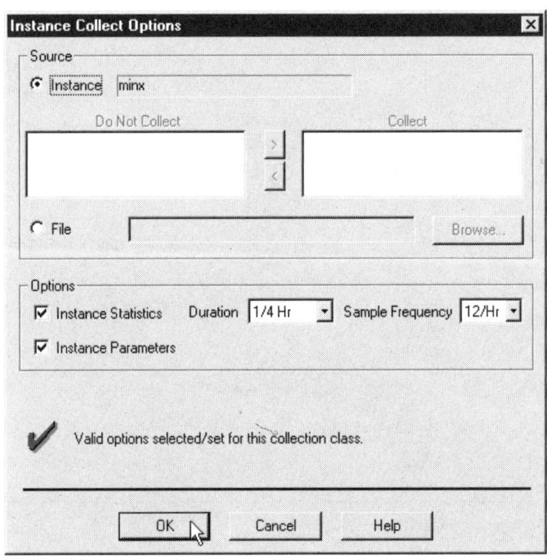

FIGURE 7-22. *Collect tab instance Options interface*

3. Click the Schema Class checkbox to collect statistics in that class. Then click on the Options button to define options. The options are shown in Figure 7-23. You should click on the Get Schemas button to obtain a list of all schemas in that database, so that you can explicitly tell Oracle Expert which schema objects it should collect statistics for. This is done by drilling down into the Schema | Object node for the schema and object you want to collect statistics for, and then by clicking on the >> button. Also, ensure that you have selected the Run Analyze Command radio button to ensure that the statistics used are based on current database activity. When finished, click OK.
4. Click the Environment Class checkbox to collect statistics in that class. This is the only class for which Oracle Expert cannot automatically capture information for you. Instead, you have to manually enter the information yourself. Click on the Options button to define options. When finished, click OK.
5. Click the Workload Class checkbox to collect statistics in that class. Then click on the Options button to define options. Figure 7-24 shows the options you have available to collect statistics from. When finished, click OK.
6. Click on the Collect button to collect your statistics. This may take a while. Oracle Expert will update you on its progress in both the Collect tab and in

Schema Collect Options
Source
Instance
minx
Get Schemas
File
Do Not Collect
Collect
MAILING_LIST
NMO_MASTER
ONRS_CONFIG
ONRS_REGION
ONRS_SERIAL
JASON
DEPT
EMP
EMPLOYEE
ERRATA
ERROR_TABLE
Options
Schema
Overwrite Existing
Schema
Table
Statistics
Collection Method
Expert Scan
Run ANALYZE Command
Read Existing ANALYZE Results
Calculation Method
Exact
Estimated/Limit:
Valid options selected/set for this collection class.
OK
Cancel
Help

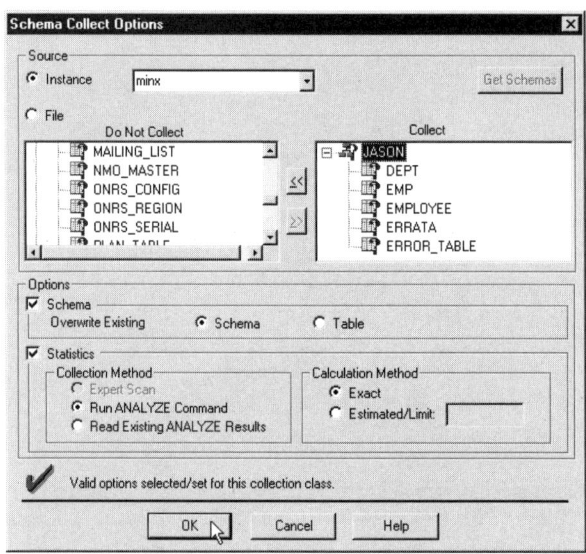

FIGURE 7-23. *Collect tab schema Options interface*

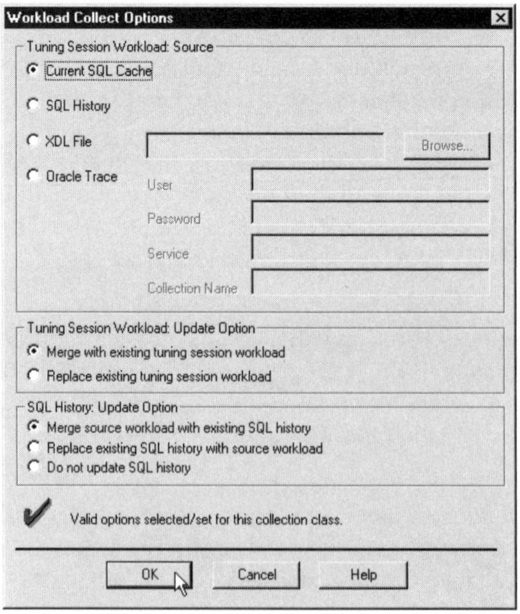

Workload Collect Options
Tuning Session Workload: Source
Current SQL Cache
SQL History
XDL File
Browse...
Oracle Trace
User
Password
Service
Collection Name
Tuning Session Workload: Update Option
Merge with existing tuning session workload
Replace existing tuning session workload
SQL History: Update Option
Merge source workload with existing SQL history
Replace existing SQL history with source workload
Do not update SQL history
Valid options selected/set for this collection class.
OK
Cancel
Help

FIGURE 7-24. *Workbook Collect Options interface*

the text box running along the lower-right side of the Oracle Expert interface. Oracle Expert collects its statistics samples in several intervals as well. Typically, Oracle Expert will pause for several minutes between collection of samples. The following illustration shows you the interface Oracle Expert will display alerting you to this fact.

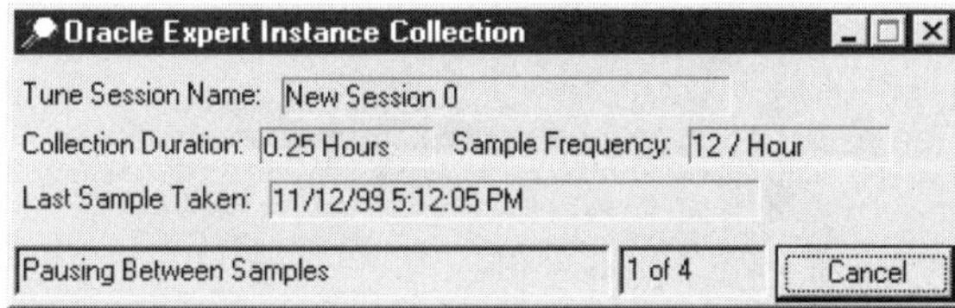

Collected Data Analysis

Once you have finished defining the scope for your data analysis collection, click on the Recommendations tab. Within that tab, click on the Generate button. Oracle Expert will then begin the process of analyzing the statistical information collected on your database. This also may take a while.

For Review

Understand how to define options for Oracle Expert tuning sessions using the Scope and Collect tab interfaces.

Reviewing and Implementing Tuning Recommendations

When Oracle Expert has finished collecting and analyzing statistics, you can view recommendations about how to boost performance on your database. These recommendations will be available in the Recommendations tab interface, shown in Figure 7-25. As you can see in the figure, the recommendations offered are available in a drill-down format. The recommendation nodes available at this point will be entirely dependent on the options you selected for Oracle Expert to analyze. You can drill to the appropriate node in this tab interface to view those recommendations.

You may also click on the View Detail button to see detailed information about Oracle Expert's recommendations in that area. For example, to see Oracle Expert's recommendations for instance configuration, you drill into the Instance Recommendations for Instance MINX node. Several recommendations will be listed right there at a glance. For example, Oracle Expert may tell you to adjust particulars having to do with SORT_AREA_SIZE initialization parameters. To view more information about Oracle Expert's recommendation, click once on the recommendation to highlight and then click on the View Detail button. Figure 7-26 shows sample output from that button. In the figure, you can see that Oracle Expert is capable of expanding its evaluation, explaining how it assesses its

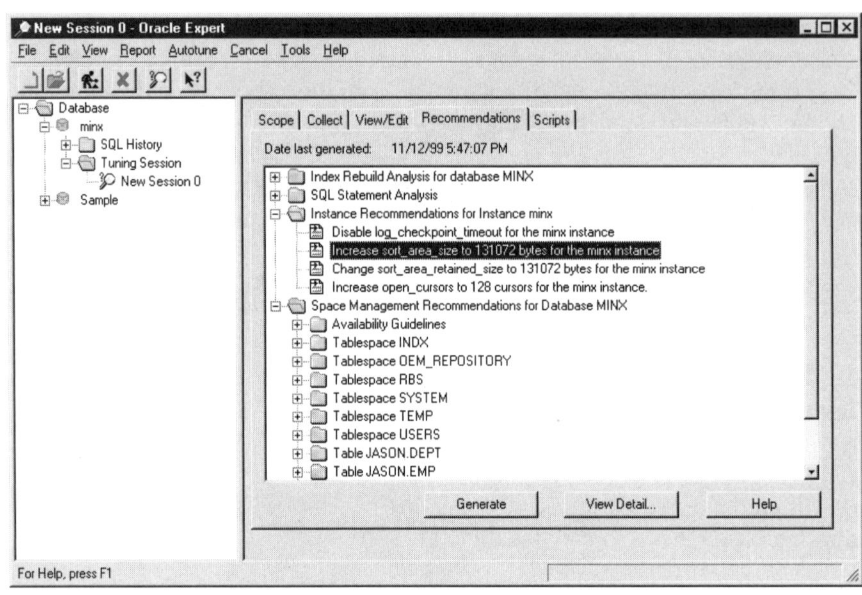

FIGURE 7-25. *Recommendations tab interface*

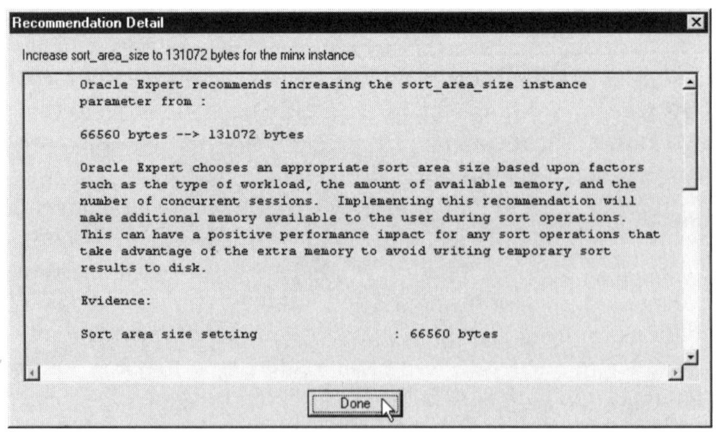

FIGURE 7-26. *Recommendation detail*

recommendations based on the information you give it. So, Oracle Expert is also an education tool, to some extent. When finished viewing the detailed recommendation, click Done.

A summary report is also available for the Oracle Expert tuning session until you run another session against the database. You can obtain the summary report by clicking on the Report | Recommendation Summary menu item in the Oracle Expert interface. Oracle Expert will then prompt you to name the summary output text report, which Oracle Expert will save on your hard drive for later perusal. You can also view the output onscreen after it has been generated, as long as the View After Creation text box in the Recommendation Summary Report interface has been selected, as shown in Figure 7-27. Oracle Expert then quickly generates a summary report of its findings, formatted into an impressive style suitable for presentation at a business meeting. A sample of Oracle Expert's output report style is included on the CD-ROM for this book in the file `summary.txt`.

Converting Analysis to Action: Implementing Recommendations

After reviewing the recommendations provided by Oracle Expert, you can have the tool help you implement its suggestions in several areas, such as by modifying your parameter file or Instance Manager parameter configuration. The Oracle Expert tool can also help you generate scripts that implement its own suggestions. You can click on the Scripts tab in the Oracle Expert interface and then click on the Generate button in that interface to have Oracle Expert generate scripts implementing its recommendations for you. Oracle Expert will notify you of the location of your scripts in the Scripts interface, such as `MINXimpl.txt` shown in Figure 7-28. You can open that file using Notepad or WordPad to see the contents. The text file

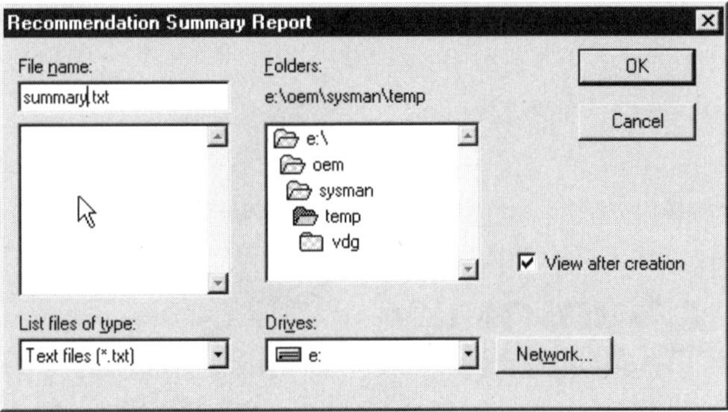

FIGURE 7-27. *Summary Recommendations report generation*

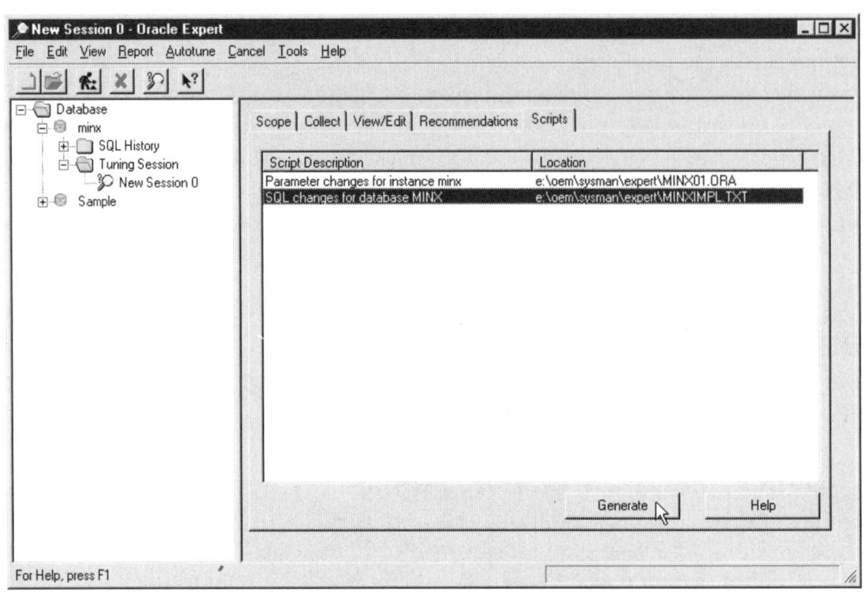

FIGURE 7-28. *Oracle Expert Scripts tab interface*

contains many SQL statements that you can then copy and paste into new files and run those files using SQL*Plus or SQL Worksheet. A copy of this file can also be found on the CD-ROM for this guide.

For Review

1. Be sure that you understand how Oracle Expert presents its findings in both a drill-down and report format.

2. Review the `summary.txt` file on the CD-ROM to familiarize yourself with the contents of a recommendations summary report.

Chapter Summary

You covered a lot of ground in this chapter and you learned many new things about troubleshooting your database, resolving blocking situations with the Oracle Lock Manager tool provided in the Oracle Diagnostics Pack, and doing high-level performance tuning using the Oracle Expert tool provided by the Oracle Tuning Pack. First, you learned about common troubleshooting situations and how to detect and avoid them. You covered how to anticipate and resolve the problems caused when the database is down, and those caused by lack of space for tablespaces and segments and over-consumption of archive and trace files. You learned about how to automate detection of problems using the OEM Job Scheduler and the OEM Event Service.

After that, the chapter covered how to detect and resolve blocking situations. You will need the Oracle Diagnostic Pack for this issue, as the standard Oracle Enterprise Manager edition does not contain Lock Manager, a key tool for performing blocking and waiting user analysis. You first covered how locks can cause blocked sessions if applications don't properly handle transaction processing. You learned by walking through examples how to create a blocking situation, which you then detected using Lock Manager. The use of Lock Manager to release blocked sessions by releasing the lock and killing the blocking session was covered as well. Finally, you covered what a deadlock is and how Oracle automatically detects deadlocks and notifies you about deadlocks occurring on the system.

The last part of this chapter covered high-level performance tuning. You learned about the use of the Oracle Expert tool in the Oracle Tuning Pack for this purpose. The chapter taught you how to perform initial setup for tuning your database using Oracle Expert and how to create a tuning session. You also learned what the steps for a tuning session were and what activities need to take place at every step of the way. Finally, you covered how to review and implement tuning recommendations offered by Oracle Expert to improve the performance of your database. Note that the CD-ROM contains reports and summaries from the Oracle Expert session illustrated as an example in this chapter for your assistance as well.

Two-Minute Drill

- OEM jobs and events can assist in diagnosing issues such as when your database is down or when tablespaces or segments run out of space.
- Some predefined events in Oracle that permit this activity include
  - **Oracle DB UpDown** Detects whether the database is up or down.
  - **Oracle Host UpDown** Detects whether the machine hosting Oracle is up or down.
  - **Oracle Listener UpDown** Detects whether the TNS listener is up or down.
  - **Oracle DB Fault** Detects faults occurring on the database, such as a blocked user.
  - **Oracle DB Resource** Detects resource issues in Oracle, such as full tablespaces.

- Be sure that you know the procedure for registering an event set for operation on a database within the OEM console.
- Three potential causes for space allocation issues on your system are listed here:
    1. A database object's maximum storage limit was set too low and has been reached.
    2. Users have added lots of data to a tablespace, the datafiles are now full, and the Auto Extend feature was not turned on.
    3. The Auto Extend feature for a tablespace's datafiles was turned on, but the disk device itself ran out of space.
- When either you or the users of the Oracle database encounter the following errors, you will know you're dealing with a space allocation issue:
    - **`ORA-01631: max # extents (`*`n`*`) reached in table`** ***`schema.name`*** An existing object's maximum number of extents has been reached, preventing the object from acquiring another extent. The cause is #1 in the previous list.
    - **ORA-01653: `Unable to extend`** ***`object schema.name`*** **`by`** ***`x`*** **`in tablespace`** ***`tbsname`*** An existing object in a tablespace cannot grow anymore. The cause could be #2 in the previous list.
    - **ORA-01658: `Unable to create INITIAL extent for segment in tablespace`** ***`name`*** A new object could not be created in a tablespace because the tablespace is out of room. This problem is most likely caused by #2 or #3 in the previous list.
- Understand that by adding too much extra space to an Oracle tablespace to accommodate growth, you also add overhead to any maintenance activities you might need to perform that involve moving those tablespace datafiles around.
- If `archivelog` mode is enabled and your archiving destination fills, Oracle will not be able to archive redo logs anymore. Online redo logs will eventually fill, and existing users will experience horrendous waits when they attempt to make changes to the database. New users will not be able to connect to the database either.
- The resolution is to clear some space in the archive destination directory by copying files to tape and removing the logs from the destination, and then performing an online redo log switch.

- Filling a trace file destination will cause Oracle to overwrite your ALERT log, causing you to lose potentially valuable alert information about your database operation.
- The resolution is to archive your trace files and clear the trace destination periodically.
- Levels of locking include row share, row exclusive, share, exclusive, share row exclusive.
- Causes of lock contention are
  - When a user process doesn't relinquish a lock it holds because transaction processing isn't performed correctly in the application
  - When a user process terminates abnormally while holding a lock in the client/server architecture
- Once a lock is acquired on a table, your session will hold that lock until you end your transaction with `commit` or `rollback`, or by ending the session. Thus, if you acquire 700 locks, your session will hold *all 700* until your transaction completes.
- Be sure you understand what a blocking situation is and how it is caused. Review the chapter content if you need to.
- A deadlock is a situation in which two sessions both need a resource that is locked by the other session, and neither session can release its own resource without acquiring the resource held by the other.
- Preventing deadlocks is done at the application level by changing the application to relinquish locks it obtains or using locks with the least amount of scope required to complete the transaction.
- Oracle errors arising from deadlocks can be found in the `alert` log, a special file the Oracle database uses to track all errors on that instance. The error `ORA-00060: deadlock detected while waiting for a resource` corresponds to a deadlock.
- Application developers can also prevent deadlocks by designing the application to acquire locks in the same order in all processes, and to use the minimum locking capability required to complete the transaction.
- Lock Manager can help you resolve blocking situations by allowing you to kill sessions blocking other sessions.

- You will want to be sure you understand the following facts about what happens when you kill a session in Lock Manager (or Instance Manager, the other OEM tool that allows you to kill sessions):
    1. The active transaction in the blocking session is rolled back.
    2. The kill won't complete until that rollback is complete.
    3. The blocking session is terminated.
    4. All locks held by the blocking session are released.
    5. The waiting session will then be able to acquire the lock it was waiting for.
- Review the SQL*Plus session transcript presented in Table 7-1 to understand deadlocking.
- Deadlocks will produce an `ORA-00060` error in the session and a trace file dump in the `USER_DUMP_DEST` directory.
- Oracle Expert is a tool that helps to diagnose and resolve tuning problems on your Oracle database. You should understand the basic usage of this tool, as covered by the chapter, before taking the OCP DBO exam.
- Oracle Expert tunes your database in the following way:
    1. You set up Oracle Expert for use and choose a database to tune.
    2. You create the tuning session.
    3. You specify scope for the tuning session. Some potential scopes you may want to limit Oracle Expert's tuning effort include application tuning, instance tuning, or storage structure tuning.
    4. Oracle Expert collects statistics. Oracle Expert collects database, instance, schema, environment, and workload information as part of this process.
    5. Oracle Expert analyzes statistics. This step can take a while.
    6. You review Oracle Expert's recommendations.
    7. You implement Oracle Expert's recommendations. You can decline some recommendations, but not all. Oracle Expert can generate scripts that will assist you in implementing those recommendations.
- Review the text to understand how to execute each tuning session step in Oracle Expert.

Chapter Questions

1. **After Oracle Expert collects statistics from the database for performance evaluation, what is the next step you will need to perform?**

   A. Tuning session setup

   B. Script generation

   C. Analysis of collected data

   D. Reviewing summary recommendation report

2. **A job has been defined that detects when a tablespace fills. Which of the following OEM console tabs would be appropriate for use in reviewing whether or not the job runs to completion?**

   A. Job

   B. Job History

   C. Job Library

   D. Recommendations

3. **A user complains that they have just received a deadlock error in their session. Where can you go to see more information about this error?**

   A. The ALERT log

   B. Trace file in BACKGROUND_DUMP_DEST

   C. Trace file in CORE_DUMP_DEST

   D. Trace file in USER_DUMP_DEST

   E. Trace file in ARCHIVE_LOG_DEST

4. **Which of the following choices correctly describes a blocking situation on an Oracle database?**

   A. A user and a batch process are updating the same row from the same table at the same time.

   B. A user is updating a table that does not exist.

   C. Two users are updating different rows from the same table.

   D. Two users are updating a row from the same table at different times, with a `commit` taking place between them.

5. **The DBO has killed a user session that was causing a blocking situation in the Oracle database. Which three of the following correctly describe actions that will occur as the result of this one?**

   A. No users will be able to access Oracle until the kill is complete.

   B. The active transaction in the blocking session is rolled back.

   C. The kill won't complete until that rollback is complete.

   D. The waiting user process will also be terminated.

   E. The blocking session is terminated.

6. **After executing Oracle Expert, the user wants to implement suggestions made to instance initialization parameters. What way can the user find out what those recommendations are?**

   A. Reviewing the Recommendations tab

   B. Reviewing the Collect tab

   C. Reviewing the Scope tab

   D. Reviewing the Scripts tab

7. **Users are complaining that performance is exceptionally slow. You believe the cause is a blocking situation. Which two of the following choices is a cause for blocking situations on a database?**

   A. A computer that crashed while trying to open the database application

   B. A batch process holding several locks needed by other users

   C. A manager who has not given users access to the application because the manager is absent today

   D. A user who left for the day without committing their work

8. **Users are complaining that the table they are trying to update is out of space. What further information would cause you to believe that the true cause is no more space available on disk?**

   A. Several other tables in the same tablespace are experiencing the same problem.

   B. The maximum number of extents allowed for that object is 5.

C. Several batch loads have put a lot of data in that table in the last month, so you turned the datafile Auto Extend feature on to avoid headaches.

D. The output from a `dir` command in the directory in which your datafiles for that tablespace are stored.

9. You are setting up event detection for segments running out of extents. Which two of the following predefined events can be used for this purpose?

A. DB UpDown

B. Tablespace Full

C. Listener UpDown

D. Maximum Extents

E. Chunk Small

10. You cannot find Lock Manager on your desktop. Which of the following Oracle Enterprise Manager products contains Lock Manager?

A. Diagnostics Pack

B. Standard OEM Pack

C. Tuning Pack

D. Change Management Pack

Answers to Chapter Questions

1. C. Analysis of collected data

Explanation After collecting data in Oracle Expert, the natural next step is to have Oracle Expert analyze it. Choice A is incorrect because tuning session setup would happen at the very beginning of the session, before any data was collected. Choice B is also incorrect because script generation would happen only after data had been collected *and* analyzed and you had reviewed the recommendations Oracle Expert provided. Finally, choice D is also incorrect because you would review the recommendations Oracle Expert made after collecting and analyzing data.

2. B. Job History

Explanation The Job History tab lists all executions of defined and submitted jobs within the database, making choice B correct. Choice A is incorrect because the Job tab only shows currently active jobs, not history. Choice C is incorrect because the Job Library tab lists all jobs stored in the OEM console for that database. Finally, Choice D is incorrect because the Recommendations tab is not even part of the OEM console; it is part of Oracle Expert.

3. B. Trace file in USER_DUMP_DEST

Explanation Deadlocks detected in user sessions cause Oracle to produce a trace file for the user's session, and these files are produced in the USER_DUMP_DEST directory. No record is written to the ALERT log, making choice A incorrect. Also, choice B is incorrect. Since user processes are not background processes, there is no reason to think the trace file would be placed in the BACKGROUND_DUMP_DEST, unless you have specified that directory to be the same as that used for USER_DUMP_DEST—a bad practice anyway. Finally, choice C is incorrect because the only things that get put into CORE_DUMP_DEST are core dumps of your Oracle SGA. Deadlock errors don't usually cause core dumps, so there is no reason for this directory to even be used.

4. A. A user and a batch process are updating the same row from the same table at the same time.

Explanation Two user processes (a batch process is considered a user process, though no "user" usually sits in front of a terminal during its execution) trying to access the same row in the same table at the same time is generally cause for a blocking situation. Choice B is incorrect because a user updating tables that don't exist usually receives an error. Choice C is incorrect because Oracle allows users to lock rows of a table for update while leaving other rows free for change by other users. Choice D is incorrect because the first user's transaction ended before the second user's transaction began, thus making it possible for two users to change the same row at different times.

5. B. The active transaction in the blocking session is rolled back.
C. The kill won't complete until that rollback is complete.
E. The blocking session is terminated.

Explanation When a blocking session is killed, the active transaction in the blocking session is rolled back. The kill also doesn't complete until that blocking session's transaction is rolled back. Finally, if a blocking session is killed, it is also terminated because terminating and killing a session are the same thing. Choice A is incorrect because users can still access the database while the kill is taking place, although some cleanup must take place to release the locks held by the blocking session before users can access the rows locked by the blocking session. Choice D is also incorrect because only the blocking session will be killed, not the waiting session.

6. A. Reviewing the Recommendations tab

Explanation To find out what recommendations have been made by Oracle, you can look at the Recommendations tab to see the recommendations online. Choice D is incorrect because reviewing the Scripts tab will only tell you where to find the scripts Oracle Expert generated to implement those recommendations. Of course, by reviewing the Scripts tab, you can reverse engineer the suggestions from how Oracle Expert is implementing them, but this takes time and thorough knowledge of the Oracle database. Choice B is incorrect because the Collect tab only helps to define statistics collection, while choice C is incorrect because the Scope tab defines tuning session scope.

7. B. A batch process holding several locks needed by other users.
D. A user who left for the day without committing his work.

Explanation Real-world reasons for blocking situations include when a batch process holds locks required by other users and when a user has not ended a transaction that holds locks required by other users. Choice A is incorrect because the computer crashed before the database application opened. Presumably, this also means that the computer crashed before the associated user session acquired any locks. Choice C is incorrect because the situation described means that fewer users can even access the system. Again, remember that to acquire locks on database information, you actually need to be connected to the database.

8. D. The output from a `dir` command in the directory in which your datafiles for that tablespace are stored.

Explanation The most conclusive evidence for knowing that the disk on which the tablespace datafiles reside is out of space is to perform a `dir` command at the DOS level to see how much space is still available on that device. Choice A is incorrect because although the situation described hints at the possibility for a full tablespace, the evidence does not rule out either that the maximum number of allowed extents is too low or that no additional room is on disk for the tablespace to grow. Choice B is incorrect because the evidence clearly suggests the possibility that the problem could really be that the maximum number of allowed extents is too low. Again, you should be looking for conclusive evidence. Choice C, though closer to the mark, is still incorrect because again you really have no information that conclusively states there is no more space left on the disk. The problem could still be one of maximum extents being set too low.

9. D. Maximum Extents.
E. Chunk Small

Explanation The two events that help detect whether maximum extents are reached for a segment are Maximum Extents and Chunk Small. Choice A is incorrect because DB UpDown detects whether the database is up or down. Choice B is incorrect because Tablespace Full simply detects whether or not a tablespace is full. Finally, choice C is incorrect because Listener UpDown detects whether or not your Net8 listener has failed.

10. A. Diagnostics Pack

Explanation The Oracle Diagnostics Pack contains Lock Manager, along with additional events that help you perform system diagnostics, and other tools that assist in monitoring the overall activities on your database. Choice B is incorrect because the Standard Management pack that comes with OEM does not contain Lock Manager. Nor does the Tuning Pack, making choice C incorrect. However, the Tuning Pack does contain Oracle Expert. Finally, choice D is incorrect because the Change Management Pack contains tools that assist in software version control and other things, but not Lock Manager.

CHAPTER 8

SQL Queries in SQL*Plus

n this chapter, you will cover the following topics regarding SQL queries in SQL*Plus:

- Looking at the Oracle RDBMS
- Basic database design
- Oracle and SQL*Plus
- Looking at SQL*Plus
- Introducing SQL commands
- Customizing queries
- Conditional clauses
- Comparison operators
- Applying multiple conditions
- Applying single-row functions
- Using single-row functions for data conversion
- Introducing table joins
- Some simple equijoins
- Using outer joins and self joins
- Group functions
- Creating and selecting groups

There's a great deal of information presented in this chapter, and it's all related to `select` statements in Oracle. You will learn all you need to know to start formulating your own queries against the Oracle database, using SQL*Plus. Some of the important things you will learn include how to create conditions limiting the data returned by the query, use of single-row functions, how to join data from one table to data in another table, and the use of group functions in Oracle. Feel free to take frequent breaks for better digestion of this important material regarding the use of Oracle `select` statements.

Instructions for Using the chapter8.sql Script

To assist you in learning this material, you may use the `chapter8.sql` script included on the CD-ROM to create the tables referred to in this chapter. However, for practice's sake, you will have to enter the queries shown yourself! To use the script, follow these instructions:

1. Put the CD-ROM from the back of this book into your CD-ROM drive.
2. Open a DOS prompt on your Windows machine.
3. Type **<DRIVE>:**, where <DRIVE> is your CD-ROM drive; open SQL*Plus; connect as a user; and use the appropriate combination of `cd` and `dir` commands to find and move into the directory containing the `chapter8.sql` script on the CD-ROM. If you cannot find that file, you can download it into any directory on your machine from www.exampilot.com.
4. From that same directory containing `chapter8.sql`, start SQL*Plus according to the instructions already provided. *The user you log in as must have the `create table` privilege granted to it!*
5. From within SQL*Plus, issue the command **@chapter8.sql** and press ENTER. Some tables will be created and populated with data.

Looking at the Oracle RDBMS

A relational database consists of many components, some of which already have been covered. These components include objects that store data, objects that aid in accessing data quickly, and objects that manage user access to data. Additionally, objects in the database contain the code that is used to manipulate and change data, to produce reports of data, and to otherwise use data to produce the desired result. Some of the objects that are part of the relational database produced by Oracle and that are used in the functions just mentioned are as follows:

- **Tables, views, and synonyms** Used to store and access data
- **Indexes and the RDBMS** Used to speed access to data
- **Triggers and integrity constraints** Used to maintain the validity of data entered
- **Privileges, roles, and profiles** Used to manage database access and usage
- **Packages, procedures, and functions** Used to code the applications that will use the database

For Review

1. What is a relational database model?
2. What are the components of a relational database? How are they used?

Basic Database Design

A relational database works on the principle of having relational data stored within tables, which can contain many columns. However, that doesn't mean that database designers can just create two or three giant tables and throw all their data in those tables, at least not if they are good database designers! Instead, the designer first models the business process flow for which the application will be used in something called an *entity relationship diagram*. This diagram, also called an ERD, focuses on business processes, not computer systems. From there, the database designer works with analysts to figure out what data must be stored for that ERD at every step of the business process. This effort is called *logical data modeling*. The resulting model, sometimes called an LDM, is used as the basis for creating tables in the Oracle database. As a database operator, you most likely will not get called in to create a data model or entity-relationship diagram. However, you might be interested in knowing what they are.

Stages of System Development

The steps involved in the software development life cycle are as follows:

- Needs assessment
- Database design
- Application development
- Performance tuning
- Database security
- Enhancements

Needs Assessment

A database system begins as an idea in someone's head. At this early stage in the game, a database application's possibilities can seem endless—however, this stage is fraught with danger. Important questions to be answered by the end of this planning stage are whether this application will support large-volume data entry, or is the fundamental point of this application to make data viewable to users. In many cases, the answer is both. By the end of needs assessment, the designer of an application should have clear answers to the following questions:

- Who will use the application?
- What use will the application fill in the organization?
- How do people plan to use the application?

Information you obtain from user-facilitated meetings can increase the likelihood of project success by involving users in important decisions early and often. By the end of needs assessment, the team developing the application should know the fundamental purpose of the application.

Database Design

The database design lays the groundwork for success in supporting the current and future needs of the application. The two steps of designing a database are these:

- Creating an entity-relationship diagram
- Translating an entity-relationship diagram into a logical data model

Creating an entity-relationship diagram and translating it into a logical data model is an involved process. The process is important, however, in ensuring correctly designed tables that can support both the user interface and the reports. Even though the users will interface with the database via the application in a controlled manner, it is still important to have a strong database design to ensure the success of the application.

Application Development

Once the users' needs are assessed and the database design is in place, the building of the application logic can begin. At this point, questions about what the application screens, Web pages, and reports will look like start to be answered. Some components of the application can be placed within the database, such as integrity constraints defining data relationships, triggers to control cascading data changes, stored procedures or packages for application logic, and tuned SQL statements to manage performance. Other components are put in separate areas, like Web servers, application servers, Java applets, or robust applications running on client hardware. Application development often involves stepwise refinement. As new needs are discovered, the application software that models business rules will undoubtedly grow more complex. PL/SQL is Oracle's procedural language extension to SQL. PL/SQL enables you to mix SQL statements with procedural constructs. With PL/SQL, you can define and execute PL/SQL program units, such as procedures, functions, and packages.

Performance Tuning

No application is harder to use than a slow one. The source of most performance issues in applications using Oracle databases is the application code itself. Particularly with proprietary software developed in-house, the application developers should explore alternative methods for providing the same data to the user interface or reports in order to maximize performance wherever possible.

However, many organizations have begun using packaged applications that do not allow the developer to get into the nitty-gritty of SQL statements. As an NT system administrator, your role as database operator may involve assessing whether a hardware upgrade might present an effective alternative to rewriting code or suffering with a slow application.

Database Security

Database security is an important factor in any database, allowing the developers and managers for the database system to handle large user populations, if necessary, and to limit database access to those users who require it. Early in the development of an application, the levels of data access that will be granted to each user or type of user in the system should be determined. Users should be divided into rough categories to determine what data they need to access to perform their tasks. Once general access and usage levels for various users are established, there are features within the Oracle database that allow the developer or the DBA to limit users to only their access level or to restrict their usage of the database to only what they need. Some key terms to know here are *privileges* and *roles* for managing user access and *resource profiles* for managing system hardware usage. Oracle8 and Oracle8*i* also provide advanced password administration features for user management.

Enhancements

Enhancements are often as important as the actual application in the minds of the users, because they represent an evolution of the business process that must be modeled by the application supporting that business process. However, in some ways, developing enhancements is often riskier than developing the original application, itself. Some of the advantages of the initial application development—such as reduced production burden on the developers of the application, a structured project plan, funding, and management attention—are lost once the application sees its first few months of successful production life. When enhancements are requested, the developers often have to do double duty—they are both the enhancement developers who have to rework existing code *and* the analysts who have to handle the production issues of the application as they arise. However, these obstacles represent an opportunity for success as much as one for failure. Strong project management in these situations generally helps the enhancement development effort succeed.

For Review

1. What are the stages of the software development life cycle?
2. What important questions should be answered before the application is developed?

Relational Database Components

Every database starts out as an entity-relationship diagram. In order to model a business process, the developers of an application must first map out the different components of a system into an ERD. The ERD consists of two different components:

- **Entity** A person, place, thing, or idea involved in the business-process flow
- **Relationship** The ties that bind entities together

In order to explain the process of creating an ERD, we'll go through an example of buying and wearing a sweater. Already in this description, a few entities have emerged in the description of the application to be created, namely, *wearer* (a person), *sweater* (things), and *bank check* (a means of payment). Some relationships have also been identified, such as *pay* and *wear,* which are activities. Figure 8-1 shows an entity-relationship diagram for this example.

A database application often begins with looking at the process as it already exists. For this example, assume there is inefficiency in the current process. You

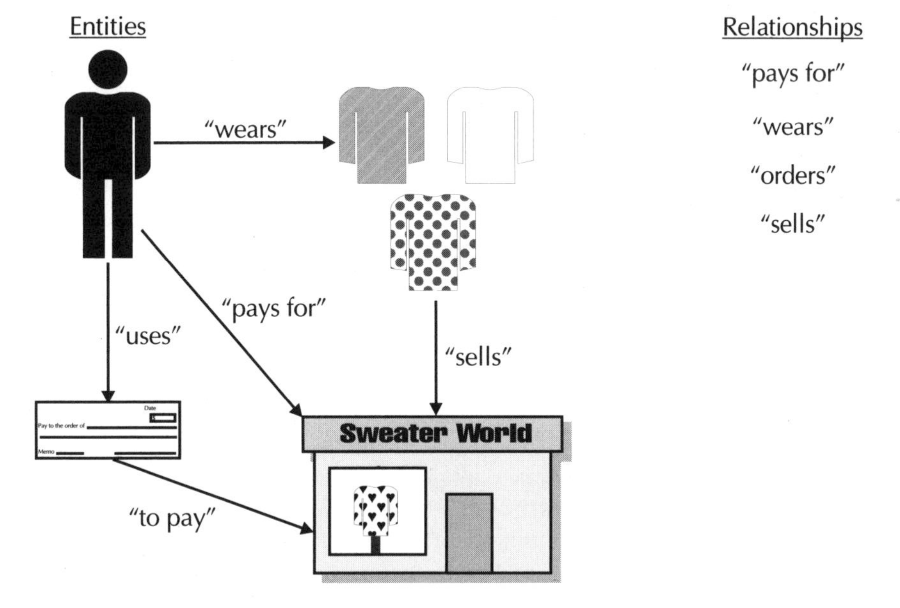

FIGURE 8-1. *An entity-relationship diagram of buying and wearing sweaters*

may have to drive a long way to get to the department store to get the sweater, only to find that the store is out of your favorite color. Also, if there is a problem with your check, the store may not know about it for several days. On top of that, it may take several more weeks for the problem to be corrected. These reasons are enough to justify the need for a more automated process, and the ERD is the mechanism to model that process.

The LDM and Data Relationships

Once an entity-relationship diagram is created, the developer must determine what data needs to be stored for each entity and relationship in the ERD in order to model the process into a logical data model. In well-constructed databases, the columns in each table relate to each other in precise and specific ways. Every table will have a main column or set of columns, whose stored values are used to identify a row in the table as unique from every other row. This main column in a table is called the table's *primary key.*

The relationship of every other column in a table to the primary key is called *functional dependency.* Functionally dependent columns relate to or modify only the primary key of the table; they do not modify a nonprimary key column. For example, a table called SWEATERS may have columns like SWEATER_ID (a unique number) as the primary key and dependent columns like SW_COLOR and SW_SIZE to indicate sweater color and size. However, the SWEATERS table would not contain a column listing the sweater wearer's mailing address, because a person's mailing address is not functionally dependent on the uniqueness of a sweater.

Functionally dependent or primary-key columns in one table may relate to primary-key columns in other tables through something called a *foreign-key relationship.* In relational databases, this relationship is often referred to as a *parent/child* relationship because in the child table, the data can appear either as part of the primary key or as a functionally dependent column, while in the parent table the referenced column *must appear in the primary key.* Foreign-key relationships are useful in situations in which users want to retrieve data stored in two or more different tables. Continuing with our example, the SW_SIZE column in table SWEATERS may have a foreign-key relationship with the primary key of a special *validation* or *lookup* table called VALID_SIZES. In this case, no row in the SWEATERS table will contain a value for the SW_SIZE column that does not correspond to a row in the VALID_SIZES table. Figure 8-2 demonstrates the primary-key, foreign-key, and functionally dependent data relationships described.

Primary-key relationships between data must be defined explicitly within the tables themselves via *integrity constraints.* However, foreign-key relationships can be defined through integrity constraints, through related database objects called *triggers* that fire every time a data change is made, or through an application. Any column that is not the primary key of the table must be functionally dependent on

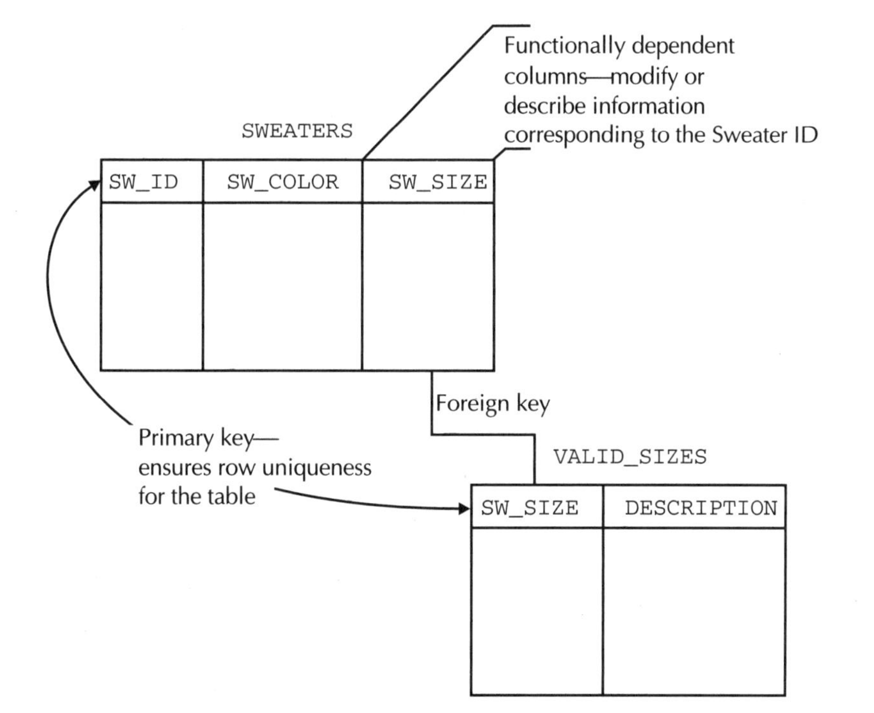

FIGURE 8-2. *Primary-key, foreign-key, and functionally dependent relationships*

the primary key for that table. To ensure that all nonprimary key columns are functionally dependent on primary keys in all tables of a database, the designer of that database must engage in what is known as the *database normalization process.* Normalization is a process that was created by E. F. Codd of IBM in the 1950s as part of the original design of databases. An often-used mantra for database designers when engaging in the normalization process is to make every column in every table dependent on "the key, the whole key, and nothing but the key (so help me Codd)!"

TIP
Data normalization is the act of separating column data into tables where each column in the table is functionally dependent on only one primary key. This process reduces data-storage costs by eliminating redundancy, and it minimizes the dependence of any column in the normalized database to only one primary key.

Role of Ordinality

Related to the discussion of foreign keys and table relationships is something called *ordinality*. The ordinality of a table relationship represents two important features about the relationship:

- Whether the relationship is mandatory or optional for these objects
- Whether one record in the table corresponds to one or to many records in the other table

The ordinality of a table relationship contains two elements and is generally represented in the logical data model as an "ordered pair," usually (0,*N*) or (1,1), or (1,*N*), or something similar. The first component in the ordered pair identifies whether the relationship is mandatory or optional. The number 1 indicates the relationship is mandatory, while 0 indicates the relationship is optional. The second component of the ordered pair indicates whether one row in this table relates to one or many rows in the other table. The number 1 indicates a one-to-one relationship, while *N* indicates a one-to-many relationship.

In some cases, the relationship between two entities may not be required. Consider the example of employees and expenses. This relationship works in two directions: from employees to expenses, and from expenses to employees. In the direction of employees to expenses, the relationship is optional. That is to say, an employee need not have ever incurred expenses on behalf of the company. However, in the other direction, from expenses to employees, the relationship is mandatory because each and every expense submitted to the employee expense system will correspond to an employee. In the direction of employees to expenses, there is a one-to-many relationship, as each employee in the company may have submitted one or more expense reports in the course of their employment, or none at all. In contrast, in the other direction, each expense submitted will always have one and only one employee who submitted it, as shown in Figure 8-3. In that figure, each ordered pair describes the relationship between the table the ordered pair is closest to and the table at the other end of the line drawn from one table to another. In the case of EMP and EXPENSE, the (1,1) ordered pair closest to table EMP indicates the mandatory one-to-one relationship of EMP rows to EXPENSE rows. The (0,*N*) ordered pair closest to the EXPENSE table on the same line indicates that in the other direction, EXPENSE rows have an optional one-to-many relationship to rows in table EMP.

Another form of notation exists for logical data models that you should be aware of. Instead of showing mandatory or optional relationships with a 1 or 0 in the first number of an ordered pair, respectively, the LDM may show mandatory relationships with a solid line connecting the two tables and a broken line to show optional relationships. Also, a one-to-many relationship will be shown with

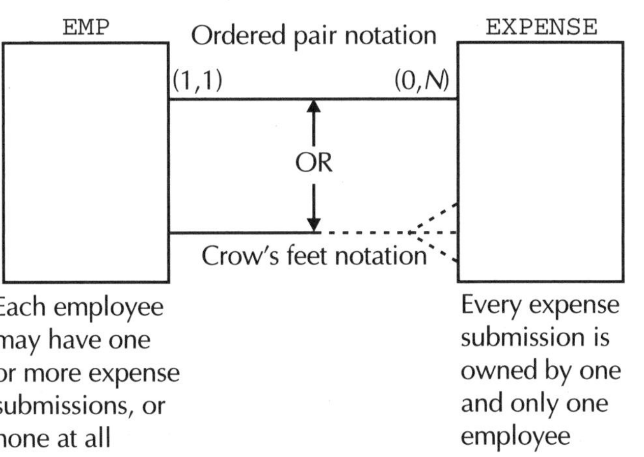

FIGURE 8-3. *The logical data model for the employee expense system*

"crows feet." Figure 8-3 shows this alternative form of data modeling notation, along with ordered pairs.

For Review

1. What is an entity-relationship diagram, and how is it read?
2. What is a logical data model? Identify some methods used to translate an entity-relationship diagram into a data model.
3. What are three types of data relationships? What is functional dependency? What is required of two tables in order for the tables to be related to one another?
4. What is ordinality, and how is it significant?

Oracle and SQL*Plus

Experience with Oracle for many DBOs begins with using an existing Oracle application in an organization. The first tool you might see for selecting data directly from the Oracle relational database management system is SQL*Plus. As you already may have surmised, however, Oracle is not "just" SQL*Plus. Oracle consists of a relational database management system, or RDBMS, which you have already learned how to install and administer. SQL*Plus is a GUI tool that helps you see the data stored in an Oracle database. Some users mistakenly refer to SQL*Plus as "Oracle." While not being completely incorrect (after all, SQL*Plus is an Oracle product!), you should remember that the data you see in SQL*Plus is not actually stored in SQL*Plus—it is stored in the Oracle database you have already learned about.

For Review

Understand the differences between SQL*Plus and the Oracle RDBMS.

Looking at SQL*Plus

When users first start SQL*Plus, they usually must enter their Oracle username and password in order to begin a session with the Oracle database. Some exceptions to this rule utilize the password authentication provided with the operating system. The following examples show how you might begin a session with Oracle from the DOS command line. From within Windows, you can instead click on Start | Programs | Oracle for Windows | SQL*Plus, or double-click the SQL*Plus icon on your desktop if one appears there.

```
C:\> plus33 jason/athena
```

or

```
C:\> plus80 /
```

After issuing the `plus33` or `plus80` command, depending on which version of Oracle you use, a SQL*Plus session with the Oracle database is started. A *session* is an interactive runtime environment in which you enter commands to retrieve data and Oracle performs a series of activities to obtain the data you ask for. The following code block shows the first text block you should see in an Oracle SQL*Plus session:

```
SQL*Plus: Release 8.0.5.0.0 - Production on Tue Feb 03 18:53:11 1999
Copyright © Oracle Corporation 1979, 1998.  All rights reserved.
Connected to: Oracle8 Release 8.0.5.1.0
With the distributed and replication options
PL/SQL Release 8.0.5.1.0 Production
SQL>
```

The first part of this code block, containing the copyright information, is a "welcome" message from SQL*Plus. If you wanted, you could suppress this information in your call to SQL*Plus from the operating system command line by entering **plus80 –s** and pressing ENTER, where the `-s` extension indicates SQL*Plus should run in silent mode. Of course, the text message appearing in the preceding code block may appear in a standalone window or within the DOS prompt window. Figure 8-4 demonstrates the SQL*Plus interface you will see running Oracle in Windows environments. Now, to get a feel for how SQL*Plus works, type **`select * from dual`**. Do not put a semicolon at the end of your current line. When finished, press ENTER. Notice that SQL*Plus now shows your cursor on a new line with a number indicating the current line number. If you press ENTER again, notice that you have now been returned to the `SQL>` prompt. The following code block illustrates:

```
SQL> select * from dual
2
SQL>
```

Oracle SQL*Plus allows you to enter SQL statements that are many lines long in this way, but makes it a little difficult to return to a previous line to correct mistakes. One way to do so is with the `change` command, which is sometimes abbreviated

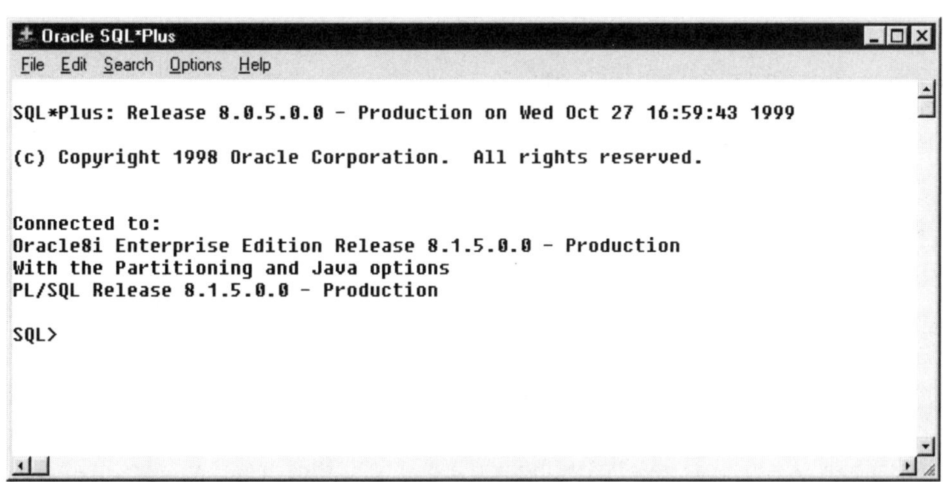

FIGURE 8-4. *SQL*Plus in Windows*

c. Observe in the following code block one way to make changes to prior lines of code using this command:

```
SQL> select *
  2  from survey
  3  where
  4  survey_name = 'GRAMMY AWARDS'
  5  and respondent = 'JASON COUCHMAN'
  6
SQL> 5
  5* and respondent = 'JASON COUCHMAN'
SQL> change/COUCHMAN/SPANKY
  5* and respondent = 'JASON SPANKY'
SQL> c/SPANKY/COUCHMAN
  5* and respondent = 'JASON COUCHMAN'
SQL>
```

Note that, after entering a SQL statement spanning multiple lines, you must first press ENTER enough times to return you to the `SQL>` prompt, then type the line number you want to change, and then use the `change` command in the format `change/`*`old`*`/`*`new`*. The abbreviated usage is shown in the code block as well. If all this line number reference and use of the `change` command seems cumbersome to you, take heart. The other way to make data changes is much simpler. After realizing you made a mistake, all you need to do is press ENTER until you get back to the `SQL>` prompt, and then type in the `edit` command (sometimes abbreviated as `ed`). The query you just entered will then appear in a text editor like Notepad, ready for you to edit, as shown in Figure 8-5. In this way, you are able to edit your SQL statements more easily using a flexible text editor you are already familiar with. You should, however, practice entering your SQL statements into SQL*Plus both ways to become familiar with the process so that you can handle entering SQL in any situation that might be called for.

Using the login.sql Script

SQL*Plus allows you to configure many aspects of your interaction with Oracle in the database session using two files that are run automatically when SQL*Plus starts. The main way to configure your session is using a special file called `login.sql`. This script usually contains many `set` commands that may be used to specify the length, format masks, and appearance qualities of columns and data in your SQL*Plus session. This script can also be used to dynamically modify the prompt message shown instead of `SQL>` while you are in SQL*Plus. You can take the time to develop your own `login.sql` script; however, this is time consuming. It is better to get one from a colleague at work, or from the Internet. A great one to use was developed by Mike Lang, and is available on http://www.geocities.com/

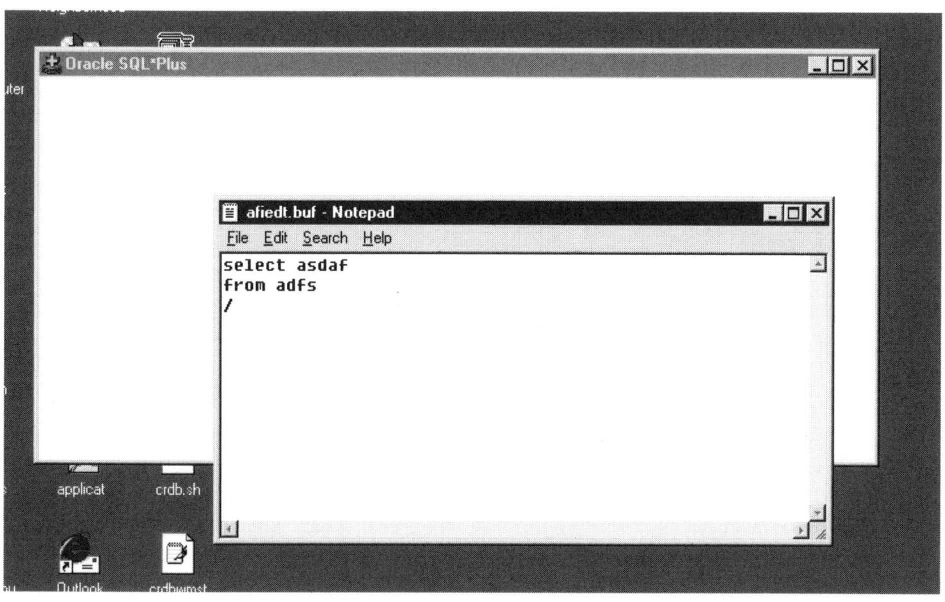

FIGURE 8-5. *Editing queries in SQL*Plus*

SiliconValley/Lakes/1261. The `login.sql` file is designed for an individual user's usage. A similar file, called `glogin.sql`, can be configured for global usage for all users on a host system. An example of a `glogin.sql` script from the Oracle8 Enterprise Edition for Windows NT, version 8.0.5 distribution software, is shown in the following code block:

```
rem SQL*Plus Global Login startup file.
Rem
rem This is the global login file for SQL*Plus.
rem Add any sqlplus commands here that are to be
rem executed when a user invokes sqlplus
rem Used by Trusted Oracle
column ROWLABEL format A15
rem Used for the SHOW ERRORS command
column LINE/COL format A8
column ERROR    format A65  WORD_WRAPPED
rem For backward compatibility
set pagesize 14
rem Defaults for SET AUTOTRACE EXPLAIN report
column id_plus_exp format 990 heading I
```

```
column parent_id_plus_exp format 990 heading p
column plan_plus_exp format a60
column object_node_plus_exp format a8
column other_tag_plus_exp format a29
column other_plus_exp format a44
```

Setting Up the login.sql File

To set up `login.sql`, you will need to follow these steps:

1. Make a `C:\sql` directory on your client machine running SQL*Plus using the `mkdir` command from a DOS prompt, or using Windows Explorer. Your `login.sql` script goes into that directory.
2. At the DOS command prompt or Run dialog window from your Start menu, execute the Windows Registry Editor by typing **`regedit`**.
3. In Registry Editor, go to `[HKEY_LOCAL_MACHINE\SOFTWARE\ORACLE]`. Append the value `C:\sql` to the string key `SQLPATH`, or create this string key if it does not exist already.

For Review

1. What commands are used to start SQL*Plus? How can you suppress the copyright information displayed at the beginning of your SQL*Plus session?
2. How are commands entered and edited in SQL*Plus?

Introducing SQL Commands

When you are in a SQL*Plus session, Oracle sits there waiting for you to issue commands, telling it what information to retrieve and how to retrieve it. You may think of this as a conversation, which in turn implies language. You communicate with Oracle using structured query language, or SQL for short. (SQL can be pronounced either as three individual letters or as "sequel.") SQL is a "functional" language, which means that you specify the types of things you want to see happen in terms of the results you want. Contrast this approach to other languages you may have heard about or programmed in, such as C++ or COBOL, which are often referred to as "procedural" programming languages because the code written in these languages implies an end result by explicitly defining the means, or the procedure, by which to get there. In contrast, SQL explicitly defines the end result, leaving it up to Oracle to determine the method by which the data is obtained. Data selection can be accomplished using the following code listing:

```
SELECT *
FROM emp
WHERE empid = 39334;
```

Data Selection in SQL*Plus

This basic SQL `select` statement asks Oracle to provide all data from the EMP table where the value in a certain column called EMPID equals 39334. The following block of code from an imaginary procedural programming language similar to C illustrates how the same function may be handled by explicitly defining the means to the end:

```
Include <stdio.h>
Include <string.h>
Include <rdbms.h>

Int *empid;
Char *statement;

Type emp_rec is record (
Int             empid;
Char[10]        emp_name;
Int             salary; )

Void main()

  Access_table(emp);
  Open(statement.memaddr);
  Strcpy("SELECT * FROM EMP WHERE EMPID = 39334",statement.text);
  parse(statement);
  execute(statement);
  for (I=1,I=statement.results,I+1)
    fetch(statement.result[I],emp_rec);
    printf(emp_rec);

  close(statement.memaddr);
```

Of course, that C-like block of code would not compile anywhere but in your imagination, but the point of the example is clear—other languages define a process, while SQL defines the result. The most common type of SQL statement executed in most database environments is the *query*, or `select` statement. `Select` statements pull requested data from tables in a database. Every select statement has two parts or "clauses," a *select* or *column* clause where you list the columns you would like to see in your output, and a *from* or *table* clause where you list the tables in which the columns are stored. In addition, sometimes Oracle developers and DBAs refer to database objects like tables as being part of something called a *schema*. A schema is a logical grouping of database objects, such as tables, specified by owner. The following code block demonstrates a `select` statement used to obtain data from the EMP table. I log into my database as myself, JASON, and I own the EMP table. Thus, the EMP table you will see is part of the JASON schema. The schema your copy of the EMP table belongs to will depend on who you logged in to Oracle as when you ran the `chapter8.sql` script. Note that the `column format` commands in the following output are designed to make the SQL*Plus output more readable.

```
SQL> column salary format a8
SQL> column lastname format a12
SQL> column firstname format a10
SQL> column dept format a6
SQL> column salary format 9999999
SQL> select * from emp;
SQL> column empid format a7
SQL> select * from emp;
EMPID   LASTNAME     FIRSTNAME    SALARY DEPT   HIRE_DATE
------- ------------ ---------- -------- ------ ---------
02039   WALLA        RAJENDRA      60000 604B   01-JAN-96
39334   SMITH        GINA          75000 604B   15-MAR-97
60403   HARPER       ROD           45000 504A   30-APR-79
49539   QIAN         LEE           90000 504A   25-MAY-99
49392   SPANKY       STACY        100000 604B   14-FEB-98
12345   BUGGY                      55000
6 rows selected.
```

TIP
A schema is a logical grouping of database objects based on the user that owns the objects.

The line in bold in the preceding excerpt illustrates the entry of a simple SQL statement. The query requests Oracle to return all data from all columns in the EMP table. Oracle replies with the contents of the EMP table. Note that you did not tell Oracle how to retrieve the data; you simply specified the data you wanted using SQL syntax and Oracle returned it. There are other types of commands in SQL for adding or modifying data in tables, as well as commands for creating tables and other database objects. For now, make sure you understand how to specify a schema owner, the table name, and the column name in a `select` statement in SQL*Plus. The following code block demonstrates proper usage:

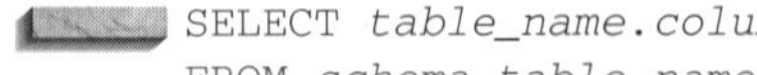

```
SELECT table_name.column_name, table_name.column_name
FROM schema.table_name;
```

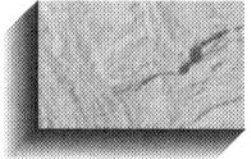

TIP
*You will usually use a semicolon (;) to end SQL statements when entering them directly into SQL*Plus. You can use a slash in some situations, such as for SQL*Plus batch scripts, as well.*

For Review

1. A `select` statement is composed of what two clauses? What are the contents of those two clauses?
2. What is the difference between a functional and procedural programming language? SQL is what type of language?
3. What is a schema?

Conditional Clauses

Obtaining all output from a table is great, but usually you must be more selective in choosing output. Most database applications contain a lot of data. How much data can a database contain? Some applications contain tables with a million rows or more, and the most recent release of Oracle8 will store up to 512 petabytes ($512*1024^5$ bytes) of data. Of course, this is only a theoretical limit; the real amount of data you can store with Oracle depends on how much disk space you give Oracle to use. But, needless to say, manipulating vast amounts of data like that requires you to be careful. Always ask for *exactly* what you want, and no more.

The where Clause

The `where` clause in Oracle `select` statements is where the really interesting things begin. This important optional clause in `select` statements allows you to single out a few rows from hundreds, thousands, or even millions like it. The `where` clause operates on a basic principle of comparison:

```
SQL> select * from emp where empid = '49392';
EMPID   LASTNAME     FIRSTNAME    SALARY DEPT   HIRE_DATE
------- ------------ ---------- -------- ------ ---------
49392   SPANKY       STACY        100000 604B   14-FEB-98
```

In the example, the Oracle RDBMS goes through every record in the EMP table, comparing the value in the EMPID column with the value 49392. If the value in the EMPID column equals 49392, then Oracle will return that row to the user. If not, the Oracle RDBMS discards that row and moves on. Oracle will keep working to find rows in which the value in the EMPID column equals 49392 until every row in the EMP table has been investigated.

Note that only columns in the table specified in the `from` clause of your SQL query may be used in `where` clause comparison operations. Consider the following example, in which table EMP has columns EMPID, LASTNAME, FIRSTNAME, and SALARY. Your `select` statement's `from` clause, containing only references to the EMP table, can use any of the columns from the EMP table in your `where` clause comparison operations, even if that column is not listed in the `select` clause.

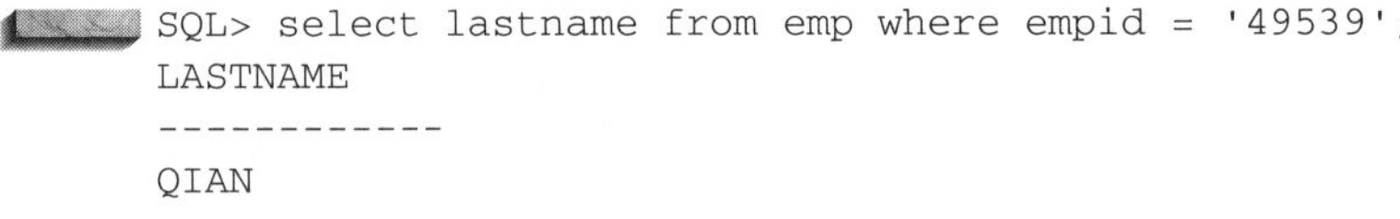

```
SQL> select lastname from emp where empid = '49539';
LASTNAME
------------
QIAN
```

For Review

1. What is a `where` clause, and how is it formulated?
2. Is a `where` clause required in a SQL query? Why or why not?

Customizing Queries

There are many ways for you to customize your queries. Options abound. For example, you can specify one or more columns, or all columns, in a table to be selected. Furthermore, you can change the output of a query to show a different heading for that column than the name of the column in the table. For example, to change the EMP table's SALARY column heading in your output to something else, such as "Pay," you can use a *column alias*. You specify that alias after the column reference in the query, optionally using the `as` keyword. The following code block illustrates the two ways to define column aliases:

```
SQL> select lastname, salary "Pay" from emp;
LASTNAME           Pay
------------ ---------
WALLA            60000
SMITH            75000
HARPER           45000
QIAN             90000
SPANKY          100000
BUGGY            55000
6 rows selected.
SQL> select lastname, salary as pay from emp;
```

```
LASTNAME           PAY
------------ ---------
WALLA            60000
SMITH            75000
HARPER           45000
QIAN             90000
SPANKY          100000
BUGGY            55000
6 rows selected.
```

Note that specifying the alias in double-quotes (" ") forces SQL*Plus to write the alias exactly as you specified it. Otherwise, Oracle will convert the alias to all capital letters. Another interesting and fun thing to do with your SQL queries is to make them dynamically modifiable using lexical substitutions. A *lexical substitution* is a special character flag that tells SQL*Plus to prompt for input for this variable. Lexical substitutions are especially handy for repeated execution of queries in SQL*Plus using different values in the `where` clause. For example, let's say you needed to check the last name of some employees for whom you had only EMPID information. You could formulate a query such as the one in the following code block to retrieve that information:

```
SQL> select lastname from emp where empid = '&empid';
Enter value for empid: 60403
old   1: select lastname from emp where empid = '&empid'
new   1: select lastname from emp where empid = '60403'
LASTNAME
------------
HARPER
```

For Review

1. What is a column alias, and how is it formulated?
2. What is a lexical substitution, and how is it formulated?

Comparison Operators

Assuming the EMPID column contains all unique values, instead of pulling all rows from EMP, Oracle pulls just one row for display. To determine what row to display, the `where` clause performs a comparison operation as specified by the query—in this case, the comparison is an equality operation, `where empid = 49392`.

However, equality is not the only means by which Oracle can obtain data. Some other examples of comparison operations are demonstrated in the following list:

`x = y`	Comparison to see if *x* is equal to *y*
`x > y`	Comparison to see if *x* is greater than *y*
`x >= y`	Comparison to see if *x* is greater than or equal to *y*
`x < y`	Comparison to see if *x* is less than *y*
`x <= y`	Comparison to see if *x* is less than or equal to *y*

`x <> y`
`x != y`
`x ^= y`
	Comparison to see if *x* is not equal to *y*

`like`	A special comparison used in conjunction with the character wildcards (`%` or `_`) to find substrings in text variables.
`soundex`	A special function used to introduce "fuzzy logic" into text string comparisons by allowing equality based on similarly spelled words.
`between`	A range comparison operation that allows for operations on dates, numbers, and characters that are similar to the following numeric comparison: *y* "is between" *x* and *z*.
`in`	A special comparison that allows you to specify multiple equality statements by defining a set of values, any of which the value can be equal to. An example of its usage may be `x in (1,2,3,4,5)`.
`is`	A special comparison used for denoting equivalence to NULL. An example of its usage is `x is null`.

Comparison Operations in Action

Here are some examples of SQL statements using alternative comparison operations in their `where` clauses:

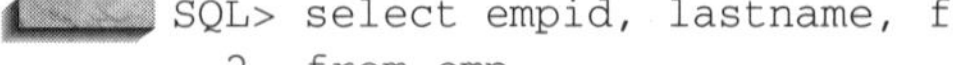

```
SQL> select empid, lastname, firstname, salary
  2  from emp
  3  where empid > '23456';
EMPID   LASTNAME     FIRSTNAME    SALARY
------- ------------ ---------- --------
39334   SMITH        GINA          75000
60403   HARPER       ROD           45000
49539   QIAN         LEE           90000
49392   SPANKY       STACY        100000
```

```
SQL> select empid, lastname, firstname, salary
  2  from emp
  3  where lastname like 'SMI%';
EMPID   LASTNAME     FIRSTNAME    SALARY
------- ------------ ---------- --------
39334   SMITH        GINA          75000

SQL> select empid, lastname, firstname, salary
  2  from emp
  3  where empid between '45039' and '70980';
EMPID   LASTNAME     FIRSTNAME    SALARY
------- ------------ ---------- --------
60403   HARPER       ROD           45000
49539   QIAN         LEE           90000
49392   SPANKY       STACY        100000

SQL> select empid, lastname, firstname, salary
  2  from emp
  3  where lastname in ('BUGGY','SMITH','SPANKY');
EMPID   LASTNAME     FIRSTNAME    SALARY
------- ------------ ---------- --------
39334   SMITH        GINA          75000
49392   SPANKY       STACY        100000
12345   BUGGY                      55000

SQL> select empid, lastname, firstname, salary
  2  from emp
  3  where empid is null;
no rows selected
```

For Review

1. What nonequality comparison operation allows you to find text string information when only part of the string is available? What are the wildcard characters you would use in this situation?
2. Which comparison operation allows you to specify a range of values between which the compared value should fall?

Applying Multiple Conditions

Every comparison between two values in Oracle boils down to one or more of the comparison operations listed in the previous discussion. However, there may come a time when you want to find data in a table according to more than one. Multiple comparisons can be placed together using the following list of operations. The operators available for piecing together multiple comparison operations in your where clauses are listed, along with the result required to fulfill the criteria based on the presence of this operator.

x and *y*	Both comparisons in *x* and *y* must be true.
x or *y*	One comparison in *x* or *y* must be true.
not *x*	The logical opposite of *x*.

Multiple Comparisons in Action

Multiple comparisons can be used any time you need to apply multiple conditions to the selection of data in a where clause of a select statement. The following example illustrates:

```
SQL> select empid, lastname, firstname, salary
  2  from emp
  3  where lastname = 'SMITH' OR empid = '49392';
EMPID   LASTNAME     FIRSTNAME    SALARY
------- ------------ ---------- --------
39334   SMITH        GINA          75000
49392   SPANKY       STACY        100000
```

Notice that both information for Gina Smith and Stacy Spanky are returned because of the use of the or keyword, joining comparison operations. However, when you change or to and, watch what happens:

```
SQL> select empid, lastname, firstname, salary
  2  from emp
  3  where lastname = 'SMITH' AND empid = '49392';
no rows selected
```

For Review

Identify all keywords in Oracle used to link comparison operations. Describe the use of each.

Applying Single-Row Functions

Oracle comes fully equipped with many different functions that can be applied to each row of data returned by the query. These functions, called *single-row functions,* handle a variety of tasks. Some functions in Oracle are designed to alter the data returned by a query. One example of this type of function is the `nvl(`*`column, sub_val`*`)` function, which accepts two variables, *`column`* and *`sub_val`*. When the value in the column specified is NULL, `nvl( )` substitutes *`sub_val`* in the return data. Let's look at a specific row in the EMP table for employee 12345, whose last name is Buggy, and who makes $55,000 per year. Let's assume we don't know Buggy's first name. The following code block shows output from a simple `select` statement, showing Buggy's employment data:

```
SQL> select empid, lastname, firstname, salary
  2  from emp
  3  where empid = '12345';
EMPID   LASTNAME     FIRSTNAME    SALARY
------- ------------ ---------- --------
12345   BUGGY                      55000
```

Notice no information is supplied in the FIRSTNAME column for this employee. Oracle stores a NULL value representing the lack of information for this column in the table. NULL stands for a nothing value. If you wanted to see the word "UNKNOWN" instead to indicate a NULL value, you could use the `nvl( )` function to make Oracle substitute the word "UNKNOWN" wherever it finds a NULL value in the FIRSTNAME column. The following code block illustrates this:

```
SQL> select empid, lastname,
  2  nvl(firstname, 'Unknown'), salary
  3  from emp
  4  where empid = '12345';
EMPID   LASTNAME     NVL(FIRSTNAME,'UNKNOWN')   SALARY
------- ------------ ------------------------ --------
12345   BUGGY        Unknown                     55000
```

Another function in this category is designed to work on the same principle as an `if-then-else` statement works in many common programming languages, including PL/SQL. It is the `decode(`*`column, value1, result1, value2, result2, ..., default`*`)` function. This function checks the value in the *`column`* specified. If the value in that column is the same as *`value1`*, then `decode( )` returns the value specified by *`result1`*, and so on. If the column does not equal any values specified, then the `decode( )` function returns whatever was specified for *`default`*. Observe the following query:

```
SQL> select lastname,
  2  decode(salary, 100000, 'OVERPAID',
  3  45000, 'UNDERPAID', salary)
  4  from emp;
LASTNAME     DECODE(SALARY,100000,'
------------ ----------------------
WALLA        60000
```

```
SMITH          75000
HARPER         UNDERPAID
QIAN           90000
SPANKY         OVERPAID
BUGGY          55000
```

Single-Row Functions for Manipulating Text

Several single-row functions in Oracle manipulate text strings. These functions are similar in concept to `nvl( )` and `decode( )` in that they can perform a change on a piece of data, but the functions in this family can change only one type of data—text.

Single-Row Text Functions in Action

Now look at some text or character function examples of single-row text functions.

`rpad( )` and `lpad( )` These two functions can be used to place additional filler characters on the right or left side of data in a column out to a specified column width. They return the column padded on the left or right side of the data in the column passed as x to a width passed as y. The optional passed value z indicates the character(s) that `lpad( )` or `rpad( )` will insert into the column. If no character is specified, a space will be used.

```
SQL> select empid, lastname, firstname,
  2  rpad(decode(dept,'604B','HR','504A',
  3  'FINANCE'),10,'-') department
  4  from emp
  5  order by empid desc;
EMPID   LASTNAME     FIRSTNAME  DEPARTMENT
------- ------------ ---------- ----------
60403   HARPER       ROD        FINANCE---
49539   QIAN         LEE        FINANCE---
49392   SPANKY       STACY      HR--------
39334   SMITH        GINA       HR--------
12345   BUGGY
02039   WALLA        RAJENDRA   HR--------
6 rows selected.
```

Output from one SQL function can be used as input for another, as demonstrated here. The `rpad( )` operation will pad the decoded SEX column out to ten characters with dashes. If the `lpad( )` operation had been used instead, the result would have been as follows:

```
SQL> select empid, lastname, firstname,
  2  lpad(decode(dept,'604B','HR','504A','FINANCE'),
```

```
  3  10, '-') department
  4  from emp
  5  order by empid desc;
EMPID   LASTNAME      FIRSTNAME  DEPARTMENT
------- ------------ ---------- ----------
60403   HARPER        ROD        ---FINANCE
49539   QIAN          LEE        ---FINANCE
49392   SPANKY        STACY      --------HR
39334   SMITH         GINA       --------HR
12345   BUGGY
02039   WALLA         RAJENDRA   --------HR
6 rows selected.
```

Other Case Translators

Some of the simpler character functions sometimes referred to as "case translators" are shown here.

`lower( ),upper( ),initcap( )` Returns the column value passed as *x* into all lowercase or uppercase characters, or changes the initial letter in the string to a capital letter, respectively.

```
SQL> select empid, lower(lastname)
  2  from emp;
EMPID   LOWER(LASTNAME)
------- ------------------------------
02039   walla
39334   smith
60403   harper
49539   qian
49392   spanky
12345   buggy
```

`length( )` This function returns the length of a text string:

```
SQL> select empid, length(lastname)
  2  as length
  3  from emp;
EMPID      LENGTH
------- ---------
02039           5
39334           5
60403           6
49539           4
49392           6
12345           5
6 rows selected.
```

TIP
Any spaces or double quotes in a text string are all counted as part of the length by the `length( )` *function!*

substr( ) This function is commonly used to extract data from a longer text string. Its first variable is the full text string. The second variable contains an integer that designates the character number at which the substring should begin. The optional third parameter specifies how many characters after the start of the substring will be included in the substring. Observe the following output to understand the effects of omitting the third parameter:

```
SQL> select lastname,
  2  substr(lastname, 2, 3)
  3  from emp;
LASTNAME     SUB
------------ ---
WALLA        ALL
SMITH        MIT
HARPER       ARP
QIAN         IAN
SPANKY       PAN
BUGGY        UGG
6 rows selected.

SQL> select lastname, substr(lastname, 2)
  2  from emp;
LASTNAME     SUBSTR(LASTNAME,2)
------------ -----------------------------
WALLA        ALLA
SMITH        MITH
HARPER       ARPER
QIAN         IAN
SPANKY       PANKY
BUGGY        UGGY
6 rows selected.
```

Single-Row Functions for Math Operations

Other functions are designed to perform specialized mathematical functions, such as those used in scientific applications, like sine and logarithm. These operations are commonly referred to as *math* or *number operations*. The functions falling into this category are listed next.

Single-Row Math Functions in Action

Math functions are frequently used in scientific applications. The following functions are not all that are available in Oracle, but rather are the most commonly used ones that will likely appear on the DBO exam.

abs( ) Shows absolute value, or how far away from zero the parameter passed lies on the number line. For example, the absolute value of –1 is 1, while the absolute value of 6 is 6.

```
SQL> select abs(25),
  2  abs(-12)
  3  from dual;
  ABS(25)  ABS(-12)
--------- ---------
       25        12
```

TIP
Sometimes in Oracle, to perform calculations on numbers that are not selected from any table, you must utilize the DUAL table. DUAL is simply a table with one column that fulfills the syntactic requirements of SQL statements like `select`, which need a table name in the `from` clause in order to work.

ceil( ) This function automatically rounds the number passed as its parameter up to the next higher integer. For example, `ceil(1.4)` = 2. Note that rounding "up" on negative numbers produces a value closer to zero (for example, `ceil(-1.6)` = –1, not –2).

```
SQL> select ceil(123.323),
  2  ceil(45),
  3  ceil(-392),
  4  ceil(-1.12)
  5  from dual;
CEIL(123.323)  CEIL(45) CEIL(-392) CEIL(-1.12)
------------- --------- ---------- -----------
          124        45       -392          -1
```

floor( ) The `floor( )` function is the opposite of `ceil( )`, rounding the value passed down to the next lower integer. This function is similar to `ceil`, except `floor` always rounds down. For example, `floor(1.6)` = 1. Note that rounding "down" on negative numbers produces a value further away from zero. For example, `floor(-1.6)` = –2, not –1.

```
SQL> select floor(123.323),
  2  floor(45),
  3  floor(-392),
  4  floor(-1.12)
  5  from dual;
FLOOR(123.323) FLOOR(45) FLOOR(-392) FLOOR(-1.12)
-------------- --------- ----------- ------------
           123        45        -392           -2
```

mod( ) This function relates to long division. It returns the remainder, or *modulus*, for a number and its divisor. The modulus of *x*, defined in long division as the integer remainder when *x* is divided by *y* until no further whole number can be produced. For example `mod(10,3)` = 1, and `mod(10,2)` = 0.

```
SQL> select mod(12,3), mod(55,4)
  2  from dual;
MOD(12,3) MOD(55,4)
--------- ---------
        0         3
```

round( ) This important function allows you to round a number off to a specified precision. Rounds *x* to the decimal precision of *y*. If *y* is negative, rounds to the precision of *y* places to the left of the decimal point. For example, `round(134.345,1)` = 134.3, `round(134.345,0)` = 134, `round(134.345,-1)` = 130.

```
SQL> select round(123.323,2),
  2  round(45,1),
  3  round(-392,-1),
  4  round(-1.12,0)
  5  from dual;
ROUND(123.323,2) ROUND(45,1) ROUND(-392,-1) ROUND(-1.12,0)
---------------- ----------- -------------- --------------
          123.32          45           -390             -1
```

sign( ) This function assists in identifying whether a number is positive or negative. If the number passed is positive, `sign( )` returns 1, and if the number is negative, `sign( )` returns –1. If the number is zero, `sign( )` returns 0.

```
SQL> select sign(-1933),
  2  sign(55),
  3  sign(0)
  4  from dual;
SIGN(-1933)  SIGN(55)   SIGN(0)
----------- --------- ---------
         -1         1         0
```

sqrt( ) This function is used to derive the square root of a number:

```
SQL> select sqrt(34),
  2  sqrt(9)
  3  from dual;
 SQRT(34)   SQRT(9)
--------- ---------
5.8309519         3
```

trunc( ) Similar to `round( )`, `trunc( )` truncates a value passed into it according to the precision that is also passed in.

```
SQL> select trunc(123.323,2),
  2  trunc(45,1),
  3  trunc(-392,-1),
  4  trunc(-1.12,0)
  5  from dual;
TRUNC(123.323,2) TRUNC(45,1) TRUNC(-392,-1) TRUNC(-1.12,0)
---------------- ----------- -------------- --------------
          123.32          45           -390             -1
```

The `trunc( )` function is particularly useful when you want to compare date values in the `where` clause of your query. This is because Oracle stores dates to the precision of seconds, and normally, you will want only to compare to the accuracy of a day. Observe that, in the following example, we are unable to obtain Stacy Spanky's information even though our query uses her hiring date:

```
SQL> select lastname, firstname
  2  from emp where
  3  hire_date = '14-FEB-98';
no rows selected
```

However, we can obtain Spanky's information once we use the `trunc( )` function, as shown here:

```
SQL> select lastname, firstname
  2  from emp
  3  where trunc(hire_date) = '14-FEB-98';
LASTNAME     FIRSTNAME
------------ ----------
SPANKY       STACY
```

vsize( ) This function is not strictly for numeric datatypes. The `vsize( )` function gives the size in bytes of any value for text, number, date, ROWID, and other columns.

```
SQL> select vsize(38438),
  2  vsize('ORANGE_TABBY'),
  3  vsize(sysdate)
  4  from dual;
VSIZE(38438) VSIZE('ORANGE_TABBY') VSIZE(SYSDATE)
------------ --------------------- --------------
           4                    12              8
```

Other Math Operations

Of course, all the basic math operations you would expect, such as +, –, *, and /, are available in Oracle. For example, to add two numbers together, you can issue

```
SQL> select 2 + 2 from dual;
      2+2
---------
        4
```

Watch Out for Parentheses!

Use of parentheses in a query can change the returned information severely! Note that, in general, Oracle resolves criteria within parentheses before it resolves criteria outside of parentheses. Notice how a subtle difference in the placement of parentheses can produce a drastically different result:

```
SQL> select 5 * 5 / 5 * 5 from dual;
  5*5/5*5
---------
       25
SQL> select (5 * 5) / (5 * 5) from dual;
(5*5)/(5*5)
-----------
          1
```

Single-Row Functions for Lists

Another category of functions discussed here is the set of list functions. These functions are actually used for many different datatypes, including text, numeric, and date.

`greatest(x,y,...)`	Returns the highest value from the list of text strings, numbers, or dates (*x*,*y*...)
`least(x,y,...)`	Returns the lowest value from the list of text strings, numbers, or dates (*x*,*y*...)

List Functions in Action

Some examples of their usage are shown here:

```
SQL> select greatest (1,2,3,4,5) from dual;
GREATEST(1,2,3,4,5)
-------------------
                  5
SQL> select least(1,2,3,4,5) from dual;
LEAST(1,2,3,4,5)
----------------
               1
```

Single-Row Functions for Dates

Another set of functions available in Oracle corresponds to dates. The functions that perform operations on dates are known as *date* functions. A special keyword, called `sysdate`, can be specified to give Oracle users the current date. In the same way that you calculated simple arithmetic using the DUAL table, so, too, can you execute a `select` statement using `sysdate` to produce today's date:

```
SELECT sysdate FROM DUAL;

SYSDATE
---------
15-MAY-99
```

add_months( ) This function takes as input a date and a number of months to be added. Oracle then returns the new date, which is the old date plus the number of months:

```
SELECT ADD_MONTHS('15-MAR-99',26)
FROM DUAL;

ADD_MONTHS('15
--------------
     15-MAY-01
```

last_day( ) This function helps determine the date for the last day in the month for the date given:

```
SELECT LAST_DAY('15-MAR-00') FROM DUAL;

LAST_DAY('15-M
--------------
     31-MAR-00
```

months_between( ) This function determines the number of months between two different dates given. The syntax of this command is tricky, so it will be presented here. The syntax of this command is `months_between(y,x)`, and the return value for this function is *y-x*:

```
SELECT MONTHS_BETWEEN('15-MAR-99','26-JUN-98') FROM DUAL;

MONTHS_BETWEEN
--------------
     8.6451613
```

new_time( ) This function accepts three parameters, the first being a date and time, the second being the time zone the first parameter belongs in, and the last parameter being the time zone you would like to convert to. Each time zone is abbreviated in the following way: *X*ST or *X*DT, where ST or DT stands for standard or daylight saving time, and where *X* stands for the first letter of the time zone (such as Atlantic, Bering, Central, Eastern, Hawaii, Mountain, Newfoundland, Pacific, or Yukon). There are two exceptions: Greenwich mean time is indicated by GMT, while Newfoundland standard time does not use daylight saving.

So far, none of the queries used to demonstrate the date functions have required that much precision, but the following example will. In order to demonstrate the full capability of Oracle in the `new_time( )` function, the format in which Oracle displays date information (also known as the National Language Set [NLS] date format) can be changed to display the full date and time for the query. The following example demonstrates both the use of `nls_date_format` to change the date format and the `new_time( )` function to convert a timestamp to a new time zone:

```
ALTER SESSION
SET NLS_DATE_FORMAT = 'DD-MON-YYYY HH24:MI:SS';

SELECT NEW_TIME('15-MAR-1999 14:35:00','AST','GMT')
FROM DUAL;

NEW_TIME('15-MAR-199
--------------------
15-MAR-1999 18:35:00
```

For Review

1. Discuss the functionality of the `decode( )` and `nvl( )` functions. Can you conceptualize the `nvl( )` function as a simplified `decode( )` operation?
2. Discuss the use of the single-row text functions presented in this section.

3. Discuss the use of the single-row number functions presented in this section. Identify the effect of parentheses on math operations Oracle may perform.
4. Discuss the use of the single-row list functions presented in this section.
5. Discuss the use of the single-row date functions presented in this section.

Using Single-Row Functions for Data Conversion

A special subset of single-row functions are designed to convert columns of one datatype to another type. These functions do not actually modify the data itself; they just return the converted values. Several different conversion functions are available in the Oracle database, as listed here:

`to_char(x)`	Converts noncharacter value *x* to character
`to_number(x)`	Converts nonnumeric value *x* to number
`to_date(x[,y])`	Converts nondate value *x* to date, using format specified by *y*
`to_multi_byte(x)`	Converts single-byte character string *x* to multibyte characters according to national language standards
`to_single_byte(x)`	Converts multibyte character string *x* to single-byte characters according to national language standards
`chartorowid(x)`	Converts string of characters *x* into an Oracle ROWID
`rowidtochar(x)`	Converts a ROWID into a string of characters *x*
`hextoraw(x)`	Converts hexadecimal (base-16) value *x* into raw (binary) format
`rawtohex(x)`	Converts raw (binary) value *x* into hexadecimal (base-16) format
`convert(x[,y[,z]])`	Executes a conversion of alphanumeric string *x* from the current character set optionally specified as *z* to the one specified by *y*
`translate(x,y,z)`	Executes a simple value conversion for character or numeric string *x* into something else based on the conversion factors *y* and *z*

The following text illustrates the most commonly used procedures for converting data in action. These are the `to_char( )`, `to_number( )`, and `to_date( )` functions. The first one demonstrated is the `to_char( )` function. In the example of `new_time( )`, the date function described earlier, the `alter session set nls_date_format` statement was used to demonstrate the full capabilities of Oracle in both storing date information and converting dates and times from one time zone to another. That exercise could have been accomplished with the use of the `to_char( )` conversion function as well. Using `to_char( )` in this manner saves you from converting `nls_date_format`, which, once executed, is in effect for the rest of your session, or until you execute another `alter session set nls_date_format` statement. Rather than using this method, you may want to opt for a less permanent option offered by the `to_char( )` function, as follows:

```
SELECT TO_CHAR(NEW_TIME(TO_DATE('15-MAR-1999 14:35:00',
'DD-MON-YYYY HH24:MI:SS'),'AST','GMT'))
FROM DUAL;

NEXT_DAY('15-MAR-9
------------------
15-MAR-99 18:35:00
```

Note that this example also uses the `to_date( )` function, another conversion function in the list to be discussed. The `to_date( )` function is very useful for converting numbers, and especially character strings, into properly formatted DATE fields. The next function to consider is `to_number( )`, which converts text or date information into a number:

```
SELECT TO_NUMBER('49583') FROM DUAL;

TO_NUMBER('49583')
------------------
             49583
```

Although there does not appear to be much difference between the output of this query and the string that was passed, the main difference is the underlying datatype. Even so, Oracle is intelligent enough to convert a character string consisting of all numbers before performing an arithmetic operation using two values of two different datatypes, as shown in the following listing:

```
SELECT '49583' + 34 FROM DUAL;

'49583'+34
----------
     49617
```

TIP
Here's an interesting fact that you probably won't need to know for OCP but can dazzle your Oracle DBA friends. The Oracle RDBMS can handle many datatype conversions implicitly, such as the one shown in the preceding code block. The component of the Oracle RDBMS that handles datatype conversions is called Two-Task Common.

For Review

1. Identify and describe the use of several conversion functions available in the Oracle database.
2. Can two functions be used in conjunction with one another? Explain.

Introducing Table Joins

The typical database contains many tables. Some smaller databases may have only a dozen or so tables, while other databases may have hundreds. The common factor, however, is that no database has just one table that contains all the data you need. Oracle recognizes that you may want data from multiple tables drawn together in some meaningful way. In order to show data from multiple tables in one query, Oracle allows you to perform *table joins*. A table join is when data from one table is associated with data from another table according to a common column in both tables.

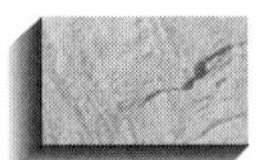

TIP
There must be at least one column shared between two tables in order to join the two tables in a `select` *statement. Recall that foreign-key relationships are defined between a column in one table and the primary key of another.*

In some cases of foreign-key relationships, a special relationship called a *master/detail* or *parent/child* relationship is created. In such relationships, the detail table contains one or more records corresponding to a record in the master table. These detail records enhance or detail the information provided in the master record. Expenses and corresponding expense items are a good example. Employees' expense reports usually contain a detailed list of expense line items, such as airfare, hotel, car rental, and other expenses. The EXPENSE table may define several important components, such as the employee's name and ID number, while the EXPENSE_DETAIL table lists each line item on the expense report, with appropriate codes for accounting for those expenses. Another good example is a customer order entry system, in which a CUSTOMER_ORDER table may identify the customer making the order, the sales representative taking it, and the total price, while the ORDER_LINE_ITEMS table lists the actual items ordered, their associated quantities, and totals. Figure 8-6 demonstrates how the relationship may work between master and detail tables identified here within the Oracle database.

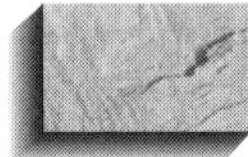

TIP
Interestingly, notice that both examples in Figure 8-6 show detail tables with composite primary keys. A table may have one or more columns acting as the primary key, the combination of all column values for the row ensuring uniqueness for the row. Often, detail tables will use a composite primary key including a column from the parent table.

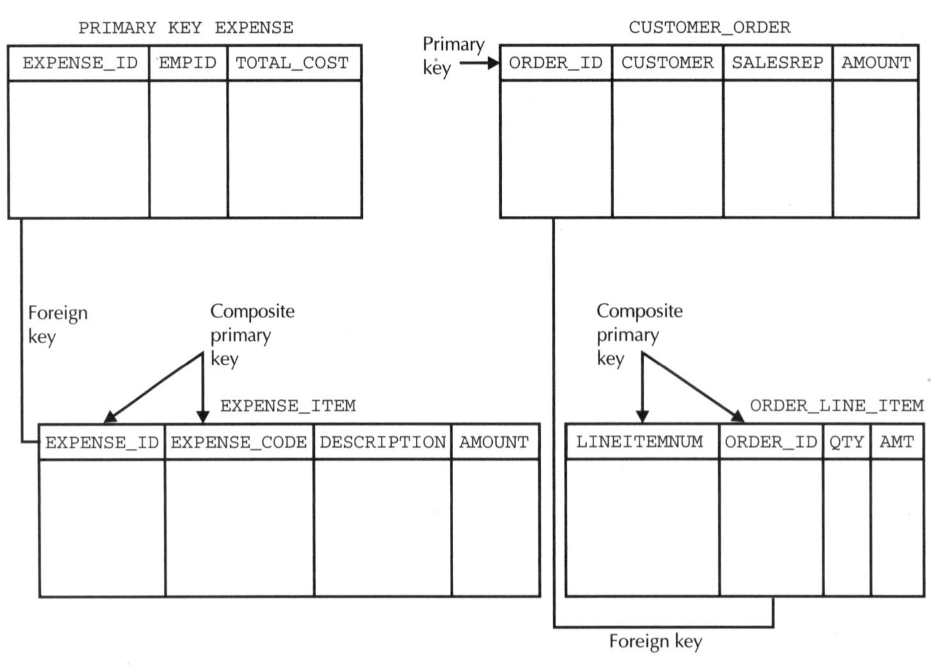

FIGURE 8-6. *Parent and child tables*

Select Statements That Join Data from More Than One Table

When a primary- or foreign-key relationship exists between several tables, it is possible to join their data. The `where` clause comparison operations in a table join statement also have another purpose—to describe how the data between two tables should be joined together, as shown in the following code:

```
SQL>  select e.empid, e.salary, d.dept_budget
  2  from emp e, dept d
  3* where e.dept = d.dept;
EMPID                   SALARY DEPT_BUDGET
-------------------- --------- -----------
02039                    60000    34000000
39334                    75000    34000000
60403                    45000       50000
49539                    90000       50000
49392                   100000    34000000
```

Many important things are happening in this sample statement, the most fundamental of which is the table join. The `from` clause in this statement is the clearest indication that a table join is taking place. In this statement, the `from` clause contains two table names, each of which is followed by a letter. Table EMP in this example is followed by the letter `e`, while table DEPT is followed by the letter `d`. This display demonstrates an interesting concept in Oracle—not only can the columns in a `select` statement have aliases, but the tables named in the `from` clause can have aliases as well.

In most cases, tables with columns in common should have the same name for those columns, because then it becomes easier to identify that they contain the same data. However, this common name can lead to ambiguity when the Oracle SQL processing mechanism (also known as the RDBMS) attempts to parse the statement and resolve all database object names. If each column isn't linked to the particular tables identified in the `from` clause, Oracle will return an error. By specifying an alias for each table in the `from` clause, and then prefixing each column name in the `select` statement with the alias, you avoid ambiguity in the SQL statements while also avoiding the need to type out a table name each time a column is specified. The following code block illustrates the extra coding necessary when referencing columns if table aliases aren't used:

```
SQL> select emp.empid, emp.salary, dept.dept_budget
  2  from emp, dept
  3* where emp.dept = dept.dept;
EMPID                   SALARY DEPT_BUDGET
-------------------- --------- -----------
02039                    60000    34000000
```

```
39334                 75000    34000000
60403                 45000       50000
49539                 90000       50000
49392                100000    34000000
```

Notice something else. Neither the alias nor the full table name need be specified before a column that appears in only one table specified by the `from` clause. Ambiguity is produced only when the column appears in two or more of the tables specified in the `from` clause. The next topic to cover in creating queries that join data from one table to data from another table is the use of comparison operations in the `where` clause of the statement. The `where` clause must include one comparison that links the data of one table to the data in the other table. Without this link, the output includes all data from both tables and is referred to as a *Cartesian product.* A Cartesian product is when Oracle joins one row in a table with every row in another table because the SQL statement joining the two tables has a malformed `where` clause or lacks one altogether. Thus, an attempt to join the EMP and DEPT tables, with 6 and 3 rows respectively, using a `select` statement with no `where` clause results in output with a whopping18 rows! The following code block illustrates:

```
SQL> select e.empid, e.salary, d.dept_budget
  2* from emp e, dept d;
EMPID                   SALARY DEPT_BUDGET
-------------------- --------- -----------
02039                    60000    34000000
02039                    60000       50000
02039                    60000   5.600E+10
39334                    75000    34000000
39334                    75000       50000
39334                    75000   5.600E+10
60403                    45000    34000000
60403                    45000       50000
60403                    45000   5.600E+10
49539                    90000    34000000
49539                    90000       50000
49539                    90000   5.600E+10
49392                   100000    34000000
49392                   100000       50000
49392                   100000   5.600E+10
12345                    55000    34000000
12345                    55000       50000
12345                    55000   5.600E+10
```

Two comparison possibilities are available in order to link the data from one table to another: *equality* comparisons and *inequality* comparisons. Joins between tables that are based on equality statements in the `where` clause are referred to as *inner joins*, or *equijoins*. An equijoin will return data when the value in one column in one table equals the value in the column of the other table. If the tables are being joined based on an inequality statement in the `where` clause, the data returned typically will have less meaning unless a range of data is specified and the actual link between the two tables is an equality statement.

```
SQL> select e.empid, e.salary, d.dept_budget
  2  from emp e, dept d
  3* where e.salary < d.dept_budget;
EMPID                   SALARY DEPT_BUDGET
-------------------- --------- -----------
02039                    60000    34000000
02039                    60000   5.600E+10
39334                    75000    34000000
39334                    75000   5.600E+10
60403                    45000    34000000
60403                    45000       50000
60403                    45000   5.600E+10
49539                    90000    34000000
49539                    90000   5.600E+10
49392                   100000    34000000
49392                   100000   5.600E+10
12345                    55000    34000000
12345                    55000   5.600E+10
```

This data is somewhat meaningless. Even though it accurately compares salaries to departmental budgets, the comparison is useless unless you already know which employees belong to what departments. The query illustrates that when an inequality operation is specified as part of the `where` clause joining data from one table to another, there is no way to guarantee that the inequality operation will be satisfied for *all* values in the column for *both* tables. There is also a high possibility that the data returned by an inequality join will look suspiciously like a Cartesian product. A better alternative for drawing data from a table that satisfies an inequality operation but does not produce a Cartesian product is to specify the inequality operation outside the comparison that produces the join, as shown here:

```
SQL> select e.empid, e.salary, d.dept_budget
  2  from emp e, dept d
  3  where
  4  e.dept = d.dept and
  5* e.salary < d.dept_budget;
EMPID                   SALARY DEPT_BUDGET
-------------------- --------- -----------
02039                    60000    34000000
39334                    75000    34000000
60403                    45000       50000
49392                   100000    34000000
```

This `select` statement will produce all results joined properly using the equality operation to link the rows of two tables in an inner join, while also satisfying the comparison needed to obtain data for only those storage boxes greater than box number three. In general, it is best to specify an equality operation for the two columns linking the tables for the join, followed by an inequality operation on the same column in *one* of the tables to filter the number of rows that will be linked in the join.

The query used to produce a table join must contain the right number of equality operations to avoid a Cartesian product. If the number of tables to be joined equals *N*, the user should remember to include at least *N*–1 equality conditions in the `select` statement so that each column in each table that exists in another table is referenced *at least once*.

TIP
For N *joined tables, you need at least* N–*1 join conditions in the* `select` *statement to avoid a Cartesian product.*

For Review

1. What must be shared between two tables in order to write join queries against those tables?
2. Generally speaking, what is the fewest number of join conditions that must be present in a query that references 12 tables to avoid Cartesian products?

Some Simple Equijoins

You have already seen some equijoin statements in the previous section. In this section, you will work through a couple of examples to become better acquainted with the process of creating simple equijoin operations. Figures 8-7 and 8-8 show Example 1 and 2 displayed pictorially.

Example 1

This first example involves two tables you might find in a business application. Table EMP has six columns: EMPID, LASTNAME, FIRSTNAME, SALARY, DEPT, and HIRE_DATE. Table DEPT has three columns: DEPT, DEPT_HEAD, and DEPT_BUDGET. Can the two tables be joined? Yes, as you have already seen, because they share the DEPT column in common, and the DEPT column is functionally dependent on EMPID in table EMP and the primary key of table DEPT.

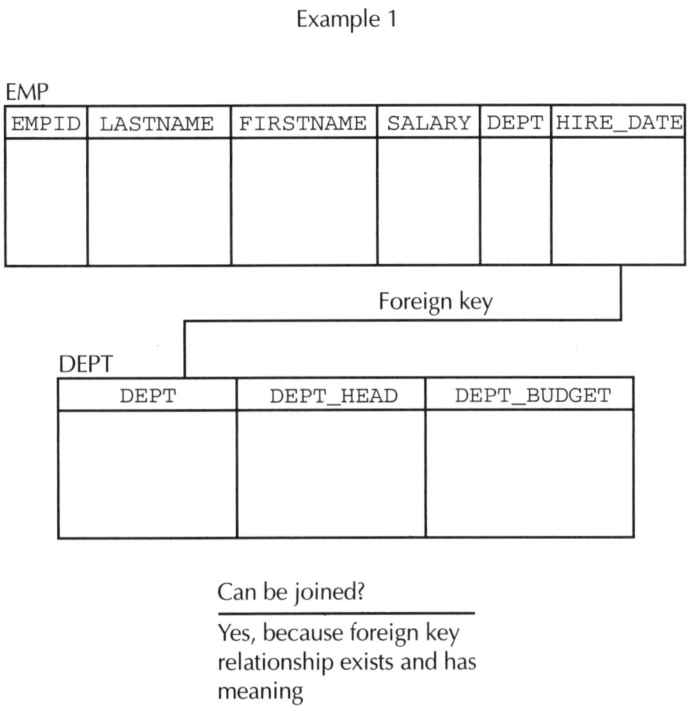

Example 1

EMP

EMPID	LASTNAME	FIRSTNAME	SALARY	DEPT	HIRE_DATE

Foreign key

DEPT

DEPT	DEPT_HEAD	DEPT_BUDGET

Can be joined?

Yes, because foreign key relationship exists and has meaning

FIGURE 8-7. *Example 1*

Example 2

The second example involves two tables you might find in a business application. Table EMP has six columns: EMPID, LASTNAME, FIRSTNAME, SALARY, DEPT, and HIRE_DATE. Table CUSTOMER has three columns, CUSTID, LASTNAME, and FIRSTNAME. Can the two tables be joined? Functionally speaking, they cannot be joined, because even though the LASTNAME and FIRSTNAME columns in both tables have the same name, they are both functionally dependent on their primary keys, and therefore not candidates for a foreign-key relationship. Table joins may be created only on tables when a foreign-key relationship exists.

For Review

What type of relationship must exist between two tables in order to create a join?

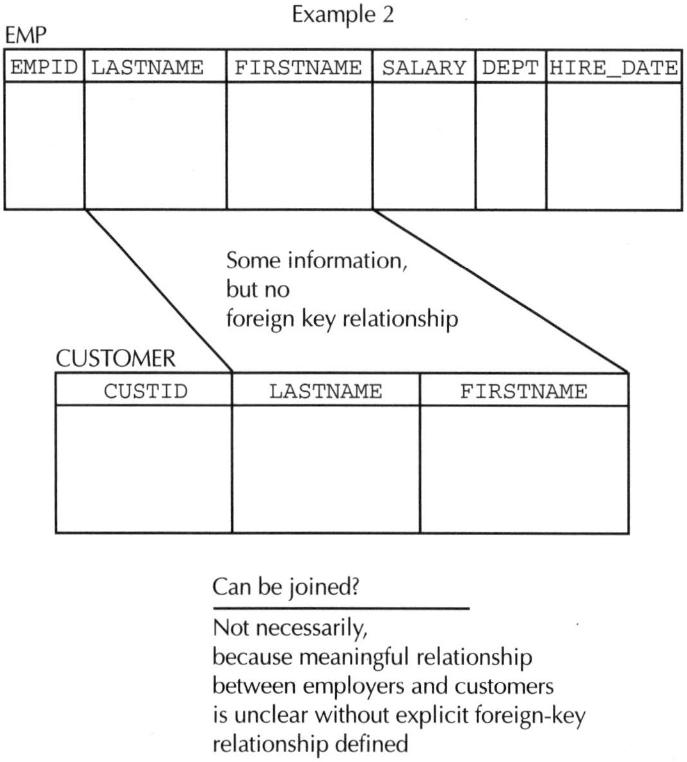

FIGURE 8-8. *Example 2*

Using Outer Joins and Self Joins

In some cases, however, you need some measure of inequality on the joined columns of a table-join operation in order to produce the data required in the return set.

Outer-Join Operations

Say, for example, that you want to see all employees not assigned to departments, as well as those who are assigned to departments. One limitation of inner-join or equijoin statements is that they will not return data from either table unless there is a common value in both columns for both tables on which to make the join.

```
SQL> select e.empid, e.lastname, e.firstname,
  2  d.dept_head
  3  from emp e, dept d
  4  where e.dept = d.dept;
EMPID   LASTNAME      FIRSTNAME  DEPT_HEAD
------- ------------ ---------- --------------------
49392   SPANKY        STACY      SMITHERS
39334   SMITH         GINA       SMITHERS
02039   WALLA         RAJENDRA   SMITHERS
49539   QIAN          LEE        ROSE
60403   HARPER        ROD        ROSE
```

Notice, only employees who have assigned a department are included in the return set. To obtain all employees and their departments, you then issue the following nonjoin query:

```
SQL> select empid, dept
  2  from emp;
EMPID                DEPT
-------------------- ---------
02039                604B
39334                604B
60403                504A
49539                504A
49392                604B
12345
```

This query hits closer to the mark, but let's say you really needed to know the employees assigned to departments *and* the employees assigned to no department, all from one query. In order to force the join to return data from one table even if there is no corresponding record in the other table, the user can specify an *outer-join* operation. The previous inner-join statement can be modified in the following way to show records in the EMP table that have no corresponding record in the DEPT table:

```
SQL> select e.empid, e.lastname, e.firstname,
  2  d.dept_head
  3  from emp e, dept d
  4  where e.dept = d.dept(+);
EMPID   LASTNAME      FIRSTNAME  DEPT_HEAD
------- ------------ ---------- ----------------
49392   SPANKY        STACY      SMITHERS
39334   SMITH         GINA       SMITHERS
02039   WALLA         RAJENDRA   SMITHERS
49539   QIAN          LEE        ROSE
60403   HARPER        ROD        ROSE
```

```
12345   BUGGY
6 rows selected.
```

Outer-join statements such as these produce result sets that are "outside" the join criteria as well as inside it. Notice the special `(+)` character string called the *outer-join operator* at the end of the comparison that forms the join. This marker denotes which column can have NULL data corresponding to the non-NULL values in the other table.

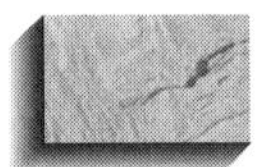

TIP
For inner joins, there must be shared values in the common column in order for the row in either table to be returned by the `select` *statement.*

Joining a Table to Itself

In special situations, it may be necessary for you to perform a join using only one table. Well, you really are using two copies of the table—you join the table to itself. This task can be useful in certain cases in which some slight difference might possibly exist between two rows that would otherwise be duplicate records. If you want to perform a self join on a table, you should utilize the table alias method, described earlier in the chapter, to specify the same table so that Oracle understands that a self join is being performed.

The following example of a self join shows how to use this technique properly. Let's look at another table called TEST_RESULTS, on which users at various locations administer a test for employees of a large corporation. Note that this table is not included in the `chapter8.sql` script; this example is primarily conceptual. The test is designed to determine whether a given employee is ready for promotion. If an employee fails the test, they must wait a full year before taking the test again. It is discovered that a bug in the system allowed some employees to circumvent the rule by taking the test at a different location. Now, management wants to find out which employees have taken the test more than once in the past year. The columns in the TEST_RESULTS table are listed as follows: EMPID, LOCATION, DATE, and SCORE. In order to determine whether an employee has taken the test twice in the last year, you could issue the following SQL `select` that uses self-join techniques:

```
SELECT a.empid, a.location, a.date, b.location, b.date
FROM test_results a, test_results b
WHERE a.empid = b.empid
AND a.location <> b.location
AND a.date > trunc(sysdate-365)
AND b.date > trunc(sysdate-365);
```

```
A.EMPID  A.LOCATION  A.DATE     B.LOCATION  B.DATE
-------  ----------  ---------  ----------  ---------
94839    St. John    04-NOV-98  Wendt       03-JAN-98
04030    Stridberg   27-JUN-98  Wendt       03-AUG-97
59393    St. John    20-SEP-98  Wendt       04-OCT-97
```

The output from this self join shows that three employees took the test in different locations within the last 12 months. The clause used to determine DATE highlights the flexibility inherent in Oracle's internal method for storing both DATE datatypes and `sysdate` as numbers representing the number of days since the beginning of the Julian calendar. The storage method Oracle uses allows you to perform simple mathematical operations on dates to obtain other dates without worrying about taking into account factors like the number of days in months between the old date and new, whether the year in question is a leap year, and so on.

Those users who must perform self joins on tables should be extremely cautious about doing so in order to avoid performance issues or Cartesian products. The required number of equality operations is usually at least *two* in the situation of self joins, simply because using only one equality condition does not usually limit the output of a self join to the degree necessary to produce meaningful information.

TIP
The number of equality operations usually needed in the `where` clause of a self join should be two or more.

It should be stated that a self join typically requires a long time to execute because Oracle must necessarily read all table data twice sequentially. Ordinarily, Oracle will read data from two different tables to perform the join, but since the operation in this case is a self join, all data comes from one table. Without a proper comparison operation set up in the `where` clause, you may wind up with many copies of every row in the table returned, which will certainly run for a long time and produce a lot of unnecessary output.

For Review

1. What performance problems are inherent in self joins, and what can you do to avoid them?
2. What is an outer-join operation and how is it constructed? What special character sequence denotes an outer join?

Group Functions

A group function allows you to perform a data operation on several values in a column of data as though the column were one collective group of data. These functions are also called *group* functions because they are often used in a special clause of `select` statements called a `group by` clause. A more complete discussion of the `group by` clause appears later in the section "Creating and Selecting Groups."

Identifying Available Group Functions

An important difference between group functions and single-row functions is that group functions can operate on several rows at a time. This allows functions to calculate figures like average and standard deviation. The list of available group functions appears here:

`avg(x)`	Averages all *x* column values returned by the `select` statement
`count(x)`	Counts the number of non-NULL values returned by the `select` statement for column *x*
`max(x)`	Determines the maximum value in column *x* for all rows returned by the `select` statement
`min(x)`	Determines the minimum value in column *x* for all rows returned by the `select` statement
`stddev(x)`	Calculates the standard deviation for all values in column *x* in all rows returned by the `select` statement
`sum(x)`	Calculates the sum of all values in column *x* in all rows returned by the `select` statement
`variance(x)`	Calculates the variance for all values in column *x* in all rows returned by the `select` statement

Using Group Functions

Examples of several of these group functions appear over the next few pages. The `avg( )` function takes the values for a single column on all rows returned by the query and calculates the average value for that column. Based on the data from the previous table, the `avg( )` function on the SALARY column produces the following result:

```
SQL> select avg(salary) from emp;
AVG(SALARY)
-----------
  70833.333
```

The second grouping function illustrated is `count( )`. This function is bound to become the cornerstone of any Oracle professional's repertoire. The `count( )`

function returns a row count for the table, given certain column names, `select` criteria, or both. Note that the fastest way to execute `count ( )` is to pass a value that resolves quickly in the SQL processing mechanism. Some values that resolve quickly are integers and the ROWID pseudocolumn.

```
SELECT COUNT(*), -- Slow
       COUNT(1), -- Fast
       COUNT(rowid) -- Fast
FROM EMP;

COUNT(*)  COUNT(1) COUNT(rowid)
--------  -------- ------------
       6         6            6
```

The asterisk (*) in the previous query is a wildcard variable that indicates all columns in the table. For better performance, this wildcard should not generally be used because the Oracle SQL processing mechanism must first resolve all column names in the table, a step that is unnecessary if one is simply trying to count rows. Notice that one of these examples uses the special pseudocolumn called ROWID. A ROWID is a special value that uniquely identifies each row. Each row in a table has one unique ROWID. The ROWID is not actually part of the table; rather, ROWID is a piece of information stored internally within Oracle indexes, not the table. This is why it is considered a pseudocolumn. Note that index-organized tables in Oracle 8.0 do not have a ROWID, although this is changing in Oracle 8.1.5.

TIP

Do not use `count (*)` to determine the number of rows in a table. Use `count (1)` or `count (ROWID)` instead. These options are faster because they bypass some unnecessary operations in Oracle's SQL processing mechanism.

The next pair of grouping functions to be covered are the `max ( )` and `min ( )` functions. The `max ( )` function determines the largest value for the column passed, while `min ( )` determines the smallest value for the column passed, as shown here:

```
SELECT MAX(salary), MIN(salary) FROM EMP;

MAX(salary)  MIN(salary)
-----------  -----------
     100000        45000
```

The final group function is used commonly in simple accounting reports. The `sum ( )` function gives the total of all values in a column.

```
SELECT SUM(salary) FROM EMP;

SUM(salary)
-----------
     425000
```

In general, the group functions will operate on columns of datatypes NUMBER and DATE because many of the functions they represent in mathematics are numeric operations. For example, it makes little sense to take the standard deviation for a set of 12 words, unless the user wants to take the standard deviation of the length of those words by combining the use of the `length( )` function with the `stddev( )` function. There is one notable exception to this general rule, though—that exception is the `count( )` function. The `count( )` function will operate on a column of any datatype.

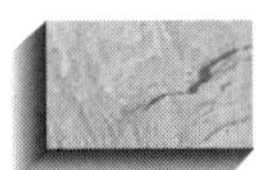

TIP
Group functions ignore NULL values by default. This is an essential piece of information you should know for OCP.

For Review

1. Identify a significant difference between single-row functions and group functions. How do group functions treat NULL values?
2. Name several group functions available on the Oracle database.

Creating and Selecting Groups

Sometimes it gives more meaning to the output of a `select` statement to collect data into logical groupings. For example, to perform calculations on the populations of several cities in the United States, you might issue a query against all records in the CITIES table. Again, you won't find the CITIES table in your database as the result of running `chapter8.sql`—this example is also provided mainly for conceptual understanding. A `select` statement containing `order by` may work well for specific queries against particular cities in this table; it could list data in order based on an alphabetized list of cities and states, as the SQL statement here shows:

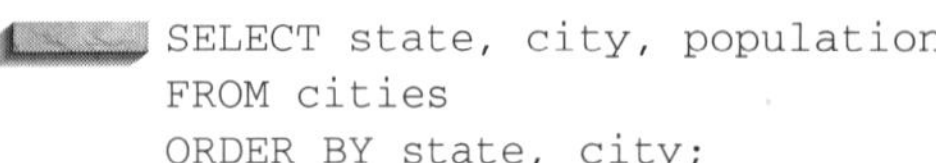

```
SELECT state, city, population
FROM cities
ORDER BY state, city;
```

```
STATE           CITY           POPULATION
--------------- -------------- ----------
ALABAMA         AARDVARK           12,560
ALABAMA         BARNARD           176,000
...
```

However, suppose you want to perform specific calculations on the cities in each state separately. For example, you want to find out the average city population for each of the states listed on the table. The preceding `select` statement works fine for producing the raw data you need in order to calculate the average city population for each state, but there is an easier way for you to make Oracle return the average city population you seek by using the `group by` clause in SQL statements.

```
SELECT state, AVG(population)
FROM CITIES
GROUP BY state;

STATE             AVG(POPULA
----------------- ----------
ALABAMA                49494
ALASKA                 14349
NEW YORK               85030
ARIZONA                35003
CALIFORNIA             65040
...
```

The `group by` clause in this example saves you from performing a great deal of work by hand. Instead, Oracle shoulders most of the work and shows only the results you need. The `group by` clause works well in many situations when you want to report calculations on data according to groups or categories.

There are some common error messages with `group by` operations. The first is shown in the following code block. The problem with this statement is that you are using a group function in a `select` statement that lacks the `group by` clause:

```
SQL> select lastname, avg(salary), empid
  2  from emp;
select lastname, avg(salary), empid
       *
ERROR at line 1:
ORA-00937: not a single-group group function
```

However, notice what happens when you add the `group by` clause:

```
SQL> select lastname, avg(salary), empid
  2  from emp
```

```
  3* group by lastname;
select lastname, avg(salary), empid
                              *
ERROR at line 1:
ORA-00979: not a GROUP BY expression
```

To solve the problem with this statement's execution, you should add the EMPID column to the `group by` clause, so that all nonaggregate columns in the `select` statement are part of the grouping expression, as shown in this code block:

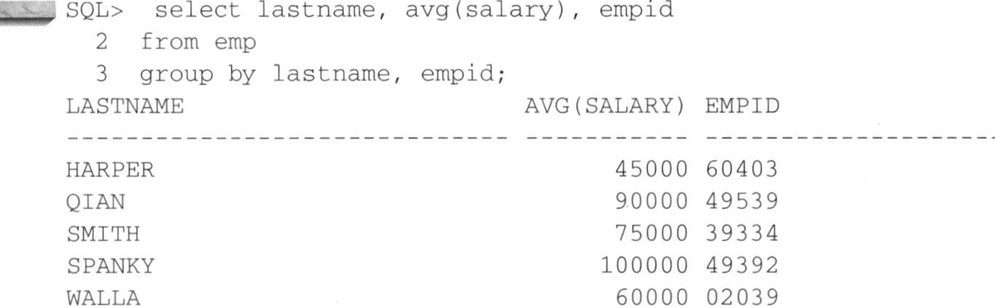

```
SQL>  select lastname, avg(salary), empid
  2  from emp
  3  group by lastname, empid;
LASTNAME                      AVG(SALARY) EMPID
------------------------------ ----------- --------------------
HARPER                               45000 60403
QIAN                                 90000 49539
SMITH                                75000 39334
SPANKY                              100000 49392
WALLA                                60000 02039
```

In this situation, however, the `group by` expression lacks meaning because all the "groups" are really just individuals with different last names. Thus, the average salary by last name and EMPID is simply an individual person's salary. To illustrate the use of `group by` in a meaningful way, assume that you want to calculate the average salary for all employees in a corporation by department. The EMP table is altered to contain the following columns: EMPID, LASTNAME, FIRSTNAME, SALARY, and DEPT. There are only two departments, 504A and 604B. Harper and Qian are part of 504A, and the rest are in 604B. The following code block illustrates how you can obtain the average employee salary by department, ordering the output from highest average salary to lowest:

```
SQL> select dept, avg(salary)
  2  from emp
  3  group by dept
  4  order by avg(salary) desc;
DEPT       AVG(SALARY)
---------- -----------
604B         78333.333
504A             67500
```

In this example, the `order by` clause was combined with the `group by` clause to create a special order for the output. This order gives the data some additional meaning. You're not limited to grouping data by only one selected column, either. If you want, more than one column can be used in the `group by` statement— provided that the same nonaggregate columns specified in the `select` clause of the query match the columns specified in the `group by` clause.

For Review

1. How is the group by clause of a select statement used?
2. Identify some situations in which statements containing the group by clause return errors.

Excluding GROUP Data with HAVING

One initial problem encountered when using the group by statement is that once the data is grouped, you must then analyze the data returned by the group by statement in order to determine which groups are relevant and which are not. It is sometimes useful to *weed out* unwanted data. For example, in the final query from the previous section, suppose you only wanted to see which departments paid an average salary of $80,000 or more per year. In effect, you would be attempting to put a where clause on the group by clause. This effect can be achieved with the use of a special clause in Oracle called having. This clause acts as a modified where clause that only applies to the resultant rows generated by the group by expression.

Consider the previous query of employee salary by department. If you want to view only those departments whose employees make an average of $80,000 or more, you could issue the following query. The having clause in this case is used to eliminate the departments whose average salary is $70,000 or less. Notice that this selectivity cannot easily be accomplished with an ordinary where clause because the where clause selects individual rows, whereas this example requires that groups of rows be selected. In this query, you successfully limit output on the group by rows by using the having clause:

```
SQL> select dept, avg(salary)
  2  from emp
  3  group by dept
  4  having avg(salary) > 70000
  5  order by avg(salary) desc;
DEPT       AVG(SALARY)
---------- -----------
604B         78333.333
```

For Review

1. What is the having clause, and what function does it serve?
2. How can the user specify values to fulfill having criteria without actually knowing what the values themselves are?

Chapter Summary

This chapter covered a variety of topics related to writing data queries in SQL*Plus. You first learned about the basics of the Oracle RDBMS relating to SQL queries. The chapter covered the basic elements of database design as well, with an emphasis on the data modeling and data management side of the application development life cycle. From there, the chapter moved on to focusing on the areas of difference between the Oracle RDBMS and SQL*Plus, which is used to find data in Oracle. You learned about basic usage and editing techniques in your Oracle database, and how to set up the `login.sql` script for customizing your SQL*Plus session.

After that, the chapter moved onto covering how to formulate commands in SQL*Plus, specifically how to formulate the `select` command. You learned about the column (`select`) and table (`from`) clauses, two mandatory parts of your SQL queries. You also learned about the conditional (`where`) clause, which is optional but important for narrowing the scope of your query to include only certain rows from tables. You learned about the use of comparison operations in the conditional clause, and that many different types of comparison operations are permitted in that clause. Multiple comparisons are also permitted, and they are set up using keywords `and` and `or`. Comparison results can also be negated using the `not` keyword. After that, you learned about single-row operations for text, math, list, and date processing, as well as for datatype conversion. You learned about group functions and the various types of table joins as well.

Two-Minute Drill

- Data is retrieved from Oracle using `select` statements.
- Syntax for a `select` statement consists of `select ... from ...;`.
- When entering a `select` statement from the prompt using SQL*Plus, a semicolon (`;`) or slash (`/`) must be used to end the statement.
- Arithmetic operations can be used to perform math operations on data selected from a table, or on numbers using the DUAL table.
- The DUAL table is a table with one column and one row used to fulfill the syntactic requirements of SQL `select` statements.
- Values in columns for particular rows may be empty or NULL.
- If a column contains the NULL value, you can use the `nvl( )` function to return meaningful information instead of an empty field.
- Aliases can be used in place of the actual column name or to replace the appearance of the function name in the header.
- Output from two columns can be concatenated using a double pipe (`||`).
- SQL commands can be entered directly into SQL*Plus on the command line.

- You can edit mistakes in SQL*Plus with the `change` command. If a mistake is made, the change (`c/`*`old`*`/`*`new`*) command is used.
- Alternatively, the `edit` (`ed`) command can be used to make changes in your favorite text editor.
- The `order by` clause in a `select` statement is a useful clause to incorporate sort order into the output of the file.
- Sort orders that can be used are `ascending` or `descending`, abbreviated as `asc` and `desc`. The order is determined by the column identified in the `order by` clause.
- The `where` clause is used in SQL queries to limit the data returned by the query.
- The `where` clauses contain comparison operations that determine whether a row will be returned by a query.
- There are several logical comparison operations, including `=`, `>`, `>=`, `<`, `<`, `<=`, `<>`, `!=`, `^=`.
- In addition to the logical operations, there is a comparison operation for pattern matching called `like`. The % and _ characters are used to designate wildcards.
- There is also a range operation called `between`.
- There is also a fuzzy logic operation called `soundex`.
- The `where` clause can contain one or more comparison operations linked together by using `and` or `or`, and preceded by `not`.
- Several SQL functions exist in Oracle.
- SQL functions are broken down into character functions, number functions, and date functions.
- A few functions can be used on many different types of data.
- Several conversion functions are also available for transforming data from text to numeric datatypes and back, numbers to dates and back, text to ROWID and back, and so on.
- `select` statements that obtain data from more than one table and merge the data together are called *joins*.
- In order to join data from two tables, there must be a common column.

- A common column between two tables can create a foreign key, or link, from one table to another. This condition is especially true if the data in one of the tables is part of the primary key—the column that defines uniqueness for rows on a table.
- A foreign key can create a parent/child relationship between two tables.
- One type of join is the inner join, or equijoin. An equijoin operation is based on an equality operation linking the data in common columns of two tables.
- Another type of join is the outer join. An outer join returns data in one table even when there is no data in the other table. The "other" table in the outer join operation is called the *outer* table.
- The common column that appears in the outer table of the join must have a special marker next to it in the comparison operation of the `select` statement that creates the table.
- The outer-join marker is as follows: `(+)`.
- If the column name is the same in both tables, common columns in tables used in join operations must be preceded either with a table alias that denotes the table in which the column appears, or the entire table name.
- The data from a table can be joined to itself. This technique is useful in determining whether the table contains rows that have slightly different values but are otherwise duplicate rows.
- Table aliases must be used in self-join `select` statements.
- Data output from table `select` statements can be grouped together according to criteria set by the query.
- A special clause exists to assist the user in grouping data together. That clause is called `group by`.
- Several grouping functions allow you to perform operations on data in a column as though the data were logically one variable.
- The grouping functions are `max( )`, `min( )`, `sum( )`, `avg( )`, `stddev( )`, `variance( )`, and `count( )`.
- These grouping functions can be applied to the column values for a table as a whole or for subsets of column data for rows returned in `group by` statements.

- Data in a `group by` statement can be excluded or included based on a special set of `where` criteria defined specifically for the group in a `having` clause.
- The data used to determine the `having` clause can either be specified at runtime by the query or by a special embedded query, called a *subquery*, which obtains unknown search criteria based on known search methods.

Chapter Questions

1. You are issuing SQL queries in SQL*Plus while connected to the Oracle database. You enter each of the following queries. Which of the following will return an error?

A. `select * from EMP where EMPID = 493945;`

B. `select EMPID from EMP where EMPID = 493945;`

C. `select EMPID from EMP;`

D. `select EMPID where EMPID = 56949 and LASTNAME = 'SMITH';`

2. A colleague asks you to revise the following query so that the salary column heading accurately describes the cost of living increase data displayed for that column. The statement to be revised is
`select empid, salary, salary*1.07 from emp;`

Which of the following correctly describes how to specify a column alias?

A. `select empid, salary, salary*1.07 from emp where user = 'CHAPMAN';`

B. `select empid, salary, salary*1.07 as cost_of_living_inc from emp;`

C. `select count(*) from emp;`

D. `select decode(salary, 55000, 'RICH', 65000, 'RICHER', 'RICHEST') from emp;`

3. You need to display a special character string every time no data is found in a column for department information on a report of the contents of the EMP table. Which of the following single-row functions may be helpful?

A. `count()`

B. `nvl( )`

C. `sum( )`

D. `to_char( )`

4. Output from a table called PLAYS with two columns, PLAY_NAME and AUTHOR, is shown next. Which of the following SQL statements produced it?

```
PLAY_TABLE
-------------------------------------
"Midsummer Night's Dream", SHAKESPEARE
"Waiting For Godot", BECKETT
"The Glass Menagerie", WILLIAMS
```

A. `select PLAY_NAME|| AUTHOR from PLAYS;`

B. `select PLAY_NAME, AUTHOR from PLAYS;`

C. `select PLAY_NAME||', ' || AUTHOR from PLAYS;`

D. `select PLAY_NAME||', ' || AUTHOR play_table from PLAYS;`

5. You need to display some results from a SQL query using a substitution of one value for another based on the contents of a tabular column. Which function can best be used for this purpose?

A. `sqrt( )`

B. `decode( )`

C. `new_time( )`

D. `rowidtochar( )`

6. You issue the following statement. What will be displayed if the EMPID selected is 60494?

```
SELECT DECODE(empid,38475, 'Terminated',60494, 'LOA',
'ACTIVE') FROM emp;
```

A. 60494

B. LOA

C. Terminated

D. ACTIVE

7. You are issuing SQL queries in SQL*Plus while connected to the Oracle database. You enter each of the following queries. Which of the following is a valid SQL statement?

A. `select to_char(nvl(sqrt(59483), '0')) from dual;`

B. `select to_char(nvl(sqrt(59483), 'INVALID')) from dual;`

C. `select (to_char(nvl(sqrt(59483), '0')) from dual;`

D. `select to_char(nvl(sqrt(59483), 'TRUE')) from dual;`

8. The appropriate table to use when performing arithmetic calculations on values defined within the `select` statement (not pulled from a table column) is

A. EMP

B. The table containing the column values

C. DUAL

D. An Oracle-defined table

9. Two tables contain data that you would like to display as the result of a query. In order to perform the join required for that query, which criteria must be true?

A. The common columns in the join do not need to have shared values.

B. The tables in the join need to have common columns.

C. The common columns in the join may or may not have shared values.

D. The common columns in the join must have shared values.

10. No search criteria for the EMP table are known. Which of the following options is appropriate for use when search criteria is unknown for comparison operations in a `select` statement? (Choose two.)

A. `select * from emp where empid = &empid;`

B. `select * from emp where empid = 69494;`

C.
```
select * from emp where empid =
(select empid from invoice where invoice_no = 4399485);
```

D. `select * from emp;`

11. **A user is setting up a join operation between tables EMP and DEPT. There are some employees in the EMP table that the user wants returned by the query, but the employees are not assigned to department heads yet. Which `select` statement is most appropriate for this user?**

    A. `select e.empid, d.head from emp e, dept d;`

    B. `select e.empid, d.head from emp e, dept d where e.dept# = d.dept#;`

    C. `select e.empid, d.head from emp e, dept d where e.dept# = d.dept# (+);`

    D. `select e.empid, d.head from emp e, dept d where e.dept# (+) = d.dept#;`

12. **You are using the `having` clause in conjunction with the `group by` statement. Which three of the following uses of the `having` clause are appropriate? (Choose three.)**

    A. To put returned data into sorted order

    B. To exclude certain data groups based on known criteria

    C. To include certain data groups based on unknown criteria

    D. To include certain data groups based on known criteria

13. **Which components are parts of an entity-relationship diagram? (Choose two.)**

    A. Referential integrity constraints

    B. Entities

    C. Relationships

    D. Triggers

14. **Which of the following choices is the strongest indicator of a parent/child relationship?**

    A. Two tables in the database are named VOUCHER and VOUCHER_ITEM, respectively.

    B. Two tables in the database are named EMPLOYEE and PRODUCTS, respectively.

    C. Two tables in the database were created on the same day.

    D. Two tables in the database contain none of the same columns.

Answers to Chapter Questions

1. D. `select EMPID where EMPID = 56949 and LASTNAME = 'SMITH';`

Explanation There is no `from` clause in this statement. Although a `select` statement can be issued without a `where` clause, no `select` statement can be executed without a `from` clause specified. For that reason, the DUAL table exists to satisfy the `from` clause in situations in which you define all data needed within the statement.

2. B. `select empid, salary, salary*1.07 as cost_of_living_inc from emp;`

Explanation An alias must be used in conjunction with the column upon which the multiplication operation is performed to give the title for the output column some meaning. Choice A simply adds a conditional clause to the existing query, which does nothing to change the column headings, only limits the data returned by the query. The other two choices simply show other examples where, without proper column aliasing, the returned data will have little meaning.

3. B. `nvl( )`

Explanation The `nvl( )` function is a simple `if-then` operation that tests column value output to see if it is NULL. If it is, `nvl( )` substitutes the specified default value for the NULL value. Since this function only operates on one row value per call to the function, choice A is incorrect because `count( )` is a group function. For this same reason, choice C is incorrect. Choice D is incorrect because `to_char( )` is a single-row conversion operation.

4. D. `select PLAY_NAME||', ' || AUTHOR play_table from PLAYS;`

Explanation This question illustrates the need to read carefully. Since the output specified for the question contained a column alias for the output of the statement, choice D is the only one that is correct, even though choice C also performed the correct calculation. Choice A is incorrect because it specified an inaccurate concatenation method, and choice B is wrong because it doesn't specify concatenation at all.

5. B. `decode( )`

Explanation The `decode( )` function is a full-fledged `if-then-else` statement that can support manipulation of output values for several different cases, along with a default. The `sqrt( )` statement simply calculates square roots, eliminating choice A. Choice C is incorrect because `new_time()` is a date function that converts a time in one time zone to a time in another time zone. Choice D is incorrect because it is a simple conversion operation.

6. B. LOA

Explanation The `decode()` statement has a provision in it that will return LOA if the EMPID in the row matches the EMPID specified for that case, which also eliminates choice D. Also, since a default value is specified by the `decode()` statement, there will never be an EMPID returned by this query. Therefore, choice A is incorrect. Choice C is also eliminated because Terminated is displayed only when 38475 is the column value.

7. A. `select to_char(nvl(sqrt(59483), '0')) from dual;`

Explanation Functions such as these can be used in conjunction with one another. Though usually the datatype of the value inserted if the column value is NULL and the column specified for `nvl()` must match, Oracle performs many datatype conversions implicitly, such as this one.

8. C. DUAL

Explanation When all data to be processed by the query is present in the statement, and no data will be pulled from the database, users typically specify the DUAL table to fulfill the syntactic requirements of the `from` clause.

9. B. The tables in the join need to have common columns.

Explanation It is possible that a join operation will produce no return data, just as it is possible for any `select` statement not to return any data. Choices A, C, and D represent the spectrum of possibilities for shared values that may or may not be present in common columns. However, joins themselves are not possible without two tables having common columns. Refer to the discussion of table joins.

10. A *and* C.

Explanation Choice A details the use of a runtime variable that can be used to have the user input an appropriate search criteria after the statement has begun processing. Choice C details the use of a subquery that allows the user to select unknown search criteria from the database using known methods for obtaining the data. Choice B is incorrect because the statement simply provides a known search criteria; choice D is incorrect because it provides no search criteria at all. Review the discussion of defining runtime variables and subqueries.

11. C. `select e.empid, d.head from emp e, dept d where e.dept# = d.dept# (+);`

Explanation Choice C details the outer-join operation most appropriate to this user's needs. The outer table in this join is the DEPT table, as identified by the (+) marker next to the DEPT# column in the comparison operation that defines the join.

12. B, C, *and* D. To exclude certain data groups based on known criteria, to include certain data groups based on unknown criteria, *and* to include certain data groups based on known criteria

Explanation All exclusion or inclusion of grouped rows is handled by the `having` clause of a `select` statement. Choice A is not an appropriate answer because sort order is given in a `select` statement by the `order by` clause.

13. B *and* C. Entities *and* Relationships

Explanation There are only two components to an entity-relationship diagram: entities and relationships. Choices A and D are incorrect because referential integrity constraints and triggers are part of database implementation of a logical data model. Refer to the discussion of entity-relationship diagrams.

14. A. Two tables in the database are named VOUCHER and VOUCHER_ITEM, respectively.

Explanation This choice implies the use of a naming convention similar to the one discussed. Although there is no guarantee that these two tables are related, the possibility is strongest in this case. Choice B implies the same naming convention; and since the two tables' names are dissimilar, there is little likelihood that the two tables are related in any way. Choice C is incorrect because the date a table is created has absolutely no bearing on what function the table serves in the database. Choice D is incorrect because two tables *cannot* be related if there are no common columns between them. Refer to the discussions of creating tables with integrity constraints, naming conventions, and data modeling.

CHAPTER 9

SQL DML and DDL in SQL*Plus

his chapter covers what you need to know as a DBO in the following areas:

- Tables, datatypes, and constraints
- Using the data dictionary
- DML operations
- Transaction processing
- Creating, managing, and using sequences
- Managing views
- Index structure and management

To pass your OCP DBO exam, you must have an understanding of how to create and manage objects in your Oracle database. These objects include tables, sequences, views, and indexes. You must also understand transaction processing and the important function it performs within an Oracle database. The Oracle data dictionary and its use is another important area to understand before you take the DBO exam. You must even know the different types of privileges that allow users to perform different tasks on the database, and how to administer and manage those privileges. This chapter will cover all these areas to help you prepare for the OCP DBO exam. This chapter is a long one, so be sure to read carefully and take lots of breaks and re-read the material when you don't understand.

Tables, Datatypes, and Constraints

The items covered in this section are

- What a table is
- Oracle datatypes
- Table pseudocolumns
- Creating basic Oracle tables
- Defining and using constraints
- The table `storage` clause
- Altering tables

Let's focus our attention on the objects containing data that you queried in the last chapter. These objects are called *tables*. You will learn about many aspects of tables in the Oracle database, from how the size of a table is determined, to how a table is defined. You will learn about Oracle datatypes and table pseudocolumns as well. The section covers more about integrity constraints, and how to use the table `storage` clause. Finally, you will learn about how to alter the tables once they are created in the Oracle database. Pay close attention now as you learn about these objects as preparation for both the DBO exam and for your career using Oracle products.

What Is a Table?

Recall that a table is an object in the Oracle database that stores data for an application. A table in Oracle is similar to a spreadsheet. Recall from the last chapter our use of the EMP table in many SQL queries. In the EMP table are columns containing data, such as EMPID, LASTNAME, FIRSTNAME, and SALARY. The table contains rows of data or information, which are associated elements of data stored in each column of the table. For example, data for employee #12345—Buggy in the EMP table—is one row of data in that table. Figure 9-1 shows a pictorial representation of a table in your Oracle database.

For Review

Make sure you understand the concept of rows and columns in tables in the Oracle database.

EMP

EMPID	LASTNAME	FIRSTNAME	SALARY	DEPT	HIREDATE
12345	Buggy				
62039	Walla	Richard	60000	604 B	01-JAN-96
60403	Harper	Rod	45000	504 A	30-APR-97
.	.	.	.	.	.
.	.	.	.	.	.
.	.	.	.	.	.

FIGURE 9-1. *Oracle tables*

Oracle Database Datatypes

Every column in Oracle tables must have an associated datatype. The datatypes available for use in the Oracle database are listed in Table 9-1. If you have done any programming in PL/SQL, you may be surprised to find that not all the datatypes available in that language are supported as column datatypes in Oracle databases. For clarity's sake, the PL/SQL datatypes aren't listed here because PL/SQL is not an area tested on the DBO exam. If you want more information about PL/SQL, check out Scott Urman's books on that language, available from Oracle Press.

There are some subtle differences between the two alphanumeric datatypes—CHAR and VARCHAR2. First, CHAR supports character strings only up to a length of 2,000 bytes for Oracle8, while the VARCHAR2 datatype supports character strings up to a length of 4,000 bytes for Oracle8. Second, when Oracle stores data

Datatype	Description
VARCHAR2(*n*)	Contains text strings of length *n*, where *n* can be up to 4,000 bytes in Oracle8 and higher
CHAR(*n*)	Contains text strings of length *n*, where *n* can be up to 4,000 bytes in Oracle8 and higher
NUMBER[(*n*[,*m*])]	Contains numeric data, of optionally defined length *n* and decimal precision *m*
DATE	Contains date data
RAW	Contains binary data of up to 2,000 bytes in Oracle8 and higher
LONG	Contains text data of up to 2 gigabytes
LONG RAW	Contains binary data of up to 2 gigabytes
ROWID	Contains the row's address for table rows
BLOB	Large binary object (Oracle8 and higher only)
CLOB	Large character-based object (Oracle8 and higher only)
NCLOB	Large single- or multibyte character-based object (Oracle8 and higher only)
BFILE	Large external file (Oracle8 and higher only)

TABLE 9-1. *Oracle Database Datatypes*

in a CHAR datatype, it will pad the value stored in the column with blanks up to the declared length of the column. In contrast, Oracle will not store padded blank spaces if the same value is stored in a column defined as datatype VARCHAR2. To illustrate, if a column called LASTNAME was defined as CHAR(50) and the value "BRADY" was assigned to it, the value Oracle would store would actually be "BRADY" with 45 blank spaces to the right of it. That same value stored in a column defined as datatype VARCHAR2 would be stored simply as "BRADY".

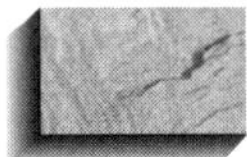

TIP
VARCHAR2 has the "2" on the end of the name because a VARCHAR datatype may be defined in future releases of Oracle. Although VARCHAR and VARCHAR2 are currently synonymous, they may not be in the future, so Oracle recommends using VARCHAR2.

The NUMBER datatype that is used to store number data can be specified either to store integers or decimals with the addition of a parenthetical precision indicator. For example, if you had a column defined to be datatype NUMBER(15,2), the number 49309.593 would be stored as 49309.59 because the number specified after the comma in the parenthetical precision definition of the datatype represents the number of places to the right of the decimal point that will be stored. The number on the left of the comma shows the total width of allowed values stored in this column, including the two places to the right of the decimal point. A column declared to be of type NUMBER(9) will not store any decimals at all. The number 49309.593 stored in a column defined in this way will appear as 49310 because Oracle automatically rounds up if the value is 5 or more in the precision area that the declared datatype will not support. You may also wonder what happens when you try to store 49309.593 in a column defined as a NUMBER(4) datatype. In this situation, Oracle returns an error—`ORA-01438: value larger than specified precision allows for this column`.

The DATE datatype stores date values in a special Oracle format represented as the number of days since December 31, 4713 B.C.E. This datatype offers a great deal of flexibility to users who want to perform date-manipulation operations, such as adding 30 days to a given date. In this case, all the user has to do is specify the column declared as a DATE datatype and add the number of days. Of course, there are also numerous functions that handle date operations more complex than simple arithmetic. Another nice feature of Oracle's method for date storage is that it is inherently millennium compliant.

Beyond these datatypes is an entire set of important type declaration options available to the developer and DBA dedicated to storage of small and large amounts of text and unformatted binary data. These datatypes include LONG, RAW, and LONG RAW. RAW datatypes in Oracle store data in binary format up to 2,000 bytes. It is useful to store graphics and sound files when used in conjunction with LONG to form the LONG RAW datatype, which can accommodate up to 2 gigabytes of data. The developer can declare columns to be of LONG datatype, which stores up to 2 gigabytes of alphanumeric text data. Only one column can be declared to be of type LONG in a table. The entire operation of storing large blocks of data has been enhanced significantly as of Oracle8, in which BLOB, CLOB, and NCLOB objects, which can contain up to 4 gigabytes of data, are used to store binary, single-byte, and multibyte character-based objects in the Oracle database. Oracle8 stores this data outside of the table, keeping pointers in the table to locate the object. This is in contrast to earlier versions of Oracle, in which the actual LONG or LONG RAW data is stored inline with the rest of the table information. However, you should note that these older methods for large data storage are included in the current version of Oracle for backward compatibility.

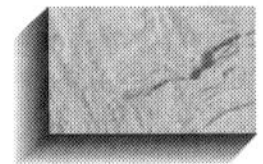

TIP
Storing data "inline" means that the data in a LONG datatype column is stored literally "in line" with the rest of the data in the row, as opposed to Oracle storing a pointer inline with row data, pointing to LONG column data stored somewhere else.

Collection, Reference, and User-Defined Types

A collection is a gathering of like-defined elements. The two types of collection types available in Oracle8 are variable-length arrays with the VARRAY type and nested tables with the TABLE type. A VARRAY can be thought of as an ordered list of objects, all of the same datatype. The VARRAY is defined to have two special attributes (in addition to those attributes within the objects the VARRAY contains). These attributes are a *count* for the number of elements in the VARRAY and the *limit* for the maximum number of elements that can appear in a VARRAY. Although the VARRAY can have any number of elements, the limit must be predefined. Each element in the VARRAY has an index, which is a number corresponding to the position of the element in the array. Constraints and default values may not be created for elements in a VARRAY, and once the VARRAY is created, the user only refers to an individual element in a VARRAY with PL/SQL (although SQL can be used to access the entire VARRAY).

The other collection type, the nested table, is a table within a table. The nested table architecture is exceptionally suited for applications that in Oracle7 have parent/child tables with referential integrity. A nested table is an unordered list of row records, each having the same structure. These rows are usually stored away from the table, with a reference pointer from the corresponding row in the parent table to the child table. Like VARRAYs, nested tables can have any number of elements, with the added bonus that you don't need to predetermine a maximum limit.

Finally, consider the reference type and user-defined types. Developers can use the reference type to define a foreign-key relationship between two objects. The reference type can reference all columns in the table for a particular row—it is a pointer to a particular object, not the object itself. User-defined types are abstract datatypes, defined by you, that are composed either of scalar, collection, or other user-defined types.

For Review

1. Name several different datatypes available in Oracle. What are some differences between the LONG and CLOB datatypes with respect to where data is stored in relation to the overall table?
2. What are some of the differences between the CHAR and the VARCHAR2 datatypes?
3. How is data stored in the DATE datatype? What is the ROWID datatype?

Table Pseudocolumns

A special datatype introduced in the prior section that was not discussed is the ROWID datatype. The ROWID datatype stores information related to the disk location of table rows. Generally, no column should be created to store data using type ROWID, but this datatype supports the ROWID virtual column associated with every table. A special pseudocolumn exists in most tables on an Oracle database that contains data of this special type. That pseudocolumn is aptly named ROWID. Check out the following code block, where ROWID information for all our rows in the EMP table is displayed:

```
SQL> select rowid, empid, lastname from emp;
ROWID              EMPID                LASTNAME
------------------ -------------------- --------------
AAAAukAAGAAAAO1AAA 02039                WALLA
AAAAukAAGAAAAO1AAB 39334                SMITH
AAAAukAAGAAAAO1AAC 60403                HARPER
AAAAukAAGAAAAO1AAD 49539                QIAN
AAAAukAAGAAAAO1AAE 49392                SPANKY
AAAAukAAGAAAAO1AAF 12345                BUGGY
```

ROWIDs are a 10-byte conglomeration of information that helps Oracle identify the physical location of row data on disk, nebulously displayed as 18 characters in base-64 (A–Z, a–z, 0–9, +, and /) format. The four components of a ROWID include object ID (first 32 bits), relative datafile number (next 10 bits), database block number (next 22 bits), and row or "slot" number in that data block (last 16 bits).

Oracle7 versus Oracle8 ROWIDs

A significant difference between Oracle7 and Oracle8 is the way ROWID information is stored. An Oracle8 ROWID is a unique identifier for every row in the Oracle database. However, ROWIDs are not addresses in memory or on disk; rather, they are identifiers that can be computed to locate a table row, and this is the fastest way to find a row in a table. Though ROWID information can be queried like other columns in a table, a ROWID is not stored explicitly as a column value.

Oracle7's ROWID format is now considered a "restricted" format because it does not store the object number. This format was acceptable in Oracle7 because the database required all datafiles to have a unique file number, regardless of the tablespace they belonged to. In contrast, Oracle8 numbers datafiles relative to the tablespace they belong to. Oracle7 ROWIDs require 6 bytes and are displayed as 18 characters in base-16 format, where the first 8 characters represent the block number, characters 10–13 are the row number, and characters 15–18 are the (absolute) file number. Characters 9 and 14 are static separator characters. Restricted ROWID format is still used to locate rows in nonpartitioned indexes for nonpartitioned tables in which all index entries refer to rows within the same segment, thus eliminating any uncertainty about relative file numbers, because a segment can be stored in one and only one tablespace.

TIP
You might think it silly, but here's how I remember the components of Oracle ROWIDs. In Oracle7, the components are block ID, row number, and file number, which shorten to the acronym "BRF." In Oracle8, the components are object ID, block ID, row number, and relative file number, which shorten to "OBRRF." To remember the acronyms, I imagine how little dogs sound when they bark.

For Review

1. Understand the ROWID pseudocolumn in Oracle tables, as well as its components.
2. Understand the differences between Oracle7 and Oracle8 ROWID formats.

Creating Basic Oracle Tables

An Oracle table is created with the `create table` command, which is part of Oracle's data definition language, or DDL. In a basic `create table` command, the table name, column names, and column datatypes must all be defined in order for Oracle to process the command correctly. Here's a basic example of this command similar to the one you already used if you ran the `chapter8.sql` script used in the last chapter to create your EMP table:

```
create table emp
( EMPID      VARCHAR2(20),
  LASTNAME    VARCHAR2(30),
  FIRSTNAME   VARCHAR2(30),
  SALARY      NUMBER,
  DEPT        VARCHAR2(10),
  HIRE_DATE   DATE );
```

There's nothing fancy about this script; it just defines the columns of your tables and the datatype Oracle can expect to store for each row in those columns. Note that the length and decimal precision for the NUMBER datatype is optional. When it does not appear, you can store real numbers up to the maximum allowed by Oracle, which varies according to the version you are using. So, the general syntax for the `create table` statement on your Oracle database is `create table (`*`column1_name column1_datatype`*`[, `*`column2_name`*` column2_datatype...]);`.

For Review

Understand the basic syntax for creating tables in your Oracle database.

Defining and Using Constraints

Tables can contain *integrity constraints*—rules that limit the type of data that can be placed in the table, row, or column. There are five types of integrity constraints, some of which you have already seen. For review, they are shown with their definitions in the following set of bullets:

- **PRIMARY KEY** Values in primary-key columns must be unique and not NULL for every row in a table. If more than one column is the primary key, the composite values for every column in the key must be unique and not NULL.
- **UNIQUE** Values in UNIQUE constraint columns must be unique for every row in a table. If more than one column has a UNIQUE constraint, the composite values for every column must be unique.

- **FOREIGN KEY** Columns in FOREIGN KEY constraints refer to primary keys in other tables called *parent tables*. All values in the constrained column must also appear in the primary key of the parent table.
- **CHECK** Values in the column with a CHECK constraint must conform to static values identified in the CHECK constraint.
- **NOT NULL** Values in the column with a NOT NULL constraint must not be NULL.

Table Constraints and Column Constraints

Two methods exist for defining constraints in table creation: the *table constraint method* and the *column constraint method*. The constraint is defined as a table constraint if the `constraint` syntax is part of the table definition, located away from the column datatype definition. The constraint is defined as a column constraint if the constraint definition syntax appears as part of a column definition. All constraints can be defined either as table constraints or as column constraints, except for NOT NULL constraints, which can only be defined as column constraints. The following code block displays two `create table` statements. The first shows definition of the primary-key constraint defined as a table constraint, while the second shows definition of the primary key as a column constraint:

```
-- Table constraint definition
CREATE TABLE employee
(empid          NUMBER(10),
lastname        VARCHAR2(25),
firstname       VARCHAR2(25),
salary          NUMBER(10,4),
CONSTRAINT      pk_employee_01
PRIMARY KEY     (empid));

-- Column constraint equivalent definition
CREATE TABLE employee
(empid          NUMBER(10) primary key,
lastname        VARCHAR2(25),
firstname       VARCHAR2(25),
salary          NUMBER(10,4));
```

The main difference between use of table and column constraint definition methods is your ability to name your constraints yourself only when you define your constraint using the table constraint method. When you use the column constraint definition method, Oracle names the constraint for you. For simplicity, throughout the rest of the chapter, you will work with constraint definitions defined as table constraints. Later in the book, you may see constraints defined both as table and column constraints.

Defining Foreign-Key Constraints When Creating Tables

You have already seen examples of defining tables with PRIMARY KEY constraints. Take another moment to review the definition that was determined for a table called BANK_ACCOUNT. The BANK_ACCOUNT table has the BANK_ACCT_NO column as its primary key because that column defines the data that is unique about each row in the table. Note also that there is a special relationship between the BANK_ACCOUNT table and the EMP table, identified by the FOREIGN KEY constraint defined.

```
CREATE TABLE bank_account
(bank_acct_no          VARCHAR2(40),
empid                  NUMBER(10),
BANK_ROUTE_NO          VARCHAR2(40),
BANK_NAME              VARCHAR2(50),
CONSTRAINT             pk_bank_acct_01
PRIMARY KEY            (bank_acct_no),
CONSTRAINT             fk_bank_acct_01
FOREIGN KEY (empid) REFERENCES employee (empid));
```

The syntax for the FOREIGN KEY constraint definition allows the column to reference another table's column, by the same or different name. But, for a FOREIGN KEY constraint to be valid, the columns in both tables must have exactly the same datatypes. The designation `FOREIGN KEY` tells Oracle that the developer would like to create referential integrity between the EMPID columns in the BANK_ACCOUNT table and the EMPLOYEE table. This fact prevents a column in the child table (BANK_ACCOUNT) from containing a value that does not exist in the referenced column in the parent table (EMPLOYEE). An option that can be specified along with the foreign key relates to the deletion of data from the parent. If someone attempts to `delete` a row from the parent table that contains a referenced value from the child table, Oracle will block the deletion unless the `on delete cascade` option is specified in the foreign-key definition of the `create table` statement. When the `on delete cascade` option is used, Oracle will not only allow the user to `delete` a referenced record from the parent table, but the deletion will cascade into the child table as well.

```
CREATE TABLE bank_acct
(bank_acct_no          VARCHAR2(40),
empid                  NUMBER(10),
BANK_ROUTE_NO          VARCHAR2(40),
BANK_NAME              VARCHAR2(50),
CONSTRAINT             pk_bank_acct_01
PRIMARY KEY            (bank_acct_no),
CONSTRAINT             fk_bank_acct_01
FOREIGN KEY (empid) REFERENCES employee (empid)
ON DELETE CASCADE);
```

Defining Other Constraints in Table Creation

The definition of a UNIQUE constraint on HOME_PHONE prevents anyone from defining a row that contains a phone number that is identical to the phone number of anyone else already in the table. There are two weaknesses in this definition. The first is that having a UNIQUE constraint on a home phone number makes it difficult to store records for employees who are spouses or roommates with the same telephone number. Another point to be made about UNIQUE constraints, and FOREIGN KEY constraints for that matter, is that no data integrity is enforced if the column data value in a row is NULL. This is a special case scenario that applies only to NULL data in columns with FOREIGN KEY, UNIQUE, and CHECK constraints defined on them.

TIP
FOREIGN KEY, CHECK, and UNIQUE integrity constraints for a column are not enforced on a row if the column data value for the row is NULL.

```
CREATE TABLE employee
(empid            NUMBER(10),
lastname          VARCHAR2(25),
firstname         VARCHAR2(25),
salary            NUMBER(10,4),
home_phone        number(15),
CONSTRAINT        pk_employee_01
PRIMARY KEY       (empid),
CONSTRAINT        uk_employee_01
UNIQUE            (home_phone));
```

CHECK constraints allow Oracle to verify the validity of data being entered on a table against a set of constants that act as valid values. For example, you could specify that the SALARY column not contain values over $500,000. If someone tries to create an employee row with a salary of $1,000,000 per year, Oracle would return an error message saying that the record data defined for the SALARY column has violated the CHECK constraint for that column.

```
CREATE TABLE employee
(empid            NUMBER(10),
lastname          VARCHAR2(25)      NOT NULL,
firstname         VARCHAR2(25)      NOT NULL,
salary            NUMBER(10,4)      CHECK(salary<500000),
home_phone        number(15),
CONSTRAINT        pk_employee_01
PRIMARY KEY       (empid),
CONSTRAINT        uk_employee_01
UNIQUE            (home_phone));
```

In this table definition, notice that *three* columns are defined to be `NOT NULL`, including the primary key. The two others are the LASTNAME and FIRSTNAME columns. The NOT NULL table constraint will be applied to the columns, preventing anyone from creating a row for this table that does not contain a first and last name for the employee. Notice also that the CHECK constraint has been created on this table. CHECK constraints have a number of limitations, all centering around the fact that the constraint can only refer to a specific set of constant values or operations on those values. A CHECK constraint cannot refer to another column or row in any table, including the one the constraint is defined on, and it cannot refer to special keywords that can have values in them, such as `user` or `sysdate`, or to the ROWID pseudocolumn. Thus, the CHECK constraint in the previous table definition is valid, but the one in the following excerpt from a table definition is not valid:

```
CREATE TABLE address
(...,
city     VARCHAR2(80)  check(city in (SELECT city FROM cities))
...);
```

TIP
Some special keywords contain information about certain database conditions. These keywords, or pseudocolumns, are `user`, `sysdate`, and `rowid`. The `user` keyword gives the username of the owner of the current session. The `sysdate` keyword gives the current date and time at the time the statement is issued. The `rowid` keyword gives the ROWID of the row specified. These keywords cannot be used in conjunction with a CHECK constraint.

For Review

1. Discuss the rules surrounding each of the five integrity constraint types.
2. Explain how integrity constraints are defined.

The Table Storage Clause

The amount of space Oracle allocates for a table to use is determined by a table's storage clause within the `create table` statement. The following code block revisits a `create table` statement from earlier, with a storage clause defined in bold:

```
CREATE TABLE SPANKY.EMPLOYEE
(empid          NUMBER(10),
lastname        VARCHAR2(25),
firstname       VARCHAR2(25),
salary          NUMBER(10,4),
CONSTRAINT      pk_employee_01
PRIMARY KEY     (empid))
TABLESPACE orgdbdata
PCTFREE    20  PCTUSED    50
INITRANS   1   MAXTRANS   255
NOCACHE        LOGGING
STORAGE ( INITIAL 100K  NEXT  150K
          MINEXTENTS 4  MAXEXTENTS  300
          PCTINCREASE 20 );
```

Let's examine the areas of the `create table` statement marked in bold, starting with the username in the first line. Recall that in Oracle, every object is owned by the user who created it. This ownership creates a logical grouping, or schema, to which the object belongs. In this case, table EMPLOYEE is part of user SPANKY's schema. Skipping down to the `tablespace` clause, this keyword indicates which tablespace Oracle should create the table in. If you do not specify this clause, Oracle will put the table in the default tablespace you were assigned to when your user was created. (More discussion on default tablespaces and user creation is offered in Chapter 5.) The next two clauses are for space utilization. `Pctfree` specifies space that Oracle leaves free when inserting rows, to accommodate growth later via updates. The `pctused` option specifies a threshold percentage of a block that the actual contents of row data must fall below before Oracle will consider the block free for new row inserts.

The next two space utilization clauses, `initrans` and `maxtrans`, control Oracle's ability to make concurrent updates to a data block. The `initrans` option specifies the initial number of transactions that can update the rows in a data block concurrently, while `maxtrans` specifies the maximum number of transactions that can update the rows in a data block concurrently. For the most part, the default values for each of these options should not be changed. For `initrans`, the default for tables is 1, while for clustered tables, the default is 2. For `maxtrans`, the default for tables is 255.

The `nocache` clause specifies that Oracle should not make these blocks persistent in the buffer cache if a `select` statement on the table results in a full table scan. In this case, `select * from EMPLOYEE` would have Oracle load blocks into the buffer cache so that those blocks will not persist for very long. If you wanted the table to stay cached in the buffer cache when `select * from EMPLOYEE` was issued, you would specify the `nocache` keyword instead. This is the default.

The next clause, `logging`, tells Oracle to track table creation in the redo log so that, in the event of disk failure, the table could be recovered. This is the default. If you didn't want the table to be recoverable, you would substitute the `nologging` keyword instead. Finally, you can specify `storage` clauses for table creation that will override the default storage settings of the tablespace you create the object in. The only tablespace default that your `storage` clause will not override is `minimum extent`.

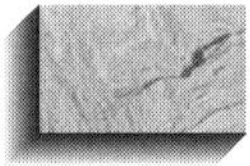

TIP
Schema Manager in Enterprise Manager is used for table creation. You can create a table either using menu options or with the Table Creation Wizard.

Observe the following rules of thumb when creating tables, and remember them for the OCP DBO exam:

- Your tables should not go in the same tablespace as your rollback segments, temporary segments, or index segments, or into the SYSTEM tablespace.
- In order to make sure there is as little fragmentation in the tablespace as possible, have a collection of standard extent sizes that are complementary for your tables, that are all multiples of 5 * `DB_BLOCK_SIZE` in size. For example, for small tables you might use 50 * `DB_BLOCK_SIZE`, and for large tables you might use 250 * `DB_BLOCK_SIZE`.
- To improve performance on full table scans like `select * from, EMPLOYEE` relates to the `DB_FILE_MULTIBLOCK_READ_COUNT` init*sid*.ora parameter. This parameter specifies the number of blocks the server process will read when performing full table scans. Set it to the number of blocks in extents on your database for tables most likely to be accessed via `select` statements without `where` clauses (these are the statements that will likely result in full table scans), up to the maximum value permitted, which is operating system specific.
- Recall that the `cache` statement will make blocks that are read into the buffer cache via full table scans persist for much longer than they otherwise would. If you have a small lookup table accessed frequently, you may want to keep it in memory by specifying the `cache` clause, or by issuing `alter table` *lookup_tblname* `cache`.

For Review

Be able to identify the components of a table storage clause.

Altering Tables

You can alter many aspects of tables after creating them. Some of the things you can change include the columns, constraints, and storage definitions for your tables. The following discussions highlight how to perform these tasks on your Oracle database using SQL*Plus.

Changing Table Columns

Columns can be added and modified in the Oracle database with ease, using the `alter table` statement and its many options for changing the number of columns in the database. A column added with a NOT NULL constraint must have data populated for that column in all rows before the NOT NULL constraint is enabled, and only one column of the LONG datatype can appear in a table in Oracle. The following code block shows an example of the `alter table` statement:

```
SQL> alter table products add (color varchar2(10));
Table altered.
```

If the developer or the DBA needs to add a column that will have a NOT NULL constraint on it, several things need to happen. The column should first be created without the constraint, and then values for all rows should be entered in the column. After all column values are not NULL, the NOT NULL constraint can be applied to it. If the user tries to add a column with a NOT NULL constraint on it, the developer will encounter an error stating that the table must be empty.

Only one column in the table may be of type LONG within a table. That restriction includes the LONG RAW datatype. However, as of Oracle8, many columns of datatype BLOB, CLOB, NCLOB, and BFILE can appear in one table. It is sometimes useful to emulate Oracle8 in Oracle7 databases by having a special table that contains the LONG column and a foreign key to the table that would have contained the column; this reduces the amount of data migration and row chaining on the database.

TIP
Row chaining and row migration occur when the Oracle RDBMS has to move row data around or break it up and save it in pieces inside the files on disk that make up an Oracle database. This activity is a concern to DBAs because it hurts database performance.

Another important aspect of table columns is the configuration of the datatype that can be stored in the column. Suppose that on a table called PRODUCTS, you have the PRODUCT_NAME column of type VARCHAR2(30). The retailer has just begun to carry a new line of products whose names are substantially longer than the names of other products the store carries. You are called in to determine whether the longer name will present a problem to the database. In order to resolve the issue, you can issue a statement that will make the column length longer.

```
SQL> alter table products modify (product_name varchar2(45));
Table altered.
```

Several conditions apply when you are modifying the existing columns' datatypes or adding columns to a table in the database. The general rule of thumb is that increases are generally okay, but decreases are usually a little trickier, although Oracle8*i* allows a bit more flexibility for removing columns in existing tables. Here are some examples of increases that are generally acceptable:

- Increases to the size of a VARCHAR2 or CHAR column
- Increases to the size of a NUMBER column
- Adding new columns to a table

Decreasing the size of various aspects of the table, including some of the column datatypes or the actual number of columns in the table, requires taking special steps. The effort usually involves making sure that the relevant column (or columns) has all NULL values in it before executing the change. In order to execute these types of operations on columns or tables that contain data, the developer must find or create some sort of temporary storage place for the data in the column. One acceptable method is creating a table using the `create table as select` statement with the `select` statement drawing data from the primary key and the column(s) that will be altered. Another method is spooling the data from the table to a flat file, and reloading it later using SQL*Loader, a utility provided with Oracle for loading data into tables from flat files.

Here are some allowable operations that decrease various aspects of the database. Note that in all the following situations, the change can be made only when you have an empty column for all rows in the table. This means that all rows that currently exist in the table must have NULL defined as the value for the column you are making this change to, or else the table must itself be empty. The operations are

- Reducing the size of a NUMBER column (empty column for all rows only)
- Reducing the length of a VARCHAR2 or CHAR column (empty column for all rows only)
- Changing the datatype of a column (empty column for all rows only)

Changing Table Constraints

Several changes can be made to constraints. These changes include altering, disabling, enabling, or removing the constraint from the column or table of the database. These processes allow the developer to create, modify, or remove the business rules that constrain data.

The first constraint-related activity that a developer may need to do is add constraints to a database. This process can be easy or difficult, depending on the circumstances. If a constraint cannot be created with the database, the simplest scenario for adding the constraint is to add it to the database before data is inserted.

```
SQL> alter table products modify (color not null);
Table altered.
SQL> create table avail_colors
  2  (color varchar2(10) primary key);
Table created.
SQL> alter table products add
  2  (constraint fk_products_02 foreign key (color)
  3  references avail_colors (color));
Table altered.
SQL> alter table products add (unique (product_name));
Table altered.
SQL> alter table products add (prod_size varchar2(10) check
  2  (prod_size in ('P','S','M','L','XL','XXL','XXXL')));
Table altered.
```

Notice that in the first statement in the preceding list of examples, the `modify` clause is used to add a NOT NULL constraint as a column constraint to the column, while the `add` clause is used to add all other types of integrity constraints as table constraints to the table. The column on which the constraint is added must already exist in the database table; no constraint can be created for a column that does not exist in the table.

Constraints That Fail on Creation

If any of the conditions for the constraints just listed are not met for the constraint to which the rule applies, then creation of the constraint *will fail.* You will need to correct the problem before attempting to create the constraint again. The following code block demonstrates a situation in which you attempt to add a primary key to a table when one already exists for that table:

```
SQL> alter table products add
  2  (constraint pk_products_01 primary key (product#))
(constraint pk_products_01 primary key (product#))
 *
ERROR at line 2:
ORA-02260: table can have only one primary key
```

The following code block illustrates another situation in which your constraint fails on creation, using an example of CHECK constraints. Here, you also see that if Oracle cannot create the constraint properly, the constraint will not exist in disabled state—it simply won't exist at all.

```
SQL> create table example_1
  2  (col1 number);
Table created.
SQL> insert into example_1 values (1);
1 row created.
SQL> insert into example_1 values (10);
1 row created.
SQL> commit;
Commit complete.
SQL> alter table example_1 add
  2  (constraint ck_01 check (col1 in (1,2,3)));
(col1 in (1,2,3)))
 *
ERROR at line 2:
ORA-02293: cannot enable (JASON.CK_01) - check constraint violated.
SQL> alter table example_1 enable constraint ck_01
  2  exceptions into exceptions;
alter table example_1 enable constraint ck_01
*
ERROR at line 1:
ORA-02430: cannot enable constraint (CK_01) - no such constraint
```

Changing the Table Storage Definition

Again, the `alter table` command is used. However, some aspects of a table's storage definition cannot be altered, including the `initial` or `initrans` settings. To change these settings, you must drop and re-create the table from scratch. An example for changing the storage definition of a table follows:

```
SQL> alter table emp
  2  storage (next 200M pctincrease 20);
Table altered.
```

Dropping Tables

Sometimes, the "cut off your toe" approach to database alteration is required to make sweeping changes to a table in the database. All the tools for taking that approach have been discussed so far, except one—eliminating the offending table. There are usually some associated objects that exist in a database along with the table. These objects may include the index that is created by the PRIMARY KEY or the UNIQUE constraint that is associated with columns in the table. If the table is dropped, Oracle automatically drops any index associated with the table as well. In order to delete a table from the database, the `drop table` command must be executed.

```
SQL> DROP TABLE test_1;
Table dropped.
```

However, dropping tables may not always be that easy. Recall from earlier in this chapter that when you disable constraints such as primary keys that have FOREIGN KEY constraints in other tables depending on their existence, you may have some errors. The same thing happens when you try to drop a table that has a primary key referenced by enabled foreign keys in another table. If you try to drop a table that has other tables' foreign keys referring to it, the following error will ensue:

```
SQL> drop table avail_colors;
drop table avail_colors
           *
ERROR at line 1:
ORA-02449: unique/primary keys in table referenced by foreign keys
```

When FOREIGN KEY constraints are on other tables that reference the table to be dropped, you can use `cascade constraints`. The constraints in other tables that refer to the table being dropped are also dropped with `cascade constraints`.

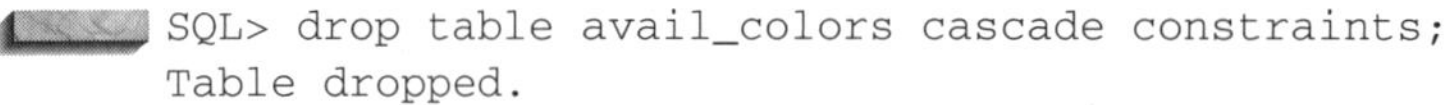

```
SQL> drop table avail_colors cascade constraints;
Table dropped.
```

Alternatively, you can disable or drop the foreign key in the other table first, by using `alter table drop constraint` *`fk_constraint_name`* syntax, and then issue the `drop table` statement without the `cascade constraints` option. However, with this method, you run the risk that many other tables having foreign keys that relate back to the primary key in the table you want to drop will each error out, one at a time, until you disable or drop every FOREIGN KEY constraint referring to the table. If there are several, your `drop table` activity may be extremely frustrating.

For Review

1. Understand how to construct statements that add columns and integrity constraints to tables using the `alter table` statement.
2. Understand how to drop tables that are referenced by FOREIGN KEY constraints. Recognize what happens when a constraint fails on creation.

Using the Oracle Data Dictionary

In this section, we will cover the following topics related to the Oracle data dictionary:

- Available dictionary views
- Querying the data dictionary

Few resources in the Oracle database are as useful as the Oracle data dictionary. Developers, DBAs, and users will find themselves referring to the data dictionary time and time again to resolve questions about object availability, roles and privileges, and performance. Whatever the information, Oracle has it all stored in the data dictionary. This discussion will introduce the major components of the data dictionary in the Oracle database, pointing out its features and highlights in order to set the groundwork for fuller discussions on the data dictionary in later chapters. It is important to understand the major data dictionary concepts before moving on, as data dictionary views will be referred to in many other areas throughout this guide.

Available Dictionary Views

There are a few basic facts about the data dictionary that you should know. First, the Oracle data dictionary consists of tables in which information about the database is stored. The SYS user in Oracle is the only user allowed to `update` those dictionary tables. Oracle processes routinely do this as part of their processing, but a user such as the DBA should never do so except to periodically `update` and `delete` records from the `SYS.AUD$` table, which stores audit trail records.

Rather than having users manipulate the dictionary tables directly, Oracle has several views on the dictionary tables through which users get a distilled look at the dictionary contents. A *view* is a database object somewhat like a "virtual table." You will learn how to create views later in this chapter, in the section "Managing Views." The data in a view is pulled from a real table by way of a `select` statement and stored in memory. The Oracle data dictionary allows users to see the available database objects to various depths, depending on their needs as users. The views of the data dictionary are divided into the following three general categories that correspond to the depth of the database users are permitted to view:

- **USER_*viewname*** These views typically allow the user to see all relevant database objects that are owned by the user accessing the view.
- **ALL_*viewname*** These views typically allow the user to see all relevant database objects that are accessible to the user.

- **DBA_*viewname*** These powerful views allow those who may access them to see all database objects appropriate to the view in the entire database.

The *viewname* component of the name for each view is usually the name of the object type itself. For example, information about tables in the database can be found in the USER_TABLES, ALL_TABLES, or DBA_TABLES views. Some other views that correspond to areas that have been or will be discussed are listed here:

- USER_, ALL_, DBA_OBJECTS Gives information about various database objects
- USER_, ALL_, DBA_TABLES Displays information about tables in the database
- USER_, ALL_, DBA_INDEXES Displays information about indexes in the database
- USER_, ALL_, DBA_VIEWS Displays information about views in the database
- USER_, ALL_, DBA_SEQUENCES Displays information about sequences in the database; a sequence is a database object that generates numbers in sequential order
- USER_, ALL_, DBA_USERS Displays information about users in the database
- USER_, ALL_, DBA_CONSTRAINTS Displays information about constraints in the database
- USER_, ALL_, DBA_CONS_COLUMNS Displays information about table columns that have constraints in the database
- USER_, ALL_, DBA_IND_COLUMNS Displays information about table columns that have indexes in the database
- USER_, ALL_, DBA_TAB_COLUMNS Displays information about columns in tables in the database

For Review

1. What is the data dictionary?
2. What are the three categories of views that a user may access in the dictionary? How much information about the database is available in each view?

3. Who owns the data dictionary? Are users allowed to access the tables of the dictionary directly? Why or why not?

Querying the Data Dictionary

We'll now look at ways for you to select data from the dictionary so you can better understand how useful the data dictionary is in Oracle. (For the purposes of this section, the ALL_ views will be used, except where noted.) Consider first the need to get information about tables. Every user should learn how to list the columns available in a table. A listing of the columns in a table can be obtained from the dictionary with the use of the describe command, often abbreviated as desc. Note that this is a SQL*Plus command, so you cannot use it in PL/SQL code.

```
DESC spanky.products

NAME                 NULL?          TYPE
---------            -----          ------
PRODUCT              NOT NULL       NUMBER
PRODUCT_NAME         NOT NULL       VARCHAR2(30)
QUANTITY                            NUMBER
```

Users can find out any information about the database tables that are available for their use with the ALL_TABLES view. ALL_TABLES displays information about who owns the table, where the table is stored in the database, and what storage parameters a table is using.

TIP
In order to apply the description of any of these ALL_ views to its counterparts in the USER_ and DBA_ families, substitute the scope "available to the user" with "created by the user" or "all those created in the database" for USER_ or DBA_, respectively.

```
SQL> SELECT owner, table_name
  2> FROM all_tables
  3> WHERE owner = 'SPANKY';
OWNER                          TABLE_NAME
------------------------------ ------------------------------
SPANKY                         PRODUCTS
```

Some of the other object views are similar to ALL_TABLES. For example, ALL_INDEXES contains information about the indexes on tables that are available to the user. Some of the information listed in this view details the features of the index, such as whether or not all values in the indexed column are unique. Other information in the view identifies the storage parameters of the index and where the index is stored.

```
SQL> SELECT owner, index_name, table_name, uniqueness
  2> FROM all_indexes
  3> WHERE owner = 'SPANKY';
OWNER      INDEX_NAME     TABLE_NAME UNIQUENESS
---------- -------------- ---------- ---------------
SPANKY     PKY_PRD_01     PRODUCTS   UNIQUE
```

The next data dictionary view represents a slight departure from the previous pattern. The ALL_VIEWS data dictionary view gives information about all the views in the database available to the user. It lists the schema owner, the view name, and the query that was used to create the view. The column containing the text that created the view is stored in LONG format. To obtain data from this column of the view, the user may need to issue the `set long` command to set the formatting that SQL*Plus uses to display a LONG column to be large enough to display the entire query used to create the view. Typically, `set long 5000` will suffice.

```
SQL> SET LONG 5000
SQL> SELECT owner, view_name, text
  2> FROM all_views
  3> WHERE owner = 'SPANKY';
OWNER      VIEW_NAME   TEXT
---------- ----------- ----------------------
SPANKY     PRD_VW      select * from products
```

The next view is the USER_USERS view. This view is used to give the current user of the database more information about their environment. Contained in this view are the default locations where objects created by the user will be stored, along with the user profile this user will abide by. Several other pieces of information will be more useful to DBAs than to developers.

```
SQL> SELECT *
  2> FROM user_users;
USERNAME                        USER_ID ACCOUNT_STATUS   LOCK_DATE
------------------------------ --------- ---------------- ---------
EXPIRY_DA DEFAULT_TABLESPACE   TEMPORARY_TABLESPACE           CREATED
--------- -------------------- ------------------------------ ---------
EXTERNAL_NAME
----------------------
SPANKY                               25 OPEN
          SPANKY               TEMPORARY                      30-MAR-99
```

The next few views are related to constraints. The first one is the ALL_CONSTRAINTS view. This view is used to display information about the constraints that have been defined in the database. It is particularly useful in determining the referenced column in cases where referential integrity constraints have been created on a table. This view gives the name of the constraint, the owner of the constraint, the name of the table the constraint is created on, and the name of the referenced table and column if the constraint created is a FOREIGN KEY.

```
SQL> SELECT constraint_name, table_name, r_owner, r_constraint_name
  2> FROM all_constraints
  3> WHERE table_name = 'PRODUCTS' and owner = 'SPANKY';
CONSTRAINT_NAME     TABLE_NAME  R_OWNER   R_CONSTRAINT_NAME
------------------ ---------- --------- ------------------
FK_PRD_01           PRODUCTS   JASON     PK_PRD_MASTER_01
PK_PRD_01           PRODUCTS
```

The next view, ALL_CONS_COLUMNS, presents information about the columns that are incorporated into constraints on a table. For example, it is possible to create a primary key for a table that uses two or more columns from the table as its unique identifier. This definition of the primary key is sometimes referred to as a *composite primary key*. The ALL_CONS_COLUMNS view gives information about the columns that are in the primary key, and in which order they appear in the composite index.

```
SQL> SELECT constraint_name, table_name, column_name, position
  2> FROM all_cons_columns
  3> WHERE table_name = 'PRODUCTS' and owner = 'SPANKY';
CONSTRAINT_NAME     TABLE_NAME   COLUMN_NAME      POSITION
------------------ ------------ --------------- --------
FK_PRD_01           PRODUCTS     PRODUCT_NAME            1
PK_PRD_01           PRODUCTS     PRODUCT                 1
```

The final dictionary view discussed in this section, ALL_IND_COLUMNS, is related to the ALL_CONS_COLUMNS view but extends the scope of that view by providing information about all the indexed columns on the database.

```
SQL> SELECT index_name, table_name, column_name, column_position
  2> FROM all_ind_columns
  3> WHERE table_name = 'PRODUCTS' and index_owner = 'SPANKY';
INDEX_NAME    TABLE_NAME    COLUMN_NAME      COLUMN_POSITION
------------- ------------- ---------------- ---------------
PK_PRD_01     PRODUCTS      PRODUCT                        1
```

For Review

1. Describe the use of object views. What purpose do the constraint views serve?
2. What is a composite index?
3. What purpose does the COLUMN_POSITION column serve in some of the dictionary views?

DML Operations

Here you will cover the following topics related to manipulating Oracle data:

- Inserting new rows into a table
- Making changes to existing row data
- Deleting data from the Oracle database

This section will introduce you to all forms of data-change manipulation. The three types of data-change manipulation in the Oracle database are updating, deleting, and inserting data. These statements are collectively known as the *data-manipulation language* of Oracle, or *DML* for short.

Inserting New Rows into a Table

The first data-change manipulation operation that will be discussed is the act of inserting new rows into a table. Once a table is created, there is no data in the table, unless the table is created and populated by rows selected from another table. Even in this case, the data must come from somewhere. This "somewhere" is from users who enter data into the table via `insert` statements.

An `insert` statement has a different syntax from a `select` statement. The general syntax for an `insert` statement is listed in the following code block, which defines several rows to be added to the PRODUCTS table owned by SPANKY. This table has three columns, titled PRODUCT#, PRODUCT_NAME, and QUANTITY. User SPANKY now wants to put some data in her table, so she executes the following statement designed to place one new row into the PRODUCTS table:

```
INSERT INTO products (product#, product_name, quantity)
VALUES (7848394, 'KITTY LITTER', 12);
```

Notice a few general rules of syntax in this statement. The insert statement has two parts. In the first part, the table to receive the inserted row is defined, along with the columns of the table that will have the column values inserted into them. The second portion of the statement defines the actual data values for the row to be added. This latter portion of the statement is denoted by the values keyword.

Oracle is capable of handling several variations on the insert statement. For example, the user generally needs to define explicit columns of the table only when data is not going to be inserted in all columns of the table. For example, if user SPANKY wanted to define only the product number and the name at the time the row was inserted, then SPANKY would be required to list the PRODUCT# and PRODUCT_NAME columns in the into clause of the insert statement. However, since she named column values for all columns in the table, the following statement would be just as acceptable as the previous one for inserting the row into the PRODUCTS table:

```
INSERT INTO products
VALUES (7848394, 'KITTY LITTER', 12);
```

One important question to ask in this situation is "how does Oracle know which column to populate with what data?" Suppose that the column datatypes are defined to be NUMBER for PRODUCT# and QUANTITY, and VARCHAR2 for PRODUCT_NAME. What prevents Oracle from placing the 12 in the PRODUCT# column? The answer is position. Position can matter in tables on the Oracle database; the position of the data in the insert statement must correspond to the position of the columns in the table. The user can determine the position of each column in a table by using the describe command or the output from the USER_TAB_COLUMNS dictionary view using COLUMN_ID to indicate position as part of the order by clause. The order in which the columns are listed in the output from the describe command is the same order in which values should be placed to insert data into the table without explicitly naming the columns of the table. The following code block shows two ways to glean positional information for table columns from the Oracle database:

```
SQL> select table_name, column_name
  2  from user_tab_columns
  3  where table_name = 'PRODUCTS'
  4  order by column_id;
 TABLE_NAME                     COLUMN_NAME
------------------------------ ------------------------------
PRODUCTS                       PRODUCT#
PRODUCTS                       PRODUCT_NAME
PRODUCTS                       QUANTITY
```

```
SQL> describe products
 Name                            Null?    Type
 ------------------------------- -------- ----
 PRODUCT#                        NOT NULL NUMBER
 PRODUCT_NAME                             VARCHAR2(30)
 QUANTITY                                 NUMBER
```

Another variation on the `insert` theme is the option to populate a table with data obtained from other tables using a `select` statement. This method of populating table data is similar to the method used by the `create table as select` statement, which was discussed earlier in the chapter. In this case, the `values` clause can be omitted entirely. However, the rules regarding column position of the inserted data still apply in this situation, meaning that if the user can `select` data for all columns of the table having data inserted into them, then the user need not name the columns in the `insert into` clause.

```
INSERT INTO products
(SELECT product#, product_name, quantity
 FROM MASTER.PRODUCTS);
```

In order to put data into a table, a special privilege must be granted from the table owner to the user who needs to perform the `insert`.

For Review

1. What statement is used to place new data into an Oracle table?
2. What are the three options available with the statement that allows new data to be placed into Oracle tables?

Making Changes to Existing Row Data

The data rows in a table often will need to be changed. In order to make those changes, the `update` statement can be used. Updates can be made to any row in a database, except in two cases. One case is when you don't have enough access privileges to `update` the data. You will learn more about access privileges in Chapter 5. The other case is when some other user on the database is making changes to the row you want to change. You will learn more about data-change control in a later section, "Transaction Processing." Otherwise, the user changes data when an `update` statement is issued, as follows:

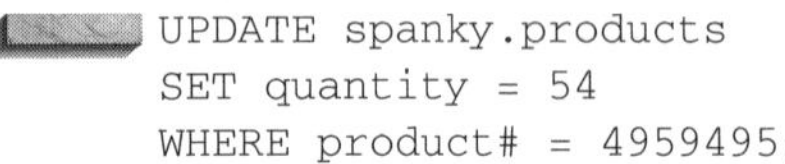

```
UPDATE spanky.products
SET quantity = 54
WHERE product# = 4959495;
```

Notice that the typical update statement has three clauses. The first is the actual update clause, in which the table that will be updated is named. The second clause is the set clause. In the set clause, all columns that will be changed by the update statement are named, along with their new values. The final clause of the update statement is the where clause. The where clause in an update statement is the same as the where clause in a select statement: it provides one or more comparison operations that determine which rows Oracle will update as a result of this statement being issued.

The update and set clauses are mandatory in an update statement. However, the where clause is not. Omitting the where clause in an update statement has the effect of applying the data change to every row that presently exists in the table. Consider the following code block that issues a data change without a where clause specified. The change made by this statement will apply to every row in the table.

```
UPDATE spanky.products
SET quantity = 0;
```

Every operation that was possible in the where clauses of a select statement is possible in the where clauses of an update. The where clause in an update statement can have any type of comparison or range operation in it and can even handle the use of the exists operation and subqueries.

For Review

What statement is used to change data in an Oracle table? What clauses in this statement are mandatory?

Deleting Data from the Oracle Database

The removal of data from a database is as much a fact of life as putting the data there in the first place. The delete statement in SQL*Plus is used to remove database rows from tables. The syntax for the delete statement is detailed in the following code block. Note that in this example, there is no way to delete data from selected columns in a row in the table; this act is accomplished with the update statement with the columns that are to be "deleted" being set to NULL by the update statement.

```
DELETE FROM spanky.products
WHERE product# = 4959394; -- all column values removed
```

As in the case of database updates, delete statements use the where clause to help determine which rows are meant to be removed. Like an update or select statement, the `where` clause in a `delete` statement can contain any type of comparison operation, range operation, subquery, or any other operation acceptable for a `where` clause. Like an `update` statement, if the `where` clause is left off the `delete` statement, the deletion will be applied to all rows in the table.

Data deletion should be undertaken with care. It can be costly to replace data that has been inappropriately deleted from the database, which is why the privilege of deleting information should be given out only to those users who really should be able to delete records from a table.

Truncating Tables—The Deletion Alternative

A special option is available in Oracle that allows certain users to delete information from a table quickly. One limitation of the `delete` statement is that it uses the transaction-processing controls like rollback segments. When the DBA or privileged developer needs to remove the data in a large table, the `delete` option is an inefficient one for accomplishing the job.

The DBA or developer may use the `truncate` statement as an alternative. The `truncate` statement is a part of the Oracle DDL, like the `create table` statement and unlike the `delete` statement, which is part of the data-manipulation language, the DML. Truncating a table removes all row data from a table quickly, while leaving the definition of the table intact, including the definition of constraints and indexes on the table. The `truncate` statement is a high-speed data deletion statement that bypasses the transaction controls available in Oracle for recoverability in data changes. Truncating a table is almost always faster than executing the `delete` statement without a `where` clause; but once it has been completed, the data cannot be recovered unless you have a backed up copy of the data.

```
TRUNCATE TABLE products;
```

TIP

Truncating tables affects a characteristic about them that Oracle calls the highwatermark. *This characteristic is a value Oracle uses to keep track of the largest size the table has ever grown to. When you truncate the table, Oracle resets the highwatermark.*

For Review

1. What are two options for deleting data from a table?
2. Is the `truncate` statement a part of DML or DDL? Explain.
3. What is a highwatermark, and how does it work?

Transaction Processing

Transaction processing is a mechanism that the Oracle database provides in order to facilitate the act of changing data. Without transaction-processing mechanisms, the database would not be able to guarantee that the users would not overwrite one another's changes in mid-process, or select data that is in the process of being changed by another user. One reality that a user of the Oracle database must understand is that a change to data made in the Oracle database is not saved immediately. Oracle allows users to execute a series of data-change statements together as one logical unit of work, terminated by either saving the work in the database or discarding it. This logical unit of work is called a *transaction*, and it begins with the user's first executable SQL statement. A transaction ends when it is explicitly committed or rolled back (both terms are discussed later in this section) by that user.

Transaction processing consists of a set of controls that allow a user issuing an `insert`, `update`, or `delete` statement to declare a beginning to the series of data-change statements they will issue. When the user has finished making the changes to the database, the user can save the data to the database by explicitly ending the transaction. Alternatively, if a mistake is made at any point during the transaction, the user can have the database discard the changes made to the database in favor of the way the data existed before the transaction.

Transactions are created with the use of two different elements in the Oracle database. The first element is the set of commands that define the beginning, breakpoint, and end of a transaction. The second element is the special locking mechanisms designed to prevent more than one user at a time from making a change to row information in a database. Locks will be discussed after the transaction control commands are defined.

The commands that define transactions are as follows:

- **`set transaction`** Initiates the beginning of a transaction and sets key features. This command is optional. A transaction will be started automatically when you start SQL*Plus, commit the previous transaction, or roll back the previous transaction.
- **`commit`** Ends the current transaction by saving database changes and starts a new transaction.
- **`rollback`** Ends the current transaction by discarding database changes and starts a new transaction.
- **`savepoint`** Defines breakpoints for the transaction to allow partial rollbacks.

set transaction

This command can be used to define the beginning of a transaction. If any change is made to the database after the `set transaction` command is issued but before the transaction is ended, all changes made will be considered part of that transaction. The `set transaction` statement is not required, because a transaction begins as soon as you log in to Oracle via SQL*Plus and execute the first command, or immediately after issuing a `rollback` or `commit` statement to end a transaction.

By default, a transaction is `read write` unless you override this default by issuing `set transaction read only`. Finally, you can set the transaction isolation level with `set transaction` as well. The `set transaction isolation level serializable` command specifies serializable transaction isolation mode as defined in SQL92. If a serializable transaction contains data-manipulation language (DML) that attempts to update any resource that may have been updated in a transaction uncommitted at the start of the serializable transaction, then the DML statement fails. The `set transaction isolation level read committed` command is the default Oracle transaction behavior. If the transaction contains DML that requires row locks held by another transaction, then the DML statement waits until the row locks are released.

```
SET TRANSACTION READ ONLY;
SET TRANSACTION READ WRITE;
SET TRANSACTION ISOLATION LEVEL SERIALIZABLE;
SET TRANSACTION ISOLATION LEVEL READ COMMITTED;
```

commit

The `commit` statement in transaction processing represents the point in time when the user has made all the changes they want to have logically grouped together, and since no mistakes have been made, the user is ready to save the work. The `work` keyword is an extraneous word in the `commit` syntax that is designed for readability. Issuing a `commit` statement also implicitly begins a new transaction on the database because it closes the current transaction and starts a new one.

It is important also to understand that an implicit `commit` occurs on the database when a user exits SQL*Plus or issues a data definition language (DDL) command, such as a `create table` statement used to create a database object or `alter table` to alter it.

```
COMMIT;
COMMIT WORK;
```

rollback

If you have at any point issued a data-change statement you don't want, you can discard the changes made to the database with the use of the rollback statement. After the rollback command is issued, a new transaction is started implicitly by the database session. In addition to rollbacks executed when the rollback statement is issued, implicit rollback statements are conducted when a statement fails for any reason or if the user cancels a statement with the CTRL-C cancel command.

```
ROLLBACK;
ROLLBACK WORK;
```

savepoint

In some cases involving long transactions or transactions that involve many data changes, you may not want to scrap all your changes simply because the last statement issued contains unwanted changes. Savepoints are special operations that allow you to divide the work of a transaction into different segments. You can execute rollbacks to the savepoint only, leaving prior changes intact. Savepoints are great for situations in which part of the transaction needs to be recovered in an uncommitted transaction. At the point the rollback to savepoint so_far_so_good statement completes in the following code block, only changes made before the savepoint was defined are kept when the commit is issued:

```
UPDATE spanky.products
SET quantity = 55
WHERE product# = 59495;

SAVEPOINT so_far_so_good;

UPDATE spanky.products
SET quantity = 504;

ROLLBACK TO SAVEPOINT so_far_so_good;
COMMIT;
```

Locks

The final aspect of the Oracle database that allows the user to perform transaction processing is the lock, the mechanism by which Oracle prevents data from being changed by more than one user at a time. All locks in Oracle are table locks. However, within the world of table locks, some locks are more restrictive than others. The types of locks in Oracle include exclusive, share, share row, exclusive row, and share row exclusive.

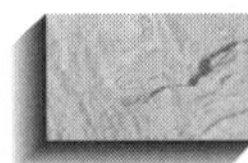

TIP

An `update` statement acquires a special row-level lock called a "row-exclusive" lock, which means that for the period of time the `update` statement is executing, no other user in the database can view or change the data in the row. The same goes for `delete` or `insert` operations. Another `update` statement, the `select for update` statement, acquires a more lenient lock called the "share row" lock. This lock means that for the period of time the `update` statement is changing the data in the rows of the table, no other user may change that row, but users may look at the data in the row as it changes.

For Review

1. What is transaction processing?
2. Identify the mechanisms that support transactions.

Creating, Managing, and Using Sequences

In this section, we will cover the following topics related to sequences:

- The role of sequences
- Creating sequences
- Using sequences
- Modifying sequence definitions
- Removing sequences

In database development, sometimes it becomes necessary to populate a column with a series of integers on an ongoing basis. These integers may be used to uniquely identify the records being entered. For example, a doctor's office may have a client tracking system that assigns each new patient a unique integer ID to identify their records. There are several ways to produce this integer ID through programmatic means, but the most effective means in Oracle is to use sequences.

Role of Sequences

A sequence is a special database object that generates integers according to rules specified at the time the sequence is created. Sequences have many purposes in database systems, the most common of which is to generate primary keys automatically. This task is common in situations where the primary key is not generally used for accessing data in a table. The common use of sequences to create primary keys has one main drawback: because it is simply a sequential number, the primary key itself and the index it creates are somewhat meaningless. But, if you only need the key to guarantee uniqueness, and don't care that you're creating a nonsense key, it is perfectly alright to do so.

Sequence Pseudocolumn Usage

Sequences are used as follows. Users `select` data from the sequence with two special keywords that denote virtual columns or *pseudocolumns* in the database. The first pseudocolumn is CURRVAL. This column can be used to see what the current value generated by the sequence is. The second pseudocolumn is NEXTVAL. This column contains the next value that the sequence will generate, according to the rules developed for it. Selecting NEXTVAL on the sequence effectively eliminates whatever value is stored in CURRVAL. Data may only be drawn from a sequence, never placed into it. These pseudocolumns are available for `select` access, but users can incorporate a call on the sequence's CURRVAL or NEXTVAL in `insert` or `update` statements so that the value in either of the two columns can be used on a row of another table.

Some restrictions are placed on the types of statements that can draw on CURRVAL and NEXTVAL. Any `update` or `insert` statement can make use of the data in a sequence. References to sequences *cannot* be used in subqueries of `select` statements (including those with `having`), views, `select` statements using set operations (such as `union` or `minus`), or any `select` statement that requires a sort to be performed.

For Review

1. What is a sequence? What are some ways a sequence can be used?
2. What are CURRVAL and NEXTVAL? What happens to CURRVAL when NEXTVAL is selected?

Creating Sequences

Many rules can be applied to sequences, allowing the developer to specify how the sequence generates integers. These rules are useful for defining sequences that produce integers in a special order, or with certain increments. There is even a feature that allows the developer to improve performance on a sequence. Sequences are created with the `create sequence` statement. Each clause in the `create sequence` statement, and some options for configuring it, is explained in the following list:

- **`start with n`** Allows the creator of the sequence to specify the first value generated by the sequence. Once created, the sequence will generate the value specified by `start with` the first time the sequence's NEXTVAL virtual column is referenced.
- **`increment by n`** Defines the number by which to increment the sequence every time the NEXTVAL virtual column is referenced. The default for this clause is 1 if it is not explicitly specified. You can set *n* to be positive for incrementing sequences, or negative for decrementing or countdown sequences.
- **`minvalue n`** Defines the minimum value that can be produced by the sequence. If no minimum value is specified, Oracle will assume the default, `nominvalue`.
- **`maxvalue n`** Defines the maximum value that can be produced by the sequence. If no maximum value is desired or specified, Oracle will assume the default, `nomaxvalue`.
- **`cycle`** Allows the sequence to recycle values produced when the `maxvalue` or `minvalue` is reached. If cycling is not desired or not explicitly specified, Oracle will assume the default, `nocycle`. You cannot specify `cycle` in conjunction with `nomaxvalue` or `nominvalue`. If you want your sequence to cycle, you must specify `maxvalue` for incrementing sequences or `minvalue` for decrementing or countdown sequences.
- **`cache n`** Allows the sequence to cache a specified number of values to improve performance. If caching is not desired or not explicitly specified, Oracle will assume the default, `nocache`.
- **`order`** Allows the sequence to assign values in the order in which requests are received by the sequence. If order is not desired or not explicitly specified, Oracle will assume the default, `noorder`.

Consider now an example for defining sequences. The integers that can be specified for sequences can be negative as well as positive. Consider the following example of a decrementing sequence. The `start with` integer in this example is positive, but the `increment by` integer is negative, which effectively tells the sequence to decrement instead of increment. When zero is reached, the sequence will start again from the top. This sequence can be useful in programs that require a countdown before an event will occur.

```
CREATE SEQUENCE countdown_20
START WITH 20
INCREMENT BY -1
MAXVALUE 20
MINVALUE 0
CYCLE
ORDER;
```

If you use the `cycle` option, you must specify a `maxvalue` for incrementing sequences or `minvalue` for decrementing sequences so that Oracle knows when it has reached the maximum or minimum value for the sequence and is supposed to cycle. If you choose to use the `nomaxvalue` and/or `minvalue` options in your sequence (or exclude them from your sequence definition, thereby making them the defaults), then you must also use the `nocycle` option, or Oracle will return an error.

For Review

1. What statement is used for creating a sequence?
2. What are the options used for sequence creation?

Using Sequences

Once the sequence is created, it is referenced using the CURRVAL and NEXTVAL pseudocolumns. The users of the database can view the current value of the sequence by using a `select` statement. Similarly, the next value in the sequence can be generated with a `select` statement. Because sequences are not tables—they are only objects that generate integers via the use of virtual columns—the DUAL table acts as the "virtual" table from which the virtual column data is pulled. As stated earlier, values cannot be placed into the sequence, only selected from the sequence. The following example demonstrates how COUNTDOWN_20 cycles when the `minvalue` is reached:

```
SQL> select countdown_20.nextval from dual;
  NEXTVAL
---------
       20
SQL> /
  NEXTVAL
---------
       19

...

SQL> /
NEXTVAL
---------
        1
SQL> /
NEXTVAL
---------
        0
SQL> /
NEXTVAL
---------
       20
```

Once the NEXTVAL column is referenced, the value in CURRVAL is updated to match the value in NEXTVAL, and the prior value in CURRVAL is lost. The next code block illustrates this point:

```
SQL> select countdown_20.currval from dual;
  CURRVAL
---------
       20
SQL> select countdown_20.nextval from dual;
  NEXTVAL
---------
       19
SQL> select countdown_20.currval from dual;
  CURRVAL
---------
       19
```

CURRVAL is undefined at sequence creation, so if you reference CURRVAL before referencing NEXTVAL, you get the following error message: `ORA-08002: sequence COUNTDOWN_20.CURRVAL is not yet defined in this session.` However, if you drop and re-create the sequence, you might encounter an interesting anomaly in Oracle—CURRVAL is set to the `start with` value until

NEXTVAL is referenced for the first time after sequence creation! After that, CURRVAL is set to the value for NEXTVAL. Every time NEXTVAL is referenced, CURRVAL changes. Interestingly, the first time you reference NEXTVAL, it gets set to the `start with` value also, so effectively the value for CURRVAL doesn't change!

Referencing Sequences in Data Changes

Sequence-value generation can be incorporated directly into data changes made by `insert` or `update` statements. This direct use of sequences in `insert` and `update` statements is the most common use for sequences in a database. For the situation in which the sequence generates a primary key for all new rows entering the database table, the sequence would likely be referenced directly from the `insert` statement. Note, however, that this approach sometimes fails when the sequence is referenced by triggers. Therefore, it is best to reference sequences within the user interface or within stored procedures. The following statements illustrate the use of sequences directly in changes made to tables:

```
INSERT INTO expense(expense_no, empid, amt, submit_date)
VALUES(countdown_20.nextval, 59495, 456.34, '21-NOV-99');

UPDATE product
SET product_num = countdown_20.currval
WHERE serial_num = 34938583945;
```

For Review

1. Identify a way to refer to a sequence with the `select` statement. Why is the DUAL table important in this method?
2. Identify a way to refer to a sequence with the `update` and `insert` statements.

Modifying Sequence Definitions

There may come a time when the sequence of a database will need its rules altered in some way. For example, you may want COUNDOWN_20 to decrement by a different number. Any parameter of a sequence can be modified by issuing the `alter sequence` statement.

```
SQL> select countdown_20.nextval from dual;
NEXTVAL
-------
     16
SQL> alter sequence countdown_20
```

```
  2  increment by -4;
Sequence altered.
SQL> select countdown_20.nextval from dual
  2  ;
  NEXTVAL
---------
       12
SQL> /
  NEXTVAL
---------
        8
```

The effect is immediate—the statement will change the COUNTDOWN_20 to decrement each NEXTVAL by 4 instead of 1. Any parameter of a sequence that is not specified by the `alter sequence` statement will remain unchanged. Thus, by altering the sequence to use `nocycle` instead of `cycle`, the COUNTDOWN_20 sequence in the following listing will run through one countdown from 20 to 0 only. After the sequence hits 0, no further references to COUNTDOWN_20.NEXTVAL will be allowed.

```
SQL> alter sequence countdown_20
  2  nocycle;
Sequence altered.
SQL> select countdown_20.nextval from dual;
  NEXTVAL
---------
        4
SQL> /
  NEXTVAL
---------
        0
SQL> /
select countdown_20.nextval from dual
*
ERROR at line 1:
ORA-08004: sequence COUNTDOWN_20.NEXTVAL goes below MINVALUE
and cannot be instantiated
```

Beware of Effects of Modifying Sequences

Modifying sequences is a simple process. However, the impact of the changes can be complex, depending on how an application uses the sequence. The main concern with changing sequences is monitoring the effect on tables or other processes that use the values generated by the sequence. For example, resetting the value returned by a sequence from 1,150 to 0 is not difficult to execute. However, if the sequence was being used to generate primary keys for a table for which several values between 0 and 1,150 had already been generated, you would encounter problems when the sequence began generating values for insert statements that depend on the sequence to create primary keys. This problem won't show up when the sequence is altered, but later inserts will have PRIMARY KEY constraint violations on the table. The only way to solve the problem (other than deleting the records already existing in the table) is to alter the sequence again.

For Review

1. What statement is used to modify a sequence definition?
2. When do changes to a sequence take effect?

Removing Sequences

When a sequence is no longer needed, it can be removed. To do so, the DBA or owner of the sequence can issue the drop sequence statement. Dropping the sequence renders its virtual columns CURRVAL and NEXTVAL unusable. However, if the sequence was being used to generate primary-key values, the values generated by the sequence would continue to exist in the database. There is no cascading effect on the values generated by a sequence when the sequence is removed.

```
SQL> DROP SEQUENCE countdown_20;
Sequence dropped.
SQL> select countdown_20.currval from dual;
select countdown_20.currval from dual
       *
ERROR at line 1:
ORA-02289: sequence does not exist
```

For Review

1. How are sequences dropped?
2. What are the effects of dropping a sequence?

Managing Views

In this section, you will cover the following topics concerning views:

- Creating simple and complex views
- Creating views that enforce constraints

- Modifying views
- Removing views

It has been said that eyes are the windows to the soul. While this may or may not be true, it is true that eyes can be used to view the data in a table. In order to make sure the right eyes see the right things, however, some special "windows" on the data in a table can be created. These special windows are called *views*. A view can be thought of as a virtual table. In reality, a view is nothing more than the results of a `select` statement stored in a memory structure that resembles a table. To the person using the view, manipulating the data from the view is just like manipulating the data from a table. In some cases, it is even possible for the user to `insert` data into a view as though the view *were* a table. The relationship between tables and views is illustrated in Figure 9-2.

Creating Simple and Complex Views

One example statement for creating a view has already been identified—the one for creating the `ALL_VIEWS` dictionary view in the Oracle database. Again, though, don't worry about understanding the minutiae of creating every Oracle data dictionary view. The most important things to remember about views can be summarized in the following points:

- Views add extra security to data (for example, a view on the EMP_SALARY table that only shows salary information for the user performing the `select` against the view).
- Views can hide data complexity by combining appropriate information from multiple tables, as discussed in "Creating Complex Views," later in this section.

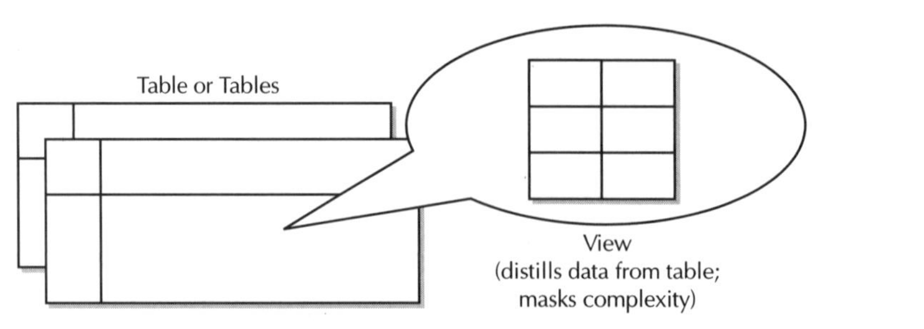

FIGURE 9-2. *Tables and views*

- Views can hide real column names that may be hard to understand and display simpler names.

Views are created by using the create view statement. Once created, views are owned by the user who created them. They cannot be reassigned by the owner unless the owner has the create any view system privilege.

Creating Simple Views

Different types of views can be created in Oracle. The first type of view is a *simple view*. This type of view is created from the data in one table. Within the simple view, all single-row operations are permitted. Options that are not allowed in a simple view include order by clauses, references to more than one table via a table join, grouping or set operations, group by clauses, hierarchical queries (those queries containing a connect by clause), and queries with the distinct keyword. The following code block demonstrates the creation of a simple view:

```
CREATE VIEW employee_view
AS (SELECT empid, lastname, firstname, salary
FROM employee
WHERE empid = 59495);
```

Users of a simple view can insert data in the underlying table of the view if the creator of the view allows them to do so, subject to the restrictions discussed next. First, though, this statement demonstrates data change via a view:

```
UPDATE employee_view
SET salary = 99000
WHERE empid = 59495;
```

Changing Data in Underlying Tables Through Simple Views: Restrictions

Users can insert data in the table underlying a simple view, subject to several restrictions. First, users may have problems inserting data into views if the underlying table has NOT NULL constraints on it. This problem can be solved by using a default value for the NOT NULL column in the table definition. The other restrictions on inserting or updating data to a table underlying a simple view are listed here:

- If the with check option is used, the user may not insert, delete, or update data on the table that the simple view is not able to select for the user.

- The user may not `insert`, `delete`, or `update` data on the table underlying the simple view if the `select` statement creating the view contains `group by` or `order by` clauses, or a single-row operation.
- No data may be inserted on the table underlying a simple view that contains references to any virtual column, such as ROWID, CURRVAL, NEXTVAL, and ROWNUM.
- No data may be inserted into tables underlying simple views that are created with the `read only` option.

Creating Complex Views

Complex views have some major differences from simple views. Complex views draw data from more than one table and can contain single-row operations and references to virtual columns. Complex views can also contain `group by` clauses. However, `insert`, `update`, and `delete` statements are not permitted on the underlying tables for complex views under most circumstances. Complex views allow complicated data models and conversion operations to be hidden behind a simple view name for the user. The following complex view presents data from multiple tables:

```
CREATE VIEW employee_view
AS (SELECT e.empid empid, e.lastname lastname, e.firstname firstname,
e.salary salary, a.address, a.city, a.state, a.zipcode
FROM employee e, employee_address a
WHERE e.empid = a.empid);
```

Updatable Join Views

Complex views usually do not allow data to be changed on the underlying table because of the join that is performed in order to obtain the result set displayed in the view. However, in some cases, you may set up a complex view that allows underlying tables to be updated, which is referred to as an *updatable join view.* (A *join view* is simply a view that contains a join.)

Fundamental to the discussion of updatable join views is the concept of a *key-preserved table.* A key-preserved table is a table in a complex view whose primary-key columns are all present in the view, and whose values are all unique and not NULL in the view. Views containing outer joins generally won't contain key-preserved tables unless the outer join generates no NULL values. Even in such a case, the updatability is dependant on your data; so for all intents and purposes, you should just assume that outer join views are not updatable. If you define a complex view that permits data changes in the underlying tables, but you don't want the underlying tables to be changed, you must specify the `read only` option on the view. You can execute data-change statements on a complex view only if all of the following conditions are met:

- The statement must affect only one of the tables in the join.
- For `update` statements, all columns changed must be extracted from a key-preserved table. In addition, if the view is created `with check option`, join columns and columns taken from tables that are referenced more than once in the view cannot be part of the `update`.
- For `delete` statements, there may only be one key-preserved table in the join. This table may be present more than once in the join, unless the view has been created `with check option`.
- For `insert` statements, all columns in which values are inserted must come from a key-preserved table, and the view must not have been created `with check option`.

Updatable Join Views: Some Examples

The easy way to determine whether you can make data changes to a complex view is by issuing the following statement: `select * from USER_UPDATABLE_COLUMNS where TABLE_NAME = 'your_complex_view'`. This view will inform you whether the data in the updatable join view's columns can be changed based on considering the key-preserved table criteria. However, even this method isn't foolproof, as demonstrated in the following code block. Also, notice in the following block that even though you can add data to the underlying table, you won't necessarily be able to see the data in the view if there is no matching information in the other table in the join. For this example, EXAMPLE_1 is the same table used earlier in this chapter, with its one column, COL1:

```
SQL> create table example_2
  2   (col_2 varchar2(30) primary key,
  3    col_3 varchar2(30),
  4    col_4 varchar2(30),
  5*   col_1 number)
Table created.
SQL>  create view example_vw as
  2  (select col1, col_3, col_4, col_1
  3  from example_1, example_2
View created.
SQL> insert into example_vw (col1) values (3);
insert into example_vw (col1) values (3)
                                      *
```

```
ERROR at line 1:
ORA-01779: cannot modify a column which maps to a non
key-preserved table
SQL> SELECT column_name, updatable
  2   FROM user_updatable_columns
  3   WHERE table_name = 'EXAMPLE_VW'
COLUMN_NAME                    UPD
------------------------------ ---
COL1                           NO
COL_3                          YES
COL_4                          YES
COL_1                          YES
SQL> insert into example_vw (col_3, col_4, col_1) values ('f','g',1);
insert into example_vw (col_3, col_4, col_1) values ('f','g',1)
            *
ERROR at line 1:
ORA-01400: cannot insert NULL into ("JASON"."EXAMPLE_2"."COL_2")
SQL> create or replace view example_vw as
  2  ((select col1, col_3, col_4, col_1
  3  from example_1, example_2
  4  where col1 = col_1);
View created.
SQL> SELECT column_name, updatable
  2  FROM user_updatable_columns
  3  WHERE table_name = 'EXAMPLE_VW';
COLUMN_NAME                    UPD
------------------------------ ---
COL1                           NO
COL_2                          YES
COL_3                          YES
COL_4                          YES
COL_1                          YES
SQL> insert into example_vw (col_2, col_3, col_4, col_1)
  2  values ('r','s','t',1);
1 row created.
SQL> select * from example_vw;
No rows selected.
```

For Review

1. What is a simple view? How does it differ from a complex view? Which view allows the user to `insert` data into the view's underlying table? Explain.

2. What is a complex view? What are the rules that determine when a complex view can be used to modify data in an underlying table?

Creating Views That Enforce Constraints

Tables that underlie views often have constraints that limit the data that can be added to a table. Views have the same limitations on data that can enter the table. In addition, the view can define special constraints for data entry. The option used to configure view constraints is `with check option`. This special constraint forces the view to review the data changes made to see if the data being changed is data the view can `select`. If the data being changed will not be selected by the view, then the view will not let the user make the data change. The following view will now guarantee that any user who tries to `insert` data into EMPLOYEE_VIEW for an employee other than EMPID# 59495 will not be able to do so:

```
CREATE VIEW employee_view
AS (SELECT empid, lastname, firstname, salary
FROM employee
WHERE empid = 59495)
WITH CHECK OPTION;
```

For Review

1. How can constraints be created and enforced on views?
2. On what principle does a view constraint operate?

Modifying Views

Sometimes, the creator of a view may need to change the view. However, views don't follow the syntax conventions of other database objects. There is an `alter view` statement in the Oracle SQL language for recompiling or revalidating all references in the view *as it exists already*, but the statement used to alter the definition of a view is the `create or replace view` statement. When a `create or replace view` statement is issued, Oracle will disregard the error that arises when it encounters the view that already exists with that name, and overwrite the definition for the old view with the definition for the new. The following code block illustrates the use of the `create or replace view` statement:

```
CREATE OR REPLACE VIEW employee_view
AS (SELECT empid, lastname, firstname, salary
FROM employee
WHERE empid = user)
WITH CHECK OPTION;
```

A view is made invalid when the underlying table is removed; this illustrates an example of object dependency in the Oracle database. That is to say, certain objects in Oracle depend on others in order to work. Some examples of object dependency that have been presented so far are indexes depending on the existence of the corresponding tables, and views depending on the existence of underlying tables.

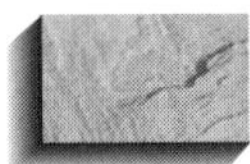

TIP
To fix a view that has become invalid due to the redefinition or deletion of a table that underlies it, the creator of the view must either re-create the underlying table and issue the `alter view` *command, or modify the view with the* `create or replace view` *statement.*

For Review

1. What statement is used to recompile or revalidate an existing view definition?
2. What statement is used to alter the definition of a view?
3. What is object dependency?

Removing Views

There may come a time when the view creator needs to remove the view, like other database objects. The command for executing this function is the `drop view` statement. There are no cascading scenarios that the person dropping a view must be aware of. The following statement illustrates the use of `drop view` for deleting views from the database:

```
DROP VIEW employee_view;
```

For Review

How are views dropped?

Index Structure and Management

In this section, you will cover the following topics on managing indexes:

- Different index types and their uses
- Creating B-tree and bitmap indexes
- Reorganizing indexes
- Dropping indexes
- Getting index information from the data dictionary

Tables can grow quite large, and when they do, it becomes difficult for users to quickly find the data they need. For this reason, Oracle offers indexes as a method of speeding database performance when accessing tables with a lot of data. Oracle provides different types of indexes for different uses, and you will learn about them here. You will also learn about the specific procedures for creating B-tree and bitmap indexes, and what sorts of situations may cause you to choose one over the other. The methods used to reorganize and drop indexes are shown here as well. Finally, you will learn where to look in the data dictionary for information about your indexes.

Different Index Types and Their Uses

An index in Oracle can be compared to the card catalog in a library. When you want to find a book, you go to the card catalog (or computer) and look up the book under author, title, or subject. When you find the card for that book, it lists the location of the book in the library according to a classification system. Looking for a book in this way reduces the time you spend looking for a book on fly-fishing in the section where autobiographies are kept. Oracle indexes work the same way. You find row data that matches your search criteria in the index first, and then use the ROWID for that row from the index to get the entire row quickly from the table.

Several criteria are used to determine what kind of index you're looking at. The first criterion is how many columns the index has. *Simple* indexes contain only one column of data through which you can search, plus the ROWID of the corresponding row in the table. *Composite* indexes store more than one column of data for you to search, plus the ROWIDs of the corresponding rows in the table. You can put up to 32 columns in a composite index, but you may be restricted from including that many if the total size of all the columns you want in the index exceeds `DB_BLOCK_SIZE` / 3. Other criteria for identifying indexes is whether the indexed column(s) contains all unique (composite) values, whether an index is partitioned or nonpartitioned, whether it is a traditional B-tree or a bitmap index, or whether the data in the index is stored in reverse order.

Oracle maintains indexes whenever user processes make data changes to tables. For example, if you `insert` a new row in a table, an associated entry is made in the index for that row's indexed column. That entry is not made to the last leaf block of the index; but, rather, the appropriate leaf block is located according to index sort order, and the entry is made there. When data is removed from the table, the corresponding index entry is marked for removal. Later, when all other rows corresponding to all index entries in the leaf node are removed, then and only then is the entire block purged of index entries. Thus, the structure of the index is preserved. An `update` statement that changes the value of a row's indexed column value is treated as a marked removal followed by an `insert`. Finally, index entries can be added to a block even past the `pctfree` threshold.

Nonpartitioned B-Tree Indexes

The B-tree index is the traditional indexing mechanism used in Oracle. It stores data in a treelike fashion, displayed in Figure 9-3. At the base of the index is the *root node,* which is an entry point for your search for data in the index. The root node contains pointers to other nodes at the next level in the index. Depending on the value you seek, you will be pointed in one of many directions. The next level in the index consists of *branch nodes,* which are similar to the root node in that they, too, contain pointers to the next level of nodes in the index. Again, depending on the value you seek, you will be pointed in one of many directions. Branch nodes point to the highest level of the index, the *leaf nodes.* In this highest level, *index entries* contain indexed column values and the corresponding ROWIDs of rows storing those column values. Each leaf node is linked to the leaf nodes on both its left and right, in order to make it possible to search up and down through a range of entries in the index.

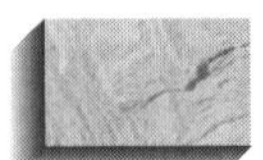

TIP

Partitioning is a feature of tables and indexes in Oracle that allows you to subdivide tables and indexes into copies containing all columns, but only some of the rows, from that table or index. Partitioning is useful for distributing tables with millions of rows in them across multiple disks for better performance, availability, and maintenance.

Within a single index entry are several elements, some of which have already been covered. The first is the *index entry header,* containing the number of columns in the entry. Following that, the entry stores the values for the column(s) in the index. Finally, the index entry stores the ROWID. No length byte is needed for this

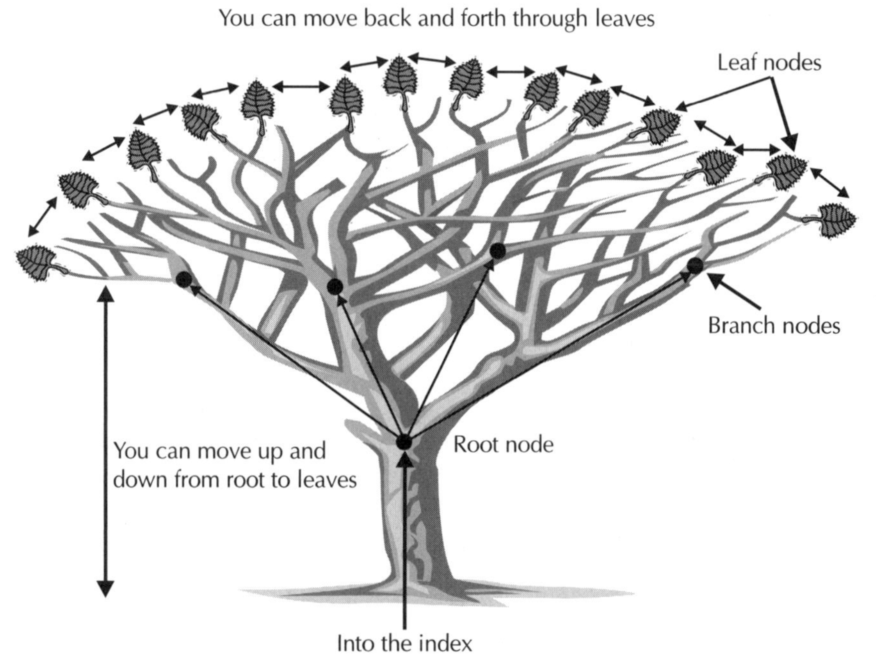

FIGURE 9-3. *B-tree index structure*

value because all ROWIDs are the same length. You should understand the following special cases of data stored in index entries:

- If the index is nonunique, and several rows contain the same value for the column, then each row with that value will have its own index entry to store each unique ROWID.
- If a row has a NULL value for the column(s) being indexed, there will be no corresponding index entry for that row.
- For nonpartitioned indexes only, since the index stores data for only one table, and since all tables can be stored in only one tablespace, the object ID number is not required to locate the row from the index. Thus, nonpartitioned B-tree indexes use restricted ROWIDs to point to row data.

B-tree indexes are used most commonly to improve performance on `select` statements using columns of unique or mostly distinct values. It is relatively easy and quick for Oracle to maintain B-tree indexes when data is changed in an indexed column, too, making this type of index useful for online transaction-processing applications. However, these indexes do a bad job of finding data quickly on `select` statements with `where` clauses containing comparison operations joined with `or`, and in situations in which the values in the indexed column are not very distinct.

Bitmap Indexes

Though all indexes in Oracle are stored with the root-branch-leaf structure illustrated in Figure 9-3, bitmap indexes are conceptualized differently. Instead of storing entries for each row in the table, the bitmap index stores an entry containing each distinct value, the start and end ROWIDs to indicate the range of ROWIDs in this table, and a long binary string with as many bits as there are rows in the table.

For example, say you are looking at a representation of a bitmap index for a table such as the one in Figure 9-4. The TYPE column indexed has only three distinct values. The bitmap index would have three entries as you see in the figure. The start and end ROWID for the object are also shown, so that you know what the potential ROWID range is. Finally, you see a binary string representing a bitmap. A position will be set to 1 for the entry if the column for that row contains the associated value; otherwise, the bit is set to 0. If an entry contains a bit set to 1, the corresponding bit in every other entry will always be set to 0.

Bitmap indexes improve performance in situations where you `select` data from a column whose values are repeated often, as is the case with employee status (for example, active, LOA, or retired). They also improve performance on `select` statements with multiple `where` conditions joined by `or`.

Bitmap indexes improve performance if data in the column is infrequently or never changed. By the same token, it is a somewhat arduous process to change data in that column. This is because changing the value of a column stored in a bitmap index requires Oracle to lock the entire segment storing the bitmap index to make the change.

Reverse-Key Indexes

Finally, consider the use of reverse-key indexes. This type of index is the same as a regular B-tree index, except for one thing—the data from the column being indexed is stored in reverse order. Thus, if the column value in a table of first names is JASON, the reverse-key index column will be NOSAJ. Typically, users of Oracle Parallel Server see the most benefit from reverse-key indexes when their `select` statements contain `where` clauses that use equality comparisons, such as `where X = 5`, but not in situations where range comparisons are used, such as `where X`

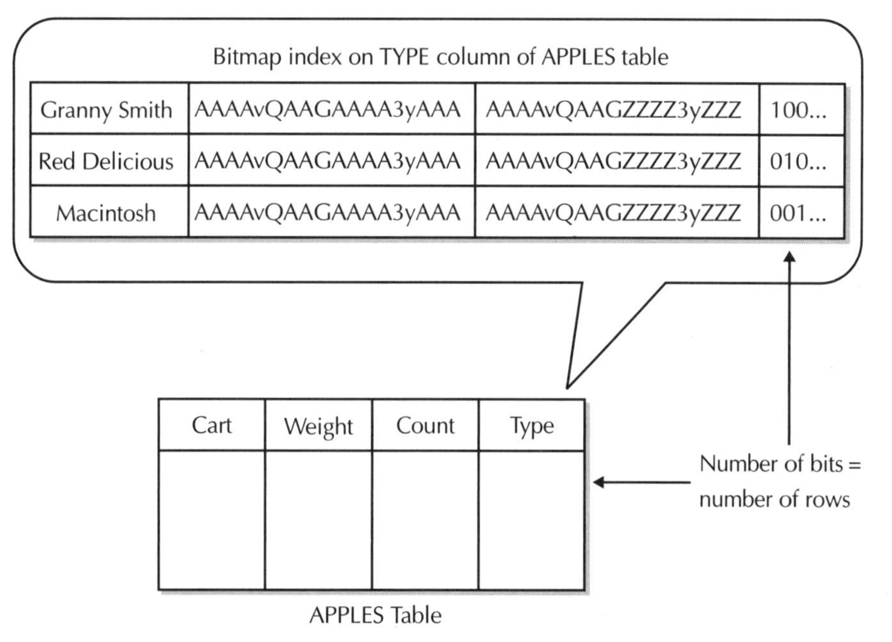

FIGURE 9-4. *Logical representation of bitmap index*

`between 4 and 6`. The value or benefit of reverse-key indexes is to assist performance in Oracle Parallel Server environments.

For Review

1. What is a unique index, and how does it compare with a nonunique index? What is the difference between a simple and composite index?
2. What is a B-tree index, and in what situations does it improve performance? When does it not improve performance? How does it compare to a bitmap index?
3. What is a reverse-key index, and when does it improve performance?

Creating B-Tree and Bitmap Indexes

The `create index` statement is used to create all types of indexes. To define special types of indexes, you must include various keywords, such as `create` unique index for indexes on columns that enforce uniqueness of every element of data, or create bitmap index for creating bitmap indexes. The following code block shows the statement for creating a unique B-tree index and also includes options for data storage and creation:

```
CREATE UNIQUE INDEX employee_lastname_indx_01
ON employee (lastname ASC)
TABLESPACE ORGDBIDX
PCTFREE 12
INITRANS 2 MAXTRANS 255
LOGGING
NOSORT
STORAGE ( INITIAL 900K
          NEXT 1800K
          MINEXTENTS 1
          MAXEXTENTS 200
          PCTINCREASE 0 );
```

TIP
In addition to allowing you to manually create indexes, Oracle automatically creates indexes that support the basic operation of PRIMARY KEY and UNIQUE constraints!

Several items in the storage definition will look familiar, such as pctfree, tablespace, logging, and the items in the storage clause. Other than pctfree, these options have the same use as they do in create table statements. Oracle uses pctfree only during the creation of the index to reserve space for index entries that may need to be inserted into the same index block.

A few other items may look unfamiliar, such as unique, asc, and nosort. You specify unique when you want the index to enforce uniqueness for values in the column. The asc keyword indicates ascending order for this column in the index, and desc (descending) can be substituted for this clause. The nosort keyword is for when you have loaded your table data in the proper sort order on the column you are indexing. In this case, it means that you have loaded data into the EMPLOYEE table sorted in ascending order on the LASTNAME column. By specifying nosort, Oracle will skip the sort ordinarily used in creating the index, thereby increasing performance on your create index statement. You might use this option if your operating system offered a procedure for sorting that was more efficient than Oracle's. Finally, pctused is not used in index definitions. Since all items in an index must be in the right order for the index to work, Oracle must put an index entry into a block, no matter what. Thus, pctused is not used.

You can create bitmap indexes with several storage specifications as well, but remember that they are used to improve search performance for low-cardinality columns, so bitmap indexes may not be unique. The following code block creates a bitmap index:

```
CREATE BITMAP INDEX employee_lastname_indx_01
ON employee (lastname)
TABLESPACE ORGDBIDX
PCTFREE 12
INITRANS 2 MAXTRANS 255
LOGGING
NOSORT
STORAGE ( INITIAL 900K
          NEXT 1800K
          MINEXTENTS 1
          MAXEXTENTS 200
          PCTINCREASE 0 );
```

The performance of commands that use bitmap indexes is heavily influenced by an area of memory specified by the `CREATE_BITMAP_AREA_SIZE` `init`*`sid`*`.ora` parameter. This area determines how much memory will be used for storing bitmap segments. You need more space for this purpose if the column on which you are creating the bitmap index has high cardinality. For a bitmap index, high cardinality might mean a dozen or so unique values out of 500,000 (as opposed to B-tree indexes, for which high cardinality might mean 490,000 unique values out of 500,000). So, in this situation, you might stick with the Oracle default setting of 8MB for your initialization parameter `CREATE_BITMAP_AREA_SIZE`.

An example of low cardinality for a column is having two distinct values in the entire table, as is the case for a column indicating whether an employee is male or female. In this case, you might size your initialization parameter considerably lower than the Oracle default, perhaps around 750K.

Sizing and Other Index-Creation Issues

Searching a large table without benefit of an index takes a long time because a full table scan must be performed. Indexes are designed to improve search performance. Unlike full table scans, whose performance worsens as the table grows larger, the performance of table searches that use indexes gets exponentially better as the index (and associated table) gets larger and larger. In fact, on a list containing one million elements, a binary search tree algorithm similar to the one used in a B-tree index finds any element in the list within 20 tries—in reality, the B-tree algorithm is actually far more efficient.

However, there is a price for all this speed, paid in the additional disk space required to store the index and the overhead required to maintain it when DML operations are performed on the table. To minimize the trade-off, you must weigh the storage cost of adding an index to the database against the performance gained by having the index available for searching the table. The performance improvement achieved by using an index is exponential over the performance of a full table scan, but the index has no value if it is never used by the application. You should also consider the volatility of the data in the table before creating an index. If the data in the indexed column changes regularly, you might want to index a more static column.

Also, consider how you are sizing `pctfree` for your index. Oracle uses `pctfree` to determine free space only when the index is first created. After that, the space is fair game, because Oracle has to keep all the items in the index in order. So, after creation, Oracle will put index records in a block right down to the last bit of space available. To determine the best value for `pctfree` on your index, consider the following. If the values in the column you are indexing increase sequentially, such as column values generated by sequences, you can size `pctfree` as low as 2 or 3. If not, you should calculate `pctfree` based on rowcount forecasts for growth over a certain time period (12 months, for example) with the following formula:

((*max_#_rows_in_period* – *initial_#_rows_in_period*) / *max_#_rows_in_period*) * 100

Finally, you should also follow the space allocation guidelines outlined in Chapter 8 for tables, such as using standard sizes for your extents that are multiples of 5 * DB_BLOCK_SIZE, and put your indexes in a tablespace separate from your tables, ideally on a separate disk resource. Also, make sure `initrans` is higher on the index than it is for the table, since index entries in a block take up less space, yielding more index entries per block. Finally, when you can, try to sort your data before initially loading the table and before creating the index. That way, you can utilize the `nosort` option and substantially increase performance on the `create index` operation.

For Review

1. Identify some of the storage clauses used for creating indexes that are not used for creating tables. How is `pctfree` used in indexes?
2. Can you define a bitmap index that is unique? Why or why not? How is the `CREATE_BITMAP_AREA_SIZE` parameter used?

Reorganizing Indexes

Reorganizing indexes is handled with the `alter index` statement. The `alter index` statement is useful for redefining storage options, such as `next`, `pctincrease`, `maxextents`, `initrans`, or `maxtrans`. You can use the `alter index` statement to change the `pctfree` value for new blocks in new extents allocated by your index as well.

Other Index-Reorganization Options

Oracle8 offers many new index-reorganization options. You can add extents manually to an index much like you do for tables, with the `alter index allocate extent` statement, specifying `size` and `datafile` optionally. You can also rid yourself of unused space below the index highwatermark with the `alter index deallocate unused` statement, optionally reserving a little extra space with the `keep` clause.

Another option for reorganizing your index is to rebuild it. This operation allows you to create a new index using the data from the old one, resulting in fewer table reads while rebuilding, tidier space management in the index, and better overall performance. This operation is accomplished with the `alter index` *`idxname`* `rebuild tablespace` *`tblspcname`* statement. All the storage options you can specify in a `create index` statement can be applied to `alter index rebuild` as well. You rebuild an index when you want to move the index to another tablespace, or when a great many rows have been `delete`d from the table, causing index entries to be removed as well. Finally, you may want to rebuild an index as a reverse-key index in Oracle Parallel Server environments to take advantage of performance gains offered by this new type of index.

TIP

You can use the `analyze index validate structure` command, as you would with tables, to check for block corruption. The `INDEX_STATS` dictionary view will then show you the number of index entries in leaf nodes in the LF_ROWS column compared to the number of deleted entries in the DEL_LF_FOWS column. Oracle recommends that, if the number of deleted entries is more than 30 percent, you should rebuild the index.

For Review

1. In what situations would you want to rebuild an index, and what is the statement for doing so?
2. What storage parameters cannot be changed as part of the `alter index` command?
3. Describe the usage of the `INDEX_STATS` dictionary view, and how it relates to the `analyze` command.

Dropping Indexes

What happens when you want to expand your index to include more columns, or when you want to get rid of columns? Can you use `alter index` for that? Unfortunately, the answer is no. You must drop and re-create the index to modify column definitions or change column order from ascending to descending (or vice versa). This is accomplished with the `drop index` *`idxname`* statement.

You may want to get rid of an index that is used only for specific purposes on an irregular basis, especially if the table has other indexes and volatile data. You may also want to drop an index if you are about to perform a large load of table data, perhaps preceded by purging all data in the table. In this way, your data load runs faster, and the index created later is fresh and well organized. You may have to re-create your index if it has a status of INVALID in the `DBA_OBJECTS` view, or if you know the index is corrupt from running DBVERIFY on the tablespace housing the index or the `analyze` command on the index itself.

For Review

Identify some reasons for dropping an index. Do you need to drop an index to add more columns to the index? Why or why not?

Chapter Summary

In this chapter, you covered many important areas of understanding the DML and DDL operations available in the Oracle database. You covered aspects of table creation, including how to define columns and their associated datatypes. You also covered declarative integrity constraints. In addition, you covered how to create sequences and indexes in this chapter. The use of the data dictionary to find information about objects in your database was explained in depth as well. You also learned about Oracle's data-manipulation language. The statements used to add, modify, or remove data from tables were explained and illustrated. You also learned about the importance of transaction control and the commands available for transaction control in SQL*Plus.

Two-Minute Drill

- A table can be created with five different types of integrity constraints: PRIMARY KEY, FOREIGN KEY, UNIQUE, NOT NULL, and CHECK.
- Referential integrity often creates a parent/child relationship between two tables, the parent being the referenced table and the child being the referring table. Often, a naming convention that requires child objects to adopt and extend the name of the parent table is useful in identifying these relationships.
- The datatypes available for creating columns in tables are CHAR, VARCHAR2, NUMBER, DATE, RAW, LONG, LONG RAW, ROWID, BLOB, CLOB, NCLOB, and BFILE.
- Indexes are created automatically in conjunction with PRIMARY KEY and UNIQUE constraints. These indexes are named after the constraint name given to the constraint in the definition of the table.
- Tables are created without any data in them, except for tables created with the `create table as select` statement. These tables are created and prepopulated with data from another table.
- Information available in the Oracle database helps users, developers, and DBAs know what objects exist in the Oracle database. The information is in the Oracle data dictionary.
- To find the positional order of columns in a table, or what columns there are in a table at all, the user can issue a `describe` command on that table. The Oracle data dictionary will then list all columns in the table being described.
- Data dictionary views on database objects are divided into three categories based on scope of user visibility: `USER_`, for what is owned by the user; `ALL_`, for all that can be seen by the user; and `DBA_`, for all that exists in the database, whether or not the user can see it.
- New rows are put into a table with the `insert` statement. The user issuing the `insert` statement can `insert` one row at a time with one statement, or do a mass `insert` with `insert into` *table_name* `(select...)`.
- Existing rows in a database table can be modified using the `update` statement. The `update` statement contains a `where` clause similar in function to the `where` clause of `select` statements.
- Existing rows in a table can be deleted using the `delete` statement. The `delete` statement also contains a `where` clause similar in function to the `where` clause in `update` or `select` statements.

- Transaction processing controls the change of data in an Oracle database.
- Transaction controls include commands that identify the beginning, breakpoint, and end of a transaction, and locking mechanisms that prevent more than one user at a time from making changes in the database.
- Tables are created with the `create table (`*`column_name datatype [column_name datatype...]`*`)` statement.
- A table column can be added or modified with the `alter table` statement.
- Columns can be added with little difficulty if they are nullable, using the `alter table add (`*`column_name datatype`*`)` statement. If a NOT NULL constraint is desired, add the column, populate the column with data, and then add the NOT NULL constraint separately.
- Column datatype size can be increased with no difficulty by using the `alter table modify (`*`column_name datatype`*`)` statement. Column size can be decreased, or the datatype can be changed, only if the column contains NULL for all rows.
- Constraints can be added to a column only if the column already contains values that will not violate the added constraint.
- PRIMARY KEY constraints can be added with a table constraint definition by using the `alter table add (constraint` *`constraint_name`* `primary key (`*`column_name`*`))` statement or with a column constraint definition by using the `alter table modify (`*`column_name`* `constraint` *`constraint_name`* `primary key)` statement.
- UNIQUE constraints can be added with a table constraint definition by using the `alter table add (constraint` *`constraint_name`* `unique (`*`column_name`*`))` statement or with a column constraint definition by using the `alter table modify (`*`column_name`* `constraint` *`constraint_name`* `unique)` statement.
- FOREIGN KEY constraints can be added with a table constraint definition by using the `alter table add (constraint` *`constraint_name`* `foreign key (`*`column_name`*`) references` *`OWNER.TABLE`* `(`*`column_name`*`) [on delete cascade])` statement or with a column constraint definition by using the `alter table modify (`*`column_name`* `constraint` *`constraint_name`* `references` *`OWNER.TABLE`* `(`*`column_name`*`) [on delete cascade])` statement.
- CHECK constraints can be added with a table constraint definition by using the `alter table add (constraint` *`constraint_name`* `check (`*`check_condition`*`))` statement or with a column constraint definition by using the `alter table modify (`*`column_name`* `constraint` *`constraint_name`* `check (`*`check_condition`*`))` statement.

- The CHECK condition cannot contain subqueries, references to certain keywords (such as `user`, `sysdate`, `rowid`), or any pseudocolumns.
- NOT NULL constraints can be added with a column constraint definition by using the `alter table modify (`*`column_name`*` NOT NULL)` statement.
- A named PRIMARY KEY, UNIQUE, CHECK, or FOREIGN KEY constraint can be dropped with the `alter table drop constraint` *`constraint_name`* statement. A NOT NULL constraint is dropped using the `alter table modify (`*`column_name`*` NULL)` statement.
- If a constraint that created an index automatically (PRIMARY KEY and UNIQUE constraints) is dropped, then the corresponding index is also dropped.
- If the table is dropped, all constraints, triggers, and indexes created for the table are also dropped.
- Removing all data from a table is best accomplished with the `truncate` command rather than the `delete from table_name` statement because `truncate` will reset the table's highwatermark and deallocate all the table's storage quickly, improving performance on `select count( )` statements issued after the truncation.
- An object name can be changed with the `rename` statement or with the use of synonyms.
- A comment can be added to the data dictionary for a database object with the `comment on` command. The comment can subsequently be viewed in `DBA_TAB_COMMENTS` or `DBA_COL_COMMENTS`.
- A sequence generates integers based on rules that are defined by sequence creation.
- Options that can be defined for sequences are the first number generated, how the sequence increments, the maximum value, the minimum value, whether the sequence can recycle numbers, and whether numbers will be cached for improved performance.
- Sequences are used by selecting from the CURRVAL and NEXTVAL virtual columns.
- The CURRVAL column contains the current value of the sequence.
- Selecting from NEXTVAL increments the sequence and changes the value of CURRVAL to whatever is produced by NEXTVAL.

- The rules that a sequence uses to generate values can be modified using the `alter sequence` statement.
- A sequence can be deleted with the `drop sequence` statement.
- A view is a virtual table defined by a `select` statement.
- Views can distill data from tables that may be inappropriate for some users and can hide the complexity of data from several tables or tables on which many operations have been performed.
- There are two types of views: simple and complex.
- Simple views are those that have only one underlying table.
- Complex views are those with two or more underlying tables that have been joined together.
- Data may be inserted into simple views except in the following cases:
  - If the `with check option` is used, the user may not `insert`, `delete`, or `update` data on the table underlying the simple view if the view itself is not able to `select` that data for the user.
  - The user may not `insert`, `delete`, or `update` data on the table underlying the simple view if the `select` statement creating the view contains `group by` or `order by` clauses, or a single-row operation.
  - No data may be inserted in simple views that contain references to any virtual column, such as ROWID, CURRVAL, NEXTVAL, and ROWNUM.
  - No data may be inserted into simple views that are created with the `read only` option.
- Data may be inserted into complex views when all of the following conditions are true:
  - The statement affects only one of the tables in the join.
  - For `update` statements, all columns changed are extracted from a key-preserved table. In addition, if the view is created with the `with check option` clause, join columns and columns taken from tables that are referenced more than once in the view are not part of the `update`.

- For `delete` statements, there is only one key-preserved table in the join. This table may be present more than once in the join, unless the view has been created with the `with check option` clause.
- For `insert` statements, all columns in which values are inserted must come from a key-preserved table, and the view must not have been created with the `with check option` clause.

- The `with check option` clause on creating a view allows the simple view to limit the data that can be inserted or otherwise changed on the underlying table by requiring that the data change be selectable by the view.
- Modifying the data selected by a view requires re-creating the view with the `create or replace view` statement, or dropping the view first and issuing the `create view` statement.
- An existing view can be recompiled by executing the `alter view` statement if, for some reason, it becomes invalid due to object dependency.
- A view is dropped with the `drop view` statement.
- Some indexes in a database are created automatically, such as those supporting the PRIMARY KEY and the UNIQUE constraints on a table.
- Other indexes are created manually to support database performance improvements.
- Indexes created manually are often on nonunique columns.
- B-tree indexes work best on columns that have high cardinality—a large number of distinct values and few duplicates in the column.
- B-tree indexes improve performance by storing data in a binary search tree, and then searching for values in the tree using a "divide and conquer" methodology outlined in this chapter.
- Bitmap indexes improve performance on columns with low cardinality—few distinct values and many duplicates on the column.
- Columns stored in the index can be changed only by dropping and re-creating the index.
- Indexes can be deleted by issuing the `drop index` statement.

Chapter Questions

1. **After creating a table on the Oracle database, you realize that several columns were mistakenly omitted. The columns to be added must accept NULL values. To increase the number of nullable columns for a table,**

   A. Use the `alter table` statement.

   B. Ensure that all column values are NULL for all rows.

   C. First, increase the size of adjacent column datatypes, and then add the column.

   D. Add the column, populate the column, and then add the NOT NULL constraint.

2. **After creating a view on the Oracle database, you realize that several columns were mistakenly omitted. The columns to be added must accept NULL values. To add the number of columns selected by a view:**

   A. Add more columns to the underlying table.

   B. Issue the `alter view` statement.

   C. Use a correlated subquery in conjunction with the view.

   D. Drop and re-create the view with references to select more columns.

3. **A user issues the statement `SELECT COUNT(*) FROM EMPLOYEE`. The query takes an inordinately long time and returns a count of zero. The most cost-effective solution to the performance issue is which of the following?**

   A. Upgrade the hardware.

   B. Truncate the table.

   C. Upgrade the version of Oracle.

   D. Define the highwatermark.

4. **You are defining a new sequence on your Oracle database. Which of the following choices are valid parameters for sequence creation?**

   A. `identified by`

   B. `using temporary tablespace`

C. `maxvalue`

D. `on delete cascade`

5. You issue the following `insert` statement against the Oracle database:

```
insert into emp (empid, lastname, salary)
values (emp_seq.NEXTVAL, 'HIGGINBOTHAM', 56000);
```

After referencing emp_seq.NEXTVAL in the statement, what happens to the value in `emp_seq.CURRVAL`?

A. Incremented by one

B. Now in emp_seq.PREVVAL

C. Equal to emp_seq.NEXTVAL

D. Unchanged

6. You are defining tables with integrity constraints in the Oracle database. Which two of the following integrity constraints automatically create an index when defined? (Choose two.)

A. FOREIGN KEY constraints

B. UNIQUE constraints

C. NOT NULL constraints

D. PRIMARY KEY constraints

7. You are attempting to determine the order of columns in constraint indexes for a table. Which of the following dictionary views gives information about the position of a column in a primary key?

A. `ALL_PRIMARY_KEYS`

B. `USER_CONSTRAINTS`

C. `ALL_IND_COLUMNS`

D. `ALL_TABLES`

8. User JANKO would like to insert a row into the EMPLOYEE table that has three columns: EMPID, LASTNAME, and SALARY. The user would like to enter data for EMPID 59694, LASTNAME Harris, but no salary. Which statement would work best?

A. `insert into EMPLOYEE values (59694,'HARRIS', NULL);`

B. `insert into EMPLOYEE values (59694,'HARRIS');`

C. `insert into EMPLOYEE (EMPID, LASTNAME, SALARY) values (59694,'HARRIS');`

D. `insert into EMPLOYEE (select 59694 from 'HARRIS');`

9. You are defining the columns that will be part of an Oracle database. Which three of the following choices are valid scalar database datatypes for Oracle tables? (Choose three.)

A. CURRENCY

B. CLOB

C. BOOLEAN

D. NUMBER

E. RAW

F. REAL

G. TEXT

H. SEQUENCE

10. You are formulating DML commands in a SQL*Plus session. Omitting the `where` clause from a `delete` statement has which of the following effects?

A. The `delete` statement will fail because there are no records to delete.

B. The `delete` statement will prompt the user to enter criteria for the deletion.

C. The `delete` statement will fail because of syntax error.

D. The `delete` statement will remove all records from the table.

11. You are creating tables in SQL*Plus on your Oracle database. Which line of the following statement will produce an error?

A. `create table GOODS`

B. `(GOODNO number,`

C. `GOOD_NAME varchar2(20) check(GOOD_NAME in (select NAME from AVAIL_GOODS)),`

D. `constraint PK_GOODS_01`

E. `primary key (GOODNO));`

F. There are no errors in this statement.

12. You are executing several DML statements against the Oracle database as a single transaction. The transaction control that prevents more than one user from updating data in a table is which of the following?

A. Locks

B. Commits

C. Rollbacks

D. Savepoints

Answers to Chapter Questions

1. A. Use the `alter table` statement.

Explanation The `alter table` statement is the only statement that allows the developer to increase the number of columns per table. Choice B is incorrect because setting a column to all NULL values for all rows simply adds an empty row of data to the table. Typically, this is not even allowed because the primary-key column for the table doesn't accept NULL values. Choice C is incorrect because increasing the adjacent column sizes simply increases the sizes of the columns without adding new columns to a table. Choice D is incorrect because the listed steps outline how to add a column with a NOT NULL constraint, when the question explicitly states you want the new columns to accept NULL values.

2. D. Drop and re-create the view with references to select more columns.

Explanation Only by dropping and re-creating the view (or using the `or replace` option) can you add columns to a view. Choice A is incorrect because adding columns to the underlying table will not add columns to the view. However, because of Oracle's dependency-checking mechanisms, redefining a table that underlies a view invalidates that view. Choice B is incorrect because the `alter view` statement simply recompiles an existing view definition, whereas the real solution here is to change the existing view definition by dropping and re-creating the view. Choice C is incorrect because a correlated subquery will likely worsen performance and underscores the real problem—a column must be added to the view. Review the discussion of altering the definition of a view.

3. B. Truncate the table.

Explanation Choices A and C may work, but remember, we're looking for the most cost-effective solution to the performance problem. An upgrade of hardware and software costs far more than taking a minute to truncate the table. Recall that the problem stems from the fact that an ordinary `delete` statement does not reset a table's highwatermark. You will notice this fact only when you remove data from extremely large (perhaps half a million rows or more) tables. Choice D is deceiving if you have studied for the DBO exam, because you will remember that some change to the highwatermark is required. However, choice D is a little too vague. It is best to stick to the choice that most accurately defines a solution on the OCP DBO exam, and thereby avoid choice D in this case.

4. C. `maxvalue`

Explanation Of the choices given, only the `maxvalue` option is valid for sequence creation. Recall that this clause defines the maximum value your sequence can obtain. Choices A and B are both part of the `create user` statement, which you learned about in Chapter 5. Choice D is a part of a constraint declaration in an `alter table` or `create table` statement. Review the discussion on creating sequences to ensure you know the clauses that are part of that statement for the OCP DBO exam.

5. C. Equal to emp_seq.NEXTVAL

Explanation Once NEXTVAL is referenced, the sequence increments the integer and changes the value of CURRVAL to be equal to NEXTVAL. Thus, choice C is the correct answer to the question. Choice A is incorrect because you can define exactly how the sequence will increment and, for this reason, should not assume that a sequence will always increment by one every time. Choice B is wrong because PREVVAL is not an actual pseudocolumn in the Oracle database associated with sequences. Choice D is wrong because referencing NEXTVAL on any sequence always changes CURRVAL on that sequence.

6. B *and* D. UNIQUE constraints *and* primary keys

Explanation Every constraint that enforces uniqueness creates an index to assist in the process. Thus, UNIQUE and PRIMARY KEY constraints will have an associated index, but FOREIGN KEY, NOT NULL, and CHECK constraints will not. These indexes are always created automatically by Oracle and will often (though not always) have a name automatically generated by Oracle. Be sure you understand at least that these two constraints have associated indexes created automatically by Oracle.

7. C. `ALL_IND_COLUMNS`

Explanation The `ALL_IND_COLUMNS` dictionary view is useful for determining the column positions in an index. Since primary keys create an index, the index created by the primary key will be listed with all the other indexed data. Choice A is incorrect because no view exists in Oracle called `ALL_PRIMARY_KEYS`. Choice B is incorrect because although USER_CONSTRAINTS lists information about the constraints in a database, it does not contain information about the index created by the primary key. Choice D is incorrect because `ALL_TABLES` contains no information related to the position of a column in an index.

8. A. `insert into EMPLOYEE values (59694,'HARRIS', NULL);`

Explanation The statement for choice A is acceptable because the positional criteria for not specifying column order is met by the data in the values clause. When you would like to specify that no data be inserted into a particular column, one method of doing so is to insert a NULL. Choice B is incorrect because not all columns in the table have values identified. When using positional references to populate column data, values must be present for every column in the table. Otherwise, the columns that will be populated should be named explicitly. Choice C is incorrect because when a column is named for data insert in the `insert into` clause, then a value must definitely be specified in the `values` clause. Choice D is incorrect because using the multiple row `insert` option with a `select` statement is not appropriate in this situation. Refer to the discussion of `insert` statements for more information.

9. B, D, *and* E. CLOB, NUMBER, *and* RAW

Explanation The valid scalar datatypes in Oracle for table columns include CLOB, NUMBER, and RAW, along with CHAR, VARCHAR2, BLOB, BFILE, DATE, LONG, LONG RAW, and ROWID. Other composite or user-defined datatypes can be created as well, but the question asks specifically for scalar types. CURRENCY, BOOLEAN, REAL, TEXT, and SEQUENCE are not valid datatypes for Oracle table columns. Although BOOLEAN and REAL are valid datatypes in PL/SQL, they aren't available on the Oracle database, meaning that you cannot create a column in a table that uses these datatypes. And don't confuse Oracle datatypes with SQL Server datatypes. CURRENCY and TEXT datatypes aren't available in Oracle at all.

10. D. The `delete` statement will remove all records from the table.

Explanation Only one effect is produced by leaving off the `where` clause from any statement that allows one—the requested operation is performed on all records in the table. As such, choice A is incorrect by default, unless your statement contains some other type of syntax error. Unless you use a lexical substitution in your DML, usually a text label preceded by an ampersand (&), SQL*Plus will not prompt you for input after you issue the DML, so choice B is also incorrect. Again, only if your DML contains a syntax error will the statement fail, and lack of a `where` clause is never a syntax error because `where` clauses are not mandatory. Thus, choice C is also incorrect.

11. C. `GOOD_NAME varchar2(20) check(GOOD_NAME in (select NAME from AVAIL_GOODS)),`

Explanation A CHECK constraint cannot contain a reference to another table, nor can it reference a virtual column, such as ROWID or SYSDATE. CHECK constraints can only reference static values. So, choice C is the correct answer for this question. The other lines of the `create table` statement contain correct syntax; so according to the phrasing of the question, the other choices are incorrect. Remember, in this question you are looking for errors.

12. A. Locks

Explanation Locks are the mechanisms that prevent more than one user at a time from making changes to the database. Thus, choice A is correct. Choices B and C are incorrect because `commit` and `rollback` statements are used to indicate the end of transactions. A `savepoint` statement indicates the end of a logical block of work within a transaction and does not ensure that two users won't overwrite data in a table the way locks do. Thus, choice D is also incorrect.

CHAPTER 10

Tips for Special Question Formats on the DBO Exam

n this chapter, you will learn some tips and techniques for answering the following special question format types on the OCP DBO exam:

- The multiple-choice question format
- The exhibit question format
- The clickable image question format
- The short-answer question format
- Tips for Oracle8*i* and beyond

As in other OCP exams, you will encounter many multiple-choice questions testing your knowledge of Oracle. You may have to select more than one answer as correct on the DBO exam as well. However, unlike many of its siblings in the Oracle Certified Professional series, the DBO exam focuses on how to utilize Oracle GUI tools. Because of this focus, the DBO exam carries several new question formats that allow for visual representation and testing of information on this exam. That said, it is important to stress that the key to passing the DBO exam is your ability to digest and retain the steps for accomplishing tasks presented in Chapters 1 through 9. Thus, you will need visual familiarity with all the tools in Oracle Enterprise Manager, particularly the Schema Manager, Lock Manager, Oracle Expert, and OEM console tools. It doesn't hurt to spend extra time before taking the exam to simply browse through those chapters and review the figures if you think you will have any difficulty in distinguishing one OEM tool from another on the exam. This chapter will help you understand both multiple-choice and non–multiple-choice format questions you may see on the DBO exam.

The Multiple-Choice Question Format

If you have read the chapters of this book in order, from Chapter 1 to this one, you already know what a multiple-choice question looks like. If you haven't, the following discussion contains a couple of examples. You will encounter two main types of multiple-choice questions in the exam. The first type is the single-answer multiple-choice question. For this format, only one answer choice must be selected. The other type is the multiple-answer multiple-choice question. In this case, you will have to select two (or even three) correct answer choices in order to receive credit for a correct answer.

Examples of Single-Answer Multiple-Choice Questions

The first example is a single-answer multiple-choice question. Note that in the absence of any text stating that more than one answer should be selected for the question at hand, the multiple-choice question has one and only one "correct" answer.

1. **Which of the following administrative tools in OEM can be used to view the initialization parameter settings for Oracle?**

   A. Schema Manager

   B. Instance Manager

   C. Security Manager

   D. Data Manager

   E. Software Manager

Despite a continued sentiment expressed by Oracle that the multiple-choice questions on the DBO exam will move to a scenario-based format, most multiple-choice questions seem to have more of a fact-based nature. Thus, it is key that you understand the facts about the usage of Oracle described in this book to answer these questions right. Incidentally, the correct answer to sample question 1 is B, Instance Manager.

The second type of question is the multiple-answer multiple-choice question. For this question format, you will see some text indicating that you must select two or three correct choices to get credit for the question. No partial credit will be given if you miss even one of the choices.

2. **You are granting `select` access on the BANK_ACCOUNT table to the `PROGRAMMER` role using Security Manager. Which of the following steps must be accomplished after selecting the BANK_ACCOUNT table in the appropriate interface? (Choose three.)**

   A. Select the role to which the privilege will be given.

   B. Click the Apply button.

   C. Move the privilege to the list of privileges granted to that role.

   D. Select the Object Privileges tab.

   E. Select the appropriate privilege from the Privilege Type list box.

The correct answers are B, C, and E. As noted previously, you must select *all* the choices that are correct to receive full credit for the question. No partial credit will be granted on the DBO exam.

For Review

Be able to recognize single- and multiple-answer multiple-choice questions and distinguish them from one another.

Tips for Answering Multiple-Choice Questions

Some preliminary items are now identified for you to take the OCP exams. The first tip is *don't wait until you're the world's foremost authority on Oracle to take the OCP exam.* The passing score for the DBO exams is approximately 47. That means you will need to get 47 or more questions correct out of 70 or so to pass the exam. So, if you are getting about five questions right out of seven on the assessment test or in the chapters, you should consider taking the OCP exam. Remember, you're certified if you pass with a 47 or a 70.

The next tip is this: *if you can't answer the question within 30 seconds, mark it with the checkbox in the upper-left corner of the OCP interface for review later.* The most significant difference between the OCP interface and the assessment test interface is a special screen that appears after you answer all the questions. This screen displays all your answers, along with a special indicator next to the questions you marked for review. This screen also offers a button you can click to review the questions you marked. You should use this feature extensively. If you spend only 30 seconds answering each question in your first pass on the exam, you will have at least an hour to review any questions you're unsure about, with the added bonus of knowing you answered first all the questions that were easiest for you.

Third, *there is no penalty for guessing.* If you answer the question correctly, your score goes up; if not, your score does not change. If you can eliminate any choices on a question, you should take the chance in the interest of improving your score. In some questions, the OCP exam requires you to specify two or even three choices—this can work in your favor, meaning you need to eliminate fewer choices to get the question right.

TIP

Here's another small difference that distinguishes single-answer multiple-choice questions and multiple-answer multiple-choice questions. In single-answer multiple-choice questions, each question choice will be accompanied by a radio button that you click to select your answer. Multiple-answer multiple-choice questions will have a checkbox next to each choice. If you select too few or too many answers for a multiple-answer multiple-choice question, the interface will prompt you to select more or fewer choices before allowing you to move to the next question.

For Review

1. Know the tips for correctly answering multiple-choice questions on the DBO exam.
2. Be sure you can recognize when the OCP exam is expecting you to provide a single answer or multiple answers.

The Exhibit Question Format

Exhibit questions are similar to multiple-choice questions, with one significant difference. The exhibit question provides a graphical exhibit that you should review as a basis for answering the question. Exhibit questions will usually also be single-answer multiple-choice questions, and at the bottom center of the screen, you will see a button labeled "Exhibit."

Examples of Exhibit Questions

The following question is an example of the exhibit-based format. Note that the question on the DBO exam may or may not mention that an exhibit is associated with the test. Ultimately, it will be up to you to verify that an exhibit is available by reviewing both question content and the bottom of the interface to see if an Exhibit button is present. See Figure 10-1 for an example exhibit.

Click on the Exhibit button to view the exhibit for the following question.

3. **You are creating user SMITH on your database and would now like to ensure that this user has the ability to create tables. Which location in the interface gives you this ability?**

   A. General

   B. Roles/Privileges

   C. Object Privileges

   D. Quotas

   E. Show SQL

You will notice that the question may include enough information to allow you to answer, provided you are familiar with the interface being tested. However, if you do not have photographic memory, this question format gives you the chance to actually look at the interface being tested. Thus, some folks might find that the exhibit question format is easier than the regular multiple-choice format.

For Review

Be sure you understand how to determine whether you are looking at an exhibit question.

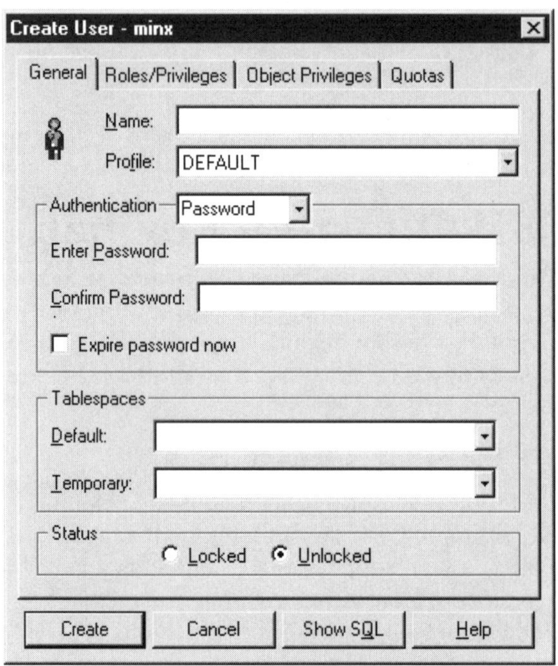

FIGURE 10-1. *Exhibit for sample question 3*

Tips for Answering Exhibit Questions

The tips for answering exhibit questions are largely the same as those for answering other multiple-choice format questions. The main difference is that you have an exhibit available to you, which you can, and probably should, use in determining the answers to your questions. The exhibit could either simplify the question for you or clarify an ambiguity, or both. Thus, use all the ammunition at your disposal for getting as many questions right as you can to pile up points. At a minimum, spend a little extra time reviewing interfaces and step-by-step instructions for various tasks using the following tools:

- Security Manager
- Lock Manager

- OEM console
- Oracle Expert
- Storage Manager
- Schema Manager

For Review

Understand the value that exhibits provide in helping you answer questions for the DBO exam.

The Clickable Image Question Format

This question format is perhaps the most interesting thing to appear in OCP exams since their inception. The clickable image question format represents Oracle's first step toward true scenario-based questioning. The basic premise is this: Since the DBO exam focuses on the use of GUI tools, the question itself should test your familiarity with these tools. Thus, the question format presents you with a question about the proper usage of some Oracle tool and then offers a graphical image display of a screenshot of that tool. Your task is either of the following:

1. Click the area on the graphical display that handles the task or activity identified in the question.

or

2. Click two or more areas on the graphical display in the appropriate order to handle the task or activity identified in the question.

Sound simple? Try your hand at some examples of clickable image questions in the next discussion.

Examples of Clickable Image Questions

Here is an example of a clickable image question that falls into the first category identified in the previous list. This example shows you a screenshot of an application you might use in Enterprise Manager for performing a task whose steps are being tested implicitly by the question.

Use the image in Figure 10-2 as the basis for answering the question.

4. **You need to grant this user additional privileges to allow them to create tables. Where is the first place you must click in order to grant this privilege?**

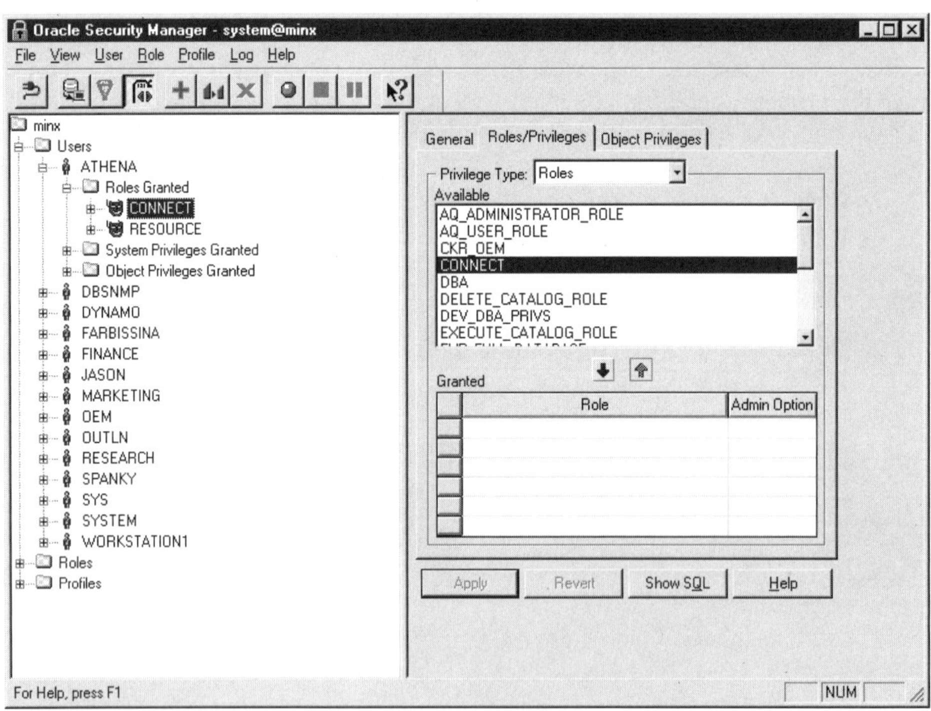

FIGURE 10-2. *Image for use in answering question 4*

Next is an example of a clickable image question that falls into the second category identified previously. This example illustrates an application available in Oracle Enterprise Manager. The question tests your knowledge of how to use this application. See if you can guess the answer.

Use the image in Figure 10-3 as the basis for answering the question.

5. **To increase the allowed number of extents the MOUSE_HOUSE table can allocate to Unlimited, where are the two places you must click in this application, and in which order?**

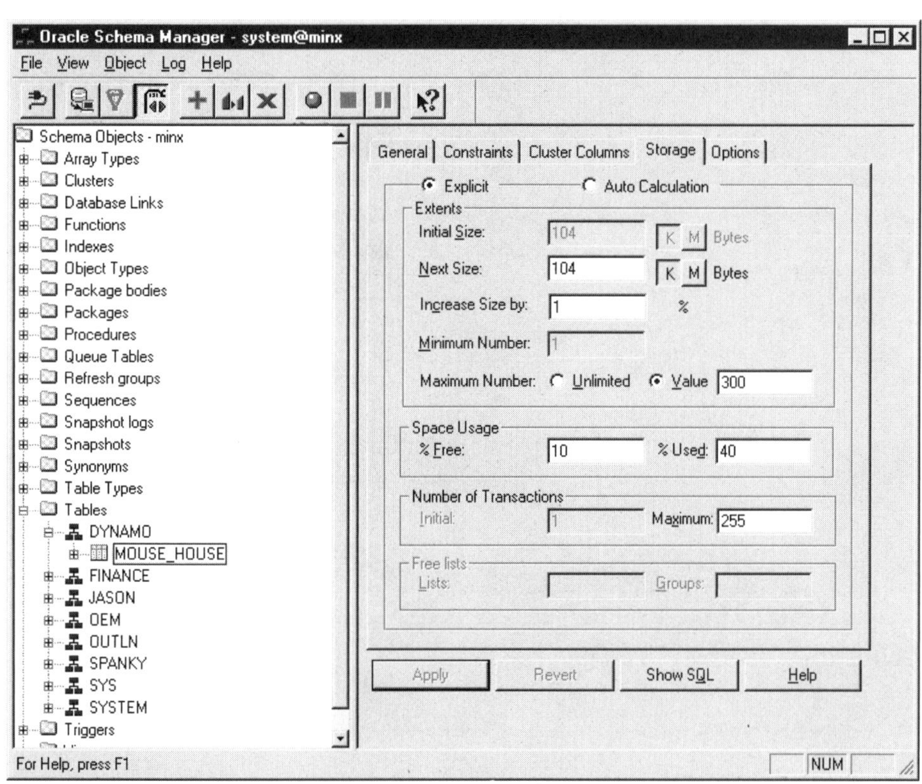

FIGURE 10-3. *Image for use in answering question 5*

The theory behind the clickable question format is to test your ability to recall how to use the applications described in this book. Hence, you can see why it was so important to cover many of these topics in step-by-step format. Did you guess the answers to questions 4 and 5? Their answers are shown in Figures 10-4 and 10-5, respectively.

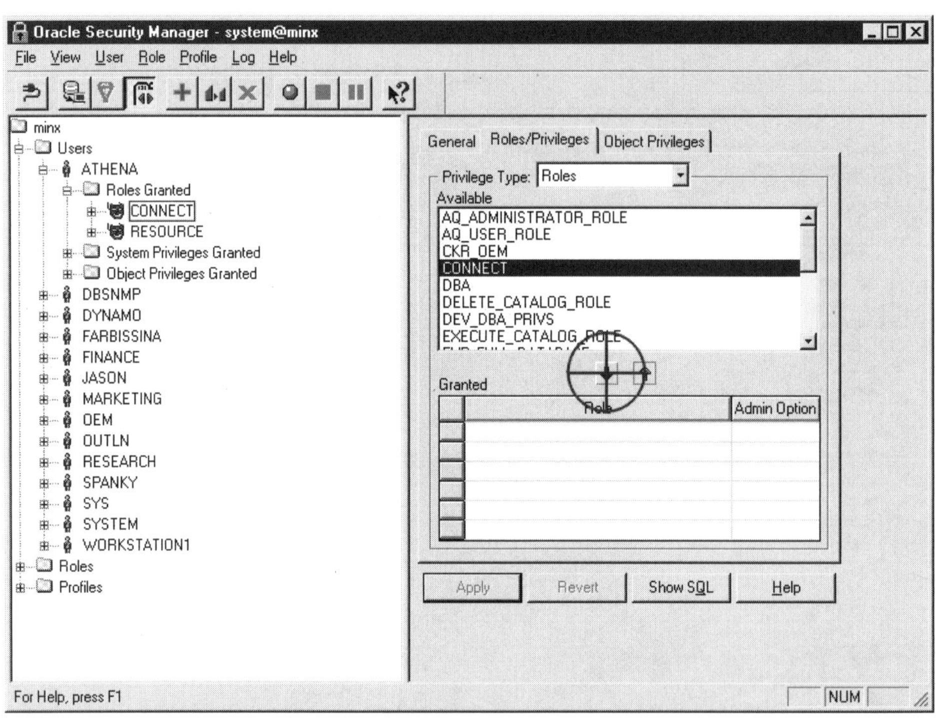

FIGURE 10-4. *Answer to question 4*

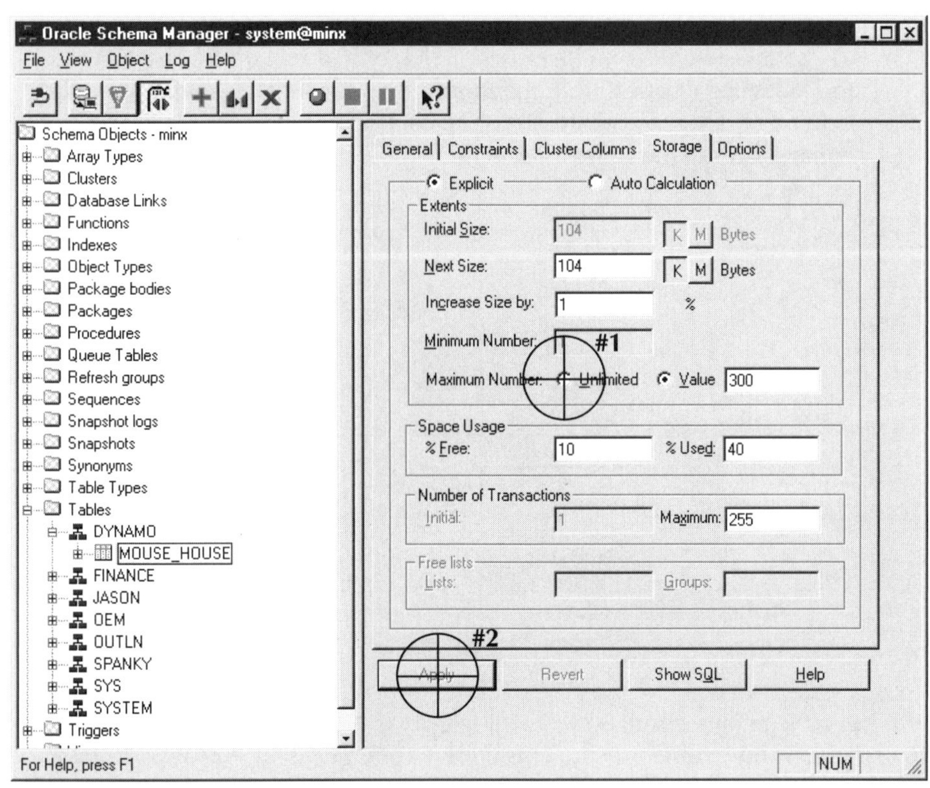

FIGURE 10-5. *Answer to question 5*

A third and less frequent format you might see on the DBO exam, that falls into the clickable image category, is the chart matchup question. This question format shows you a chart of items listed in two columns. The object of the question is for you to click on one item in the left column and drag it to the corresponding item in the right column. Following is an example.

Use the information in the illustration to answer the following question.

6. Match the specific item identified in the left column of the chart shown in the following illustration to the more general category shown in the right column of that same chart. Do so by clicking and dragging from the left column item to the right column item.

COLUMN 1	COLUMN 2
CREATE SESSION	PRIVILEGE
SELECT CATALOG_ ROLE	
DBA	ROLE
CREATE ROLLBACK SEGMENT	

On test day you may not draw actual lines from the items in the left column to the items in the right column. So you will have to trust your instincts on whether you marked the question correctly. This third question type appears less frequently than the other two. If you get stuck, remember that this is only one question among dozens on the DBO exam. You need to answer about 50 questions correctly to pass, so be sure you spend adequate time answering every question. Incidentally, the correct answer for question 6 is shown here.

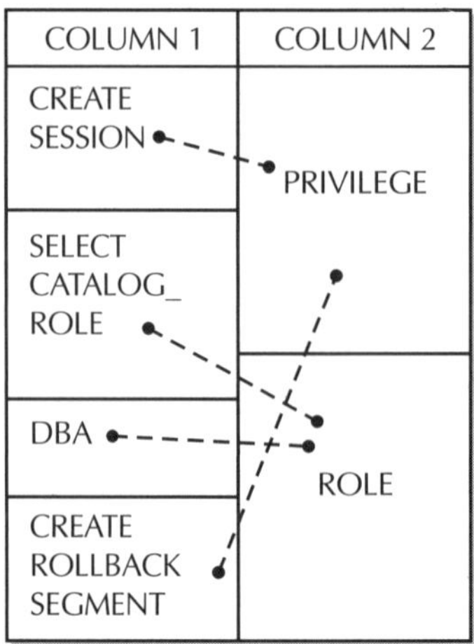

Important Points to Understand About Clickable Image Questions

First, make sure that you understand how to answer these questions. These questions contain no multiple-choice selections, so you won't be able to guess by eliminating choices. Instead, the answer depends on your ability to maneuver the mouse pointer to the appropriate position on the screen to allow for the functionality being tested. Second, when you click on the area of the screen you believe represents the correct answer, the test engine will draw a marker on the screen (as you saw in Figures 10-4 and 10-5).

This marker represents your answer. When you reach the end of the exam, you will see these markers listed as your answers to the clickable image questions on the exam. Behind the scenes, the test has also captured the location on the screen where you placed the marker. If you place your marker and then later decide to move it, you need only to click the marker again to make it go away or click on a new place on the image to redraw the marker in that new place. As in the game of horseshoes, getting close to the target counts, so make sure you are as near to what you believe is the correct answer as you can get. And remember, you can always mark the question for later review if you're running short on time.

For Review

1. Know how to identify a clickable image question.
2. Know how to answer clickable image questions, as the methods are not the same as those used for multiple-choice questions.

Tips for Answering Clickable Image Questions

This is as close to a true "scenario-based" format as Oracle has achieved thus far in the Oracle Certified Professional program, so be sure you're up for the task of answering these types of questions. Essentially, this question tests your ability to perform the following tasks, in order:

1. Identify the Enterprise Manager application displayed.
2. Recall all steps involved in performing a particular task with that tool.
3. Determine where you are in the execution of that task.
4. Identify and select the appropriate part of the interface allowing you to perform that step.

Thus, the best tactic you can take to maximize your chances for success on this question format is to break down your review of the materials presented in Chapters

1 through 9 into the four tasks. So, to master identification of the OEM application displayed, review the application figures shown throughout the book to be sure you can visually distinguish Schema Manager from Lock Manager, User Manager from Oracle Expert, and so on. Of course, a little hands-on exposure to the use of these tools will go a long way toward preparing you for this question type as well.

Regarding mastery of the steps involved in performing particular tasks with a particular tool, this book an excellent tool at your disposal for mastering this segment of the material. You have seen countless examples of the step-by-step tasks necessary to complete certain activities. You may have read but not examined thoroughly each of the steps in a given process—by skimming through the contents of a particular set of instructions. By all means, be sure that you carefully review each and every set of instructions given in this book before taking the DBO exam, or else you may encounter some scenario-based questions you cannot answer. Even better, follow through the instructions in the book with Oracle Enterprise Manager and Oracle8 Server on your computer at work or home. Obviously, this exercise will help you with being able to determine where you are within a set of instructions to choose the correct answer to the question.

For Review

Understand the four required tasks for answering the clickable image questions on the DBO exam.

The Short-Answer Question Format

The final type of question format appearing on the DBO exam that is new for the OCP curriculum is the short-answer question format. As its name implies, your answer must be given as a short, fill-in-the-blank format, thus making it impossible for you to guess the correct answer based on the answer choices listed for the question. These questions are usually fact based, rather than scenario based, but they are more challenging than fact-based multiple-choice questions because you have to know the material tested on the DBO exam thoroughly. Does this mean you need to sit down for weeks on end, memorizing every detail presented in this book? By all means, *no*! Fortunately for DBO exam takers, only a limited amount of questions on the DBO exam are given in short-answer question format. On any given exam, you can expect to see maybe five questions in this format.

Examples of Short-Answer Questions

Let's look at a sample with the format described. The following question is similar to the short-answer questions you will see on the DBO exam:

Answer the question by filling in the answer in the blank space given. Be sure to spell out your answer.

7. **You are defining a table column for a user that will store numeric information. The format of the information will be either 999-99-9999 or 9-9999-9999-9999. You want to be able to store the dashes as well as the numbers themselves in the table column. What is the Oracle datatype you would use for defining this table column?**

   ____

The test interface will actually use a text box on the screen, where you will enter your answer. Unfortunately, spelling counts on this question format, so make sure that when you enter the correct answer (which, in this case, is VARCHAR2) you spell the answer correctly and include any important information (such as the 2 on the end of VARCHAR2).

Here's another example:

Answer the question by filling in the answer in the blank space given. Be sure to spell out your answer.

8. **Which table constraint type in Oracle is a combination of two other constraints, one for enforcing that every column entry is different, the other enforcing that a NULL entry is disallowed for the column?**

   ____

Note also that the interface will likely show your answer keyed in uppercase characters. This is fine. Thus, for this example, the correct answer is PRIMARY KEY. Incidentally, don't signal blanks between the words of your answer using the underscore character (_) unless you are explicitly instructed to do so by the question. Usually, as with the examples shown here, the short-answer questions will appear with associated instructions, so don't worry about returning to an instruction section. However, as with other exams such as the GMAT or LSAT, it is a good idea to go into the DBO exam with an idea of the types of questions you are being asked so that you don't waste time reading instructions at the beginning or throughout the test.

For Review

Understand the short-answer question format and what is expected in order for you to receive full credit for a test answer.

Tips for Answering Short-Answer Questions

Since these questions are fact based and require that you know the material cold to achieve full credit, no techniques will help you "bluff" or guess the correct answer. So, you'll have to spend extra time before taking the exam to learn the correct answers. That said, you might find the following tips helpful as you determine on which areas to focus for test preparation. Remember, these questions are fact based, not scenario based, so the time you spend memorizing steps that you need to execute a task will not be beneficial here (though that effort will help with the clickable image format questions, so you're not wasting your time in doing so). Consider focusing on the following areas in preparation for answering short-answer questions:

1. Know the five types of table constraints in Oracle.
2. Know the different datatypes in Oracle.
3. Know the purpose of every OEM tool.
4. Know the different types of roles created automatically when you install a database.

For Review

Review the relevant areas of the book where the topics mentioned in this section are covered in detail.

Chapter Summary

In this chapter, you reviewed the multiple-choice question formats and the non-multiple-choice question formats that appear on the DBO exam. You learned about exhibit questions, clickable image questions, and short-answer questions. Examples of each new question type were presented, along with tips for answering that type of question. The remainder of the chapter will focus on giving you hands-on exposure to answering these types of questions.

Two-Minute Drill

- Review material on how to answer multiple-choice questions.
  - Use the 30/60 method to ensure you answer every question on the exam.
  - Guess if you don't know the answer.

    - Don't wait until you think you can score 100 percent on the exam—you'll pass with as few as 47 out of 70 correct answers.
- Review material on how to answer exhibit questions.
    - Understand how exhibit questions differ from other multiple-choice questions.
- Review material on how to answer clickable image questions. Specifically, be sure you know how to perform the following tasks with Enterprise Manager tools, in order:
    1. Identify the Enterprise Manager application displayed.
    2. Recall all steps involved in performing a particular task with that tool.
    3. Determine where you are in the execution of that task.
    4. Identify and select the appropriate part of the interface allowing you to perform that step.
- Review material on how to answer short-answer questions. Specifically, focus your preparation for these question formats by reviewing the following topics:
    1. Know the five types of table constraints in Oracle.
    2. Know the different datatypes in Oracle.
    3. Know the purpose of every OEM tool.
    4. Know the different roles created automatically when you install a database.

Chapter Questions

Answer the question by filling in the answer in the blank space below the question. Be sure to spell out your answer.

1. To allow user SMITH access to the database, the DBO issues the GRANT CONNECT TO SMITH statement from within SQL Worksheet. Which OEM tool could the DBO have also used to grant this access?

____

Use the information in Figure 10-6 to answer the following question.

2. **Your R01 rollback segment is currently online. Which two places in the interface shown do you need to click in order to take it offline, and in which order?**

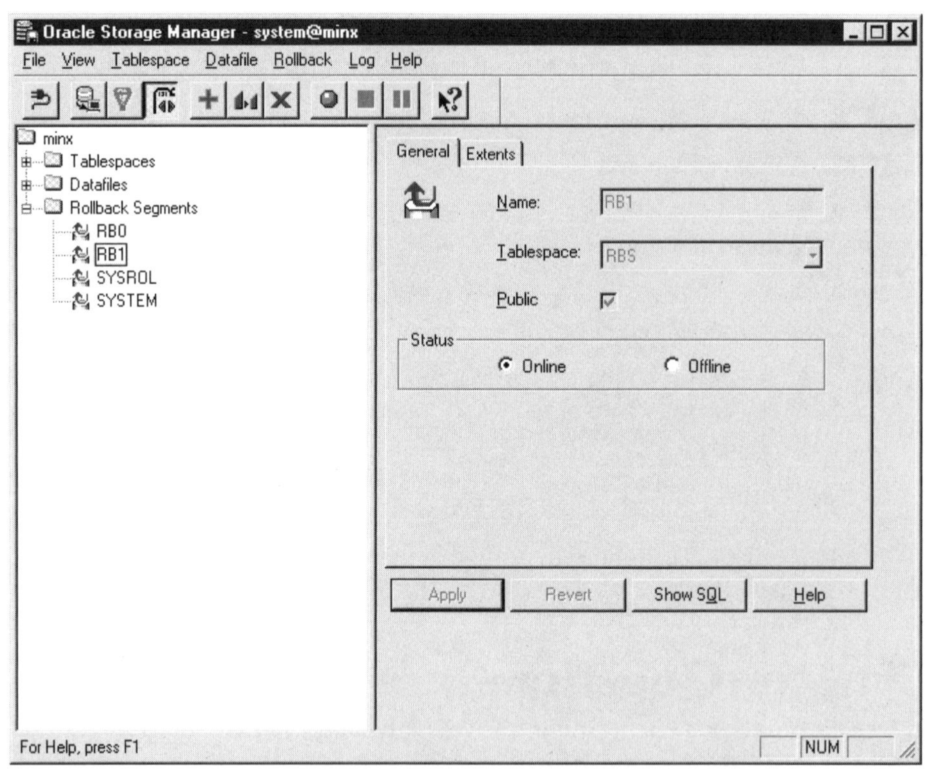

FIGURE 10-6. *Image for use in answering question 2*

Use the information in Figure 10-7 to answer the following question.

3. In tuning your database, you determine that you want to set up some workload tuning parameters. Where would you click in the interface shown to configure this option?

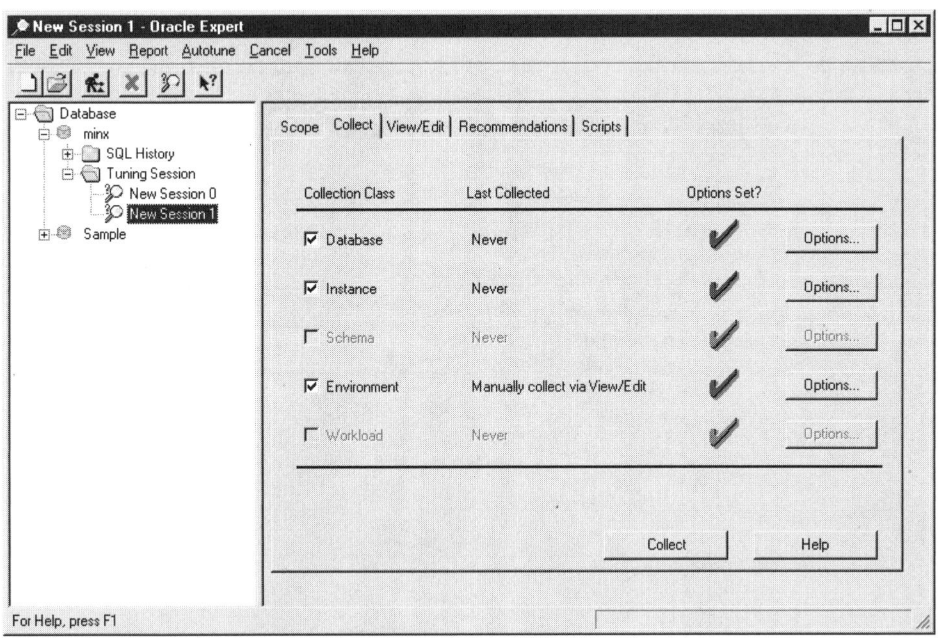

FIGURE 10-7. *Image for use in answering question 3*

Use the exhibit in Figure 10-8 to answer the following question.

4. **You want to create user JONES and assign the ability for JONES to create rollback segments all in one operation. Which of the following tab interfaces would you click on to give user JONES the ability to create rollback segments?**

   A. General

   B. Roles/Privileges

   C. Object Privileges

   D. Quotas

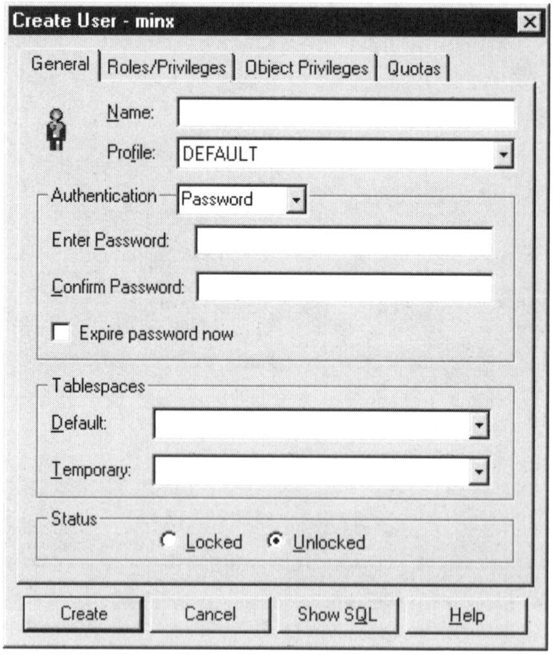

Create User - minx

General | Roles/Privileges | Object Privileges | Quotas

Name:

Profile: DEFAULT

Authentication: Password

Enter Password:

Confirm Password:

Expire password now

Tablespaces

Default:

Temporary:

Status

Locked Unlocked

Create | Cancel | Show SQL | Help

FIGURE 10-8. *Image for use in answering question 4*

Answer the question by filling in the answer in the blank space given. Be sure to spell out your answer.

5. **Your database has only one tablespace, SYSTEM. How many rollback segments do you need to create in conjunction with this database to open it?**

____

Use the information in Figure 10-9 to answer the following question.

6. **User JASON needs to have the ability to run the FIND_MOUSE( ) procedure, owned by user SPANKY. What two places on the interface shown in Figure 10-9 would you click on to give user JASON this ability, and in which order?**

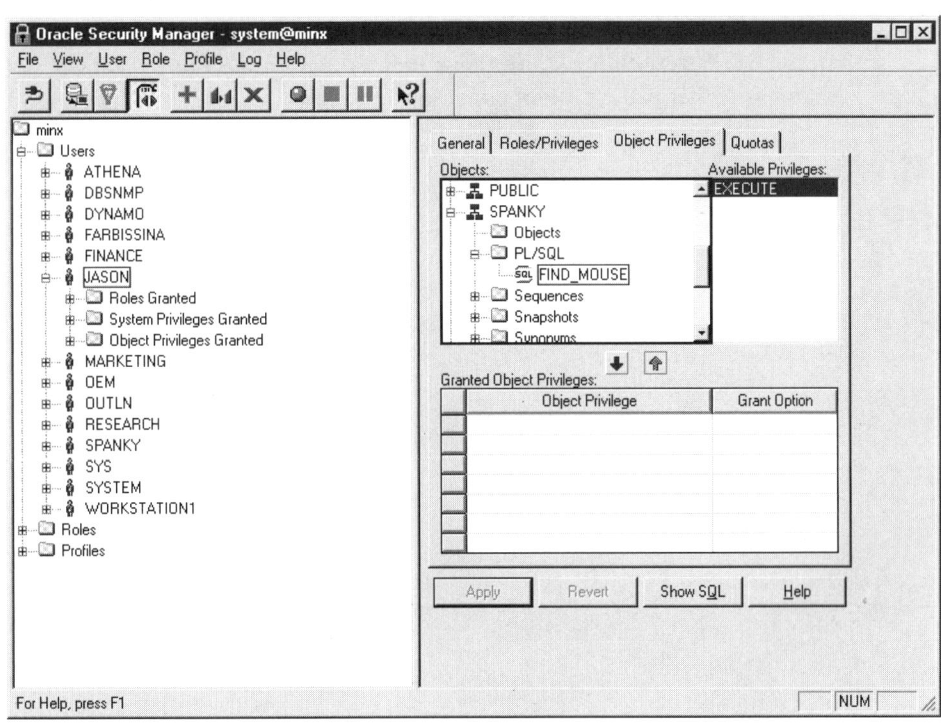

FIGURE 10-9. *Image for use in answering question 6*

Use the information in the illustration to answer the following question.

7. Match the specific items in Column 1 of the chart shown to the more general categories listed in Column 2 of the same chart.

COLUMN 1	COLUMN 2
Datafiles	Physical storage structures
Tablespaces	
Segments	Logical storage structures
Blocks	

Answer the question by filling in the answer in the blank space given. Be sure to spell out your answer.

8. You define a constraint on a table that prevents information from being entered if it falls within a static range defined within the table creation statement. What is the type of constraint created?

____

Answers to Chapter Questions

1. Security Manager

Explanation The Security Manager interface is used for granting privileges to users. Review the overall text to be sure you understand the use of OEM tools. See Chapter 5 for more information.

2. Review Figure 10-10 to see the answer.

Explanation First, you must click on the Offline radio button to specify offline status for your rollback segment. Next, you must click the Apply button to enable that status. See Chapter 4 for more information.

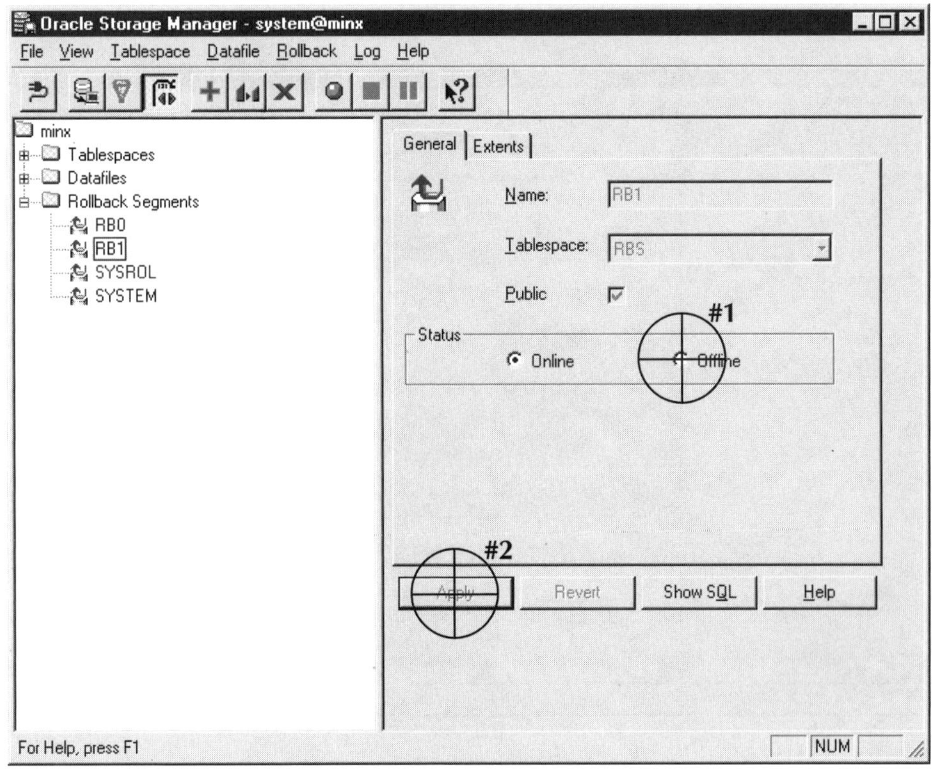

FIGURE 10-10. *Answer to question 2*

3. Review Figure 10-11 to see the answer.

Explanation You must click on the Scope tab interface in order to select the scope of your tuning session. This selection, in turn, defines the collection classes enabled in the Collect tab interface. See Chapter 7 for more information.

4. B. Roles/Privileges

Explanation The Roles/Privileges tab allows you to grant roles and system privileges to the user you are defining. Choice A is incorrect because the General tab is used to define basic components of the user ID, while Choice C is incorrect because the Object Privileges tab allows you to define object privileges for the user. Finally, Choice D is incorrect because the Quotas tab interface is used for defining tablespace quotas or storage limits for this user. See Chapter 5 for more information.

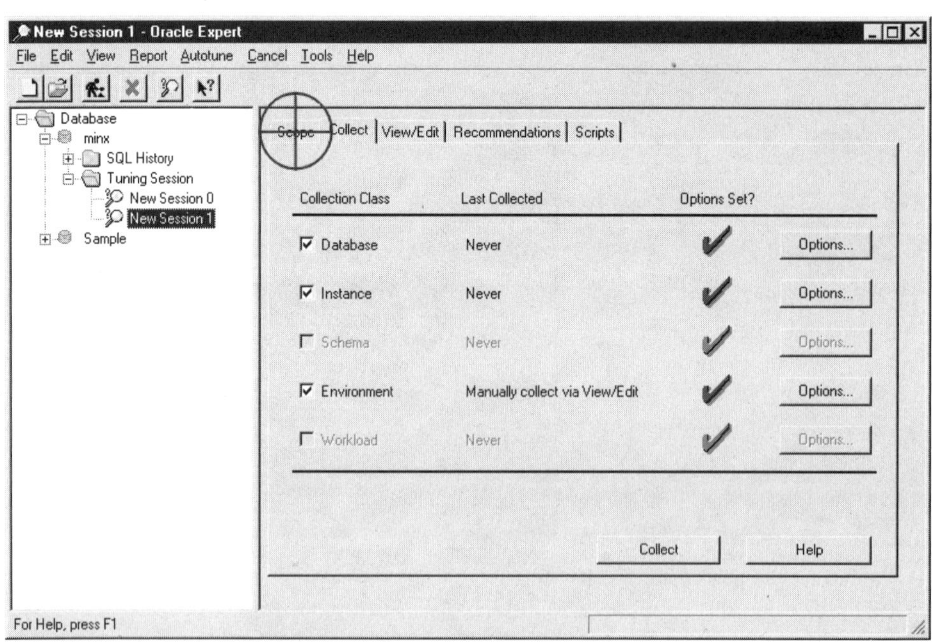

FIGURE 10-11. *Answer to question 3*

5. ONE

Explanation Only one rollback segment is required to start an Oracle database consisting of only a SYSTEM tablespace. For all databases having more than the SYSTEM tablespace, you must have two rollback segments. See Chapter 4 for more information.

6. Review Figure 10-12 to see the answer.

Explanation First, you click on the down arrow button in the interface to move the selected `EXECUTE` privilege on the `find_mouse( )` procedure, highlighted in the upper-right corner of the interface. Because it is already highlighted, you don't need to click on it again. Then you click on the Apply button to grant this privilege to the user. See Chapter 5 for more information.

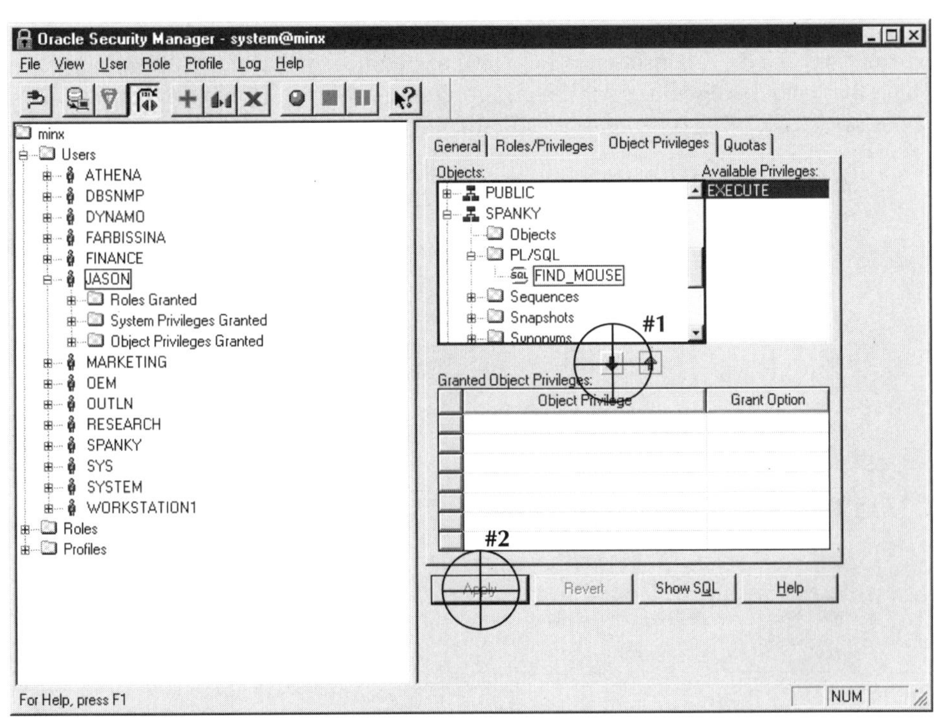

FIGURE 10-12. *Answer to question 6*

7. Review the illustration to see the answer.

COLUMN 1	COLUMN 2
Datafiles	Physical storage structures
Tablespaces	
Segments	Logical storage structures
Blocks	

Explanation Datafiles and blocks are physical storage structures on an Oracle database. Tablespaces and segments are logical storage structures. See Chapter 4 for more information.

8. CHECK

Explanation CHECK constraints allow you to define a static set of values, within which the value being added for the column must conform. The several limits on values set for CHECK constraints are identified in Chapter 9.

Index

A

B

D

F

G

H

I

N

O

P

Q

R

S

T

U

V

W

☐ **YES! Please send me a FREE subscription to Oracle Magazine.** ☐ **NO, I am not interested at this time.**

If you wish to receive your free bimonthly subscription to *Oracle Magazine,* you must fill out the entire form, sign it, and date it (incomplete forms cannot be processed or acknowledged). You can also subscribe at our Web site at **www.oramag.com/html/subform.html** or fax your application to *Oracle Magazine* at **+847.647.9735.**

SIGNATURE (REQUIRED) ✓ ______ **DATE** ______

NAME ______ TITLE ______

COMPANY ______ E-MAIL ADDRESS ______

STREET/P.O. BOX ______

CITY/STATE/ZIP ______

COUNTRY ______ TELEPHONE ______

You must answer all eight questions below.

1 What is the primary business activity of your firm at this location? *(circle only one)*
- 01 Agriculture, Mining, Natural Resources
- 02 Architecture, Construction
- 03 Communications
- 04 Consulting, Training
- 05 Consumer Packaged Goods
- 06 Data Processing
- 07 Education
- 08 Engineering
- 09 Financial Services
- 10 Government—Federal, Local, State, Other
- 11 Government—Military
- 12 Health Care
- 13 Manufacturing—Aerospace, Defense
- 14 Manufacturing—Computer Hardware
- 15 Manufacturing—Noncomputer Products
- 16 Real Estate, Insurance
- 17 Research & Development
- 18 Human Resources
- 19 Retailing, Wholesaling, Distribution
- 20 Software Development
- 21 Systems Integration, VAR, VAD, OEM
- 22 Transportation
- 23 Utilities (Electric, Gas, Sanitation)
- 24 Other Business and Services ______

2 Which of the following best describes your job function? *(circle only one)*

CORPORATE MANAGEMENT/STAFF
- 01 Executive Management (President, Chair, CEO, CFO, Owner, Partner, Principal)
- 02 Finance/Administrative Management (VP/Director/Manager/Controller, Purchasing, Administration)
- 03 Sales/Marketing Management (VP/Director/Manager)
- 04 Computer Systems/Operations Management (CIO/VP/Director/Manager MIS, Operations)
- 05 Other Finance/Administration Staff
- 06 Other Sales/Marketing Staff

IS/IT Staff
- 07 Systems Development/Programming Management
- 08 Systems Development/Programming Staff
- 09 Consulting
- 10 DBA/Systems Administrator
- 11 Education/Training
- 12 Engineering/R&D/Science Management
- 13 Engineering/R&D/Science Staff
- 14 Technical Support Director/Manager
- 15 Webmaster/Internet Specialist
- 16 Other Technical Management/Staff

3 What is your current primary operating platform? *(circle all that apply)*
- 01 DEC UNIX
- 02 DEC VAX VMS
- 03 Java
- 04 HP UNIX
- 05 IBM AIX
- 06 IBM UNIX
- 07 Macintosh
- 08 MPE-ix
- 09 MS-DOS
- 10 MVS
- 11 NetWare
- 12 Network Computing
- 13 OpenVMS
- 14 SCO UNIX
- 15 Sun Solaris/SunOS
- 16 SVR4
- 17 Ultrix
- 18 UnixWare
- 19 VM
- 20 Windows
- 21 Windows NT
- 22 Other ______
- 23 Other UNIX ______

4 Do you evaluate, specify, recommend, or authorize the purchase of any of the following? *(circle all that apply)*
- 01 Hardware
- 02 Software
- 03 Application Development Tools
- 04 Database Products
- 05 Internet or Intranet Products

5 In your job, do you use or plan to purchase any of the following products or services? *(check all that apply)*

	Use	Plan to buy
SOFTWARE		
01 Business Graphics	☐	☐
02 CAD/CAE/CAM	☐	☐
03 CASE	☐	☐
04 CIM	☐	☐
05 Communications	☐	☐
06 Database Management	☐	☐
07 File Management	☐	☐
08 Finance	☐	☐
09 Java	☐	☐
10 Materials Resource Planning	☐	☐
11 Multimedia Authoring	☐	☐
12 Networking	☐	☐
13 Office Automation	☐	☐
14 Order Entry/Inventory Control	☐	☐
15 Programming	☐	☐
16 Project Management	☐	☐
17 Scientific and Engineering	☐	☐
18 Spreadsheets	☐	☐
19 Systems Management	☐	☐
20 Workflow	☐	☐
HARDWARE		
21 Macintosh	☐	☐
22 Mainframe	☐	☐
23 Massively Parallel Processing	☐	☐
24 Minicomputer	☐	☐
25 PC	☐	☐
26 Network Computer	☐	☐
27 Supercomputer	☐	☐
28 Symmetric Multiprocessing	☐	☐
29 Workstation	☐	☐
PERIPHERALS		
30 Bridges/Routers/Hubs/Gateways	☐	☐
31 CD-ROM Drives	☐	☐
32 Disk Drives/Subsystems	☐	☐
33 Modems	☐	☐
34 Tape Drives/Subsystems	☐	☐
35 Video Boards/Multimedia	☐	☐
SERVICES		
36 Computer-Based Training	☐	☐
37 Consulting	☐	☐
38 Education/Training	☐	☐
39 Maintenance	☐	☐
40 Online Database Services	☐	☐
41 Support	☐	☐
42 **None of the above**	☐	☐

6 What Oracle products are in use at your site? *(circle all that apply)*

SERVER/SOFTWARE
- 01 Oracle8
- 02 Oracle7
- 03 Oracle Application Server
- 04 Oracle Data Mart Suites
- 05 Oracle Internet Commerce Server
- 06 Oracle InterOffice
- 07 Oracle Lite
- 08 Oracle Payment Server
- 09 Oracle Rdb
- 10 Oracle Security Server
- 11 Oracle Video Server
- 12 Oracle Workgroup Server

TOOLS
- 13 Designer/2000
- 14 Developer/2000 (Forms, Reports, Graphics)
- 15 Oracle OLAP Tools
- 16 Oracle Power Object

ORACLE APPLICATIONS
- 17 Oracle Automotive
- 18 Oracle Energy
- 19 Oracle Consumer Packaged Goods
- 20 Oracle Financials
- 21 Oracle Human Resources
- 22 Oracle Manufacturing
- 23 Oracle Projects
- 24 Oracle Sales Force Automation
- 25 Oracle Supply Chain Management
- 26 Other ______
- 27 **None of the above**

7 What other database products are in use at your site? *(circle all that apply)*
- 01 Access
- 02 BAAN
- 03 dbase
- 04 Gupta
- 05 IBM DB2
- 06 Informix
- 07 Ingres
- 08 Microsoft Access
- 09 Microsoft SQL Server
- 10 Peoplesoft
- 11 Progress
- 12 SAP
- 13 Sybase
- 14 VSAM
- 15 **None of the above**

8 During the next 12 months, how much do you anticipate your organization will spend on computer hardware, software, peripherals, and services for your location? *(circle only one)*
- 01 Less than $10,000
- 02 $10,000 to $49,999
- 03 $50,000 to $99,999
- 04 $100,000 to $499,999
- 05 $500,000 to $999,999
- 06 $1,000,000 and over

OMG

WARNING: BEFORE OPENING THE DISC PACKAGE, CAREFULLY READ THE TERMS AND CONDITIONS OF THE FOLLOWING COPYRIGHT STATEMENT AND LIMITED CD-ROM WARRANTY.

Copyright Statement

This software is protected by both United States copyright law and international copyright treaty provision. Except as noted in the contents of the CD-ROM, you must treat this software just like a book. However, you may copy it into a computer to be used and you may make archival copies of the software for the sole purpose of backing up the software and protecting your investment from loss. By saying, "just like a book," The McGraw-Hill Companies, Inc. ("Osborne/McGraw-Hill") means, for example, that this software may be used by any number of people and may be freely moved from one computer location to another, so long as there is no possibility of its being used at one location or on one computer while it is being used at another. Just as a book cannot be read by two different people in two different places at the same time, neither can the software be used by two different people in two different places at the same time.

Limited Warranty

Osborne/McGraw-Hill warrants the physical compact disc enclosed herein to be free of defects in materials and workmanship for a period of sixty days from the purchase date. If the CD included in your book has defects in materials or workmanship, please call McGraw-Hill at 1-800-217-0059, 9am to 5pm, Monday through Friday, Eastern Standard Time, and McGraw-Hill will replace the defective disc.

The entire and exclusive liability and remedy for breach of this Limited Warranty shall be limited to replacement of the defective disc, and shall not include or extend to any claim for or right to cover any other damages, including but not limited to, loss of profit, data, or use of the software, or special incidental, or consequential damages or other similar claims, even if Osborne/McGraw-Hill has been specifically advised of the possibility of such damages. In no event will Osborne/McGraw-Hill's liability for any damages to you or any other person ever exceed the lower of the suggested list price or actual price paid for the license to use the software, regardless of any form of the claim.

OSBORNE/McGRAW-HILL SPECIFICALLY DISCLAIMS ALL OTHER WARRANTIES, EXPRESS OR IMPLIED, INCLUDING BUT NOT LIMITED TO, ANY IMPLIED WARRANTY OF MERCHANTABILITY OR FITNESS FOR A PARTICULAR PURPOSE. Specifically, Osborne/McGraw-Hill makes no representation or warranty that the software is fit for any particular purpose, and any implied warranty of merchantability is limited to the sixty-day duration of the Limited Warranty covering the physical disc only (and not the software), and is otherwise expressly and specifically disclaimed.

This limited warranty gives you specific legal rights; you may have others which may vary from state to state. Some states do not allow the exclusion of incidental or consequential damages, or the limitation on how long an implied warranty lasts, so some of the above may not apply to you.

This agreement constitutes the entire agreement between the parties relating to use of the Product. The terms of any purchase order shall have no effect on the terms of this Agreement. Failure of Osborne/McGraw-Hill to insist at any time on strict compliance with this Agreement shall not constitute a waiver of any rights under this Agreement. This Agreement shall be construed and governed in accordance with the laws of New York. If any provision of this Agreement is held to be contrary to law, that provision will be enforced to the maximum extent permissible, and the remaining provisions will remain in force and effect.

NO TECHNICAL SUPPORT IS PROVIDED WITH THIS CD-ROM.